KIDS LOVE Guide ®

2nd Edition

KIDS LOVE INTERSTATE 75

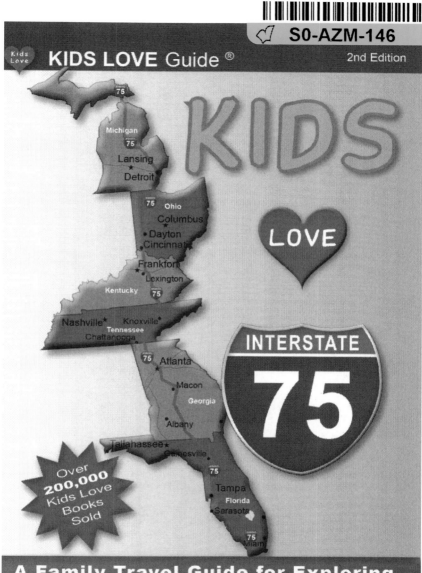

Over 200,000 Kids Love Books Sold

A Family Travel Guide for Exploring the Best Kid-Tested Places Along I-75 - from Michigan to Florida

Michele Darrall Zavatsky

Dedicated to the Families traveling 75

In a Hundred Years...It will not matter, The size of my bank account...The kind of house that I lived in, the kind of car that I drove...But what will matter is...That the world may be different Because I was important in the life of a child.

- author unknown

For the latest major updates corresponding to the pages in this book visit our website:

www.KidsLoveTravel.com

Although the authors have exhaustively researched all sources to ensure accuracy and completeness of the information contained in this book, we assume no responsibility for errors, inaccuracies, omissions or any other inconsistency herein. Any slights against any entries or organizations are unintentional.

- **REMEMBER:** Museum exhibits change frequently. Check the site's website before you visit to note any changes. Also, HOURS and ADMISSIONS are subject to change at the owner's discretion. If you are tight on time or money, check the attraction's website or call before you visit.
- **INTERNET PRECAUTION**: All websites mentioned in KIDS LOVE I-75 have been checked for appropriate content. However, due to the fast-changing nature of the Internet, we strongly urge parents to preview any recommended sites and to always supervise their children when on-line.
- **EDUCATORS**: There are suggestions for finding FREE lessons plans embedded in many listings as helpful notes for educators.

ISBN-13: 978-0-6923545-5-1

KIDS ♥ I-75 ™ Kids Love Publications, LLC

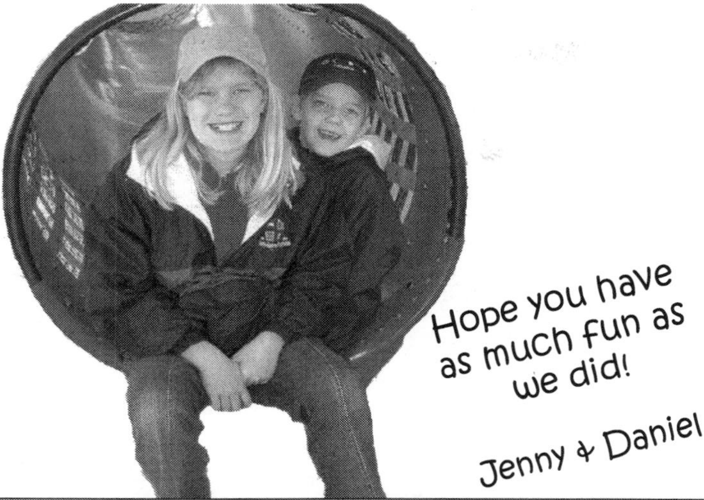
Hope you have as much fun as we did!
Jenny & Daniel

TABLE OF CONTENTS

Nearly 1,800 miles of America awaits you...

Why we wrote this book?

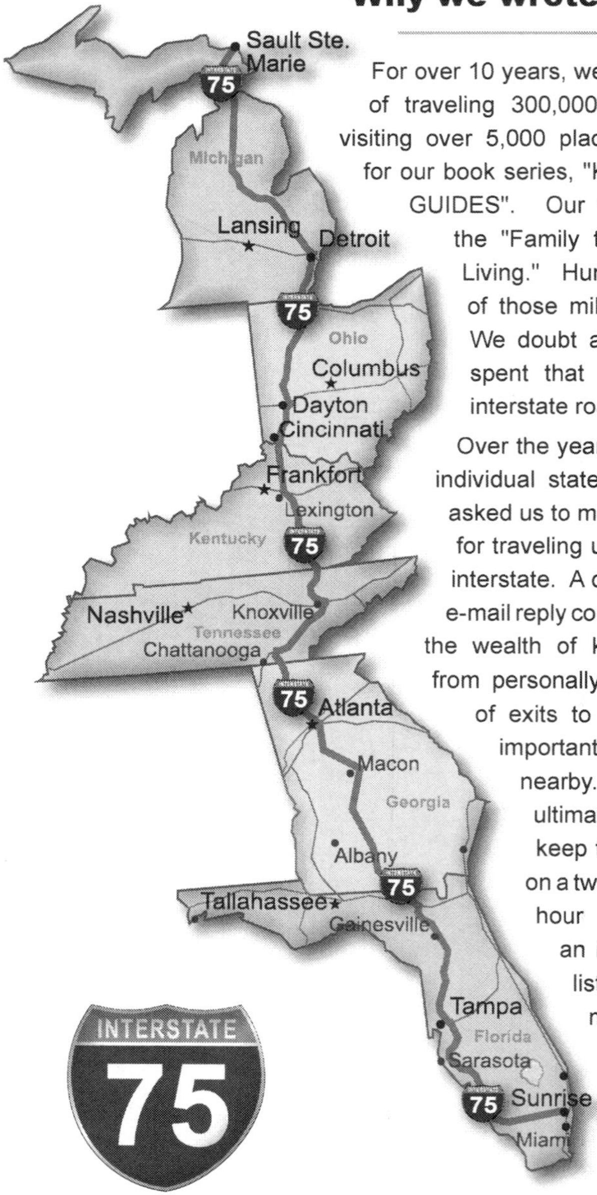

For over 10 years, we've had the privilege of traveling 300,000 miles as a family visiting over 5,000 places to kid-test them for our book series, "KIDS LOVE TRAVEL GUIDES". Our family is known as the "Family that Vacations for a Living." Hundreds of thousands of those miles were along I-75. We doubt any other family has spent that much time on one interstate road!

Over the years, folks who use our individual state travel guides have asked us to map out an action plan for traveling up and down a major interstate. A quick conversation or e-mail reply could not possibly cover the wealth of knowledge we have from personally stopping at 1,000s of exits to eat, rest and most importantly, visit attractions nearby. So, this book is the ultimate answer to how to keep the any family happy on a two hour trip or a twenty hour trip traveling along an interstate! All of the listings are within 10 miles of I-75, most are just minutes from an exit. The best part – **THIS IS THE STUFF A GPS DOESN'T TELL YOU!**

Do KIDS LOVE I-75?

Who Can Benefit from this Book... A new way to travel - Sidetripping

Every year, thousands of families load up their minivans and drive I-75 to visit family and friends or vacation destinations. I-75 has also become the "driveway" to Orlando, the most visited vacation area in the United States. While most kids would agree they can't wait to get to their destination, many feel boredom or cause stress on the way there. But, road trips don't need to be tense or difficult to plan. "Getting there" can be half the fun - if you know what family-friendly places are along the way. And, you can trust our advice as the best-selling "Family Travel Parents" who have been there, done that - wrote the books. We don't just do internet research, we actually kid-test most every site we list, weeding out the bad and highlighting favorites. We also share clues on how to make the visit more valuable...even on a budget. We did the busy work so you don't have to...

HOW TO USE THIS BOOK

Here are a few hints to make your adventures run smoothly:

BEFORE YOU LEAVE:

- Each chapter represents a state that I-75 traverses through. The chapter begins with an introduction and **Quick Tour** of favorites within the chapter. The listings are by Exit Number and then by proximity to the exit (places closest listed first). Each listing has tons of important details (pricing, hours, website, etc.) and a review noting the most engaging aspects of the place. Our popular **Activity Index** (at the beginning of each state/chapter) is helpful if you want to focus on a particular type of attraction (i.e. History, Tours, Outdoor Exploring, Animals & Farms, Suggested Lodging and Dining, etc.).

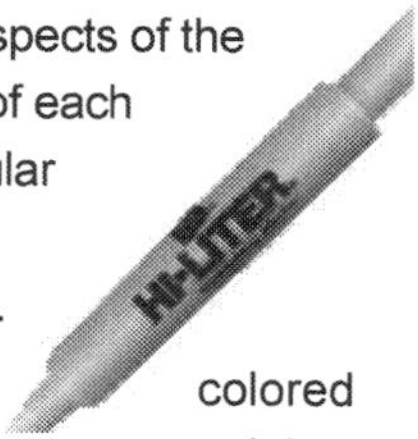

- Begin by assigning each family member a different colored highlighter (for example: Daniel gets blue, Jenny gets pink, Mommy gets yellow and Daddy gets green). At your leisure, begin to read each review and put a highlighter "check" mark next to the sites that most interest each family member or highlight the features you most want to see. Now, when you go to plan a quick trip - or a long van ride - you can easily choose different stops in one day to please everyone.

HOW TO USE THIS BOOK

BEFORE YOU LEAVE (cont.)

- Know directions and parking. Use a GPS system or print off directions from websites.
- Most attractions are closed major holidays unless noted.
- When children are in tow, it is better to make your lodging reservations ahead of time. Every time we've tried to "wing it", we've always ended up at a place that was overpriced, in a unsafe area, or not super clean. We've never been satisfied when we didn't make a reservation ahead of time.
- Campers? The best reference you may find to make campsite reservations is: www.i-75-rv-guide.com.
- If you have a large family, or are traveling with extended family or friends, most places offer group discounts. Check out the company's website for details.
- For the latest critical updates corresponding to the pages in this book, visit our website: www.kidslovetravel.com. Click on ***Updates.***

EASILY REMEMBER YOUR TRIP:

- Make a family "treasure chest". Decorate a big box or use an old popcorn tin. Store memorabilia from a fun outing, journals, pictures, brochures and souvenirs. Once a year, look through the "treasure chest" and reminisce.

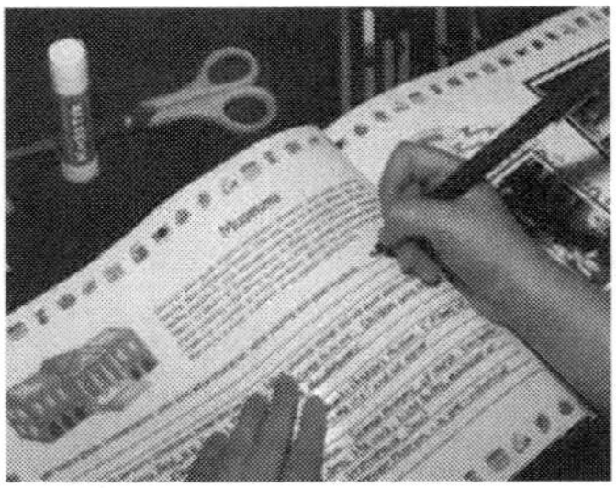

Trip Notes:

WAYS TO SAVE MONEY:

- MEMBERSHIPS - many children's museums, science centers, zoos and aquariums are members of associations that provide FREE or Discounted reciprocity to other such museums across the country. AAA Auto Club cards offer discounts to many of the activities and hotels in this book. If grandparents are along for the ride, they can use their AARP card and get discounts. Be sure to carry your member cards with you as proof to receive the discounts.
- SUPERMARKET CUSTOMER CARDS - national and local supermarkets often offer good discounted tickets to major attractions in the area.
- INTERNET HOTEL RESERVATIONS - if you're traveling with kids, don't take the risk of being spontaneous with lodging. Make reservations ahead of time. We don't use non-refundable, deep discount hotel "scouting" websites (ex. Hotwire) unless we're traveling on business - just adults. You can't cancel your reservation, or change them, and you can't be guaranteed the type of room you want (ex. non-smoking, two beds). Instead, stick with a national hotel chain you trust and join their rewards program (ex. Choice Privileges) to accumulate points towards FREE night stays.
- STATE TRAVEL CENTERS - as you enter a new state, their welcome centers offer many current promotions.
- HOTEL LOBBIES - often have a display of discount coupons to area shops and restaurants. When you check in, ask the clerk for discount pizza coupons they may have at the front desk.
- ATTRACTION ONLINE COUPONS - check the websites listed with each review for possible printable coupons or discounted online tickets good towards the attraction.

Trip Notes:

ON THE ROAD:

- Consider the child's age before you stop at an exit. Some attractions and restaurants, even hotels, are too formal for young ones or not enough adventure for teens. Read our trusted reviews first.
- Estimate the duration of the trip and how many stops you can afford to make. From our experience, it is best to stop every two hours to stretch your legs or eat/snack or maybe visit an inexpensive attraction. Some of our favorite stops on the way are little BBQ or ice cream diners that keep the kids looking forward to the journey, not just the final destination. We also indicate **Playlands, Rest Areas and Welcome Centers** when available at most exits.
- Pace yourself. Each map is 20 miles long and gives you a sense of "traveling with the book" in small increments which breaks up the monotony of long journeys. It's also great for estimating how far you've come and how much farther you have to go.
- Allow kids to bring their favorite music and personal electronics. Bring along a small portable DVD player, too. Decide family rules for how much time you allow electronics on while traveling BEFORE you leave.
- Bring along travel books and games for "quiet time" in the van. (see tested travel products on www.kidslovetravel.com) As an added bonus, these "enriching" games also stimulate conversation - you may get to know your family better and create memorable life lessons.

- In between meals, we offer the family snacks like: pretzels, whole grain chips, nuts, water bottles, bite-size (dark) chocolates, carrots, grapes, dried fruit, string cheese and apples. None of these are messy and all are healthy. Keep these in a small cooler or backpack near the front of the vehicle.
- Plan picnics along the way. Many Historical sites and State Parks are scattered along the highway. Kids can run around outside and release some energy. Allow time for a rest stop or a scenic byway to take advantage of these free picnic facilities.
- Safety - we indicate Hospital or major Health Care facility exits.

A QUICK TOUR OF THE MAPS

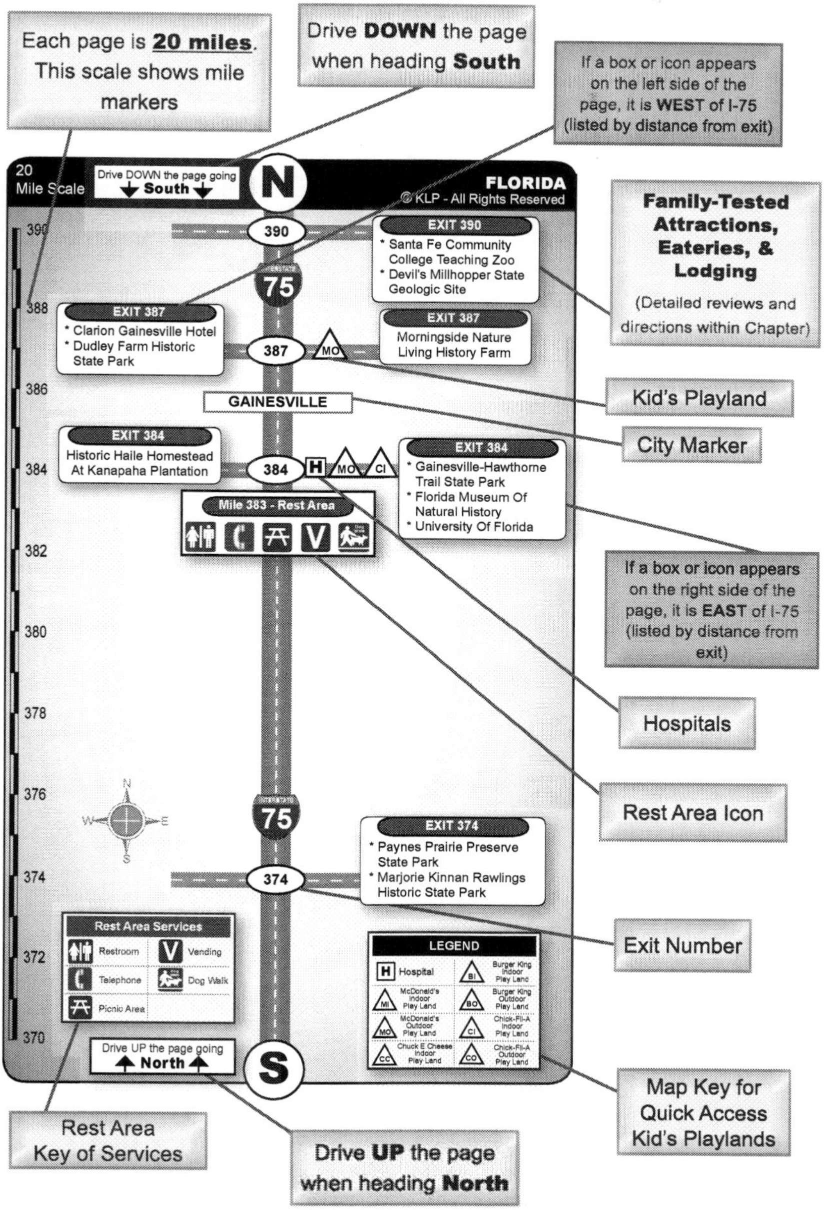

Travel Journal & Notes:

Chapter 1
MICHIGAN

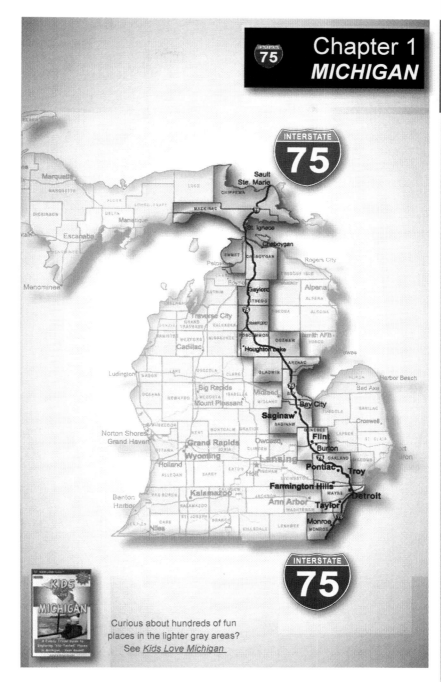

Curious about hundreds of fun places in the lighter gray areas? See *Kids Love Michigan*

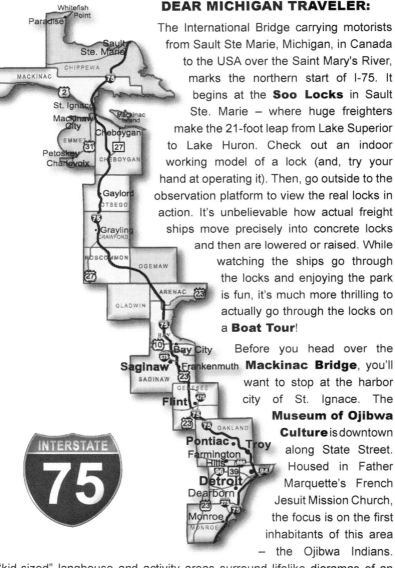

MICHIGAN

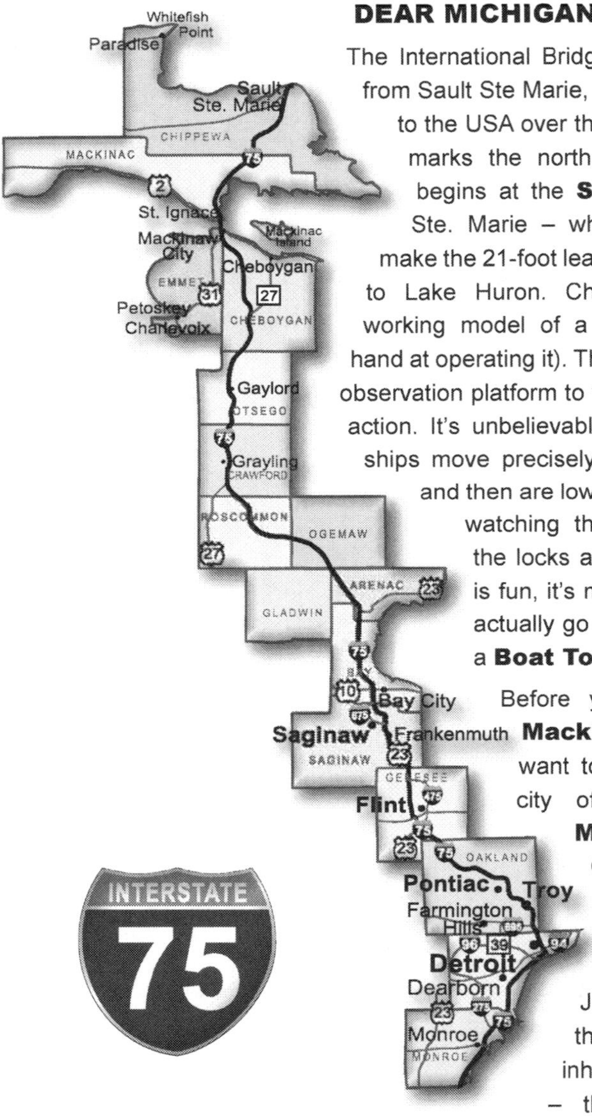

DEAR MICHIGAN TRAVELER:

The International Bridge carrying motorists from Sault Ste Marie, Michigan, in Canada to the USA over the Saint Mary's River, marks the northern start of I-75. It begins at the **Soo Locks** in Sault Ste. Marie – where huge freighters make the 21-foot leap from Lake Superior to Lake Huron. Check out an indoor working model of a lock (and, try your hand at operating it). Then, go outside to the observation platform to view the real locks in action. It's unbelievable how actual freight ships move precisely into concrete locks and then are lowered or raised. While watching the ships go through the locks and enjoying the park is fun, it's much more thrilling to actually go through the locks on a **Boat Tour**!

Before you head over the **Mackinac Bridge**, you'll want to stop at the harbor city of St. Ignace. The **Museum of Ojibwa Culture** is downtown along State Street. Housed in Father Marquette's French Jesuit Mission Church, the focus is on the first inhabitants of this area – the Ojibwa Indians. A "kid-sized" longhouse and activity areas surround lifelike dioramas of an Ojibwa family network. Outside, you can't miss the giant longhouse or the realistic teepee with weaved bark mats. **Castle Rock** is just a few minutes away. See and climb the 189 steps of the limestone "sea stack" – nearly 200 feet tall – that Native Americans once used as a lookout.

For a little slower pace, take a ferry over to **Mackinac Island**. Since motor vehicles aren't permitted on the island, we suggest you take a guided carriage tour or rent bicycles for a 5-6 mile self-guided tour around the entire island. Your kids will like the adventure of being on an island without the fear of cars and trucks – just cobblestone streets and coastline roads sprinkled with carriages and bikes. Many young families may just opt to day trip here but if you stay the night and want to make it special – the Grand is grand and Mission Point is full of activities for kids.

As soon as you cross the Bridge, your family ends up in a magical place – Mackinaw or Mackinac (pronounced Mac-eh-naw). **Mackinaw City** has Lake Michigan on its west and north sides and Lake Huron on its east side. This is at the south end of the Mackinac Bridge. European fur traders and settlers established a stockade village on the Straits of Mackinac, a key strategic point in the Upper Great Lakes. This settlement is now preserved in time as **Colonial Michilimackinac**. Outside of the settlement, today's Mackinaw City offers visitors a 'resort town' environment that allows walking to most every attraction on the mainland. In the mix of old and new there are three other National Historic Sites: **Old Mackinac Point Lighthouse**, **Historic Mill Creek, and Fort Mackinac**. When it's time to return to the present you will find a Family Waterpark, parks, beaches, and over 100 shops and dining to delight you... all within the backdrop of the Mighty Mackinac Bridge. Can't decide what to do first? We highly recommend the **Mackinaw Trolley Tours** to get an overall picture of the area. Let your kids ring the trolley bell!

If the Lower Peninsula of Michigan is a mitten, you're in for a cozy ride, folks. Cities of note are Bay City, Dearborn, Detroit, Flint, Frankenmuth, Grayling, Mackinaw, and Saginaw. The main theme: See what living during the age of Industry - near the water was really like!

Michigan is defined not only by its waters but also by the forests once used for logging. Rivers and lakes for water sports, and thousands of miles of hiking trails thread their way among some 100 species of trees. The Mackinaw State Forest and Huron National Forest dominate the majority of Northeast Michigan.

Gaylord has Otsego Lake which has an abundance of beautiful, white, sandy beaches. And, just northeast of Grayling, is **Hartwick Pines State Park**, where visitors can participate in a number of outdoor activities and learn about Michigan's logging history at the Hartwick Pines Logging Museum. Some call it an "outdoor cathedral of nature," walking along the Old Growth Forest Foot

Trail as it winds through the forest behind the Visitor Center (full of "talking" trees and loggers).

The town of Frankenmuth offers up old world charm and its famous family style chicken dinners...and now, two different Indoor **Waterparks**. When you're waterlogged or stuffed full of chicken dinner, try walking off some calories on South Main Street. We've all seen freshly shaven sheep and probably own wool clothing – but how is it processed? At the **Frankenmuth Woolen Mill**, you'll watch them wash, air dry (it gets really fluffy that way) and card fresh wool. You can watch first from the observation windows, and then handle some wool yourself. Across the street is the **Frankenmuth Cheese Haus**. Ever tried "chocolate" or "strawberry" CHEESE? Watch a video of the cheesemaking process, or, if you time it right, actually see the ladies make it from scratch. There are plenty of other shops, amusements and a historical museum to peek in, too. Be sure to catch the night lights at **Bronners** every evening – it's Christmas year-round there.

Travel a little further south to the town of Flint, the birthplace of General Motors. Probably our favorite special events attraction in the region is **Crossroads Village**. The 1860's era living village is a collection of 30 authentic buildings that form a town bigger than Walnut Grove (Little House of the Prairie)! Dad could get a shave while the kids shop for toys in the General Store (no batteries required toys!) and Mom tries on bonnets. When your feet get tired, hop on a riverboat or the Huckleberry Railroad train.

I-75 heads right into the mouth of Detroit. Detroit, the largest metropolitan area in Michigan, boasts one of the Midwest's great **Zoos**, the home of the Motown sound and a revitalized theater and arts district, homes & factories of the "Auto Barons," major league sports, and America's most popular indoor/outdoor history museum complex – **The Henry Ford** and **Greenfield Village**. If you want to capture the history of the city, a great family river tour is aboard **Diamond Jacks**. Ride a Model T, get welded and painted at the **Rouge**, watch the polar bears play in the Arctic, feed a giraffe, help captain a boat or "drive a train...then, eat at sports café before you catch a show or a ballgame – all within a twenty mile radius!

Want a farm setting near the city? Try a day trip to a real farm at **Calder Dairy** (Detroit area). With all the city influences abundant is this region, you may not think there is a place for nature. Well, there are scattered recreation areas around big cities. Camping, fishing and mountain bike trails can be found at **Pontiac Lake State Recreation** area in Pontiac. Look for "beach" parks, too.

ACTIVITIES AT A GLANCE

AMUSEMENTS

Exit - 344 - *Mystery Spot*
Exit - 144 - *Junction Valley Railroad*
Exit - 144 - *Bavarian Inn*
Exit - 144 - *Riverplace*
Exit - 144 - *Zehnder's Splash Village Hotel & Waterpark*
Exit - 144 - *Bronner's Christmas Wonderland*

ANIMALS & FARMS

Exit - 344 - *Deer Ranch*
Exit - 344 (Take Ferry) - *Original Butterfly House*
Exit - 344 (Take Ferry) - *Wings Of Mackinac*
Exit - 256 - *Grayling Fish Hatchery*
Exit - 150 / I-675 Exit 2 - *Saginaw Children's Zoo*
Exit - 144 - *Grandpa Tiny's Farm*
Exit - 136 - *Wilderness Trails Animal Park*
Exit - 61 / I-696 Exit 16 - *Detroit Zoo*
Exit - 20 / I-275 Exit 5 - *Calder Dairy Farm*

HISTORY

Exit - 344 (Take Ferry) - *Fort Mackinac State Historic Park*
Exit - 339 - *Col. Michilimackinac State Historic Park*
Exit - 339 - *Old Mackinac Point Lighthouse*
Exit - 339 - *Icebreaker Mackinaw Maritime Museum*
Exit - 338 - *Historic Mill Creek Discovery Park*
Exit - 326 - *Cheboygan County Historical Museum*
Exit - 254 - *Wellington Farm Park*
Exit - 244 - *North Higgins Lake State Park*

HISTORY *(cont.)*

Exit - 162A - *Bay County Museum*
Exit - 144 - *Frankenmuth Historical Museum*
Exit - 125 / I-475 Exit 13 - *Crossroads Village & Huckleberry RR*
Exit - 53A - *Detroit Historical*
Exit - 46 - *Historic Fort Wayne*
Exit - 41 - *The Henry Ford*
Exit - 41 - *Greenfield Village*
Exit - 14 - *River Raisin Battlefield Visitor's Center*

MUSEUMS

Exit - 394 - *Soo Locks Park*
Exit - 394 - *Tower Of History*
Exit - 394 - *River Of History*
Exit - 394 - *Museum Ship Valley Camp*
Exit - 345 - *Museum Of Ojibwa Culture*
Exit - 339 - *Mackinac Bridge Museum And "Mighty Mac" Bridge*
Exit - 282 - *Call Of The Wild*
Exit - 254 - *Bottlecap & Diner*
Exit - 118 - *Flint Children's*
Exit - 118 - *Flint Cultural Center*
Exit - 78 - *Chrysler Museum*
Exit - 74 - *Cranbrook Art And Science Museums*
Exit - 53A - *Museum Of African-American History*
Exit - 50 - *Motown Historical*
Exit - 41 - *Automobile Hall Of Fame*

OUTDOOR EXPLORING

Exit - 348 - *Castle Rock*
Exit - 344 (Take Ferry) - *Mackinac Island State Park*
Exit - 343 - *Straits State Park*
Exit - 326 - *Cheboygan State Park*

MICHIGAN

ACTIVITIES AT A GLANCE

OUTDOOR EXPLORING *(cont.)*

Exit - 310 - *Burt Lake State Park*
Exit - 270 - *Ostego Lake State Park*
Exit - 239 - *South Higgins Lake State Park*
Exit - 168 - *Bay City State Recreation Area*
Exit - 149 - *Shiawassee National Wildlife Refuge*
Exit - 125 / I-475 Exit 13 - *Genesee Recreation Area*
Exit - 122 - *For-Mar Nature Preserve & Arboretum*
Exit - 101 - *Seven Lakes State Park*
Exit - 101 - *Holly Recreation Area*
Exit - 101 - *Ortonville Recreation Area*
Exit - 93 - *Pontiac Lake Recreation Area*
Exit - 81 - *Bald Mountain Recreation Area*
Exit - 77 - *Drayton Plains Nature Center*
Exit - 77 - *Dodge No. 4 State Park*
Exit - 47A - Belle Isle
Exit - 15 - Sterling State Park

SCIENCE

Exit - 259 - *Hartwick Pines State Park*
Exit - 162A - *Delta College Planetarium & Learning Center*
Exit - 53A - *Michigan Science Center*

SPORTS

Exit - 93 - *The Fridge*

SUGGESTED LODGING & DINING

Exit - 344 (Take Ferry) - *Grand Hotel*
Exit - 344 (Take Ferry) - *Mission Point*
Exit - 50 - *Hockeytown Café*
Exit - 41 - *Best Western Greenfield*
Exit - 41 - *Holiday Inn Express Hotel & Suites Allen Park/Dearborn*

THE ARTS

Exit - 160 - *Marshall M. Fredericks Sculpture Gallery*
Exit - 150 / I-675 Exit 3 - *Saginaw Art Museum*
Exit - 53A - *Detroit Institute of Arts*
Exit - 47A - *Pewabic Pottery*

TOURS

Exit - 394 - *Soo Locks Boat Tours*
Exit - 344 (Take Ferry) - *Mackinac Island Ferry Services*
Exit - 344 (Take Ferry) - *Mackinac Island Carriage Tours*
Exit - 339 - *Mackinaw Trolley Tours*
Exit - 144 - *Frankenmuth Cheese Haus*
Exit - 144 - *Frankenmuth Woolen Mill*
Exit - 144 - *Bavarian Belle Riverboat Tours*
Exit - 84 - *Rainforest Café Educational Tours*
Exit - 50 - *Ford Field Tours*
Exit - 50 - *Diamond Jack's Tours*
Exit - 41 - *Ford Rouge Factory*

WELCOME CENTERS

Exit - 394 - *Michigan Welcome Center (Far North)*
Exit - 344 Mile - *Michigan Welcome Center*
Exit - 338 - *Michigan Welcome Center*
Exit - 47 - *Michigan Welcome Center*
Exit - 10 Mile - *Michigan Welcome Center (Far South)*

GENERAL INFORMATION

Contact the services of interest. Request to be added to their mailing lists.

- ☐ DNR PARKS & RECREATION - www.michigan.gov/dnr. (517) 373-9900 or (800) 44-PARKS.
  - State Park Explorer Programs: Each summer, state park explorer programs are offered to campers and day visitors at 41 of Michigan's 97 state parks. Armed with field guides, animal skins, bug boxes and other hands-on materials, state park explorer guides lead informal programs and hikes that feature each location's unique natural, cultural and historic resources.
  - Fishing in the Park Programs: The instruction and fishing is FREE! Persons under age 17 don't need to have a license. Plus, you're welcome to bring your own equipment, but if you don't have a rod and reel, don't worry. The Fishing in the Parks program supplies everything you need to get started.
- ☐ Fisheries Division - (517) 373-1280
- ☐ Fishing Hotline - (800) 275-3474
- ☐ Skiing - www.ultimateskiguide.com
- ☐ Snowmobiling, Skiing and Cross-Country Skiing - www.michigan.org. (888) 78-GREAT
- ☐ Michigan Festivals and Events Association - www.mfea.org.
- ☐ Michigan Association of Recreational Vehicles and Campgrounds, MARVAC - (800) 422-6478, www.MARVAC.org
- ☐ Michigan Association of Private Campground Owners (MAPCO) - www.michcampgrounds.com
- ☐ Travel Michigan - (888) 784-7328 or www.michigan.org
- ☐ Mackinaw Area Visitors Bureau (800) 666-0160 or www.mackinawcity.com
- ☐ Detroit CVB (800) Detroit or www.visitdetroit.com

Travel Journal & Notes:

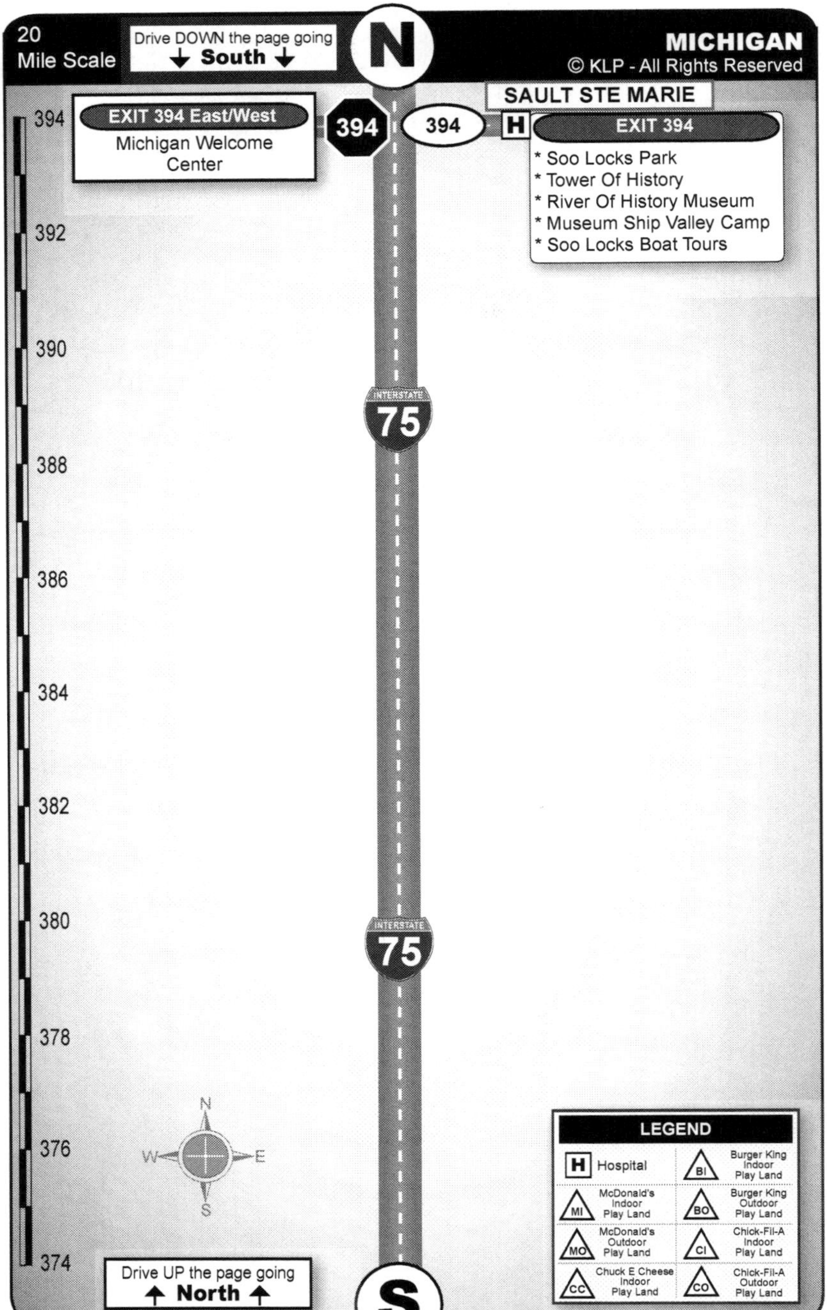
20
Mile Scale
Drive DOWN the page going
South
N
MICHIGAN
© KLP - All Rights Reserved
SAULT STE MARIE
EXIT 394 East/West
Michigan Welcome Center
394
394
H
EXIT 394
* Soo Locks Park
* Tower Of History
* River Of History Museum
* Museum Ship Valley Camp
* Soo Locks Boat Tours
394
392
390
388
386
384
382
380
378
376
374
INTERSTATE 75
INTERSTATE 75
N
W
E
S
LEGEND
H Hospital
BI Burger King Indoor Play Land
MI McDonald's Indoor Play Land
BO Burger King Outdoor Play Land
MO McDonald's Outdoor Play Land
CI Chick-Fil-A Indoor Play Land
CC Chuck E Cheese Indoor Play Land
CO Chick-Fil-A Outdoor Play Land
Drive UP the page going
North
S

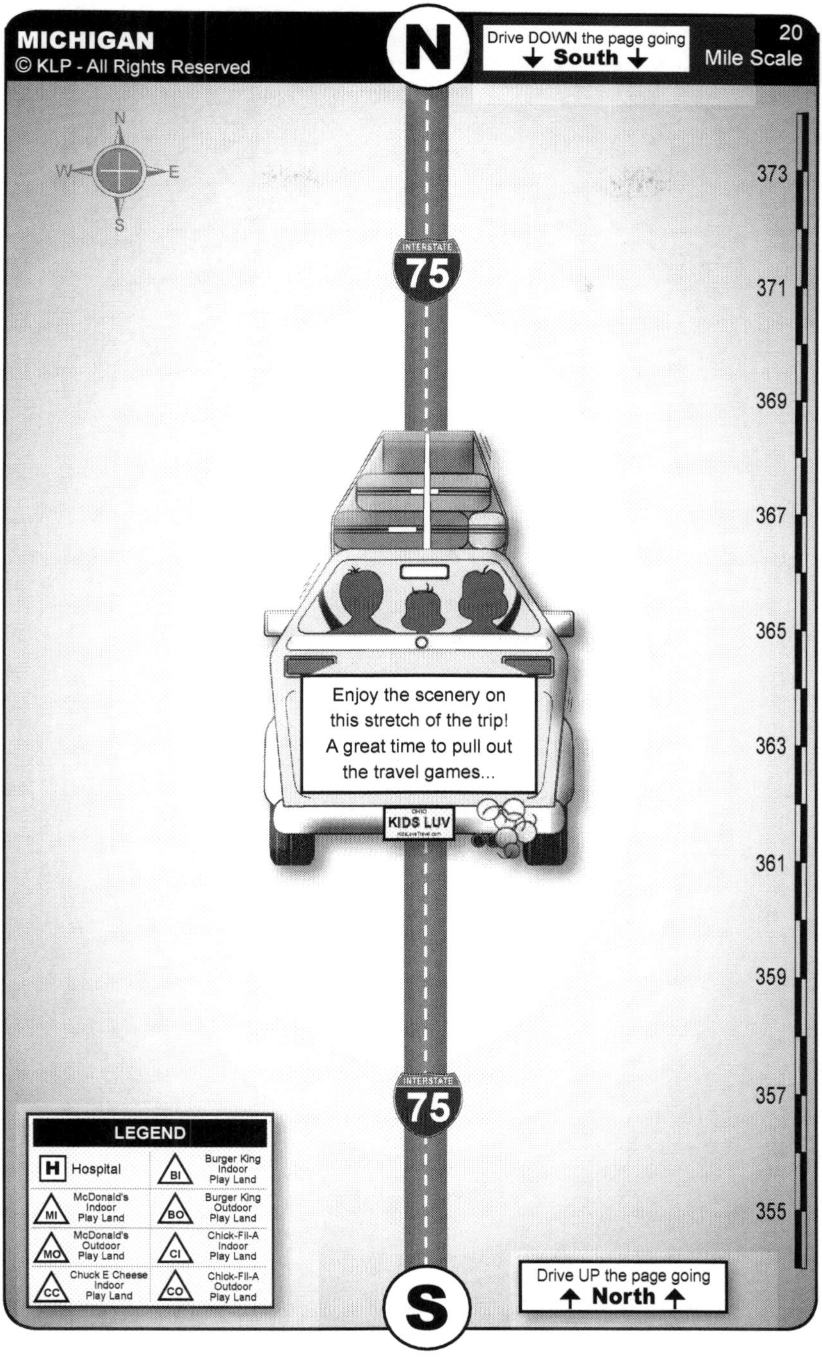
MICHIGAN
© KLP - All Rights Reserved
N
Drive DOWN the page going
South
20
Mile Scale
N
W
E
S
373
371
369
367
365
363
361
359
357
355
75
Enjoy the scenery on
this stretch of the trip!
A great time to pull out
the travel games...
KIDS LUV
75
LEGEND
H Hospital
BI Burger King Indoor Play Land
MI McDonald's Indoor Play Land
BO Burger King Outdoor Play Land
MO McDonald's Outdoor Play Land
CI Chick-Fil-A Indoor Play Land
CC Chuck E Cheese Indoor Play Land
CO Chick-Fil-A Outdoor Play Land
S
Drive UP the page going
North

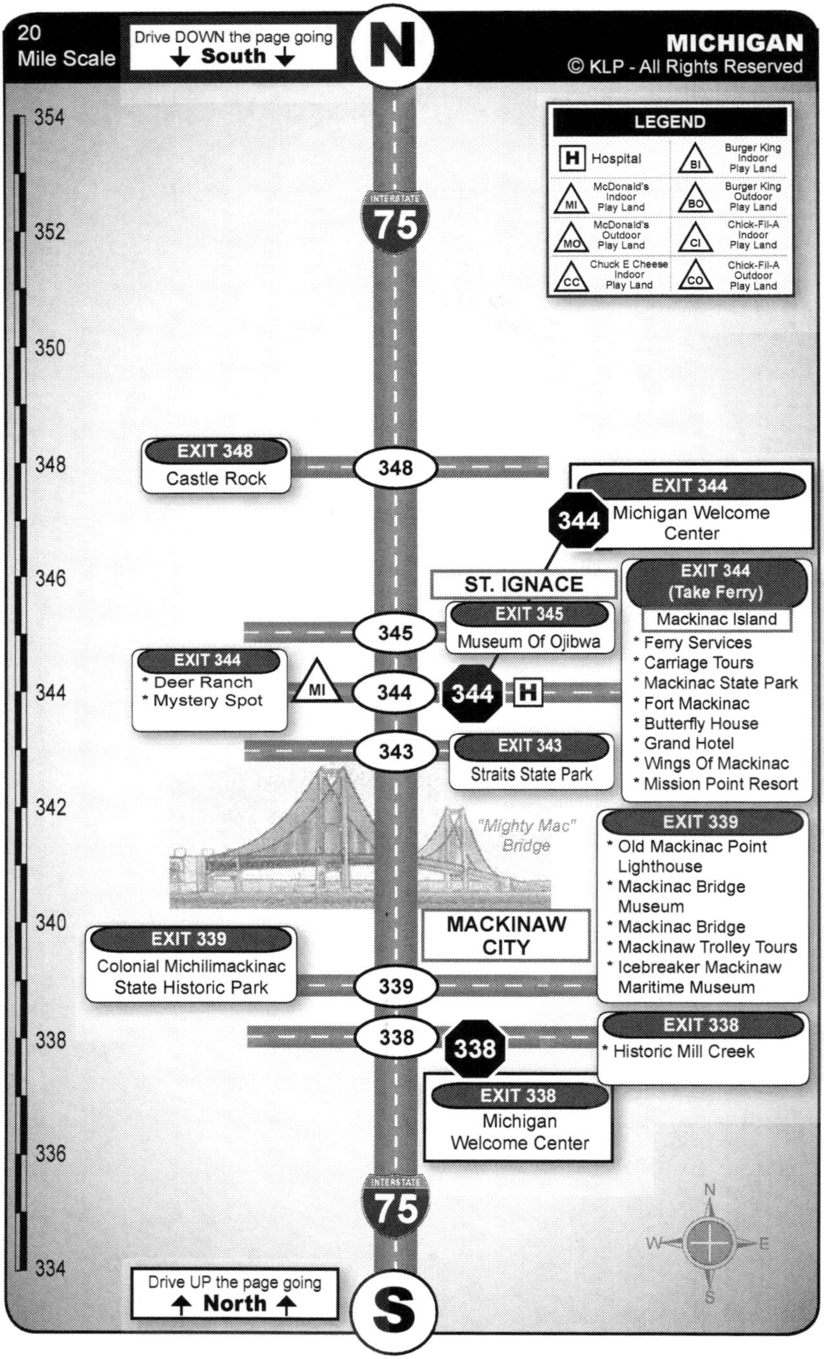
20 Mile Scale
Drive DOWN the page going ↓ South ↓
N
MICHIGAN
© KLP - All Rights Reserved
LEGEND
H Hospital
BI Burger King Indoor Play Land
MI McDonald's Indoor Play Land
BO Burger King Outdoor Play Land
MO McDonald's Outdoor Play Land
CI Chick-Fil-A Indoor Play Land
CC Chuck E Cheese Indoor Play Land
CO Chick-Fil-A Outdoor Play Land
354
352
350
348
346
344
342
340
338
336
334
INTERSTATE 75
EXIT 348
Castle Rock
348
EXIT 344
Michigan Welcome Center
344
ST. IGNACE
EXIT 344 (Take Ferry)
Mackinac Island
* Ferry Services
* Carriage Tours
* Mackinac State Park
* Fort Mackinac
* Butterfly House
* Grand Hotel
* Wings Of Mackinac
* Mission Point Resort
345
EXIT 345
Museum Of Ojibwa
EXIT 344
* Deer Ranch
* Mystery Spot
MI
344
344
H
343
EXIT 343
Straits State Park
"Mighty Mac" Bridge
EXIT 339
* Old Mackinac Point Lighthouse
* Mackinac Bridge Museum
* Mackinac Bridge
* Mackinaw Trolley Tours
* Icebreaker Mackinaw Maritime Museum
MACKINAW CITY
EXIT 339
Colonial Michilimackinac State Historic Park
339
338
338
EXIT 338
* Historic Mill Creek
EXIT 338
Michigan Welcome Center
INTERSTATE 75
N
W
E
S
Drive UP the page going ↑ North ↑
S

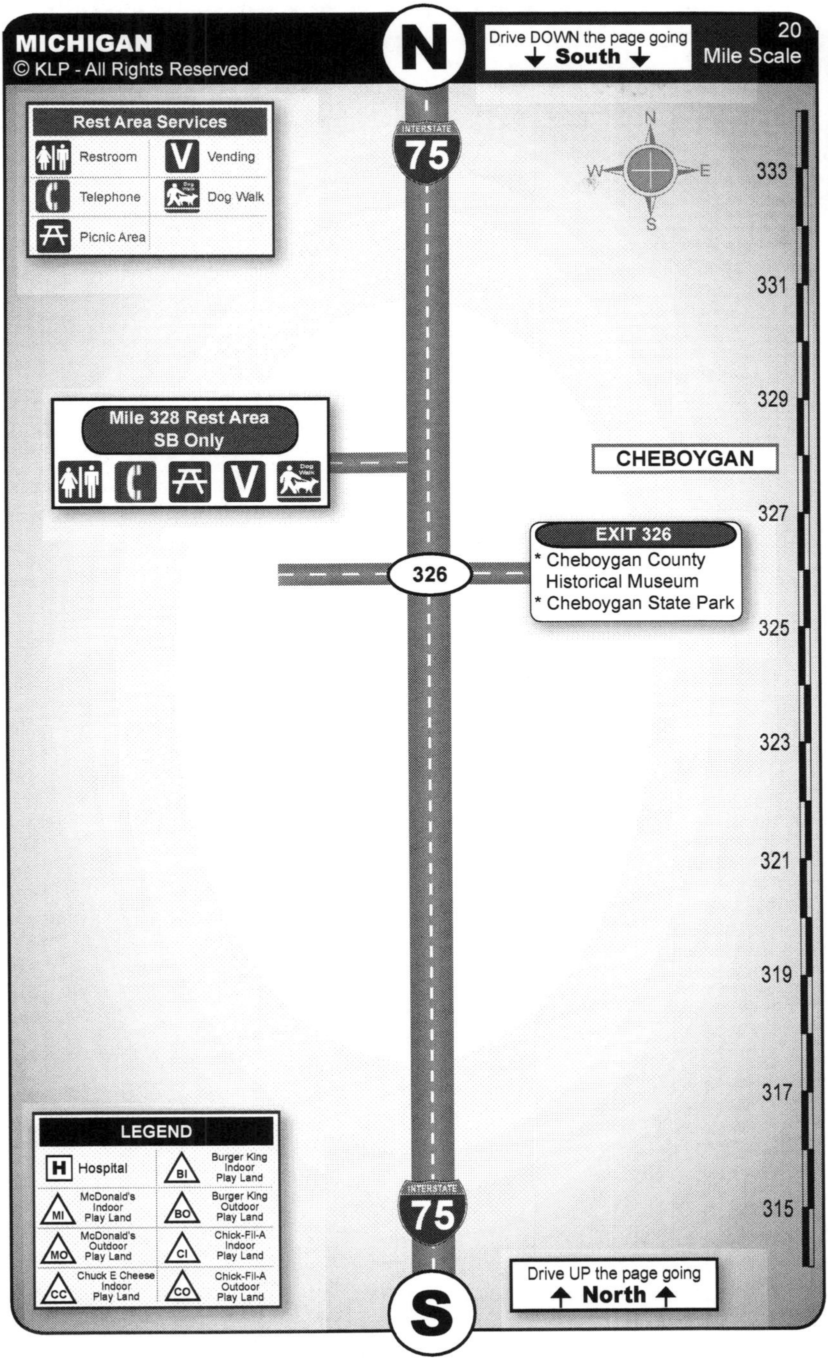
MICHIGAN
© KLP - All Rights Reserved
N
Drive DOWN the page going
South
20
Mile Scale
Rest Area Services
Restroom
Vending
Telephone
Dog Walk
Picnic Area
75
333
331
329
327
325
323
321
319
317
315
Mile 328 Rest Area
SB Only
CHEBOYGAN
EXIT 326
* Cheboygan County
Historical Museum
* Cheboygan State Park
326
LEGEND
Hospital
Burger King Indoor Play Land
McDonald's Indoor Play Land
Burger King Outdoor Play Land
McDonald's Outdoor Play Land
Chick-Fil-A Indoor Play Land
Chuck E Cheese Indoor Play Land
Chick-Fil-A Outdoor Play Land
75
S
Drive UP the page going
North

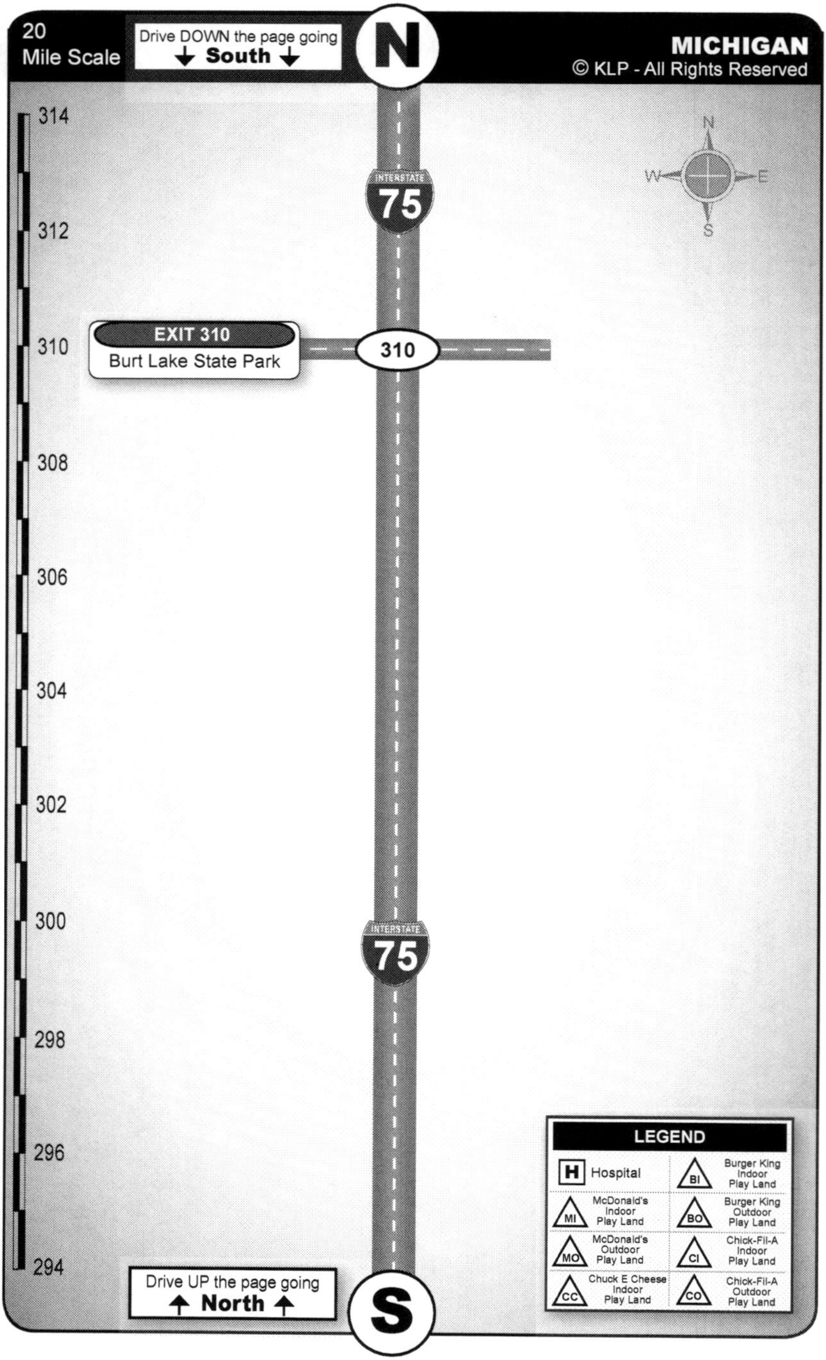
20
Mile Scale
Drive DOWN the page going
South
N
MICHIGAN
© KLP - All Rights Reserved
314
312
310
308
306
304
302
300
298
296
294
INTERSTATE
75
EXIT 310
Burt Lake State Park
310
N
W
E
S
Drive UP the page going
North
S
LEGEND
H Hospital
BI Burger King Indoor Play Land
MI McDonald's Indoor Play Land
BO Burger King Outdoor Play Land
MO McDonald's Outdoor Play Land
CI Chick-Fil-A Indoor Play Land
CC Chuck E Cheese Indoor Play Land
CO Chick-Fil-A Outdoor Play Land

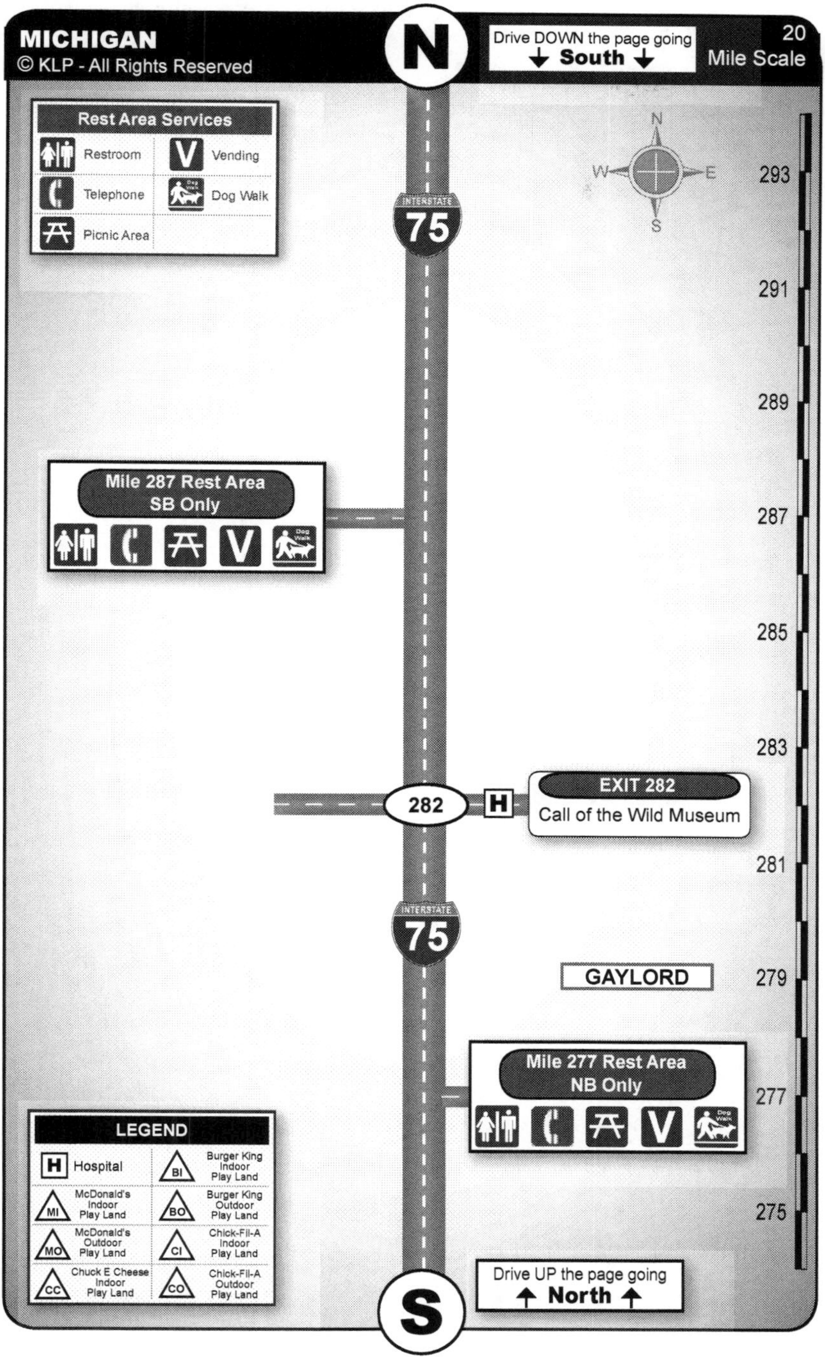
MICHIGAN
© KLP - All Rights Reserved
N
Drive DOWN the page going
South
20
Mile Scale
Rest Area Services
Restroom
Vending
Telephone
Dog Walk
Picnic Area
INTERSTATE
75
293
291
289
Mile 287 Rest Area
SB Only
287
285
283
282
H
EXIT 282
Call of the Wild Museum
281
GAYLORD
279
Mile 277 Rest Area
NB Only
277
275
LEGEND
H Hospital
BI Burger King Indoor Play Land
MI McDonald's Indoor Play Land
BO Burger King Outdoor Play Land
MO McDonald's Outdoor Play Land
CI Chick-Fil-A Indoor Play Land
CC Chuck E Cheese Indoor Play Land
CO Chick-Fil-A Outdoor Play Land
S
Drive UP the page going
North

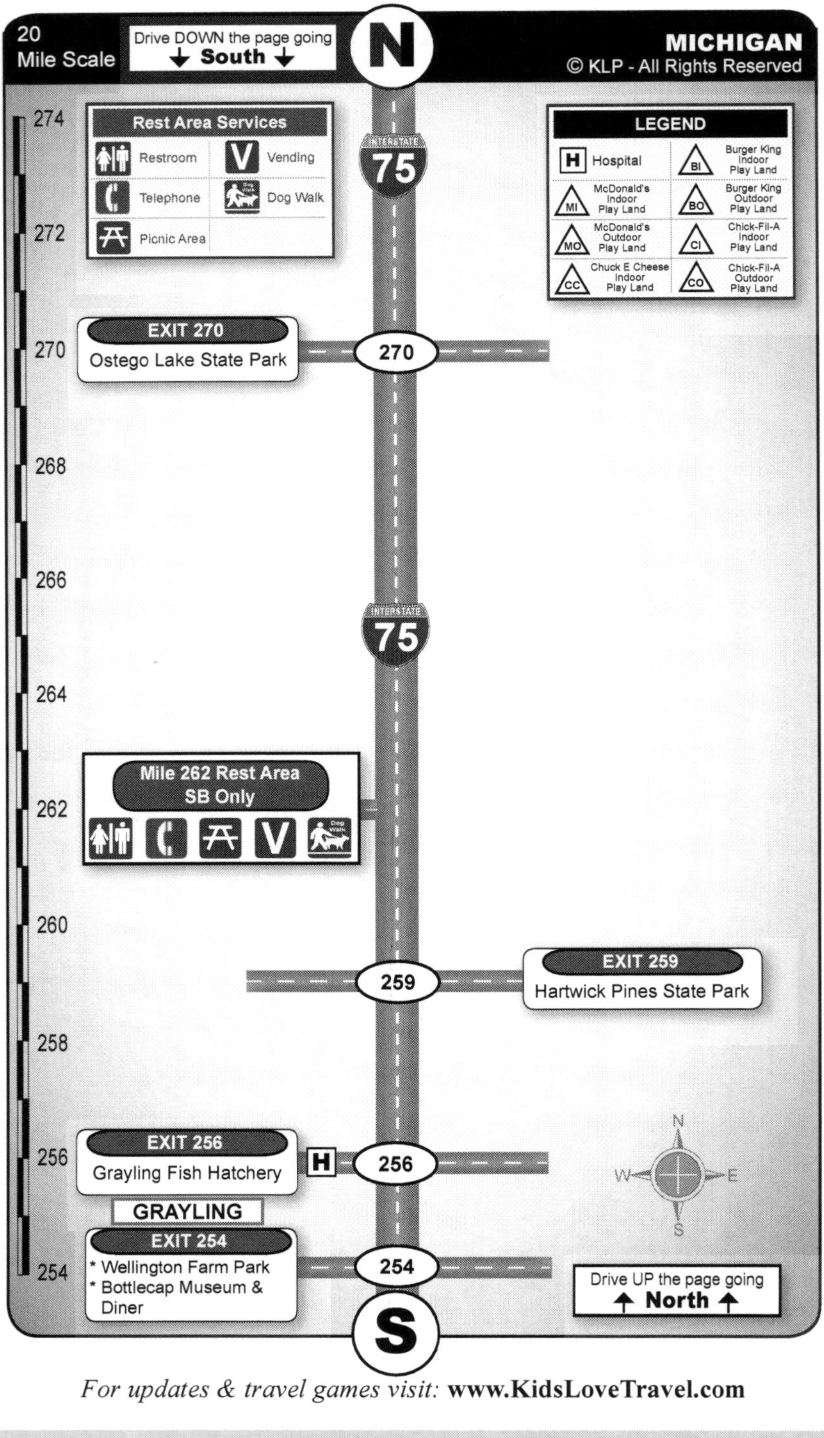

20 Mile Scale
Drive DOWN the page going South
N
MICHIGAN
© KLP - All Rights Reserved
Rest Area Services
Restroom
Vending
Telephone
Dog Walk
Picnic Area
LEGEND
Hospital
Burger King Indoor Play Land
McDonald's Indoor Play Land
Burger King Outdoor Play Land
McDonald's Outdoor Play Land
Chick-Fil-A Indoor Play Land
Chuck E Cheese Indoor Play Land
Chick-Fil-A Outdoor Play Land
274
272
270
268
266
264
262
260
258
256
254
EXIT 270
Ostego Lake State Park
Mile 262 Rest Area SB Only
EXIT 259
Hartwick Pines State Park
EXIT 256
Grayling Fish Hatchery
GRAYLING
EXIT 254
* Wellington Farm Park
* Bottlecap Museum & Diner
Drive UP the page going North
S

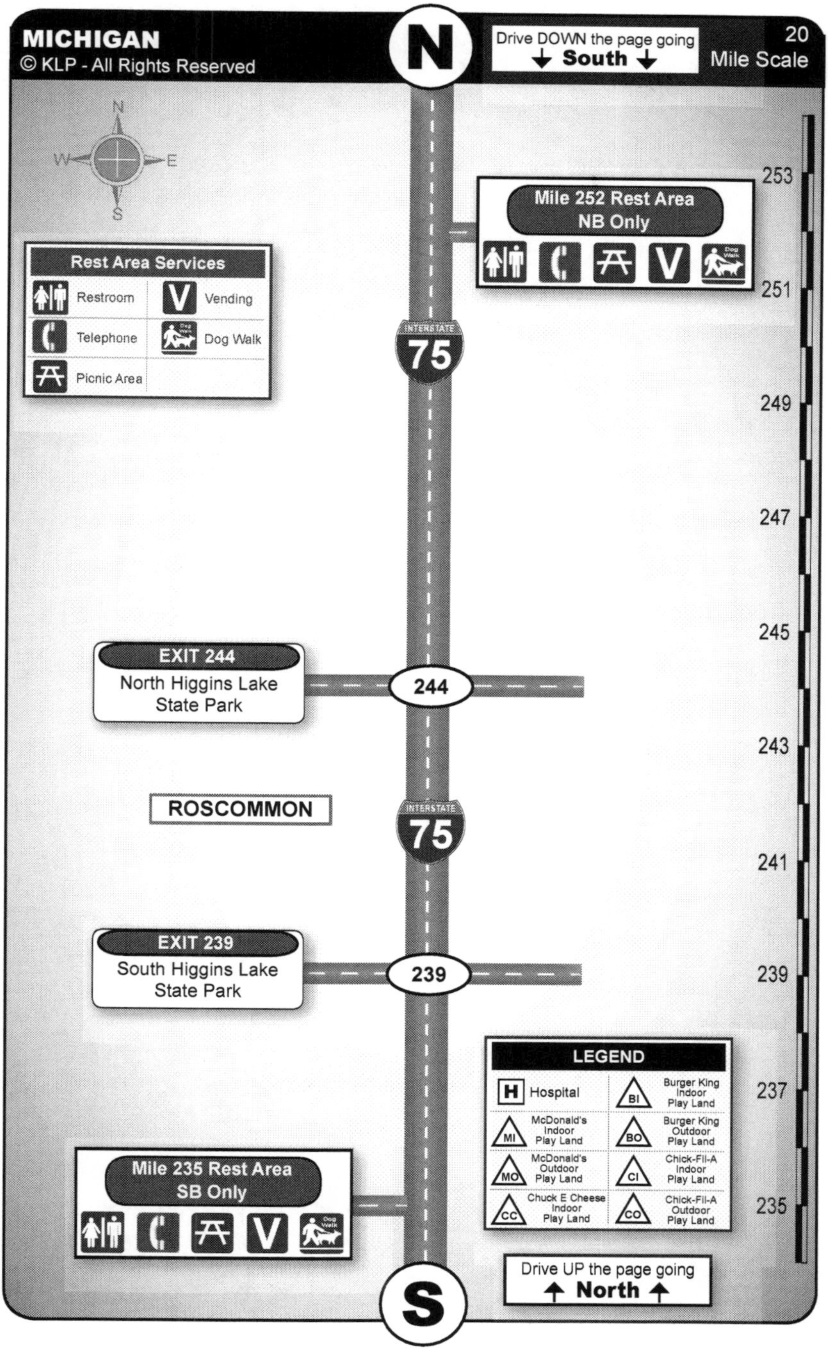
MICHIGAN
© KLP - All Rights Reserved
N
Drive DOWN the page going
South
20
Mile Scale
N
W
E
S
Mile 252 Rest Area
NB Only
Rest Area Services
Restroom
Vending
Telephone
Dog Walk
Picnic Area
INTERSTATE
75
253
251
249
247
245
243
241
239
237
235
EXIT 244
North Higgins Lake
State Park
244
ROSCOMMON
EXIT 239
South Higgins Lake
State Park
239
LEGEND
H Hospital
BI Burger King Indoor Play Land
MI McDonald's Indoor Play Land
BO Burger King Outdoor Play Land
MO McDonald's Outdoor Play Land
CI Chick-Fil-A Indoor Play Land
CC Chuck E Cheese Indoor Play Land
CO Chick-Fil-A Outdoor Play Land
Mile 235 Rest Area
SB Only
Drive UP the page going
North
S

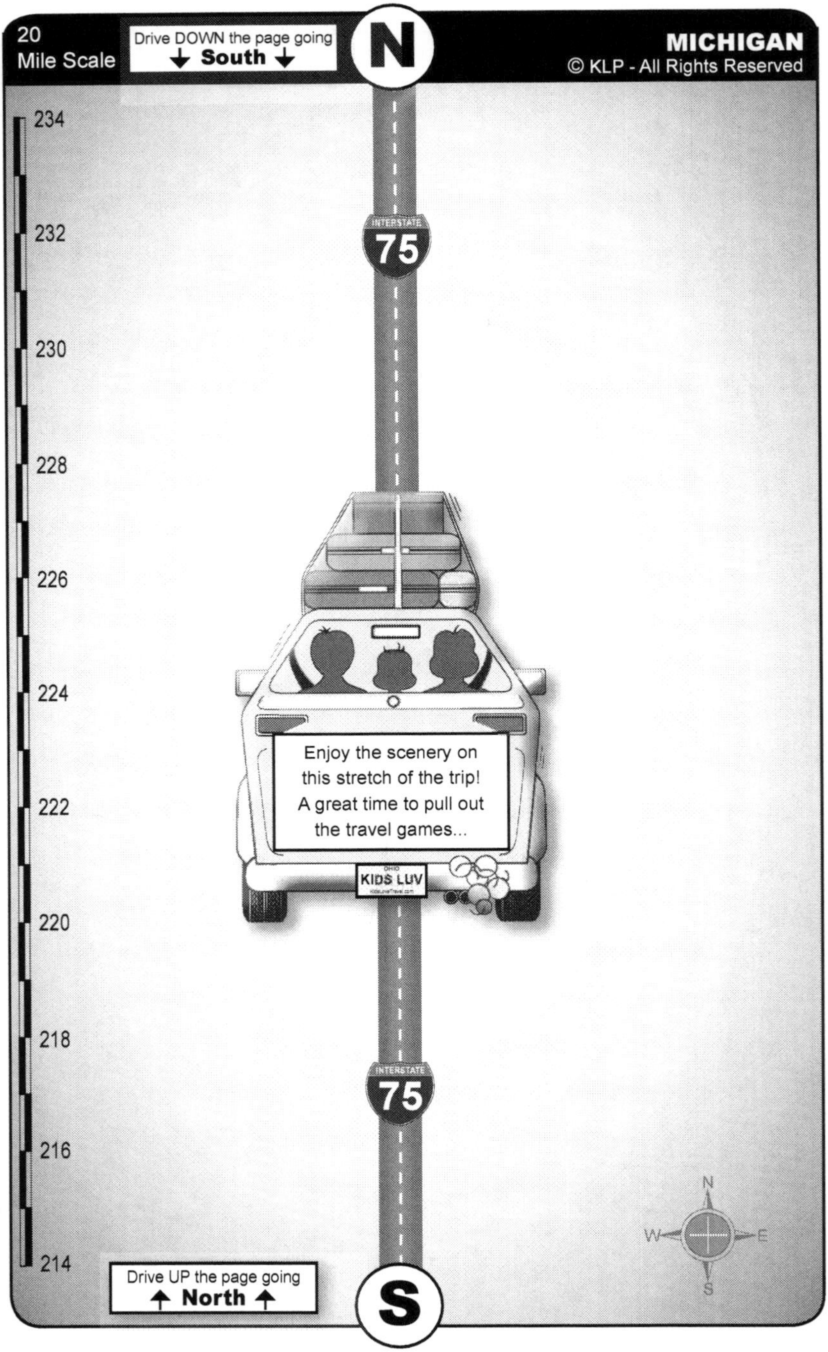

20
Mile Scale
Drive DOWN the page going
South
N
MICHIGAN
© KLP - All Rights Reserved
234
232
230
228
226
224
222
220
218
216
214
75
Enjoy the scenery on
this stretch of the trip!
A great time to pull out
the travel games...
KIDS LUV
75
N
W
E
S
Drive UP the page going
North
S

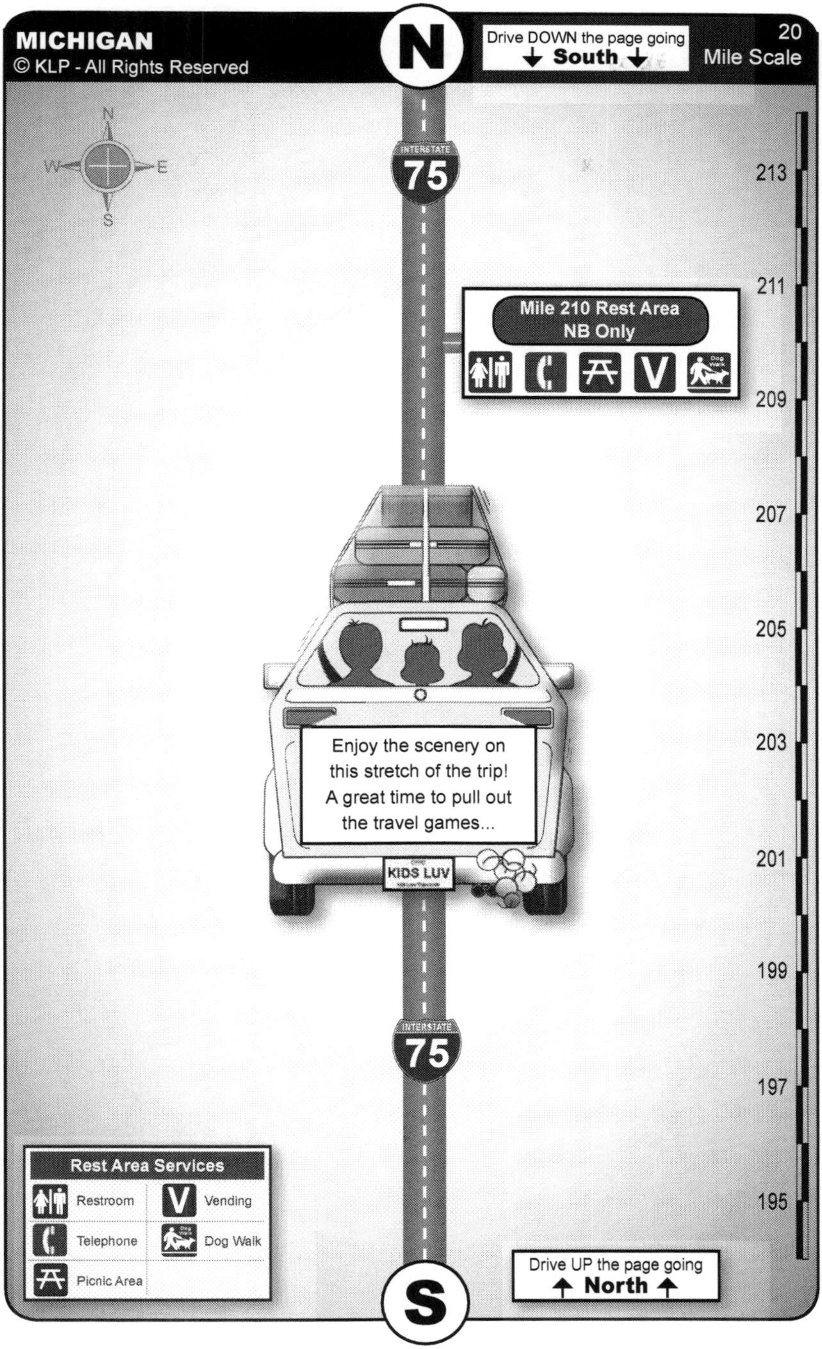
MICHIGAN
© KLP - All Rights Reserved
N
Drive DOWN the page going
South
20
Mile Scale
N
W
E
S
INTERSTATE
75
213
211
Mile 210 Rest Area
NB Only
209
207
205
Enjoy the scenery on
this stretch of the trip!
A great time to pull out
the travel games...
203
KIDS LUV
201
199
INTERSTATE
75
197
195
Rest Area Services
Restroom
Vending
Telephone
Dog Walk
Picnic Area
Drive UP the page going
North
S

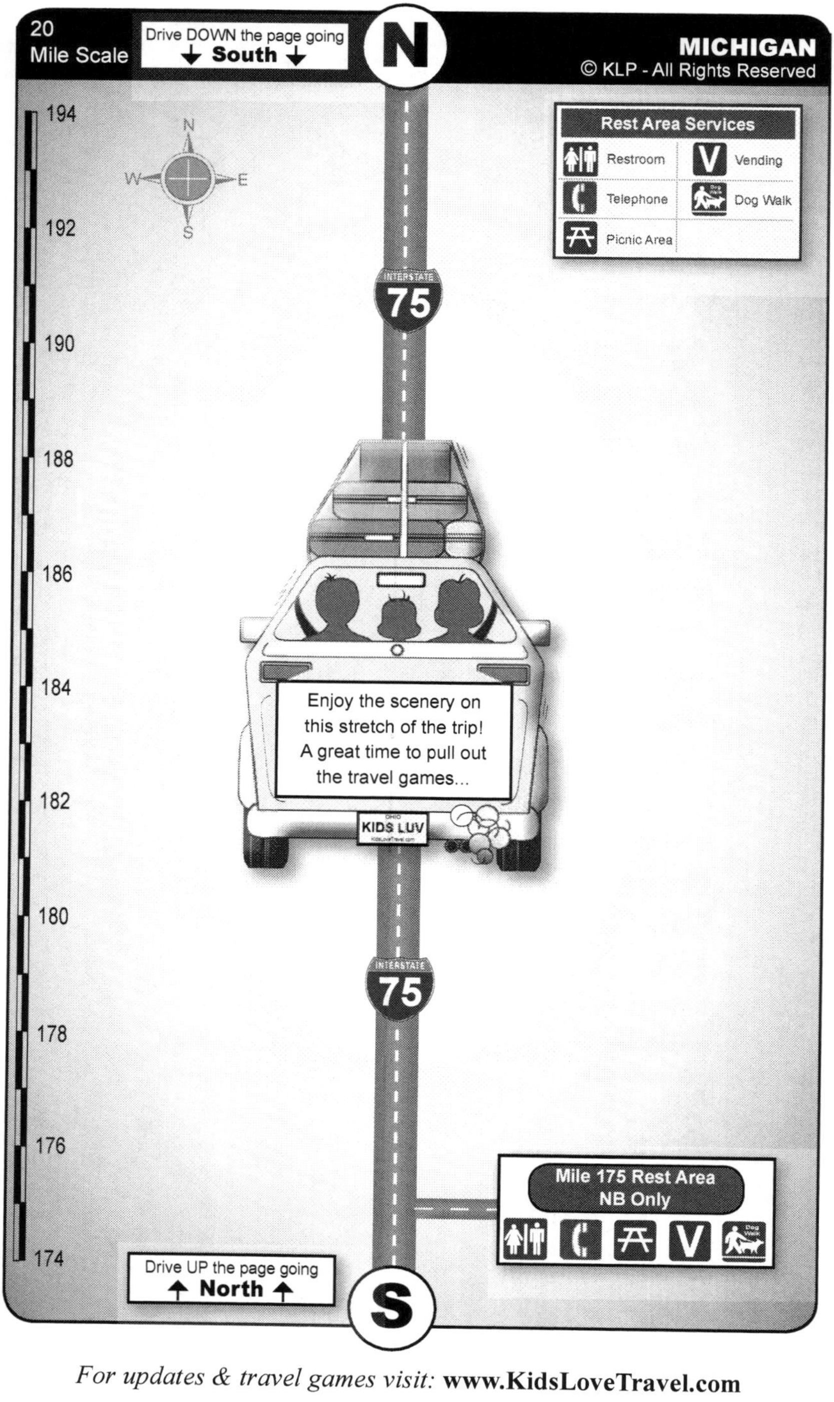
20
Mile Scale
Drive DOWN the page going
South
N
MICHIGAN
© KLP - All Rights Reserved
Rest Area Services
Restroom
Vending
Telephone
Dog Walk
Picnic Area
194
192
190
188
186
184
182
180
178
176
174
75
Enjoy the scenery on
this stretch of the trip!
A great time to pull out
the travel games...
KIDS LUV
Mile 175 Rest Area
NB Only
Drive UP the page going
North
S

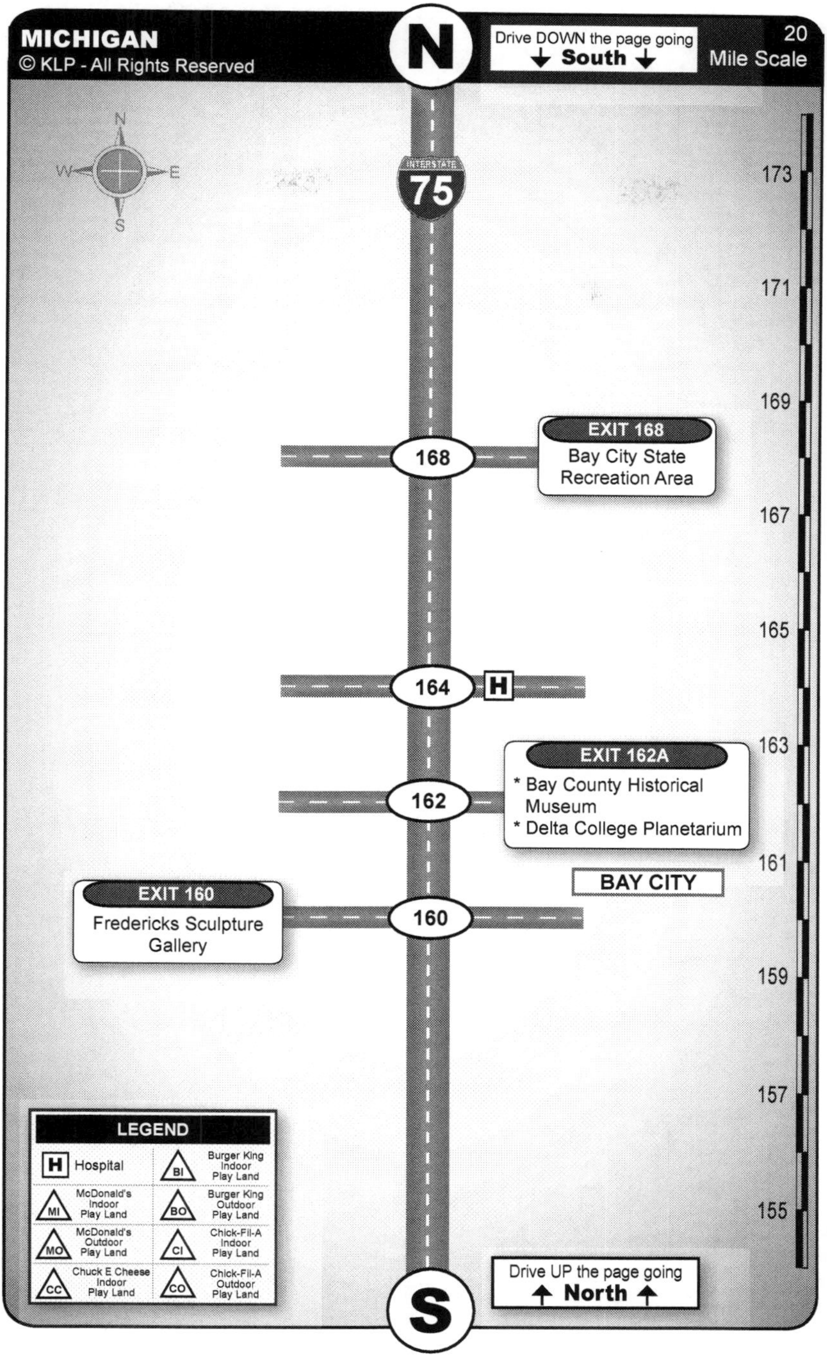
MICHIGAN
© KLP - All Rights Reserved
N
Drive DOWN the page going
South
20
Mile Scale
N
W
E
S
INTERSTATE
75
173
171
169
EXIT 168
Bay City State
Recreation Area
168
167
165
164
H
163
EXIT 162A
* Bay County Historical
Museum
* Delta College Planetarium
162
161
BAY CITY
EXIT 160
Fredericks Sculpture
Gallery
160
159
157
155
LEGEND
H Hospital
BI Burger King Indoor Play Land
MI McDonald's Indoor Play Land
BO Burger King Outdoor Play Land
MO McDonald's Outdoor Play Land
CI Chick-Fil-A Indoor Play Land
CC Chuck E Cheese Indoor Play Land
CO Chick-Fil-A Outdoor Play Land
Drive UP the page going
North
S

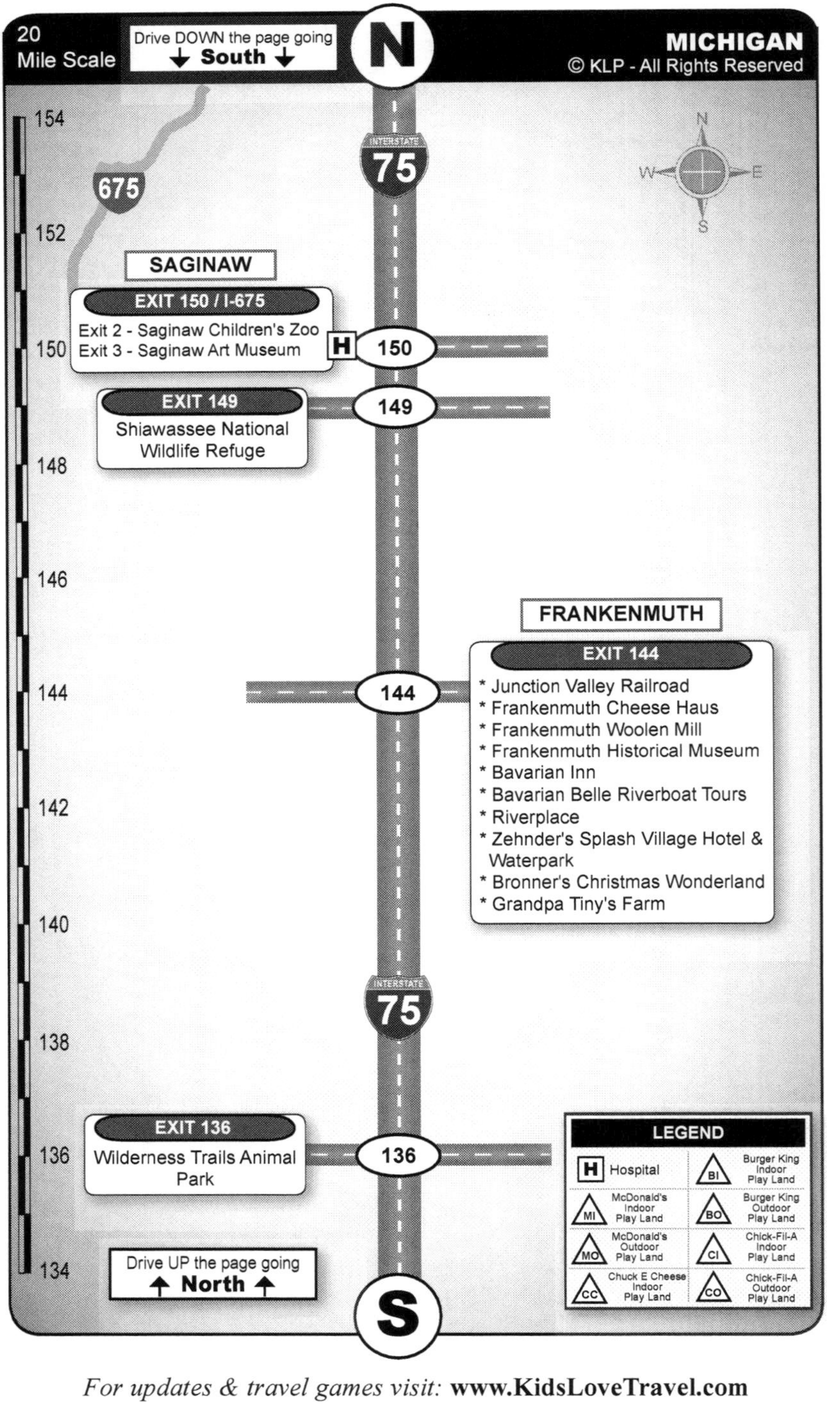
20
Mile Scale
Drive DOWN the page going
South
N
MICHIGAN
© KLP - All Rights Reserved
154
152
150
148
146
144
142
140
138
136
134
675
75
SAGINAW
EXIT 150 / I-675
Exit 2 - Saginaw Children's Zoo
Exit 3 - Saginaw Art Museum
H
150
EXIT 149
Shiawassee National Wildlife Refuge
149
FRANKENMUTH
EXIT 144
* Junction Valley Railroad
* Frankenmuth Cheese Haus
* Frankenmuth Woolen Mill
* Frankenmuth Historical Museum
* Bavarian Inn
* Bavarian Belle Riverboat Tours
* Riverplace
* Zehnder's Splash Village Hotel & Waterpark
* Bronner's Christmas Wonderland
* Grandpa Tiny's Farm
144
EXIT 136
Wilderness Trails Animal Park
136
LEGEND
H Hospital
BI Burger King Indoor Play Land
MI McDonald's Indoor Play Land
BO Burger King Outdoor Play Land
MO McDonald's Outdoor Play Land
CI Chick-Fil-A Indoor Play Land
CC Chuck E Cheese Indoor Play Land
CO Chick-Fil-A Outdoor Play Land
Drive UP the page going
North
S

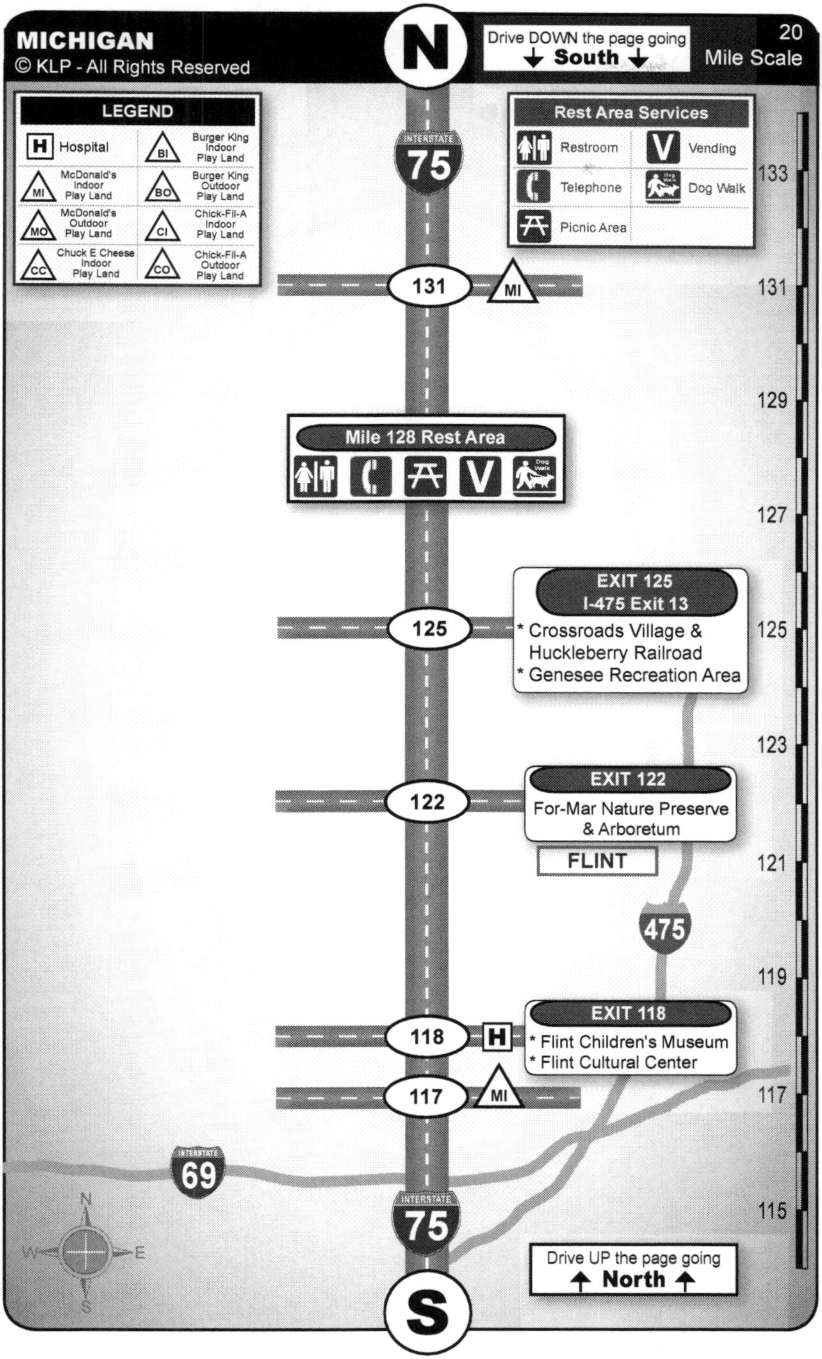
MICHIGAN
© KLP - All Rights Reserved
N
Drive DOWN the page going
South
20
Mile Scale
LEGEND
H Hospital
BI Burger King Indoor Play Land
MI McDonald's Indoor Play Land
BO Burger King Outdoor Play Land
MO McDonald's Outdoor Play Land
CI Chick-Fil-A Indoor Play Land
CC Chuck E Cheese Indoor Play Land
CO Chick-Fil-A Outdoor Play Land
Rest Area Services
Restroom
Vending
Telephone
Dog Walk
Picnic Area
INTERSTATE 75
133
131
MI
129
Mile 128 Rest Area
127
EXIT 125
I-475 Exit 13
* Crossroads Village & Huckleberry Railroad
* Genesee Recreation Area
125
123
EXIT 122
For-Mar Nature Preserve & Arboretum
122
FLINT
121
475
119
EXIT 118
* Flint Children's Museum
* Flint Cultural Center
118
H
117
MI
INTERSTATE 69
INTERSTATE 75
115
N
W
E
S
Drive UP the page going
North
S

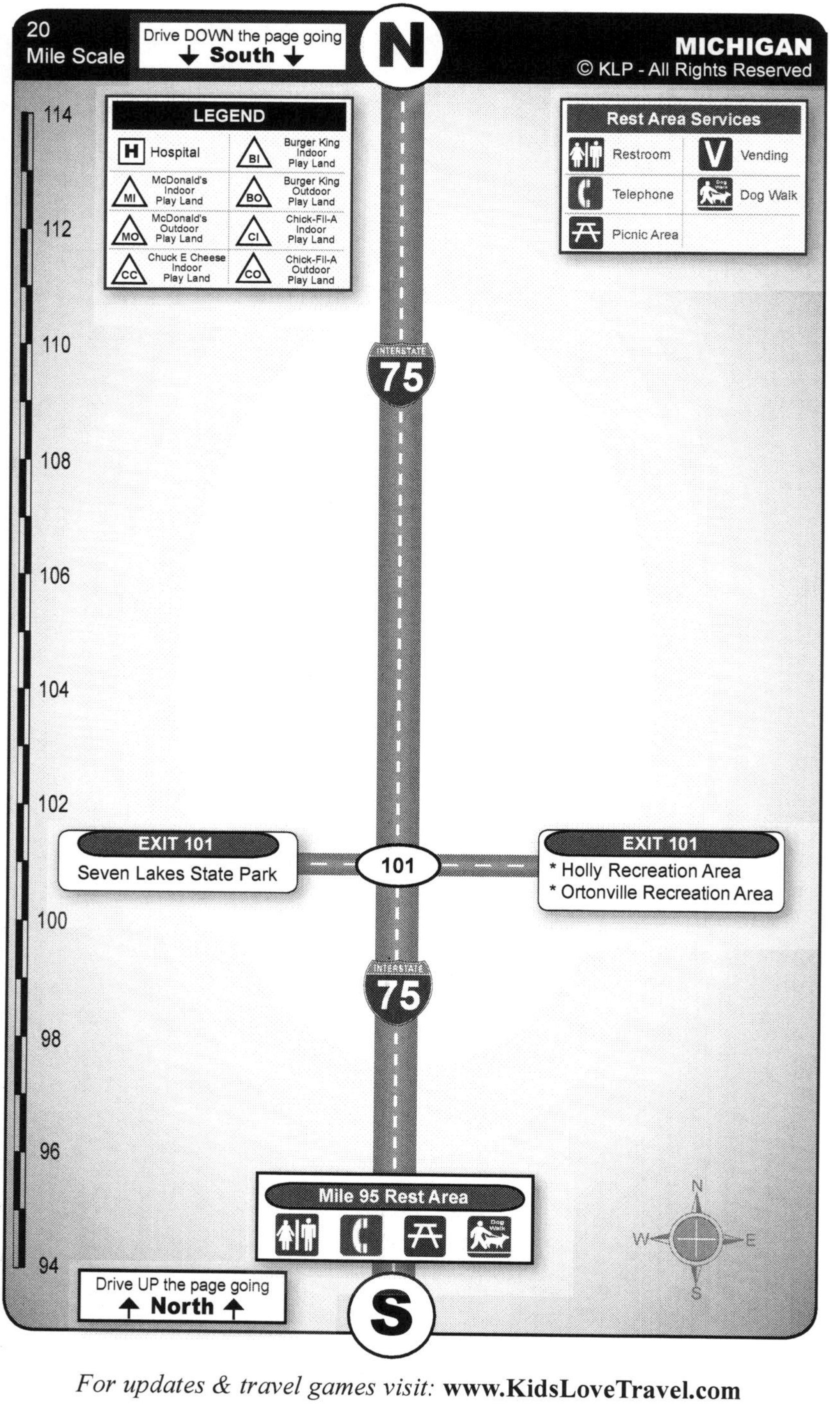
20 Mile Scale
Drive DOWN the page going South
N
MICHIGAN
© KLP - All Rights Reserved
114
112
110
108
106
104
102
100
98
96
94
LEGEND
H Hospital
BI Burger King Indoor Play Land
MI McDonald's Indoor Play Land
BO Burger King Outdoor Play Land
MO McDonald's Outdoor Play Land
CI Chick-Fil-A Indoor Play Land
CC Chuck E Cheese Indoor Play Land
CO Chick-Fil-A Outdoor Play Land
Rest Area Services
Restroom
V Vending
Telephone
Dog Walk
Picnic Area
INTERSTATE 75
EXIT 101
Seven Lakes State Park
101
EXIT 101
* Holly Recreation Area
* Ortonville Recreation Area
INTERSTATE 75
Mile 95 Rest Area
N
W
E
S
Drive UP the page going North
S

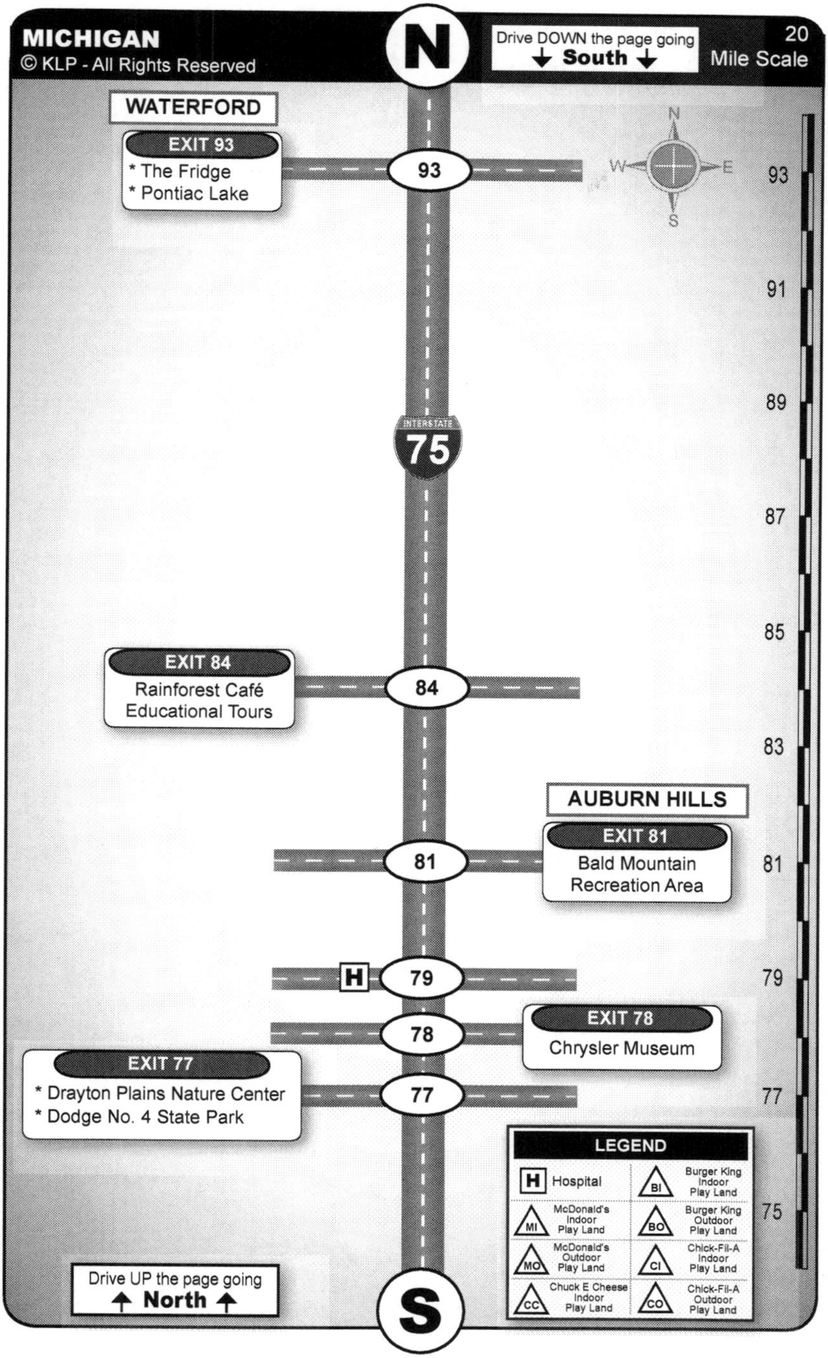
MICHIGAN
© KLP - All Rights Reserved
N
Drive DOWN the page going
South
20
Mile Scale
WATERFORD
EXIT 93
* The Fridge
* Pontiac Lake
93
N
W
E
S
93
91
89
INTERSTATE
75
87
85
EXIT 84
Rainforest Café
Educational Tours
84
83
AUBURN HILLS
EXIT 81
Bald Mountain
Recreation Area
81
81
H
79
79
78
EXIT 78
Chrysler Museum
EXIT 77
* Drayton Plains Nature Center
* Dodge No. 4 State Park
77
77
LEGEND
H Hospital
BI Burger King Indoor Play Land
MI McDonald's Indoor Play Land
BO Burger King Outdoor Play Land
MO McDonald's Outdoor Play Land
CI Chick-Fil-A Indoor Play Land
CC Chuck E Cheese Indoor Play Land
CO Chick-Fil-A Outdoor Play Land
75
Drive UP the page going
North
S

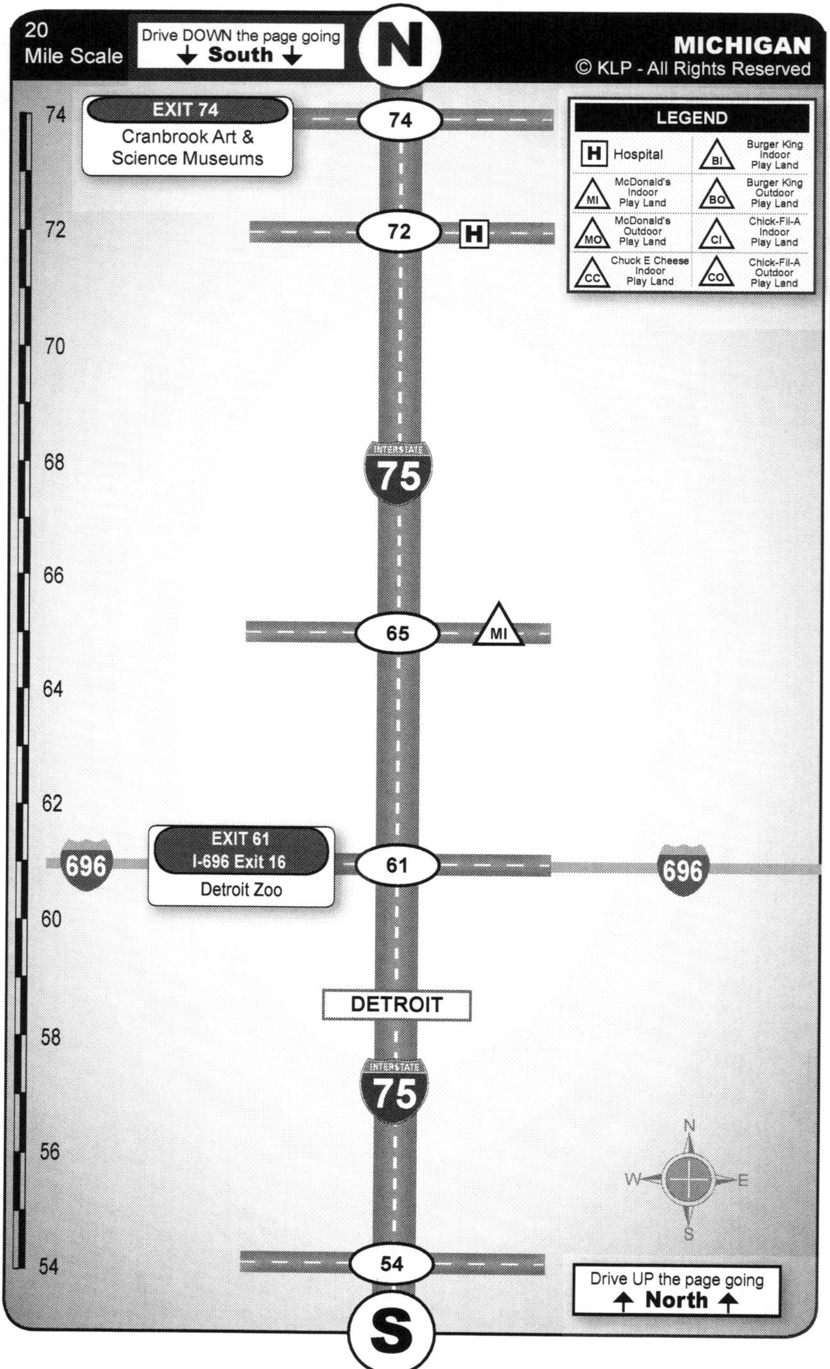
20
Mile Scale
Drive DOWN the page going
South
N
MICHIGAN
© KLP - All Rights Reserved
LEGEND
Hospital
Burger King Indoor Play Land
McDonald's Indoor Play Land
Burger King Outdoor Play Land
McDonald's Outdoor Play Land
Chick-Fil-A Indoor Play Land
Chuck E Cheese Indoor Play Land
Chick-Fil-A Outdoor Play Land
EXIT 74
Cranbrook Art & Science Museums
74
72
H
70
68
75
66
65
MI
64
62
EXIT 61
I-696 Exit 16
Detroit Zoo
61
696
60
DETROIT
58
56
54
Drive UP the page going
North
S

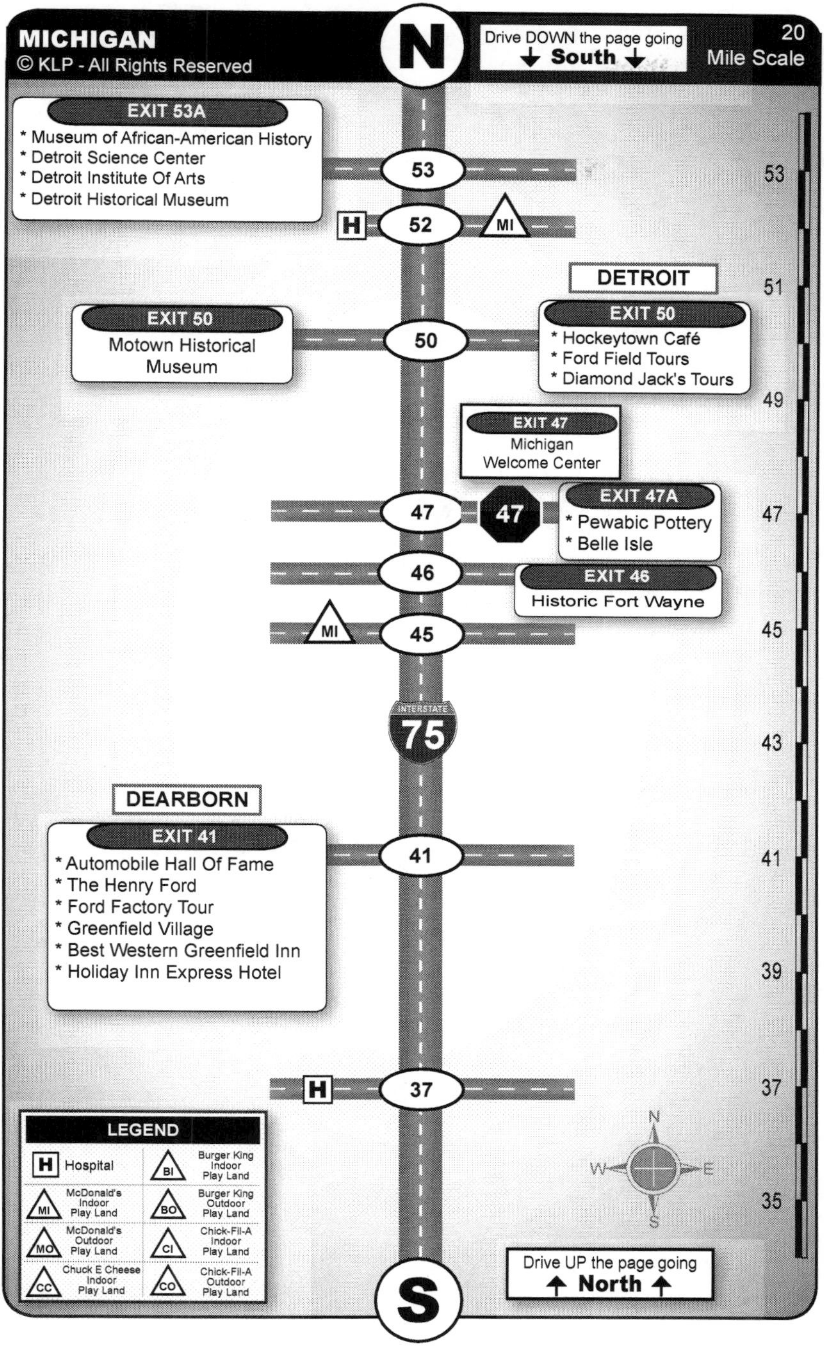
MICHIGAN
© KLP - All Rights Reserved
N
Drive DOWN the page going ↓ South ↓
20 Mile Scale
EXIT 53A
* Museum of African-American History
* Detroit Science Center
* Detroit Institute Of Arts
* Detroit Historical Museum
53
H
52
MI
DETROIT
EXIT 50
Motown Historical Museum
50
EXIT 50
* Hockeytown Café
* Ford Field Tours
* Diamond Jack's Tours
EXIT 47
Michigan Welcome Center
47
47
EXIT 47A
* Pewabic Pottery
* Belle Isle
46
EXIT 46
Historic Fort Wayne
MI
45
INTERSTATE 75
DEARBORN
EXIT 41
* Automobile Hall Of Fame
* The Henry Ford
* Ford Factory Tour
* Greenfield Village
* Best Western Greenfield Inn
* Holiday Inn Express Hotel
41
H
37
53
51
49
47
45
43
41
39
37
35
LEGEND
H Hospital
BI Burger King Indoor Play Land
MI McDonald's Indoor Play Land
BO Burger King Outdoor Play Land
MO McDonald's Outdoor Play Land
CI Chick-Fil-A Indoor Play Land
CC Chuck E Cheese Indoor Play Land
CO Chick-Fil-A Outdoor Play Land
N
W
E
S
Drive UP the page going ↑ North ↑
S

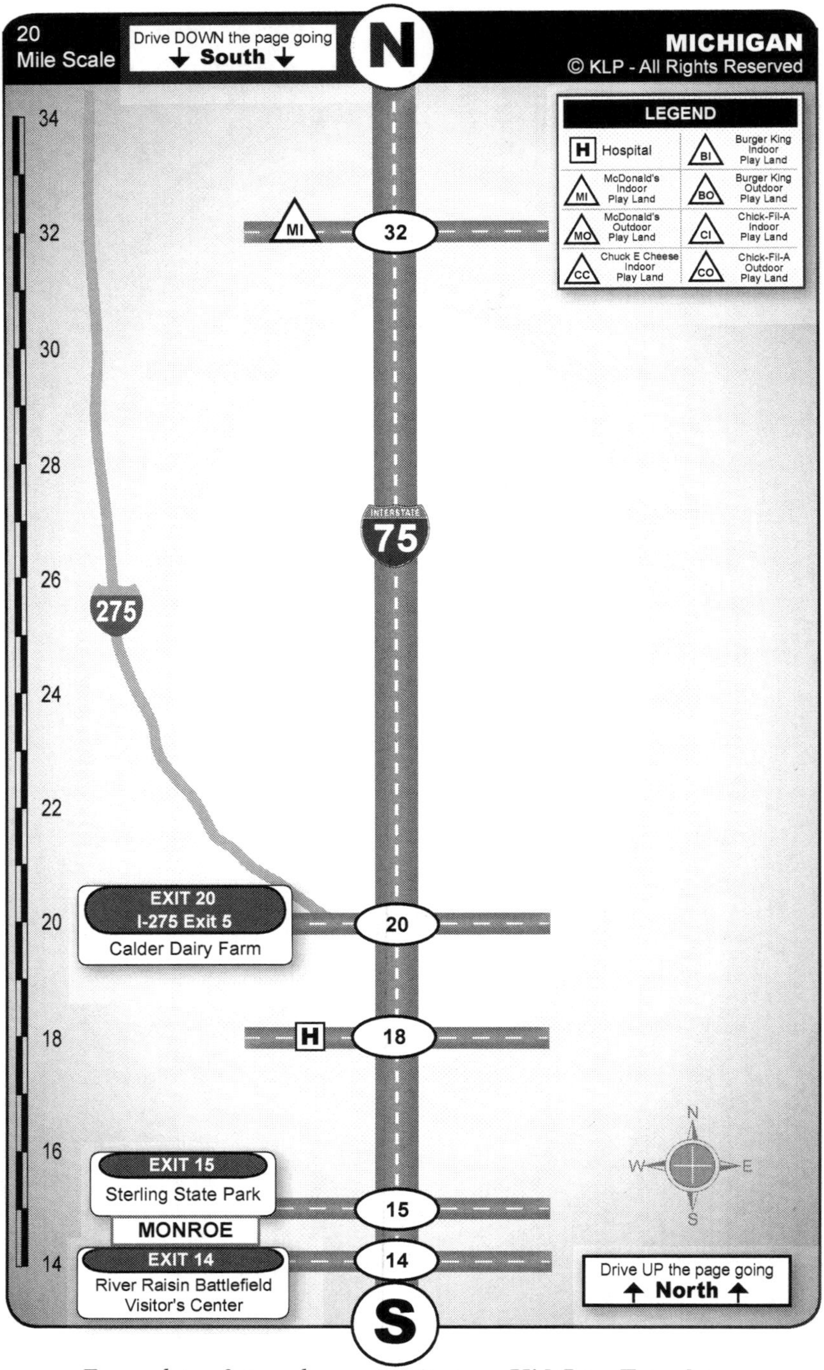
20
Mile Scale
Drive DOWN the page going
South
N
MICHIGAN
© KLP - All Rights Reserved
LEGEND
H Hospital
BI Burger King Indoor Play Land
MI McDonald's Indoor Play Land
BO Burger King Outdoor Play Land
MO McDonald's Outdoor Play Land
CI Chick-Fil-A Indoor Play Land
CC Chuck E Cheese Indoor Play Land
CO Chick-Fil-A Outdoor Play Land
34
32
MI
32
30
28
INTERSTATE 75
26
275
24
22
EXIT 20
I-275 Exit 5
Calder Dairy Farm
20
20
18
H
18
16
EXIT 15
Sterling State Park
15
MONROE
14
EXIT 14
River Raisin Battlefield Visitor's Center
14
N
W
E
S
Drive UP the page going
North
S

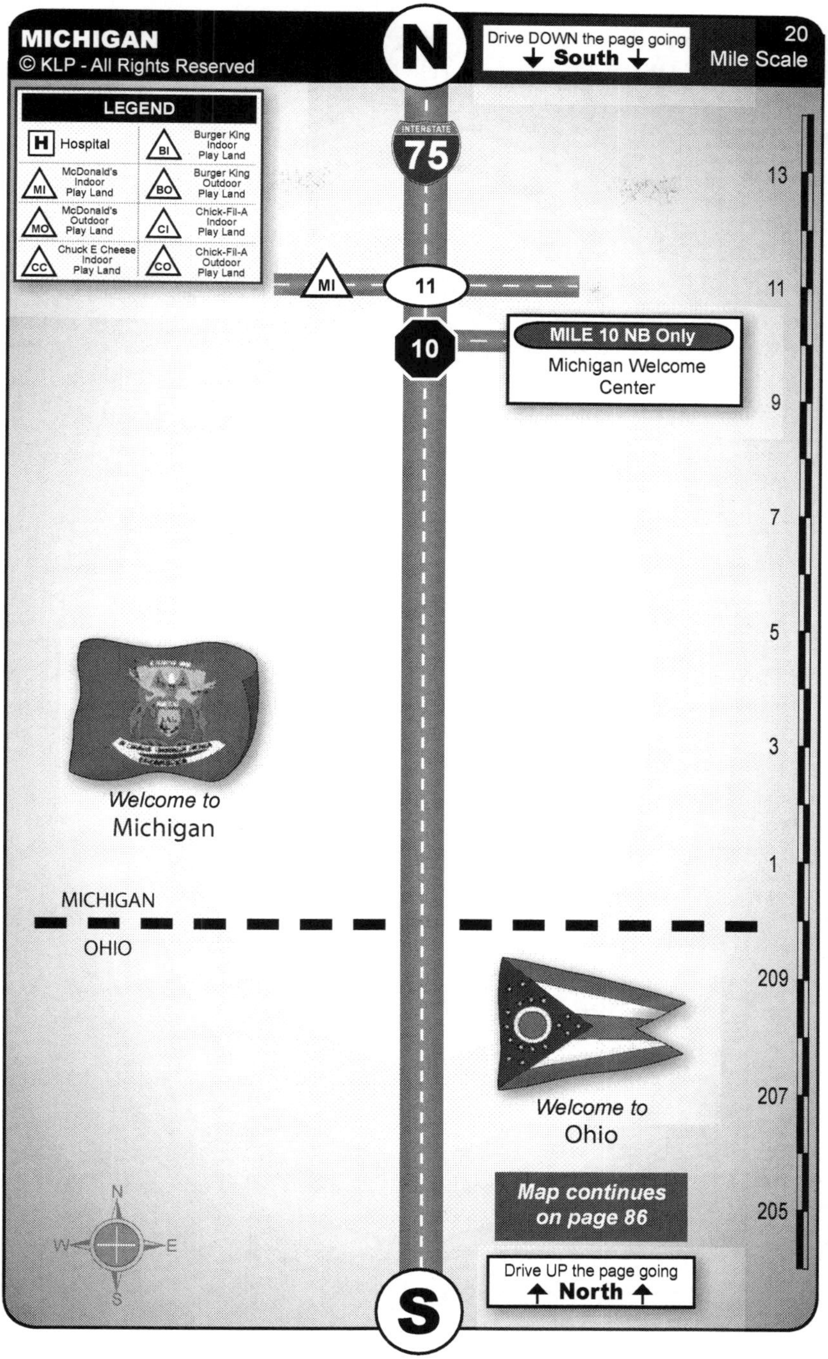
MICHIGAN
© KLP - All Rights Reserved
N
Drive DOWN the page going
South
20
Mile Scale
LEGEND
H Hospital
BI Burger King Indoor Play Land
MI McDonald's Indoor Play Land
BO Burger King Outdoor Play Land
MO McDonald's Outdoor Play Land
CI Chick-Fil-A Indoor Play Land
CC Chuck E Cheese Indoor Play Land
CO Chick-Fil-A Outdoor Play Land
INTERSTATE
75
13
MI
11
11
10
MILE 10 NB Only
Michigan Welcome Center
9
7
5
3
Welcome to Michigan
1
MICHIGAN
OHIO
209
207
Welcome to Ohio
Map continues on page 86
205
N
W
E
S
Drive UP the page going
North
S

Sites and attractions are listed in order by Exit Number (North to South) and distance from the exit (closest are listed first). Symbols indicated represent:

Restaurants Lodging

Exit - 394 (west of I-75)

MICHIGAN WELCOME CENTER (FAR NORTH)

Sault Ste. Marie - ***(I-75 exit 394, turn right onto Portage Avenue) 49783. Emergency Contact Number: (906) 632-8242. www.michigan.org/welcome-centers/default.aspx. Hours: Open year round, 9:00am-5:00pm. During summer travel season, these hours will be extended to meet demands of the season. Restroom facilities are open 24 hours a day.***

This site has public restrooms, pet walk areas, picnic areas, public phones, weather updates and tourism information.

Exit - 394 (east of I-75)

SOO LOCKS PARK

Sault Ste. Marie - ***Downtown. 312 W Portage Avenue (Within view of International Bridge. Follow signs off I-75) 49783. www.saultstemarie.com/soo-locks-46/. Phone: (906) 253-9290. Hours: Daily 9:00am-9:00pm (mid-May to mid-October). Admission: FREE. Note: Run by the US Army Corp of Engineers. Theater showing film on history of operations. Online cam views of the lock.***

HUGE freighters pass through here everyday...

The highlights at Soo Locks Park are:

OBSERVATION PLATFORM - 2nd level or Riverside view of the locks. It's unbelievable how actual freight ships move precisely into concrete locks and then are lowered or raised to the level of the next part of the lake. How do they do it? (Learn how...and they do not use pumps). Now the longest in the world, they are still the largest waterway traffic system on earth. A public address system lets visitors know which vessels are coming through the locks and what their size, cargo, nationality and destination are. You would have to sign on-board as a crew member to get any closer than this. A beautiful, multi-colored lighted fountain, surrounded by park benches is found here as well. The fountain and lights dance in time to background music providing a pleasant backdrop to this gorgeous park. Dress appropriately for weather outside because you'll want to watch the large freighters rise up in the water before your eyes!

WORKING MODEL OF A LOCK (with real water moving a model boat) is inside the museum building and best to watch before outdoor viewing.

TOWER OF HISTORY

Sault Ste. Marie - ***326 East Portage Avenue (I-75 exit 394 into downtown along waterfront) 49783. www.saultstemarie.com/tower-of-history-416/. Phone: (906) 632-3658. Hours: Daily 10:00am-5:00pm (mid-May to mid-October). Admission: $7 adult, $3.50 child (5-17).***

A 21-story tower offering a panoramic view of the Soo Locks, the St. Mary's River Rapids, and many historical homes. The tower museum has Native American artifacts and a video show depicting the history of the Great Lakes and Sault Ste. Marie. The Lower Level features museum exhibits. The Upper Level, in addition to the view, features descriptions of the surrounding area. You ride to the top by elevator.

RIVER OF HISTORY MUSEUM

Sault Ste. Marie - ***531 Ashmun Street (I-75 exit 394 into downtown along waterfront) 49783. Phone: (906) 632-1999. www.riverofhistory.org. Hours: Monday-Saturday 11:00am-5:00pm (mid-May to mid-October). Admission: $3.50-$7.00 (age 6+).***

St. Mary's River history through exhibit galleries of sight and sound. Join the River as she tells her story of the events she has witnessed, people she has met, and changes wrought along her shores and waters. Follow Chippewa Indians to French fur traders to modern industry. Kids can step into a French fur trader's cabin and try on clothes and other hands-on items. Trip motion sensors activate spoken stories as visitors enter each room. The sound of locks and canals being built is one of the audio enhanced exhibits.

Exit - 394 (east of I-75)

MUSEUM SHIP VALLEY CAMP

Sault Ste. Marie - ***501 East Water Street (I-75 exit 394 into downtown along waterfront, east of locks) 49783. www.saulthistoricsites.com/museum-ship-valley-camp/ Phone: (906) 632-3658 or (888) 744-7867. Hours: Daily 10:00am-5:00pm (mid-May to mid-October). Admission: $13.00 adult, $7 child (5-17).***

Walk-in tours are offered of the 1917 steam powered freighter containing the world's largest Great Lakes maritime museum. Many come to see the Edmund Fitzgerald Exhibit - two lifeboats from the actual boat along with multimedia shows of the tragic event. Several mechanical (dormant) parts of the ship are touchable. A long aquarium is along one wall with marine life found in the area. After seeing the large freighters and their crew go through the locks, kids will love to see an actual ship's pilot house, dining rooms and crew's quarters.

SOO LOCKS BOAT TOURS

Sault Ste. Marie - ***Dock #1: 1157 E. Portage Ave; Dock #2: 515 E. Portage Ave. (I-75 exit 394 into downtown along waterfront) 49783. Phone: (906) 632-6301 or (800) 432-6301. www.soolocks.com. Hours: Daily 9:00am-4:30pm (mid-May to early-October). Later hours on summer weekends. Admission: $26.00 adult, $11 child (5-12).***

While watching the ships go through the locks and enjoying the park is fun, it's much more thrilling to actually go THROUGH the locks on a ship. On the Soo Locks Tour, you'll be in for a two-hour live narrated excursion that will actually take you through the Locks, right alongside the big freighters. Your tour boat will ride the water as it is raised twenty-one feet, straight up, to the level of Lake Superior. You will then cruise under the International Bridge and railroad bridge before crossing into Canadian waters where you'll see one of Canada's largest steel plants in operation. You will return to the lower harbor through the historic "newly restored" Canadian Lock and cruise past the St. Mary's Rapids.

See HUGE freighters...up close!

Exit - 348 (west of I-75)

CASTLE ROCK

St. Ignace - ***N2690 Castle Rock Road (I-75 to exit 348) 49781. Phone: (906) 643-8268. www.castlerockmi.com Hours: Daily 9:00am-9:00pm. (early May to mid-October) Admission: 50 cents to climb the rock trails.***

See and climb (189 steps) the legendary Castle Rock (a limestone "sea stack" - nearly 200 feet tall) that Native Americans once used as a lookout. Be sure to check out Paul Bunyan and Babe! A great piece of history and what a view for a half dollar! There are lots of Native American gifts in the shop below. This is a difficult climb, aerobically, so take your time and don't plan on carrying the kids up...everyone will have to climb the stairs on their own (you'll feel like "Rocky" when you reach the top)! Don't worry, the walk down is much easier.

Exit - 345 (east of I-75)

MUSEUM OF OJIBWA CULTURE

St. Ignace - ***500-566 North State Street (I-75 exit 345 at the north end of the boardwalk, downtown, across from waterfront) 49781. Phone: (906) 643-9161. www.museumofojibwaculture.net Hours: Daily 9:00am-5:00pm (Memorial weekend - October). Admission: $1.00-$2.00 general, $5.00 family. Note: Native American Museum Store. Marquette Mission Park adjacent is supposed site of grave of missionary Father Marquette and also site of archeological discoveries.***

The museum is housed in Father Marquette's French Jesuit Mission Church and dedicated to his focus on Ojibwa Indians, the first inhabitants of this region. Learn traditions of the peoples through an 8-minute video presentation, dioramas of an Ojibwa family network, and frequent demonstrations by Native American interpreters (esp. outside in the giant longhouse or the realistic teepee with weaved bark mats). There is a "kid-sized" longhouse indoors where kids can play, then walk diagonally over to the Interactive Kids Area: color drawings of Ojibwa symbols or make a paper canoe or scroll stories. The easy to follow descriptions and activities really help you understand their way of life, they often relate it to modern life.

Exit - 344 (west of I-75)

DEER RANCH

St. Ignace - ***1540 US Highway 2 West (US 2, 4 miles west of Big Mac Bridge) 49781. Phone: (906) 643-7760. www.deerranch.com. Admission: $4.50 (age 4+)***

Gift Shop featuring Deer skin products including many sizes of moccasins. They have a nature trail where you can feed and photograph native Michigan Whitetail Deer and fawns. (May-October)

MYSTERY SPOT

St. Ignace - ***150 Martin Lake Road (US-2 West, 5 miles west of Mackinac Bridge) 49781. Phone: (906) 643-8322. www.mysteryspotstignace.com. Hours: Daily 9:00am-dusk (mid May - mid October). Admission: $6.00-$8.00 per activity (age 5+). Add $20 for Zipline.***

O.K. - Illusion or reality? Reality or illusion? That's up for you to decide, but one thing's for sure…you'll sure have fun doing it. See the laws of physics as we know them…and why they don't apply to the "Mystery Spot". The kids will love this science lesson. There's also mini-golf, new ziplines, and a maze on the premises.

Mile - 344 (east of I-75)

MICHIGAN WELCOME CENTER

St. Ignace - ***(I-75 mile marker 344, Just past toll booths on north east side of bridge) 49781. Emergency Contact Number: (906) 643-6979. www.michigan.org/welcome-centers/default.aspx. Hours: Open year round, 9:00am-5:00pm. During summer travel season, these hours will be extended to meet demands of the season. Restroom facilities will be open 24 hours a day.***

This site has public restrooms, pet walk areas, picnic areas, public phones, weather updates and tourism information.

Exit - 344 (take ferry) (east of I-75)

MACKINAC ISLAND FERRY SERVICES

Mackinaw Island - ***(Stops/Dock Pickups are clearly marked in either St. Ignace or Mac city) 49757.***

Call for season schedules. Rain or shine. (early May - mid to late October). Note: Budget $23.00 for adults, about 1/2 price for kids. Save $1.00-$2.00

with online prices. (Round Trip)

- **ARNOLD LINE FERRY**. (800) 542-8528 or www.arnoldline.com. Smooth trips, large ships, comfortable seats and cabins. Restrooms.
- **SHEPLER'S FERRY**. (800) 828-6157 or www.sheplersferry.com. Fast trips with very courteous and efficient staff. Restrooms. Narrative on the way over.
- **STAR LINE FERRY**. (800) 638-9892 or www.mackinacferry.com. Newest fleet. Most scheduled daily departures. Restrooms.

MACKINAC ISLAND CARRIAGE TOURS

Mackinac Island - ***(Across from Arnold Ferry Dock - Main Street, Downtown) 49757. Phone: (906) 847-3307. www.mict.com. Hours: Daily 9:00am-5:00pm (mid - June - Labor Day). Daily 9:00am-4:00pm (mid-May to mid-June and Labor Day to October 1st). Daily 9:00am-3:00pm (rest of October). Admission: $28 adult, $11 child (5-12). Tours: 1 hour & 45 minutes. You also have on/off privileges at several "hot spots".***

Step Back In Time...
Since motor vehicles aren't permitted on the Island, this is one fun way to leisurely see the sites. It keeps the island quaint to hear the clip-clop sound of carriages - we think you'll agree!

It's guaranteed you'll hear amusing stories of the history (past & present) of the island. The multi-seated carriages stop at all of these highlights: Arch Rock (which story of formation do you believe?), Skull Cave, the Governor's Mansion, Grand Hotel, Fort Mackinac, Surrey Hill shops and snacks (including Wings of Mackinac Butterfly House), and the horse's stable area. Look for several "parking lots" full of bikes and carriages! We recommend this tour on your first trip to the island.

Exit-344 (take ferry) (east of I-75)

MACKINAC ISLAND STATE PARK

Mackinac Island - ***(at docks, head southeast one block, downtown) 49757. Phone: (906) 847-3328. www.mackinacparks.com. Hours: Park open 24/7. Visitors Center open every season 9:00am-4:00pm, except winter. Admission: FREE for center. Tours of historic homes require fee of $3.00-$5.00 (age 5+). Tours: Summers- guided tours w/ costumed interpreters. Beaumont Memorial (dedicated to the studies of human digestion), Blacksmith, Biddle House (crafts), McGulpin House, Indian Dorm are off premises but part of package fee in the summer. Many archeological digs take place every few years.***

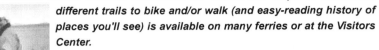

Note: Visitors Center located downtown on waterfront. Maps of numerous different trails to bike and/or walk (and easy-reading history of places you'll see) is available on many ferries or at the Visitors Center.

Most of Mackinac Island is preserved as a state park. Stretching eight miles around the island's perimeter, M-185 is a scenic shoreline road and the nation's only state highway without motor vehicle traffic. There are 70 miles of roads and trails within Mackinac Island State Park, most of which are wooded inland trails for hikers, bikers and horseback riders in spring, summer and fall. There are 1,800 acres under canopies of cedars, birches and crossings of creatures like butterflies. The prehistoric geological formations, Arch Rock and Sugar Loaf, are natural limestone wonders that tower over the Straits. These can be viewed from below on biking trails or from a walking overview. Fort Holmes features a panoramic view of the Fort Mackinac and the Straits of Mackinac at the island's highest point - 320 feet above Lake Level. Look for historic caves and nature trails around most every turn.

FORT MACKINAC STATE HISTORIC PARK

Mackinac Island - ***(on the bluff above downtown Mackinac Island) 49757. Phone: (906) 847-3328. www.mackinacparks.com. Hours: Daily 9:30am-7pm (early June to Labor Day). Daily until 5pm (May to early June and early September through October). Admission: $12 adult, $7 youth (5-12). Combo tickets for Fort Mac, Colonial Michi and Mill Creek are available at great discounts. Note: Food available at Tea Room (lunch). Pets are welcome.***

Soldier Daniel ready for duty...

Your carriage is greeted by a period dressed soldier inviting strangers to visit. Families will want to see the short audio visual presentation in the Post Commissary Theater. Next, if it's close to the top of the hour, be sure to check out the kid-friendly, wonderfully amusing, cannon firing and rifle firing demonstrations. Maybe volunteer to help the soldiers (check out the funny, pointed hats). The Post Hospital and Officer's Quarters (costumes/hands-on or "Hanging with Harold") and Blockhouses (short narrative by an animatronic figure) will intrigue the kids. In the new exhibit space, Military Medicine, you can hear through a giant stethoscope, visit with a virtual Post Surgeon on rounds, and take a look at a frostbitten foot! On your way in or out of the complex, be sure to visit the Soldier's Barracks exhibits featuring "Mackinac: An Island Famous in These Regions". Mackinac Island history from Furs (touch some) to Fish (step on a dock and listen to the fishermen come into port) to No Cars (1898 law) to Fudge! Oh, by the way, be sure to check and see if your ancestor was a Victorian soldier at Fort Mackinac. Well done, folks.

ORIGINAL BUTTERFLY HOUSE

Mackinac Island - ***1308 McGulpin Street (Huron Street north to Church Street west to McGulpin) 49757. www.originalbutterflyhouse.com. Phone: (906) 847-3972. Hours: 10:00am-7:00pm (Summer), 10:00am-6:00pm (Labor Day- late October). Admission: $9 adult, $4.50 child (4-11).***

See several hundred live butterflies from Asia, Central and South America and the United States in free flight. You will be amazed at the size of the insects that live in the tropical regions of the world. 14" Walking Sticks, and 6" Centipedes along with the world's largest Cicada and Heaviest Bug are on display, while live reptiles and amphibians living in their natural habitats help keep things fun for the kids. Kids of all ages will love the new interactive displays and their "Turtle Adventure Park". A great setting of tropical gardens. One of America's first butterfly houses featured in popular magazines.

Exit - 344 (take ferry) (east of I-75)

GRAND HOTEL

Mackinac Island - ***(from the ferry docks, head west one-half mile). 49757. Phone: (906) 847-3331 or (800) 33-GRAND. www.grandhotel.com.***

At 660 feet, Grand Hotel's Front Porch (full of white rockers) is the world's largest. Self-guided grounds tours are $10.00 per person if not a hotel guest.

Wow...the front porch is over 600 feet long!

The kitchen staff of 100 serves as many as 4,000 meals per day. Their gourmet food is unforgettable! Ask to take a Kitchen Tour to see how they do it. Kids won't believe the large number of plates, pies and potatoes they use. (Kitchen tours by pre-arrangement only or at special events). Recreational activities include: golf, tennis, croquet, bocce ball, swimming (outdoor pool), bicycling, saddle horses, carriage tours, duck pin bowling and a game room.

Children's Programs (day or evening-3 hours) include "kids-style" lunches or dinners and fun group games, arts and crafts or a hike or tour. Rebecca's Playroom is open daily for families to enjoy games, crafts, videos and play when they are not conducting a paid program. Off-peak or special family rates begin at around $400.00 per night (includes full breakfast and five-course dinner and gratuities). Watch the movies "Somewhere in Time" (Christopher Reeve/Jane Seymour) or "This Time for Keeps" (Esther Williams) before your visit to get the feel for the place. If you forget, they have a TV/VCR in every room and a copy of "Somewhere in Time" ready to watch. Remnants of these movies are found throughout the grounds (i.e.. Esther Williams pool or "Is it you?" twin trees). Believe it or not, this place is not stuffy...just casually elegant...best for a special treat or occasion.

WINGS OF MACKINAC

Mackinac Island - ***(Surrey Hill Shops, just past Grand Hotel) 49757. Phone: (906) 847-WING. www.wingsofmackinac.com. Open (mid-May to early October). Admission: $8 adult, $5 child (5-12).***

The all-glass Conservatory holds beautiful lush plants surrounded by hundreds of butterflies, dancing around you to gentle instrumental music. See exotic butterflies from around the world including: White Peacocks, Long-Tailed Skippers, Painted Ladies, Spice Bush Swallowtails, Graphium Decolors, Ruddy Daggerwings, Blue Morphos, Tiger Swallowtails and Monarchs. Curators available to answer questions.

MISSION POINT RESORT

Mackinac Island - ***(from the ferry docks, head southeast one-half mile). 49757. Phone: (906) 847-3312 or (800) 833-7711.. www.missionpoint.com.***

This is truly a "family-friendly" resort and with the features they keep adding... it's a destination to stay at for a few days. You can just hang out around the grounds with amenities like: outdoor heated pool, tennis, croquet, horseshoes, video arcade/game room and lawn bowling. Or, sign up for a one hour Island sail or Ferry tour. Now, rent bikes or in-line skates and explore the 8 mile Island trail. They have four eateries and kids 12 & under eat FREE (most restaurants). They have hayrides, picnic games, poolside bingo and Sundae parties, too. Probably the best feature is their children's program: Mac The Moose Kid's Club, open to all youngsters ages 12 and under. Character meets, parties and tuck-in services are available for a fee. The Discovery

Club Center has themes like "Space Day", "Nature Day", "Under the Sea", or "Wild West Day". They have a Tweeners club, too (ages 11-14). Rates: Start at $149.00 per night. Open May - October.

Exit - 343 (east of I-75)

STRAITS STATE PARK

***St. Ignace** - 720 Church Street (I-75, exit 343 onto Graham, right on Church) 49781. Phone: (906) 643-8620. www.michigan.gov/straits. Season: March - October. Admission: $6.00-$8.00 per vehicle.*

Great views from an observation platform of the Mackinac Bridge and the Straits of Mackinac. A hiking trail runs through the park. One end has a viewing platform with an overlook of the Straits of Mackinac and Mackinac Bridge. The other end has a different view of the Mackinac Bridge. Camping/mini-cabins, picnicking, boating, fishing, swimming and winter sports. A visitor's center highlights Father Marquette exploration in the area.

The FATHER MARQUETTE NATIONAL MEMORIAL tells the story of that 17th-century missionary-explorer and the meeting of French and Native American cultures deep in the North American wilderness. Explore the National Memorial and an outdoor interpretive trail. (access to the Memorial is free, it is not necessary to pay the vehicle admission fee to view it)

Exit - 339 (west of I-75)

COLONIAL MICHILIMACKINAC STATE HISTORIC PARK

***Mackinaw City** - 102 Straits Ave (Downtown under the south side of Mackinac Bridge - Exit 339 off I-75) 49701. Phone: (231) 436-5563. www.mackinacparks.com. Hours: Daily 9:00am-5:00pm (May to early October). Extended hours until 7:00pm (mid-June to Labor Day). Admission: $11 adult, $6.50 youth (5-17). Combo tickets for Fort Mac, Colonial Michi and Mill Creek are available at great discounts. Note: Many festivals are held here including encampments and Colonial weddings. Pets are welcome.*

"Join the Redcoats. Watch a Dig. Dance a Jig". In the Summer, costumed docents (in character) demonstrate musket /cannon firing, cooking, blacksmithing, barracks living, church life, and trading. Pies cook near fireplaces, chickens roam free, and an amusing soldier leads you on a tour of the village. Originally occupied by the French, then the British, even the Indians - an audiovisual program will explain the details. Archeological digs are held in the summer to look for ongoing significant finds. What you see today is a reconstruction of how the fortified village appeared in the 1770s. Be sure to check out the updated "Treasure From the Sand" exhibit as it takes you to a unique underground tunnel display of subterranean artifacts recovered. In the Soldiers Barracks hands-on building: Dress up, stir the pot, lie in a bunk, try on coats, play a game or go into the "Black Hole" - a dark "time-out". Many areas of this park engage the kids interest - how cool to play in a real fort!

Exit - 339 (east of I-75)

OLD MACKINAC POINT LIGHTHOUSE

Mackinaw City - ***(just east of the Colonial Michilimackinac Visitor's Center in Mackinaw City near the south end of the Mackinac Bridge) 49701. Phone: (231) 436-4100. www.MackinacParks.com. Hours: Daily 9:00am-4:30pm (May to mid-October). Extended until 5:30pm in summer. Admission: $7.50 adult, $4.50 youth (5-17). Combo tickets for Fort Mac, Colonial Michi and Mill Creek are available at great discounts. Tours: Tours to the top of the lighthouse tower are available. The climb is about 4 stories via 51 steps and an 11-rung, vertical ladder through a narrow access opening. You should be over 4 feet tall and wear shoes that have no chance of falling off your feet while climbing the stairs and ladder (no bare feet or flip-flops). Note: Pets are welcome on the park grounds.***

Visitors will see original artifacts from the station, including the brass and glass Fresnel lens that lit the Straits of Mackinac for more than 60 years. Built in 1892, the light guided ships through the dangerous straits until the navigation lights from the Mackinac Bridge rendered it obsolete. Take a peek at the restored, fully furnished kitchen of the keeper's dwelling in its 1910 appearance. Hands-on exhibits let you test your nighttime navigation skills, light up a miniature Fresnel lens, and try on a lighthouse keeper's clothing. Guides in historic costumes are stationed within the lighthouse to provide historical information, conduct tours of the grounds and lead small groups up the tower. Enjoy a panoramic view of the Mackinac Straits with unique photographic perspectives of the Mackinac Bridge and Mackinac Island.

MACKINAC BRIDGE MUSEUM AND "MIGHTY MAC" BRIDGE

Mackinaw City - ***231 East Central Avenue (Downtown within view of bridge) 49701. www.mackinacbridge.org and www.facebook.com/MamaMiasMackinaw Phone: (231) 436-5534. Hours: Daily 8:00am-Midnight (May-October). Bridge open 24 hours. FREEBIES: www.mackinacbridge.org/kids-corner-35/ has coloring and puzzle pages.***

Go to the upstairs museum at Mama Mia's Pizza (donations only). Watch the all new digitally re-mastered movie covering the history and construction of the Mackinac Bridge back in the mid-1950's. Why build the longest bridge ever - the "bridge that couldn't be built"? When you see the black & white photos of the long lines, staging cars to get on ferry boats to cross over the lake to the Upper Peninsula, you'll see the reason. On display, are the original spinning wheels that spun and ran cable (41,000 miles of it!) across the bridge; the original wrench (9-10 feet long) used to tighten anchor bolts on the towers; and most interesting, the hard hats of the numerous iron workers. Now, pay the $2.50 toll and cross the 5 mile long steel super-structure! P.S. On a windy day the bridge bows or swings out to the east or west as much as 20 feet!

A mega-bridge that is 5 miles long - wow!

Exit - 339 (east of I-75)

MACKINAW TROLLEY TOURS

Mackinaw City - ***(pickup at hotels downtown) 49701. Phone: (231) 436-7812. www.mackinactrolley.com. Tours: off peak season general transport tours of the city only: Narrated $5.95 historical tour is priced just right for everyone looking to see Mackinaw's timeless historical sites, including the Mackinac Bridge, Colonial Michilimackinac, Old Mackinac Point Lighthouse, & the Coast Guard Icebreaker Mackinaw. Note: Kids of all ages get to ring the trolley bell (and get a sticker, too). Peak season Tours: If you climb Castle Rock, you get a sticker for that, too! This is a wonderfully organized tour with amusing stories and enough stops along the way to keep the kids attention from wandering. Try a different trip each visit!***

Here are some of the best trolley tours for families:

HISTORICAL TOUR OVER THE BRIDGE: Ride through history on the Mackinaw Trolley as they narrate happenings and events along the way. Fort Michilimackinac area, Old Mackinac Point Lighthouse, Train and Car Ferry Docks, The Mackinac Bridge, Father Marquette's Mission and Grave Site at St. Ignace, Indian lore at Ojibwa Museum and the magnificent view from Castle Rock. 2½ hours. Departs evenings (mid-May to mid-October). $9.95.

ICEBREAKER MACKINAW MARITIME MUSEUM

Mackinaw City - ***(Chief Wawatam railroad dock, near ferry docks) 49701. Phone: (231) 436-9825. www.themackinaw.org. Admission: $11.00 adult, $6.00 child (6-17). Hours: Daily 9am-5pm (Mid-May to Mid-October)***

When commissioned, Mackinaw was the most powerful and capable icebreaker in the world. During World War 2, the Mackinaw had a crew of 140 and broke ice 24 hours. She is still the standard by which other icebreakers are measured. Hop aboard and take a look around. Visit the Mess Deck, Captains Quarters, Bridge, Engine Room, Ward Room, Sick Bay and much more. Hear the story of the Mackinaw's 62-year career breaking ice on the Great Lakes and serving as a goodwill ambassador throughout the region. Note the narrow spacing in the ship's steel ribs that distinguish her as an icebreaker.

Exit - 338 (east of I-75)

MICHIGAN WELCOME CENTER

Mackinaw City - ***(I-75 exit 338 on Nicolet Street) 49701. Emergency Contact Number: (231) 436-5566. www.michigan.org/welcome-centers/default.aspx. Hours: Open Winter 9:00am-5:00pm, Summer, 8:00am-6:00pm. During summer travel season, these hours will be extended to meet demands of the season. Restroom facilities will be open 24 hours a day. Staffed Tourist Info Center. Open Memorial Day, July 4th, and Labor Day. Closed all other holidays.***

This site has public restrooms, pet walk areas, picnic areas, public phones, weather updates and tourism information.

HISTORIC MILL CREEK DISCOVERY PARK

Mackinaw City - ***South US 23 (I-75 exit 338, head east on US 23 south, 5 minutes southeast of town)***

49701. Phone: (231) 436-7301. www.mackinacparks.com. Hours: Daily 9:00am-6pm (mid-June to mid-August). Daily 9:00am-5pm (May to mid-June) & (Labor Day to late September). Admission: $8.00 adult, $5 youth (5-17). Good combo rates when add Fort Michilimackinac, Old Lighthouse or Fort Mackinac. Add $8.00 per person for the Adventure Tour. Note: Cook house Snack Pavilion. Museum Store. Forest trails with working beaver dam.

As you walk along wooden planked paths, notice the different tree names - Thistleberry, Ironwood, etc. You'll have an opportunity to see a replica 18th century industrial complex - the oldest sawmill yard to provide finished lumber - in the Great Lakes Region. Water-powered sawmill and saw pit demos are given daily (Summers -lumberjack demos). Participants can help demo old & "newer", easier techniques to saw wood (which would you rather do?). There's also a reconstructed millwrights' house on site along with a museum. The audiovisual orientation is only 12 minutes long and is a great way to understand Michigan lumber history. Did you know a local amateur historian discovered this site, accidentally, in 1972? Creatures of the Forest is a naturalist outdoor "forest" talk - dress up as a beaver (why the raincoat?) and learn how creatures and trees co-exist. Next try the high ropes nature experience - the Adventure Tour. Soar like an eagle down the Eagle's Flight Zip Line. Walk through the treetops on the Forest Canopy Bridge. For the youngest adventurers, exercise body and mind by exploring the Water Power Station and fostering interaction in the Forest Friends Children's Play Area. Now they have something for toddlers through teens.

Exit - 326 (east of I-75)

CHEBOYGAN COUNTY HISTORICAL MUSEUM

Cheboygan - ***404 South Huron Street (I-75 exit 326 east on C66 into downtown) 49721. Phone: (231) 627-9597. www.cheboyganhistory.org. Hours: Tuesday-Saturday 1:00-4:00pm (Memorial Day - September) Admission: $2.00 adult (18+).***

The county sheriff used to call this place home from 1882 - 1969 - it even was the area jail complete with 8 cells. Today, these cells have become exhibit areas featuring local history including: lumbering, farming, and lifestyle. Walking down the corridor of REAL jail cell displays intrigues the kids. See a recreated late 1800's "parlor room", a barber shop (look for old-fashioned curling irons), bedrooms, and even a schoolroom. Look for the old tv's and record players. The log cabin on site was part of a Native American village on Burt Lake built in the late 1800's.

CHEBOYGAN STATE PARK

Cheboygan - ***4490 Beach Road (I-75 exit 326, east on C66 thru town, then southeast on US 23) 49721. Phone: (231) 627-2811. www.dnr.state.mi.us/parksandtrails/Details.aspx?id=441&type=SPRK. Admission: $6.00-$8.00 per vehicle.***

Cheboygan State Park is open all year for a variety of activities. A system of well-marked trails through the park provides access to scenic Lake Huron vistas, glimpses of rare wildflowers and the lake shore species. Modern camping, rustic cabins, and teepees are all available within the park. The Little Billy Elliot Creek flows through the park and is known for its trout. Fishing is also plentiful in Duncan Bay. Several well-marked cross-country skiing trails provide expansive winter vistas of the Lake Huron shoreline and inland natural areas. One of the main highlights of the park is the Cheboygan Point Light or the Duncan Bay Beach.

Exit - 310 (west of I-75)

BURT LAKE STATE PARK

Indian River - 6635 State Park Drive (I-75 exit 310 west to SR 68 to Old US 27) 49749. Phone: (231) 238-9392. www.michigan.gov/burtlake. Admission: $6.00-$8.00 per vehicle or Rec Pass.

Burt Lake State Park is open from April to November (depending on the snowfall). It is located on the southeast corner of Burt Lake with 2,000 feet of sandy shoreline. Shoreline fishing is available on the northern boundary of the park along the Sturgeon River. Great beaches on the state's third largest lake, the park has numerous campsites and cabins, boating and rentals, swimming, and winter sports.

Exit - 282 (east of I-75)

CALL OF THE WILD MUSEUM

Gaylord - ***850 South Wisconsin Avenue (I-75 exit 282, then east on Main Street, then south on Wisconsin) 49735. www.gocallofthewild.com. Phone: (989) 732-4336 or (800) 835-4347. Hours: Daily 9am-9pm. (mid-June-Labor Day), Daily 9:30am-6:00pm. (Rest of year). Admission: $4.50-$7.00 (age 5+). Note: Also at location are Bavarian Falls Adventure Golf, Go Carts, Krazy***

Kars Tot Ride (additional fee). Gift shop.

The museum is full of dioramas of over 60 North American Animals in natural settings. As you look over displays of elk, moose, black bear, timber wolves, etc., you'll learn about their behavior and habitat and sounds. The Michigan History area has stories recounted by an early fur trapper named Joseph. The Four Seasons Display of Michigan changes as you watch. They have an observation beehive there, too. Before you begin your adventure into the museum, make sure you pick up an activity sheet to help you discover a little more as you go through. Once you are finished going through the museum, you can turn in each activity sheet for a prize.

Exit - 270 (west of I-75)

OSTEGO LAKE STATE PARK

Gaylord - ***7136 Old 27 South (I-75 to the village of Waters, Exit 270, and go west to Old 27. Go north on Old 27 five miles to park) 49735. Phone: (989) 732-5485. www.dnr.state.mi.us/parksandtrails/Details.aspx?id=482&type=SPRK Admission: $6.00-$8.00 per vehicle.***

"The Alpine Village." The park is shaded with large oak, maple and pine. The park encompasses 62 acres and provides more than a half mile of sandy beach and large sites near or within sight of the lake. For those without a boat, the park has an accessible fishing pier. The Otsego Lake Park Store offers hand-dipped ice cream, soda, candy, pizza, subs along with T-shirts and sweatshirts. The store is open from Memorial Day weekend to Labor Day weekend. Camping/mini cabin, boating, swimming (mid-April to early November).

Exit - 259 (east of I-75)

HARTWICK PINES STATE PARK

Grayling - ***4216 Ranger Road (I-75 exit 259 - on M-93) 49738. Phone: (989) 348-2537 center or (989) 348-7068 park. www.michigan.gov/loggingmuseum. Hours: Park open 8:00am-10:00pm. Museum buildings 9:00am-4:00pm (May-October) and for special events. Logging Museum is closed November - April. Admission: $6.00-$8.00 per vehicle admission to park. Museum is free.***

See remnants of ancient forests that used to populate Michigan - over 300 years old!

Note: Bike trails, Braille trails, hiking, camping, fishing, picnic areas, winter sports, small gift shop. Summers- living history programs along the Forest Trail.

Some call it an "outdoor cathedral of nature", walking along the Old Growth Forest Foot Trail as it winds through the forest behind the Visitor Center. A paved trail through the forest leads visitors to the 300-year-old Monarch pine, a remnant of the ancient forests that once covered most of northern Michigan. Along the 1¼ mile long trail, you can stop at the Logging Museum (open May-October only). Depending on the event, you'll see logging wheels and other logging equipment, a steam sawmill, plus logger's quarters in use. Be sure to stop in the Visitor Center before your walk out into the pines. See the history of logging - both past cut and run phases - and modern conservation forestry. The self-guided tour takes the visitor on a journey through time that begins with the Ice Age and ends with a look at how Michigan's healthy forest lands of today are growing more each year than is harvested. Did you know, today, there is more paper recycled than made from trees cut down? Find hands-on exhibits on computer (Forest Management Simulation), dioramas (Reading the Rings, Sounds of Birds), and the talking "Living Tree"... or talking Loggers and Rivermen displays. Their guides and programs have a great reputation.

Exit - 256 (west of I-75)

GRAYLING FISH HATCHERY

Grayling - ***4890 W. North Down River Road (I-75 to exit 256) 49738. Phone: (989) 348-9266. www.graylingfishhatchery.com. Hours: Wednesday-Sunday Noon-6:00pm (Memorial Day-Labor Day). Admission: $2.50 adult, $1.50 child (5-12).***

It's always fun to watch kid's eyes light up at a "fish farm". See 11 ponds that contain more than 40,000 trout. See fish ranging from tiny aquarium size (2 inches long) to several pounds (28 inches long), and yes, you can even buy some to take home (priced by the inch). Fish food is available from dispensers for a nominal fee and is a great way to really bring the fish to life. Entertainment and demos every Sunday at 2:00pm.

Exit - 254 (west of I-75)

WELLINGTON FARM PARK

Grayling - ***97 Michigan Avenue (west end) (I-75 exit 254, heading west) 49738. Phone: (989) 348-4461. www.wellingtonfarmpark.org. Hours: Daily 10:00am-5:00pm (Memorial Day weekend thru October). Seasonal festivals throughout the year focus on old-fashioned farming themes. Admission: $1.50 per person.***

Wellington Farm, USA is a 60-acre open-air interpretive museum designed to provide an educational opportunity for visitors to experience life as it was in rural mid-America during The Great Depression. Located in the former Michigan Central Depot, the museum details local history from Camp Grayling military history to lumbering and fire fighting. You can walk through historic buildings, see them in operation when scheduled, and usually be fortunate enough to sample some freshly prepared food/goodies inside their sumptuous Summer Kitchen. The museum also has a railroad caboose, farm shed, trapper's cabin and a display dedicated to the greatest archer of all time - Fred Bear.

BOTTLECAP MUSEUM & DINER

Grayling - ***231 Michigan Avenue (uptown Grayling, Dawson & Stevens Classic 50's Diner) 49738. www.bottlecapmuseum.com.***

Lunch and dinners are served in this 50s motif restaurant and museum. More than 7,000 pieces of Coca-Cola memorabilia once housed in Sparr have been placed in the diner. The oldest pieces in the collection are bottles dating back to the 1890s. Among the original owners favorite pieces is a driver's hat from the 1930s. While you're waiting on your burgers and fries, take a look at the various displays behind glass around the store. Serving breakfast, lunch and dinner.

Exit - 244 (west of I-75)

NORTH HIGGINS LAKE STATE PARK

Roscommon - ***11252 North Higgins Lake Drive (I-75 exit 244-take SR200) 48653. www.mi.gov/cccmuseum. Phone: (989) 821-6125 or (989) 373-3559 (CCC Museum). Hours: Park open dawn to dusk. Museum open summers 11:00am-4:00pm. Admission: $6.00-$8.00 per vehicle.***

Over 400 acres available for camping/cabins, picnicking, hiking, boating, fishing, swimming, and winter sports. Most people find the Civilian Conservation Corps Museum is the reason for their trip here. During the Great Depression, many men without work were enrolled to perform conservation and reforestation projects throughout Michigan. CCC planted trees, taught and practiced fire fighting, constructed trails, built bridges and even built buildings (some are still standing). Housed in replica barracks, the museum has displays of highlights and techniques of their work. Interpretive, outside walks are available too.

Exit - 239 (west of I-75)

SOUTH HIGGINS LAKE STATE PARK

Roscommon - ***106 State Park Drive (I-75 at Roscommon Road south, exit 239) 48653. www.dnr.state.mi.us/parksandtrails/Details.aspx?id=496&type=SPRK Phone: (989) 821-6374. Admission: $6.00-$8.00 per vehicle or Rec Pass.***

Voted some of the most beautiful lakes in the world, this park caters to families. The park contains almost one mile of shoreline along Higgins Lake, which is a large spring-fed body of water known for its clarity and fishing potential. The beaches are family-friendly and there's plenty of camping sites. As the second largest campground in a state park, the park's 400 modern camp sites are situated in a hardwood-shaded area. The park is very popular during the summer months and reservations must be made early. Hiking trails, fishing, and winter sports are there too. For information on canoe and boat rentals call (989) 821-5930.

Exit - 168 (east of I-75)

BAY CITY STATE RECREATION AREA

Bay City - ***3582 State Park Drive (I-75 exit 168 east to Euclid Avenue) 48706. Phone: (989) 684-3020. www.dnr.state.mi.us/parksandtrails/Details.aspx?id=437&type=SPRK Admission: $6.00-$8.00 per vehicle or Rec Pass.***

Lots of camping (tent and cabins) plus a swimming beach free from sharp zebra mussels found in the area, make this an attraction. Also find boating, fishing, trails, winter sports. Another highlight is the Saginaw Bay Visitors Center which focuses on the importance of wetlands to the bay. It's open Tuesday - Sunday, Noon - 5:00pm. A great spot for birding, you'll also learn from the 15 minute video presentation, boardwalks and observation trails. More than seven miles of trails help visitors explore the wetlands close-up. Includes over three miles of paved accessible pathways, three observation towers, boardwalks, viewing platforms and shoreline spotting scopes. Bicycles and rollerblades are welcome.

Exit - 162A (east of I-75)

BAY COUNTY HISTORICAL MUSEUM

Bay City - ***321 Washington Avenue (I-75, take exit 162A to Downtown) 48708. Phone: (989) 893-5733. www.bchsmuseum.org. Admission: FREE Hours: Monday-Friday 10:00am-5:00pm, Saturday & Sunday Noon-4:00pm. Note: Every***

Saturday at 2:00pm, a trolley leaves from the Museum for a 75-minute tour.

Visitors will experience maritime history from the geological formation of the Great Lakes and the Saginaw River to the completion of the area's first lighthouse. Exhibits focus on the shipbuilding and lumbering industries. Visitors enter a re-creation of the tug wheelhouse, experience what the docks were like, and view an interactive shipwreck exhibit. A series of seven period rooms compares and contrasts life in the 1880s to the early 1930s. You can also learn about Native Americans and the fur trade and early Bay County settlers. Many industries such as agriculture, lumbering and manufacturing will highlight the recent history section of the gallery.

DELTA COLLEGE PLANETARIUM & LEARNING CENTER

Bay City - ***100 Center Avenue (I-75 exit 162A, head into town, left on N. Madison, right on Center) 48708. Phone: (989) 667-2260. www.delta.edu/planet/. Hours: Call or visit website for schedule. Note: Show lengths vary. Allow a one hour. Pre- and post-visit materials are available for selected shows. Admission: $5-$7.00.***

A wonderful place to teach children the fun of star-gazing. The planetarium is state-of-the-art and the rooftop observatory seats over 100 people. The audience actually gets to choose what to see in the solar system. Look for programs about sky pirates or cowboys or Garfield.

Exit - 160 (west of I-75)

MARSHALL M. FREDERICKS SCULPTURE GALLERY

Saginaw - ***7400 Bay Road (SR84), University Center (I-75 exit 160, take M-84 south to Arbury Fine Arts Center on Saginaw Valley State University) 48710. Phone: (989) 790-5667. www.svsu.edu/mfsm/. Hours: Monday-Friday 11am-5pm, Saturday Noon-5:00pm. Closed university holidays. Admission: FREE. K-12 tours are free. $2.00 per student hands on activity fee. Adult tours are $3.00 per person.***

Home to more than 200 sculptures by the same artist. He is known nationally and internationally for his impressive monumental figurative sculpture, public memorials and fountains, portraits, medals, and animal sculptures. Free-standing sculptures, drawings and portraits, and photos of bronze pieces are displayed. Plaster models used to cast the sculptor's work in bronze constitute the bulk of the collection indoors. There's a sculpture garden and fountain, too.

Exit - 150 (west of I-75) / I-675 exit 2

SAGINAW CHILDREN'S ZOO

Saginaw - *1730 South Washington (I-75 exit 150 to I-675 to 5th/6th Exit to Celebration Square) 48601. Phone: (989) 759-1408. www.saginawzoo.com. Hours: Monday-Saturday 10:00am-5:00pm, Sunday & Holidays 11:00am-6:00pm. (Mother's Day weekend - September). Weekends only in October. Admission: $5.00 per person (age 1+). Carousel $1.00 extra.*

This "kid-sized" zoo features all the fun animals including: monkeys, bald eagles, alligators, and farm animals.The zoo's Amphitheater holds regular shows, each highlighting 3 animals such as pygmy goats, river otters or kangaroos. Take a miniature train or pony ride and then a chance to see and ride a unique, locally built carousel. After choosing your mount (from horses, rabbits, ponies or sea horses), enjoy the views of hand-painted panels depicting scenes of Saginaw's history.

Exit - 150 (west of I-75) / I-675 exit 3

SAGINAW ART MUSEUM

Saginaw - *1126 North Michigan Avenue (I-75 exit 150 to I-675 exit 3 toward M-58/ Michigan Ave.) 48602. Phone: (989) 754-2491. www.saginawartmuseum.org. Hours: Tuesday-Saturday 10:00am-5:00pm. Closed holidays. Admission: $5.00 adults (age 16+), $3.00 senior (65+) and student.*

Housed in an early 1900's mansion, you'll mostly find 19th and 20th century American art. The Vision area Hands-On Room is the best place to spend time with kids (make easy art jewelry, prints or art science - uninstructed play).

Exit - 149 (west of I-75)

SHIAWASSEE NATIONAL WILDLIFE REFUGE

Saginaw - *Green Point Environmental Learning Center is at 3010 Maple Street in town. (I-75 exit 149 into town. Refuge is 6 miles south of town, west of SR13) 48601. www.fws.gov/refuge/Shiawassee/. Phone: (989) 777-5930 or (989) 759-1669 (Learning Center). Hours: Dawn to Dusk.*

The 9000 acre Refuge provides food and rest for a variety of birds and other wildlife. This includes 250 species of birds, 10 miles of observation trails to walk, two observation decks with scopes, and The Green Point Environmental

Learning Center. The Center offers 2.5 miles of hiking trails, indoor exhibits and many displays. For Shiawassee Flats "Michigan Everglades" Boat Trips, call Johnny Panther Quests (listed on previous page).

Exit - 144 (east of I-75)

JUNCTION VALLEY RAILROAD

Bridgeport - ***7065 Dixie Highway (I-75 exit 144 south - Just before you turn to head into Frankenmuth) 48722. Phone: (989) 777-3480. www.jvrailroad.com. Hours: Monday-Saturday 10:00am-4:00pm, Sunday 1:00-5:00pm. (Memorial Day Weekend-Labor Day Weekend). Weekends Only (September & October & Special events). Admission: $5.00-$6.00 per person (age 2+). Note: Picnic area and playground. You'll pull into a business parking lot, but the ride into the woods is cute, especially over the trestles.***

See and ride the world's largest ¼ scale railroad. Voyage on rides through the woods, past miniature buildings, through a 100 foot long tunnel, and over 865 feet of trestles (one has diamonds underneath). Look for the roundhouse with a turntable and the 5-track switch yard.

FRANKENMUTH CHEESE HAUS

Frankenmuth - ***561 South Main Street (I-75 exit 144 east towards downtown) 48734. Phone: (989) 652-6727. www.frankenmuthcheesehaus.com. Hours: Daily 9:30am-6:00pm. Open until 9:30pm (summer). Admission: FREE.***

Lots of tasting going on here! Ever tried "Chocolate" or "Strawberry" cheese? Not only will you sample some...you can also try cheese spreads (smooth, creamy and fresh tasting) or over 140 different kinds of cheese. Watch a video of the cheesemaking process, or if you time it right, actually see the ladies make it from scratch. They have giant photographs of each step of the process, so if the kids can't see it all they can still understand the process from the pictures. Yummy samples of cheese spreads in varieties from Garden Vegetable to Jalapeno! You will want some to take home (although this souvenir will soon be eaten with a box of crackers!)

Exit - 144 (east of I-75)

FRANKENMUTH WOOLEN MILL

Frankenmuth - ***570 South Main Street (I-75 to Frankenmuth Exit - Follow signs to downtown) 48734. Phone: (989) 652-8121. www.frankenmuthwoolenmill.com. Hours: Daily 10:00am-9:00pm (Summer). Daily 10:00am-6:00m (Winter). Admission: FREE.***

> A video of wool processing plays continuously when workers aren't in, but the store is open.

We've all seen freshly shaven sheep and probably own wool clothing. But how is it processed? Here's your unique chance to see how it all happens. They began here in 1894 and the mill has produced over 250,000 hand-made, wool-filled comforters since then. See the mill in action where you can begin by looking through a window of the wash basins (great viewing for smaller children) where they clean wool brought in from farmers. Washed fleece is then air dried (it gets really fluffy that way) and then put through a "carding machine". The wool passes through wire-spiked rollers until it is untangled and meshed together to form a sheet. Comforters are assembled according to Bavarian tradition (hand-tied). Throughout the tour, your guide will let you handle samples of wool at different stages of the process. This "hands-on" activity keeps their interest throughout the demonstration.

FRANKENMUTH HISTORICAL MUSEUM

Frankenmuth - ***613 South Main Street (I-75 to Frankenmuth Exit - Next to the Visitor's Center, Fischer Hall) 48734. www.frankenmuthmuseum.org. Phone: (989) 652-9701. Hours: Monday-Thursday 10:00am-5:00pm, Friday & Saturday 10:00am-8:00pm, Sunday Noon-6:00pm. (April-December). Shorter hours (January-March). Closed winter holidays. Admission: $1.00-$2.00 per person. Note: Museum Gift Shop with folk art and toy objects.***

Frankenmuth Historical Museum is a small, easily navigated exhibit space geared specifically toward the history of Frankenmuth. Exhibits depict the area's German history from Indian mission days to a town called "Michigan's Little Bavaria". Begin onboard the immigrants' ship traveling from Bavaria to the Saginaw Valley. There are a number of hands on exhibits for kids. Test your strength by lifting two water buckets on a yoke. Feel the different pelts of native animals. All the exhibits have extensive placarding, and there is also an audio narrative as you walk through the different rooms. Perhaps the most interesting of the exhibits for school students are the actual letters that these early settlers wrote to their families and friends back in Germany. You can find them in the "Outgoing Mail" section of the Post Office exhibit. The museum is small, and you can easily go through it in about half an hour, more if you read all the letters.

BAVARIAN INN

Frankenmuth - ***713 South Main Street (I-75 exit 144 into town, head south on Main) 48734. Phone: (800) BAVARIA. www.bavarianinn.com.***

A famous Frankenmuth restaurant (established in 1888) offering family style dinners. An authentically dressed server will help introduce your kids to all the menu offerings they will like such as potato pancakes, veal cutlets, baked chicken, etc. (except maybe the sauerkraut). None of the food is over-seasoned...all kid friendly...but the adults may want to use extra all purpose seasonings available at each table. Also see the Glockenspiel Clock Tower (with performances telling the Pied Piper of Hamelin story in music) and the Doll and Toy Factory (see dolls created before your eyes).

The Lodge has five pools and overnight accommodations. Inside the Lodge you'll find: an indoor waterpark (including one courtyard pool and whirlpool especially for adults, a water cannon & lazy river pool, waterfall pool & whirlpool, fun center pool & whirlpool, plus a wading pool for little ones), 100+ video and redemption games, 18-hole indoor miniature golf, Children's Play Village, exercise room, and plenty of sitting areas for you to relax in comfort with your family. Hours: Daily Lunch, Dinner or Overnight.

BAVARIAN BELLE RIVERBOAT TOURS

Frankenmuth - ***925 South Main Street (RiverPlace) (I-75 exit 144 into town, follow signs for Riverplace) 48734. www.bavarianbelle.com. Phone: (866) 808-BOAT. Hours: Departures 11:00am until dusk (May thru mid-October). Admission: $10.00 adult, $4.00 child (3-12).***

One hour sightseeing cruises narrated about the Cass River folklore and history. Learn about the local covered bridge, the beginnings of the shops and Bavarian Inn and a brief background on the boat itself. Open air canopied upper deck and enclosed lower salon (air-conditioned and heated). Snack bar and restrooms on board.

RIVERPLACE

Frankenmuth - ***925 South Main Street (I- 75 exit 144 into downtown area by river) 48734. Phone: (800) 600-0105. www.frankenmuthriverplace.com. Hours: Sunday-Thursday 10:00am-7:00pm, Friday-Saturday 10:00am-9:00pm (September-***

December, May). Slightly more limited hours (January-April). Daily 10:00am-9:00pm (June-August). Admission: Varies with activity. Gameroom, toy stores and treats shops, too.

A-MAZE-N-MIRRORS - life size maze of mirrors and glass. MOONWALK MAN'S HOUSE - bounce inflatable playplace. BAVARIAN BELLE - see separate listing. LIGHTS FANTASTIC - nightly laser-light shows in amphitheater. FREE.

ZEHNDER'S SPLASH VILLAGE HOTEL & WATERPARK

Frankenmuth - ***1365 S. Main Street (next to Bronner's Christmas Wonderland) 48734. Phone: (800) 863-7999. www.zehnders.com. Admission: Room packages are most appealing. Seasonal room and waterpark inclusive rates range: $109.00-$409.00 per night. Note: Zehnder's offers a full-service menu that features all-you-can-eat family-style chicken dinners, seafood, steaks, fresh baked goods and European desserts. Dinners range from $15.25 to $21.50, with children's portions and special event menus available. Their luncheon menu is available Monday through Saturday from 11:00am-2:00pm. Zehnder's is open seven days a week.***

The Zehnder family transformed its Bavarian Haus Motel into the Splash Village Hotel and Waterpark. Zehnder's Splash Village offers 152 deluxe accommodations including 63 new suites. Enjoy over 30,000 sq. ft. of indoor aquatic fun with Splash landing play area, dumping bucket, giggling gorge and Perilous plunge-a four story tube slide. Relax in the whimsical whirl hot tub or just float along the Crooked Brook Creek lazy river. For the landlubber have fun at our new arcade or lunch at Elf hollow café. A towering 26-foot tree is a prominent feature in the hotel lobby with a large gas fireplace built into the trunk. Zehnder's Splash Village includes elves and fairies as part of the waterpark and hotel's overall theme. Complimentary shuttle service is available to Zehnder's Restaurant and the Fortress golf course.

BRONNER'S CHRISTMAS WONDERLAND

Frankenmuth - ***25 Christmas Lane (I-75, exit 144 - follow signs off Main Street M-83) 48734. Phone: (989) 652-9931 or (800) ALL-YEAR. www.bronners.com. Hours: Monday-Saturday 9:00am-5:30pm, Sunday Noon-5:30pm, Open Friday until 9:00pm (January-May). Monday-Saturday 9:00am-9:00pm, Sunday Noon-7:00pm (June-December). Closed Winter holidays including Easter and Good Friday. Admission: FREE. Note: "Season's Eatings" snack area.***

A visit to Michigan wouldn't be complete without seeing the "World's Largest

Christmas Store" that hosts over 2,000,000 visitors each year! View nativity scenes, 260 decorated trees, and 200 styles of nutcrackers. As dusk approaches, drive through "Christmas Lane" that sparkles with over 40,000+ lights. While you're there be sure to check out the "World of Bronners" (an 18 minute multi-image slide show) that highlights the design and production of their selection of trains. Visit "Bronner's Silent Night Memorial Chapel" - named after the famous song (the chapel was originally made in Austria). Kids seem to be most fascinated with the "It Feels Like Christmas" drive around the vast parking lot and the animated displays of seasonal bears, elves, and children playing around the upper perimeter of each theme room. Be sure to get at least one ornament to keep - but "oh" - how to decide!

Holding Gigantic ornaments...!

Exit - 144 (east of I-75)

GRANDPA TINY'S FARM

Frankenmuth - ***7775 Weiss Street (across from Bronners) 48734. Phone: (989) 652-KIDS (5437). www.grandpatinysfarm.com. Hours: Daily 10:00am-5:00pm (April-October) Admission: $5.00 (age 3+). Maximum Family Price $20.00 (Price includes horse drawn wagon ride.)***

Step back in time at this working Historical Farm and Petting Farm. Hold cuddly baby bunnies and chicks. Watch playful lambs and goats. Feed and play with the farm animals, gather your own eggs and take a horse-drawn wagon ride! Enjoy seasonal demonstrations of draft horses plowing, planting and harvesting. Special activities are scheduled, weather permitting.

Exit - 136 (west of I-75)

WILDERNESS TRAILS ANIMAL PARK

Birch Run - ***11721 Gera Road - M-83 (I-75 to Birch Run Exit) 48415. Phone: (989) 624-6177. www.wildernesstrailszoo.org. Hours: Monday-Saturday 10:00am-6:00pm, Sunday 11:00am-5:00pm (summer). Open until 5:00pm (May, September, October). Admission: $11.75 adult, $9.00 senior (60+), $8.50 child (3-15). Note: Picnic area. Playground.***

One of the most popular privately owned animal exhibits in the state, Wilderness Trails offers over 50 acres and 60 different types of animals. See lions, a Siberian tiger and bear, bison, elk, black bears, and deer. Two gravel walking trails wind through park or a horse drawn covered wagon is available for a small charge. Kids can have fun touching the alpaca, watching the flirting butterflies, and feeding the baby animals in the petting area.

Exit - 125 (east of I-75) / I-475 exit 13

CROSSROADS VILLAGE & HUCKLEBERRY RAILROAD

Flint ***- 6140 Bray Road (I-75 exit 125 to I-475, exit 13 - follow signs) 48505. www.geneseecountyparks.org/pages/crossroads. Phone: (810) 736-7100 or (800) 648-PARK. Hours: Wednesday-Sunday, Holidays 10:00am-5:00pm (mid-May to early September). Weekends in October and December for seasonal events. Admission: $10.00 adult, $9.00 senior (60+), $8.00 child (2-12) - Village Only. Add $2.00-$3.00 more for Train OR Boat Ride. Note: Mill Street Warehouse, Cross Roads Café, Concessions, Carousel, Venetian Swing, Ferris Wheel and Wagon Rides (pulled by mechanical ponies) - rides additional charge. Seasonal events keep the village open throughout the year.***

The 1860's era CROSSROADS Living Village is a collection of 30 authentic buildings that were relocated here to form a village. Friendly, costumed villagers fill you in on the events of the day and answer questions. For example, the barber shop (still operational) staff will share their charges for a cut, shave or bath. We learned that they let a dental patient (yes, they were the town dentist then) take a swig of vanilla extract (full tilt variety!) before they extracted a tooth. The fellas at the cider and sawmill will remind you of characters from "Little House on the Prairie" as they demonstrate their craft. Be sure to buy a cup of cider there - all natural with no added sugar. You'll also meet the town blacksmith, printer (try your hand printing a souvenir off the "kissing" press), doctor, storekeeper at the General Store (with cute, old-fashioned novelties for sale), and toymaker (try your hand walking on stilts - we have a video and George did it!). Before you leave, take a relaxing slow ride on the HUCKLEBERRY RAILROAD: The original line went so slow that passengers claimed they could get off - pick huckleberries along the tracks (still growing plentifully today) and catch the caboose a few minutes later. Watch out for the playful train robber skit...

GENESSEE BELLE: a paddle-wheel riverboat, offers scenic cruises on unspoiled Mott Lake. The Genesee Belle has an open-air upper deck for unobstructed sightseeing and the lower deck is climate-controlled in summer and fall. Although the Genesee Belle is a replica of the steamboats that traveled during the era of Mark Twain, it is very safe and especially designed for sightseeing and relaxation. 45 minute cruises on the lake.

Exit - 125 (east of I-75) / I-475 exit 13

GENESEE RECREATION AREA

Flint - ***(I-75 exit 125 to I-475 exit 13) 48506. www.geneseecountyparks.org. Phone: (800) 648-7275.***

This area includes Stepping Stone Falls on Mott Lake on Branch Road which are lit with color evenings between Memorial Day and Labor Day. Genesee County's first Splash Pad Spray Ground shoots water in a timed sequence from the ground and from various play structures on the Splash Pad. There is no charge to use the Splash Pad Spray Ground. You can also find camping, hiking, boating, fishing, beach swimming, bicycle trails, and winter sports. Hours vary by activity (mostly dawn to dusk). (Memorial Day-October).

Exit - 122 (east of I-75) / I-475 exit 8

FOR-MAR NATURE PRESERVE & ARBORETUM

Flint (Burton) - ***2142 North Genesee Road (I-75 exit 122 to I-475 exit 8 east on Davison, north on Genesee) 48509. Phone: (810) 789-8567 or (800) 648-7275. www.geneseecountyparks.org/pages/formar Hours: Wednesday-Sunday 8:00am-5:00pm. Trails 8:00am -Sunset. Special programs on Saturdays.***

A 380 acre preserve with 7 miles of trails. There are hundreds of wonderful things to see and learn at For-Mar Nature Preserve and Arboretum. To help you experience everything nature has to offer, For-Mar now loans Discovery Backpacks. There are three types of Discovery Backpacks : Michigan Naturalist, Basic Birding and Insect Investigator. Each backpack offers different tools and materials that will help you and your family enrich your outdoor experience. These backpacks may be borrowed for up to two hours with a valid driver's license from an adult, 18 years of age or older. Visitor Center with Gift Shop. Cross-country skiing in winter. Guided programs charge admission.

MICHIGAN

Exit - 118 (east of I-75)

FLINT CHILDREN'S MUSEUM

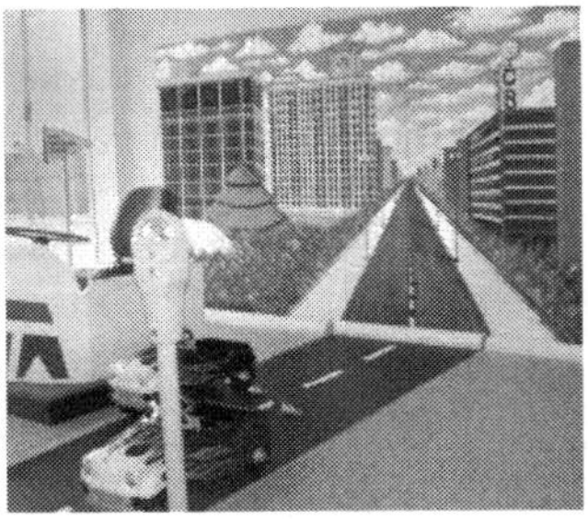

Flint - ***1602 West 3rd Avenue, Kettering University Campus (I-75 exit 118 - Corunna Rd. east. Left on Ballenger Hwy., right on Sunset Drive, turns into 3rd) 48504. Phone: (810) 767-5437. www.thefcm.org Hours: Tuesday-Friday 9:00am-5:00pm, Saturday 10:00am-5:00pm. Closed major holidays. Admission: $4.00 general (age 1+). Note: Recommended for ages 2-10. Gift shop.***

Over 40 exhibits focused on science, technology, and the arts. Kids' favorites are the Crazy Mirrors and the Lego table. Be sure to check out the different theme rooms: Mr. Bones, showing how our skeletons work as you take a bicycle ride together; Our Town, where they can shop for groceries at the Smart Mart or visit Frac-tions Pizza Parlor; a picnic lunch in Sproutside; and Center Stage, where young performers can act out anything they imagine with puppets and costumes. The parent-friendly exhibit signs helps adult chaperones to guide children's understanding of each concept from simple machines to math to health and safety.

FLINT CULTURAL CENTER

Flint - ***1221 East Kearsley Street (I-75 exit 118 east on SR 21 thru town to I-475, exit 8A) 48503. www.flintculturalcenter.com. Phone: (810) 237-7330 or (888) 8CENTER. Hours: Museum: Monday-Friday 10:00am-5:00pm, Saturday & Sunday Noon-5:00pm. Admission: $9.00 adult, $8.00 senior, $6.00 child (4-11). $2.00 off coupon online. Combo prices. Note: Museum Store. Café.***

Institutions on the Flint Cultural Center campus include Sloan Museum, Buick Gallery & Research Center, Longway Planetarium, The Whiting, Flint Youth Theatre, Flint Institute of Arts and Flint Institute of Music.

SLOAN MUSEUM - (810-237-3450 or www.sloanmuseum.org) highlights include: "FLINT AND THE AMERICAN DREAM" - 20th Century Flint beginning with the birth of General Motors, United Auto Workers, and then neon colorful advertising. Also 1950's - 70's typical household furnishings. Check out the 1950's station wagon. "HOMETOWN GALLERY" - the area's early history with displays on fur trading, pioneer life, lumbering, and carriage making. Look for the 10,000 year old mastodon and Woodland Indian wigwam. "SCIENCE DISCOVERY CENTER" - hands-on science, weekends only.

Also in the same complex (recommended for grade school and up):

- **FLINT INSTITUTE OF ARTS** - 1120 East Kearsley. (810) 234-1695. Free.
- **LONGWAY PLANETARIUM** - 1310 East Kearsley. (810) 237-3400 or www.longway.org. Monday - Friday 9:00 am-4:00pm, Saturday & Sunday 1:00-4:30pm. Free displays. $4.00-5.00 for light & astronomy shows. The largest planetarium in Michigan and in the north-central U.S.! 282 seats under a 60 foot dome. Check out the planetarium shows - the Sky Theater has been completely renovated with a new Digistar 2 projector, seats, sound system, and video projection system. Enjoy laser light shows featuring both rock music and family oriented fare. Popular hands-on science activities provide families with opportunities to have fun while learning about science.
- **SHOWCASE SERIES, (THE)** - Whiting Auditorium. Broadway, dance, classic theater & holiday shows. www.flintyouththeatre.com

Exit - 101 (west of I-75)

SEVEN LAKES STATE PARK

Holly - ***14390 Fish Lake Road (I-75, exit 101 west on Grange Hall Rd., just before town) 48442. Phone: (248) 634-7271. www.michigan.gov/sevenlakes. Admission: $6.00-$8.00 per vehicle or Park Pass.***

The dam, constructed by the developers, formed one large lake from seven small lakes (historically known as the DeCoup Lake) hence the name Seven Lakes State Park. Their trail system is used by hikers, cross country skiers, snowmobilers (when there is four or more inches of snow) and mountain bikers. About 230 acres of water with several miles of shoreline await the park user. Boat rentals of row boats, canoes, paddle boats and your-motor-on boats are available from mid-May to mid-September. Camping, hiking trails, fishing, swimming, bicycle trails, and winter sports.

Exit - 101 (east of I-75)

HOLLY RECREATION AREA

Holly - ***8100 Grange Hall Road (I-75 exit 101 east) 48442. Phone: (248) 634-8811. www.michigan.gov/holly. Admission: $6.00-$8.00/vehicle or Park Pass.***

Approximately 10 miles of hiking and cross country ski trails are in the central portion of the recreation area. Although mountain bikes are prohibited on these trails, there is an extensive mountain bike trail system located in the

Holdridge Lakes area of the park, ranging in terrain from easy to advanced. The rolling woodland and prairies that dominate this landscape, are featured in the development in the Holly Woods Disc Golf Course. Offering both 9 and 18 hole routes, this course offers a variety of challenges and fun for all skill levels. Camping, hiking, boating, fishing, swimming, bicycle trails and winter sports.

ORTONVILLE RECREATION AREA

Ortonville *- 5779 Hadley Road (follow state park signs off interstate) 48462. Phone: (248) 627-3828. www.michigan.gov/ortonville.*

Fishing is allowed throughout the recreation area with access sites located on Algoe, Davidson, Round and Today lakes. The lakes and streams may produce a wide variety of fish such as pike, bass, and perch. The equestrian trails offer 6.5 miles of designated trails wandering through Hadley Hills. The 6.5-mile Equestrian trail is also open for snowmobiling with sufficient snow. Camping, cabins, hiking trails, boating, swimming and winter sports.

Exit - 93 (west of I-75)

PONTIAC LAKE RECREATION AREA

Waterford *- 7800 Gale Road (I-75 exit 93, head southwest on US 24 to Williams Lake Rd. to Gale on right) 48327. www.michigan.gov/pontiaclake. Phone: (248) 666-1020. Admission: $6.00-$8.00 per vehicle or Park Pass.*

Archery ranges and horse trails/rentals make this park unique. Designated trails meandering throughout the recreation area are available for horseback riding, hiking and mountain biking. The 11-mile mountain bike trail has been ranked as one of the "Top 100 Trails" in the United States. Two new universally accessible fishing piers are located at the Pontiac Lake Beach Area. Camping, boating, fishing, swimming, and winter sports.

Exit - 84 (west of I-75)

RAINFOREST CAFÉ EDUCATIONAL TOURS

Detroit (Auburn Hills) *- 4310 Baldwin Road (I-75, exit 84 - Great Lakes Crossing) 48326. Phone: (248) 333-0280. www.rainforestcafe.com. Hours: Daily, Lunch and Dinner. Tours: Usually begin at 10:00am and include lunch. Must be scheduled in advance.*

A theme restaurant and wildlife preserve filled with live and mechanical animals; ongoing rainstorms (even thunder and lightning); a talking rainforest tree; giant "walk-through" aquarium (really cool!); hand-sculpted "cave like" rock everywhere. Preschoolers and younger love the fish tank but are a little uneasy with the motorized large gorillas and elephants (request seating on the other side of the dining room). Did you know they give Educational Group Tours? The Fun Field Trip Adventure uncovers why elephants have big ears & why the Café's resident crocodile collects pennies for charity. You can also include a group lunch afterwards in your plans (for an ~$8.00 per person fee). Nibble on Jurassic Tidbits and Paradise Pizza plus other kid-friendly food, drink and dessert. Although your food bill will be above moderate - it's the epitome of a theme restaurant.

Exit - 81 (east of I-75)

BALD MOUNTAIN RECREATION AREA

Lake Orion - ***1330 Greenshield (I-75 exit 81 on SR 24 north approximately 7 miles) 48360. Phone: (248) 693-6767. www.michigan.gov/baldmountain. Admission: $6.00-$8.00 per vehicle.***

Bald Mountain Recreation Area consists of 4,637 rolling acres. The picturesque park area has some of the steepest hills and most rugged terrain in southeastern Michigan. Two accessible piers makes fishing available to everyone. One pier is located East Graham and one at Lower Trout Lake. Beginning with a great kiddie beach at Lower Trout Lake, the park also features hiking trails, fishing, boating, horseback riding, winter sports, and cabins for camping.

Exit - 78 (east of I-75)

CHRYSLER MUSEUM, WALTER P.

Detroit (Auburn Hills) - ***1 Chrysler Drive (I-75 exit 78, follow signs to northwest corner of Featherstone & Squirrel Roads on Daimler-Chrysler campus) 48326. Phone: (888) 456-1924 or (248) 944-0001. www.chryslerheritage.com. Hours: Tuesday-Saturday 10:00am-6:00pm, Sunday Noon-5:00pm. Admission: $8.00 adult, $7.00 senior (62+), $4.00 child (6-12). Online discounts. Kids Corner.***

The Museum contains 55,000 square feet and displays 75 vehicles. It tells the stories of Walter P. Chrysler and his love of trains, brothers John and Horace Dodge and their mechanical genius. It covers everything from the Detroit Tank Arsenal to Roadrunners, Vipers and Prowlers. Several interactive displays explain brake systems, aerodynamics, power steering, platform team design and more. Interactive computer kiosks timeline the decades from 1920-1980 using vintage news footage, classic commercials and audio clips.

Exit - 77 (west of I-75)

DRAYTON PLAINS NATURE CENTER

Waterford - *2125 Denby Drive (near Dixie Hwy. & M-59. Turn onto Edmore off of Hatchery Road) 48329. www.dpnaturecenter.org. Phone: (248) 674-2119. Hours: Grounds open 8:00am-9:00pm (April -October). Only open until 6:00pm rest of year. Interpretive Center open Tuesday - Friday 11:00am - 2:00pm and Weekends Noon - 4:00pm. Admission: FREE.*

An old fish hatchery is now the Drayton Plains Nature Center. The grounds include woods, ponds, streams, and a prairie. 137 acres of trails along the Clinton River plus a nice Interpretive Center. In the center are displays of mounted animals in re-created scenes of their natural habitats.

DODGE NO. 4 STATE PARK

Waterford - *4250 Parkway Drive (I-75 exit 77, west off M-59 west to Cass Elizabeth Road) 48328. Phone: (248) 682-7323. www.michigandnr.com/parksandtrails/. Admission: $6.00-$8.00 per vehicle or Park Pass.*

A white sandy beach and a one-mile shoreline on Cass Lake makes Dodge #4 State Park an excellent location for summer and winter water activities. Dodge #4 has recently added a universally accessible fishing pier on Cass Lake. Camping, fishing, boating, swimming and winter sports.

Exit - 74 (west of I-75)

CRANBROOK ART AND SCIENCE MUSEUMS

Detroit (Bloomfield Hills) - *1221 North Woodward Avenue (I-75 exit to Square Lake Road (West) to Woodward, I-696 exit - Woodward) 48303. Phone: (877) GO-CRANB. www.cranbrook.edu. Hours: Art: Wednesday-Sunday 11:00am-5:00pm. Science: Tuesday-Saturday 10:00am-5:00pm. Weekends until 10:00pm, Sunday Noon-4pm. Admission: Science: $9.50-$13.00. Other areas: $3.00-$5.00. Note: Picnic areas. Live Bat Programs $4.00 extra. Café. Gift shop. Seasonal gardens.*

What makes Cranbrook an extraordinary place to visit is the wide selection of arts and entertainment it offers. Not only can you visit the Cranbrook Art Museum, but there is also the Cranbrook Institute of Science. The Institute of Science has programs for kids and adults, a planetarium and observatory, special group programs, summer camps and fun weekend events for the entire family throughout the year. Different areas to check out are: Our Dynamic Earth (15 foot T-Rex, woolly mastodon), Gem & Mineral Hall, Nature Place (live reptiles, turtles, and bugs - native to Michigan), Art (metalwork, realism sculpture "Body Builder", outdoor sculpture), and Physics Hall (hands-on experiments about lasers and light, movement, water and air). The museum grounds feature a life-sized statue of a stegosaurus, as well as a koi pond.

Exit - 61 (west of I-75) / I-696 exit 16

DETROIT ZOO

Detroit (Royal Oak) - ***8450 West Ten Mile Road (I-75 to I-696 West - Woodward Avenue Exit 16) 48068. Phone: (248) 398-0900 info. http://detroitzoo.org. Hours: Daily 10:00am-5:00pm (April - October). Daily 10:00am-4:00pm. (November-March). Admission: $14.00 adult, $10.00 senior (62+), child (2-14). $6.00 Parking fee. Note: Picnic areas and playground. Strollers and Adult roller chairs available for rent. Giraffe Feedings (seasonal - $5.00 per person) offer personal food feedings off the new platforms! 4D Theater $5.00.***

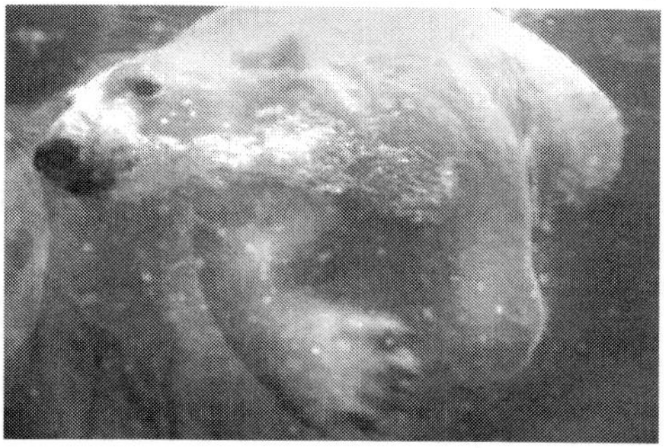

Simply put...your family is in for a real day of adventure and fun when visiting the Detroit Zoo. The world's largest polar bear exhibit, the Arctic Ring of Life, is a lifelike trek to the North Pole's tundra, open sea and ice mountains. Start outside and curve around the exhibit to the spectacular 70 foot long clear tunnel (Polar Passage) which takes visitors underneath diving and swimming polar bears and seals. Their antics and casual behavior will entertain you for most of the visit (plan 45 minutes to one hour just at this exhibit)! What a fun learning experience for the kids to see the Inuit peoples and their interaction w/ Arctic animals. Here's a few of the other, constantly changing exhibits that you'll see: The Wilson Aviary Wing (30 species of birds in a large free-flying building - much like an indoor jungle - there is even a waterfall), The Penguinarium (love that name! - see underwater views of these birds that cannot fly), The Chimps of Harambee (a forest setting with rock habitats... what a show!), and The Wildlife Interpretive Gallery (huge aquarium, theater, hummingbird and butterfly garden).

Instead of looking through glass or over a moat, patrons will have the chance to get face to face with 19 red kangaroos – from inside the Australian Outback Adventure exhibit! Visitors move along a winding path bordered by knee-high cables on both sides, while the kangaroos are free to bound wherever they want. The simulated outback is complete with re-created settlement buildings, termite mounds, and Aboriginal artifacts. Can you leap as far as the kangaroo can? And if all this wasn't enough...take an excursion on the famous Detroit Zoo Miniature Railroad (it transports over 500,000 passengers a year).

Exit - 53A (west of I-75)

MUSEUM OF AFRICAN-AMERICAN HISTORY

Detroit - ***315 East Warren Avenue (I-75, next to Detroit Science Center at Brush Street corner) 48201. Phone: (313) 494-5800. http://thewright.org. Hours: Tuesday-Saturday: 9:00am-5:00pm, Sunday: 1:00pm-5:00pm. Admission: $8.00 adult, $5.00 senior (62+) and child (3-12). Note: Vending area.***

A tribute to the history and culture of Detroit's African-American community. The exhibit, "And Still We Rise" traces the history and operations of the slave trade. Learn also that Detroit was one of the most active stops in the "Underground Railroad". Once reaching Detroit, they could cross the Detroit River into Canada. See the space suit worn by Mae Jemision, the first African-American woman to travel in space in 1992. Twenty-six interactive stations make up a three-dimensional "dictionary" designed for children from pre-school through fourth grade in A is for Africa. Other fun and educational exhibits trace the history of African music and how it transformed present American music including the famous Detroit's "Motown Sound".

MICHIGAN SCIENCE CENTER

Detroit - ***5020 John R Street (I-75 - Warren Ave. Exit heading west to John R St.) 48202. Phone: (313) 577-8400. www.mi-sci.org. Hours: Monday-Friday 10:00am-3:00pm, Saturday 10:00am-6:00pm, Sunday Noon-6pm. Increased hours during school holidays and occasional Fridays. Admission: $21.00-$24.00 per person (age 2+). IMAX is additional $4.00. Note: Café.***

Just a block away from the Detroit Institute of Arts is another wonderful example of what learning "outside of the books" is all about. Located in the heart of Detroit's Cultural Complex (park once and visit maybe 4-5 museums), the museum still has the IMAX Dome Theatre and Digital Dome Planetarium plus new, dynamic exhibits. Space Laboratory takes you into the sky via space shuttle or telescope. Visitors can pedal a bicycle "at the speed of the space shuttle" to discover how long will it take to reach the moon, Mars and beyond and position each planet the correct scale distance from the sun. Motion Lab has a "stadium" Science Stage and lots of pulling, pushing physics comparing motion, speed and direction (little engineers thrive here). The Life Science Lab focuses on similarities between the rainforest and city ecosystems. The Matter and Energy Lab has a "caged" Sparks Theatre and exhibits exploring electricity, magnetism, energy conversion, etc. Power a light bulb with a hand-crank generator—then see how much less effort is required to light a fluorescent tube of the same intensity. Or, create a tornado! Surf the phenomena of everyday light and sound in the Waves and Vibrations Laboratory - just look for all the funky lights and sounds. There's even an area for the younger set to explore all the things their older siblings are playing with on a larger scale. Everyday objects become boats and water movers in a water feature surrounded by aquariums and plants. A quiet area provides families with a space where children can work on computers and infants can receive special care. Children can create treasures to take home in the Make and Take area, a space designed as a "science through art" studio. The Greenhouse introduces children to seeds, plants and how things grow.

DETROIT INSTITUTE OF ARTS (DIA)

Detroit - 5200 Woodward Avenue (I-75, follow signs to Cultural Center) 48202. Phone: (313) 833-7900. www.dia.org. Hours: Tuesday-Friday 9:00am-4:00pm, Saturday and Sunday 10:00am-5:00pm. Friday nights until 10:00pm. Admission: $12.50 adult, $8.00 senior, $4.00 child (6-17). Local residents are FREE. Tours: 1:00pm Wednesday - Saturday. 1:00 & 2:30pm, Sunday. Guided tours are $5.00 per person. Note: CaféDIA and the Kresge Court Coffee Stop.

A great place for kids of all ages to interact and explore. Most exhibits are "kid-friendly" and interactive and there is even a booklet: Animal & Creatures Abound, that encourages kids to "want to discover" the museum and its treasures. See exhibits such as "The American House", "The Spiral Staircase" and even "The Donkey" (which invites kids to hang, climb, and burn up excess energy) while at the museum. Fun, interactive computer programs also entertain and teach. The Great Hall features many suits of armor from the 13th to 18th century. But, above all, the masked mummy (kept safely in a display case) in the Egyptian art and artifacts exhibit is always a way to get the kids to say "wow" or "wooooo".

DETROIT HISTORICAL MUSEUM

Detroit - ***5401 Woodward Avenue (Woodward and Kirby. SR 1) 48202. Phone: (313) 833-1805. www.detroithistorical.org. Hours: Tuesday-Friday 9:30am-4:00pm, Saturday & Sunday 10:00am-5:00pm. Admission: FREE. Parking is $7.00 per car. Educators: Encyclopedia of Detroit www.detroithistorical.org/learn/encyclopedia-of-detroit.***

After you've wondered through Frontiers to Factories: Detroiters at Work before the Motor City; and the Streets of Old Detroit, be sure to plan most of your time in the Motor City exhibits. See the first car in Detroit - a horseless carriage that was driven down Woodward Avenue. Then, around the corner, you can crank up a Model T and then sit in it (great photo op!). The best part of this exhibit has to be the Body Drop! First, watch it happen on video (actual footage from a Ford Assembly plant). Then see the 70 foot section of actual assembly plant and the performance as some mannequins are in the pits below, some workers are above one floor as they "drop" the car body onto the chassis below. Did you know that Mr. Cadillac's full name is Antoine de la Mothe Cadillac? - No wonder they're so fancy!

Exit - 50 (west of I-75)

MOTOWN HISTORICAL MUSEUM

Detroit - ***2648 West Grand Blvd. (I-75 exit 50 north on M-10 to West Grand Blvd. Exit) 48208. Phone: (313) 875-2264. www.motownmuseum.com. Hours: Tuesday-Saturday, 10:00am-6:00pm. (Closed holidays, Mondays and Sundays). Open Summer Mondays. Admission: $12-$15.00$10 senior (62+) adult, $8.00 child (12 and under).***

In two homes that are next to each other, the music world was changed forever by Berry Gordy, composer and producer. The original recording studio "A" not only helped to build the "Motown" sound, but discovered and built the careers of the Stevie Wonder, the Temptations, the Four Tops, Diana Ross, and Marvin Gaye, just to name a few. A great stop in musical history.

Exit - 50 (east of I-75)

HOCKEYTOWN CAFÉ

Detroit - ***2301 Woodward, downtown, next to Fox Theatre (Proceed on the FisherFreeway service drive across Grand River Avenue. Turn right on Woodward Avenue) 48201. Phone: (313) 965-9500. www.hockeytowncafe.com.***

Near all the sporting action is a good stop for food and sports themed meals. You're greeted by the 1962 Zamboni (ice resurfacing machine) and while you're waiting on your food, take a stroll around and gander at the Statues, The Walk of Fame, or the Ring of Honor. Look for your favorite player's showcase. Both the outdoor video screen and televisions throughout the Hockeytown Café carry the live in-arena video and audio of Red Wings games directly from Joe Louis Arena. The kids meals are around the $5.00 range. The adult entrees were delicious and a great value. Ample, well-lit parking nearby in lots or garages. Many "kid-friendly" shows next door at Fox Theatre, too. Lunch and Dinner.

FORD FIELD TOURS

Detroit - ***2000 Brush Street (just south of I-75 (Fisher Freeway) and directly across Brush Street from Comerica Park) 48226. www.fordfield.com. Phone: (313) 262-2100. Tours: Each 25-person group tour will start from the Ticket Office on the second level, and will last approximately one hour. Tour tickets may be purchased at the Ford Field Ticket Office. Admission $5.00-$7.00 per person. Walk Up Tours: Join public walk-up tours at 11:00am and 1:00pm on the following days: (June-December) Mondays, Thursdays & Fridays; (January-May) Mondays & Fridays only. Reservations & advance purchase not required for walk-up tours.***

A behind-the-scenes glimpse at Detroit's crown jewel and the home of the Detroit Lions & Super Bowl XL. Get a peek at a Ford Field suite, an NFL locker room, walk down the tunnel to the field and stand on the turf for a player's view of the stadium.

DIAMOND JACK'S RIVER TOURS

Detroit (Grosse Ile) - ***25088 Old Depot Court (take Lodge freeway (SR 10) til it ends at Hart Plaza, foot of Woodward, downtown) 48138. Phone: (313) 843-9376. www.diamondjack.com. Hours: Thursday-Sunday (early June-Labor Day). Admission: $19.00 adult, $17.00 senior (60+), $15.00 child (6-16). Tours: 2-hour leisurely narrated cruise departs at 1:00pm and 3:30pm. Note: Snacks and beverages available on board. Safest parking available at the Renaissance Center.***

The 65-foot "mini-ship" cruises down the Detroit River around Belle Isle and back to Ambassador Bridge. This is the world's busiest international waterway along the U.S. and Canadian shorelines. There's a good chance that large freighters and ocean ships will pass by. You'll see a great view of both the Detroit and downtown Windsor, Canada skylines and pass by (with stories told by captain) the historic Warehouse District, Mayor's Residence (if he's out back, he'll wave), Yacht Clubs, Islands, Bridges and a Fireboat. See the world's only marble Art Deco lighthouse or one of only two International Marine Mailboats in the world. The mailboat has it's own zip code and delivers mail to freighters by a pail on a pulley.

Exit - 47A (east of I-75)

PEWABIC POTTERY

Detroit - 10125 E. Jefferson Avenue (across from Waterworks Pk) (Take EXIT 47A toward M-3/Clark Ave. East on SR3. 1.5 miles east of the Belle Isle Bridge) 48214. Phone: (313) 822-0954. www.pewabic.org. Gallery Hours: Monday-Saturday 10:00am-6:00pm. Admission: FREE. Tours: Self-guided tours of the pottery's kiln room and other production areas are during regular business hours. Groups must call ahead to make reservation ($5.00 fee per person for 20 minimum groups).

Pewabic is nationally renowned for its handcrafted ceramic vessels and architectural tiles and its unique glazes. Being Michigan's only historic pottery, it continues to operate in a 1907 Tudor Revival building as a non-profit educational institution. The word Pewabic is derived from the Ojibwa (or Chippewa) word for the color of copper metal (or perhaps the clay from which copper came) and specifically referring to the "Pewabic" Upper Peninsula copper mine. They make a wide range of vases, candlesticks and unique embossed tiles. Four of the 13 People Mover stations are adorned with ceramic murals created at Pewabic. Guided Tours are suitable for children ages 12 years and older. Younger children appreciate a more interactive visit so we suggest a Pewabic Workshop or just a free look around visit.

BELLE ISLE

Detroit (Belle Isle) - ***100 Strand Drive (I-75 to Take EXIT 47A toward M-3/Clark Ave., then along Jefferson. Take MacArthur Bridge over to the Isle on the Detroit River) 48207. www.michigandnr.com/parksandtrails/Details.aspx?id=736&type=SPRK. Phone: (313) 852-4075. Hours: Dawn to Dusk. See specific hours for special parks within the Isle. Note: FREE admission to Trails, Picnic areas, beach, Nature Centers and museums. There's also a wild animal hospital and playgrounds. In Winter: Ice skating and sledding & 30-foot ice sculpture.***

The island is situated on America's busiest inland waterway and provides spectacular views of Detroit, Canada, freighter traffic and the Ambassador Bridge. Once on the island, you may get about by car or take a leisurely walk along the many miles of trails, paths and roadways that connect all of Belle Isle's points of interest. The well-used 1000 acre park and playground, still in site of the skyscrapers of Detroit offers:

- **CONSERVATORY** - (313) 852-4141. Hours: Wednesday-Sunday 10:00am-4:00pm. FREE. The conservatory explores plants and flowers mostly in desert and tropical settings. It has a continuous display of blooming plants during the six major flower seasons of the year. Aquarium also.
- **BELLE ISLE NATURE ZOO** - Wednesday-Sunday 10am-4pm. FREE. Deer feedings. Honeybee Hive. Snakes, fish, and turtles.
- **DOSSIN GREAT LAKES MUSEUM** - (South Shore of Belle Isle). www.detroithistorical.org/aboutus/dossin.asp. (313) 833-1805. Hours: Saturday - Sunday, 11:00am-4:00pm. Admission: FREE. You're greeted by two Battle of Lake Erie cannons and the actual anchor recovered from the Edmund Fitzgerald shipwreck. The Miss Pepsi, one of the fastest hydroplane racing boats of all time. Stand in the pilot house of an ore carrier. As the marine radio sends out requests, turn the ship wheel to steer it on course or use the periscope. The 1912 Great Lakes Luxury Steamer Lounge Room is handsome (all oak carvings) - reminiscent of scenes in the movie "Titanic".
- **BELLE ISLE BEACH AND WATERSLIDE** - As the summer heats up, stay cool at the Belle Isle Water Slide, Wednesday-Sunday (mid-June through Labor Day). $1.00 per slide.

Exit - 47 (east of I-75)

MICHIGAN WELCOME CENTER

Detroit - ***(I-75 NB (Bagley Ave. and 21st Street) 48214. Emergency Contact Number: (313) 962-2360. www.michigan.org/welcome-centers/default.aspx. The center is available for travel assistance & information 7 days/wk, 9:00am-5:00pm.***

This site has new/clean restrooms, family restrooms, weather updates and tourism information.

Exit - 46 (east of I-75)

HISTORIC FORT WAYNE

Detroit - ***6325 West Jefferson (I-75 exit 46. Livernois towards river, ends at Jefferson-riverfront) 48209. www.historicfortwaynecoalition.com/visitors.html. Phone: (313) 833-1805. Hours: Saturday and Sunday 10:00am-4:00pm. Admission: Secured parking is $5.00 per vehicle. Tours: $5***

Enjoy optional guided tours of the Historic Fort Wayne grounds at a price of $5.00 per person. Leaving regularly from the Fort's Visitors Center, the tours will include the Star Fort built in the 1840s, the Commanding Officer's House, and the Spanish-American War Guardhouse. Picnic lunches and coolers are permitted on the Fort grounds, which offer a nice view of the Detroit River, the Ambassador Bridge and Canada. However, alcohol, grills, pets and fishing are not permitted.

Exit - 41 (west of I-75)

AUTOMOBILE HALL OF FAME

Dearborn - ***21400 Oakwood Blvd. (I-75 exit 41 northbound M39 eight miles. Oakwood Blvd exit #4. Next to Greenfield Village) 48121. Phone: (313) 240-4000. www.automotivehalloffame.org. Hours: Wednesday-Sunday 9:00am-5:00pm. Closed major winter holidays. Admission: $10 adult, $6 senior(62+) & student (13-18), $4 youth (5-12).***

A 60-seat theatre giant-screen theatre features a short film, "The Driving Spirit", that takes an amusing look at the individuals responsible for the creation of the automotive industry (follow the "Spirit-ed" boy on this video journey and through the rest of the museum). Before you leave, be sure to start up a replica of the first gasoline-powered car, listen in on a meeting that led to forming the world's largest corporation, look into the Ransom Olds workshop, and visit a classic 1930's showroom.

THE HENRY FORD

Dearborn - ***20900 Oakwood Blvd. (I-75 exit 41 to SR 39 north to Oakwood) 48124. Phone: (313) 982-6001 or (800) 835-5237. www.thehenryford.org. Hours: Daily 9:30am-5:00pm. Closed Thanksgiving & Christmas Days. Admission: $20.00 adult, $18.00 senior (62+), $15.00 child (5-12). Combo discounts available for Ford Factory tour or Greenfield Village. IMAX Theatre (800-747-IMAX) where you'll learn of fascinating innovations and interesting modern science ($7.50-$10 per movie). Freebies: Themed itineraries & Curriculum online (grades 4th-12th). CAFÉ - Check out the Weiner Mobile (make a Mold-A-Rama w/ the kids or grab a snack at the Weiner Mobile Café).***

America's largest indoor-outdoor museum examines our country from rural to industrial societies. A special focus is placed on accomplishments and inventions of famous Americans. The Henry Ford Museum highlights:

- HOME ARTS - evolution of home appliances. Were those the "good ole days?"
- PRESIDENTIAL LIMOUSINES - Among the nationally renowned artifacts of the Museum are the vehicles in which 20th-century American presidents traveled. The Kennedy limo is unforgettable.

President Kennedy's car...

- MADE IN AMERICA - production of goods in the USA.
- INNOVATION STATION - interactively be an innovator or team project player. Really hands-on! Furniture Fun Packs.
- YOUR PLACE IN TIME - explore the 1900's from your own life history experiences. Kids find it silly to see what was considered "technology" years ago. For example, The Dymaxion House was built and sold in the mid-1900's as a solution to the need for a mass-produced, affordable, easily transportable and environmentally efficient house. The house was shipped in it's own metal tube and used tension suspension from a central point. From the outside, it looks like a mutated Airstream or flying saucer! A Sales Rep greets you at the entrance and shares the features of the efficient home with your family – want to buy one?

- HEROES OF THE SKY - With a blend of education and entertainment, it literally allows visitors to become a wingwalker at the county fair, see just how far the Wright Brothers flew on their first flight, or test the principles of aviation as you prepare and test flight your special paper plane. Fifteen historic airplanes interpret storylines that bring to life the lofty accomplishments of America's pioneering aviators.
- WITH LIBERTY & JUSTICE FOR ALL - Lincoln's Chair (the rocking chair he was assassinated in) and Rosa Park's Bus (the one that started the Civil Rights movement). They will stop you in your tracks!

Compared to our visits as children years ago, we noticed a much more interactive, kid-friendly environment.

FORD ROUGE FACTORY TOUR

Dearborn - ***(The Henry Ford Museum departures out front) 48124. Phone: (313) 982-6001. www.thehenryford.org. Hours: Monday-Saturday 9:30am-5:00pm. Closed Thanksgiving and Christmas Days. Admission: Timed tickets: $16.00 adult, $14.50 senior, $12.00 child (3-12).***

Tours: While they cannot guarantee you will see the assembly line in full operation, you will still be able to visit the assembly line area temporarily suspended in mid-operation. They will not be building vehicles during daily breaks, shift changes, Saturdays, Sundays, holidays and during the first two weeks of July. Either way, the tour offers unique experiences with full walking access above the factory assembly area. FREEBIES: Activities for educators online.

Tell the kids to look and listen. Your tour bus actually drives through the Steel Stamping Plant. Next, visitors are led to the Legacy Theater where you view a 12-minute film made from historic photos and films, which tells the story of both Henry Ford and the Ford Rouge complex (great Industrial Revolution learning here, parents). A short walk away, visitors enter the next theater, the Art of Manufacturing. This 360-degree, multi-screen theatre-in-the-round gives viewers the sensation of actually being a part of the manufacturing process through the film which incorporates the traditional visual experience with sound, touch and scent (new car smell)! Visitors feel the heat of the blast furnace and the gentle mist of the paint shop. Get stamped and welded, too! Station Three, the eighty-foot high Observation Deck, offers an impressive view of the entire Rouge Center, including the world's largest living roof covering much of the Dearborn Truck Plant. Finally, visitors take a walkway to the Ford F-150 truck assembly plant for a panoramic, self-guided view of the modern industrial factory (stroller accessible). Along the one-third of a mile walk (with rest stops and potty breaks, if needed) through the plant, you'll see key points in the final assembly process. Meet actual team leaders (by video) and hopefully Bumper and Blinker are working hard installing windshields. Because it's both entertaining and industrial (not super technical), both parents and kids will enjoy this tour.

GREENFIELD VILLAGE

Dearborn - ***20900 Oakwood Blvd. (exit 41 to SR 39 north to Oakwood Blvd.) 48124. Phone: (313) 982-6100 or (313) 982-6150 info. www.thehenryford.org. Hours: Daily 9:30am-5:00pm (April 15 - early November). Friday-Sunday 9:30am-5:00pm (November-December). Open New Year's Day. Closed Thanksgiving and Christmas Days. Admission: $25.00 adult, $22.50 senior (62+), $18.75 child (5-12) (Combo prices and additional attractions available). Carriage rides, Model T rides, sleigh rides, steam train or steamboat rides available for additional fee. Note: Dining options and snacks sold throughout complex.***

When a new road forced Henry Ford's beloved birthplace from its original location, Ford decided not only to move it, but to restore and refurnish it to match his boyhood recollections. The restoration received so much press that

Ford was inundated with requests to save other buildings. Soon after, the idea for Greenfield Village was born. The American Experience examines so much of American history it's hard to believe it's all in one village. Henry Ford's was genius in choosing the best authentic and reproduced historic buildings. Greenfield Village Highlights:

- HENRY FORD BIRTHPLACE - he certainly loved and cherished his mother. See what he played with as a boy.
- FORD COMPANY - the hostess recommends you don't buy the model A, but wait for the Model C (better radiator).
- COHEN MILLINERY - try on hats of olden days.
- GEORGE WASHINGTON CARVER - PEANUTS! A great look at the possibilities of products made with peanuts. Carver helped find industrial uses for peanuts to help poor Southerners find new crops to grow and new uses for the crops they had. Summers, you'll often find "Mr. Carver" making some clever concoctions.
- WRIGHT BROTHERS CYCLE SHOP & HOME - just think of the boys "tinkering" around the shop.
- MATTOX HOUSE - Recycling before the work existed! Newspaper wallpaper, license plate shingles, and layered cardboard ceilings.

- EDISON'S MENLO PARK LAB - Learn about Edison's brilliant and showy sides. Using a loud child as a volunteer, they demonstrate a real Edison phonograph (it really worked) and souvenir piece of tin foil used as the secret to the phonograph's success.
- TASTE OF HISTORY RESTAURANT -Choose from favorites such as Abraham Lincoln's Chicken Fricassee or George Washington Carver's dish-of-choice. Or, try a Railroaders Lunch made with hobo bread just like 19th century railroad workers ate - round raisin nut bread filled with turkey and cheese.

The guides and actors really are skilled at engaging the kid's curiosity and use kids, not adults, as part of their demos.

BEST WESTERN GREENFIELD INN

Dearborn (Allen Park) - ***3000 Enterprise Drive (I-75 exit 41, north on M39 to exit 4. Head southeast on Oakwood to I-94 underpass) 48101. Phone: (313) 271-1600. www.bestwesterngreenfield.com.***

Amenities: Spacious rooms (some w/ frig), large heated indoor pool & jacuzzi, fitness center, coffee makers, cookies at night, in-room VCRs, and Special price tickets available to The Henry Ford/Greenfield Village.

HOLIDAY INN EXPRESS HOTEL & SUITES ALLEN PARK/DEARBORN

Dearborn (Allen Park) - ***3600 Enterprises Drive (I-75 exit 41, north on M39 to exit 4. Head southeast on Oakwood to I-94 underpass) 48101. Phone: (313) 323-3500. www.ihg.com.***

The Family Suites have bunk beds w/ Redwing décor and the continental breakfast is massive. The indoor pool area is clean and kid-friendly, too.

Exit - 20 (west of I-75) / I-275 exit 5

CALDER DAIRY FARM

Carleton - ***9334 Finzel Road (I-275 exit 5 - Telegraph Road Exit (south), to Stoney Creek Road - West to Finzel Road South - follow signs) 48117. Phone: (734) 654-2622. www.calderdairy.com. Hours: Daily 10:00am-7:00pm. Winter hours vary. Admission: FREE. Tours: Pre-arranged @ $6.00 per person (includes hayride and ice cream cone). Minimum group is 15. Note: Farm Store and Ice Cream Shop. Main Store - watch milk arriving and fed through series of pipes for processing. Cow milkings at 4:00pm each afternoon.***

See how luscious ice cream is made - right from the Brown Swiss Cow's milk! Calder Dairy has 37 flavors of New England Style Ice Cream which is hand packaged on the farm. At the farm: Pet the Holstein and Swiss Cows plus numerous other animals that you're likely to see on a farm (pigs, ducks, sheep). They make creamy ice cream, chocolate milk, eggnog, plus milk right from the cows - fresh in glass bottles. Check out the milking machines behind the store to see cows milked by the dozen. (Calder's Dairy also continues to make home deliveries of bottled milk as it has since it opened. Their trucks are unmistakable with big Holstein black markings and the Calder logo). Take a tour in a hay wagon (horse driven) and you'll see fields of llamas, deer and bright peacocks. A family of Ducks and Geese can be fed corn that can be purchased at the store. At the end of your visit to the land of "Babe", be sure to buy a generous souvenir cup of fresh ice cream!

Exit - 15 (east of I-75)

STERLING STATE PARK

Monroe - ***2800 State Park Road (off I-75, exit 15, east on SR 50) 48161. Phone: (734) 289-2715. www.michigan.gov/sterling. Admission: $6.00-$8.00 per vehicle or Park Pass.***

Walleye are plentiful in Lake Erie. Shore fishing is possible at Sterling's three lagoons, three fishing piers and at its access to River Raisin. A total of seven miles of trails provide opportunities for hiking, biking and exploring. The 2.9-mile paved Marsh Trail circles one of the marsh lagoons in the park. A 0.6-mile hiking trail follows the Lake Erie shoreline. These trails include interpretive stations, an observation deck and a covered pavilion with spotting scopes. Camping, boating, and swimming. Boat Rentals Memorial Day - Labor Day. Row boats, canoes, paddle boats.

Exit - 14 (west of I-75)

RIVER RAISIN BATTLEFIELD VISITOR'S CENTER

Monroe - ***1403 East Elm Street (I-75, exit 14) 48161. Phone: (734) 243-7136. www.nps.gov/rira. Hours: Daily 9am-5pm. Admission: FREE (donations accepted)***

An important stop for interesting regional history, this visitor's center focuses on the battle (during the War of 1812) that was the worst defeat for the Americans. The British and Chief Tecumseh's Indians killed over 800 settlers during this battle. A 10 minute presentation summarizes the importance of who was in control of the Great Lakes. The display includes dioramas & full-size British & American soldiers, as well as a fiber-optic map presentation on the Battle of the River Raisin.

Mile - 10 mile (east of I-75)

MICHIGAN WELCOME CENTER (FAR SOUTH)

Monroe - ***(I-75 exit 10 mile marker heading north) 48161. Phone: (734) 242-1768 emergency number. www.michigan.org/welcome-centers/default.aspx. Hours: Year round 9:00am-5:00pm - tourism, plus extended summer hours during peak demand. Restroom facilities open 24 hours a day.***

Monroe not only has over 4,000 brochures to meander through, but the kids will love the fully accessible playground for kids to enjoy. Parents will enjoy relaxing in the special outdoor rock garden.

Chapter 2
OHIO

Curious about hundreds of fun
places in the lighter gray areas?
See *Kids Love Ohio*

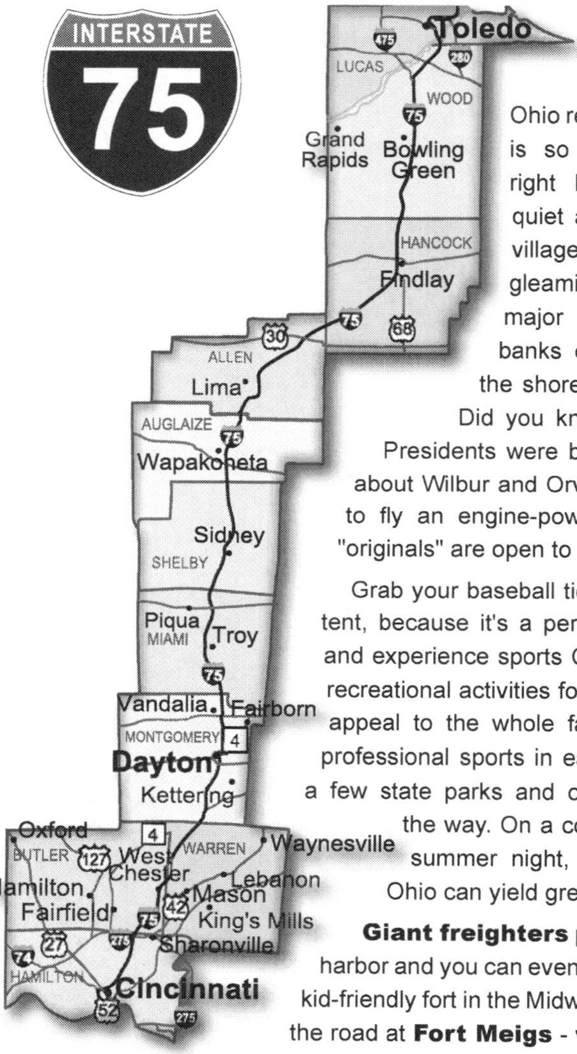

DEAR OHIO TRAVELER:

A trip through Ohio reminds us that there is so much of America right here. Ohio is the quiet and beauty of rural villages and it is also the gleaming glass towers of major cities. Ohio is the banks of great rivers and the shores of a Great Lake. Did you know that eight U.S. Presidents were born in Ohio? What about Wilbur and Orville Wright, the first to fly an engine-powered aircraft? The "originals" are open to visit in Ohio.

Grab your baseball tickets, tackle box or tent, because it's a perfect day to get out and experience sports Ohio. The state has recreational activities for every season that appeal to the whole family, with exciting professional sports in each major city, and a few state parks and campgrounds along the way. On a cool fall day or a hot summer night, getting off I-75 in Ohio can yield great adventures.

Giant freighters pour into the Toledo harbor and you can even tour one. The most kid-friendly fort in the Midwest is located down the road at **Fort Meigs** - with plenty of dress up clothes to try on and green space to run on. Built up an appetite for some crazy food? Stop by the original **Tony Packo's** and take a bite of a Packo's Hungarian Hot Dog while viewing framed hot dog buns signed by celebrities. We told you crazy stuff...

Do your kids love candy? What about spending the day sampling chocolates, ice cream and hard candies? You're in the right place! This region of the state has **Dietsch Brothers** (Findlay) old-fashioned ice cream and chocolates.

Tours are not too hard to coordinate (weekdays) or tag along on. Try wacky flavors like "Everything but the Kitchen Sink" or "Snick-a-Ripple" flavors. You can't miss on these visits – just be sure to brush your teeth soon after!

Canals, not planes, are the hot topic at **Piqua Historical Area**. Ever tried to churn butter by hand? Trying some ice cream or butter freshly made by costumed 1800s-period folks? Then, take a "slow ride" on the canal with mules leading the way.

Meet the inventors of flight and the pilots of space in the Dayton area. The dream of flight was imagined by many, but achieved by Orville and Wilbur Wright, two brothers from Dayton who built and flew the first mechanically powered airplane. Their **Wright Cycle Company and Carillon Park** are probably the most kid-friendly sites to catch a glimpse of their genius. Walk on the same workshop floors of these famous folks who wouldn't stop at a "no" until they had a "yes". The **National Museum of the U.S. Air Force**, located just east of Dayton, also tells the story of the 100-plus years of flight, from its beginning to today's stealth age. ..and it's a FREE attraction. The world's only B-2 stealth bomber on public display is here, too. North of Dayton in Wapakoneta is the **Armstrong Air & Space Museum** where you'll see another form of aviation. Astronaut Neil Armstrong has permitted display of many space artifacts and a wonderful interactive area that immerses kids into "space."

Dayton is host to some other great sites like the **Boonshoft Museum of Discovery** where interactive techno exhibits combined with a zoo and planetarium make for more than a day's worth of fun. Their sister location nearby is **Sunwatch** – an ancient Indian village recreated from actual archeological digs in the area. What did they find and where did the Indians go?

The first major-league pro baseball team was the Cincinnati Red Stockings, but the Cincinnati area has many more "major-league" attractions to offer. Spend the weekend exploring four great places in one historic building at the Cincinnati Museum Center at Union Terminal. Walk through the Ice Age and a recreated limestone cave at the **Museum of Natural History and Science** or let kids explore The Woods, an interactive adventure in the wilderness, at the **Duke Energy Children's Museum**. A Hands-on **Cincinnati History Museum** and an IMAX theatre are located here, too. But that's not all there is to do for family fun. In the city you can climb down a real fire pole (**Cincinnati Fire Museum**). On the water you can **Ride the Ducks** and get Quacky with it. In the water, the greater Cincinnati area has two indoor waterparks and two outdoor waterparks.

There are some pretty neat places just a little ways north of downtown Cincinnati that are so worth fitting into your next trip. A small pioneer village bustles with activity most every weekend at **Heritage Village** in Sharonville. Try your hand at churning butter or marching a Civil War battle drill at special events throughout the year. Off the northern tip of the outerbelt you'll find a grocery store adventure at **Jungle Jim's**. Adventure? This store is – a supermarket that's a tourist attraction in Fairfield. Foodies and kids love the animals that greet you outside and the whimsical dioramas inside. Look for the Amish buggy, a shrimp boat, the Big Cheese, Elvis, a fire truck and even a walk through Sherwood Forest.

Sometimes, planning a vacation that appeals to the whole family can be problematic. In Ohio, the only problem might be trying to fit everything in. Creating and sharing memories on a budget is easy in this fun-filled, family-friendly state. We hope you enjoy your drive through Ohio, the Buckeye State.

ACTIVITIES AT A GLANCE

AMUSEMENTS

Exit - 192 / I-475 Exit 6 - *Splash Bay Resort*

Exit - 22 - *Entertrainment Junction*

Exit - 16 / I-275 Exit 41 - *Jungle Jim's International Market*

ANIMALS & FARMS

Exit - 201 (NB Only)/202A (SB Only) - *Toledo Zoo*

Exit - 73 - *Idle Hour Ranch*

Exit - 6 - *Cincinnati Zoo And Botanical Gardens*

HISTORY

Exit - 199 - *National Museum of the Great Lakes*

Exit - 192 / I-475 Exit 2 - *Fort Meigs*

Exit - 192 / I-475 Exit 4 - *Wolcott House Museum Complex*

Exit - 125B - *Allen County Museum*

Exit - 83 - *Lockington Locks*

Exit - 83 - *Piqua Historical Area Tour*

Exit - 61A / I-70 Exit 38 - *Carriage Hill Farm And Museum*

HISTORY *(cont.)*

Exit - 54C - *National Museum Of The USAF*

Exit - 53A - *Wright Cycle Company Complex*

Exit - 53A - *Dunbar House*

Exit - 51 - *SunWatch*

Exit - 51 - *Carillon Historical Park, Dayton History At*

Exit - 44 - *Miamisburg Mound*

Exit - 44 - *Wright B. Flyer*

Exit - 16 / I-275 Exit 46 - *Heritage Village Museum*

Exit - 1D - *Cincinnati History Museum*

Exit - 1A - *National Underground Railroad Freedom Center*

MUSEUMS

Exit - 206 - *Toledo Firefighters Museum*

Exit - 199 - *Imagination Station*

Exit - 179 - *Snooks Dream Cars Museum*

Exit - 53A - *Citizens Motorcar Packard Museum*

Exit - 1D - *Duke Energy Children's Museum*

Exit - 1C - *Cincinnati Fire Museum*

OUTDOOR EXPLORING

Exit - 208 / I-280 Exit 9 - *Maumee Bay State Park*
Exit - 204 / I-475 Exit 19 - *Toledo Botanical Gardens*
Exit - 164 - *Van Buren Lake State Park*
Exit - 99 - *Lake Loramie State Park*
Exit - 53B - *Riverscape*
Exit - 50B - *Cox Arboretum*
Exit - 1C - *Carew Tower*

SCIENCE

Exit - 210 - *Fossil Park*
Exit - 179 - *BG Wind Farm*
Exit - 111 - *Armstrong Air And Space Museum*
Exit - 73 - *Brukner Nature Center*
Exit - 63 - *Aullwood Audubon Center And Farm*
Exit - 57B - *Boonshoft Museum Of Discovery*
Exit - 1D - *Museum Of Natural History And Science*

SUGGESTED LODGING & DINING

Exit - 208 / I-280 Exit 9 - *Tony Packo's Café*
Exit - 199 - *Real Seafood Co.*

THE ARTS

Exit - 203B - *Toledo Museum Of Art*
Exit - 159 - *Mazza Collection Museum*
Exit - 54B - *Dayton Art Institute*
Exit - 1C - *Taft Museum Of Art*

TOURS

Exit - 201B (NB Only) / 202A (SB Only) - *Sandpiper Canal Boat*
Exit - 161 - *Northwest Ohio Railroad Preservation*
Exit - 157 - *Dietsch Brothers Fine Chocolates & Ice Cream*
Exit - 102 - *Airstream Factory Tour*

WELCOME CENTERS

Exit - 178 - *Ohio Travel Information Center*
Exit - 28 - *Ohio Travel Information Center*

GENERAL INFORMATION

Contact the services of interest. Request to be added to their mailing lists.

- ☐ Ohio Department of Natural Resources, www.dnr.state.oh.us/odnr (877) 4BOATER or (800) WILDLIFE.
- ☐ Ohio Campground Owner's Association (614) 764-0279 or www.ohiocamper.com
- ☐ National Camping Information www.gocampingamerica.com
- ☐ Ohio State Parks (614) 466-0652 or www.dnr.state.oh.us/parks
- ☐ Ohio State Park Lodges & Resorts www.dnr.state.oh.us/parks/overnightfacilities or (800) 282-7275.
- ☐ Ohio's Agricultural Fairs, www.ohioagriculture.gov. (614) 728-6200. Schedules available through the Ohio Department of Agriculture.
- ☐ Ohio Division of Travel & Tourism (800) BUCKEYE or www.discoverohio.com
- ☐ Greene County CVB (800) 733-9109 or www.greenecountyohio.org
- ☐ Cincinnati CVB (800) CINCYUSA or www.cincyusa.com

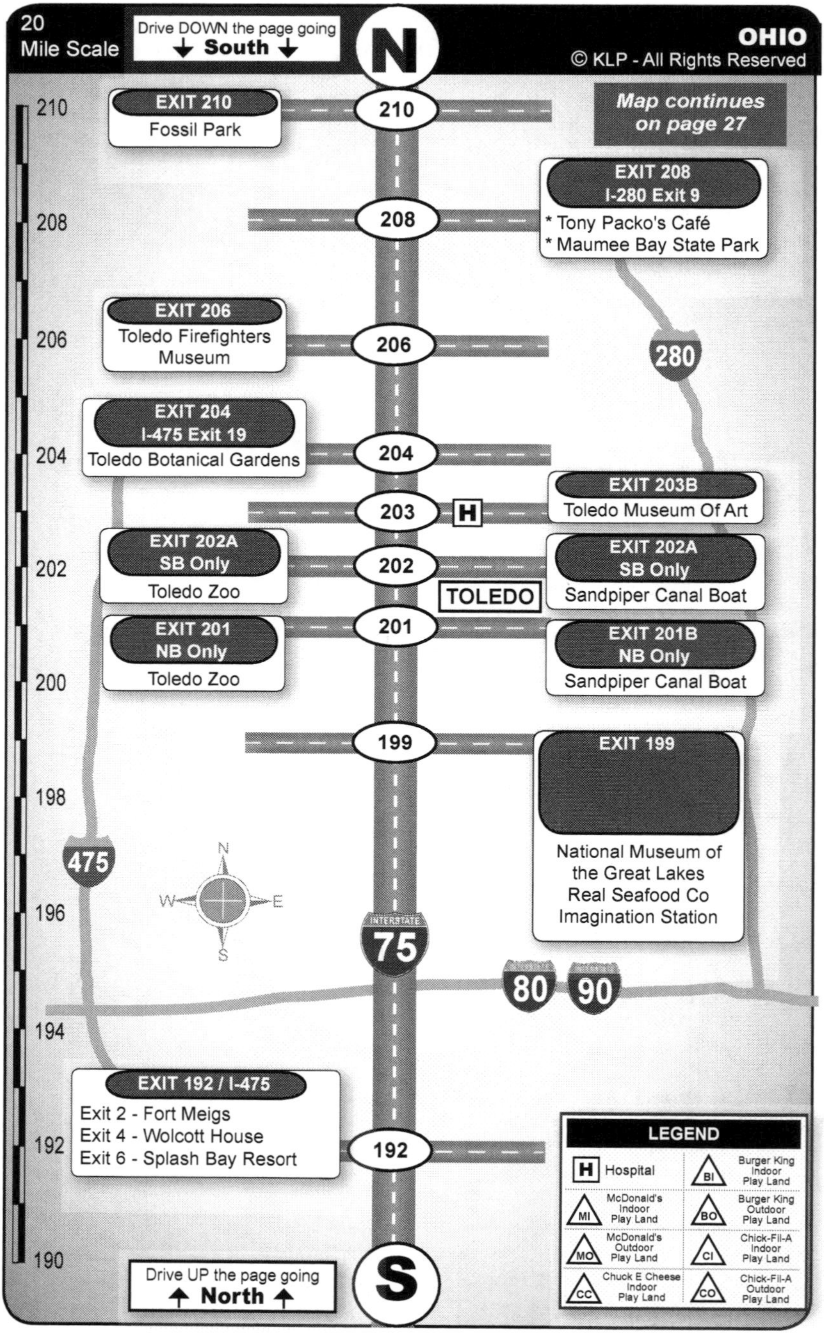
20
Mile Scale
Drive DOWN the page going
South
N
OHIO
© KLP - All Rights Reserved
Map continues on page 27
EXIT 210
Fossil Park
EXIT 208
I-280 Exit 9
* Tony Packo's Café
* Maumee Bay State Park
EXIT 206
Toledo Firefighters Museum
EXIT 204
I-475 Exit 19
Toledo Botanical Gardens
EXIT 203B
Toledo Museum Of Art
EXIT 202A
SB Only
Toledo Zoo
EXIT 202A
SB Only
Sandpiper Canal Boat
TOLEDO
EXIT 201
NB Only
Toledo Zoo
EXIT 201B
NB Only
Sandpiper Canal Boat
EXIT 199
National Museum of the Great Lakes
Real Seafood Co
Imagination Station
210
208
206
204
203
202
201
199
192
280
475
75
80
90
N
W
E
S
210
208
206
204
202
200
198
196
194
192
190
EXIT 192 / I-475
Exit 2 - Fort Meigs
Exit 4 - Wolcott House
Exit 6 - Splash Bay Resort
LEGEND
H Hospital
BI Burger King Indoor Play Land
MI McDonald's Indoor Play Land
BO Burger King Outdoor Play Land
MO McDonald's Outdoor Play Land
CI Chick-Fil-A Indoor Play Land
CC Chuck E Cheese Indoor Play Land
CO Chick-Fil-A Outdoor Play Land
Drive UP the page going
North
S

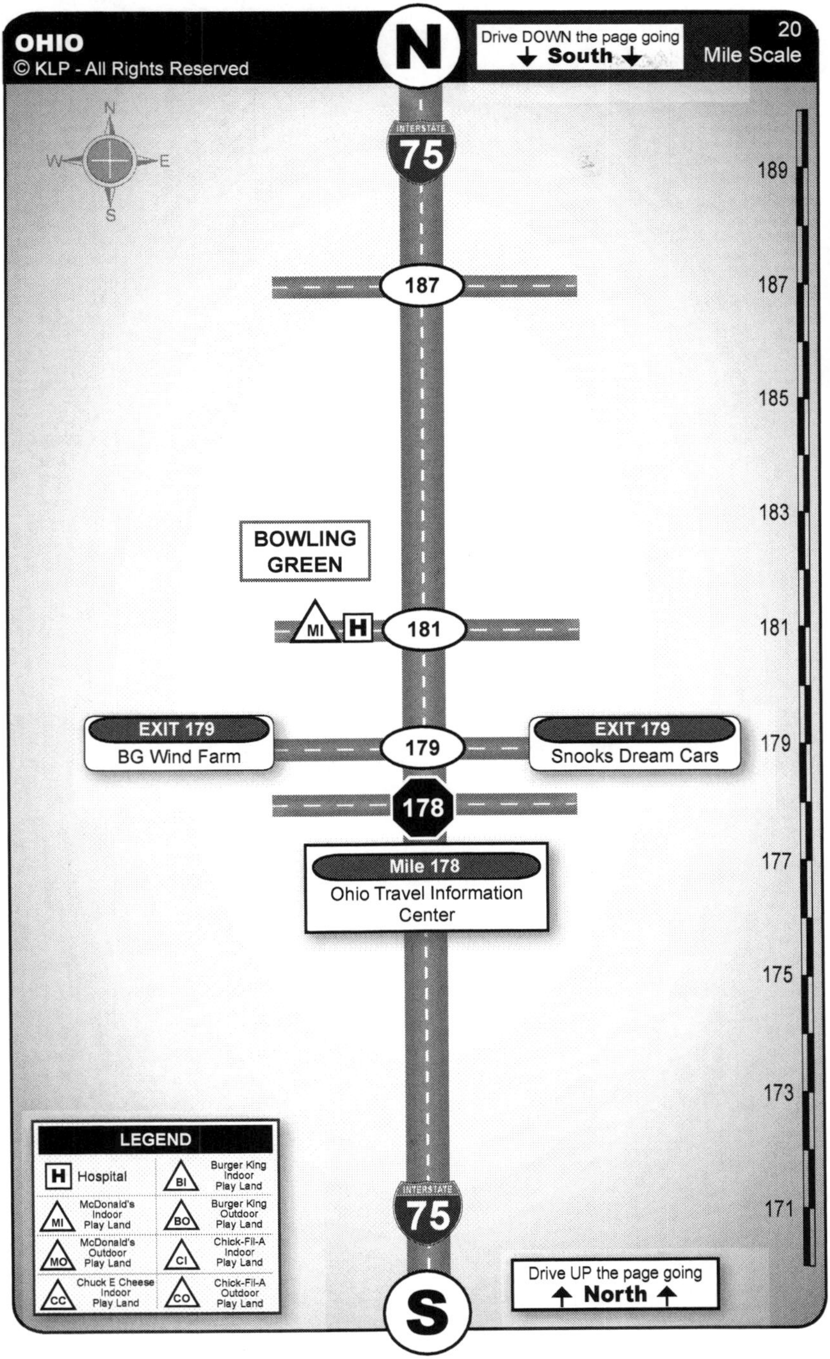
OHIO
© KLP - All Rights Reserved
N
Drive DOWN the page going
South
20
Mile Scale
75
189
187
185
183
181
179
177
175
173
171
BOWLING
GREEN
MI
H
EXIT 179
BG Wind Farm
EXIT 179
Snooks Dream Cars
178
Mile 178
Ohio Travel Information
Center
LEGEND
Hospital
Burger King Indoor Play Land
McDonald's Indoor Play Land
Burger King Outdoor Play Land
McDonald's Outdoor Play Land
Chick-Fil-A Indoor Play Land
Chuck E Cheese Indoor Play Land
Chick-Fil-A Outdoor Play Land
75
S
Drive UP the page going
North

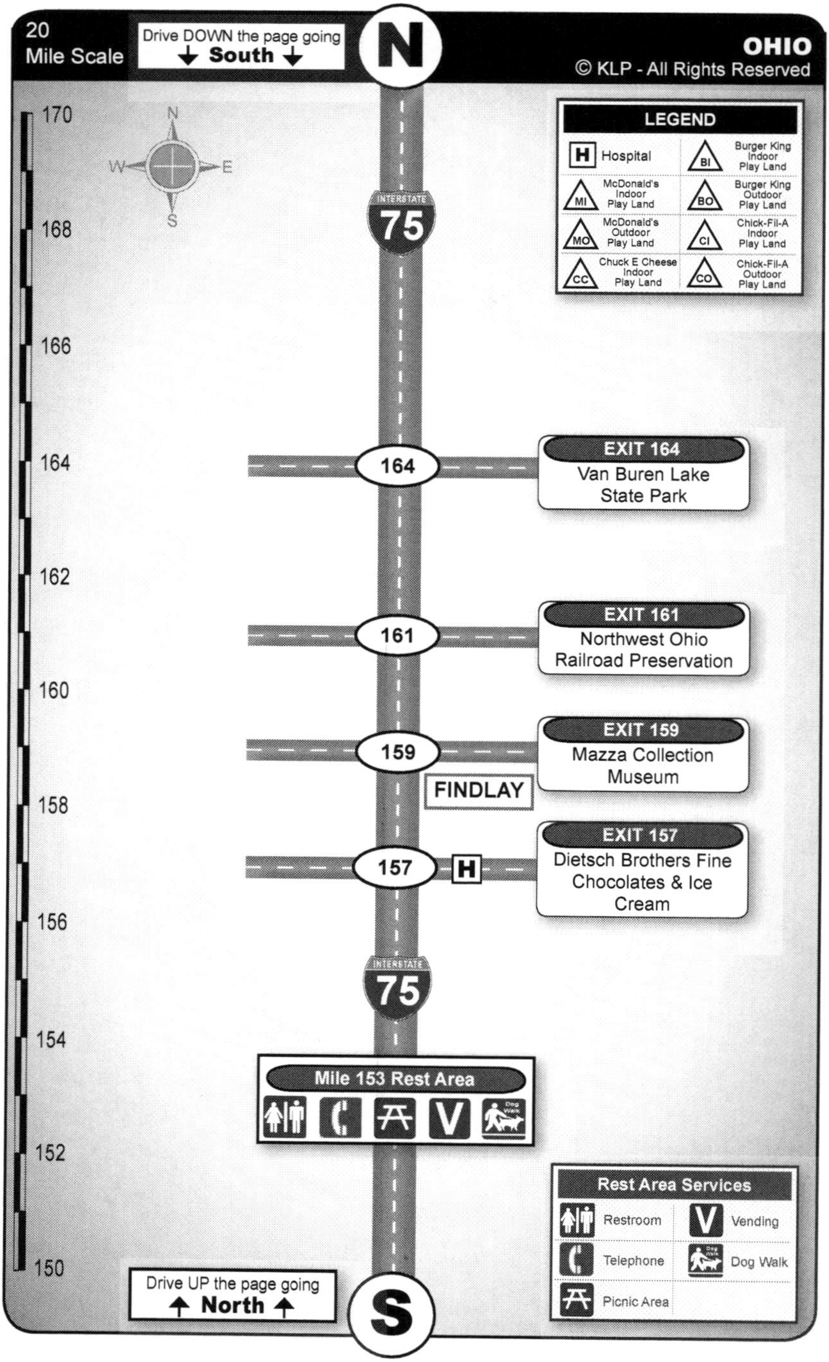

20 Mile Scale
Drive DOWN the page going ↓ South ↓
N
OHIO
© KLP - All Rights Reserved
LEGEND
H Hospital
BI Burger King Indoor Play Land
MI McDonald's Indoor Play Land
BO Burger King Outdoor Play Land
MO McDonald's Outdoor Play Land
CI Chick-Fil-A Indoor Play Land
CC Chuck E Cheese Indoor Play Land
CO Chick-Fil-A Outdoor Play Land
170
168
166
164
162
160
158
156
154
152
150
N
W
E
S
INTERSTATE 75
164
EXIT 164
Van Buren Lake State Park
161
EXIT 161
Northwest Ohio Railroad Preservation
159
EXIT 159
Mazza Collection Museum
FINDLAY
157
H
EXIT 157
Dietsch Brothers Fine Chocolates & Ice Cream
INTERSTATE 75
Mile 153 Rest Area
Dog Walk
Rest Area Services
Restroom
Vending
Telephone
Dog Walk
Picnic Area
Drive UP the page going ↑ North ↑
S

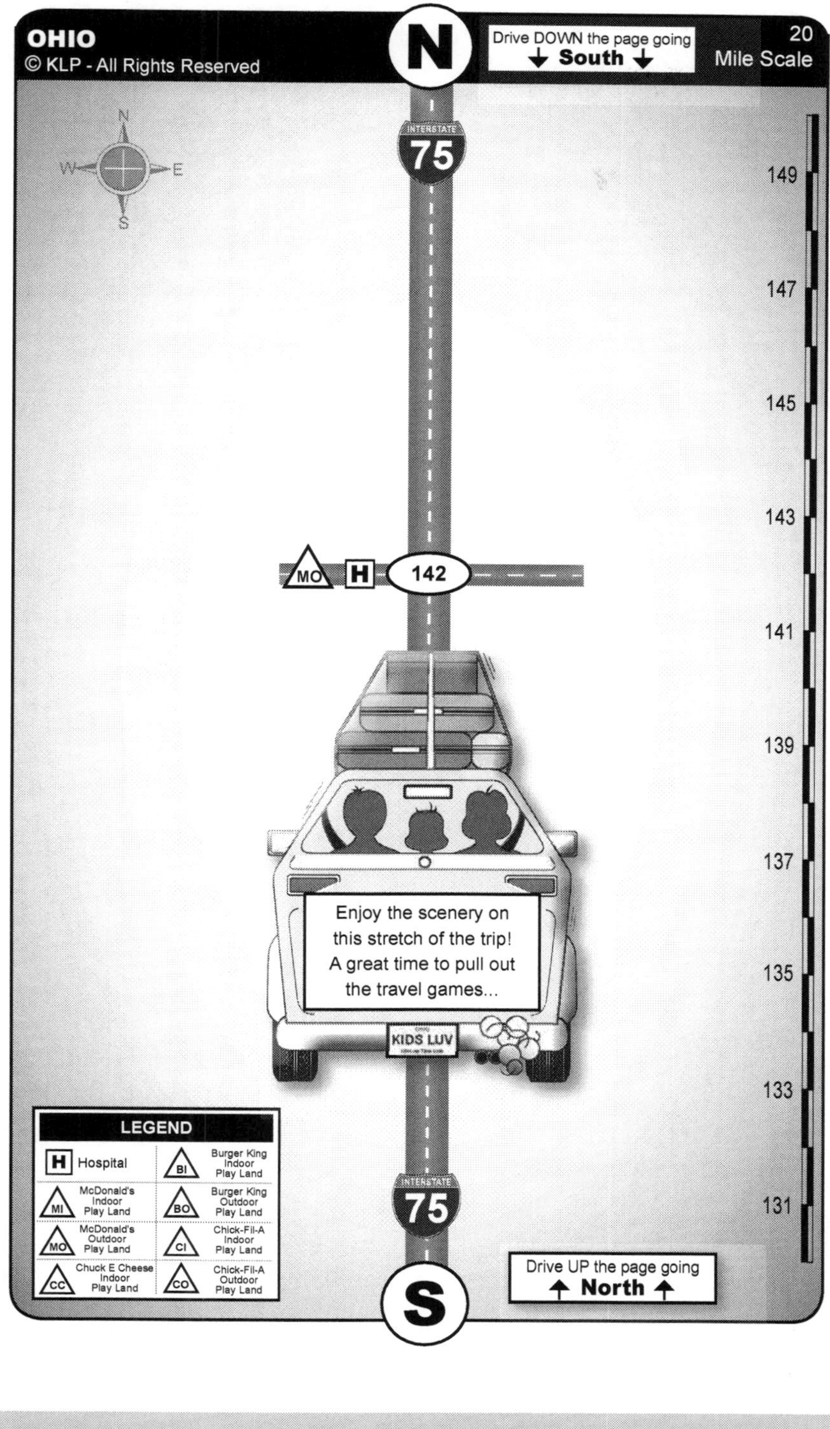
OHIO
© KLP - All Rights Reserved
N
Drive DOWN the page going
South
20
Mile Scale
INTERSTATE
75
149
147
145
143
MO
H
142
141
139
137
Enjoy the scenery on
this stretch of the trip!
A great time to pull out
the travel games...
135
KIDS LUV
133
131
LEGEND
H Hospital
BI Burger King Indoor Play Land
MI McDonald's Indoor Play Land
BO Burger King Outdoor Play Land
MO McDonald's Outdoor Play Land
CI Chick-Fil-A Indoor Play Land
CC Chuck E Cheese Indoor Play Land
CO Chick-Fil-A Outdoor Play Land
INTERSTATE
75
Drive UP the page going
North
S

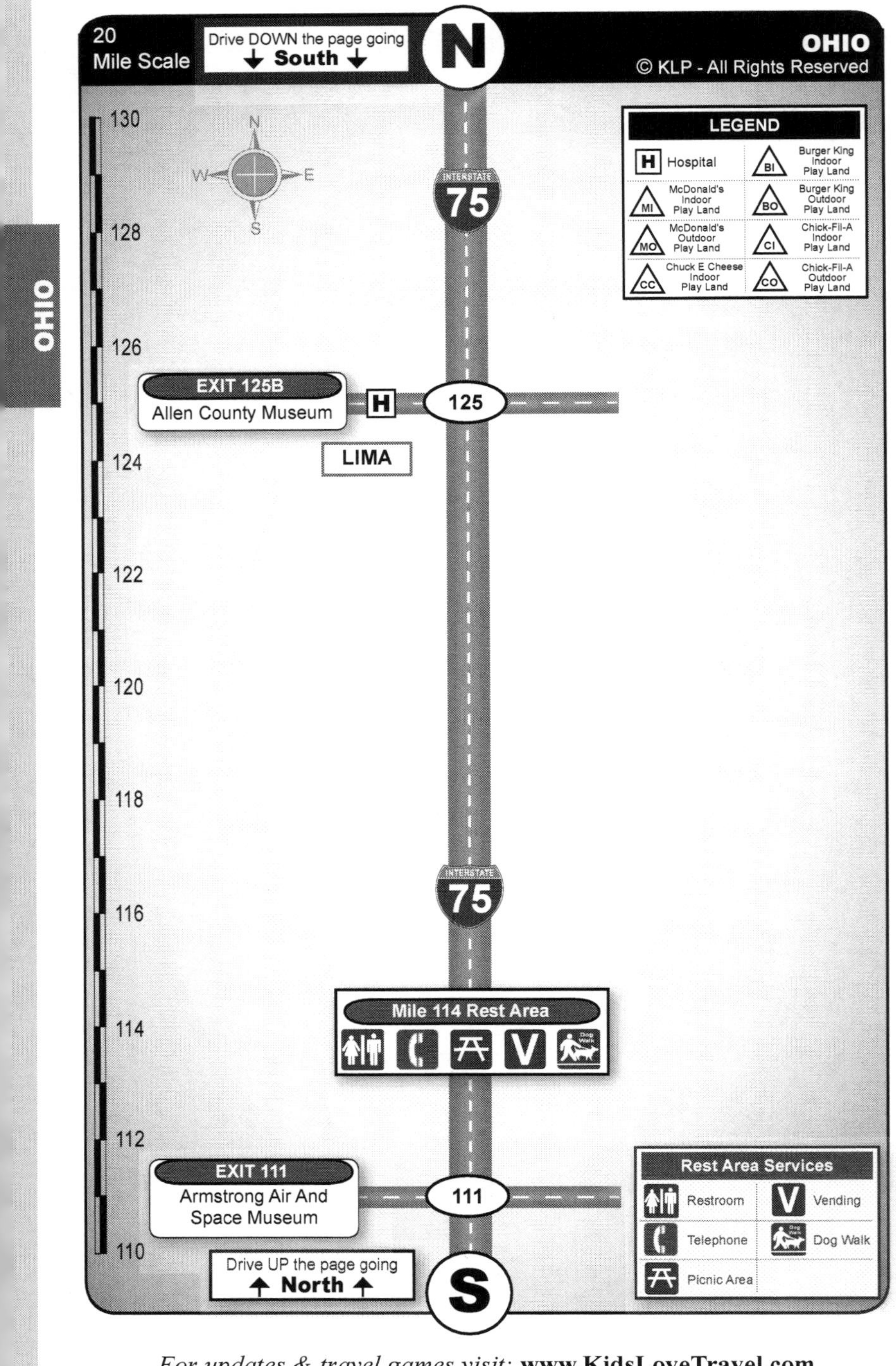
20
Mile Scale
Drive DOWN the page going
South
N
OHIO
© KLP - All Rights Reserved
130
128
126
124
122
120
118
116
114
112
110
N
W
E
S
75
LEGEND
H Hospital
BI Burger King Indoor Play Land
MI McDonald's Indoor Play Land
BO Burger King Outdoor Play Land
MO McDonald's Outdoor Play Land
CI Chick-Fil-A Indoor Play Land
CC Chuck E Cheese Indoor Play Land
CO Chick-Fil-A Outdoor Play Land
EXIT 125B
Allen County Museum
H
125
LIMA
75
Mile 114 Rest Area
V
Dog Walk
EXIT 111
Armstrong Air And Space Museum
111
Rest Area Services
Restroom
Vending
Telephone
Dog Walk
Picnic Area
Drive UP the page going
North
S

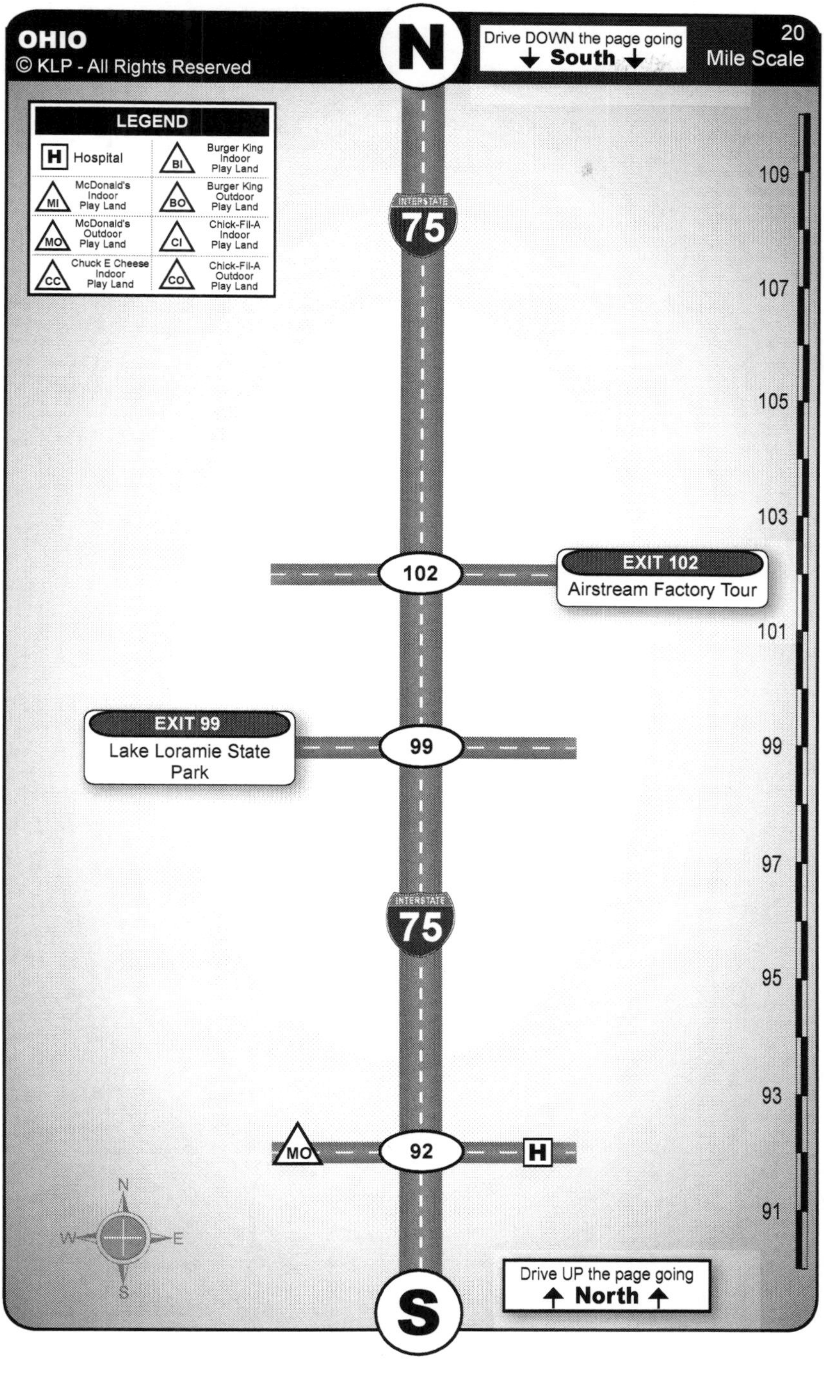
OHIO
© KLP - All Rights Reserved
N
Drive DOWN the page going
South
20
Mile Scale
LEGEND
H Hospital
BI Burger King Indoor Play Land
MI McDonald's Indoor Play Land
BO Burger King Outdoor Play Land
MO McDonald's Outdoor Play Land
CI Chick-Fil-A Indoor Play Land
CC Chuck E Cheese Indoor Play Land
CO Chick-Fil-A Outdoor Play Land
INTERSTATE 75
109
107
105
103
102
EXIT 102
Airstream Factory Tour
101
EXIT 99
Lake Loramie State Park
99
97
95
93
MO
92
H
91
N
W
E
S
Drive UP the page going
North
S

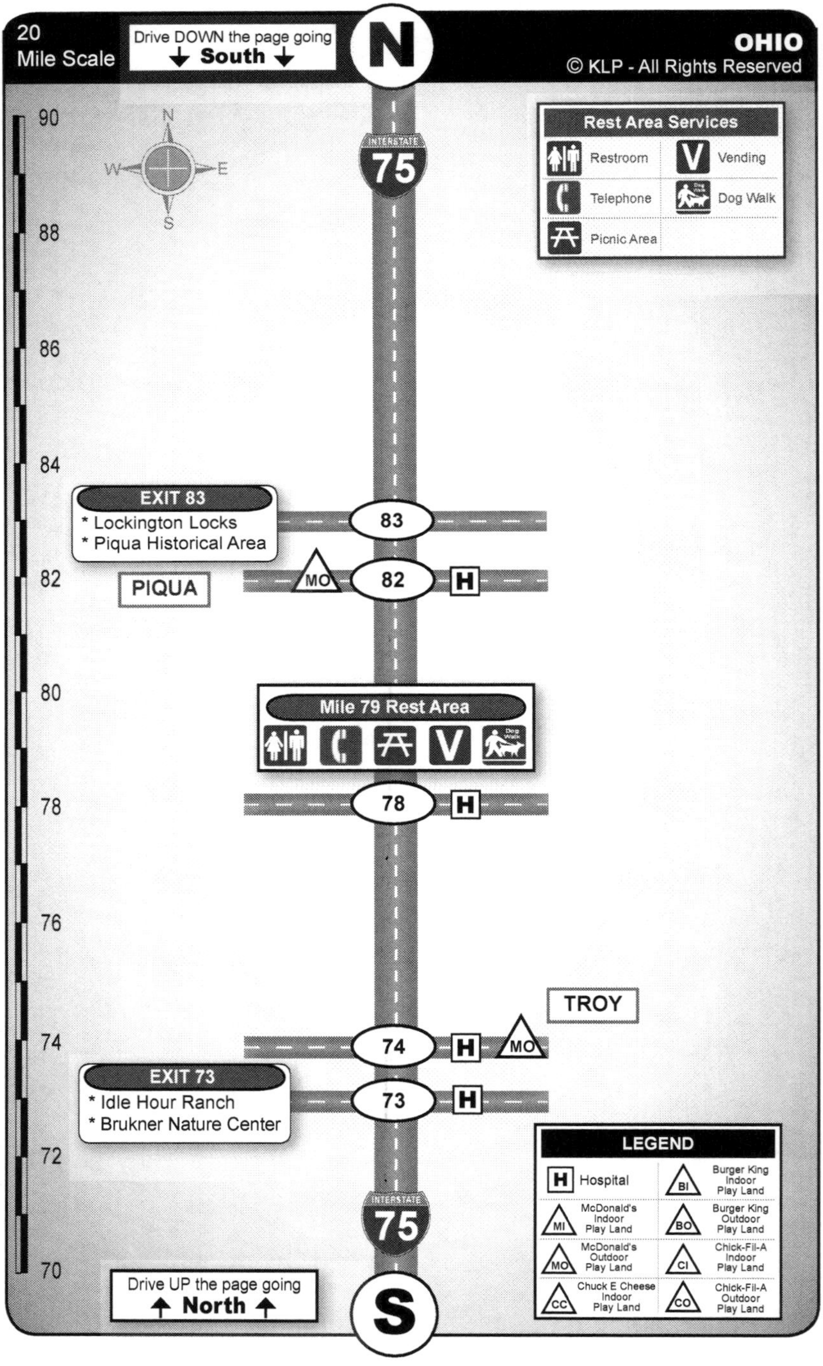
20
Mile Scale
Drive DOWN the page going
South
N
OHIO
© KLP - All Rights Reserved
90
88
86
84
82
80
78
76
74
72
70
N
W
E
S
INTERSTATE
75
Rest Area Services
Restroom
Vending
Telephone
Dog Walk
Picnic Area
EXIT 83
* Lockington Locks
* Piqua Historical Area
83
PIQUA
MO
82
H
Mile 79 Rest Area
V
78
H
TROY
74
H
MO
EXIT 73
* Idle Hour Ranch
* Brukner Nature Center
73
H
LEGEND
H Hospital
BI Burger King Indoor Play Land
MI McDonald's Indoor Play Land
BO Burger King Outdoor Play Land
MO McDonald's Outdoor Play Land
CI Chick-Fil-A Indoor Play Land
CC Chuck E Cheese Indoor Play Land
CO Chick-Fil-A Outdoor Play Land
INTERSTATE
75
Drive UP the page going
North
S

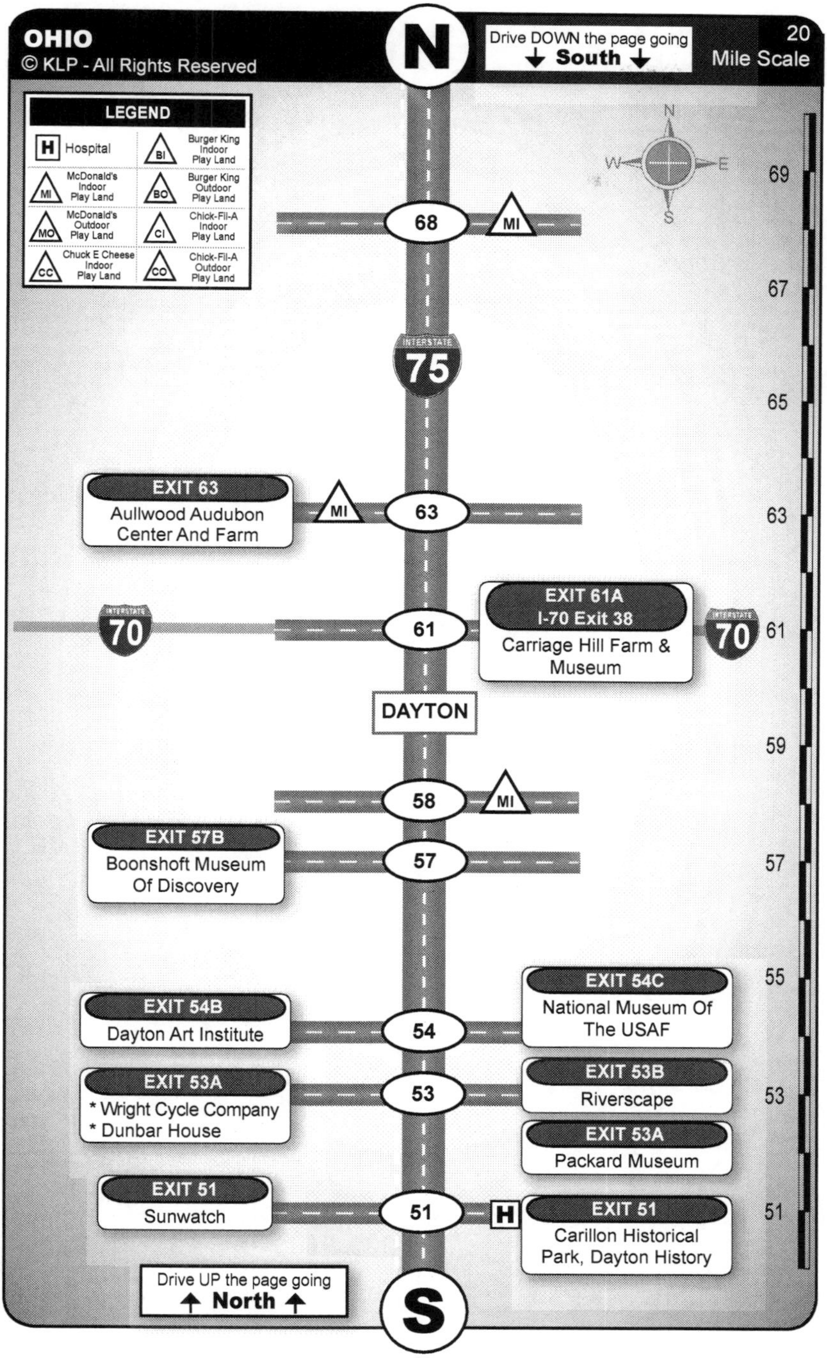
OHIO
© KLP - All Rights Reserved
N
Drive DOWN the page going
↓ South ↓
20
Mile Scale
LEGEND
H Hospital
BI Burger King Indoor Play Land
MI McDonald's Indoor Play Land
BO Burger King Outdoor Play Land
MO McDonald's Outdoor Play Land
CI Chick-Fil-A Indoor Play Land
CC Chuck E Cheese Indoor Play Land
CO Chick-Fil-A Outdoor Play Land
N
W
E
S
69
68
MI
67
INTERSTATE 75
65
EXIT 63
Aullwood Audubon Center And Farm
MI
63
63
INTERSTATE 70
61
EXIT 61A
I-70 Exit 38
Carriage Hill Farm & Museum
INTERSTATE 70
61
DAYTON
59
58
MI
EXIT 57B
Boonshoft Museum Of Discovery
57
57
55
EXIT 54C
National Museum Of The USAF
EXIT 54B
Dayton Art Institute
54
EXIT 53A
* Wright Cycle Company
* Dunbar House
53
EXIT 53B
Riverscape
53
EXIT 53A
Packard Museum
EXIT 51
Sunwatch
51
H
EXIT 51
Carillon Historical Park, Dayton History
51
Drive UP the page going
↑ North ↑
S

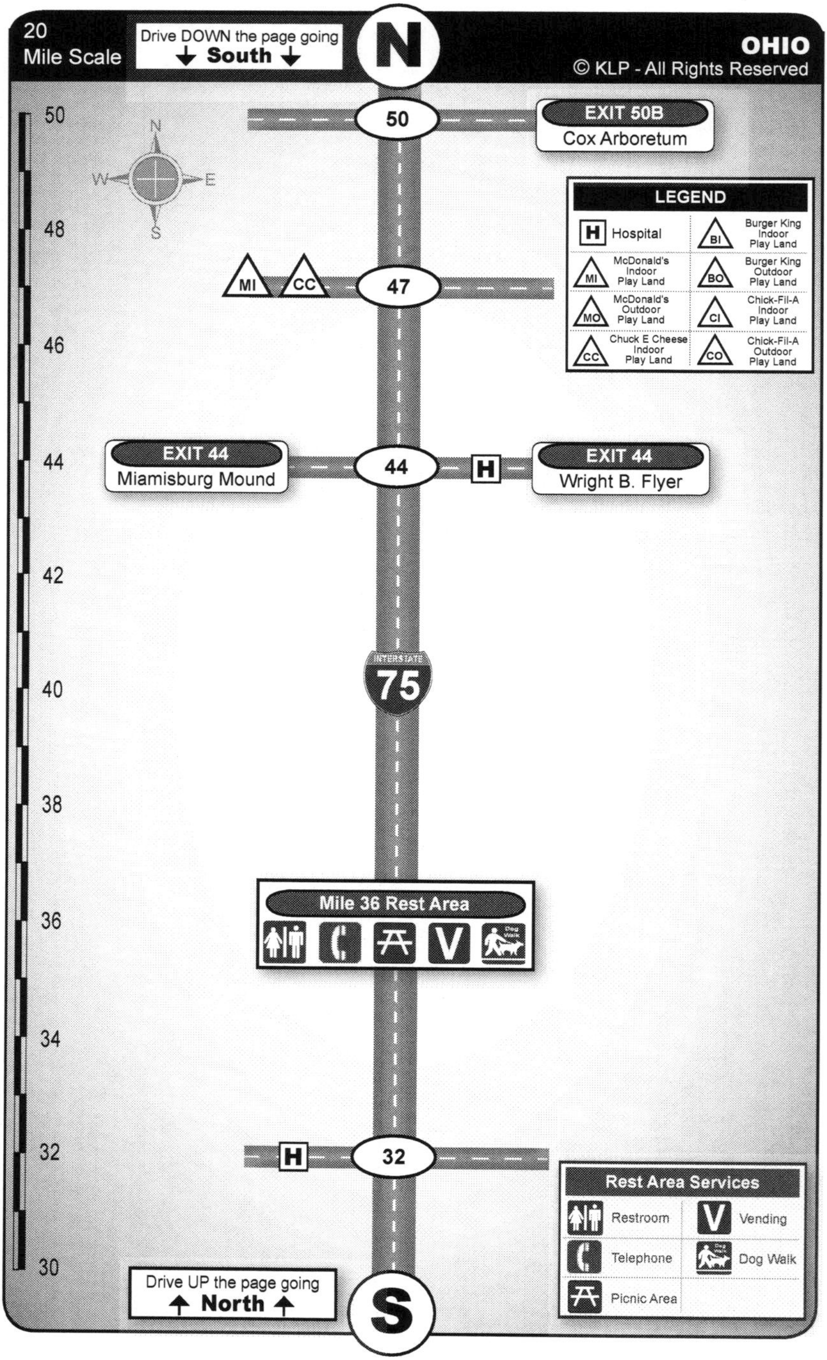
20
Mile Scale
Drive DOWN the page going
South
N
OHIO
© KLP - All Rights Reserved
50
48
46
44
42
40
38
36
34
32
30
N
W
E
S
50
EXIT 50B
Cox Arboretum
LEGEND
H Hospital
BI Burger King Indoor Play Land
MI McDonald's Indoor Play Land
BO Burger King Outdoor Play Land
MO McDonald's Outdoor Play Land
CI Chick-Fil-A Indoor Play Land
CC Chuck E Cheese Indoor Play Land
CO Chick-Fil-A Outdoor Play Land
MI
CC
47
EXIT 44
Miamisburg Mound
44
H
EXIT 44
Wright B. Flyer
INTERSTATE
75
Mile 36 Rest Area
Dog Walk
H
32
Rest Area Services
Restroom
Vending
Telephone
Dog Walk
Picnic Area
Drive UP the page going
North
S

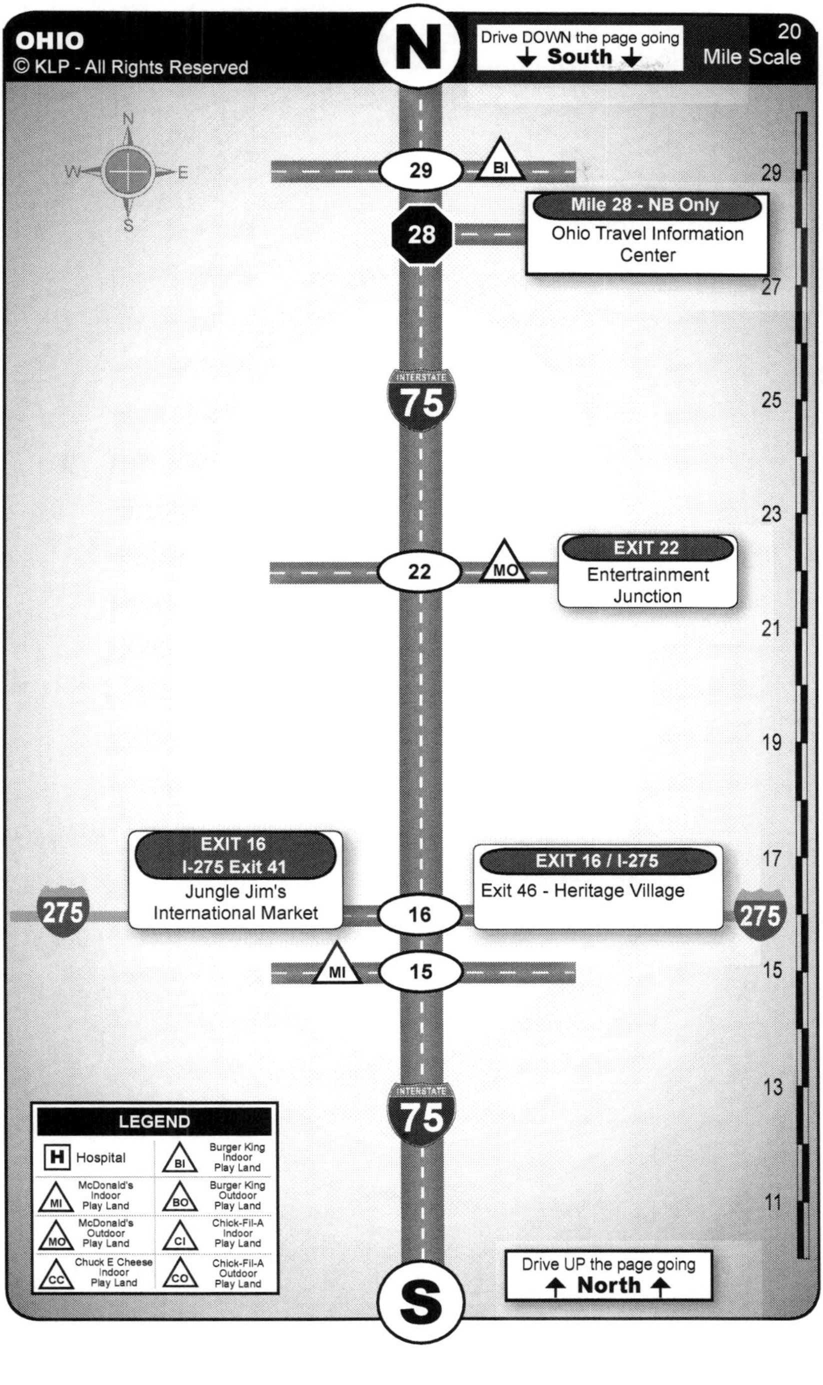
OHIO
© KLP - All Rights Reserved
N
Drive DOWN the page going
↓ South ↓
20
Mile Scale
N
W
E
S
29
BI
Mile 28 - NB Only
Ohio Travel Information Center
28
75
22
MO
EXIT 22
Entertrainment Junction
EXIT 16
I-275 Exit 41
Jungle Jim's International Market
275
16
EXIT 16 / I-275
Exit 46 - Heritage Village
275
15
MI
75
29
27
25
23
21
19
17
15
13
11
LEGEND
H Hospital
BI Burger King Indoor Play Land
MI McDonald's Indoor Play Land
BO Burger King Outdoor Play Land
MO McDonald's Outdoor Play Land
CI Chick-Fil-A Indoor Play Land
CC Chuck E Cheese Indoor Play Land
CO Chick-Fil-A Outdoor Play Land
S
Drive UP the page going
↑ North ↑

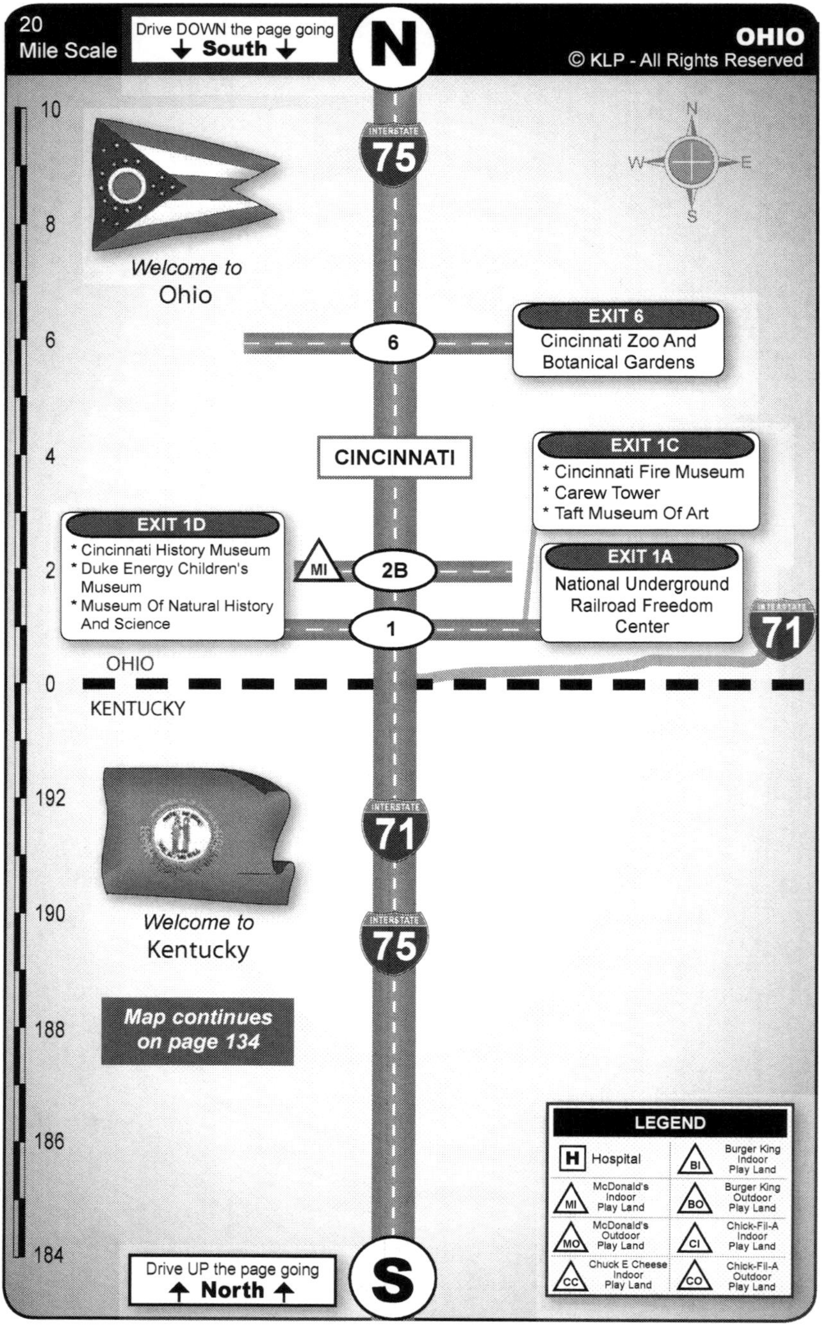
20
Mile Scale
Drive DOWN the page going
South
N
OHIO
© KLP - All Rights Reserved
10
8
6
4
2
0
192
190
188
186
184
INTERSTATE
75
N
W
E
S
Welcome to
Ohio
EXIT 6
Cincinnati Zoo And
Botanical Gardens
6
CINCINNATI
EXIT 1C
* Cincinnati Fire Museum
* Carew Tower
* Taft Museum Of Art
EXIT 1D
* Cincinnati History Museum
* Duke Energy Children's
Museum
* Museum Of Natural History
And Science
MI
2B
EXIT 1A
National Underground
Railroad Freedom
Center
1
71
OHIO
KENTUCKY
INTERSTATE
71
Welcome to
Kentucky
INTERSTATE
75
Map continues
on page 134
LEGEND
H Hospital
BI Burger King Indoor Play Land
MI McDonald's Indoor Play Land
BO Burger King Outdoor Play Land
MO McDonald's Outdoor Play Land
CI Chick-Fil-A Indoor Play Land
CC Chuck E Cheese Indoor Play Land
CO Chick-Fil-A Outdoor Play Land
Drive UP the page going
North
S

Sites and attractions are listed in order by Exit Number (North to South) and distance from the exit (closest are listed first). Symbols indicated represent:

Restaurants Lodging

Exit - 210 (west of I-75)

FOSSIL PARK

Sylvania - ***5705 Centennial Road (I-75 exit 210 west on SR 184) 43560. Phone: (419) 882-8313. Hours: Saturday 10:00am-6:00pm, Sunday 11:00am-6:00pm (Memorial Day -late October).***

Fossil Park, located in an abandoned quarry in Sylvania, Ohio, is an unusual destination for travelers who are interested in rocks, quarries or mines. The park contains some of the best fossils from the Devonian period in the world; even little tyke diggers can easily find corals, brachiopods, echinoderms and trilobites . Visitors are allowed to break the fossils from the soft shale and keep any fossils that they find...but, No tools are allowed. FREE Admission.

Exit - 208 (east of I-75) / I-280 exit 9

TONY PACKO'S CAFÉ

Toledo - ***1902 Front Street (I-280 exit 9) 43605. www.tonypackos.com. Phone: (419) 691-6054.***

Built up an appetite for some crazy food? After seeing the "macho" life of "shipmen" near the Toledo port, try some fiery or authentic ethnic Hungarian food at Tony Packo's Café. The original restaurant is part dining, part museum. Sample a Packo's Hungarian Hot Dog, made famous by Corporal Klinger on the TV show "M.A.S.H." Be sure to look for the 100's of hot dog buns signed by TV stars that have visited the café. Other unique dishes are a Chili Sundae (chili and toppings served in a sundae glass with chips); Fried Pickles; Cabbage Rolls; and Chicken Paprikas.

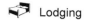

Exit - 208 (east of I-75) / I-280 exit 9

MAUMEE BAY STATE PARK

Toledo (Oregon) - ***1400 Park Road #1 (I-280 exit 9 - head north, then 8 miles east off State Route 179) 43618. Phone: (419) 836-7758 park, (419) 836-1466 Lodge or (419) 836-9117 Nature Center. www.maumeebaystateparklodge.com***

Resort cottages and rooms, golf, racquetball, sauna, whirlpool, fitness, tennis, volleyball and basketball are available. The lodge, cottages and golf course are nestled among the scenic meadows, wet woods and lush marshes teeming with wildlife.

The park boasts two sand beaches - one on the Lake Erie shore, while the other lines the park's inland lake. Developed hiking trails in the park include the Mouse Trail, a 3-mile diverse trail winding through meadows and young woodlands, and several miles of paved combination trails for bicycling and cross-country skiing. Hikers will discover acres of meadow, marshland and woodland. A 2-mile boardwalk traversing swamp and marsh wetlands has interpretive signs, an observation blind and tower, and wheelchair accessible loop. 1,845 acres of camping, hiking trails, boating, fishing, swimming and winter sports.

Exit - 206 (west of I-75)

TOLEDO FIREFIGHTERS MUSEUM

Toledo - ***918 Sylvania Avenue (I-75 exit 206) 43612. www.toledofiremuseum.com. Phone: (419) 478-FIRE. Hours: Saturday Noon-4:00pm.***

Feel what 150 years of history of fire-fighting must have meant to the fireman. Learn fire safety tips. In Jed's Bedroom, children are taught how to roll out of bed, keep low in case of smoke, and feel the door for heat with the back of their hand. See actual vintage pumpers, uniforms, and equipment used that trace the growth of the Toledo Fire Department. Located in the former No. 18 Fire Station. Always FREE.

Exit - 204 (west of I-75) / I-475 EXIT 19

TOLEDO BOTANICAL GARDENS

Toledo - ***5403 Elmer Drive (I-475/US23 exit 19, head west on SR120, off North Reynolds Road) 43615. Phone: (419) 936-2986. www.toledogarden.org. Hours: Open 8:30am-5:30pm.***

Fifty-seven acres of meadows and gardens. Outdoor sculpture and storybook garden appeal to kids. A scavenger hunt can be picked up at the Administrative Office for families to enjoy while discovering the Garden. Gallery and gift store. FREE except for special events. Family Nights are held each season (fee).

Exit - 203B (east of I-75)

TOLEDO MUSEUM OF ART

Toledo - ***2445 Monroe at Scottwood (off I-75) (I-75 exit 203 east, follow signs, located parallel to highway) 43620. www.toledomuseum.org. Phone: (419) 255-8000. Hours: Tuesday-Saturday 10:00am-4:00pm, Sunday 11:00am-5:00pm. Open Friday evening til 10:00pm.***

Discover treasures from the riches of the medieval, the splendors of a French chateau and the tombs of Egypt. Also glass, sculpture, paintings. Drop in to the Family Center for themed activities that enliven the world of art for kids of all ages (even those in grown-up guise). The Glass Pavilion is—in itself—a work of art. All exterior and nearly all interior walls consist of large panels of curved glass, resulting in a transparent structure that blurs the boundaries between interior and exterior spaces. You are greeted by a clear glass "fish-looking" Chihuly sculpture and then drawn in further by the live glass-blowing artists at work.

Exit - 201B (east of I-75) (NB only) 202A (SB only) SANDPIPER CANAL BOAT

Toledo - ***2144 Fordway, Riverfront (Jefferson Street Docks in Promenade Park, I-75 exit 201B or 202A) 43606. Phone: (419) 537-1212. www.sandpiperboat.com. Admission: Range of $7.00-$15.00. Basically double the price for lunch cruises.***

Replica of a Miami and Erie Canal boat. Educational or historical Cruise up river past riverside estates, downtown or down river. See busy ports, shipyards and dry docks. Public and group tours average 2-4 hours. Mostly weekends (morning/lunchtime). Some evening cruises. Seasonal Fireworks and Fall Cruises. Bring a picnic. Reservations suggested. (May-October)

Exit - 201 (west of I-75) (NB only) 202A (SB only)

TOLEDO ZOO

Toledo - *2700 Broadway (I-75 to US 25 west - 3 miles South of downtown) 43609. Phone: (419) 385-5721. www.toledozoo.org. Hours: Daily 10:00am-5:00pm (May-Labor Day). Daily, 10:00am-4:00pm (Rest of the Year). Admission: $17.00 adult, $14.00 senior (60+) and child (2-11). Parking fee $7.00. Military, County residents and special promotion discounts updated seasonally on the website. Note: Carnivore Cafe. Children's Zoo - petting zoo and hands on exhibits. Wagon/ stroller rentals.*

Immerse yourself in the heart of Africa on the Safari Railway through a 5-acre African habitat teeming with giraffes, zebra and all the wilds of Africa. Grab lunch at the Carnivore Café before enjoying your whirlwind trip through the Arctic Encounter, Hippoquarium, Nature's Neighborhood, Museum of Science and Aquarium…your journey is endless! The new aquarium was funded by locals, so it's their pride and joy. I particularly loved that the zoo keeps many old structures and recycles them. For instance, the old lion and tiger cages are now the Carnivore Café – indoor seating in actual barred cages! They have areas typical of a zoo but they are known for their Hippoquarium (the world's first underwater viewing of the hippopotamus) along with a small enough acreage that is manageable with little ones in tow.

Exit - 199 (east of I-75)

NATIONAL MUSEUM OF THE GREAT LAKES

Toledo - *1701 Front Street, Toledo, OH 43605 (I-75 to US 25 west - on the river) Phone: (419) 214-5000. www.inlandseas.org. Hours: Tuesday-Saturday 10:00am-5:00pm, Sunday Noon-5pm. Admission: $8.00 adult, $7.00 senior (65+) and child (6-18). Add $4.00 for touring the Schoonmaker.*

The National Museum of the Great Lakes reveals the haunting and fascinating history of our treasured Great Lakes that happen to make up 84 percent of the fresh surface water in North America. The main emphasis is on the new museum at the Toledo Maritime Center with a complete experience for visitors of all ages to include: original artifacts (some from horrific shipwrecks like the Edmund Fitzgerald); over 40 hands-on exhibits (for example: direct your own submersible through the wreckage of a lost freighter or keep your own ship afloat by operating a real bilge pump); the real life-size S.S. Col. James M. Schoonmaker Museum Ship sits outside the museum for touring. The Schoonmaker freighter depicts how ships of the Great Lakes worked in the early to mid-1900s. Visitors are awed by the massive engine room and the galley. And for waterside wonderers - A beautifully landscaped 3.5 acre maritime-themed park.

IMAGINATION STATION

Toledo - ***One Discovery Way (corner of Summit & Adams Streets on riverfront) 43604 (I-75 to US 25 west) Phone: (419) 244-2674. www.imaginationstationtoledo.org. Hours: Tuesday-Saturday 10am-5pm, Sunday Noon-5pm. Admission: $10.00 adult, $8.00 child (3-12). Note: Store & Cafe.***

Classics like the High Wire Cycle and the BOYO along with Grow U agriculture and farming. Energy Factory allows kids to program a robot or command an oil refinery. In Water Works you'll find the Hurricane Chamber and water play. Smash your food and take on the Wheel of Fire in Eat It Up. They do a bang up job involving kids in life-applicable experiments downstairs.

REAL SEAFOOD CO.

Toledo - ***22 Main Street 43605. www.realseafoodcorestaurant.com. Phone: (419) 691-6054.***

Take a break and relax with a view of the beautiful downtown Toledo skyline at one of several restaurants located at the Docks. Enjoy the picturesque riverfront on the outdoor patio of Real Seafood for an afternoon nibble and a cold drink. They bring in fresh seafood from the Atlantic, Pacific and Great Lakes. Many rave about their crab cakes. I liked their selection of locally caught Perch or Walleye. Lunch runs $10-$13. Dinner runs about double. Entrees include two sides. I recommend you try their blue cheese vinaigrette coleslaw with any fish entrée. All kids meals include a beverage and the entrees (shrimp, burger, tenders, spaghetti, etc) run $5.95. On a nice day, try to get a patio seat. Really good view.

Exit - 192 (west of I-75) / I-475 exit 2

FORT MEIGS

Toledo (Perrysburg) - ***29100 West River Road (1 mile Southwest of State Route 25, I-475 to exit 2) 43552. www.fortmeigs.org. Phone: (419) 874-4121. Hours: Wednesday-Saturday 9:30am-5:00pm. Sunday & Holidays Noon-5:00pm (April-October). Visitor Center ONLY remains open year-round. Admission: $8.00 adult, $7.00 senior (60+), $4.00 child (6-12). Note: Military History Center with Gift Shop at the stone shutterhouse describes role of Ohioans at War. Monthly summer weekend reenactments. Educators: Printable activity sheets (word search and scavenger hunts) are online under Education. FREEBIES: games and puzzles are found here: www.fortmeigs.org/kids***

A War of 1812 era authentic castle-like log and earth fort with seven blockhouses that played an important role in guarding the Western frontier against the British. William Henry Harrison built Fort Meigs on the Maumee River in 1813 to protect northwest Ohio and Indiana from British invasion. The remodeled museum with authentically restored fort is a child's dream! The museum has many unique artifacts, easily displayed with a large gift shop attached. But, the fort's blockhouses, earthen mounds and cannon holes are major "role-playing" spaces! Each blockhouse exhibits a "theme" and the re-enactors add flare to the scene. March like a soldier or try the Wheel of Disease. The walls of the blockhouses are 2 feet thick with 4-inch deep windows and cannon hole ports on the second floor. See actual cannons fired as the air fills with smoke. Notice how much manpower was needed to "run" a fort. Our favorite fort in the Midwest!

Exit - 192 (west of I-75) / I-475 exit 4

WOLCOTT HOUSE MUSEUM COMPLEX

Toledo (Maumee) - ***1031 River Road (I-475/23 to exit 4, Rte. 24 east) 43537. Phone: (419) 893-9602. www.wolcotthouse.org. Hours: Thursday-Sunday Noon--4:00pm (April-December). Admission: $6.00 adult, $5.00 senior (60+), $2.50 student. Educators: Teacher Tour Activities online.***

Life in the mid-1800's in the Maumee Valley. Costumed guides lead you through a building complex of a log home, depot, church and gift shop.

Exit - 192 (west of I-75) / I-475 exit 6

SPLASH BAY RESORT

Toledo (Maumee) - *1705 Tollgate Drive (I-75 exit 192, I-475 to exit 6, head east towards turnpike) 43537. www.splashbayresort.com. Phone: (419) 897-5555. Hours: Vary by season. Generally open weekends only. Check calendar as they close some months. Admission: Day Passes are $19.00-$29.00 per person. Spectator Passes $6.00. Overnight packages begin around $179.00 / night with waterpark passes included that work on the day of check-in and check-out.*

The 35,000 square foot domed waterpark features a kiddy pool, lazy river, a giant playspace with bucket, and water slides that weave in and out of the building (still covered while outside, of course). The tube slides and body bowl are favorites with many kids. Cute, local names for rides like: Fort Meigs Deck Top and Walleye River Run add to the fun. There is also an arcade to satisfy your dry time gaming urges and a snack bar in the park.

Exit - 179 (west of I-75)

BG WIND FARM

Bowling Green - *Corner of Route 6 & Tontogany Rds. (I-75 exit 179) 43402. Phone: (419) 354-6246.*

Visit the only wind farm in the state of Ohio (Daily from 9:00am-6:00pm). Four wind turbines swirl through the air to generate electricity to BG and it's electric co-op. An informational computerized kiosk is available for visitors to see how these towering turbines were erected.

Exit - 179 (east of I-75)

SNOOKS DREAM CARS MUSEUM

Bowling Green - *13920 County Home Road, Twp 172 (I-75 exit 179, east on US 6) 43402. Phone: (419) 353-8338. www.snooksdreamcars.com. Hours: Weekdays 9:00am-4:00pm. Admission: $4.00-$6.00 per person.*

Begin in a 1940's era Texaco filling station, featuring "automobilia" - everything from hood ornaments to backseat games to seat covers. Operational mechanics area leads to coin-operated amusement games (even a Model T kiddie ride). Remember pedal cars? The showroom has dream cars showcased in themed rooms from the 30's-60's. "We like to consider this a living museum," says Jeff, co-owner, "since all the cars on display are in working condition. My father and I drive one or another of them around town on a regular basis."

Mile - 178

OHIO TRAVEL INFORMATION CENTER

Bowling Green - ***(milepost 178 off I-75 either direction). www.dot.state.oh.us. Hours: 9:00am-5:00pm daily.***

The centers are staffed by professional travel counselors to assist the public with any travel-related need. Visitors may obtain brochures and maps and seek advice in reaching their destinations in Ohio. This rest area also has restrooms, a dog walk, vending and picnic areas.

Exit - 164 (east of I-75)

VAN BUREN LAKE STATE PARK

Van Buren - ***State Route 613 (1 mile East of Van Buren, I-75 exit 164) 45889. Phone: (419) 832-7662. www.dnr.state.oh.us.***

Hiking trails circle the lake. Hikers, horseback riders, and mountain bikers are welcome on 6 miles of multiple-use trails traversing steep ravines and gentler terrain in scenic woodlands. 296 acres of camping, hiking trails, boating, fishing, and winter sports.

Exit - 161 (east of I-75)

NORTHWEST OHIO RAILROAD

Findlay - ***11600 County Rd. 99 (northeast corner of I-75 exit #161 east and County Rd. 99, north end of Findlay) 45840. www.nworrp.org. Phone: (419) 423-2995. Hours: Generally weekends 1:00-4:00pm (April-December) plus evenings during peak seasonal excursions. Diesel on Saturdays and Steam on Sundays. Admission: $1.00-$2.00 per person.***

Experience the thrill of a coal-burning steam train ride on the nearly 1/2 mile of 15" gauge track layout. Tours of their B&O caboose are the first Sunday of each month, April-September. Kids eyes gleam at the Lionel Toy Train layout.

Exit - 159 (east of I-75)

MAZZA COLLECTION MUSEUM

Findlay - ***1000 North Main Street (University of Findlay Campus, I-75 EXIT 159 SR 224) 45840. www.mazzacollection.org. Phone: (419) 424-4777 or (800) 472-9502. Hours: Wednesday-Friday Noon-5:00pm, Sunday 1:00-4:00pm. Closed all***

holidays. Admission: FREE Tours: Tuesday-Thursday between 9:00am-2:00pm and Friday 9:00am-Noon. $2.00 per student, $1.00 extra for craft.

This is the world's first and largest teaching museum devoted to literacy and the art of children's picture books. All the artwork here is based on children's storybooks and the teaching units include such exhibits as printmaking, the Mother Goose Corner, a borders section, the book-making process, an historical art gallery, and an art media exhibit. After a tour, some groups opt to have an art activity where the students get to use the ideas they saw in the galleria to produce their own artwork.

Exit - 157 (east of I-75)

DIETSCH BROTHERS FINE CHOCOLATES & ICE CREAM

Findlay - ***400 W. Main Cross Street (I-75 exit 157, State Route 12) 45839. Phone: (419) 422-4474. http://dietschs.com/. Hours: Store open daily except Mondays. Tours: Wednesday & Thursday mornings (1st grade & up). (Fall & Spring). Reservations please.***

Three brothers (2nd generation) run an original 1937's candy and ice cream shop. In the summer, see ice cream made with real cream. They make 1500 gallons per week. Fall, heading into the holidays, is the best time to see 500 pounds of chocolate treats made daily. Try some wacky flavors like "Everything but the Kitchen Sink" or "Snick-a-Ripple."

Exit - 125B (west of I-75)

ALLEN COUNTY MUSEUM

Lima - ***620 West Market Street (I-75 exit 125 on SR117/309 west) 45801. Phone: (419) 222-9426. www.allencountymuseum.org. Hours: Tuesday-Sunday 1:00-4:00pm. Closed holidays & Mondays. Children's Museum only open in summer and by appointment in the school year. Admission: Suggested donation of $5.00 per adult. MacDonell House $3.00.***

Note: While in town, stop for lunch or dinner at the Old Barn Out Back (3175 W. Elm St - www.oldbarnoutback.com) serving country-style food - known for their fried chicken and cinnamon rolls.

Indian and pioneer artifacts. Antique automobiles and bicycles. Barber Shop, Doctor's office, country store, log house on grounds. Next door is MacDonell House (wall of purses). Lincoln Park Railroad exhibit locomotive and Shay Locomotive (huge train) is something the kids will love.

The most unusual display is a collection of objects that people have swallowed (ex. Bolts, diaper pins). Each year, they present a new theme in the Children's Discovery Center where kids can assemble and operate exhibit interactives based on relevant themes (ex. Railroads). Experiment with other means of communication. Try your hand at sign language. Learn how to read and write Braille. Play checkers blindfolded. Send signals with flags. Write with hieroglyphs like an ancient Egyptian. Try to decipher a secret code. Make a craft or art project to take home with you.

Exit - 111 (west of I-75)

ARMSTRONG AIR AND SPACE MUSEUM

Wapakoneta - ***500 South Apollo Drive (I-75 to Exit 111) 45895. Phone: (419) 738-8811 or (800) 860-0142. http://armstrongmuseum.org/ Hours: Tuesday-Saturday 9:30am-5:00pm. Sunday Noon – 5:00pm. Closed Winter Holidays. Open Mondays (April-September). Admission: $8.00 adult, $4.00 student (6-12).***

The museum honors Neil Armstrong (a Wapakoneta native) and other area aeronauts (like the Wright Brothers) and their flying machines. After greeted by a NASA Skylaneer flown by Armstrong in the early 1960's, trace the history of flights from balloons to space travel. Look at the Apollo crew spacesuits, a real moon rock, or watch a video of lunar space walks. In the Astro Theater, pretend you're on a trip to the moon. Try a lunar or shuttle landing interactive. Look at Space Food, even dessert! Another favorite is the Infinity Cube – 18 square feet covered with mirrors that make you feel like you've been projected into space. Interactives and videos are abundant. Blast OFF! ...The Eagle has landed.

Exit - 102 (east of I-75)

AIRSTREAM FACTORY TOUR

Jackson Center - ***419 West Pike Street (I-75 exit 102, SR 274 east) 45334. Phone: (937) 596-6111. www.airstream.com. Tours are: Monday- Friday at 2:00pm. Friday Tours are after normal production hours. This is a walking tour approximately ¾ of a mile in length. The tour begins in the Service Lobby and travels outside to the production facility. Eye protection and hearing protection are required. No sandals or open toe shoes.***

Airstream's founder Wally Byam said, "Let's not make any changes – let's only make improvements!" Airstream, the world's leader in travel trailers and motor coaches, are completely manufactured and assembled in Jackson Center, Ohio. This is your chance to come see how it's done. From chassis assembly through final quality assurance, you'll be able to witness it all, first hand. These travel trailers and motor homes are custom assembled, by hand, in stages throughout the manufacturing process. You won't believe your eyes as you watch them come together in this 90-minute tour.

Exit - 99 (west of I-75)

LAKE LORAMIE STATE PARK

Minster - ***4401 Ft. Loramie Swanders Road (3 miles Southeast of Minster off State Route 66) 45865. Phone: (937) 295-2011. http://parks.ohiodnr.gov/lakeloramie***

One of the original canal feeder lakes, Lake Loramie State Park offers visitors a quiet retreat in rural Ohio. Swim from the sandy beach, hike along the old canal towpath, stay a night in a shaded campsite or boat the lazy waters of Lake Loramie. The hiking opportunities at Lake Loramie include more than eight miles of trail. A portion of the trail system follows the Miami-Erie Canal from the park to Delphos. This route is also a part of the Buckeye Trail and the North Country National Scenic Trail.

Exit - 83 (west of I-75)

LOCKINGTON LOCKS

Lockington - ***5 miles North of Piqua-Lockington Road (I-75 to exit 83 West on State Route 25A) 45356. www.ohiohistory.org. Phone: (800) 686-1535. Hours: Daily Dawn to Dusk. Admission: FREE.***

These stair step locks, among the best preserved in Ohio, were part of the Miami and Erie Canal System, which opened for navigation in 1845 and connected Cincinnati and the Ohio River to Toledo and Lake Erie. For several decades, the canal provided Ohio with valuable transportation and waterpower. View portions of five original locks (elevation adjusters for canal boats) and the aqueduct that lowered boats 67 feet into the Miami-Erie Canal.

JOHNSTON FARM & INDIAN AGENCY

Piqua - ***North Hardin Road (I-75 to exit 83 County Road 25A West to State Route 66 North) 45356. www.ohiohistory.org/visit/museum-and-site-locator/johnston-farm-and-indian-agency. Phone: (937) 773-2522.***

***Hours:** Thursday-Friday 10am-5pm (June-August). Saturday, Sunday and Holidays Noon-5:00pm (April-October). **Admission:** $9.00 adult, $4.00 child (6-12). Includes canal boat ride. **Note:** Canal rides a few times during the afternoon in the summer.*

The historical site celebrates two thousand years of Ohio's rich history from prehistoric Indians to Ohio's canal era. The focal point of the peaceful 200-acre park is John Johnston - farmer, public official, and United States Indian Agent for western Ohio from 1812 to 1829. Tour the Johnston Farm which includes an 1808 massive log barn which is probably the oldest such barn in Ohio. In the farmhouse, the kids will be most interested in the beds made of rope and hay filled sacks. Eight girls slept in one room (ages 2-20) and three boys in another. Many youth games of that time period are displayed. The Winter Kitchen is also very interesting – especially the size of the walk-in fireplace. The Farm buildings have costumed guides describing and interacting with youth as they demonstrate chores on the farm.

Ride the General Harrison canal boat...

Before you visit the canal, stop in the museum where excellent exhibits, inside and out, explain the treacherous job of building a canal and why. The General Harrison canal boat is powered by two mules which pull the boat down and back on a section of the Old Miami-Erie Canal (Cincinnati to Toledo). The cargo boat was once used to transport produce and meat at a speed limit of 4 MPH. Once the railroads came, canals became obsolete.

Exit - 73 (west of I-75)

IDLE HOUR RANCH

Troy *- 4845 Fenner Road (I-75 exit 73 west, turn right onto Fenner) 45373. Phone: (937) 339-9731. www.idle-hourranch.com. **Hours:** Saturday & Sunday Noon-6:00pm (June - October). **Admission:** $12.00 adult, $10.00 child (3-12) and seniors (65+).*

Ever want to hitch a ride with a kangaroo? See the world from a giraffe's point of view? Unlike a zoo, IHR allows you to get up close & personal with the animals. Interact with & see over 200 animals including: Camels, Kangaroo, Wallabies, Cougar, Zebu, Llamas, Alpaca, Reindeer, Nilgai, Yak, Wolves, Cavies, Horses, farm animals and many, many more! Special areas included: the North American River Otter Exhibit, the Giraffe Observation Deck & the Farm Market. Otter feeding at 3:00pm. Look for "babies" every now and then.

BRUKNER NATURE CENTER

Troy - ***5995 Horseshoe Bend Rd. (Exit # 73 off of I-75, west on SR 55 3 miles, then right on Horseshoe) 45373. Phone: (937) 698-6493. www.facebook.com/BruknerNatureCenter Hours: Monday-Saturday 9:00am-5:00pm, Sunday 12:30-5:00pm. Admission: Small admission charged on Sundays.***

This 164 acre nature preserve's attractions include 6 miles of hiking trails, a wildlife rehabilitation center and the interpretive center. The 1804 Iddings log house was built by the first settlers in Miami County. The Center's animal rehabilitation has over 65 permanent residents on display. The top floor contains a glass-enclosed vista room for watching and listening to birds as they feed. A ground-level viewing station for mammals also is available. They are best known for their Night Hikes, Star Gazes, Wild Journeys and Seasonal events.

Exit - 63 (west of I-75)

AULLWOOD AUDUBON CENTER AND FARM

Dayton - ***1000 Aullwood Road (I-75 exit 63, follow signs) 45414. Phone: (937) 890-7360. http://aullwood.center.audubon.org. Hours: Monday-Saturday 9:00am-5:00pm, Sunday 1:00-5:00pm. Closed holidays. Admission: $5.00 adult, $2300 child (2-18).***

The Discovery Room has more than 50 hands-on exhibits. Visitors can begin walks on five miles of hiking trails here. Around the building are special plantings of prairie and woodland wildflowers and a butterfly - hummingbird garden. The nearby Farm (9101 Frederick Pike) is the site of many special events. Cows, pigs, horses, chickens, turkeys, sheep, goats and barn swallows can all be found here if you come at the right time. The sugar bush, organic garden, herb garden and access to the trails are here. The glacial erratics are the start of the Geology trail. On it, you can explore the recent erosion of the land and the water cycle, the leavings of the continental glacier, and the old bedrock with its load of Ordovician fossils.

Exit - 61A (east of I-75) / I-70 exit 38

CARRIAGE HILL FARM AND MUSEUM

Dayton (Huber Heights) - ***7800 East Shull Road (I-70 to Exit 38 - State Route 201 north) 45424. Phone: (937) 278-2609. www.metroparks.org/parks/carriagehill/. Hours: Tuesday-Saturday 10:00am-5:00pm, Sunday Noon-5:00pm (April-October). Tuesday-Sunday Noon-4pm (Nov-March). Admission: Donation. Note: Picnic area, fishing, horseback riding, cross country skiing, hayrides and bobsled rides. No bikes on trails, though.***

Farm life in the 1880s comes alive at Carriage Hill Farm. Stop at the Visitor Center for exhibits highlighting lifestyles of a century ago, a children's interactive center and the Country Store gift shop. The self-guided tour of an 1880's working farm is a great benefit to the community. The farm includes a summer kitchen, workshop, black smith and barns. Household chores and farming are performed as they were 100 years ago and a variety of farm animals fill the barn.

Exit - 57B (west of I-75)

BOONSHOFT MUSEUM OF DISCOVERY

Dayton - ***2600 DeWeese Parkway (North of downtown I-75 to exit 57B, follow signs) 45414. Phone: (937) 275-7431. www.boonshoftmuseum.org. Hours: Monday-Saturday 9:00am-5:00pm, Sunday Noon-5:00pm. Closed major winter holidays. Admission: $13 adult, $11 senior & $10 child (3-16). $4-$6.00 additional for Space Theater. Note: With modest memberships purchased at this location, you also can get free or discounted admissions to many museums in Ohio and surrounding states. Vending area. Discovery Shop.***

A Children's Museum, a Science Center, Nature Center AND Planetarium all in one place! Interactive technology exhibits combined with a zoo and planetarium make for more than a day's worth of fun. Here's highlights of each space:

A treehouse of discovery...

DISCOVERY CENTER - mastodon bones, desert animals (daytime vs. nighttime creatures using flashlights!), touch tide pool (ever seen a red sea cucumber? Touch one!), rainforest and treehouse within campsite and binoculars window views.

DISCOVERY ZOO – An indoor tree house & zoo with small animals in natural surroundings. Visit the den of bobcat Van Cleve or a coyote, river otter, groundhog, fox or turtle. A Falcon nest Web Cam is a popular area - something new is always happening with that family. Both parents will tend to the chicks so keep an eye out for both Mercury and Snowball at the nest.

ANCIENT WORLD – Egyptian artifacts with 3000 year old mummy, a replica of the Rosetta Stone and some African jewelry.

SCIENCE CENTRAL – Inventions stations (water table w/ sticky water, airfort and force (tubes & funny windbag blower machines), chemistry lab, and a climbing discovery tower (nets, tubes & slide) provides hands on adventures.

SPLASH - explore the story of water in the Miami Valley...from dams to water treatment.

KIDS' PLAYCE - baby garden, pioneer cabin, dig, slide & little creatures. Dress up spot.

Exit - 54C (east of I-75)

NATIONAL MUSEUM OF THE USAF

Dayton (Fairborn) - ***Wright Patterson Air Force Base, 1100 Spaatz Street (I-75 to State Route 4 East to Harshman Road Exit) 45433. www.nationalmuseum.af.mil/. Phone: (937) 255-3286. Hours: Daily 9:00am-5:00pm. Closed Thanksgiving, Christmas and New Years. Admission: FREE. Tours: The free USAF Heritage Tour begins at 1:30pm Monday through Friday. Saturdays 10:30am & 1:30pm. No reservation required. Educators: Scavenger Hunt - click on Education, then Educators for printable links. Note: Largest Gift Shop imaginable. Concessions.***

3D THEATRE - 6 story with hourly 40 minute space/aviation films - feel like you're flying with the pilots. Fee. (937-253-IMAX. Morphis MovieRide Theater - actually move, tilt and shout. extra fee).

HUFFMAN PRAIRIE FIELD - Rte. 44 (937-257-5535). See where The Wright Brothers first attempted flight.

This museum tells the story of the 100-plus years of flight, from its beginning to today's stealth age.You'll have a real adventure exploring the world's oldest and largest military aviation museum that features over 50 vintage WWII aircraft (even the huge 6-engine B-36) and 300 other aircraft and rockets. See everything from presidential planes, to Persian Gulf advanced missiles and bombs, the original Wright Brothers wind tunnel, to the original Apollo 15 command module. Look for the observation balloon (easy to find—just look up ever so slightly), Rosie the Riveter and "Little Vittles" parachuted goodies. Discovery Hangar Five follows a common museum trend and focuses on the interactive learning of why things fly and different parts of airplanes. Continuous films played at stations throughout the complex (with chairs-take a break from all the walking). This attraction houses more than 400 total aircraft and missiles, including the world's only B-2 stealth bomber on public display. National Aviation Hall of Fame is next door.

Exit - 54B (west of I-75)

DAYTON ART INSTITUTE

Dayton - ***456 Belmonte Park North (I-75 exit 53B or 54B) 45405. Phone: (937) 223-5277 or (800) 296-4426. www.daytonartinstitute.org. Hours: Tuesday-Saturday 11am-5pm, Sunday Noon-5pm. Thursday nights until 8:00pm. Admission: FREE.***

Overlooking the Great Miami River and downtown Dayton, The Dayton Art Institute's Italian Renaissance-style building houses an extensive permanent collection of American, European, Asian and African art. Experiencenter (features 20 hands-on activities) encourages interaction with art and experimentation with artistic elements of line, pattern, color, texture and shape. A gallery bag and an alphabet book are also available at the Entrance Rotunda desk allowing families to further explore featured special exhibits through the use of games and learning activities.

Exit - 53B (east of I-75)

RIVERSCAPE

Dayton - ***111 E. Monument Avenue (MetroPark's RiverScape, I-75 exit 53B) 45402. Phone: (937) 278-2607. www.riverscape.org.***

Enjoy the RiverScape landscaped gardens, a free summer concert, major community festivals and family walks and bike rides along the river corridor recreation trails. A focal point of RiverScape is the Five Rivers Fountain of Lights, a series of five fountains that shoot water upwards of 200 feet and 400 feet across at the confluence of the Great Miami and Mad Rivers (May through October). And, don't forget your bathing suit. A popular spot for visitors looking to cool off on hot summer days is the Interactive Fountain where multiple fountain jets shoot water as high as 15 feet into the air choreographed to the sounds of family friendly music. And, the fun isn't over when it gets cold -MetroParks' invites you to come "Skate the Scape" as RiverScape becomes home to the regions only outdoor ice skating rink, festive light displays and other family winter activities. Concessions available.

Exit - 53A (west of I-75)

WRIGHT CYCLE COMPANY COMPLEX

Dayton - ***16 South Williams Street (I-75 exit 53A, off West 3rd Street) 45407. Phone: (937) 225-7705. www.nps.gov/daav/. Hours: Daily 9am-5:00pm except major winter holidays. Admission: Donation. Tours: Join a ranger for a walking tour of the historic Wright-Dunbar Village, the neighborhood of the Wright brothers and Paul Laurence Dunbar. (offered daily during summer).***

This is the neighborhood in which the Wright brothers started their printing business, entered into the bicycle business and became involved with the mystery of flight. The Wright Cycle Company complex consists of the Wright Cycle Company building and the Wright–Dunbar Interpretive Center (the restored Hoover Block building) or the Aviation Trail Visitor Center and Museum. In this location, the Wrights edited and published newspapers for the West Side patrons, including the Dayton Tattler, written by Paul Laurence Dunbar. The bicycle craze in America began in 1887 with the introduction from England of the safety bicycle (two wheels of equal size). It made the freedom of cycling accessible to a much wider market. This building is the actual site where the Wright Brothers had a bicycle business from 1895-1897 and developed their own brand of bicycles. On this site, they also developed ideas that led to the invention of flight almost 7 years later. The dream of flight was imagined by many, but achieved by Orville and Wilbur Wright - just two brothers from Dayton who happened to fly

Learn the bicycle history of the Wright Brothers

OHIO

> **Did You Know?**
> On September 7, 1904, the Wright brothers use a catapult launching device for the first time at Huffman Prairie Flying Field, Dayton, Ohio.

the first mechanically powered airplane. You'll walk on the same floorboards that the brothers did and see actual plans for a flying bicycle!

DUNBAR HOUSE

Dayton - ***219 North Paul Lawrence Dunbar Street (2 blocks north of 3rd Street, east of US35) 45401. www.nps.gov/daav/. Phone: (937) 224-7061. Hours: Friday, Saturday and Sunday 10am-4pm. Admission: FREE. FREEBIES: word games are online - click on Site Education Programs.***

The restored home of the first African American to achieve acclaim in American literature. From a young poet at age 6 to a nationally known figure (until his death at age 33 of tuberculosis), the guide helps you understand his inspiration especially from his mother and her stories of slavery. Personal belongings like his bicycle built by the Wright Brothers and a sword presented to him by President Roosevelt lead you to his bedroom where he wrote 100 novels, poems and short stories.

"We smile, but, O great Christ, our cries
To thee from tortured souls arise.
We sing, but oh the clay is vile
Beneath our feet, and long the mile;
But let the world dream otherwise,
We wear the mask!"

- Paul Laurence Dunbar, from the poem, We Wear the Mask

Exit - 53A (east of I-75)

CITIZENS MOTORCAR PACKARD MUSEUM

Dayton - ***420 South Ludlow Street - Downtown (I-75 to US 35 exit, head east a few blocks) 45402. Phone: (937) 226-1917. www.americaspackardmuseum.org. Hours: Monday-Friday Noon-5:00pm, Saturday and Sunday 1:00-5:00pm. Open Every Day except Easter, Thanksgiving, Christmas, and New Years Day. Admission: $6.00 adult, $5.00 senior, $4.00 student.***

See the world's largest collection of Packard automobiles in an authentic showroom. The art deco Packard dealership interior exhibits are spread through 6 settings, including the service area and period salesman's office.

Exit - 51 (west of I-75)

SUNWATCH

***Dayton** - 2301 West River Road (I-75 to Exit 51, west on Edwin C. Moses Blvd., cross South Broadway, turn left) 45418. www.sunwatch.org. Phone: (937) 268-8199. Hours: Tuesday-Saturday 9:00am-5:00pm. Sunday and Holidays Noon – 5:00pm. Closed major winter holidays. Admission: $6.00 adult, $4.00 child (6-16) & senior (60+). Tours: Guided tours daily at 1:30pm. (Summer). Note: Occasional Flute Circle weekends offer music, storytelling and food like Bison burgers, Indian tacos and summer Indian corn. Visitor's are welcome to carry-in their own food. A beverage vending machine is available.*

SunWatch Indian Village/Archaeological Park is a partially reconstructed Fort Ancient period Native American village along the Great Miami River. Here visitors can explore Dayton's first neighborhood, walk in reconstructed houses, hear the intriguing history of the Fort Ancient people, and discover the role the sun played in daily life. Archaeological excavations at a site near the Great Miami River uncovered evidence of an 800-year-old village built by the Fort Ancient Indians. The reconstructed 12th Century Indian Village has self-guided tours of the thatched huts, gardens and artifacts of the lifestyle of a unique culture. In the museum exhibits, study the trash pits - you can learn a lot from people's trash. Some activities include story telling, archery, toys and games, harvesting, a multi-media presentation, and best of all, learn to tell time by charting the sun. See how the Indians used flint and bone to create jewelry and tools - then buy some as souvenirs. This is a nice family-friendly introduction to ancient Indian lifestyles - be sure to view the orientation film first.

Exit - 51 (east of I-75)

CARILLON HISTORICAL PARK

***Dayton** - 1000 Carillon Blvd. (I-75 to Exit 51) 45409. www.daytonhistory.org/destinations/carillon-historical-park/ Phone: (937) 293-2841. Hours: Monday-Saturday 9:30am-5:00pm. Sunday & Holidays Noon - 5:00pm, closed on Thanksgiving, Christmas, New Year's. Admission: $8.00 adult, $7.00 senior, $5.00*

child (3-17). Note: Museum Store sells period toys, snacks and candy. Wooded park with Ohio's largest bell tower, the Carillon Bell Tower (57 bells), also has many shaded picnic areas. CULP'S CAFE, reminiscent of Culp's Cafeteria located in downtown Dayton in the 1930s and 1940s, serves soup, salads, and sandwiches, ice cream and sodas. (937) 299-2277.

A must see - very comfortable and educational - over 65 acres of historical buildings and outdoor exhibits of history, invention and transportation. Called the "Little Greenfield Village" in Miami Valley and we definitely agree! Inventions like the cash register, innovations like flood control, and industries like Huffy Corporation are represented throughout the Park. Many of the oldest buildings from the early 1800's are represented too (tavern, home, school). As you enter most buildings, a costumed guide will orient you to colorful stories of the famous people who once occupied them. The highlight of the collections is the 1905 Wright Flyer III, the world's first practical airplane. Our favorites are the Deed's Barn (learn about the Barn Gang and the big companies they started) and the rail cars that you can actually board- the Barney & Smith is ritzy!

Exit - 50B (east of I-75)

COX ARBORETUM

Dayton - ***6733 Springboro Pike (I-75 exit 50B to OH 74 south) 45449. Phone: (937) 434-9005. www.metroparks.org. Hours: Daily 8:00am to dusk. Visitor Center weekdays 8am-5pm and weekends 11:00am-4:00pm.***

Cox Arboretum MetroPark is a hands-on landscaping arboretum. Best family features are: Water Garden & Rock Garden; the Bell Children's Maze; and the Butterfly House and Garden (Butterfly House is a seasonal display). 170 acres total including the nationally recognized Edible Landscape Garden. Every season has something special to offer, from spring's splashes of bright color to winter's textures. In addition to exploring gardens, hike trails through mature forests and colorful meadows. FREE admission.

Exit - 44 (west of I-75)

MIAMISBURG MOUND

Dayton (Miamisburg) - ***(I-75 to State Route 725 exit 44, follow signs) 45342. Phone: (937) 866-5632. www.ohiohistory.org. Hours: Daily Dawn to Dusk. Admission: FREE. Note: Park, Picnic tables and playground.***

Take the 116 stairs up a 68-foot high and 1.5 acre wide mound built by American Indians. This is the largest conical burial mound in Ohio. Archaeological investigations of the surrounding area suggest that it was constructed by the prehistoric Adena Indians (800BC - AD100). The mound measures 877 feet in circumference.

Exit - 44 (east of I-75)

WRIGHT B. FLYER

Dayton (Miamisburg) - ***10550 Springboro Pike (I-75 exit 44, State Route 741 – Dayton Wright Airport) 45342. www.destinationdayton.com/wrightb/hanger.html. Phone: (937) 885-2327. Hours: Tuesday, Thursday, and Saturday 9:00am-2:00pm. Admission: There is no charge for the museum or to look at the aircraft. Aircraft ride certificates may be purchased for $150.00. This entitles the certificate bearer to an orientation ride replicating the Wright Brothers' original flight patterns over Huffman Prairie! Otherwise, only donations.***

A group decided to build a flying replica of the first production aircraft ever built - the Wright Brothers B Model Airplane. The result is a fully operational flying aircraft that closely resembles the original Wright B Model that flew over Huffman Prairie in 1911. This hangar houses a flyable replica of the 1911 plane built by Wilbur and Orville Wright. They also have a half scale model of the plane and other aviation exhibits and souvenirs.

Mile - 28 (east of I-75) (NB Only)

OHIO TRAVEL INFORMATION CENTER

Monroe - ***(milepost 28 off I-75 heading north only). www.dot.state.oh.us. Hours: 9:00am-5:00pm daily.***

The centers are staffed by professional travel counselors to assist the public with any travel-related need. Visitors may obtain brochures and maps and seek advice in reaching their destinations in Ohio. There are also restrooms, vending, a dog walk and picnic areas.

Exit - 22 (east of I-75)

ENTERTRAINMENT JUNCTION

Cincinnati (West Chester) - *7379 Squire Court (I-75 exit 22 toward Mason) 45069. Phone: (513) 898-8000. www.entertrainmentjunction.com. Hours: Monday - Saturday 10:00am-6:00pm, Sunday Noon-6:00pm. Closed only Easter, Thanksgiving and Christmas. Admission: $13.95 adult, $11.95 senior (65+), $9.95 child (3-12). There is a separate charge of $2.50 for the Kids' Express hand-cranked locomotives; open seasonally (June-Labor Day), weather permitting. Seasonal Journey prices run $9.95 extra.*

EnterTrainment Junction offers the largest interactive indoor G-scale layout known, with more than two miles of track and 90 trains, depicting every era of American railroading (called the Train Journey). Start in the early days (pre-Civil War) up to the present. Each train car (over 1,200 of them!) is about the size of a loaf of bread. Even though they're big, they're not all at eye level - some are below and some even high in the air. Actual water flows through canals and rivers into a large lake with a huge waterfall backdrop. Lots of tunnels, small towns, trestles and trains shine with lights. There's also an American Railroading Museum and a 5,000-square-foot play area for kids called "Imagination Junction," that includes a climbing structure and interactive games.

SEASONAL JOURNEY:

- AMAZE N FUNHOUSE (January-September): old-time amusement park fun house.
- JACK-O-LANTERN JUNCTION (fall): well-lit mazes through an old Victorian village that is slightly haunted. Mirror mazes, clown rooms, chain-link mazes, and a wind tunnel.
- CHRISTMAS AT THE JUNCTION (winter): walk-thru either A Christmas Carol scene or a Journey to the North Pole.

Exit - 16 (west of I-75) / I-275 exit 41

JUNGLE JIM'S INTERNATIONAL MARKET

Cincinnati (Fairfield) - *5440 Dixie Highway (Route 4) (I-75 exit 16 west on I-275 to exit 41 north) 45014. Phone: (513) 674-6000. www.junglejims.com. Hours: Open daily 8:00am-10:00pm.*

A grocery store is an adventure? This store, selling exotic foods is! This Fairfield, Ohio landmark is as popular a supermarket as it is a tourist attraction. Ohio's

Famous Playground for Food Lovers (Foodies) allows customers to shop in four acres of food from all around the world all under one roof. Plastic animals and giant fruits greet you. Once inside, the store is divided into theme areas. Visit Amish Country, The Ocean, Europe, South America, India and the Middle East. Does the Big Cheese ever change? Try some new food like medallions of alligator! Their fish are so fresh, they keep them in holding ponds and tanks in the store until they are ready to be purchased. You can view this tanks and a mezzanine walkway near the indoor ponds. Spicy food is inside a walk-thru firetruck - hot. Food from England lies under a moving display of Robinhood and friends in the Sherwood Forest. Tea and crumpets, anyone? Even Elvis is here and will occasionally sings a tune while you choose pastries.

Exit - 16 (east of I-75) / I-275 exit 46

HERITAGE VILLAGE MUSEUM

Cincinnati (Sharonville) - ***11450 Lebanon Pike, Sharon Woods Park (I-75 exit 16 east to US 42, 1 mile south of I-275 exit 46) 45241. www.heritagevillagecincinnati.org. Phone: (513) 563-9484. Hours: Wednesday-Saturday 10:00am-5:00pm, Sunday 1:00-5:00pm. (May-October). Guided Tours: $5.00 adult, $3.00 child (5-11). Note: Dressed interpreters. Bicycle rental, hiking trails. $2.00 entry into Sharon Woods park (per vehicle). Many picnic and shelter areas, mostly wooded for shade. General Store with many pioneer hand-make items and lots of American Girl clothes and books for sale. Educators: Click on the Teachers Page under Education Programs or rent a History to Go program.***

See 18th Century Ohio. Nine actual buildings from Southwest Ohio including: The Elk Lick House - "fancy house", learn about the gothic Ohio clock and why the "mouse ran up the clock"; the Train Station - with its treasure trunk hands-on pieces to play with; Kemper Log House - look for Isabella's sampler (Little House on the Prairie theme here) and the "Y" staircase; the kitchen and smokehouse - during festivals they cook here; and the medical office - see Civil War medical and pharmaceutical equipment- amputation city! Their Kids History Camps are wonderfully organized and a great way to "participate" in history.

Exit - 6 (east of I-75)

CINCINNATI ZOO AND BOTANICAL GARDENS

Cincinnati - *3400 Vine Street (I-75 to exit 6, Mitchell Ave) 45220. Phone: (513) 281- 4700 or (800) 94-HIPPO. www.cincinnatizoo.org. Hours: Daily 9:00am-6:00pm (Summer); 9:00am-5:00pm (Winter), 9:00am-8:30pm (Summer Saturdays). Admission: $18.00 adult, $12.00 child (2-12). Children's Zoo and rides are $2.00-$6.00 additional. Parking Fee $9. Advance online tickets save $1.00-$3.00 per person. Note: Safari Restaurant. Concessions. Tram and train rides, 4D Theater, & Carousel (additional fee), Children's Zoo & Animal Nursery. Wildlife Theatre. Stroller rentals. FREEBIES: Self-Guided Scavenger Hunts.*

Ranked one of the top 5 zoos in the United States, its highlight is the successes in breeding white Bengal tigers and other rare wild animals. Komodo dragons (10 feet long and 300 lbs!) and endangered Florida Manatees are some of the large, unusual animals there. Visitors can pass into the underwater world of the manatee in a freshwater spring habitat. The Lords of the Arctic area features polar bears on land and nose-to-nose through underwater glass panels, too. Dramatic waterfalls and a polar bear cave, with educational interactives complement the exhibit. The zoo added to its furry family the first-ever Mexican wolf pups born in 2007 - now exploring Wolf Woods in the Children's Zoo. And, you'll find a new eye level experience - Giraffe Ridge. This 27,000 square-foot exhibit, complete with an elevated viewing platform, provides an amazing interactive experience, bringing guests eye-to-eye with a herd of giraffes. Their landscaped gardens duplicate the animals' world and the Jungle Trails exhibit even has a tropical rainforest. The first Insectarium (you guessed it!) in the nation is also here.

Exit - 1D (west of I-75)

CINCINNATI HISTORY MUSEUM

See a miniature Cincinnati...

Cincinnati - *1301 Western Avenue, Cincinnati Museum Center (I-75 exit 1D, US 50 W. River Road. Exit left to Gest St., Right onto Gest, right on Freeman, then follow signs. I-75 south follow signs off hwy) 45203. www.cincymuseum.org. Phone: (513) 287-7000. Hours: Monday-Saturday (& Holidays) 10:00am-5:00pm, Sunday*

11:00am-6:00pm. Closed Thanksgiving and Christmas. Admission: $8.50-$10.50 per person. Toddler (age 1-2) rates are slightly lower. Combo prices with other museums in the Center are well worth the few extra dollars if you have the whole day to explore. Parking fee. Note: Gift Shops - Worth a good look! OmniMax Theatre on premises has several shows daily (a movie fee is charged per person). Educators: look for a wide list of pdf Teachers Guides on current and past exhibits: www.cincymuseum.org/educators/resources.

As you enter the museum, your eyes will race around the Cincinnati in Motion model of the city (from 1900-1940) with interactive computer booths and most of the transportation moving (planes, trains, cars, etc). Such an easy and fun way to learn about historical buildings in town or, just reminisce or admire the fascinating layout. Next, you'll visit with The Flynns (ring the doorbell first) talking about life at home during World War II. Hop on board a streetcar with the conductor telling news of the war. Moms and grandmothers will have to check out the "Leg Makeup Bar" (clue: there was a stocking shortage during the war). Now, walk through a life-like forest with shadows and birds wrestling and singing. Then, walk through re-created streets of Cincinnati. Visit the Fifth Street Market and Millcreek Millery - try on hats of the early 1900's and then shop next door at the pretend open air market. The kids can play in a miniature cabin and flat boat, then actually board a steamboat and pretend you're the captain. Very authentically presented, clever displays throughout the whole museum. Cincinnati folks should be proud.

Exit - 1D (west of I-75)

DUKE ENERGY CHILDREN'S MUSEUM

Cincinnati - *Cincinnati Museum Center, 1301 Western Avenue (I-75 exit 1D, US 50 W. River Road. Exit left to Gest St., Right onto Gest, right on Freeman, then follow signs. I-75 south follow signs off hwy) 45203. www.cincymuseum.org. Phone: (800) 733-2077 or (513) 287-7000. Hours: Monday-Saturday (& Holidays) 10:00am-5:00pm, Sunday 11:00am-6:00pm. Closed Thanksgiving and Christmas. Admission: $8.50-$10.50 per person. Toddler (age 1-2) rates are slightly lower. Combo prices with other museums in the Center are well worth*

the few extra dollars if you have the whole day to explore. Parking fee. Note: Gift Shops - Worth a good look! Snack Bar. OmniMax Theatre on premises has several shows daily (a movie fee is charged per person). Educators: look for a wide list of pdf Teachers Guides on current and past exhibits: www.cincymuseum.org/educators/resources.

Start in the Woods, kiddies. The dim lighting adds mystery to the slides, tunnels, rope climbing mazes and walls, and treehouses. The Energy Zone has kids move plastic balls along a conveyor to a gigantic dump bucket. It's actually a gigantic physics experiment in this Zone - lots of machines and tubes to move balls. Kids At Work lets them make real-life and pretend structures from blocks, pebbles and Legos. They can even use a 12 foot crane to move and lift blocks. Other highlights are the Little Sprouts Farm (age 4 and under), Water Works, Kids Town (pretend town), or Animal Spot (lots of unusual skeletons). Each area is so interactive and so different from the other. We liked how most areas required friend's/parent's participation to complete a task.

MUSEUM OF NATURAL HISTORY & SCIENCE

Cincinnati - ***1301 Western Avenue, Cincinnati Museum Center (I-75 exit 1D, US 50 W. River Road. Exit left to Gest St., Right onto Gest, right on Freeman, then follow signs. I-75 south follow signs off hwy) 45203. www.cincymuseum.org. Phone: (513) 287-7000 or (800) 733-2077. Hours: Monday-Saturday (& Holidays) 10:00am-5:00pm, Sunday 11:00am-6:00pm. Closed Thanksgiving and Christmas. Admission: $8.50-$10.50 per person. Toddler (age 1-2) rates are slightly lower. Combo prices with other museums in the Center are well worth the few extra dollars if you have the whole day to explore. Parking fee. Note: Gift Shops - Worth a good look! OmniMax Theatre on premises has several shows daily (a movie fee is charged per person). Educators: look for a wide list of pdf Teachers Guides on current and past exhibits: www.cincymuseum.org/educators/resources.***

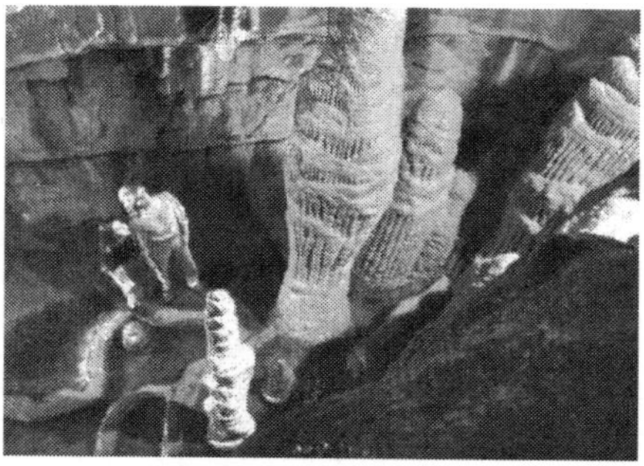

The caves seemed so real....

Want to know a lot about the Ohio Valley's Natural and Geological history? The Glacier and Cavern simulated areas are both wonderful walk-thru reproductions that are so real, it's almost spooky. Start at the Ice Age of fossils and re-created walk-through glaciers. Maybe try to solve the Ice Age mystery or change the landscape of glaciers. The Paleo Lab (within the Ice Cave) is the place to watch actual scientists at work on lots of fossils.

On to the simulated Limestone Cavern with underground waterfalls and a live bat colony (behind glass!). (There are two routes - one that is challenging and involves much climbing and navigating, and the other that is wheelchair or stroller accessible). Look for lots of dino skeletons in Dinosaur Hall. Find out "All About You" as you explore inside, outside and beneath your great body. Brush a huge tooth, see under the skin of your hand, pretend in the office of doctors and dentists, or maybe play pinball as your "food ball" goes through the digestive system. Plan a few hours at this extremely well done museum - we promise it will engage you and you'll learn many new things...easily!

Exit - 1C (east of I-75)

FIRE MUSEUM OF GREATER CINCINNATI

Cincinnati - ***315 West Court Street, near Plum, Downtown (I-75 exit 1C follow signs for 5th Street) 45202. Phone: (513) 621-5553. www.cincyfiremuseum.com. Hours: Tuesday-Saturday 10:00am-4:00pm. Closed holidays. Admission: $8.00 adult, $7.00 senior (65+), $5.00 child (7-17).***

From the minute you walk in the restored fire station, the kids will be intrigued by the nation's first professional fire department exhibits. Displays chronicle

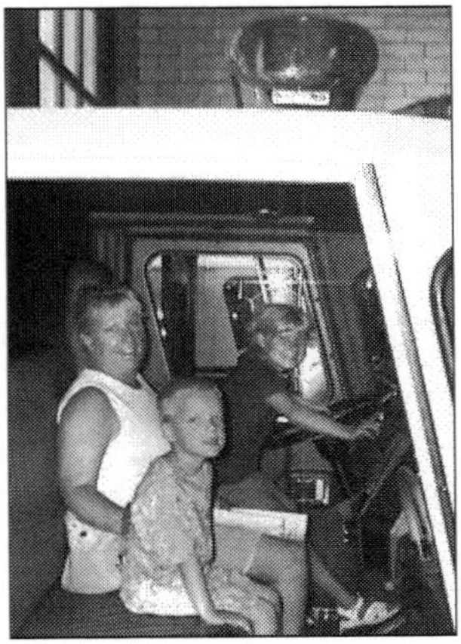

fire fighting history from antique equipment to the cab of a newer fire truck where you can actually pull levers, push buttons, ring bells, operate the siren and flash emergency lights. The history of Cincinnati in frontier days comes to life as the children participate in a "hands-on" bucket brigade and take a turn on an old style hand pumper. Three interactive computers are fun and tell you all about today's firefighting and fire safety. The museum has an emphasis on fire safety with "Safe House" models (touch and demo area) and a video about fire fighting dangers. Before you leave be sure you slide down the 5-foot fire pole or ring the old fire bell. Let's Stop, Drop and Roll. Everyone can do it! This is the most kid-friendly fire museum in the Midwest!

CAREW TOWER

Cincinnati - ***441 Vine Street (5th and Vine, across from Fountain Square, Downtown, I-75 exit 1C) 45202. Phone: (513) 241-3888. Hours: Monday-Thursday 9:30am-5:30pm, Friday 9:00am-6:00pm, Saturday/Sunday 10:00am - 7:00pm.***

An 1930's Art Deco building that is the tallest building downtown. The building itself is a study in old and new. Modern elevators passing renovated plush office floors transport guests only as high as the 45th floor. A trip to the observation deck requires a ride in a rickety, phone booth-sized elevator to the 48th floor. The Observation deck has a panoramic view. Small admission fee per person ($1.00-2.00).

TAFT MUSEUM OF ART

Cincinnati - ***316 Pike Street (Broadway to Fifth to Pike Sts, I-75 exit 1C) 45202. Phone: (513) 241-0343. www.taftmuseum.org. Hours: Wednesday-Sunday 11:00am-4:00pm, weekends until 5pm. Admission: $10 adult, $8 senior (60+) and youth (12-17). Kids are FREE. The museum is FREE to all on Wednesdays. Note: Café and gift shop. Educators: Lesson plans online under Education icon.***

See works of European and American painters, Chinese porcelains, Limoges enamels displayed in a federal period mansion. At the greeter's desk on the second floor, pick up one of the Family Gallery Guides or, before you go, download themed Self-Guided Family Tours from their website (ex. Animals, Children). Select Saturdays "Families Create!" programs combine storytelling and games with art-making activities. If you need an action break, Lytle Park is across the street and is a great play space.

Exit - 1A (east of I-75)

NATIONAL UNDERGROUND RAILROAD FREEDOM CENTER

Cincinnati - ***50 East Freedom Way (Cincinnati waterfront, I-71 exit 2nd street, I-75 exit 1A) 45202. Phone: (513) 333-7500. www.freedomcenter.org. Hours: Tuesday-Saturday 11:00am-5:00pm. Admission: $15.00 adult, $13.00 senior (60+), $10.50 child (3-12). Note: Audio tours, one for adults and another for children, are available free of charge with paid admission. NorthStar Cafe.***

Ohio's involvement in guiding slaves to freedom is commemorated in a museum that helps tell the story of the Underground Railroad. The Center is made up of three buildings that symbolize the cornerstones of freedom - it's a warm art museum with an historical twist. A dynamic presentation, the "moving painting" titled "Suite for Freedom" takes visitors on an emotional journey from freedom to un-freedom. Next, move on to the Slave Pen - used to "warehouse" slaves being moved further south for sale. ESCAPE! This child-friendly gallery uses storytelling and hands-on interaction. Probably the only area designed for kids, time can be spent listening to choices slaves must make, then testing YOUR decisions as a computer-interactive slave yourself. Your choices reveal a lot about your character. From Slavery to Freedom takes the visitor on a journey from the slaves' arrival in the New World through the Colonial period to the Civil War. The Concluding Experience area is designed to help each visitor put into personal perspective all that he or she has just experienced. What does freedom mean today? To you? To all of us? Visitors can participate in individual polling based on "what would you do" scenarios. This is serious stuff, be sure your children are prepared to think about their reactions to the material. The site would be an excellent student post-study of Pre-and-Post Civil War era history. Some pre-study of the Underground Railroad is helpful. The Center leaves an enduring impression on those who "get it."

Travel Journal & Notes:

Chapter 3
KENTUCKY

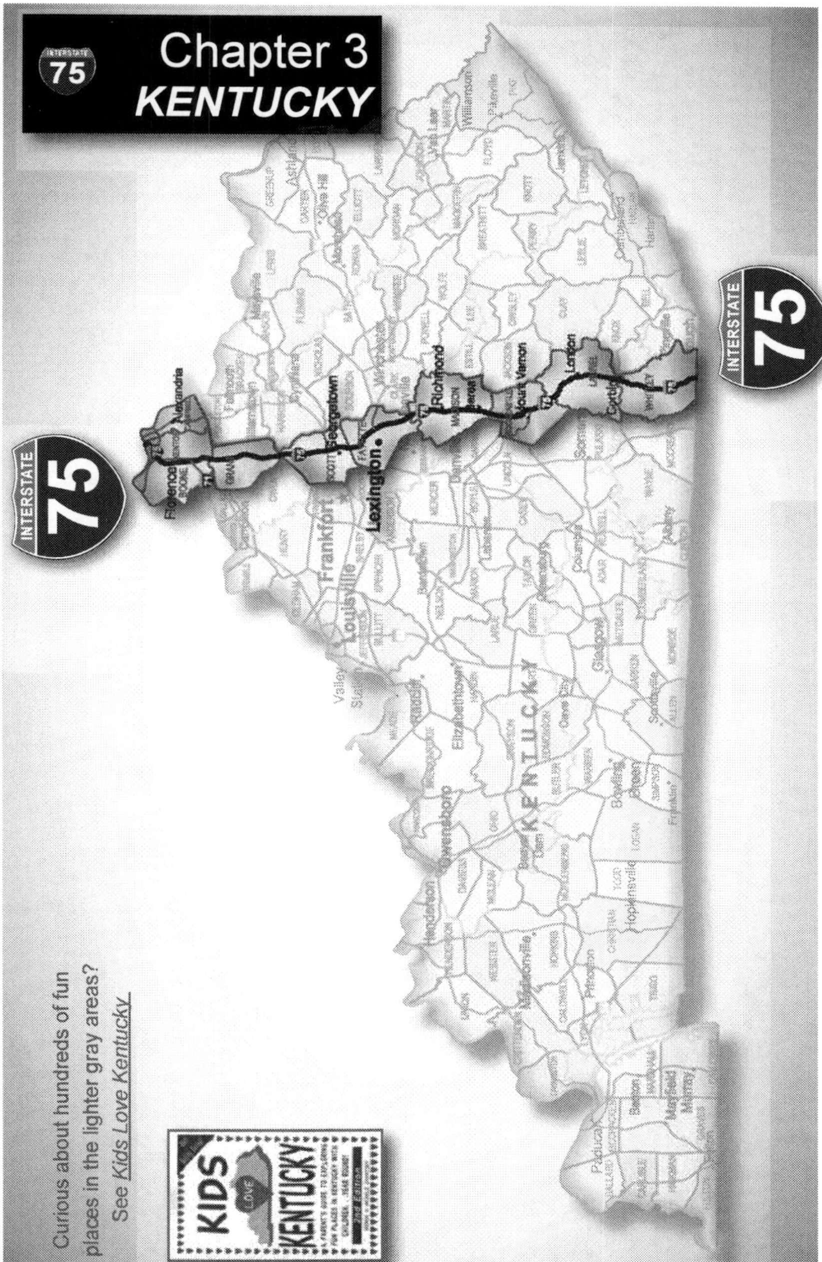

Curious about hundreds of fun places in the lighter gray areas? See <u>*Kids Love Kentucky*</u>

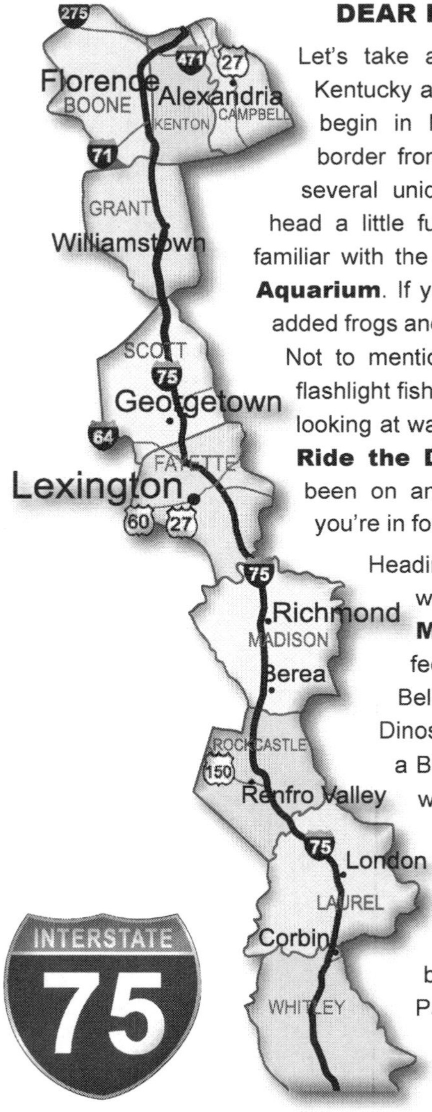

DEAR KENTUCKY TRAVELER:

Let's take a trip down the I-75 Corridor of Kentucky and look for family sites to see. We begin in Northern Kentucky, just over the border from Cincinnati, Ohio. Covington has several unique little museums, but most will head a little further east to Newport. Many are familiar with the oceanic adventures at **Newport Aquarium**. If you haven't visited recently, they've added frogs and the sharks are still waiting for you! Not to mention, the penguins, the pirates, the flashlight fish and elegant jelly fish. If you're tired looking at water, try now going IN the water (on **Ride the Ducks Newport**). If you haven't been on an amphibious Duckie boat before, you're in for a treat.

Heading further south on I-75, take I-275 west a few exits to the **Creation Museum**. The site's 60,000 square feet of family fun logo is: "Prepare to Believe", and it's true! Some call it a Dinosaur Museum - it's true. Some call it a Bible Museum - it's true. You decide which interactive science story you believe is the right one...

Back on I-75 heading south, you won't want to miss **Big Bone Lick State Park**. This is the birthplace of American Vertebrate Paleontology...the greatest ice age graveyard ever found! Erosion may still reveal bones (look for them while hiking), especially along the creek. A live buffalo herd now roams the property and your kids can touch Mastodon teeth!

Heading towards Lexington, you first come upon the suburb of Georgetown. This is the home of **Toyota Manufacturing Plant Tours**. Interact and "test drive" in the museum, then take a scheduled tram tour of a real working car plant. From one type of horsepower to another, everyone's next stop is the most popular in the state – **Kentucky Horse Park**. Unless you're planning to stay in Lexington a few overnights, it's impossible to visit and stop at all the horse farms scattered throughout this region. Here, at one park, you can view the most beautiful horses, magnificent scenery, expert shows and a whole lot of history. Afterwards, make your way to downtown Lexington and catch a few hours at **Explorium**. Brushing giant teeth, making a tornado or walking on the moon sound fun to you?

Driving south of Lexington to another suburb, you come upon another town of intriguing sites. Richmond is home to the **Hummel Planetarium** and Space Theater at Eastern Kentucky University with many family shows simulating the night sky with over 10,000 stars, moons, planets, etc. – all operating simultaneously with surround sound. Richmond has a driving **Civil War Tour** and the home of Cassius Marcellus Clay (a fervent emancipationist and friend to Abraham Lincoln), White Hall. The home is rather progressive for it's time...they had running water and central heating. A State Park that includes a beach, pool, mini-golf and the real historic **Fort Boonesborough** is a short ways off exit 95. Great place to wear your kids out with activities! Before you leave the area, your family must witness the "shopping ritual" at **Bybee Pottery**.

Now that we're talking about pottery, let's visit the craft capital of Kentucky – **Berea**. They've been making brooms here for 80 years and weaving even longer. Visit the working studios of woodworkers, weavers, furniture makers and broom craft. The tours are well worth the time and you'll find lots of questions to ask as you go along.

Our last stop down I-75 is Corbin. Two of the most unique sites in Kentucky are here. Take a side trip around lunchtime at the **Harland Sanders Café** and Museum and "Eat where it all began"! See Kentucky Fried Chicken Colonel's kitchen where he developed his secret recipe. Now, purchase some KFC fast food and munch on it sitting next to a statue of Colonel Sanders.

Also in Corbin is the site of the famous moonbow (arch of light and color), a phenomena not found anywhere else in the Western Hemisphere! **Cumberland Falls State Park**, the "Niagara of the South," is a 125-foot wide curtain of water falling 60 feet – dramatic night and day. To try to catch a moonbow, it is best to visit when there's a full moon...

In southern Kentucky, I-75 has to go over each mountain so it is up and down like a yoyo. Once in awhile I-75 will sneak through a pass, along side a river. But, at least, there is nothing boring about driving on this part of I-75.

KENTUCKY

ACTIVITIES AT A GLANCE

AMUSEMENTS

Exit - 185 / I-275 Exit 79 - *Totter's Otterville @ Johnny's Toys*

Exit - 11 - *Kentucky Splash Water Park*

ANIMALS & FARMS

Exit - 192 - *Newport Aquarium*

Exit - 120 - *Kentucky Horse Park*

Exit - 95 - *Raven Run Nature Sanctuary*

HISTORY

Exit - 113 - *Mary Todd Lincoln House*

Exit - 95 - *White Hall State Historic Site*

Exit - 95 - *Fort Boonesborough State Park*

MUSEUMS

Exit - 191 - *Behringer / Crawford Museum*

Exit - 189 - *Railway Exposition Museum*

Exit - 181 - *Dinsmore Homestead*

Exit - 113 - *Explorium Of Lexington*

Exit - 113 - *Hunt-Morgan House*

Exit - 110 - *Aviation Museum Of Kentucky*

Exit - 108 - *Waveland State Historic Site*

Exit - 104 - *Ashland, The Henry Clay Estate*

Exit - 62 - *Kentucky Music Hall Of Fame Museum*

Exit - 29 - *Harland Sanders Café & Museum*

OUTDOOR EXPLORING

Exit - 192 - *World Peace Bell Exhibit Center*

Exit - 175 - *Big Bone Lick State Park*

Exit - 115 - *McConnell Springs*

Exit - 38 - *Levi Jackson Wilderness Road State Park*

Exit - 15 - Cumberland Falls State Resort Park

SCIENCE

Exit - 185 / I-275 Exit 11 - *Creation Museum*

Exit - 87 - *Hummel Planetarium & Eastern Kentucky University*

SUGGESTED LODGING & DINING

Exit - 110 - *Parkette Drive-In*

Exit - 110 - *Keeneland Track Kitchen*

Exit - 76 - *Boone Tavern*

Exit - 15 - *Cumberland Falls State Resort Park Lodge*

THE ARTS

Exit - 192 - *Mainstrasse Village*

Exit - 62 - *Renfro Valley Entertainment Center*

TOURS

Exit - 192 - *BB Riverboats*

Exit - 192 - *Ride The Ducks Newport*

Exit - 126 - *Toyota Motor Manufacturing Kentucky*

Exit - 113 - *University Of Kentucky*

Exit - 110 - *Old Kentucky Chocolates*

Exit - 87 - *Richmond Civil War Driving Tour*

Exit - 76 - *Berea College Log House*

WELCOME CENTERS

Exit - 177 Mile SB Only - Kentucky Welcome Center

Exit - 1 Mile NB Only - Kentucky Welcome Center

GENERAL INFORMATION

Contact the services of interest. Request to be added to their mailing lists.

- Canoe Kentucky (800) K-CANOE -1 or www.canoeky.com
- Kentucky Roadside Farm Markets www.kyfb.com/roadside.htm
- Kentucky State Parks - www.state.ky.us/agencies/parks/parkhome.htm or (800) 255-Park
- Kentucky Tourism Council www.kentuckytourism.com or (800) 225-8747
- Lexington CVB (800) 845-3959 or www.visitlex.com

Travel Journal & Notes:

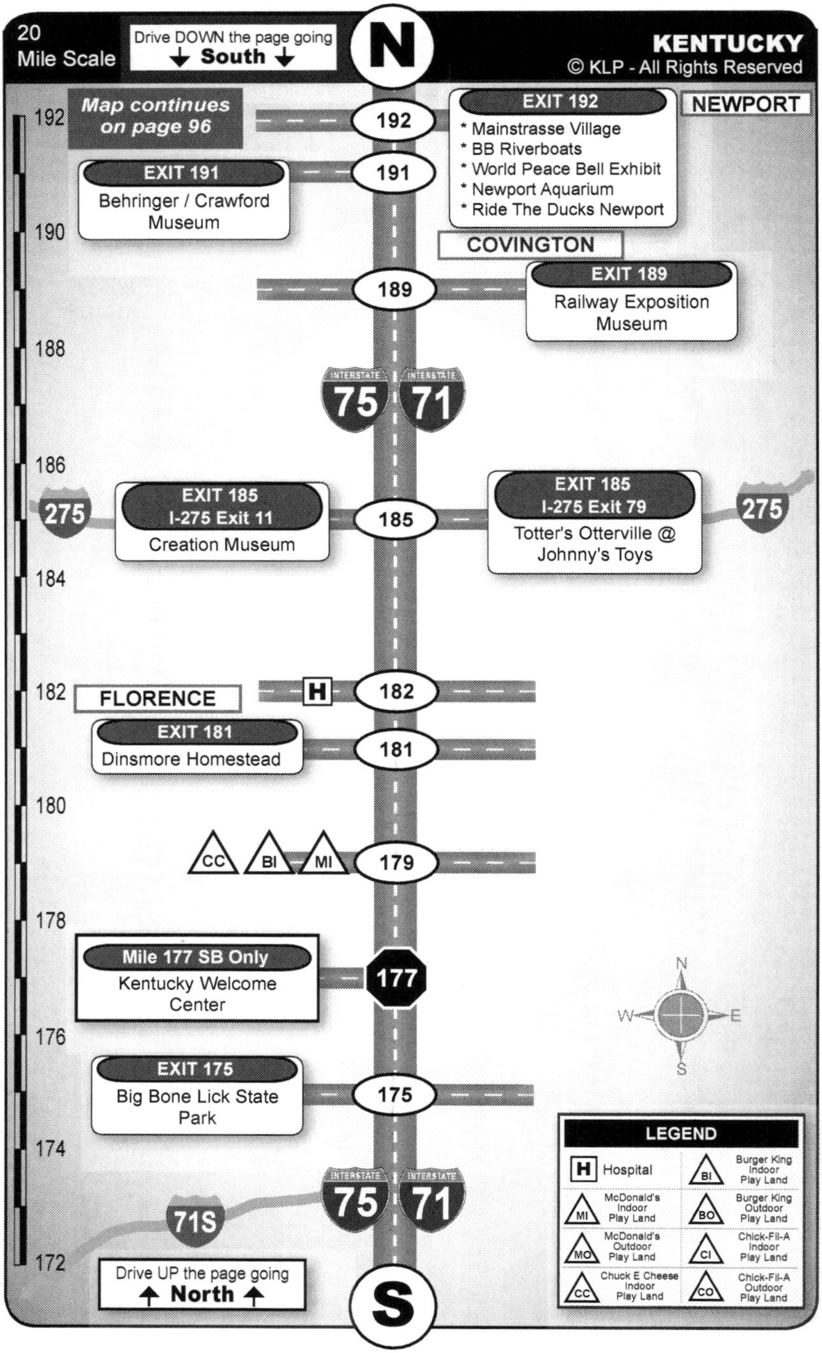
20
Mile Scale
Drive DOWN the page going
South
N
KENTUCKY
© KLP - All Rights Reserved
Map continues
on page 96
192
EXIT 192
NEWPORT
* Mainstrasse Village
* BB Riverboats
* World Peace Bell Exhibit
* Newport Aquarium
* Ride The Ducks Newport
191
EXIT 191
Behringer / Crawford
Museum
190
COVINGTON
189
EXIT 189
Railway Exposition
Museum
188
INTERSTATE 75
INTERSTATE 71
186
275
EXIT 185
I-275 Exit 11
Creation Museum
185
EXIT 185
I-275 Exit 79
Totter's Otterville @
Johnny's Toys
275
184
182
FLORENCE
H
182
EXIT 181
Dinsmore Homestead
181
180
CC
BI
MI
179
178
Mile 177 SB Only
Kentucky Welcome
Center
177
N
W
E
S
176
EXIT 175
Big Bone Lick State
Park
175
174
LEGEND
H Hospital
BI Burger King Indoor Play Land
MI McDonald's Indoor Play Land
BO Burger King Outdoor Play Land
MO McDonald's Outdoor Play Land
CI Chick-Fil-A Indoor Play Land
CC Chuck E Cheese Indoor Play Land
CO Chick-Fil-A Outdoor Play Land
71S
INTERSTATE 75
INTERSTATE 71
172
Drive UP the page going
North
S

KENTUCKY

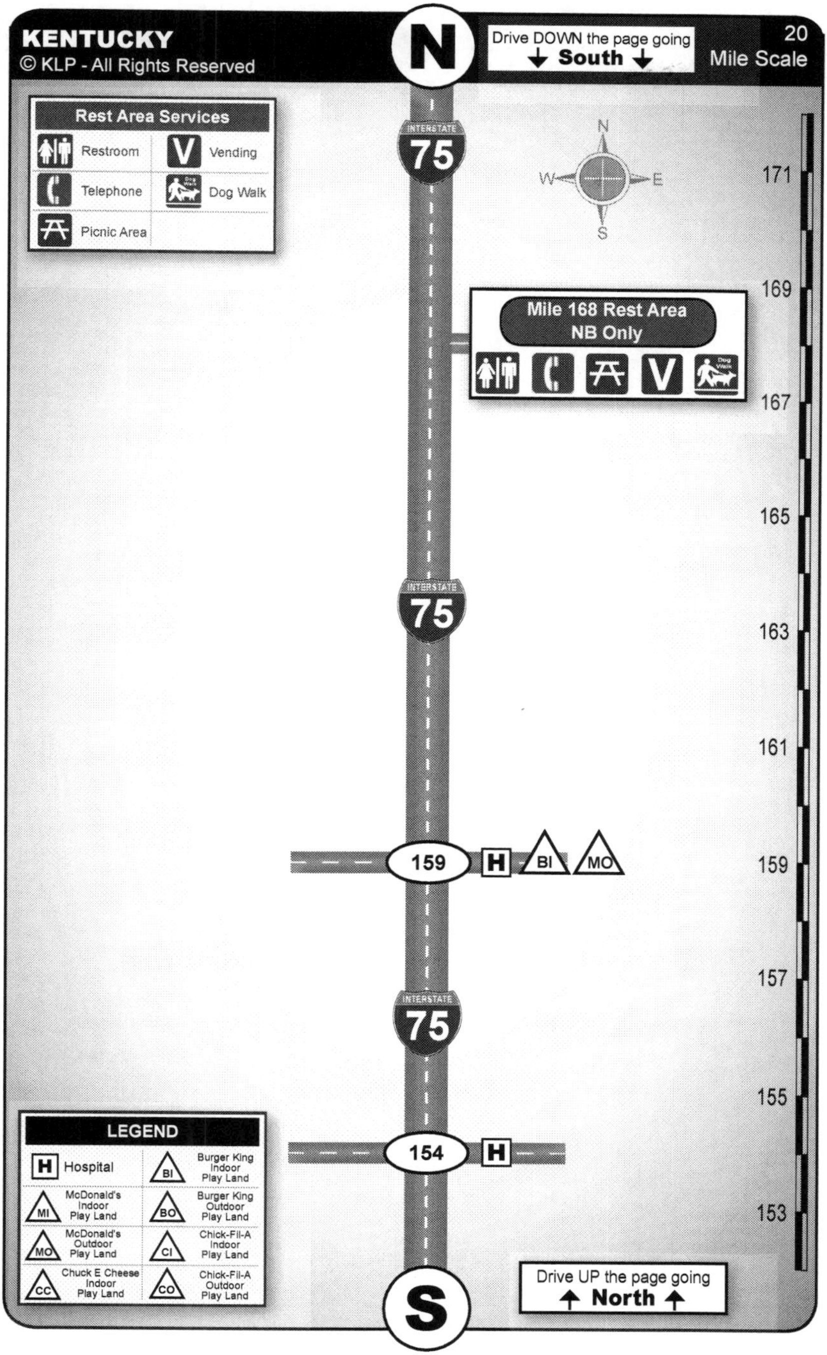
KENTUCKY
© KLP - All Rights Reserved
N
Drive DOWN the page going
South
20
Mile Scale
Rest Area Services
Restroom
Vending
Telephone
Dog Walk
Picnic Area
INTERSTATE
75
N
W
E
S
171
169
Mile 168 Rest Area
NB Only
167
165
INTERSTATE
75
163
161
159
H
BI
MO
159
157
INTERSTATE
75
155
154
H
153
LEGEND
H Hospital
BI Burger King Indoor Play Land
MI McDonald's Indoor Play Land
BO Burger King Outdoor Play Land
MO McDonald's Outdoor Play Land
CI Chick-Fil-A Indoor Play Land
CC Chuck E Cheese Indoor Play Land
CO Chick-Fil-A Outdoor Play Land
S
Drive UP the page going
North

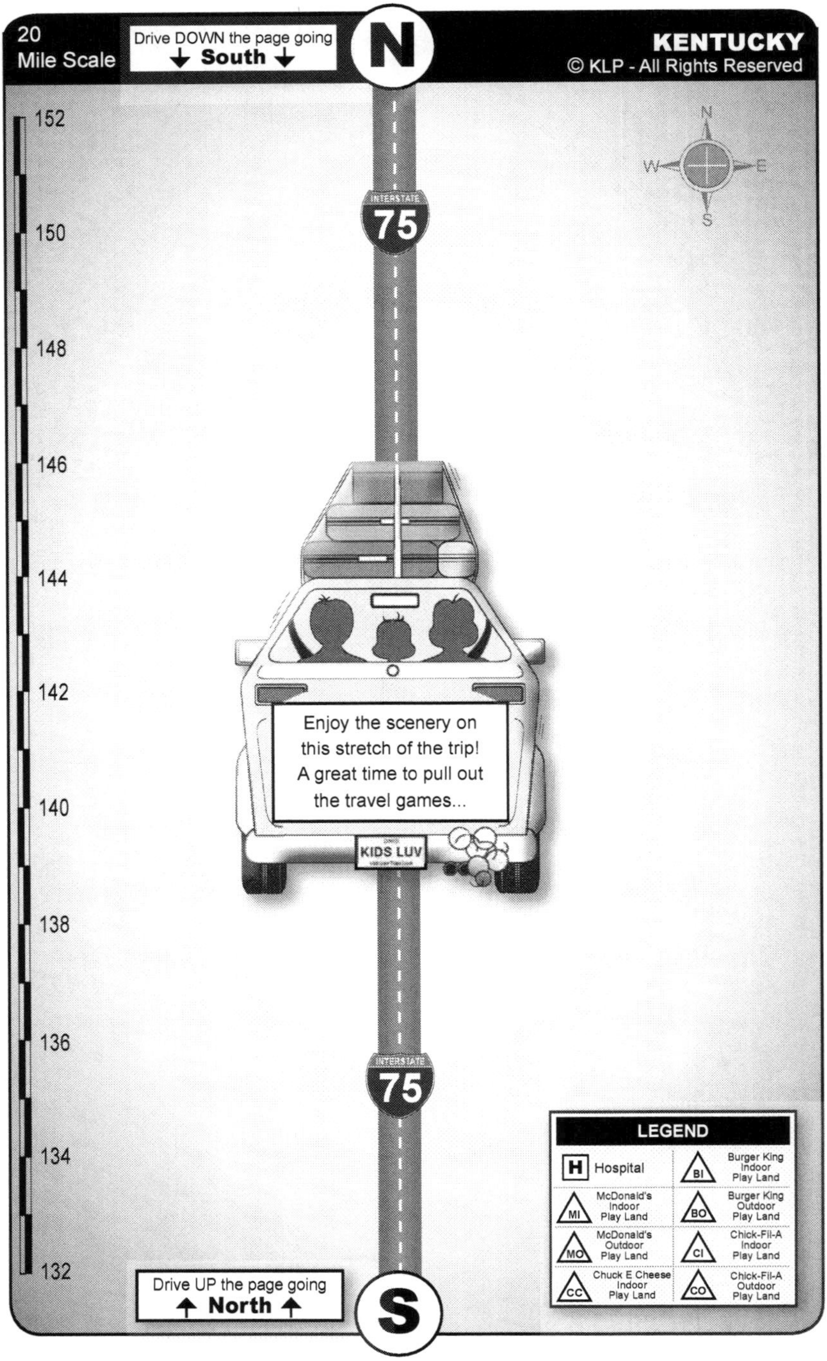
20
Mile Scale
Drive DOWN the page going
South
N
KENTUCKY
© KLP - All Rights Reserved
152
150
148
146
144
142
140
138
136
134
132
N
W
E
S
INTERSTATE
75
Enjoy the scenery on
this stretch of the trip!
A great time to pull out
the travel games...
KIDS LUV
INTERSTATE
75
Drive UP the page going
North
S
LEGEND
H Hospital
BI Burger King Indoor Play Land
MI McDonald's Indoor Play Land
BO Burger King Outdoor Play Land
MO McDonald's Outdoor Play Land
CI Chick-Fil-A Indoor Play Land
CC Chuck E Cheese Indoor Play Land
CO Chick-Fil-A Outdoor Play Land

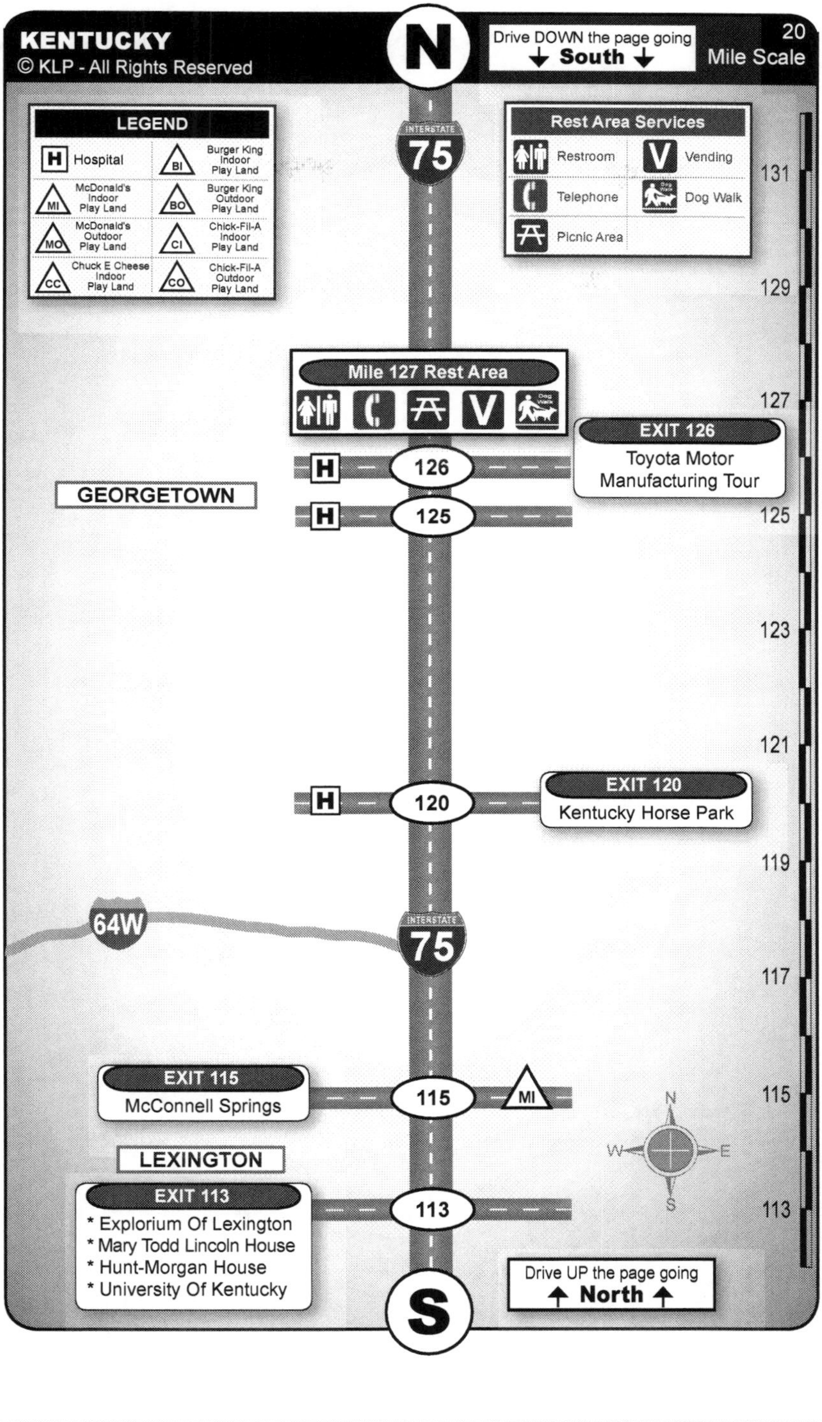
KENTUCKY
© KLP - All Rights Reserved
N
Drive DOWN the page going
South
20
Mile Scale
LEGEND
Hospital
Burger King Indoor Play Land
McDonald's Indoor Play Land
Burger King Outdoor Play Land
McDonald's Outdoor Play Land
Chick-Fil-A Indoor Play Land
Chuck E Cheese Indoor Play Land
Chick-Fil-A Outdoor Play Land
BI
MI
BO
MO
CI
CC
CO
75
Rest Area Services
Restroom
Vending
Telephone
Dog Walk
Picnic Area
131
129
Mile 127 Rest Area
127
EXIT 126
Toyota Motor
Manufacturing Tour
126
GEORGETOWN
125
123
121
EXIT 120
Kentucky Horse Park
120
119
64W
75
117
EXIT 115
McConnell Springs
115
MI
LEXINGTON
EXIT 113
* Explorium Of Lexington
* Mary Todd Lincoln House
* Hunt-Morgan House
* University Of Kentucky
113
N
W
E
S
Drive UP the page going
North
S

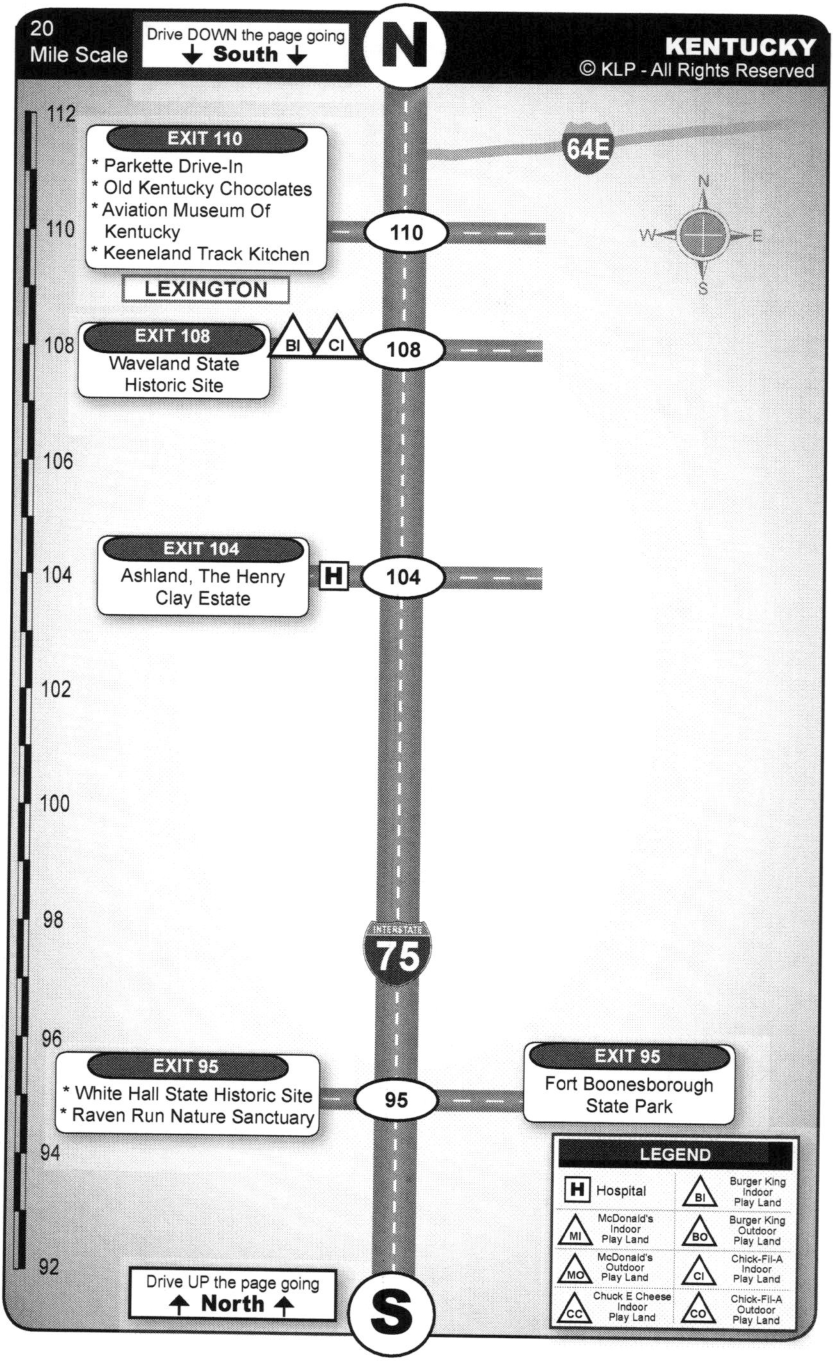
20 Mile Scale
Drive DOWN the page going ↓ South ↓
N
KENTUCKY
© KLP - All Rights Reserved
112
64E
EXIT 110
* Parkette Drive-In
* Old Kentucky Chocolates
* Aviation Museum Of Kentucky
* Keeneland Track Kitchen
110
LEXINGTON
N
W
E
S
108
EXIT 108
Waveland State Historic Site
BI
CI
106
EXIT 104
Ashland, The Henry Clay Estate
H
104
102
100
98
INTERSTATE 75
96
EXIT 95
* White Hall State Historic Site
* Raven Run Nature Sanctuary
95
EXIT 95
Fort Boonesborough State Park
94
92
LEGEND
H Hospital
BI Burger King Indoor Play Land
MI McDonald's Indoor Play Land
BO Burger King Outdoor Play Land
MO McDonald's Outdoor Play Land
CI Chick-Fil-A Indoor Play Land
CC Chuck E Cheese Indoor Play Land
CO Chick-Fil-A Outdoor Play Land
Drive UP the page going ↑ North ↑
S

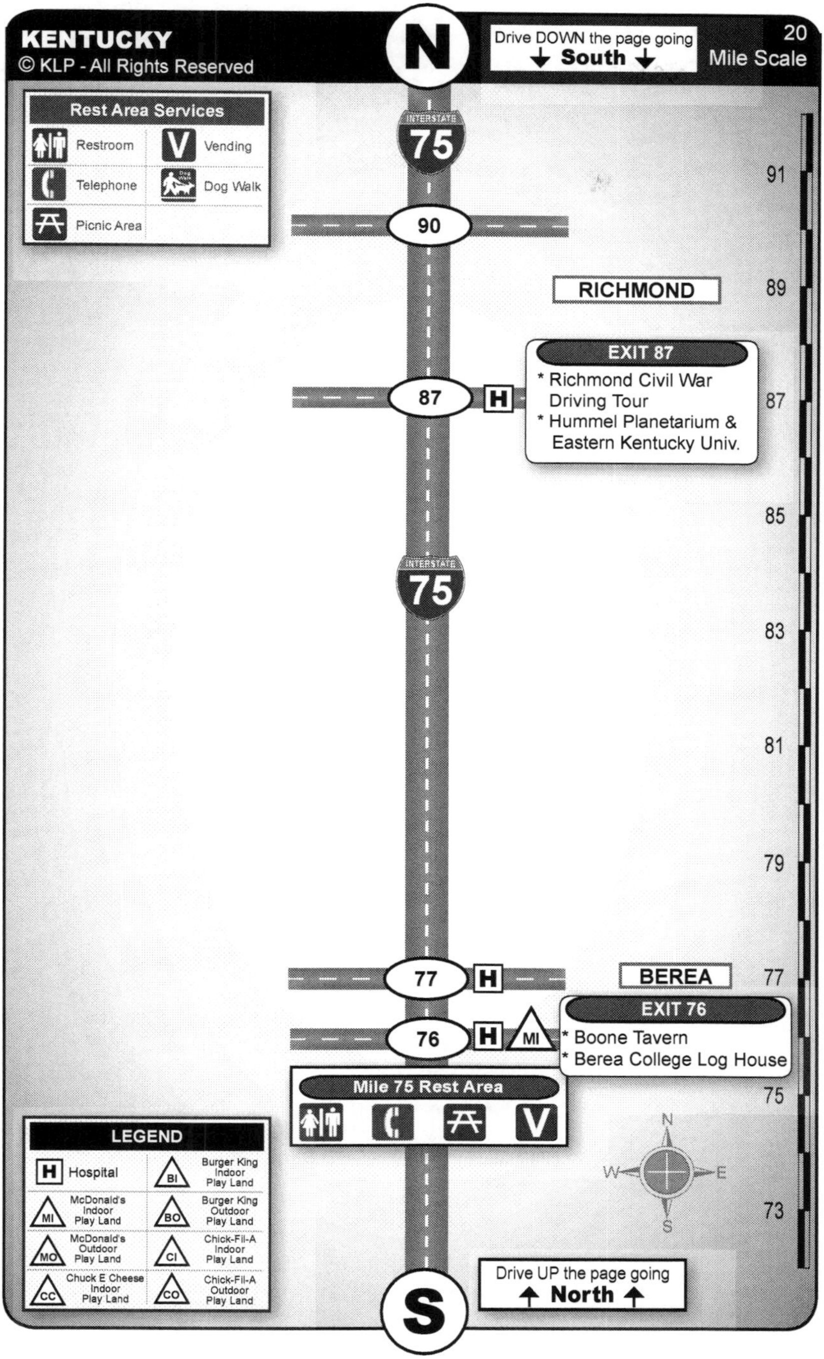
KENTUCKY
© KLP - All Rights Reserved
N
Drive DOWN the page going
South
20
Mile Scale
Rest Area Services
Restroom
Vending
Telephone
Dog Walk
Picnic Area
INTERSTATE 75
91
90
RICHMOND
89
EXIT 87
* Richmond Civil War Driving Tour
* Hummel Planetarium & Eastern Kentucky Univ.
87
H
85
INTERSTATE 75
83
81
79
77
H
BEREA
EXIT 76
* Boone Tavern
* Berea College Log House
76
H
MI
Mile 75 Rest Area
75
73
N
W
E
S
LEGEND
H Hospital
BI Burger King Indoor Play Land
MI McDonald's Indoor Play Land
BO Burger King Outdoor Play Land
MO McDonald's Outdoor Play Land
CI Chick-Fil-A Indoor Play Land
CC Chuck E Cheese Indoor Play Land
CO Chick-Fil-A Outdoor Play Land
S
Drive UP the page going
North

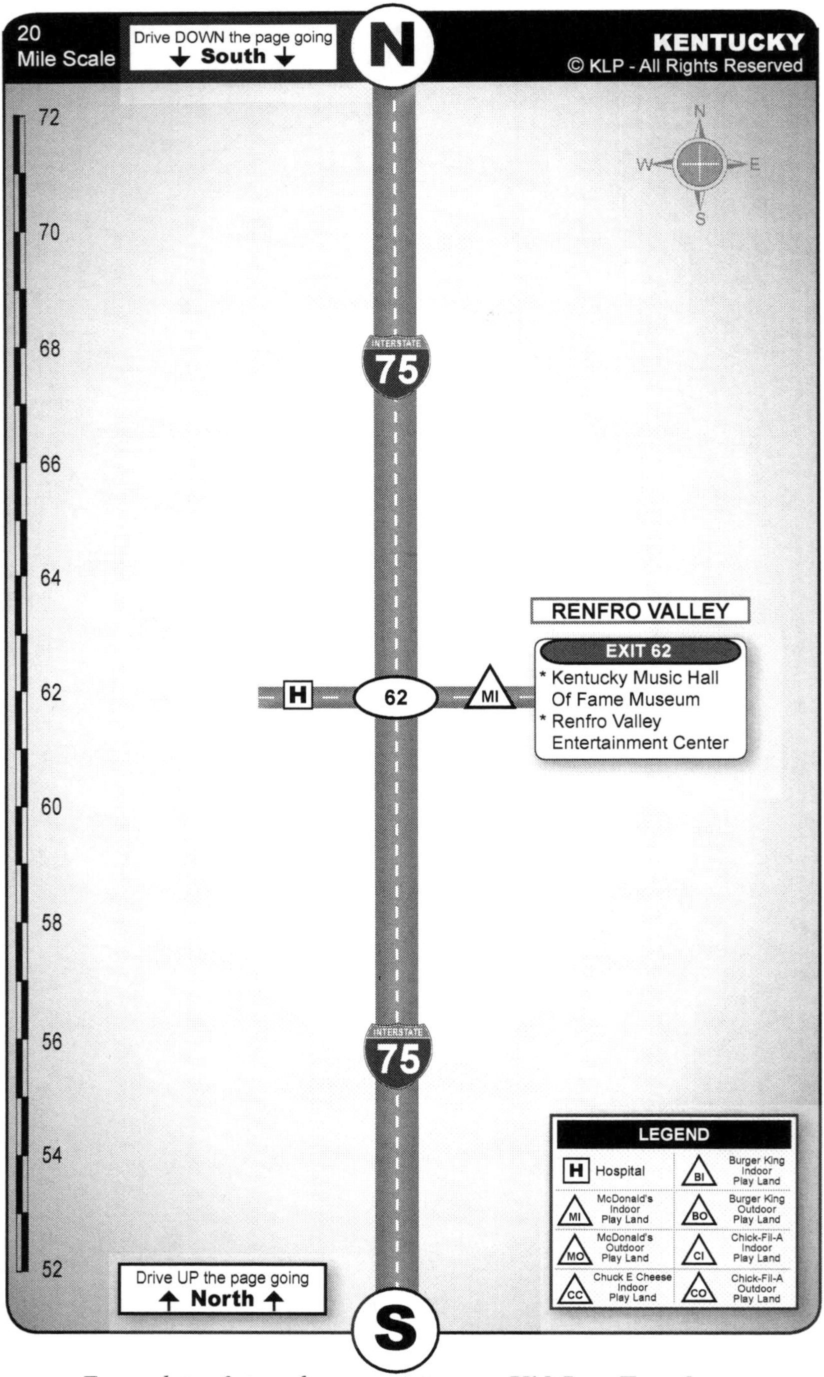

20 Mile Scale

Drive DOWN the page going
↓ South ↓

N

KENTUCKY
© KLP - All Rights Reserved

KENTUCKY

72
70
68

INTERSTATE
75

66
64

RENFRO VALLEY

62

H — **62** — △MI

EXIT 62
* Kentucky Music Hall
 Of Fame Museum
* Renfro Valley
 Entertainment Center

60
58
56

INTERSTATE
75

54

LEGEND

H Hospital		△BI Burger King Indoor Play Land	
△MI McDonald's Indoor Play Land		△BO Burger King Outdoor Play Land	
△MO McDonald's Outdoor Play Land		△CI Chick-Fil-A Indoor Play Land	
△CC Chuck E Cheese Indoor Play Land		△CO Chick-Fil-A Outdoor Play Land	

52

Drive UP the page going
↑ North ↑

S

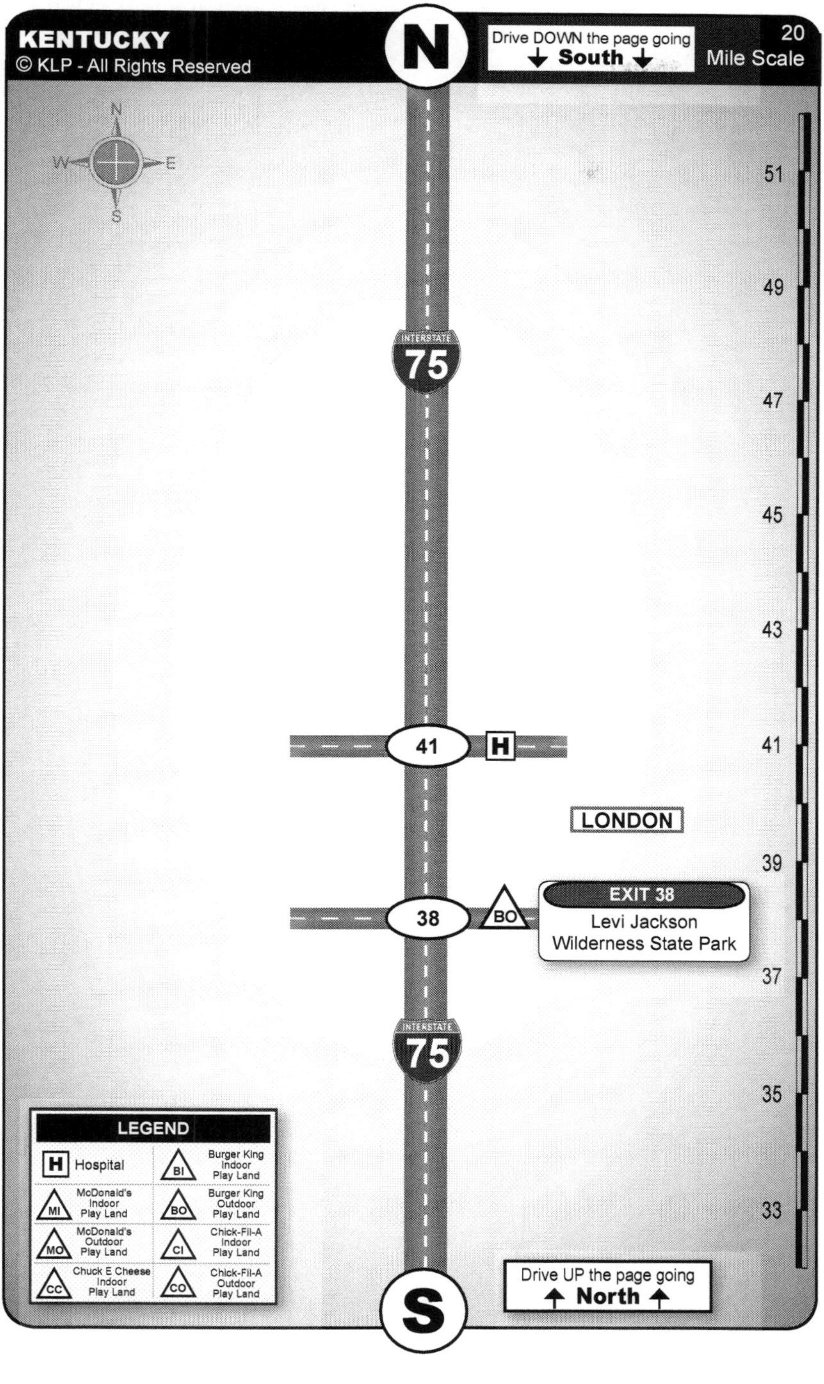
KENTUCKY
© KLP - All Rights Reserved
N
Drive DOWN the page going
South
20
Mile Scale
N
W
E
S
51
49
INTERSTATE
75
47
45
43
41
41
H
LONDON
39
EXIT 38
Levi Jackson
Wilderness State Park
38
BO
37
INTERSTATE
75
35
33
LEGEND
H Hospital
BI Burger King Indoor Play Land
MI McDonald's Indoor Play Land
BO Burger King Outdoor Play Land
MO McDonald's Outdoor Play Land
CI Chick-Fil-A Indoor Play Land
CC Chuck E Cheese Indoor Play Land
CO Chick-Fil-A Outdoor Play Land
Drive UP the page going
North
S

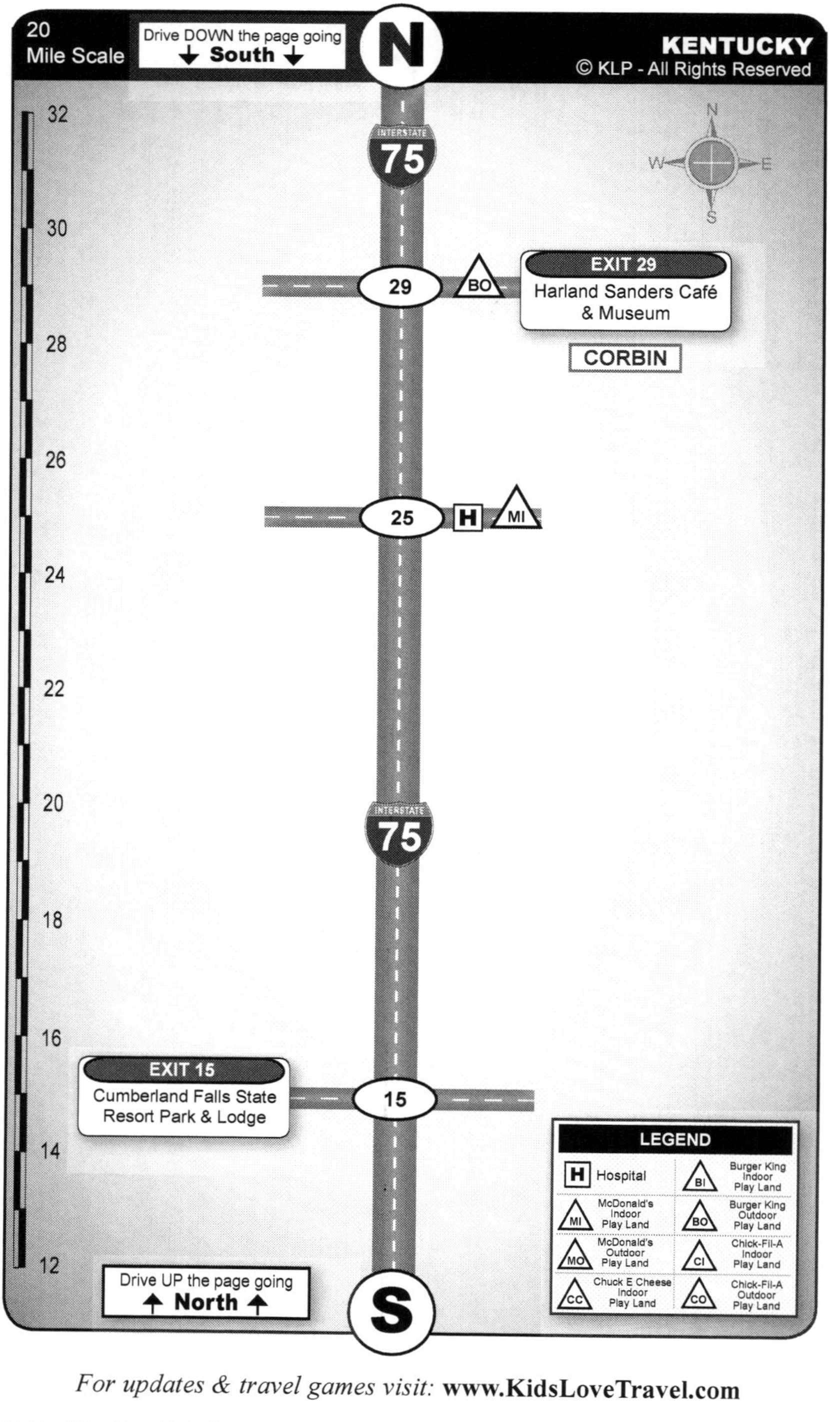
20
Mile Scale
Drive DOWN the page going
South
N
KENTUCKY
© KLP - All Rights Reserved
32
30
28
26
24
22
20
18
16
14
12
75
N
W
E
S
29
BO
EXIT 29
Harland Sanders Café
& Museum
CORBIN
25
H
MI
75
EXIT 15
Cumberland Falls State
Resort Park & Lodge
15
LEGEND
H Hospital
BI Burger King Indoor Play Land
MI McDonald's Indoor Play Land
BO Burger King Outdoor Play Land
MO McDonald's Outdoor Play Land
CI Chick-Fil-A Indoor Play Land
CC Chuck E Cheese Indoor Play Land
CO Chick-Fil-A Outdoor Play Land
Drive UP the page going
North
S

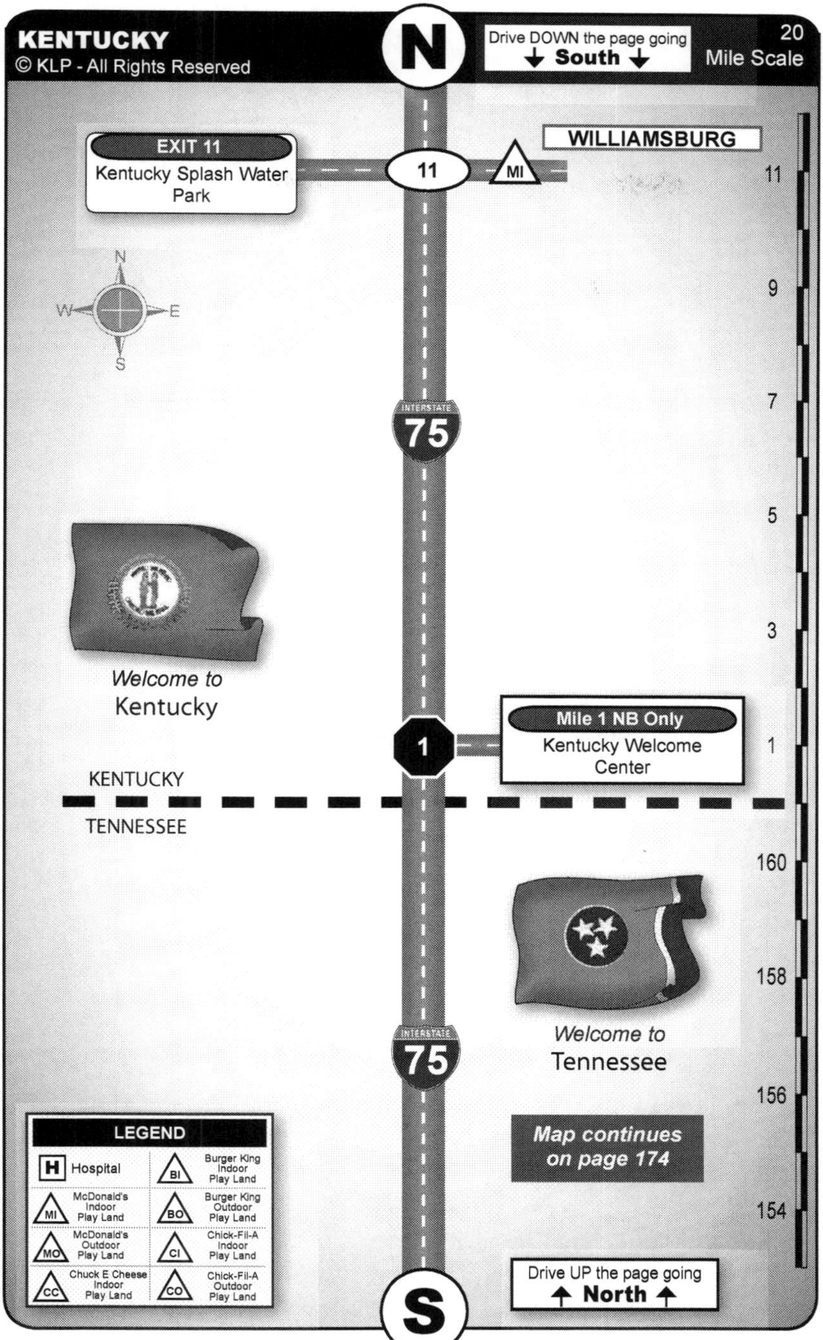
KENTUCKY
© KLP - All Rights Reserved
N
Drive DOWN the page going
↓ South ↓
20
Mile Scale
WILLIAMSBURG
EXIT 11
Kentucky Splash Water Park
11
MI
11
9
7
5
3
1
INTERSTATE
75
Welcome to
Kentucky
Mile 1 NB Only
Kentucky Welcome Center
KENTUCKY
TENNESSEE
160
158
156
154
Welcome to
Tennessee
Map continues on page 174
LEGEND
H Hospital
BI Burger King Indoor Play Land
MI McDonald's Indoor Play Land
BO Burger King Outdoor Play Land
MO McDonald's Outdoor Play Land
CI Chick-Fil-A Indoor Play Land
CC Chuck E Cheese Indoor Play Land
CO Chick-Fil-A Outdoor Play Land
S
Drive UP the page going
↑ North ↑

Sites and attractions are listed in order by Exit Number (North to South) and distance from the exit (closest are listed first). Symbols indicated represent:

Restaurants Lodging

Exit - 192 (east of I-75)

MAINSTRASSE VILLAGE

Covington - ***616 Main Street (I-75 exit 192) 41011. Phone: (859) 491-0458 or (800) STAY-NKY. www.mainstrasse.org. Note: Northern Kentucky Visitors Center next to bell tower. Goose Girl bronze sculpture 2 blocks east of tower.***

Ongoing restoration and revitalization of a 30 block area in west Covington is now a village with shops and restaurants (try some sweets at the Bakery Shop near the Tower). A favorite with kids is the Carroll Chimes Bell Tower in Goebel Park. The 100 foot bell tower with a 43 bell carillon plays on the hour, from 9:00am-dusk, spring thru Christmas. The bell tower contains one of the 2 American-made animated clocks in the world, with 21 figures performing "The Pied Piper of Hamelin".

BB RIVERBOATS

Covington - ***Covington Crossing, just over the blue suspension bridge (I-75 exit 192 to Riverboat Row) 41071. Phone: (800) 261-8586. www.bbriverboats.com. Admission: $16-$22.00 just sightseeing. Add $6-$16.00 if meal served. Children nearly half price. Tours: 1 1/2 hour sightseeing cruises on the Ohio River. Several times daily (best to call for schedule). Reservations Required (May-October). Concessions on board.***

Docked at the foot of Madison Street see the Modern "Funliner", "Mark Twain" sternwheeler or steamboat "Becky Thatcher". Also theme cruises like Pirates or year-round holiday tours. Many cruises offer additional lunch, brunch and dinner cruise options with live entertainment.

WORLD PEACE BELL EXHIBIT CENTER

Newport - ***425 York Street 41071. Phone: (859) 261-2526.***

The World Peace Bell is the world's largest free swinging bell. It weighs 66,000 lbs., is 12 feet in diameter and 12 feet high. Its clapper alone weighs an amazing 6,878 pounds. The yoke in which it swings weighs an additional 16,512 pounds. This magnificent bell rings with a powerful, awe-inspiring, deep resonant tone that is truly a majestic symbol of freedom and peace. Bell swings and rings each day at noon. When we say quick stop, this really is.

NEWPORT AQUARIUM

Newport - *One Aquarium Way (Newport on the Levee, I-75 exit 192 or I-275 east to I-471 south exit 5 (Rt. 8) to parking garage). 41011. Phone: (859) 261-7444 or (888) 491-FINS. www.newportaquarium.com. Hours: Daily 10:00am-7:00pm (Summers), Daily 10:00am-6:00pm (Fall/Winter/Spring). Admission: $23.00 adult, $15.00 child (2-12). Note: Sharky's Café, Gift shop. No strollers past the entrance.*

As you take the escalator down into the ocean, you'll read thru a brochure that invites you to explore one million gallons of water. They use clear, seamless acrylic walls and tunnels that truly make you want to reach out and touch the fish. Everywhere you go, remember to look up, look down and keep your ears open - it truly is a place you have to see with all your senses. 60 different exhibits take you places you'd probably never go! Rivers of the World (knifefish); The Bizarre and Beautiful (flashlight fish); Pirate Theatre (a movie ship - Yo, Ho, Ho!); Shore Gallery (touch pool where visitors can feel & examine creatures like Mermaid's Purses or tickle a Horseshoe Crab); Kingdom of Penguins - 16 King Penguins from Japan are set in a winter setting theatre with video monitor close-ups. Occasionally baby penguins are hatched and grown in the nursery here! If your knowledge of frogs is limited, hop over to the Frog Bog - an exhibit space featuring 30 species of frogs and a new Frogger-type video game with an interactive pad that lets kids do the jumping. The absolute highlight is the Surrounded by Sharks exhibit - 85 feet under water! The tunnels take you thru a shark home - as your child presses his nose against the acrylic tube - wait - for the first shriek when a shark is sighted and comes right at you! Don't worry, it's a total thrill that's completely safe.

This is definitely the closest you'll ever get while staying dry...wow!

Exit - 192 (east of I-75)

RIDE THE DUCKS NEWPORT

Newport - ***One Aquarium Way (Newport on the Levee, I-75 exit 192, head east on W. 5th St. or I-275 East to I-471 North. Newport Exit) 41011. Phone: (859) 815-1439. http://newport.rideducks.com. Admission: $19.00 adult, $14 child (2-12). Tours: Summer hours daily 10:00am-8:00pm. Fall/Spring hours generally daily Noon - 5:00pm (subject to weather and groups).***

Quack-Tastic Fun! Ride The Ducks Newport is a 40-minute amphibious sightseeing experience. Travel on land and water in one amazing vehicle. Tour the streets and then SPLASH into the Ohio River. From the water, explore the historic waterfronts of Newport, Covington, and Cincinnati. See the World Peace Bell, Newport Aquarium, Historic Riverside Drive, Great American Ballpark, Paul Brown Stadium and much more. Your Captain will en-tour-tain you with stories of past and present. Learn about Newport and Ohio history, the Ohio River, its famous personalities and its impact on the state and our nation. Find out about Greater Cincinnati's role in film, song and sports too. Use the famous Wacky Quacker to become a part of the show as you roam the streets. Free with every ride, the Wacky Quacker will grab locals' attention and get the Duck rocking as you roll through the city streets. We always suggest Duck tours for kids to have fun with historical cities and never get bored because they're having too much fun quacking - they never realize they're learning.

Exit - 191 (west of I-75)

BEHRINGER / CRAWFORD MUSEUM

Covington - 1600 Montague Road (I-75, exit either 5th Street or 12th Street/Pike, head west on Montague) Street, follow signs to Devou Park) 41011. Phone: (859) 491-4003. www.bcmuseum.org/#_=_ Hours: Tuesday-Saturday 10:00am-5:00pm, Sunday 1:00-5:00pm. Closed holidays. Admission: $9.00 adult, $8.00 senior (60+), $5.00 child (3-17).

Permanent exhibits include galleries focusing on: Paleontology; Archaeology - detailing prehistoric Native American cultures; Kentucky, Naturally! focusing on local wildlife; 19th Century History featuring home life, politics, Underground Railroad & the Civil War; and River Heritage specializing in steamboats and tugs. All permanent exhibits include touchable objects to supplement learning. Additionally, special activities and exhibits include historic toys and trains available for play. Kids, look for the shrunken head!

Exit - 189 (east of I-75)

RAILWAY EXPOSITION MUSEUM

Covington - *315 West Southern Avenue 41011. Phone: (859) 491-7245. Hours: Saturday-Sunday 12:30-4:30pm (May-October) Admission: $4.00 general.*

Interiors of railroad cars, railroad memorabilia and locomotives are displayed at this educational museum. Guided tours of pullman sleepers, diner, business cars, training cars, caboose, engine cars, kitchen cars, postal cars, and troop carriers.

Exit - 185 (west of I-75) / I-275 exit 11

CREATION MUSEUM

Petersburg - *2800 Bullittsburg Church Road (I-75 exit 185 (I-275 west) to exit 11 south) 41080. Phone: (888) 582-4253. www.creationmuseum.org. Hours: Monday-Friday 10:00am-6:00pm, Saturday 9:00am-6:00pm, Sunday Noon-6:00pm. Petting Zoo hours are slightly shorter. Closed most Christian holidays. Winter hours may be earlier close time. Admission: $29.95 adult, $23.95 senior (60+), $15.95 child (5-12). Military personnel FREE with paid adult admission. Price includes Exhibits, Theaters and Petting Zoo and 2 days admission. FREEBIES: The sister website, www.answersingenesis.org/kids, has some fun puzzles, coloring and the parents page link if you want to download study guides. Note: The Planetarium Creation simulation shows are outstanding and worth the extra admission if you can afford to add it in - $7.95 per person. Mining Company Sluice interactive mining experience is $6.00 more. Open Friday & Saturday afternoons. Zip line tours extra.*

The site's 60,000 square feet of family fun logo is: "Prepare to Believe", and it's true! Some call it a Dinosaur Museum- it's true. Some call it a Bible Museum - it's true. "Much of the experience features displays that would be similar to what you would find in a natural history museum, so you will see exhibits on par with some of the fine science museums around the world," said director, Mark Looy. "Because we're taking our visitors on a walk through history from Genesis to Revelation, it is a biblical museum combining Scripture with the best of what science can present."

KENTUCKY

Begin in the senses-shattering (and maybe beliefs-shattering) Men in White Special Effects Theater. A satire, two hip angels expose common myths about God and Creation thru thunder, rain, wind and lightning effects that you actually feel! Next, kids can take their own route through a Canyon into the Dino dig site. The museum then uses a series of realistic dioramas to explore Biblical relevance - Old scholars and contemporaries. Walk through a Time Tunnel into the Six Days of Creation Theater for yet another opportunity to sit down and visually stimulate your mind. Now, walk thru a simulated Garden of Eden, past the Tree of Life. Help Noah and his family prepare at the giant Ark Construction Site. After the flood came Confusion at Babylon yet redemption at the Last Adam Theater (again, another great spot to sit down and take it all in). The final areas are all about kids - Dino Den, the Dragon Theater (yes, dragons were real!) and an interactive Children's Play Area.

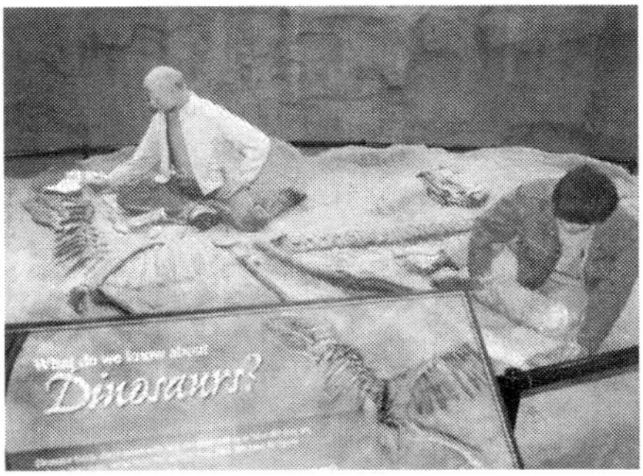

What do we really know about dinosaurs?

Building Noah's Ark...

Finally, grab a snack or ice cream treat and walk the winding trails outside including two swinging bridges and a misty swamp area. The Petting Zoo is open, too. Guests are able to watch sheep and llama shearing, hoof trimming and get up close with all kinds of animals.

All will find answers to perplexing questions like: Why am I here? How old is the Earth? What really happened to the Dinosaurs? We all learned so much, so easily - I think our kids, the most. Well worth the admission price "investment", friends.

Exit - 185 (east of I-75) / I-275 exit 79

TOTTER'S OTTERVILLE @ JOHNNY'S TOYS

Covington - ***4314 Boron Drive (I-75 exit 185 to I-275 exit 79, Taylor Mill/Covington exit. Head north, at fourth traffic light, turn left) 41015. Phone: (859) 491-1441. www.tottersotterville.com. Hours: Monday-Saturday 10:00am-5:00pm. Friday-Saturday open until 8:00pm. Sunday 11:00am-5:00pm. Holiday schedule varies - see website. Admission: $8.95 child (ages 1 year up to 10 years). Adults FREE. Note: Totter's Otterville is inside Johnny's Toys. A café is on the premises with many common kiddie foods like pizza, hot dogs, nuggets but also wraps & subs and snacks. They do not fry anything here - all baked.***

As you enter Johnny's Toys, you'll notice lots of color, lots of toys and so many trains. Kids can begin by playing at the train tables scattered in the store. After paying admission, young families can enter Totter's Otterville. Here, even more trains, a mini toy section with toy animals and dollhouses, a ball pit or climbing zone, a water play area, and a pretend play area with dress up clothes and props. In the seasonal outdoor area, kids can play on a gym structure, dig for dino bones, ride a mini trolley or try to solve the walk-thru maze.

Exit - 181 (west of I-75)

DINSMORE HOMESTEAD

Burlington - ***5656 Burlington Pike (I-75/71 exit 181 to KY 18 west) 41005. Phone: (859) 586-6117. www.dinsmorefarm.org. Hours: Wednesday, Saturday, Sunday 1:00-5:00pm (April thru mid-December). Last tour leaves at 4:00pm. Admission: $5.00 adult, $3.00 senior (60+), $2.00 student (5-17). FREEBIES: Biographies of the folks that lived here throughout history are online. Might want to check it out on your laptop before or after a visit.***

What is The Dinsmore Homestead? The Dinsmore Homestead is a unique historic site where visitors can learn what rural life was like in the 19th and early 20th centuries. Nature enthusiasts enjoy the hiking trails developed in cooperation with the Kentucky Nature Conservancy and County Parks Department. Kids can relieve boredom by experiencing a historical place both inside and outside - where they can run about and explore their own way. This Living History Farm, with a museum and nature center on the farm, was the property of the Dinsmore family who originally came from the deep south. Learn of their benevolent treatment of slaves. Discovery Days or School Living History (hands-on) Tours are your best bet to take advantage of this facility (usually weekends).

Mile - 177 (SB Only)

KENTUCKY WELCOME CENTER

(mile marker 176.8 heading south on I-75) . http://511.ky.gov/rest/home.htm.

The facility has tourism staff on hand during business hours; 1000s of brochures; restrooms; public phones; vending; a dog walk and picnic areas.

Exit - 175 (west of I-75)

BIG BONE LICK STATE PARK

Union - ***3380 Beaver Road (I-75 AND KY 338, exit 175, follow signs) 41091. Phone: (859) 384-3522. http://parks.ky.gov/parks/historicsites/big-bone-lick/ Hours: Museum daily 8:30am-4:00pm (April-October). Monday-Friday 9am-3pm (November-March). Discovery Trail open daily dawn til dusk. Admission: FREE. Fee for campground and mini-golf. Note: Campground, Gift shop, Pool, 2.5 miles of Hiking Trails, Tennis, Mini Golf, Picnicking.***

Huge mastodon and wooley mammoth recreations await you...

The birthplace of American Vertebrate Paleontology. A premier archeological site because great herds of giant mastodons, mammoths, and bison came to the warm salt springs (the springs still bubble today). Some became trapped in the marshy ground and died here, leaving skeletons that have been uncovered from prehistoric times. A walking diorama, the outdoor museum hosts these beasts displayed in their natural habitat. Erosion may still reveal bones (look for them on your hike) especially along the creek. Great buffalo herds once roamed this area and provided food, clothing and shelter for the Indians and pioneers. Hunted to near extinction, the last wild buffalo was seen in Kentucky around 1800. A live buffalo herd now roams the property and your kids can touch Mastodon teeth!

The greatest ice age graveyard ever found!

Exit - 126 (east of I-75)

TOYOTA MOTOR MANUFACTURING KENTUCKY

Georgetown - ***1001 Cherry Blossom Way (I-75 exit 126 east - US 62 E, follow signs to "Visitor's Entrance") 40324. Phone: (502) 868-3027 or (800) TMM-4485. http://toyotaky.com/tour.asp. Hours: Visitor Center - 8:30am-3:30pm weekdays; to 6:00pm on Thursdays only. Admission: FREE Public Tours: Monday-Friday, 9:30am, 11:30am, and 1:30pm; with additional 6:00pm tour on Thursday only. Closed major holidays and 3rd week of July. Reservations strongly encouraged. Children must be at least 1st graders and accompanied by an adult.***

Can you imagine a building so BIG that it could house over 156 football fields side by side! Begin your tour at the Visitor's Center where you get a great taste of what to expect through several interactive exhibits that teach you all about the Toyota JIT (Just in Time) manufacturing philosophy. During your visit, don't hesitate to slam a few doors, climb inside and test the reclining seats or flip a few knobs on the instrument panel.

See the "insides" of a Toyota before you begin your tour...

After viewing a short informational film, you'll board an electric tram (complete with headphones – no loud factory noises here!), to take you on your journey. See steel coils weighing over 34,000 lbs. pressed into body panels and over 700 robots working in precision to create both sedans and mini-vans at this plant. In fact, this is the only manufacturing facility in the world where you will see both vans and cars on the same assembly line at the same time (how do they do that!). Kids will especially love the welding robots that send sparks flying to the factory ceiling (viewed from a safe distance). There are over 4000 welds in each vehicle made. Make sure you tell your kids to watch for the "flying assembly workers" who float in and out of vehicles on specially made chairs (on long booms).

Exit - 120 (east of I-75)

KENTUCKY HORSE PARK

Lexington - ***4089 Iron Works Parkway (I-75 exit 120) 40511. Phone: (859) 233-4303 or (800) 678-8813. www.kyhorsepark.com. Hours: Daily 9:00am-5:00pm (March 15-October). Closed on Mondays and Tuesdays (November-March 14). Closed Thanksgiving, Christmas, and New Years. Admission: $12.00-$16.00 adult, $6.00-$8.00 child (6-12). Additional special exhibit fees may be added on during peak season (late spring thru late summer). Children 5 and under free when accompanied by paying adult. The lowest pricing is offered for the Winter Season (less activities available). Tickets include admission to the world renowned International Museum of the Horse, the American Saddlebred Museum, trolley tour and equine presentations throughout the day. Note: Clubhouse Restaurant, Campgrounds, Gift Shop, Horseback rides ($25+), Pony rides ($5.00+). Nearly 60 horse shows are held here yearly. Visits with Mares and Foals daily presentation in June/July. Educators: wonderful curriculum on the history of the horse is online under: Educational Opportunities/ ATQH Curriculum.***

Do you have a real horse lover in the family? This is a horse-lover's dream

park. It's Kentucky's tribute to one of its famous industries from tiny minis to large draft houses to retired racing stars. Begin with the Visitor Info Center - wide screen film "Thou Shalt Fly Without Wings" - depicting man's special relationship with horses both at work and play. Now, go next door to the International Museum of the Horse. Before long, take the horse-drawn trolley tour. Then catch a show at the Hall of Champions - home of retired "equine millionaires" (3x daily). They tell you funny stories about famous horses. Also be sure to catch a show at the Parade of Breeds - show of dozens of breeds of horses with their riders in native costume with music accompaniment (2x daily). Some are used for rugged terrain, pulling, cowboy riding, cavalry, or trailing. Fill the time between shows at the Big Barn (talk with trainers), Draft and Breeds and Carriage Barns, Farrier's and harness maker's shops. The American Saddle Horse Museum - is a multi-image show and exhibit hall located on the premises near the parking lots. (800) 829-4438.

Exit - 115 (west of I-75)

MC CONNELL SPRINGS

Lexington - ***416 Rebmann Lane (I-75 exit 115, south on Newtown Pike, west on New Circle to Old Frankfort Pike, exit 6 south, follow signs) 40504. Phone: (859) 225-4073. www.mcconnellsprings.org. Hours: Daily 9:00am-5:00pm.***

In June 1775, William McConnell and his fellow frontier explorers camped at a natural spring in the wilderness of the Virginia territory known as Kentucky. Word came from nearby Fort Boonesboro that the first battle of the American Revolution had been fought in Lexington, Massachusetts. In honor of the battle, the group named their future settlement "Lexington". McConnell Springs is the site where Lexington was founded. McConnell Springs has over two miles of trails that wander past historic foundations, stone fences, an old farm pond and lush vegetation. The new Education Center is equipped with a lab with sinks and counter space allowing students to conduct hands-on experiments. There's a bird-watching window too. Colonial Fests are good time to visit.

Exit - 113 (west of I-75)

EXPLORIUM OF LEXINGTON

Lexington - ***440 West Short Street (I-75 exit 113, take US 27 into town. Victorian Square, corner of W. Short and Algonquin Streets) 40507. Phone: (859) 258-3253. www.explorium.com. Hours: Tuesday-Saturday 10:00am-5:00pm, Sunday 1:00-5:00pm. Closed Mondays except some holidays and breaks. Closed Easter, week after Labor Day, Thanksgiving and Christmas. Admission: $8.00 per person (age 1+). Free parking for up to 3 hours in Victorian Square Garage. FREEBIES: While you're downtown, stop by Thoroughbred Park on Main Street where 7 life size bronze statues of horses racing are available to climb on for great photo ops!***

Hands-on exhibits cover science, nature, history, civics and ecology. Little ones can visit Wonder Woods (under age 3 - hear, touch and see nesting areas). Everyone will love to make huge bubbles in the Bubble Zone; go Home to world geography and culture; "Walk on the Moon" and even sit in a crater!; make a Quake; be a Turtle; Greet the Brainzilla (giant brain that talks to you);

Walk thru a Human Heart with many "chamber" rooms; make Me and My Shadow; or brush some giant teeth. Extremely well done exhibits include descriptions that are easy to follow and teach to the children. Exhibits change each season, so there is something new to explore. Look for occasional new Dino, horse or bubble themed exhibits. Have fun!

Exit - 113 (west of I-75)

MARY TODD LINCOLN HOUSE

Lexington - ***578 West Main Street (I-75 exit 113. Take US 27 towards downtown. just a block down from the Rupp Arena) 40507. www.mtlhouse.org. Phone: (859) 233-9999. Hours: Monday-Saturday 10:00am-3:00pm (mid-March -November). Closed holidays. Admission: $10.00 adult, $5.00 child (6-12). Guided, one hour tours. FREEBIES: Printable Word Search, Math Word Problems online under: Educational.***

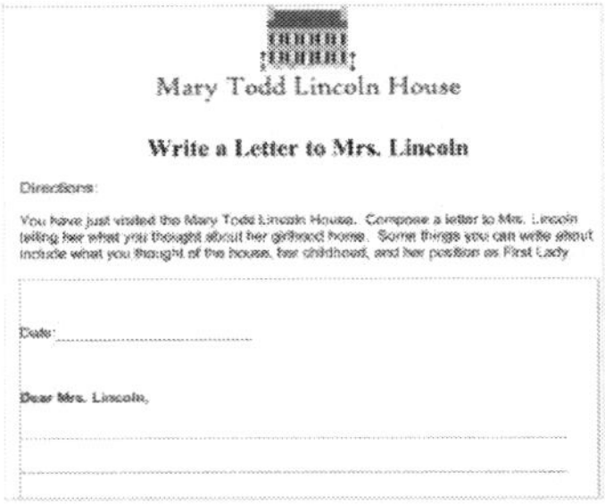
Mary Todd Lincoln House

Write a Letter to Mrs. Lincoln

Directions:

You have just visited the Mary Todd Lincoln House. Compose a letter to Mrs. Lincoln telling her what you thought about her girlhood home. Some things you can write about include what you thought of the house, her childhood, and her position as First Lady

Date: ____________

Dear Mrs. Lincoln,

Write a letter to Mrs. Lincoln...

The girlhood home of Abraham Lincoln's wife, Mary. The two story, beautiful brick 1803 Georgian-style house is furnished with period furniture from Mary's collection and personal articles of the Lincoln-Todd families. Kids like hearing stories about a famous adults' life as a child. Do you know how many brothers and sisters Mary had (15) or that she had a formal education of 12 years (vs. her husband who really had very little)? Opposites attract.

HUNT-MORGAN HOUSE

Lexington - ***201 North Mill Street (I-75 exit 113, head west on US 27 into town, near 2nd Street, downtown) 40508. www.bluegrasstrust.org/hunt-morgan.html. Phone: (859) 253-0362 or 233-3290. Admission: $10.00 adult, $4.00 student with ID. Tours: Guided tours Wednesday-Friday 1:00-4:00pm, Saturday 10am-3pm, Sunday 1:00-5:00pm (mid-March to mid-December). Closed Thanksgiving. Tours begin ¼ past the hour.***

An 1800's Federal-style prominent family home of the Hunt-Morgan families. John Wesley Hunt was the first millionaire of the west (and built this home), John Hunt Morgan was the "Thunderbolt of the Confederacy" and Thomas Hunt Morgan was the "father of modern genetics" and a Nobel Prize winner. The architecture of a fan-light doorway and cantilevered staircase mixed with original furnishings and Civil War memorabilia, make this a piece of history based on it's inhabitants.

UNIVERSITY OF KENTUCKY

Lexington - ***South Limestone Street (I-75 exit 113, head west on US 27 into town. Follow signs to Visitor Center at UK Student Center - near Euclid Ave. and Rose Street) 40506. Phone: (859) 257-9000. www.uky.edu (campus guide/ map). Admission: FREE. Tours: Walking tours are conducted Monday-Friday at 10:00am and 2:00pm (also Saturday at 11:00am during the academic year). Guided tours of the campus depart from the visitors center in the Student Center on Euclid Avenue across from Memorial Coliseum. Note: a good stop to catch some Wildcat Fever or just stretch your legs admiring exhibits, inside or outside. Admission is FREE!***

The 625 acre campus was established in 1865 and enrolls 24,000 students.

UK ART MUSEUM - Singletary Center for the Arts at the corner of Euclid and Rose Streets. Changing shows of permanent and traveling exhibits. Tours available. Tuesday-Sunday, Noon-5:00pm. Closed July 4, Thanksgiving, and Christmas thru New Years. (859) 257-5716.

WEBB MUSEUM OF ANTHROPOLOGY - Lafferty Hall, center of campus. Traces history of humans in Kentucky. Other displays highlight the artistry, ingenuity and technology of present-day cultures from around the world. Monday-Friday 8:00am-4:30pm. Closed holidays. (859) 257-7112.

UNIVERSITY OF KENTUCKY (cont.)

COLDSTREAM & MAINE CHANCE FARMS - Newtown Park. Used by UK for crop and livestock research. North of downtown near I-64/75.

ARBORETUM PARK - "A Walk Across Kentucky" showcases state vegetation grouped by region. Open dawn to dusk. Children's Garden - Alphabet plants and plantings in old tennis shoes. Master Gardener - demo Veggie Garden, Fish Pond, plants for KY gardens. Be sure to get a colorful map and have fun playing the Arboretum Garden Game. (859) 257-9339.

Exit - 110 (west of I-75)

PARKETTE DRIVE-IN

Lexington - ***1230 E. New Circle Road (I-75 exit 110 head west on US 60 to south on New Circle Road a couple miles on the right) 40505. Phone: (859) 254-8723. http://theparkette.com/. Hours: Monday-Thursday 11:00am-10:30pm; Friday & Saturday 11:00am-11:30pm.***

Very economically priced (combo meals are under $4.00), this place is a step back in time. Since 1951, this "drive-in" ordering eatery is right out of scenes of "Happy Days". After placing your order over the microphone, a delivery girl or boy (adorned in Parkette cap and t-shirt or poodle skirt of the 50's) delivers you order window-side. Their menu includes burgers, fried chicken, seafood and the famous "Kentucky Poor Boy" sandwich (double-decker burgers dressed with toppings to the hilt!). Memories meet the pavement when (on Friday nights) the Parkette is host to classic cars and motorcycles. They serve 12,000 customers a week.

OLD KENTUCKY CHOCOLATES

Lexington - ***450 Southland Drive (I-75 exit 110 west on Rte. 60 to New Circle Rd exit 19, head north on US 27, left onto Southland) 40503. Phone: (859) 278-4444 or (800) 786-0579. www.oldkycandy.com. Admission: FREE. Tours: Monday-Friday 10:00am and 2:00pm. 45 minutes. Best to call ahead for production hours. 8 to 50 people for tours. Reservations please. Miscellaneous: if you don't reserve a tour ahead of time, you can still enjoy the viewing and especially the sampling!***

Hopefully you'll go on a day when you can watch them make Kentucky Derby Mints or UK molded chocolates. Plenty of samples follow the tour that includes verbal and photo explanations.

AVIATION MUSEUM OF KENTUCKY

Lexington - ***4316 Hanger Drive (Off Airport Rd) (Exit 110 head 2 miles west off New Circle Rd. on US 60 to Bluegrass Airport Road) 40510. Phone: (859) 231-1219. www.aviationky.org. Hours: Tuesday-Saturday 10:00am-5:00pm, Sunday 1:00-5:00pm (April-December). Closed Thanksgiving, Christmas and New Years. Admission: $5.00-$8.00 (age 6+).***

Most interesting to kids is the cockpit you can sit in, the supersonic trainer, and the "Women in Aviation" display. There's also lots of uniforms, model airplanes, actual aircraft (helicopters, a Skyhawk II, and a Quadraplane). There is a lot of walking around, inside and out, in places like this so enjoy the exit from the vehicle and get some exercise.

KEENELAND TRACK KITCHEN

Lexington - ***4201 Versailles Road (I-75 exit 110 west on US 60 west-near the barn area, look for the black water tower) 40592. www.keeneland.com. Phone: (859) 253-0541. Hours: "Breakfast with the Works" buffet served during morning workouts during seasonal race months (usually April and October) daily 6:00am-10:30am and again for lunch (times vary). Otherwise, open daily except major holidays at 6:00am. May be Closed Monday, Tuesday and Easter. Admission: Reasonably priced buffet.***

Meet and greet and eat with trainers and jockeys at breakfast during morning workouts. You don't have to be a horseman to enjoy the food at Keeneland's track kitchen - but you might end up sitting near a famous jockey, trainer or owner when you do. What's on the buffet? Pure Kentucky southern breakfast of meats, biscuits, eggs, potatoes, grits and assorted light fare. To walk off your breakfast, try wondering the paddock in the morning when its serene (unless its race month - then it's a hub of activity). Race months, morning walks give fans one last look at the magnificent horses before they run the race of their lives.

Exit - 108 (west of I-75)

WAVELAND STATE HISTORIC SITE

Lexington - ***225 Waveland Museum Lane, 225 Higbee Mill Road (Man O War Blvd. West 8 miles to US 27 south. Off US 27, south of downtown) 40514. Phone: (859) 272-3611. http://parks.ky.gov/parks/historicsites/waveland/. Hours: Wednesday-Saturday 10:00am-5:00pm, Sunday 1:00-5:00pm (March-December). Admission: $7.00 adult, $6.00 senior, $4.00 student (age 6+). Tours: On the hour, last tour 4:00pm. Tours last approximately 1.5 hours. Note: Picnic grounds. Country Picnic and tours (meal and tour several days each week in June, small additional fee for food).***

This beautiful 1847 Greek Revival home was built by Joseph Bryan, a grand-nephew of Daniel Boone. Tours focus on the everyday lives of the Bryan Family and the African-Americans who lived and worked there. Waveland exemplifies plantation life in Kentucky in the 19th-century; from the acres of grain and hemp waving in the breeze (hence the Waveland name), to the raising and racing of blooded trotting horses. Included are the icehouse, smokehouse and servants quarters.

Exit - 104 (west of I-75)

ASHLAND, THE HENRY CLAY ESTATE

Lexington - ***120 Sycamore Road (I-75 exit 104, turn northwest toward Lexington, go 7.5 miles. Look for big brown sign.) 40502. www.henryclay.org. Phone: (859) 266-8581. Hours: Tuesday-Saturday 10:00am-4:00pm, Sunday 1:00-4:00pm. Closed Sundays (November-March). Closed January, February and holidays. Admission: $10.00 adult, $5.00 child (6-18). Tours: one hour long - guided, given on the hour. Note: Food is available in the Ginkgo Tree Café on the brick patio outside, is open for lunch and snacks. Museum Store.***

Henry Clay (1777-1852) was named The Great Compromiser, Harry of the West, Candidate for President and quoted "I'd rather be right than president". For more than forty years, Henry Clay lived at Ashland, the place he loved best. When he was at home he could be seen frequently pacing the "Henry Clay Walk" that still runs through the trees behind the main house. Many of the great speeches which he delivered in Congress were composed along these peaceful walks. Living here most of his adult life, the 18 room mansion is furnished with Clay family possessions. The tour begins with a videotape historical review. On tour, there are also outbuildings on the grounds like the icehouse, smokehouse, dairy cellar, privy/laundry and keepers cottage - all in a park-like setting.

Exit - 95 (west of I-75)

WHITE HALL STATE HISTORIC SITE

Richmond - ***500 White Hall Shrine Road (I-75 exit 95) 40475. Phone: (859) 623-9178. http://parks.ky.gov/parks/historicsites/white-hall/ Hours: Monday-Saturday 9am-5pm, Sunday Noon-4pm (April-October). No mansion tours on Mondays and Tuesdays. Admission: $8.00 adult, $7.00 senior and $4.00 for students of any age. Tours: One hour long. Note: Gift shop, picnicking.***

The home of Cassius Marcellus Clay: emancipationist, newspaper publisher, Minister to Russia, and friend to Abraham Lincoln. Overall, he was quite a character and lived grandly. The restored 44 room Italianate mansion is 200 years old and has period and heirloom furnishings, a working cookhouse, outside slave/servant quarters, and many unique features for its day. They had running water and central heating (look for the outlets hidden in fireplaces and behind

> In 1920, Laura Clay (Cassius' daughter) became the first woman to be nominated for U.S. President by a major political party.

little doors). How were orators (like Clay) similar to our superstars today?

RAVEN RUN NATURE SANCTUARY

Lexington - ***5888 Jacks Creek Road (I-75 exit 95. Take SR 3055 west to Jacks Creek Road. near US 25/421 south) 40515. Phone: (859) 272-6105. www.ravenrun.org. Hours: Daily 9:00am-5:00pm. Trails close 30 minutes before park closing. Closed Thanksgiving and Christmas. Admission: FREE.***

Follow trails lined with native flora and fauna, rock fences, an historic home, meadow, forest and creeks leading to views of the Kentucky River palisades. The park is also known for the waterfalls, wildflowers and nature center.

Exit - 95 (east of I-75)

FORT BOONESBOROUGH STATE PARK

Richmond - ***4375 Boonesborough Road (I-75 exit 95, follow signs to KY 627) 40475. Phone: (859) 527-3131. http://parks.ky.gov/parks/recreationparks/fort-boonesborough/default.aspx Hours: Wednesday-Sunday 9:00am-5:00pm (April-October). Friday-Sunday 10:00am-4:00pm (rest of year). Closed Thanksgiving and Christmastime. Admission: $5.00-$8.00 (age 6+) (April-October). November-March admission is minimal as the property is not staffed with re-enactors. Admission includes entrance to both the fort and museum. Additional fee for some activities. Note: Campground, Marina/Boat Launch, Pool, some Hiking Trails, Mini-Golf, Picnicking, and Sandy beach.***

After several skirmishes with Indians and rough terrain, Daniel Boone and his men reached the Kentucky River on April 1, 1775 and began laying out Kentucky's 2nd settlement. For many years this was a fortress, stopping point and trade center. The fort they constructed has been reconstructed as a working fort complete with cabins, blockhouses and period furnishings. Resident artisans share pioneer experiences and demonstrate pioneer crafts like pottery, candle-making, weaving and cooking. Riverside trails pass native plants and unusual geological sites.

Begin your visit watching a film showing the struggles of the fort - esp. withstanding a 9-day attack by Indians and Frenchmen later known as "The Great Siege". Why are the names Blackfish and Henderson also important here? Look for interesting artifacts like the Clock Rotisserie, giant corn mill, walking spinning wheel or "Pop goes the Weasel". The Kentucky River Museum has numerous displays of prehistoric fishing to locks (some working models) and dams. Steamboats and showboats passed along this River...it's visitors and river rats are all explored in this new museum.

Exit - 87 (east of I-75)

RICHMOND CIVIL WAR DRIVING TOUR

Richmond - ***345 Lancaster Avenue (Richmond Visitor Center) 40475. Phone: (859) 626-8474 or (800) 866-3705. www.trailsrus.com/civilwar/region4/richmond.html. Admission: Small fee charged for brochure and tape available (for purchase) at the visitor's center.***

Follow Confederate troops on a 2 hour driving tour of the battle route of August 1862. There are six tour stations established in the approximate order the battle took place. Begin at the Top of Big Hill and on to places like Mt. Zion Church (used as a Union Hospital) to the Madison County Courthouse. After the Confederate advance, they later marched in triumph into Lexington and then took Frankfort. This was the only time in the war that the capitol of a Union state fell to Southern forces.

Exit - 87 (east of I-75)

HUMMEL PLANETARIUM & EASTERN KENTUCKY UNIVERSITY

Richmond - Lancaster Avenue (off KY 876 to Kit Carson Drive at traffic light#7, turn right and follow signs) 40475. http://planetarium.eku.edu/. Phone: (859) 622-1000. Note: You might want to ask the staff a clever question like: Has anyone ever been hit by a meteorite? Like to look at the sky online, go to www. skyviewcafe.com and take a look!

HUMMEL PLANETARIUM AND SPACE THEATER - (859) 622-1547, Kit Carson Drive, Eastern Bypass. The 13th largest planetarium in the US with space science gift shop. Admission around $3.00-$4.00/person. Public Programs Saturdays. A visit to the Hummel Planetarium is a trip through the universe. Planetarium equipment stimulates the night sky by using a giant star ball with the capacity of projecting over 10,000 stars, multiple projections of five planets, a sun, the moon, etc. - all of these operating simultaneously with surround sound. You can also travel throughout space and see the planets from other planets besides earth. At the end of each program, see the Kentucky night sky as it will look that night - look for your favorite constellations.

MEADOWBROOK FARM PROGRAM - (859) 622-1310. Meadowbrook Road (off KY 52). Agricultural production, diary cattle, beef cattle, sheep, swine and cropping operations. Welcome during normal business hours or tours by appointment.

ATHLETIC TICKET OFFICE - (859) 622-2122. Eastern Bypass. Over ten varieties of sports including Collegiate basketball and football.

GREENHOUSE - (859) 622-2228, Eastern Bypass. Foliage propagation and production, rose and carnation beds.

Exit - 76 (east of I-75)

BOONE TAVERN

Berea - ***100 Main Street N, College Square (I-75 exit 76 east into the town square) 40404. Phone: (800) 366-9358. www.boonetavernhotel.com. Hours: Thursday, Friday and Saturday lunch and dinner. Reservations suggested. Breakfast and Sunday- Wednesday lunch/brunch hours vary by season. Closed school breaks.***

Combine crafts in town with helpings of traditional KY fare at Boone Tavern restaurant operated by the college's student industries since 1909. Signature items include spoonbread, Chicken Flakes in Bird's Nest (creamed chicken served in a crisp basket of fried potatoes) or maybe try some black-eyed peas, fried green tomatoes or corn pudding. The slightly formal furnishings mean children should be on their best behavior. Dress code: tastefully casual. Entrees start at $8.00 with children's portion pricing - may we suggest lunchtime is best.

BEREA COLLEGE LOG HOUSE

Berea - ***210 Center Street, College Square (I-75 exit 76, follow signs for college) 40404. Phone: (859) 985-3220. www.bereacollegecrafts.com. Hours: Monday-Saturday 8:00am-6:00pm, Sunday 1:00-5:00pm (April-December). Extended summer hours. Admission: FREE. Tours: Walk along the Square as storefront studios invite you to enter and watch and ask questions of students crafting.***

> All students of this college work on campus in lieu of paying tuition and board - their crafts are featured at this gallery.

They've been making brooms here for 80 years and weaving even longer! Visit the working studios of woodworkers (see them make the famous "Berea Basket" with all wood and paper product used), weavers (several students will make one piece - it takes two hours just to string the loom), furniture makers and broom craft (use the stalk and husk of "broom corn" - see a broom made before your eyes, then purchase it if you like). Master craftsmen supervise and teach. We were very impressed with the school's philosophies and students' attitudes about work and study! The tours are well worth the time and you'll find lots of questions to ask as you go along.

Exit - 62 (east of I-75)

KENTUCKY MUSIC HALL OF FAME MUSEUM

Renfro Valley - ***2590 Richmond Road (I-75 exit 62, east on Hwy 25) 40473. Phone: (606) 256-1000 or (877) 356-3263. www.kentuckymusicmuseum.com. Hours: Monday-Saturday 10:00am-5:00pm. Admission: $7.50 adult, $7.00 senior, $4.50 child (6- 12).***

The Hall of Fame includes exhibit cases for artifacts, instruments and costumes of honored inductees. You'll see and hear hundreds of entertainers like...Patty Loveless, Loretta Lynn, Bill Monroe, Rosemary Clooney, Billy Ray Cyrus, Ricky Skaggs and the Judds. Also included in the Museum is an instrument room (visitors touch, hear and perform); a sound booth where you can actually sing and record; and a timeline of KY Music from front porch jamboree to radio to major public event concerts.

RENFRO VALLEY ENTERTAINMENT CENTER

Renfro Valley - ***Richmond Road (I-75 exit 62, US 25) 40473. Phone: (606) 256-2638 or (800) 765-7464. www.renfrovalley.com. Hours: Afternoon and evening shows. Sunday Renfro Valley Gatherin" at 8:30am. Barn Dance on Saturday nights at 7:00pm. Village open March-December. Admission: Varies with production. Best to get on their mailing list for program offerings. Note: RV Park. Renfro Valley***

Lodge Motel & Cabins.

Country music, family comedy and headliner concerts and festivals. "Kentucky's Country Music Capital" has an average of 12 shows weekly, Country restaurants, and Brush Arbor Log Shopping Village.

Exit - 38 (east of I-75)

LEVI JACKSON WILDERNESS ROAD STATE PARK

London - ***998 Levi Jackson Mill Road (I-75 exit 38, head south on US 25) 40744. Phone: (606) 878-8000. http://parks.ky.gov/parks/recreationparks/Levi-Jackson/. Hours: Park open 24 hours. Mill grounds open 8:00am-4:30pm in the summer. Museum open daily 9:00am-4:30pm (April-October). Everything closed the week of Christmas. Admission: FREE. Seasonal pool and mini-golf charge admission. Note: Campground, Gift Shop, Pool (nice, w/ two water slides and a children's pool), Mini-golf, Picnicking, and Archery range.***

Begin with historic trails - the Wilderness Road (30 foot wide wagon road used by pioneers) and Boone's Trace. Over 200,000 eastern settlers forged into Kentucky wilderness between 1774 and 1796 for the promise of fertile land, abundant game, clear streams and rivers. They faced many dangers - McNitt's Defeat (worst Kentucky Indian massacre) occurred here on the Wilderness Road in 1796. The Mountain Life Museum is a log building with pioneer artifacts such as kitchen utensils, weapons and furniture. At McHargue's Mill you'll see a working reproduction mill dating back to the late 1700s with authentic interior works. "The people went and gathered it and ground it in mill" - Numbers 11:8.

See the largest display of millstones in the country.

Exit - 29 (east of I-75)

HARLAND SANDERS CAFÉ & MUSEUM

Corbin - ***US 25W (I-75 exit 29, US 25E south to US 25W) 40701. www.corbinkycityguide.com/kfc/kfc.htm. Phone: (606) 528-2163. Hours: Open daily 10:00am-10:00pm. Admission: FREE.***

Eat where it all began! The original Kentucky Fried Chicken Restaurant serves KFC products in the large restored dining room. See the Colonel's kitchen as it was in 1940 (early dishwashers, French fry press) when he developed his secret recipe.

The business flourished because he combined good cooking, hard work and showmanship. Be sure to look in the display case for the cooking clock with the third hand. Also see his office, model motel room he rented and much of his marketing strategies. Do you know how many herbs and spices are in his chicken recipe? Did you know it was his honor system franchise concept (that he sold across country) that, at age 65+, made him money - and not his own restaurant?

Hangin' out with the Colonel...

Exit - 15 (west of I-75)

CUMBERLAND FALLS STATE RESORT PARK

Corbin - ***7351 State Route 90 (I-75 exit Corbin to US 25W, then to SRKY 90) 40701. Phone: (606)528-4121. http://parks.ky.gov/parks/resortparks/cumberland-falls/default.aspx Hours: 6:00am-Midnight. Until 3:00am the 2 days before, after and including a full moon. Eastern Time. Admission: FREE. Charge for boat rides or rentals. Tours: Rainbow Mist Ride to the Base of Falls (mid-May thru Labor Day). Sheltowee Trace Outfitters raft trips www.ky-rafting.com. Note: Dupont Lodge with dining, Cottages, Campground, Gift Shop, Pool, Horseback Riding, Tennis, Picnicking, Rafting.***

The "Niagara of the South" is a 125 foot wide curtain of water falling 60 feet - dramatic night and day. But, the accomplishment is to have been touched by a moonbow! (Moonbow Dates listed on website) Finally, we arranged an overnight so we and a few hundred others, could walk in the quiet, moonlit night (about 8:45pm) towards the Falls. After a few seconds stare . . . we captured the white spray arch that then turned into a rainbow of color the longer you watched. How outstanding and romantic (esp. for night owls)! Dawn to dusk viewing is better for photos and safety.

Eagle Falls are nearby and are a beautifully high stream of water (vs. a roaring gush). There's also a Nature Preserve and the Moonbow Trail connects to

The famous moonbow (a rainbow arch of light and colors best during a full moon), is a phenomena not found anywhere else in the Western Hemisphere!

the Daniel Boone National Forest. We find many families like to stay overnight at the lodge (very family friendly with family activities throughout the first floor Great Room area) and wander or hike in the daytime. The Falls are within long walking distance for grade-schoolers and strollers, but there are some hills.

CUMBERLAND FALLS STATE RESORT PARK LODGE

Corbin - ***7351 State Route 90 (I-75 exit Corbin to US 25W, then to SRKY 90) 40701. Phone: (800) 325-0063 reservations. http://parks.ky.gov/parks/resortparks/cumberland-falls/default.aspx.***

Now, off to the Lodge. Solid hemlock beams and knotty pine paneling complement the massive stone fireplaces. The rooms have been updated and their rates begin at $63.00! The buffet offers classic southern dishes and there is a reasonable a la carte menu. Our favorite memory is playing ping-pong and checkers while other families sat around and played cards. Visit the gift shop, featuring a large selection of Kentucky handcrafts and souvenirs. There's also a snack shop and visitors center, both located in the falls area. Inside the center, a three-dimensional map outlines major park facilities. Other exhibits show the area's history and illustrates Native American life. Guided tours (30 minutes long) leave from the Center most weekends and summer days.

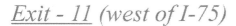

Exit - 11 (west of I-75)

KENTUCKY SPLASH WATER PARK

Williamsburg - ***1050 Hwy 92 West (I-75 exit 11) 40769. Phone: (606) 549-6065. www.kentuckysplash.com. Hours: Daily, except Sundays 11:00am-7:00pm (Memorial Day weekend thru mid-August). Sundays 12:30-6:00pm. Extended hours for indoor activities. Admission: Waterpark: $10.00(age 3+).***

All Event: $26.95. Dry activities: $2.00-$5.00 each.

The Hal Rogers Family Entertainment Center is home to the Kentucky Splash Water Park. The park includes an 18,000 square ft. wave pool, a drift river, a kiddy activity pool, a triple slide complex, a go-kart track, a championship miniature golf course, an arcade, a batting cage and even a café and gift shop. Changing rooms/lockers are available.

Mile - 1 (NB Only)

KENTUCKY WELCOME CENTER

(mile marker 1 heading north on I-75). http://511.ky.gov/rest/home.htm.

The facility has tourism staff on hand during business hours; hundreds of brochures; restrooms; public phones; vending; a dog walk and picnic areas.

Travel Journal & Notes:

Chapter 4
TENNESSEE

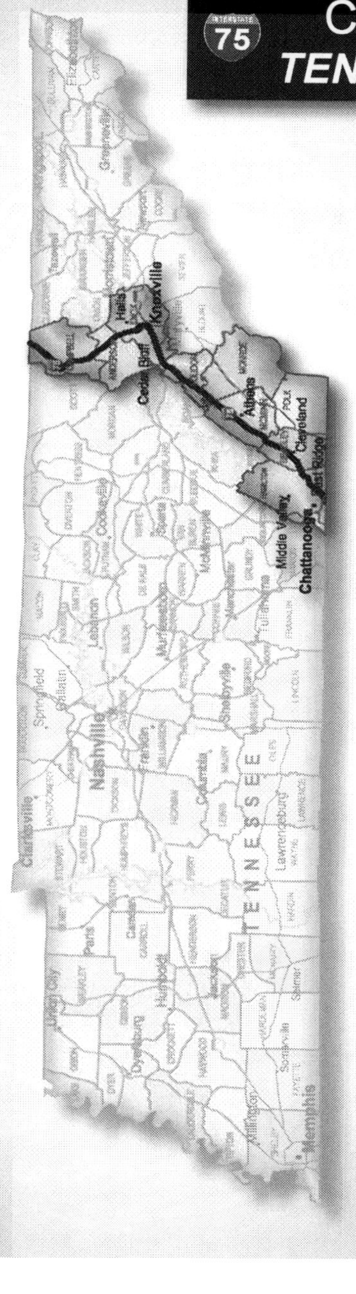

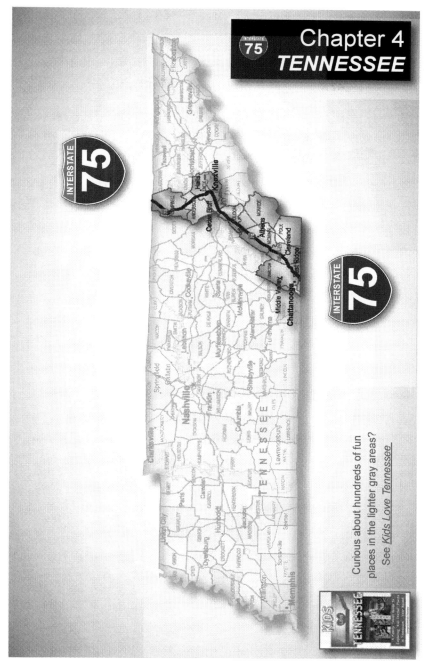

Curious about hundreds of fun places in the lighter gray areas? See *Kids Love Tennessee*

DEAR TENNESSEE TRAVELER:

One of the striking features about I-75 in Tennessee is its routing. This part of the United States is very mountainous. While creeks and rivers have cut passes in many directions, generally it's like a roller coaster ride across a series of minor mountain ranges. For most of the way passengers can look down at the valley floor, 1,000 feet below, and see the coal trails creeping along the Norfolk Southern railroad track.

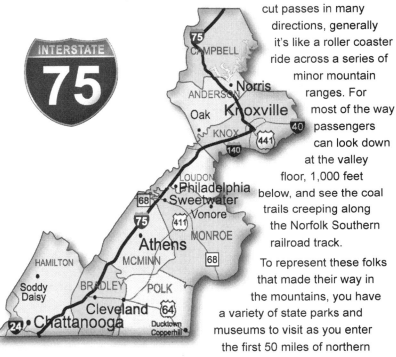

To represent these folks that made their way in the mountains, you have a variety of state parks and museums to visit as you enter the first 50 miles of northern Tennessee. Probably the best stops close to the interstate are **Norris Dam State Park** and the **Museum of Appalachia**. Norris Dam State Park's most notable feature may be the first dam built in the TVA system, but this area is also home to a walking trail park leading to either the cabins and rec center or the Clear Creek Trail. The Creek trails run along the stream feeding the Rice Grist Mill and the Lenoir Museum. Both are modest museums to peak into but the real fun is exploring the scenic, meandering trail…look for trout jumping! Just a few exits south is the classic Appalachian village called the Museum of Appalachia. The title may fool you as this museum is actually an open-air history complex of mostly authentic pioneer Appalachian buildings and artifacts. Of special interest to kids is the Children's Corner quirky gadgets and the cabin used as Daniel Boone's Home during the TV series.

Back on the highway, just as you exit the tall mountains is an oasis of some flat land. On the water, or on the town and all around...get ready for good times in Knoxville! Knoxville reminds us of many other family-oriented towns in the Midwest. Shoot a few hoops or enjoy interactive exhibits at the **Women's Basketball Hall of Fame**. Right across the street, walk into a totally different era of early pioneers at the **James White Fort**. World-class sporting events rule at the University of Tennessee. Spend a relaxing day on the water at Volunteer Landing & Marina. Play in the fountains, rent a paddleboat, or enjoy a boat cruise or a scenic train ride. Visit the area around the World's Fair Park for a variety of family activities.

After you navigate the notorious Knoxville traffic out of town, you may want to stop after a while and grab a leisurely snack. Well, two food factory locations are well within reach on your way to Chattanooga. **Sweetwater Valley Farm** in Philadelphia boasts the best farmstead cheese in the state with names like Tennessee Aged Cheddar and Volunteer Jack. Look for cows, curds and whey here...and, of course, free samples. Grab some cheese and crackers for a picnic at the **Lost Sea**, nearby. Hungry for something sweet now? Get a "scoop" on how things operate at **Mayfield Dairy Farms** in Athens. Don a hair net and watch all the swirling and twirling and spinning and turning and churning of jugs and cartons of milk and ice cream. Or, just stop for a taste of some of their ice cream creations for sale (one scoop is only $1.00!).

Chattanooga has a grandiose welcome when you enter the city gates. This is a fun town with a lot of things to see and do. Take exit 2 west towards the many downtown attractions. Start by taking a Chattanooga trolley or duck boat tour around the town to get a feel for which attraction you definitely want to do on this stop. Maybe it's the heart of the staff and the engagement of the exhibits at the **Creative Discovery Museum** or the wonder of the rivers and the ocean at the **Tennessee Aquarium**. Not only do they have frogs, seahorses, and sharks – but even penguins!

You've been seeing billboards and barns advertising **Lookout Mountain** for miles. This is a special place and, if you haven't seen it yet, you really shouldn't pass it by. Here is "America's deepest cave, largest underground waterfall accessible to the public and the world's steepest passenger railway". You also have a view of seven states, including the next state on our I-75 tour, Georgia!

ACTIVITIES AT A GLANCE

AMUSEMENTS

Exit - 107 - I-275 Exit 1 - *Historic Candy Factory And Worlds Fair Park Sites*

Exit - 2 - I-24 Exit 184 - *Lake Winnepesaukah Amusement Park*

Exit - 2 - I-24 Exit 178 - *Coolidge Park And Walnut Street Bridge*

ANIMALS & FARMS

Exit - 68 - *Sweetwater Valley Farm*

Exit - 2 - I-24 Exit 181 - *Chattanooga Zoo At Warner Park*

Exit - 2 - I-24 Exit 178 - *Tennessee Aquarium*

Exit - 2 - I-24 Exit 175 - *Chattanooga Nature Center & Reflection Riding*

HISTORY

Exit - 122 - *Museum Of Appalachia*

Exit - 107 - I-275 Exit 1 - *Blount Mansion*

Exit - 107 - I-275 Exit 1 - *James White Fort*

Exit - 107 - I-275 Exit 1 - *East Tennessee History Center*

Exit - 20 - *Museum Center At 5ive Points*

Exit - 2 - I-24 Exit 178 - *Battles For Chattanooga Electric Map & Museum*

Exit - 2 - I-24 Exit 178 - *Lookout Mountain Battlefield @ Point Park*

Exit - 2 - I-24 Exit 178 - *Chattanooga African-American History Museum/ Bessie Smith Hall*

Exit - 2 - I-24 Exit 178 - *Chattanooga History Center*

Exit - 107 - I-275 Exit 1 - *University Of Tennessee Campus*

MUSEUMS

Exit - 107 - I-275 Exit 1 - *Women's Basketball Hall Of Fame*

Exit - 2 - I-24 Exit 178 - *International Towing & Recovery Hall Of Fame Museum*

Exit - 2 - I-24 Exit 178 - *Creative Discovery Museum*

OUTDOOR EXPLORING

Exit - 160 - *Indian Mountain State Park*

Exit - 134 - *Cove Lake State Park*

Exit - 128 - *Norris Dam State Park*

Exit - 107 - I-275 Exit 1 - *Volunteer Landing*

Exit - 4 - *Booker T. Washington State Park*

Exit - 3A - *Audubon Acres*

Exit - 2 - I-24 Exit 178 - *Rock City*

SCIENCE

Exit - 107 - I-275 Exit 1 - *Ijams Nature Center*

Exit - 376 - *American Museum Of Science And Energy*

SUGGESTED LODGING & DINING

Exit - 107 - I-275 Exit 1 - *Holiday Inn Select - Downtown Knoxville*

Exit - 107 - I-275 Exit 1 - *Calhoun's On The River*

Exit - 378 - *Best Western Cedar Bluff*

Exit - 2 - I-24 Exit 178 - *Chattanooga Choo Choo Holiday Inn Resort*

THE ARTS

Exit - 107 - I-275 Exit 1 - *Knoxville Museum Of Art*

Exit - 2 - I-24 Exit 178 - *Bluff View Art District*

ACTIVITIES AT A GLANCE

TOURS

Exit - 107 - I-275 Exit 1 - *Knoxville Trolley*

Exit - 107 - I-275 Exit 1 - *Star Of Knoxville, TN Riverboat Company*

Exit - 107 - I-275 Exit 1 - *Three Rivers Rambler*

Exit - 81 - *Secret City Scenic Excursion Train*

Exit - 60 - *Lost Sea*

Exit - 52 - *Mayfield Dairy Farms Tours*

Exit - 4 - *Tennessee Valley Railroad*

TOURS *(cont.)*

Exit - 2 - I-24 Exit 178 - *Lookout Mountain Incline Railway*

Exit - 2 - I-24 Exit 178 - *Ruby Falls*

Exit - 2 - I-24 Exit 178 - *Chattanooga Ducks Tours*

Exit - 2 - I-24 Exit 178 - *Chattanooga Riverboat Co. Southern Belle*

WELCOME CENTER

Exit - 1 - *Tennessee Welcome Center*

GENERAL INFORMATION

Contact the services of interest. Request to be added to their mailing lists.

- ☐ Tennessee's Civil War Heritage Trail: A Path Divided. Tennessee Historical Commission, Nashville. www.state.tn.us/environment/hist/ or (615) 532-1550
- ☐ Pick Tennessee Products @ www.picktnproducts.org.
- ☐ Whitewater Rafting/Kayaking @ www.chattanoogafun.com
- ☐ Tennessee Department of Tourist Development, Nashville. (800) GO2-TENN or www.tnvacation.com
- ☐ Tennessee Historical Commission, Nashville. (615) 532-1550
- ☐ Tennessee Wildlife Resources Agency, Agriculture Center, Nashville. (615) 781-6500 or (800) 372-3928
- ☐ Tennessee State Parks, Nashville. www.tnstateparks.com or (888) TN-PARKS
- ☐ Knoxville Tourism & Sports Corporation, Knoxville. (800) 727-8045 or www.knoxtsc.com
- ☐ Chattanooga Area CVB. www.chattanoogafun.com. (800) 322-3344.

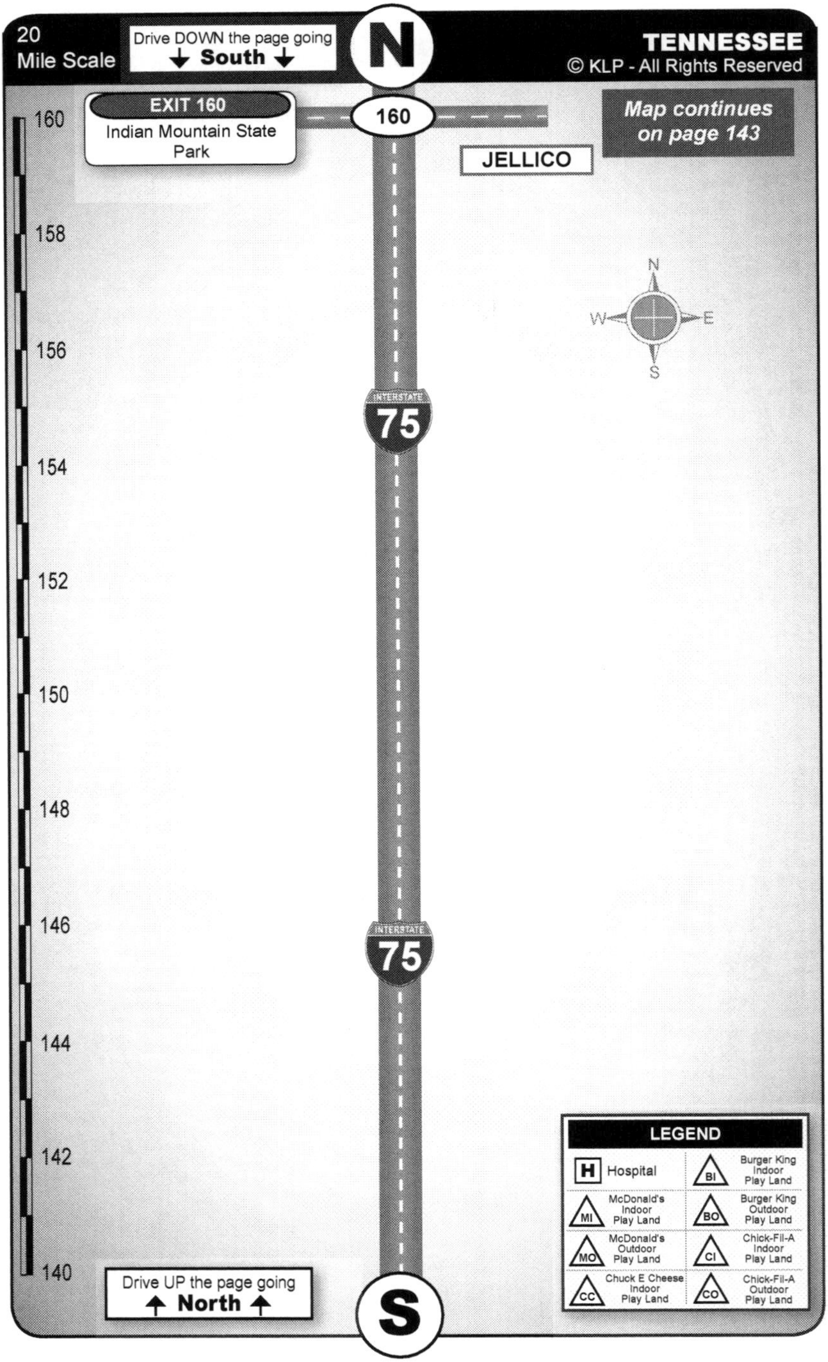

20 Mile Scale

Drive DOWN the page going
↓ **South** ↓

N

TENNESSEE
© KLP - All Rights Reserved

160

EXIT 160
Indian Mountain State Park

160

Map continues on page 143

JELLICO

158

N
W ⊕ E
S

156

INTERSTATE
75

154

152

150

148

146

INTERSTATE
75

144

LEGEND

H Hospital		△BI	Burger King Indoor Play Land
△MI	McDonald's Indoor Play Land	△BO	Burger King Outdoor Play Land
△MO	McDonald's Outdoor Play Land	△CI	Chick-Fil-A Indoor Play Land
△CC	Chuck E Cheese Indoor Play Land	△CO	Chick-Fil-A Outdoor Play Land

142

Drive UP the page going
↑ **North** ↑

140

S

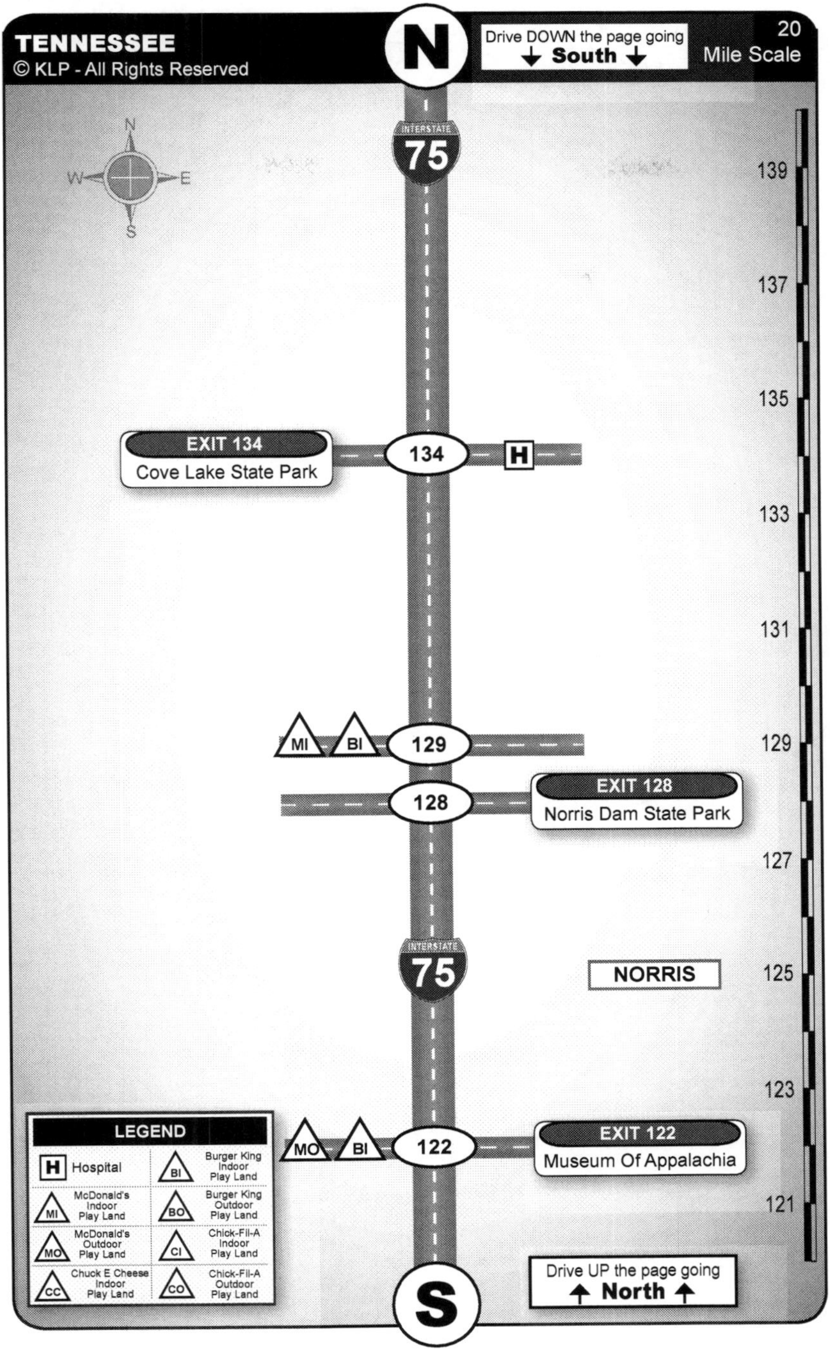
TENNESSEE
© KLP - All Rights Reserved
N
Drive DOWN the page going
South
20
Mile Scale
N
W
E
S
INTERSTATE
75
139
137
135
EXIT 134
Cove Lake State Park
134
H
133
131
MI
BI
129
129
128
EXIT 128
Norris Dam State Park
127
INTERSTATE
75
NORRIS
125
123
LEGEND
H Hospital
BI Burger King Indoor Play Land
MI McDonald's Indoor Play Land
BO Burger King Outdoor Play Land
MO McDonald's Outdoor Play Land
CI Chick-Fil-A Indoor Play Land
CC Chuck E Cheese Indoor Play Land
CO Chick-Fil-A Outdoor Play Land
MO
BI
122
EXIT 122
Museum Of Appalachia
121
S
Drive UP the page going
North

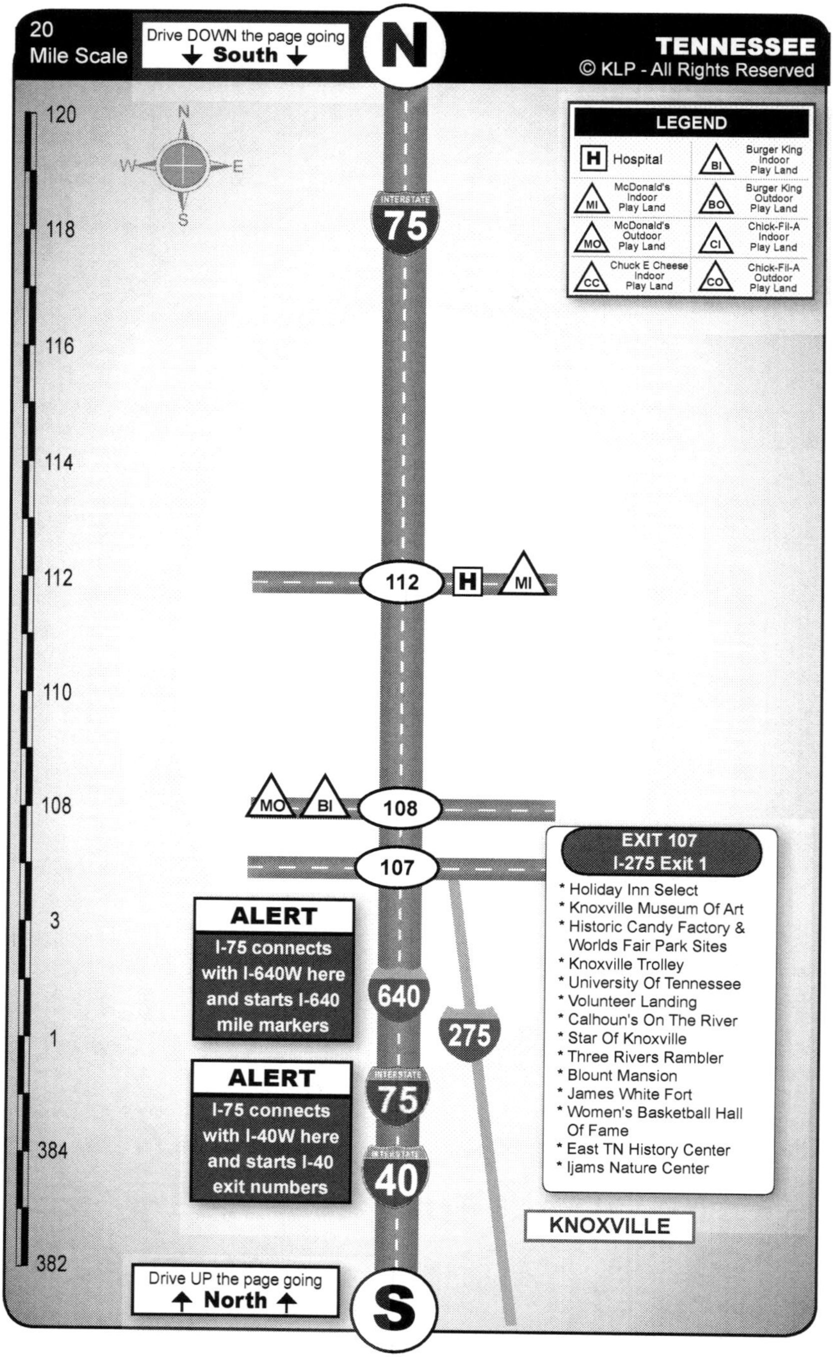
20
Mile Scale
Drive DOWN the page going
South
N
TENNESSEE
© KLP - All Rights Reserved
LEGEND
Hospital
Burger King Indoor Play Land
McDonald's Indoor Play Land
Burger King Outdoor Play Land
McDonald's Outdoor Play Land
Chick-Fil-A Indoor Play Land
Chuck E Cheese Indoor Play Land
Chick-Fil-A Outdoor Play Land
120
118
116
114
112
110
108
3
1
384
382
75
112
108
107
EXIT 107
I-275 Exit 1
* Holiday Inn Select
* Knoxville Museum Of Art
* Historic Candy Factory & Worlds Fair Park Sites
* Knoxville Trolley
* University Of Tennessee
* Volunteer Landing
* Calhoun's On The River
* Star Of Knoxville
* Three Rivers Rambler
* Blount Mansion
* James White Fort
* Women's Basketball Hall Of Fame
* East TN History Center
* Ijams Nature Center
ALERT
I-75 connects with I-640W here and starts I-640 mile markers
ALERT
I-75 connects with I-40W here and starts I-40 exit numbers
640
275
40
KNOXVILLE
Drive UP the page going
North
S

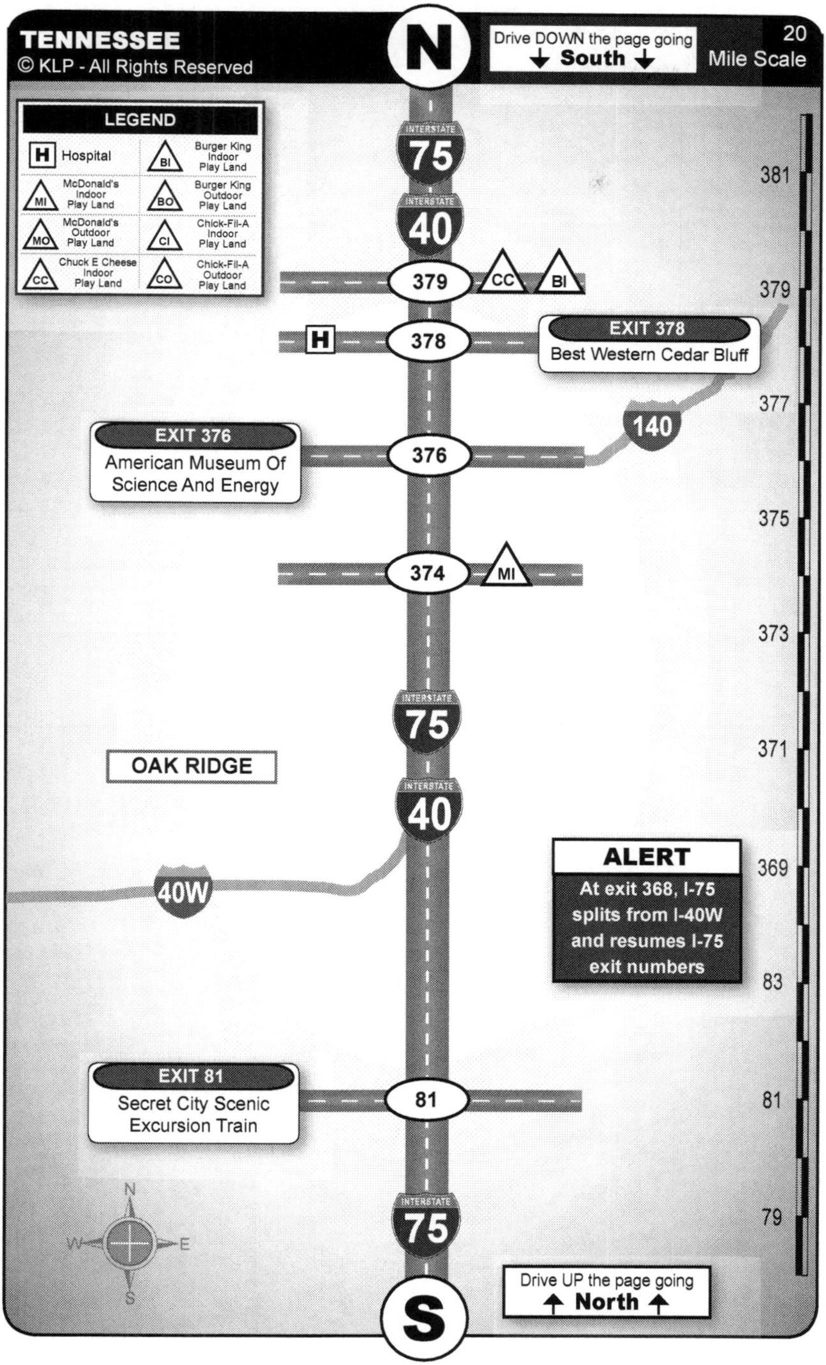
TENNESSEE
© KLP - All Rights Reserved
N
Drive DOWN the page going
South
20
Mile Scale
LEGEND
H Hospital
BI Burger King Indoor Play Land
MI McDonald's Indoor Play Land
BO Burger King Outdoor Play Land
MO McDonald's Outdoor Play Land
CI Chick-Fil-A Indoor Play Land
CC Chuck E Cheese Indoor Play Land
CO Chick-Fil-A Outdoor Play Land
INTERSTATE 75
INTERSTATE 40
381
379
CC
BI
379
H
378
EXIT 378
Best Western Cedar Bluff
377
140
EXIT 376
American Museum Of Science And Energy
376
375
374
MI
373
INTERSTATE 75
371
OAK RIDGE
INTERSTATE 40
369
40W
ALERT
At exit 368, I-75 splits from I-40W and resumes I-75 exit numbers
83
EXIT 81
Secret City Scenic Excursion Train
81
81
79
INTERSTATE 75
N
W
E
S
Drive UP the page going
North
S

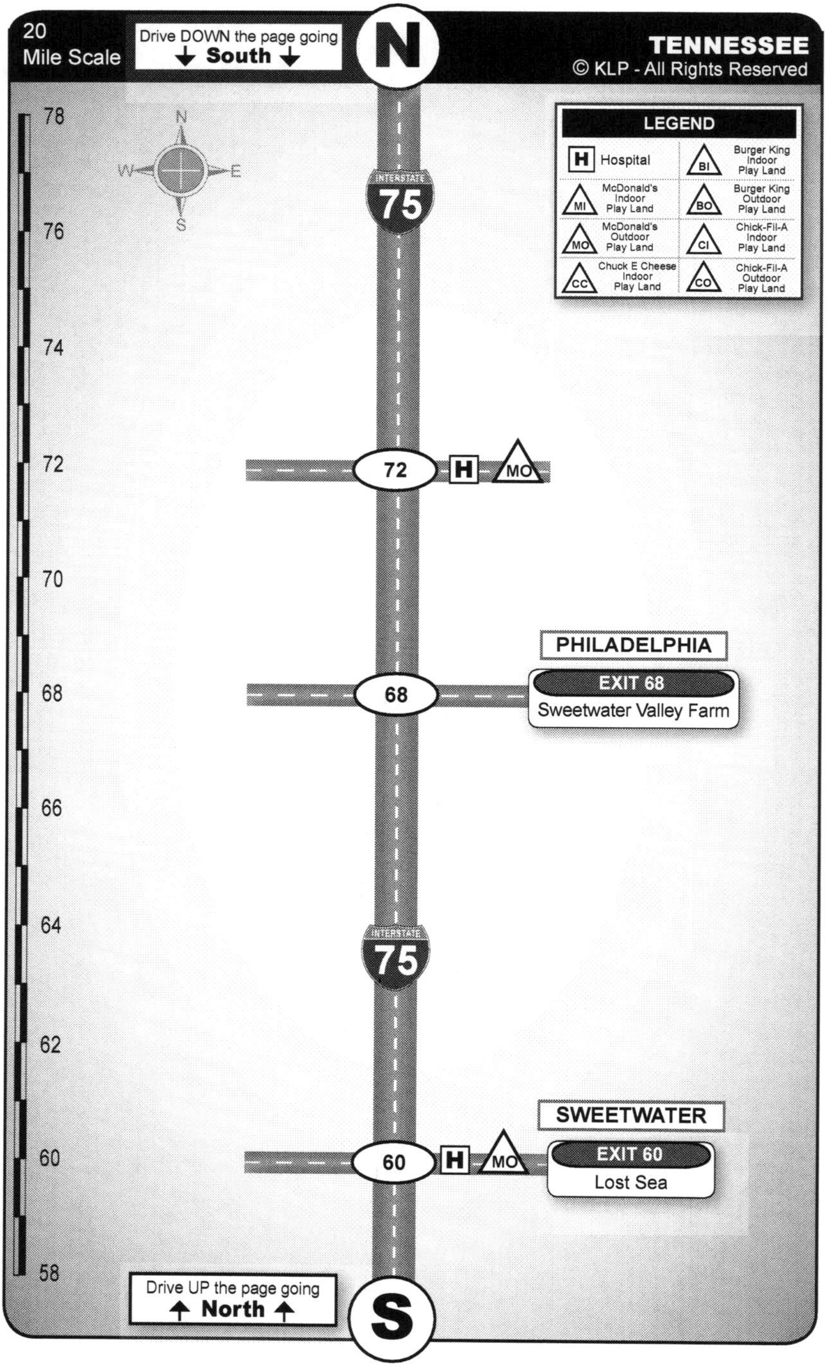
20
Mile Scale
Drive DOWN the page going
South
N
TENNESSEE
© KLP - All Rights Reserved
LEGEND
Hospital
Burger King Indoor Play Land
McDonald's Indoor Play Land
Burger King Outdoor Play Land
McDonald's Outdoor Play Land
Chick-Fil-A Indoor Play Land
Chuck E Cheese Indoor Play Land
Chick-Fil-A Outdoor Play Land
78
76
74
72
70
68
66
64
62
60
58
INTERSTATE 75
72
PHILADELPHIA
68
EXIT 68
Sweetwater Valley Farm
SWEETWATER
60
EXIT 60
Lost Sea
Drive UP the page going
North
S

TENNESSEE

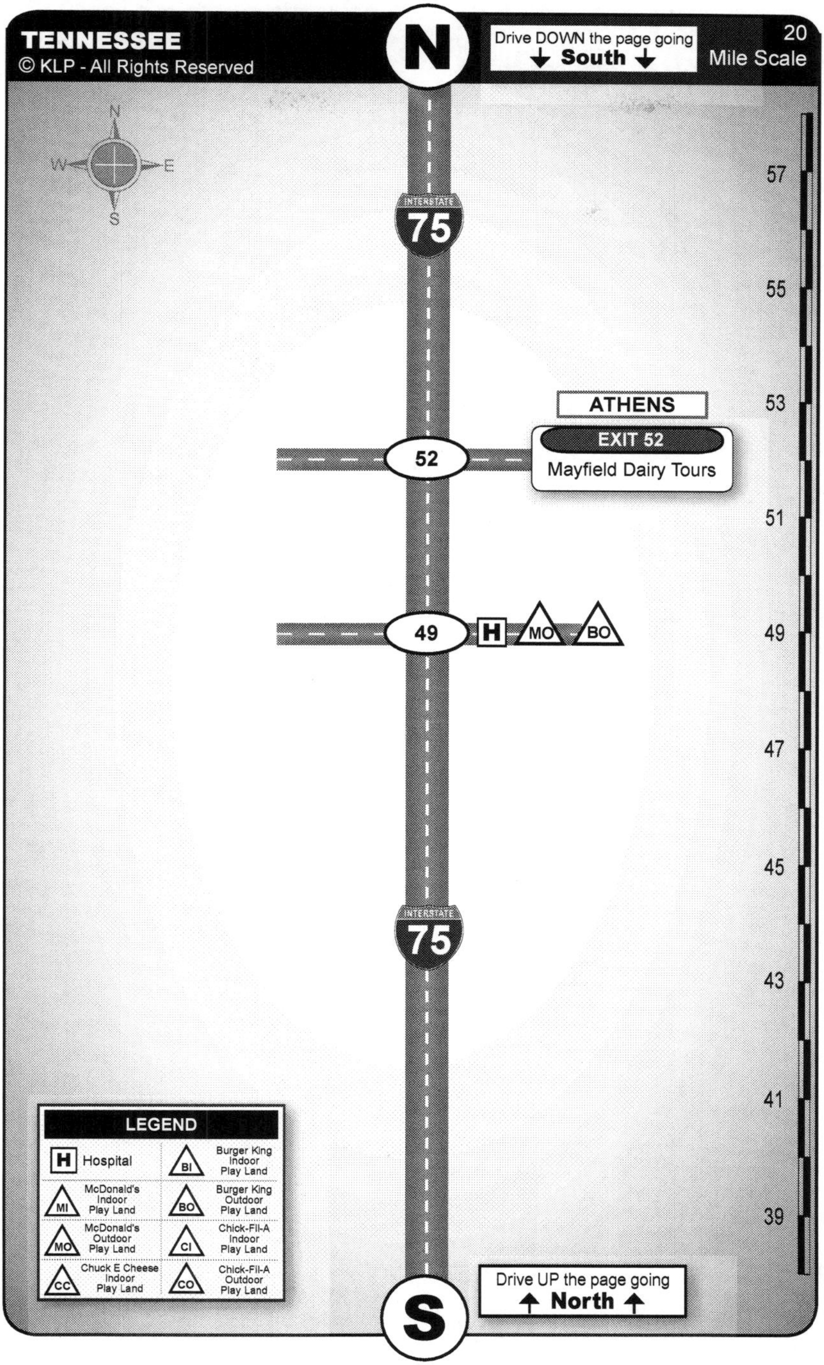
TENNESSEE
© KLP - All Rights Reserved
N
Drive DOWN the page going
South
20
Mile Scale
N
W
E
S
INTERSTATE
75
57
55
ATHENS
53
EXIT 52
Mayfield Dairy Tours
52
51
49
H
MO
BO
49
47
45
INTERSTATE
75
43
41
39
LEGEND
H Hospital
BI Burger King Indoor Play Land
MI McDonald's Indoor Play Land
BO Burger King Outdoor Play Land
MO McDonald's Outdoor Play Land
CI Chick-Fil-A Indoor Play Land
CC Chuck E Cheese Indoor Play Land
CO Chick-Fil-A Outdoor Play Land
Drive UP the page going
North
S

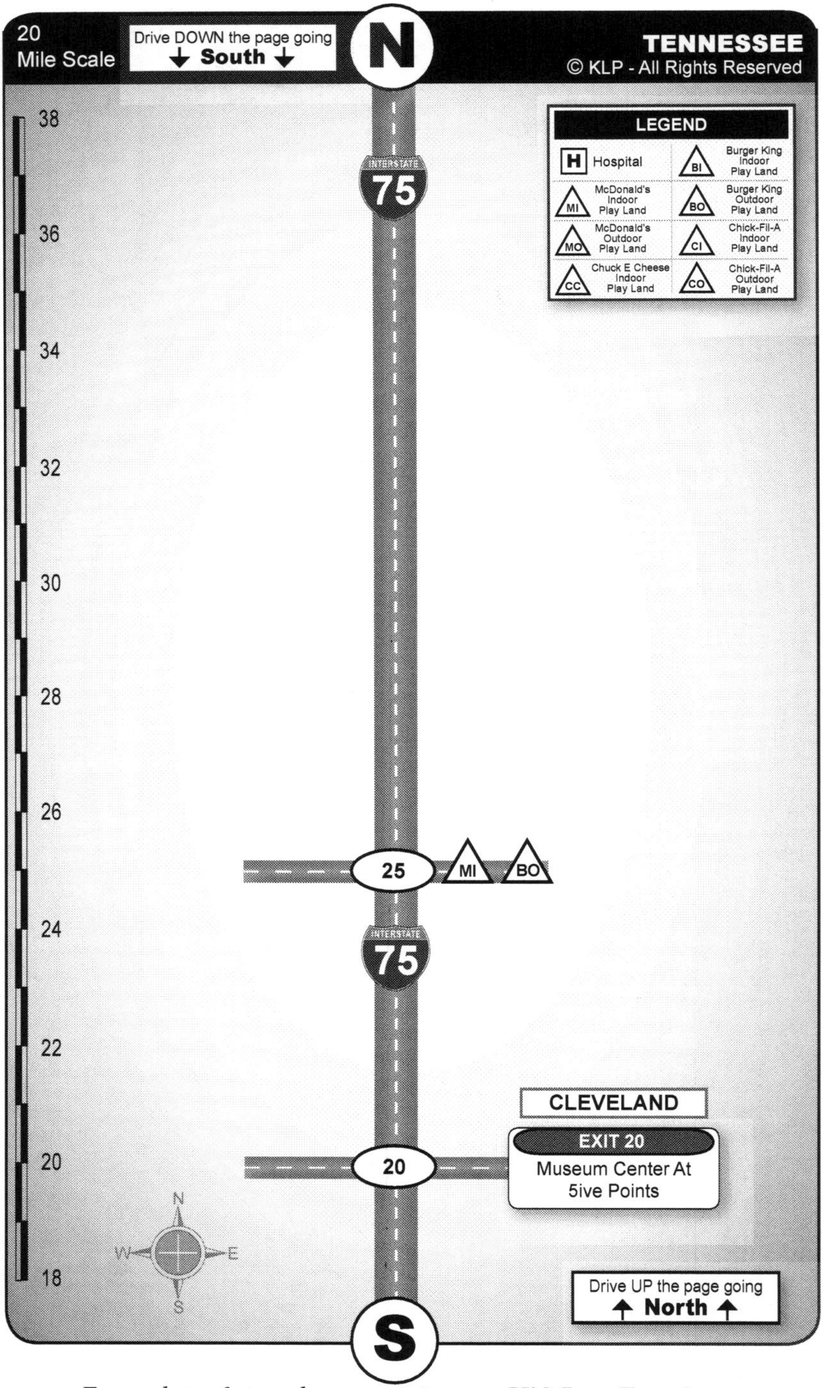
20
Mile Scale
Drive DOWN the page going
South
N
TENNESSEE
© KLP - All Rights Reserved
LEGEND
Hospital
Burger King Indoor Play Land
McDonald's Indoor Play Land
Burger King Outdoor Play Land
McDonald's Outdoor Play Land
Chick-Fil-A Indoor Play Land
Chuck E Cheese Indoor Play Land
Chick-Fil-A Outdoor Play Land
38
36
34
32
30
28
26
25
MI
BO
24
22
CLEVELAND
EXIT 20
Museum Center At 5ive Points
20
18
Drive UP the page going
North
S

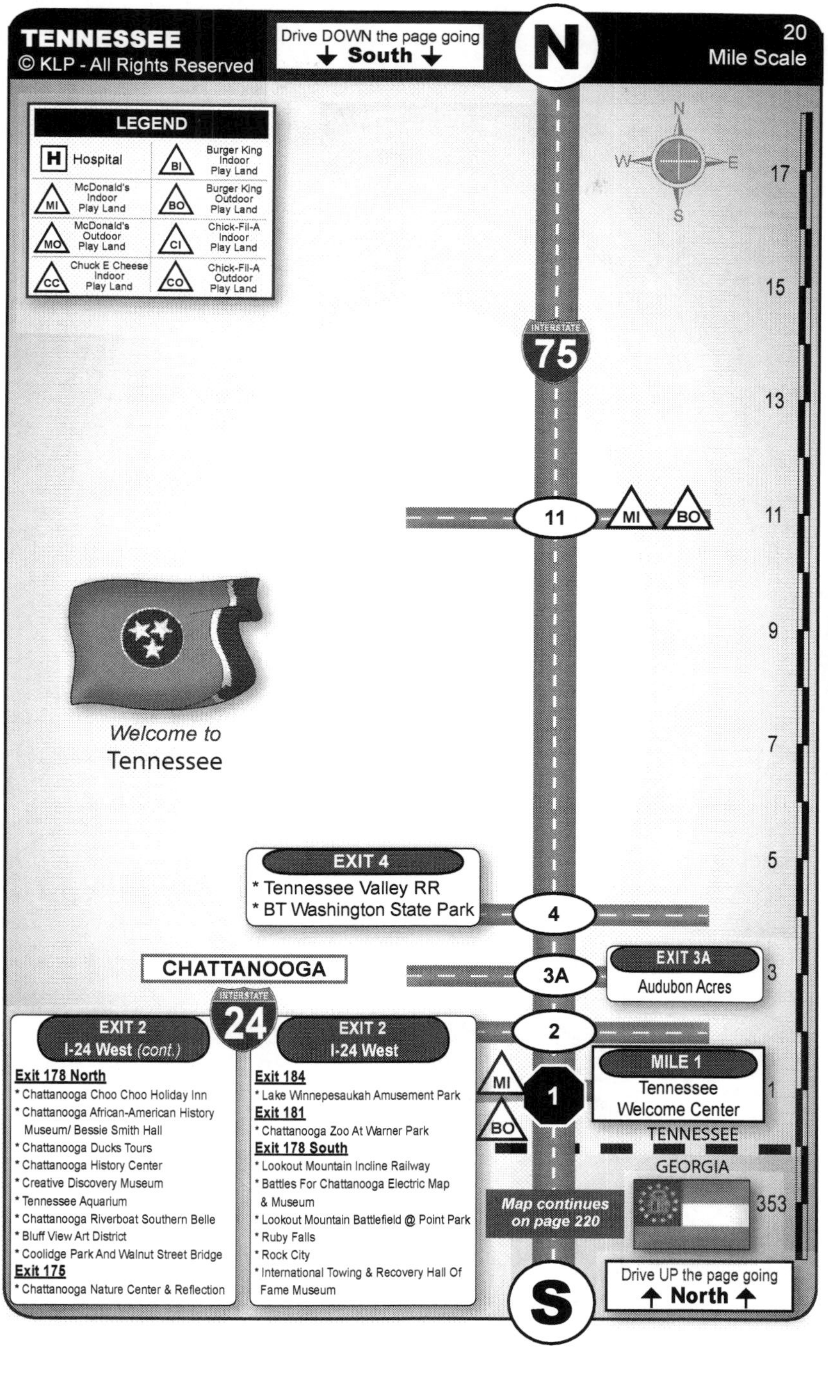
TENNESSEE
© KLP - All Rights Reserved
Drive DOWN the page going
South
N
20
Mile Scale
LEGEND
H Hospital
BI Burger King Indoor Play Land
MI McDonald's Indoor Play Land
BO Burger King Outdoor Play Land
MO McDonald's Outdoor Play Land
CI Chick-Fil-A Indoor Play Land
CC Chuck E Cheese Indoor Play Land
CO Chick-Fil-A Outdoor Play Land
N
W
E
S
INTERSTATE 75
17
15
13
11
MI
BO
9
7
5
3
1
Welcome to Tennessee
EXIT 4
* Tennessee Valley RR
* BT Washington State Park
4
CHATTANOOGA
3A
EXIT 3A
Audubon Acres
INTERSTATE 24
2
EXIT 2
I-24 West (cont.)
Exit 178 North
* Chattanooga Choo Choo Holiday Inn
* Chattanooga African-American History Museum/ Bessie Smith Hall
* Chattanooga Ducks Tours
* Chattanooga History Center
* Creative Discovery Museum
* Tennessee Aquarium
* Chattanooga Riverboat Southern Belle
* Bluff View Art District
* Coolidge Park And Walnut Street Bridge
Exit 175
* Chattanooga Nature Center & Reflection
EXIT 2
I-24 West
Exit 184
* Lake Winnepesaukah Amusement Park
Exit 181
* Chattanooga Zoo At Warner Park
Exit 178 South
* Lookout Mountain Incline Railway
* Battles For Chattanooga Electric Map & Museum
* Lookout Mountain Battlefield @ Point Park
* Ruby Falls
* Rock City
* International Towing & Recovery Hall Of Fame Museum
MI
BO
1
MILE 1
Tennessee Welcome Center
TENNESSEE
GEORGIA
Map continues on page 220
353
S
Drive UP the page going
North

Sites and attractions are listed in order by Exit Number (North to South) and distance from the exit (closest are listed first). Symbols indicated represent:

Restaurants Lodging

Exit - 160 (west of I-75)

INDIAN MOUNTAIN STATE PARK

Jellico - ***Indian Mountain Road (I-75 exit 160, go north on U.S. Hwy. 25 to State Hwy. 297, make a right on London and a left on Dairy Street) 37762. Phone: (423) 784-7958. www.tnstateparks.com/parks/about/indian-mountain. Hours: Daily 7:00am-sunset.***

Located at the base of the Cumberland Mountains, this park is popular with campers. Park visitors can enjoy fishing at the two small lakes, picnicking, camping, and two walking trails (one paved and one unpaved). The park has a 80' x 42' swimming pool that is open from Memorial Day through late summer. Individual picnic areas are equipped with tables and grills.

Exit - 134 (west of I-75)

COVE LAKE STATE PARK

Caryville - ***110 Cove Lake Lane (I-75 exit 134 take Hwy 25W) 37714. Phone: (423) 566-9701. www.tnstateparks.com/parks/about/cove-lake. Hours: Daily 8:00am-sunset.***

Situated in a mountain valley setting on the eastern edge of the Cumberland Mountains, there are scenic nature trails and bike trails leading through the open grasslands and woodlands. In the winter, several hundred Canadian Geese make this lakeshore their feeding ground. Nearby is the Devil's Race Trace whose steep pinnacle rock affords a panoramic view. There is a 3.5 mile paved hiking trail that is also used for biking. Other activities: camping, swimming, recreation center, boating and fishing. Rowboats and pedal boats are available for rent on the lake, but no personally owned boats are permitted. No gas powered motors are allowed but you may bring your own electric trolling motor to put on the fishing boats. Boat rental is year-round. There are 112 picnic tables and grills to serve the Cove Lake day-user. Most sites are located adjacent to the lake. Playgrounds, playfields, restrooms and water are conveniently located to serve picnickers. Picnic areas are not covered but they are situated in shady locations.

Exit - 128 (east of I-75)

NORRIS DAM STATE PARK

Norris - ***125 Village Green Circle (From I-75, take exit 128 and go 2.5 miles south on Hwy. 441 to the entrance of the park) 37769. Phone: (865) 426-7461. www.tnstateparks.com/parks/about/norris-dam. Hours: Park Hours: Summer 8:00am-10:00pm. Winter 8:00am-Sundown. Lenoir Museum Hours: Wednesday-Sunday 9:00am-5:00pm. Note: Picnic areas are available on both the east and west sections. Each area is equipped with tables and grills, with playground and restrooms.***

The first dam built in the TVA system, this area provided part of the electricity for the now historic Manhattan Project. The park recreation center is located at the Village Green Complex. A fee paid outdoor pool (only open June - early August), badminton, volleyball, basketball and many other activities are available to park visitors. Norris Lake is a sportsman's paradise offering 800 miles of shore-line for camping, boating, fishing and more. The park has 19 rustic vacation cabins and 10 three-bedroom deluxe cabins. All are located in quiet, wooded settings and are completely equipped for housekeeping including electrical appliances, cooking and serving utensils, and linens. Guided activities include a nice morning lake cruise, wildlife tours, critter scavenger hunts and crafts or owl/bat walks.

18TH CENTURY RICE GRIST MILL - Originally constructed in 1798 along Lost Creek, this mill was operated by four generations of the Rice family. At times, the mill was also rigged to power a sawmill, a cotton gin, a trip hammer, and even to operate a dynamo that supplied electrical lights for the Rice home in 1899. Clear Creek Trail runs along the stream feeding the mill... very scenic...look for trout.

LENOIR MUSEUM - display of pre-industrial revolution equipment and products. When you visit the Museum, make sure and get a close look at the antique barrel organ. The organ plays ten different tunes with 110 wood pipes to make the music. In all, 44 figures are in action. These figures include dancers dancing, a clown clowning, foot soldiers marching, a woman churning and a blacksmith hard at work. Also, ask about the collection of antique mouse traps.

Exit - 122 (east of I-75)

MUSEUM OF APPALACHIA

Norris - ***Highway 61 (I-75 exit 122) 37769. www.museumofappalachia.org. Phone: (865) 494-7680. Hours: Year Round during daylight hours, generally 8:30am-6:00pm except reduced hours each winter (November - March). Closed only on Christmas and Thanksgiving. Admission: $18.00 adult (19-64), $15.00 senior (65+), $10.00 youth (13-18), $6.00 child (5-12).***

Want quirky amusement without the glitz of rides? Discover the pre-WWII heritage of the area at this 65-acre Appalachian history complex. John Rice Irwin's open-air museum is called "the most authentic and complete replica of pioneer Appalachian life in the world." The museum contains over 250,000 pioneer everyday relics including 30 log structures - a chapel, a schoolhouse, cabins and barns. There's even a restaurant and craft center. Of special interest to kids is the Mark Twain Family Cabin, Uncle John's dirt floor cabin (used as Daniel Boone's TV Home), and the Children's Corner in the Hall of Fame building. Look for a shoe carved from coal and a lot of whittlers and fiddlers who used their spare time to create famous works or just plain weird works of art? (i.e. A ukulele made from matchsticks or a "ukuweewee" – a "bed pan" banjo). A great, leisurely day trip…with lots to look see.

Exit - 107 (east of I-75) / I-275 exit 1

HOLIDAY INN SELECT - DOWNTOWN

Knoxville - ***525 Henley Street, Convention Center (Downtown @ World's Fair campus. At the I-275/I-40 interchange, bear right onto 441 South) 37902. Phone: (865) 522-2800. www.ihg.com***

First of all, if staying overnight…and, you want to be in the middle of it all…we might suggest this property, located at beautiful World's Fair Park, home of the 1982 Worlds Fair. They offer seasonal Family Packages (see www.knoxville.org) and have a mini-fridge in the room. Their indoor pool/whirlpool was clean and warm. Kids eat free with paying adults in their restaurant. The best part is its location. Rooms start around $89.

KNOXVILLE MUSEUM OF ART

Knoxville - ***1050 World's Fair Park Drive (Downtown @ World's Fair campus. At the I-275/I-40 interchange, bear right onto 441 South) 37996. Phone: (865) 525-6101. www.knoxart.org. Hours: Tuesday-Saturday 10:00am-5:00pm, Sunday 1:00-5:00pm. Closed major holidays. Admission: FREE.***

> In World's Fair Park is the Sunsphere, the 266-foot tall steel tower with a golden globe that was built for the 1982 World's Fair.

Highlighted in the permanent collection are works of American art created during and after the 1960s. The museum also contains five galleries, a Sculpture Terrace, and a Creative Corner. In Exploratory, "put your face on" or walk into portraits, work on paper, abstract paint and read art-related books and games. The space is designed for pre-kindergarten and elementary school groups during weekdays, and self-directed for parents and children on weekends and holidays.

HISTORIC CANDY FACTORY AND WORLD'S FAIR PARK SITES

Knoxville - ***1060 World's Fair Park Drive (Downtown @ World's Fair campus. At the I-275/I-40 interchange, bear right onto 441 South) 37996. Phone: (865) 546-5707. www.worldsfairpark.org. Note: Across the street is Fort Kid playground. www.knoxchox.com is Bradleys Chocolate Factory website.***

A collection of shops and galleries featuring the works of local and regional artists. Also, home to a working chocolate factory (watch the ooey-gooey folks dipping chocolates by hand), near a children's playground called Fort Kid. Food cafes with light lunchtime snacks available. The Art Museum, Sunsphere and playful water fountains are in this square block area. The 4th level of the Sunsphere houses the Observation Deck. It offers a 360-degree view of the original 1982 World's Fair site, downtown Knoxville, the Tennessee River, the University of Tennessee, and the Smoky Mountains. There is no admission charge to visit the Observation Deck and access is limited to the double elevators facing the lake at the base of the Sunsphere and the Convention Center level.

KNOXVILLE TROLLEY

Knoxville - ***(several downtown locations for pickup, look for signs) 37902. Phone: (800) 727-8045. www.katbus.com. Hours: Monday-Friday 7:00am-6:00pm.***

Knoxville Trolley Lines, a downtown trolley service, provides a convenient way to see all the attractions in the downtown area.

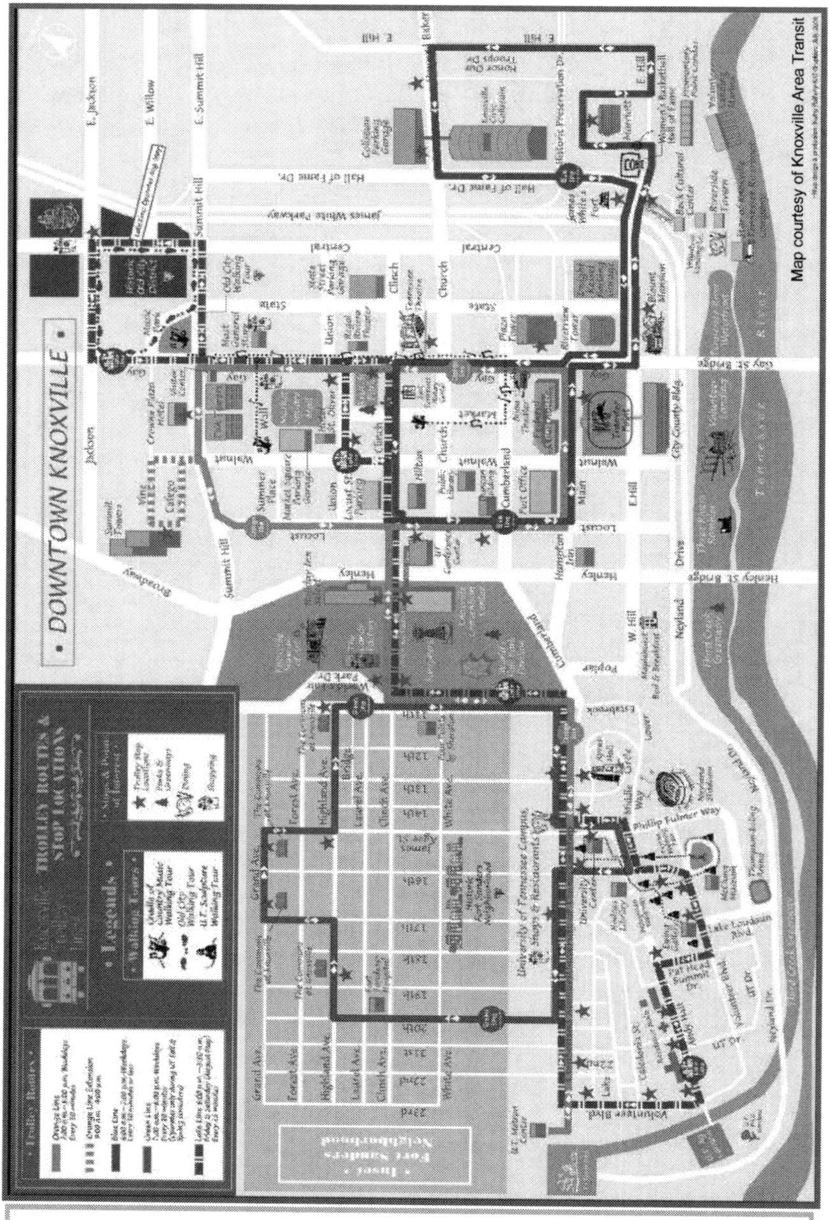

Visit www.Katbus.com for the latest fares and trolley routes as they are updated annually.

The trolley service also connects to the City's regular bus service Knoxville Area Transit (KAT) for trips outside of the downtown area, including malls, parks and other attractions. In addition, a Late Line Trolley operates every 15 minutes on Friday and Saturday nights (8:00pm-2:00am) with service to Knoxville's historic Old City, the Knoxville Convention Center and other entertainment spots. Go online for a trolley map. Maps are also available at the downtown Visitors Center.

Exit - 107 (east of I-75) / I-275 exit 1

UNIVERSITY OF TENNESSEE CAMPUS

Knoxville - ***(off interstate, proceed south, following campus signs - most off or near Volunteer Blvd running thru the heart of campus) 37996. www.utk.edu***

Some sites you want to see include:

- **FOOTBALL HALL OF FAME**: (865-974-5789). 1704 Johnny Majors Drive, Neyland Thompson Sports Center. Monday-Friday 8:00am-5:00pm. FREE. The museum stands as a tribute to the student athletes who shaped 100+ years of Volunteer Football.
- **McCLUNG MUSEUM**: (865-974-2144). 1327 Circle Park Drive, next to Visitors Info & Parking. FREE. http://mcclungmuseum.utk.edu. Monday-Saturday 9:00am-5:00pm, Sunday 1:00-5:00pm. Closed holidays. The Geology and Fossil History of Tennessee exhibition focuses on the many years of the state's geologic past and explores, thru graphics and animation, formations and drift. Special features are six life-size dioramas of life forms at various times with actual fossils of creatures, a replica of a giant dinosaur marine lizard or T-rex, and actual dino eggs. Also, Ancient Egypt and a Freshwater Mussels exhibit. Look for the many unusual fossils, both on display or under "walk-on windows" at your feet. A video portrays the journey of Cherokee through the ages. Free stroller tours offered monthly.

- **GARDENS**: (865) 974-7324). Neyland Drive at the Agriculture Campus. Daily sunrise to sunset. FREE. More than 1400 varieties of herbs and plants, the All-America Flower Trials and TenneSelect program.
- **MCKENZIE SCULPTURE OF ATHLETES**: (865-974-1250). 1801 Volunteer Blvd., Thornton Athletic Student Life Center. FREE. 8:00am-4:00pm, Monday-Friday. Over 100 sculptural works including statuettes, bas-reliefs, medals, portrait medallions and plaques, which celebrate athletic achievement.
- **UNIVERSITY OF TENNESSEE ATHLETICS**: NCAA baseball, basketball, cross-country, golf, swimming, track, volleyball & football. (800) 332-VOLS.

Exit - 107 (east of I-75) / I-275 exit 1

VOLUNTEER LANDING

Knoxville - ***Volunteer Landing, downtown (At the I-275/I-40 interchange, bear right onto 441 South. Follow signs onto Gay to Neyland Dr. Park is on shoreline) 37915. http://worldsfairpark.org/volunteer-landing-attractions.html. Phone: (865) 971-4440 or (800) 727-8045. Hours: Daylight hours. Admission: FREE. Note: The Star of Knoxville Riverboat & the Three Rivers Rambler train have depots here.***

Volunteer Landing offers attractions and eateries on the Tennessee River. At the Marina paddle, pontoon, and houseboats are available for rental (865-633-5004 or www.volunteermarina.com). There are numerous historical markers along the one-mile riverwalk, including interactive displays that tell of the historic significance of the river (waterfalls & fountains, too). The sprouting fountains on Neyland Drive are great for the kids to play in on hot summer days. You'll notice some families picnicking and others fishing from the docks. This is the place to start your visit in town because you really get a handle on the historical and fun attractions around town and in East Tennessee.

CALHOUN'S ON THE RIVER

Knoxville - ***400 Neyland Drive, Volunteer Landing (follow directions to Volunteer Landing) 37915. Phone: (865) 673-3355. www.calhouns.com.***

Try the "Best Ribs in America!" and their chicken so you can get an idea of what the locals rave about. Then, move on to other temptations like Buffalo Wings or Fried Green Tomatoes, to the enticing steak or catfish with their own recipe flavors. Some unique signature items include: White Chili, Turkey Creek Salad, Creamy Country Slaw, Smoky Mountain Baked Beans and Spinach Maria sides. Land a sweet ending with freshly made seasonal Strawberry Shortcake or Key Lime Pie. Calhoun's is accessible by boat and has its own dock for mooring your vessel. There is an outside deck as well as an enclosed deck with a panoramic view of the Tennessee River. They are proud to be the Taste of Tennessee. Daily lunch and dinner.

STAR OF KNOXVILLE, TENNESSEE RIVERBOAT COMPANY

Knoxville - ***300 Neyland Drive (Volunteer Landing) 37902. Phone: (865) 525-7827 or (800) 509-BOAT. http://tnriverboat.com.***

The authentic, Mississippi-style paddlewheel boat offers a view of Knoxville from the water on a brunch, luncheon, dinner (includes food & entertainment) or sightseeing cruise ($12.50-$17) per person, departs 3:00pm, Thursday-Sunday, May-October). Join the sightseeing cruise for a look at original historic sights along the beautiful Tennessee River. During the history commentary, the Captain will show points of interest along the river. The lunch tour is great if you want to combine a fair price ($15.95-$26.75) for yummy buffet food along with a nice historic commentary of the sites/events along the river. The Star of Knoxville is fully air-conditioned and heated. Their staff is very friendly and their food is wonderful!

THREE RIVERS RAMBLER

Knoxville - ***2560 University Commons Way (adjacent to the Univ of Tenn) 37901. Phone: (865) 524-9411. www.threeriversrambler.com. Hours: Saturdays 1:00pm and 4:00pm (April-October). Christmas Express trains run weekends (Thanksgiving thru days before Christmas) Admission: $26.50 adult, $25.50 senior (55+), $15.50 child (3-12). Special Trains are a few dollars higher (ex. Christmas Express).***

Crossing the river trestle...

This vintage steam engine train takes guests on a 90-minute excursion to the Forks of the River and back, through some historic and scenic countrysides. On the trip back, stop for a while on the trestle bridge to feel like the train is flying in mid-air. Learn a little of the history of the town and famous folks who helped build it. An open air rail car is available to ride and each car is supplied with a uniformed conductor who explains the sites and is available for questions. At the Asbury Quarry, the train makes a brief stop where the locomotive is switched to return back to the depot. Note: If it's very hot (90° F.+), definitely pay the extra for the air-conditioned luxury car.

BLOUNT MANSION

Knoxville - ***200 West Hill Avenue (downtown, corner of Gay St & Hill Ave, near Volunteer Landing) 37902. www.blountmansion.org. Phone: (865) 525-2375. Hours: Tuesday-Friday 9:30am-5:00pm, Saturday 10am-2pm. Closed major holidays and UT home games. Admission: $7.00 adult, $4.00 child (6-17).***

This National Historic Landmark is the 1792 home of Territorial Governor William Blount (and signer of the US Constitution), the first and only governor of the Territory Southwest of the River Ohio.

It is also the birthplace of Tennessee statehood in 1796. The frontier capital still stands on the original site. Known by the Cherokee Indians as "the house with many eyes," Blount Mansion has watched American history parade through its rooms and on the streets outside. Start with a short introduction video that focuses on William Blount's diplomacy with the Cherokee.

Hear about the many changes to the house. Look for the elegant original Blount shoe buckles and the children's toys. See the room where the state Constitution was signed. Interesting details shared throughout the tour about Blount family life, too.

Exit - 107 (east of I-75) / I-275 exit 1

JAMES WHITE FORT

Knoxville - ***205 East Hill Ave. (Volunteer Landing area - see listing for directions - just up the street) 37915. www.jameswhitefort.org. Phone: (865) 525-6514. Hours: Monday-Friday 10:00am-4:00pm (December-March), Monday-Saturday 9:30am-5:00pm (April-November). Admission: $7.00 adult, $3.00 child (6-12).***

Located on a bluff above the Tennessee River near downtown, the fort was built in 1786 by General James White, Knoxville's founder. General White brought his wife and children across the mountains from North Carolina to claim land given to him for his service in the American Revolution. Originally it consisted of his home, three cabins and the stockade wall used to protect the families from Indian attacks and the threat of wild animals. What would the pioneers eat? How would you cook? What are your chores? The guides here really ask questions and engage the kids in what pioneer life was like.

WOMEN'S BASKETBALL HALL OF FAME

Knoxville - ***700 Hall of Fame Drive (Follow directions to Volunteer Landing. Then, follow Hall of Fame Drive to corner of Hill Ave) 37915. Phone: (865) 633-9000. www.WBHOF.com. Hours: Monday-Saturday 10:00am-5:00pm (summers). Tuesday-Friday 11:00am-5:00pm & Saturday 10:00am-5:00pm (rest of year). Closed on Sundays & Mondays except during special game event days.***

Closed Christmastime, Thanksgiving Day, New years eve/day, Summer holidays and Easter with abbreviated hours on some holidays. Admission: $7.95 adult, $5.95 senior (62+) & child (6-15).

The world's most interactive Hall of Fame brings college, Olympic and Pro teams' history to life. The facility features three indoor courts, an interactive locker room where visitors can hear a coach's halftime talk, and an area called "In the Huddle" pep talk with the coach (great photo ops). Put yourself in a Hall of Fame's induction pics or sit on benches amongst players. See the world's largest basketball or try your skills on the Ballgirl Athletic Playground. Dioramas feature an early basketball scene and the Red Heads actual touring car. Tip-Off Theater's inspirational film packs all the emotion of more than 100 years of history of women's basketball into 15 minutes. A very inspiring and exciting museum!

The world's largest basketball is located on the north end of the Hall, weighs 10 tons and sits on top of a glass staircase that resembles a basketball net.

EAST TENNESSEE HISTORY CENTER

Knoxville - ***601 South Gay Street, downtown (Follow directions to Volunteer Landing. Right onto Gay, then corner of Gay & Clinch Avenue, downtown) 37901. Phone: (865) 215-8830. www.easttnhistory.org. Hours: Monday-Saturday 10:00am-4:00pm, Sunday 1:00-5:00pm. Admission: FREE.***

A visit to the Center will bring you face to face with the region's history makers. Here you will find larger than life figures, such as David (Davy) Crockett, Nancy Ward, and Sgt. Alvin C. York. Visitors enter in the year 1750 and follow the road to statehood in 1796 in a streetscape exhibit featuring a recreated drugstore and restored streetcar. The signature exhibit, Voices of the Land, covers narratives of many important characters. The legacy of the Cherokee Indians' "Trail of Tears" is illustrated, as well as an overcoat made by President Andrew Johnson, an East Tennessee tailor by trade. The Children's area is called Davy's Attic with a small log cabin full of clothing like Davy Crockett wore, books and puppets. The Museum also has "hold-it" boxes stationed everywhere. The boxes contain items that children can pick up and examine that relate to the period. Find out why a Governor's battle was called the "War of the Roses" or why Oak Ridge is called the "Secret City".

Exit - 107 (east of I-75) / I-275 exit 1

IJAMS NATURE CENTER

Knoxville - *2915 Island Home Avenue (head south all the way into downtown & riverfront. Cross over the Tennessee River and take the Sevier Ave. / Hillwood Dr. exit) 37920. Phone: (865) 577-4717. www.ijams.org. Hours: Monday-Saturday 9:00am-5:00pm. Sunday 11:00am-5:00pm (March-November only). Grounds open 8:00am until sunset. Admission to park: FREE.*

The regional environmental education center is surrounded by more than 150 acres of beautiful forests, meadows, ponds and gardens connected by 5 miles of trails. Special events include evening walks in the park, canoe trips, junior naturalist workshops, Bug Night, Invasive Species Movie Marathon and Music in the Park. We noticed unique exhibits like the Bird's Nests (even spider nests!), a live beehive and the Conservation Cottage (great ways to apply new recycle habits to your home as you walk thru the pretend house). Of the Hiking Trails, we liked the Tennessee River boardwalk best. The winding boardwalk runs along the River Trail on the banks of the Tennessee River. You'll find many little critters, even Great Blue Herons, and even a small cave. Jo's Grove - whimsical nature playscape with fairy house and knome home. Navitat Knoxville's tree-based zipline adventure park at Ijams Nature Center has more than 60 adventure elements – from ziplines and bridges to swings, nets, elevated tunnels, and more! ($45-$49 fee)

Exit - 378 (east of I-75)

BEST WESTERN CEDAR BLUFF

Knoxville - *420 Peters Road North (I-40/75 exit 378) 37922. Phone: (865) 539-0058 or (800) 348-2562.. www.bwcedarbluff.com.*

They have reasonable, clean, spacious rooms with an outdoor pool and hot breakfast. Each room has a refrigerator and recliner. The king rooms also offer a microwave and a loveseat sofa bed. Located on the west side of town with loads of restaurants nearby. Family Vacation Pkg starts at $89.

Exit - 376 (west of I-75)

AMERICAN MUSEUM OF SCIENCE AND ENERGY

Oak Ridge - ***300 South Tulane Avenue (I-75/I-40 exit 376, Hwy 162 turns into Hwy 62, Oak Ridge Pkwy to traffic light #10. OR, I-40 exit 376, Rte. 162N) 37830. Phone: (865) 576-3200. www.amse.org. Hours: Monday-Saturday 9:00am-5:00pm, Sunday 1:00-5:00pm. Closed Christmas, Thanksgiving And New Years. Admission: $5.00 adult, $4.00 senior (65+) and $3.00 child (6-17). Note: Best for kids nearing middle school age and older, mostly because they have studied some of the science behind atomic energy. FREEBIES: Ask for the Scavenger Hunt –Search each exhibit area in the museum for clues to the answers for this pictorial scavenger hunt.***

What a fun way to learn about science!

About one-third of the museum is devoted to the World War II Manhattan Project that created the secret city of Oak Ridge...enriching uranium that is used in nuclear bombs. One-third highlights basic science and technology and one-third is devoted to fossil fuels and alternative energy sources. There are live demonstrations for audience participation, hands-on activities, and models and devices to explore, experiment and discover more about how the world works through science. Key spots are the: Solar Energy Project, Cold War/Civil Defense - model of atomic plant, sample lab diorama, and try-on assembly lab equipment, Real Robots, and Science & Tech Career Centers - modern uses for old technology facilities. Atoms and Atom Smashers - This is a regularly scheduled demonstration (2-3 times daily) that combines a discussion of basic atomic structure with a "hair raising" demonstration of static electricity. Volunteer to become a very positively charged person! Funny and fun!

Exit - 81 (west of I-75)

SECRET CITY SCENIC EXCURSION TRAIN

Oak Ridge - ***Hwy 58, East TN Technology Park Heritage Park (I-75 exit 81, northwest on Rte 321, continue NW on SR 95 for 6 miles. Then southwest on SR 58 2 miles) 37830. www.secretcityrailroad.com. Phone: (865) 241-2140. Hours: Spring, Summer and Fall season schedules. Regular Trips June - September depart on the 1st & 3rd Saturday each month at 11:00am, 1:00pm, 3:00pm. General Admission: $19.00 adult, $15.00 child (under 12).***

The northern portion of the route was featured in the movie October Sky

Ride the Atomic Train on a 12-mile tour through the once secret K-25 Manhattan Project site and enjoy the scenic beauty of the Blair Community. Each round trip travels approximately 14 miles and lasts about one hour. Trains are pulled by 1950's vintage Alco diesel locomotives. Seating is in an air-conditioned coach and a dining car, both restored from the 1940's era of passenger railroading. An open-air concession car has souvenirs and snacks for sale. They celebrate pretty much every holiday with a themed train ride so this might be a good attraction to plan ahead for, make reservations, and take a few hours out of your journey to relax and let someone else do the driving.

Exit - 68 (east of I-75)

SWEETWATER VALLEY FARM

Philadelphia - ***17988 West Lee Highway (I-75 exit 68, SR 323 east to Hwy 11, turn left) 37846. Phone: (865) 458-9192 or (877) 862-4332. www.sweetwatervalley.com. Hours: Monday-Saturday 9:00am-5:00pm. Extended store hours seasonally. Tours: Monday-Saturday 9:00am (summer). Saturdays at 10:00am & 2:00pm (spring). Pre-arranged group tours include an activity pack for each child (sm. Fee). Note: If you just stop in you can watch a video and sample - 15 minutes.***

Ever seen curds and whey?

Sweetwater Valley Farms boasts the best farmstead cheese in the state with names like Tennessee Aged Cheddar and Volunteer Jack. Their cows and what they eat are part of their secret. Stop in and see how cheese is made while tasting delicious samples. The phrase "curds and whey" turns into reality when visitors are able to observe cheesemaking thru a viewing window.

"Cheddar" becomes a verb which describes the process of pasteurization, culturing (ugh!), slabbing, draining, milling, blocking and aging.

They usually make cheese from January through June, occasionally during the summer, and then less frequently September through December. On the days they do make cheese, they have our fresh cheese curds bagged and ready to sell by 4:00 p.m. If you opt for the farm tour, you'll get a close view of the Feed Shed. Cows have 4 stomachs and need lots of food (it takes 100 lbs of feed and 50 gallons of water to make just 10 gallons of milk). They serve them 8 different grain blends made from things like cottonseed and tofu! Very interesting agricultural tour!

Exit - 60 (east of I-75)

LOST SEA

Sweetwater - ***140 Lost Sea Road (I-75 exit 60, Rte. 68, between Madisonville & Sweetwater) 37874. Phone: (423) 337-6616. www.thelostsea.com. Hours: Open daily 9:00am until 5:00pm (winter), until 6:00pm (September, October, March, April), until 7:00pm (May, June, August), until 8:00pm (July). Closed Christmas Day. Admission: $18.95 adult, $9.95 Child (5-12). Note: Level walkways on dirt floors, however some steep hills. Stroller/wheelchair accessible. Asthmatic persons may experience breathing difficulty.***

Walk thru a metal tunnel into the unbelievable site of the giant Indian council chamber (600 ft x 120 ft). Indians used the calcium deposits as toothpaste and Confederate soldiers mined the cave for saltpeter. "America's Largest Underground Lake" is home to rare Cave Flowers and cascade formations. The earliest known visitor to the cave was a saber-toothed tiger, whose fossilized remains are now in the Museum of Natural History. A guided walk to the bottom of the cavern is rewarded upon entering the lake room, where you will board large glass bottom boats for a trip into the Lost Sea. While on the trip, you will observe some of the largest rainbow trout in the United States (but, why do they taste like liver?) and learn about the 4 acre lake underground. It's hard to believe what you see here!

A giant, metal, bright yellow tunnel... not a typical cave entrance...

Before or after your tour, enjoy the relaxed atmosphere East Tennessee is famous for at the "Old Sweetwater Village." Step back in time and enjoy shaded walkways leading to authentic log cabins. Meander through a General Store, Ice Cream Parlor, Gem Mine and Glassblower. The Cavern Kitchen cafe, offers sandwiches and real pit barbeque to hungry visitors. Ample picnic facilities and a nature trail are also available. Shops in the "Old Sweetwater Village" may not be open depending on the season.

Exit - 52 (east of I-75)

MAYFIELD DAIRY FARMS TOURS

Athens - ***4 Mayfield Lane (I-75 exit 52, Mt. Verd. Turn east on Hwy 305 4.3 miles) 37303. Phone: (423) 745-2151 or (800) Mayfield. www.mayfielddairy.com. Hours: Monday-Friday 9:00am-5:00pm (CLOSED WEDNESDAYS), Saturday 9:00am-2:00pm. Admission: FREE. Tours: Tours begin every top of the hour, last about 40 minutes. Last tour is one hour before closing. Wear comfortable, non-slip shoes. Some stairs on tour. Note: Gift shop and ice cream parlor. FREEBIES: click on the link to: Fun & Learning - For Teachers - to print some fun puzzles and games.***

Get the "scoop" on the history of this dairy through a film presentation followed by a plant tour that includes how ice cream treats are made and how milk is bottled. Begin by donning a hair net and watch all the swirling and twirling and spinning and turning and churning of jugs and cartons of milk and ice cream. This fun tour includes a great look at how they make plastic milk jugs, home-made, from a handful of tiny pellets...melted and molded. It's amazing to see ice cream sandwiches made by one machine! After this excellent guided visual tour - taste some of their ice cream creations for sale (one scoop is only $1.00!). Try unique Yellow Brick Road or Turtle Tracks. This is a must-see, easy to understand, colorful factory tour! Note: if you don't have time for the tour, just sampling ice cream and buying a cheap treat is just fine...

Exit - 20 (east of I-75)

MUSEUM CENTER AT 5IVE POINTS

Cleveland - *200 Inman Street East (I-75 exit 20, follow US 11 to Inman St. east) 37311. Phone: (423) 339-5745. www.museumcenter.org. Hours: Tuesday-Friday 10:00am-5:00pm, Saturday 10:00am-3:00pm. Closed holidays. Admission: $5.00 adult, $4.00 senior & students. FREEBIES: Ask for a treasure hunt paper you complete using clues numbered throughout the museum.*

A regional history museum of the Ocoee Region. "The River of Time" core exhibit includes seven time periods dating from prehistory to today and interprets how people of this region lived, worked and played. Using video and displayed artifacts, you can meet "Fallen Sky" (an aging Cherokee), a traveling missionary, a child (petrified pants, stiff shoes, swinging washer and butter churn), a railroad conductor (progress), a black teacher, or a TVA carpenter. Great stories with hands-on activities at each station. Did you know Cleveland, Tennessee is the stove capital of the world?

Exit - 4 (west of I-75)

TENNESSEE VALLEY RAILROAD

Chattanooga - *4119 Cromwell Road (Grand Junction depot:near the Jersey Pike Exit off Highway 153 (past airport); 1 mile from I-75) 37421. Phone: (423) 894-8028 or (800) 397-5544. www.tvrail.com. Admission: $16.00 adult, $10.00 child (age 3-12). Tours: Trains run everyday, March through October; Weekends through Thanksgiving. December special theme trains only. Departures 2 to 5 times daily. Approx. one hour trip. Note: The Station has a full deli with indoor or picnic seating.*

"Missionary Ridge Local Service" is a six-mile, 50-minute roundtrip from Grand Junction Station to East Chattanooga Depot, crossing Chickamauga Creek, CSX mainline (ex-W&A), Tunnel Boulevard and Awtry Street bridges and passing through pre-Civil War Missionary Ridge Tunnel (over 950 ft. long built in 1858). If you ride the last car, you can stand out on the porch when going thru the tunnel for the best view. Passengers detrain in East Chattanooga for a layover which includes viewing the locomotive rotate on a turntable and a tour through the railyard and into the restoration shop to see work in progress before reboarding the train for the return trip. This stop looks just like a giant Thomas depot on the Island of Sodor! In the depot, a conductor may help you send a message.

Exit - 4 (west of I-75)

BOOKER T. WASHINGTON STATE PARK

Chattanooga - ***5801 Champion Road (I-75 exit 4, Hwy 153. Take exit Hwy 58, go 5 miles) 37416. Phone: (423) 894-4955. http://tnstateparks.com/parks/about/booker-t-washington. Hours: 7:00am-dark.***

Named for famous educator, Booker T. Washington, this 352-acre park is located on the shores of TVA's Chickamauga Reservoir. They have a year-round lodge and seasonal boat-launching ramp. The park has a large olympic size pool with diving board and a childrens' wading pool. The pool is open from early summer through Labor Day. Park recreation activities include biking trail (single track on 6-mile loop), hiking, field games, playgrounds, basketball, badminton, horseshoes, volleyball and board games. The park has 30 or more individual picnic sites to choose from. Sites are located by the lake, ball courts, pool and there are several in wooded areas. Each is equipped with grills and water spigots nearby. Picnic areas are wheelchair accessible.

Exit - 3A (east of I-75)

AUDUBON ACRES

Chattanooga ***(East Brainerd) - 900 North Sanctuary Road (From I-75, take Exit 3A to E. Brainerd Road – East) 37421. www.chattanoogaaudubon.org. Phone: (423) 892-1499. Hours: Monday-Saturday 9:00am - 5:00pm, Sunday 1:00pm-5pm. Admission: Visitors Center is FREE. General admission to grounds and trails: $4.00 adult, $2.00 child (5-12).***

Over 100 acres of wildlife sanctuary with 4 miles of trails, a pedestrian suspension bridge over the South Chickamauga Creek and a reconstructed Cherokee cabin (dates back to the 1700s and is said to be the birth place of Cherokee naturalist, Spring Frog). Little Owl Village is the location of a Mississippian Era Native American village in the 1400's and 1500's. This village is believed to be the location of the first contact between local Native Americans and Spanish explorers. It is being slowly restored as records indicate it was burned to the ground when the explorers invaded in the 1500's. The Visitor Center has a timeline exhibit and a gift shop.

Exit - 2 (west of I-75) / I-24 exit 184

LAKE WINNEPESAUKAH AMUSEMENT PARK & SOAK YA WATERPARK

Chattanooga - *Lakeview Drive (I-24 East to the Moore Road (exit 184) and go straight to the 2nd traffic light and turn right onto McBrien Road) 37412. Phone: (877) LAKE-WIN. www.lakewinnie.com. Hours: Weekends 10:00am-8:00 or 10:00pm (April-mid-September). Open Wednesday-Friday also (May-early August). Admission: $5.00 (age 3+). $27.00 unlimited rides wristband. Individual Ride Tickets are available for $1.00 each. (rides range from 2-5 tickets).*

Free concerts featuring Christian, Country or Rock music artists are regular items on the Lake Winnie calendar of events. Thirty rides with exciting rides like the Cannon Ball Roller Coaster and the Pipeline Plunge, an intense water ride featuring a five-story maze of pipes that lead to a wet and wild final splash. Kiddie Land at Lake Winnie has dozens of attractions designed for the youngest of your family members. The Stay and Play Hideaway is like a giant fort with "manual" fun - no gears or gizmos - just climbing and sliding. Wholesome and old-fashioned.

Soakya has a floating river, soak-n-slide, splish-n-splash, waterworks and Zoom flume.

Exit - 2 (west of I-75) / I-24 exit 181

CHATTANOOGA ZOO AT WARNER PARK

Chattanooga - *301 North Holtzclaw Avenue (exit 181 off I-24, right at end of ramp, left on 23rd St. for .8 miles, right on Holtzclaw) 37404. Phone: (423) 697-1322. www.chattzoo.org. Hours: 9:00am-5:00pm (April-October). Closed: Christmas Day, New Year's Day, Martin Luther King Day, Thanksgiving Day. Admission: $8.95 adult, $6.95 senior (65+), $5.95 child (3-12). FREEBIES: Education page has activities to do while visiting the zoo (scroll to bottom of page).*

A 5-acre zoo offering exotic animals and an animal contact area. The Warner Park Ranch Exhibit invites visitors to directly interact with the 'ranch' animals. The Gombe Forest features chimpanzees, the Himalayan Passage features red pandas, the highly endangered "Bali-Mynahs", and Asian Elongated tortoises, and the Zoo's newest exhibit, the Cougar Express, features Mountain Lions. Newer exhibits feature lively chimps, a spider monkey habitat, and an African Aviary home to Crowned Cranes, a Camel encounter and Pygmy Goats kids can pet.

Exit - 2 (west of I-75) / I-24 exit 178 South

LOOKOUT MOUNTAIN INCLINE RAILWAY

> The 72.7% grade of the track near the top gives the Incline the unique distinction of being the steepest passenger railway in the world!

Chattanooga (Lookout Mtn) - ***827 E. Brow Road/3917 St. Elmo Ave. (Lower Station) (near I-24, 3 blocks south of Hwy. 11, 41, 64 or 72 on Hwy. 58) 37350. www.ridetheincline.com. Phone: (423) 821-4224. Hours: Saturday/Sunday 9am-7pm. Monday-Friday 9:00am - 6:00pm - last round trip leaves one hour before closing time. Closed Christmas Day only. Admission: Tickets may be purchased at either the Lower or Upper Station and at the Chattanooga Visitors Center. Round trip $15.00 adult, Half price child (3-12) and senior (65+). $1.00 discount for one way fares. Combo prices with other Lookout Mountain Attractions offered. Tours: Approximately 10 minutes, one way. Note: Candy Connection, Snack Shoppe at Upper Station. Seasonal gift shop at Lower Station.***

"America's Most Amazing Mile" delights guests as the Incline climbs historic Lookout Mountain. Chattanooga's surrounding mountains and valleys come in full view as the trolley-style railcars carry you high. The free observation deck at the Upper Station is the highest overlook on Lookout Mountain. While at the upper station, be sure to visit the Incline's machine room where the giant gears and cables are put into motion. Be sure to check out the Incline Centennial Exhibits, too. And while you are traveling on the Incline, you will pass another Incline car on the single track. At the halfway point of the track, the two Incline cars pass along side each other. The "switch" allows the two cars to travel on a single track system. Make sure you wave to the folks in the other car. At 600 steep feet per minute, this is really cool!

BATTLES FOR CHATTANOOGA ELECTRIC MAP & MUSEUM

Chattanooga (Lookout Mtn) - *1110 E. Brow Road (I-24 W exit 178, Lookout Mtn., to Broad St. S (Hwy. 41), follow signs) 37350. Phone: (423) 821-2812 or (423) 821-7786 (Point Park). www.battlesforchattanooga.com. Hours: Daily 9:00am-6:00pm (summer). 10:00am-5:00pm (rest of year). Admission: $6-$8.00.*

The kids' favorite feature will be the three-dimensional electronic battle map presentation of Chattanooga's Civil War history featuring 5,000 miniature soldiers, 650 lights, sound effects and exceptional details of the major battles which were fought here in November of 1863. Hear and see about Chattanooga's Battle Above the Clouds and Sherman's assault on Missionary ridge before his historic March To the Sea. This is just long enough to help you visually see the battle from afar and understand the strategies involved without getting boring.

Lights tell the story of the battles

LOOKOUT MOUNTAIN BATTLEFIELD

Chattanooga (Lookout Mtn) - *East Brow Road (atop Lookout Mountain) 37350. www.nps.gov/chch/.Phone: (706) 866-9241Ranger or (423) 821-7786 Visitor Center. Hours: Daily 8:30am-5:00pm except Christmas. Admission: $5.00 per each adult (age 16+) for Point Park entrance gate. Pay by the honor system. Note: Hiking and horse trails. Ranger guided talks and Civil War era demonstrations are conducted during the summer season.*

In the fall of 1863, two armies clashed in an effort to gain control of vital transportation hubs. The battle was fought over a four square mile area that was covered with dense woods and thick underbush, unlike most battles that occur in open fields. Both sides were winning at different points. After you learn about the battles, be sure to take a walk over to POINT PARK - site of the famous Battle Above the Clouds (learn why it's called that...two kinds of fog that day) & preserved/interpreted portions of the Chickamauga battlefields - the battles that sealed the fate of the Confederacy. The Visitors Center is home to the large mural, the "Battle of Lookout Mountain" with an audio presentation that helps you visually locate the

See the sites of the "Battle Above the Clouds"

details of this enormous mural painted by an eye-witness. Cravens' House (open for touring) was the site of some of the fiercest fighting, serving as headquarters for both sides. Why did soldiers and reporters take the house apart to stay warm?

Exit - 2 (west of I-75) / I-24 exit 178

RUBY FALLS

Tip: Be sure to have the kids use the restroom before touring - only one way in and out.

Chattanooga (Lookout Mtn) - ***1720 S. Scenic Hwy. (I-24 exit 178, follow signs to Lookout Mtn.) 37409. Phone: (423) 821-2544. www.rubyfalls.com. Hours: Daily 8:00am-8:00pm. Closed Christmas Day. Admission: $18.95 adult, $10.95 child (3-12). Combo prices with other Lookout Mountain Attractions offered. Tours: Minimum time for caverns tour is 1-1/2 hours. Guided tours take you on a one mile easy hike. Note: Lookout Mountain Tower (stairs), the Fun Forest Playground, and gift shops/snack bar.***

The thundering 145 foot waterfall inside historic Lookout Mountain is the world's highest underground waterfall. A powerful earthquake, or more likely a series of them, caused the layers of rock in the Mountain to bend or fold upwards... cracks or crevices then occurred. Take a descending elevator tour that opens to cave paths of the Lookout Mountain Caverns. Look for rock formations that resemble steak and potatoes, an elephant's foot or an angel's wing. These caves were once used by Native Americans and Civil War troops for living space and as a hideout for the outlaws. The 1/2 hour walk is worth it as you enter the Falls room! The "light & sound" show that magically, spiritually occurs once you're by the Falls is awesome! Lots of oohs and aahs here...

ROCK CITY

Chattanooga (Lookout Mtn) - ***1400 Patten Road (I-24 exit 178 south, follow signs to Lookout) 30750. Phone: (706) 820-2531 or (877) 820-0759. www.seerockcity.com. Hours: 8:30am - 5:00pm every day except Christmas. Open later in the summer***

and peak shoulder seasons. Admission: $19.95 adult, $11.95 child (3-12). Combo prices with other Lookout Mountain Attractions offered. Tours: Self-guided tours take 60-90 minutes. The trail includes Fairyland Caverns and Mother Goose Village for kids. Note: Cornerstone Station soda fountain.

The Grand Corridor welcomes you to unusual rock formations carved by nature. Look for the quiet, enchanted gnomes and elves around many corners...there's a wonderful outdoor family adventure ahead! Start at the Needles Eye - narrow passage. Deer Park - observe rare white Fallow deer in the wild – descendants of species transported here from Europe in the 1930s (our family thought they looked right out of a storybook!). Swing-A-Long Bridge - provides visitors with both a challenge and a breathtaking view. This engineering marvel stretches a full 180 feet through the blue sky. Lover's Leap - do you believe the stories of Indian braves and maidens thrown from this cliff? Seven States Flag Court - from the time of the Civil War, people noted you could see 7 states from this lookout - Alabama, Georgia, Kentucky, North Carolina, South Carolina, Tennessee, and Virginia. Fat Man's Squeeze - think thin! And, the 1,000 Ton Balanced Rock - how does it stay up? Amusing Gnomes hang out near Fairytale scenes. Garnet Carter and his wife first developed this land and, because of some construction delays, ended up inventing miniature golf and creating a "rock" park!

Exit - 2 (west of I-75) / I-24 exit 178

INTERNATIONAL TOWING & RECOVERY HALL OF FAME MUSEUM

Chattanooga - ***3315 Broad Street (north of Lookout Mtn. Incline) 37408. Phone: (423) 267-3132. www.internationaltowingmuseum.org. Hours: Monday-Saturday 9:00am-5:00pm, Weekends 11:00am-5:00pm. Shorter winter hours on weekdays.***

Closed major holidays. Admission: $10.00 adult, $9.00 senior (55+) and $6.00 child (6-14).

Enjoy restored antique wreckers and equipment, industry-related displays of tools, unique equipment, and pictorial histories of manufacturers who pioneered a worldwide industry. Model T's & Model A's with cranes and wreckers are fun to see. Chattanooga was chosen as the museum's home because the industry's first wrecker was fabricated a few blocks away from the museum at the Ernest Holmes Company. Understand the engineering behind a wrecker with exhibits like the drapery rod example. Tons of toy & collectible tow trucks are on display and available to purchase - a little boy's dream.

Exit - 2 (west of I-75) / I-24 exit 178

CHATTANOOGA CHOO CHOO HOLIDAY INN RESORT

The FREE shuttle bus to downtown is right next door and highly recommended for any downtown site visits.

Chattanooga - ***1400 Market Street (I-75 exit 2 to I-24 exit 178, take ramp towards downtown onto Market and travel .4 mile to hotel) 37402. Phone: (423) 266-5000 or (800) TRACK-29. www.choochoo.com.***

"It's a train. It's a song. It's a hotel." This is the hotel made famous in the Glenn Miller song (hear it on their website). The 30-acre vacation family complex includes a 1900's train station (now a lobby and restaurant), three pools (one indoors) with waterfalls and slides, casual restaurants (like the Silver Diner car) and snackeries, shops, an arcade and overnight lodging in regular rooms, suites or actual Victorian parlor cars on the property. They have a trolley ride ($0.50) you can take thru the complex and the kids will like the largest

model railroad museum in the South display (very small admission). The water garden is filled with more than 400 fish. Try the Station House Restaurant where your server is taking your order one minute, on stage singing the next. Maybe make it more special by ordering a Shirley Temple for the kids with dinner. Their pools and train station environment make this the perfect family stay in Chattanooga! Admission: Rooms and great family packages from $99.00 - $229.00, depending on time of year and type of room, plus amount of perks included.______________________________________

BESSIE SMITH CULTURAL CENTER

Chattanooga - ***200 East Martin Luther King Jr. Blvd. (I-75 exit 2, follow I-24 west to exit 178 east into downtown. Turn right a few blocks past the Chatt Choo Choo hotel) 37403. Phone: (423) 266-8658. www.bessiesmithcc.org. Hours: Monday-Friday 10:00am-5:00pm, Saturday Noon-4:00pm. Admission: $7.00 adult, $5.00 senior & student, $3.00 child (6-12).***

The exhibits begin with a "Wall of Respect", dedicated to African-Americans who have achieved first in their professional endeavors. After passing the "Wall", the visitor travels through an authentic African dwelling and a section with a variety of statues, tools and artifacts depicting the life, work, art and worship of Africans before they came to America. There are other displays of Chattanooga African-American Civil War involvement, their achievements in sports and performing arts, portrayals of family and professional life and even a focus on the Civil Rights movement. The achievements of Bessie Smith are remembered at the annual Riverbend Festival and throughout the museum.

Exit - 2 (west of I-75) / I-24 exit 178

CHATTANOOGA DUCKS TOURS

Chattanooga - ***503 Market Street (5th & Market) 37402. Phone: (423) 756-DUCK. www.chattanoogaducks.com. Admission: $22.00 adult, $20.00 senior, $11.00 child (3-12). Tickets are available at the Visitors Center or on board. Tours: Best to call for reservations first. 45 minute tours. Ducks leave hourly from 10:00am-dusk. Sundays Noon-8:00pm. (May-October). Generally, weekends only, 1:00-5:00pm, weather pending (March, April). Note: Command Post Museum: check out how East Tennessee heroes contributed to the largest wars in world history.***

The Chattanooga Duck's are unique ex-military amphibious vehicles made for the US Army to land troops on beaches during wartime. The Ducks are equally at home on land as well as water. Begin downtown with a "quacky" tour of famous sites. Then, hit the water as they tell you about Maclellan Island,

the Tennessee River and places of natural and historical interest...most only accessible by boat. Hopefully, you'll observe a Great Blue Heron or migrating Warblers. The birds live among squirrels, rabbits, raccoons, beaver, fox, ducks, geese and other waterfowl. Good tour to do before you explore the city...they point out many sites along the way that might interest you. Buy a "Duck Quacker" whistle before you tour so you can "quack all the day"!

CHATTANOOGA HISTORY CENTER

Chattanooga - ***2 West Aquarium Way 37402. Phone: (423) 265-3247. www.chattanoogahistory.org.***

UPDATE: CURRENTLY IN MIDDLE OF EXPANSION. CENTER IS NOT OPEN TO PUBLIC AS OF LATE 2015. Check their website for grand re-opening dates. The Chattanooga Regional History Museum is the place you'll meet the region's peoples. Events are illustrated in five historical periods: Early Land, Early People; The Cherokee Nation; Growth & Conflict; The New South; and The Dynamo of Dixie. Did you know Coca-Cola's bottling franchise, Moon Pies and Little Debbie's were first made here?

CREATIVE DISCOVERY MUSEUM

Chattanooga - ***321 Chestnut Street (Riverfront District) (I-24 to downtown, or then US 27 N to exit 1-C, 4th Street to Chestnut) 37402. Phone: (423) 756-2738. www.cdmfun.org. Hours: Daily 9:30am-5:30pm (summer). Daily 10:00am-5:00pm (September-May). Closed Wednesdays (September-February). Last ticket sold one hour prior to closing. Closed Thanksgiving and Christmastime. Admission: $12.95 general (age 2+) or $9.95 per person (show Aquarium ticket or military ID). Note: Great gift shop for educational toys.***

Learning through play...Love It!

Specially designed for children ages 2-12, this museum is full of hands-on discoveries in art (where you can sculpt, print and puppet). See your face as a Dali or a Warhol painting. Let your kids' imaginations run wild digging for dino bones or making music. Play giant instruments. Sing in a canyon, a shower or a concert hall! This place has the widest variety of musical instruments to try. And, with each sound, a simple description of the people behind the music (this is our favorite part of the site and the best we've ever seen)! In the Inventors Clubhouse learn about local inventors, then make your own inventions. "RiverPlay" has a two story climbing structure consisting of nets, slides, a spiral staircase, and even a lift to provide access for visitors who use wheelchairs. A multi-level riverboat is nearby - a pilot's cabin and crane lift are there. Underneath the climbing structure is a watercourse where kids can sail boats, learn about dams and locks, create river currents, and use water pressure to spin wheels and tip buckets. Can you climb all the way to the crows nest and raise the mast...it's high! Kids can visit the Little Yellow House or soon, climb up to the Rooftop Fun Factory. Explore the world of simple machines as you enjoy sound, movement and fun high up on the rooftop.

Exit - 2 (west of I-75) / I-24 exit 178

TENNESSEE AQUARIUM

Chattanooga - ***One Broad Street (I-24 to downtown, follow I-27 N to exit 1C, turn left at 2nd light) 37401. Phone: (423) 267-FISH. www.tnaqua.org. Hours: Daily 10:00am-6pm (ET). IMAX shows begin at 11:00am. Closed Thanksgiving and Christmas. Extended hours on weekends, holidays and summertime. Admission: $29.95 adult, $18.95 child (3-12). IMAX tickets extra $6.00. FREEBIES: Downloadable Activities like penguin quizzes, a treasure map and scavenger hunts are printable from: KidsTeachers/DownloadableActivities. Educators: guides on specific themes are on same page. Note: Tennessee Aquarium River Gorge Explorer tours - 70 passenger high-speed catamaran cruising into the Tennessee River Gorge. Aquarium naturalist leads you into this protected habitat, pointing out wildlife and historic points of interest along the way. ($21-27.00 extra per person).***

The Tennessee Aquarium tells the story of fresh water ecosystems. You follow the Tennessee River from its Appalachian beginnings through the swampwaters of the Mississippi River and into the Gulf of Mexico (lots of colorful fish), making side trips to some of the world's other great rivers. Our favorite area was Discovery Hall - pet a fish!-what does it feel like? Look for baby alligators in the nursery. Along the way, visitors travel through a 60-foot canyon and two living forests. In the rivers, you'll see the only mammals on-site...river otters and their playful antics. A look at the creepy alligator snapping turtle (prehistoric) or side-necked turtles is a highlight, too.

The Tennessee Aquarium has expanded (as have most all the museums on the riverfront). The addition presents a saltwater adventure that explores the mysteries of the ocean. Ocean Journey is the place to touch sharks and sting rays. Immerse yourself in the Butterfly Garden (very friendly creatures) or dive into a secret cave reef and discover the weird world of boneless beauties. A funny site are the live penguins on Penguin Rock.

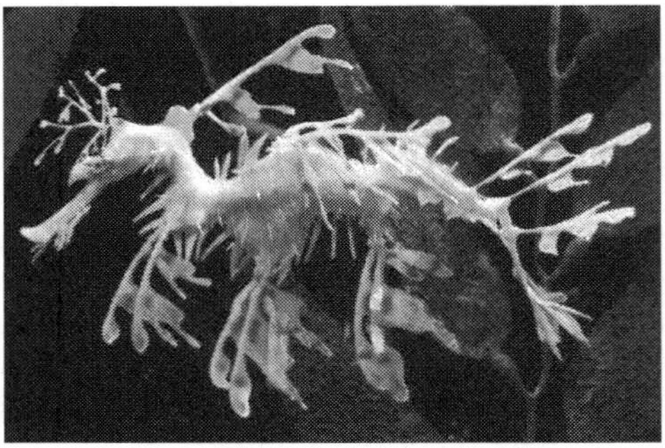

A Sea Dragon...amazing - looked like a living, leafy, SALAD...

The jelly fish and giant crab were big hits with the kids.

Be sure to go online to the KidsTeachers icon and download some fun games and activity sheets to occupy your drive to Chattanooga. Once here, trust us you will find loads of educational toys to purchase in their giant gift shop.

TENNESSEE

Exit - 2 (west of I-75) / I-24 exit 178

CHATTANOOGA RIVERBOAT CO. SOUTHERN BELLE

Chattanooga - *201 Riverfront Pkwy, Pier 2 @ the Landing (Ross's Landing down from Aquarium) 37402. www.chattanoogariverboat.com. Phone: (423) 266-4488 or (800) 766-2784. Admission: (see brochure or online schedule) Sightseeing Cruises run $7.00-$15.00, Breakfast and Lunch Cruises run $13.00-$25.00. Family Nite Dinner Cruise and Monday nite Pizza Cruises are more. Tours: Boarding 30 minutes before departure (April-December). Basically 1-3 departures in the afternoon, one in the evening for dinner.*

Enjoy the informative commentary on the city's history as you float down the beautiful Tennessee River. Familiar sights like Lookout Mountain and Chattanooga's skyline are leisurely viewed as you snack or eat a meal. Entertainment on many evening dinner cruises includes magicians and dance bands. Look for "themed" special events. If you're going on a meal cruise, be sure to bring along travel games (cards, coloring books, crayons) while the kids wait for food. The atmosphere is relaxed so it's a nice cruise for a lazy day along the river.

BLUFF VIEW ART DISTRICT

Chattanooga - *Corner of High & East 2nd Street (I-24, take Hwy 27 N, exit 1C to 4th St. to Art District) 37403. www.bluffviewartdistrict.com. Phone: (423) 265-5033.*

Love to get out and stretch, sample treats and notice some modern art? Peer through the windows of The Chocolate Kitchen, the Courtyard & Pastry Kitchen, or the Bakery and Pasta Kitchen to get a sneak peek at the delicious concoctions being served at the District's fine restaurants. Now, grab a snack, dessert or meal at a café or restaurant in the area. If you still want more art...head over to the Hunter Museum of Art to view changing and permanent

exhibits of regional fame (along the Tennessee River Walk, 423-267-0968 or ***www.huntermuseum.org***, Open daily, Admission). The "Big Julie" and the "Fundraiser" sculptures are of interest (one is a life-like in the main lobby... amazing). Much of the modern glassworks are colorful with unusual shapes.

COOLIDGE PARK AND WALNUT STREET BRIDGE

Chattanooga - ***Tennessee Riverpark (across the river from the Tenn. Aquarium) 37405. Phone: (423) 757-2142. www.hamiltontn.gov/tnriverpark/. Hours: Park: sunrise to midnight. Carousel: Monday-Saturday 11:00am-6:00pm, Sunday 1:00-6:00pm. Fountains: Daily 8:00am-10:30pm (April-October). Admission: Carousel rides: $1.00 adult, $0.50 senior and child (13 & under). Miscellaneous: Park anywhere downtown and pick up the trolley or walk to the Bluff View District - then walk over the bridge with a picnic basket or take out lunch from one of the assorted local cafes.***

The Walnut Street Bridge is a fun way to take a stroll...

Once downtown by the river, start your excursion by popping the top of a cold cola and snacking on Moon Pies (locally made) while you walk the WALNUT STREET pedestrian BRIDGE over to COOLIDGE PARK. Check out the Sculpture Garden outside the HUNTER MUSEUM as you enter the bridge. This is truly Americana at it's best. Stroll across the world's longest pedestrian bridge, play in the Park's interactive water fountain and on the Walnut Wall Climbing Facility, or ride on the antique carousel. The carousel was made by another favorite, HORSIN AROUND CARVING SCHOOL in nearby Soddy Daisy. People will be seen walking, biking, Frisbee throwing, playing badmitten or volleyball, splashing in the fountains or just picnicking on the grass. Water spurts from both ground-level jets, and to the surprise and delight of their targets, the mouths and snouts of stone animals (lions, tigers & bears). The park hosts open-air performances and has a Chattanooga Theatre Centre presenting regular plays.

Exit - 2 (west of I-75) / I-24 exit 175

CHATTANOOGA NATURE CENTER & REFLECTION RIDING

Chattanooga - ***399 Garden Road (I-24W to exit 175, turn left onto Brown's Ferry, go to Cunnings Hwy, turn left; follow signs) 37419. www.reflectionriding.org/nature-center/. Phone: (423) 821-1160. Hours: Wednesday-Saturday 9:30am-4:00pm. Sundays 12:30pm-4:00pm. Open Tuesday each Autumn. Closed winter weekdays. Admission: $10.00 adult, $7.00 senior (65+) and child (4-11). Note: While visiting the***

Center, children can learn what its like to be a real naturalist by checking out one of the Discovery Forest Backpacks (rental $3.50). Packed with study and field guides, binoculars, a microscope, and more...your child's next visit will become much more than a walk through the woods.

Need a little break from the city? Go just past Lookout Mountain to an area where you can get out and walk or drive! Either way, its winding trails take you to a hidden place of discovery for kids and a nice break for parents. DISCOVERY FOREST TREEHOUSE is a structure built among the arms of a 100-year-old Overcup Oak

in the heart of the Nature Center's lowland forest wetlands. Stained glass works and many more pieces make it one of the most unique treehouses in the world. WILDLIFE WANDERLAND exhibit area: The centerpiece of this area is the Red Wolf exhibit where daily programming educates visitors. Unlike a zoo, the Wanderland holds only native birds and animals that are unable to be released because of their injuries and/or extensive human contact. If you have time, enter the REFLECTION RIDING Garden area (by car, bike or walking). The three-mile driving road (which gives the Riding its name) invites visitors to "ride" through the changes each season. Labels and signs tell of the horticulture, geology, history and geography of the area.

Mile - 1 (east of I-75)

TENNESSEE WELCOME CENTER

Hamilton - ***(0.7 miles north of GA state line). Phone: (423) 894.6399. All welcome centers are open and staffed 24 hours a day, 365 days a year. Business Hours has tourism staff on hand. Otherwise, plenty of brochures on display and to take. Public restrooms and vending machines are available at all times.***

No dump stations are located at any of these locations. No overnight parking is allowed. There is a two-hour parking limit. NO REST AREAS OPEN in Tennessee off I-75!

Chapter 5 GEORGIA

Curious about hundreds of fun places in the lighter gray areas? See *Kids Love Georgia*

DEAR GEORGIA TRAVELER:

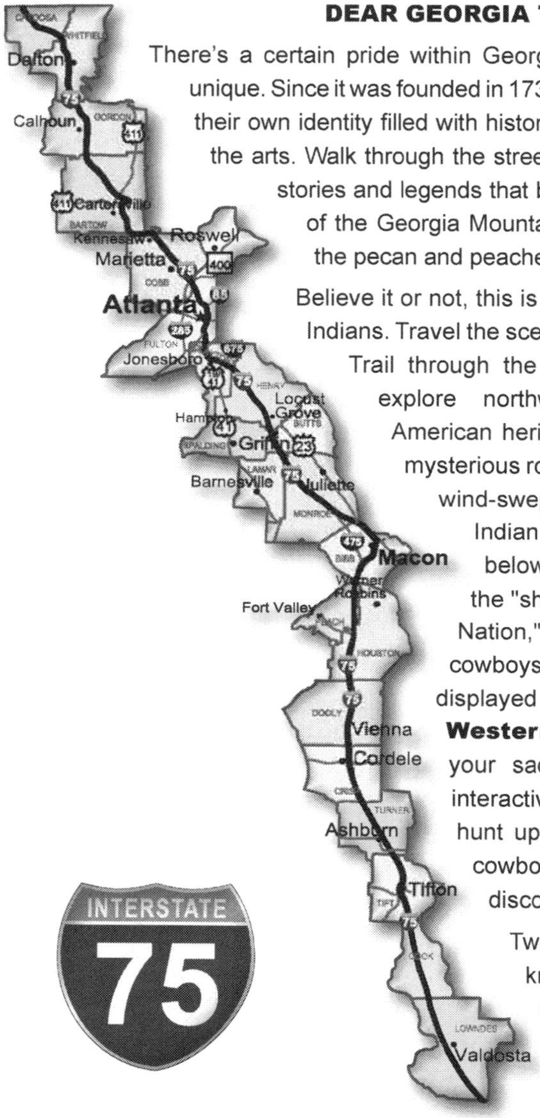

There's a certain pride within Georgia that makes this state unique. Since it was founded in 1733, Georgians have sought their own identity filled with history, modern museums, and the arts. Walk through the streets and be inspired by the stories and legends that blow from the sweet pines of the Georgia Mountains to the wetland soil of the pecan and peaches in the South.

Believe it or not, this is the land of Cowboys and Indians. Travel the scenic route of the Chieftains Trail through the Appalachian foothills to explore northwest Georgia's Native American heritage. Follow a path from mysterious rock formations high atop a wind-swept summit and ceremonial Indian mounds on the river bank below (**Etowah Mounds**), to the "showplace of the Cherokee Nation," **New Echota**. And the cowboys – well they are proudly displayed in art form at **Booth Western Art Museum**. Grab your saddlebag and go on an interactive art journey scavenger hunt upstairs, then play pretend cowboy or cowgirl in the clever discovery room downstairs.

Two things Atlanta is most known for are: Coca-Cola and fish? Yes, the **World Of Coca-Cola** and the **Georgia Aquarium** are both in downtown Atlanta and worth a definite stop. After a brief orientation, guests are let loose exploring the land of cola at Bottle Works production line, meeting a soda jerk and ending your tour at Taste It – sampling galore! Beluga whales, whale sharks, 8 million gallons of water – oh my! The world's largest aquarium is separated into different "worlds" so every child can change his attention to the overwhelming new waters and sea critters in each world without burning out too fast. Expend whatever energy is left in the playspace area full of climbing and touching interactives that let kids act like fish swimming upstream...

Visit the **Center for Puppetry Arts** if you are looking for an outrageous or mildly eccentric show. Parents love the concept of the Puppetry center as it seeks to take the child through a process of creativity – some hands on. First, view famous puppets, then watch a flawless puppet show, and finally create your own puppet to take home.

From the battlefields of the Civil War to the center of the Civil Rights Movement, Atlanta has been making history. In the 1860's, history took a turn for the worse with the advent of the Civil War. To get a feel for the state's pitied soul, plan a visit to **Margaret Mitchell's House** (the author of *Gone with the Wind)* in downtown Atlanta. She was quite a character. Another charismatic Georgian came forward 100 years after the Civil War. The transition from the Civil War era to the era of Civil Rights was successfully carried out by people like Atlanta native **Dr. Martin Luther King Jr**., (National Historic Site) a Nobel Peace Prize winner, who preached for justice and social change.

Two more tours that are unique to Atlanta: CNN Studio Tours and Turner Field Tours. For children four and older, the **CNN Studio Tour** is an exciting way to discover how a newsroom operates. Listen to behind-the-scenes action of the actual newsroom, see what it takes to put a news broadcast together and even learn how the weather map works. Another behind the scenes tour is open at the Atlanta Braves home field: **Turner Field Tours**. Go through the museum and then explore the ball park from the tippy top to deep into the locker rooms.

If you're staying overnight in Atlanta, here's a recommendation: Stay at populated exits with many hotels, restaurants and RV parks to choose from. Heading northbound, be sure to stay in a suburb like Marietta (so you avoid rush hour traffic in the morning). Heading southbound, stay in a suburb just south of the airport.

Begin your tour of Middle Georgia at a truly Southern place – the **Whistle Stop Café** in Juliette. A national forest, wildlife refuge and state parks surround this sleepy little town and this famous little café. Get out and stretch your legs or sit on the porch and rock awhile before you try some old-fashioned specialties like homemade Fried Green Tomatoes. Remember, the secret's in the sauce...

Next, take the outerbelt <u>around</u> Macon if you are passing through, stay on I-75 if you want to go <u>into</u> Macon. Start your adventure at the beginning—

Ocmulgee National Monument is one of the nation's most important archaeological sites. Survey the landscape from atop ancient Indian mounds, step inside a 1,000 year-old ceremonial earthlodge, hike along mysterious river trails and study artifacts dating back 10,000 years! Then, shoot baskets and kick field goals at the **Georgia Sports Hall of Fame** in Macon. See how Georgia geography, mathematics, science and history relate to sports on themed computer programs, and watch Georgia sports greats on a huge screen! Pretty much every exhibit here is visitor interactive so plan on being active.

As you progress south you'll notice the terrain changes some and you start to see more orchards along the highway. You'll find many vendors at the exits, even in the gas stations. Yes, Georgia Grown products like peaches and pecans really do grow along the highway and are sold by many roadside markets. See for yourself at **Lane Southern Orchards** in Fort Valley - a fourth generation family farm with a Roadside Market featuring Georgia's seasonal produce in a giant Peachy gift shop and Café (guess what flavor ice cream they serve most?). From mid-May through mid-August, sweet Georgia peaches are in season. This is the best chance to see those little peaches line up like soldiers and get washed, dried and pruned on the colorful packing lines. It's all about pecans from October through January.

"All Aboard!" Georgia's rolling park. The **SAM Shortline** Train's 1949 railcars travel past pecan groves and country farms with stops in towns along the way. We highly recommend this as the preferred method to explore President Jimmy Carter's hometown and the Habitat for Humanities Global Village. You can pick the train up at **Georgia Veterans State Park** & the Lake Blackshear Resort in Cordele (pronounced Core-Deal). Rent an overnight room or condo to base from this well-maintained and active property that offers many family deals.

As you get to Tifton, site of Georgia's **Agrirama** - 'Georgia's Living History Center' - you have an excellent opportunity to stop, stretch your legs and see some very interesting exhibits. The area's wetland soil is unique and very productive for crop farming. After Tifton, the landscape becomes fields of crops and glimpses of swamps all the way to Florida. Most people make a pit stop in Valdosta, home to a favorite amusement and waterpark – **Wild Adventures** Theme Park.

ACTIVITIES AT A GLANCE

AMUSEMENTS

Exit - 265 - *Whitewater Park, Six Flags*
Exit - 265 - *The Big Chicken*
Exit - 82 - *World's Largest Peanut*
Exit - 13 - *Wild Adventures Theme Park*

ANIMALS & FARMS

Exit - 248C - *Georgia Aquarium*
Exit - 246 - *Zoo Atlanta*
Exit - 218 - *Southern Belle Farm*
Exit - 212 - *Noah's Ark Animal Rehabilitation Center*

HISTORY

Exit - 350 - *Chickamauga National Military Park*
Exit - 317 - *New Echota Historic Site*
Exit - 288 - *Bartow History Center*
Exit - 288 - *Etowah Indian Mounds Historic Site*
Exit - 273 - *Southern Museum Of Civil War & Locomotive History*
Exit - 269 - *Kennesaw Mountain National Battlefield Park*
Exit - 255 - *Atlanta History Center*
Exit - 249A (SB Only) / 248B (NB Only) - *Apex Museum*
Exit - 248D - *Martin Luther King Jr. National Historic Site*
Exit - 248C - *Jimmy Carter Library And Museum*
Exit - 248A (SB Only)/248B (NB Only) - *Georgia State Capitol & Museum*
Exit - 246 - *Atlanta Cyclorama*
Exit - 165 / I-16 Exit 2 - *Ocmulgee National Monument Indian Mounds*
Exit - 165 / I-16 Exit 2 - *Tubman African American Museum*
Exit - 101 - *Georgia Veterans State Park*
Exit - 63B - *Agrirama*

MUSEUMS

Exit - 250 - *Paper Museum At IPST*
Exit - 250 - *Federal Reserve Bank Of Atlanta Visitors Center & Monetary Museum*
Exit - 248C - *Imagine It! The Children's Museum Of Atlanta*
Exit - 146 - *Museum Of Aviation*
Exit - 109 - *Georgia Cotton*
Exit - 82 - *Crime And Punishment Museum & Last Meal Café*

OUTDOOR EXPLORING

Exit - 285 - *Red Top Mountain State Park*
Exit - 278 - *Cauble Park*
Exit - 250 - *Atlanta Botanical Garden*
Exit - 248C - *Centennial Olympic Park*
Exit - 233 - *Reynolds Memorial Nature Preserve*
Exit - 198 - *High Falls State Park*
Exit - 39 - *Reed Bingham State Park*

SCIENCE

Exit - 293 - Tellus Northwest Georgia Science Museum
Exit - 248C - Fernbank Museum Of Natural History
Exit - 164 - Museum Of Arts & Sciences

SPORTS

Exit - 165 / I-16 Exit 2 - *Georgia Sports Hall Of Fame*

SUGGESTED LODGING & DINING

Exit - 333 - *Hampton Inn Dalton*
Exit - 333 - *Dalton Depot Restaurant*
Exit - 249D - *The Varsity*
Exit - 186 - *Whistle Stop Café - Fried Green Tomatoes*
Exit - 169 - *Courtyard By Marriott*
Exit - 164 - *Nu-Way Weiners*
Exit - 109 - *Ellis Brothers Pecans*
Exit - 101 - *Lake Blackshear Resort*

ACTIVITIES AT A GLANCE

THE ARTS

Exit - 288 - *Booth Western Art Museum*

Exit - 250 - *Margaret Mitchell House & Museum*

Exit - 250 - *Center For Puppetry Arts*

Exit - 249D - *High Museum Of Art*

Exit - 164 - *Sidney Lanier Cottage*

TOURS

Exit - 333 - *Dalton Carpet Mill Tours / Visitors Center*

Exit - 252 - *Georgia Dome Tours*

Exit - 248C - *World Of Coca-Cola*

Exit - 248C - *CNN Studio Tour*

Exit - 246 - *Atlanta Braves Museum / Turner Field Tours*

TOURS *(cont.)*

Exit - 218 - *Atlanta Motor Speedway Tours*

Exit - 165 / I-16 Exit 2 - *Around Town Tours - Macon*

Exit - 142 - *Lane Southern Orchards*

Exit - 101 - *S A M Shortline Excursion Train*

WELCOME CENTERS

Exit - 352 Mile - *Georgia Visitor Information Center*

Exit - 2 Mile - *Georgia Visitor Information Center*

GENERAL INFORMATION

Contact the services of interest. Request to be added to their mailing lists.

- ☐ Georgia State Parks (800) 864-7275 www.gastateparks.org
- ☐ Georgia Travel Information (800) VISIT GA or www.exploregeorgia.org
- ☐ Macon-Bibb County Convention & Visitors Bureau - www.maconga.org
- ☐ Atlanta Convention & Visitors Bureau - (800) Atlanta or www.atlanta.net
- ☐ Cartersville Area Tourism - www.notatlantaga.org

Travel Journal & Notes:

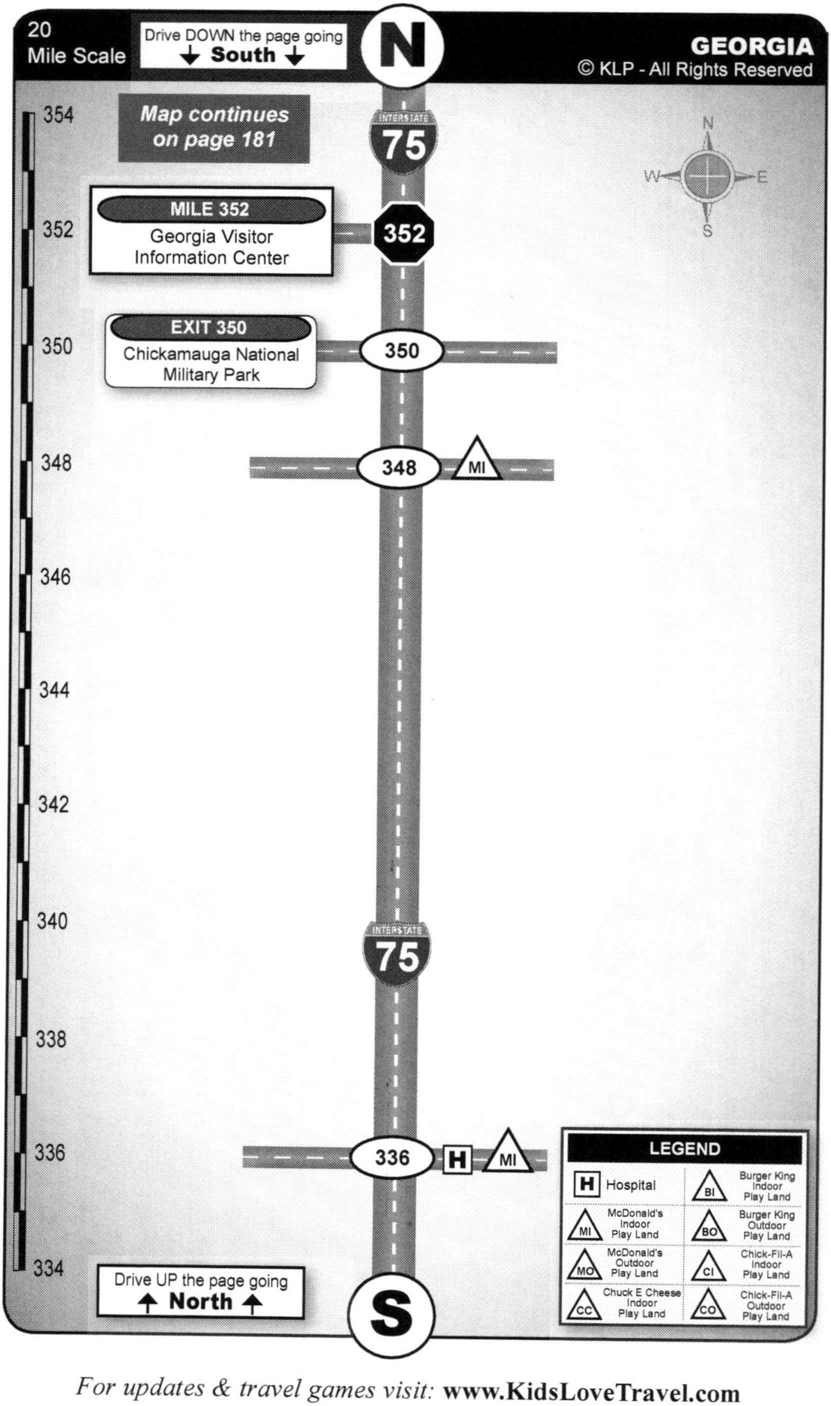
20 Mile Scale
Drive DOWN the page going ↓ South ↓
N
GEORGIA
© KLP - All Rights Reserved
Map continues on page 181
INTERSTATE 75
N
W
E
S
354
352
350
348
346
344
342
340
338
336
334
MILE 352
Georgia Visitor Information Center
352
EXIT 350
Chickamauga National Military Park
350
348
MI
INTERSTATE 75
336
H
MI
LEGEND
H Hospital
BI Burger King Indoor Play Land
MI McDonald's Indoor Play Land
BO Burger King Outdoor Play Land
MO McDonald's Outdoor Play Land
CI Chick-Fil-A Indoor Play Land
CC Chuck E Cheese Indoor Play Land
CO Chick-Fil-A Outdoor Play Land
Drive UP the page going ↑ North ↑
S

GEORGIA

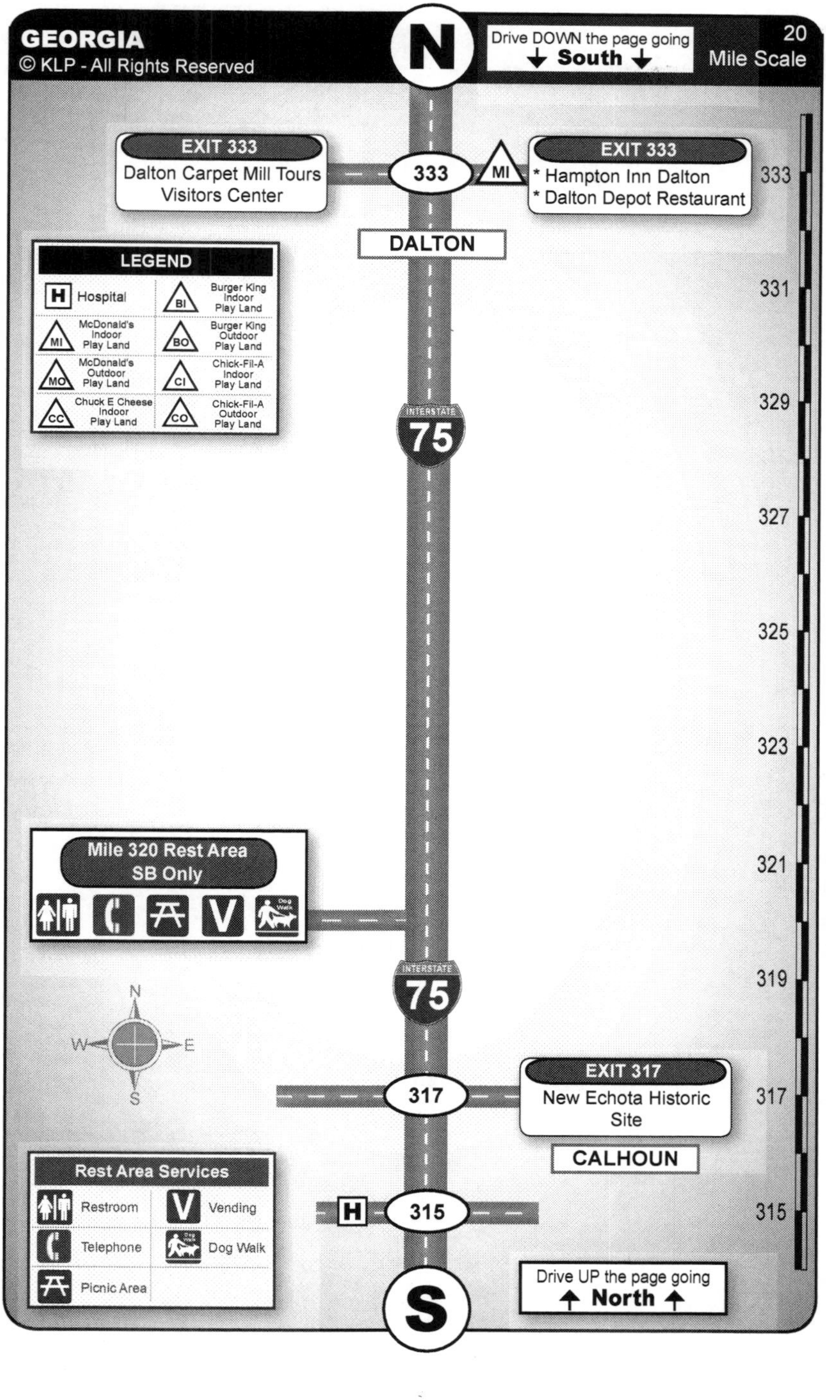
GEORGIA
© KLP - All Rights Reserved
N
Drive DOWN the page going
South
20
Mile Scale
EXIT 333
Dalton Carpet Mill Tours
Visitors Center
333
MI
EXIT 333
* Hampton Inn Dalton
* Dalton Depot Restaurant
333
DALTON
LEGEND
H Hospital
BI Burger King Indoor Play Land
MI McDonald's Indoor Play Land
BO Burger King Outdoor Play Land
MO McDonald's Outdoor Play Land
CI Chick-Fil-A Indoor Play Land
CC Chuck E Cheese Indoor Play Land
CO Chick-Fil-A Outdoor Play Land
331
Interstate 75
329
327
325
323
Mile 320 Rest Area
SB Only
V
321
Interstate 75
319
N
W
E
S
317
EXIT 317
New Echota Historic
Site
317
CALHOUN
Rest Area Services
Restroom
V Vending
Telephone
Dog Walk
Picnic Area
H
315
315
Drive UP the page going
North
S

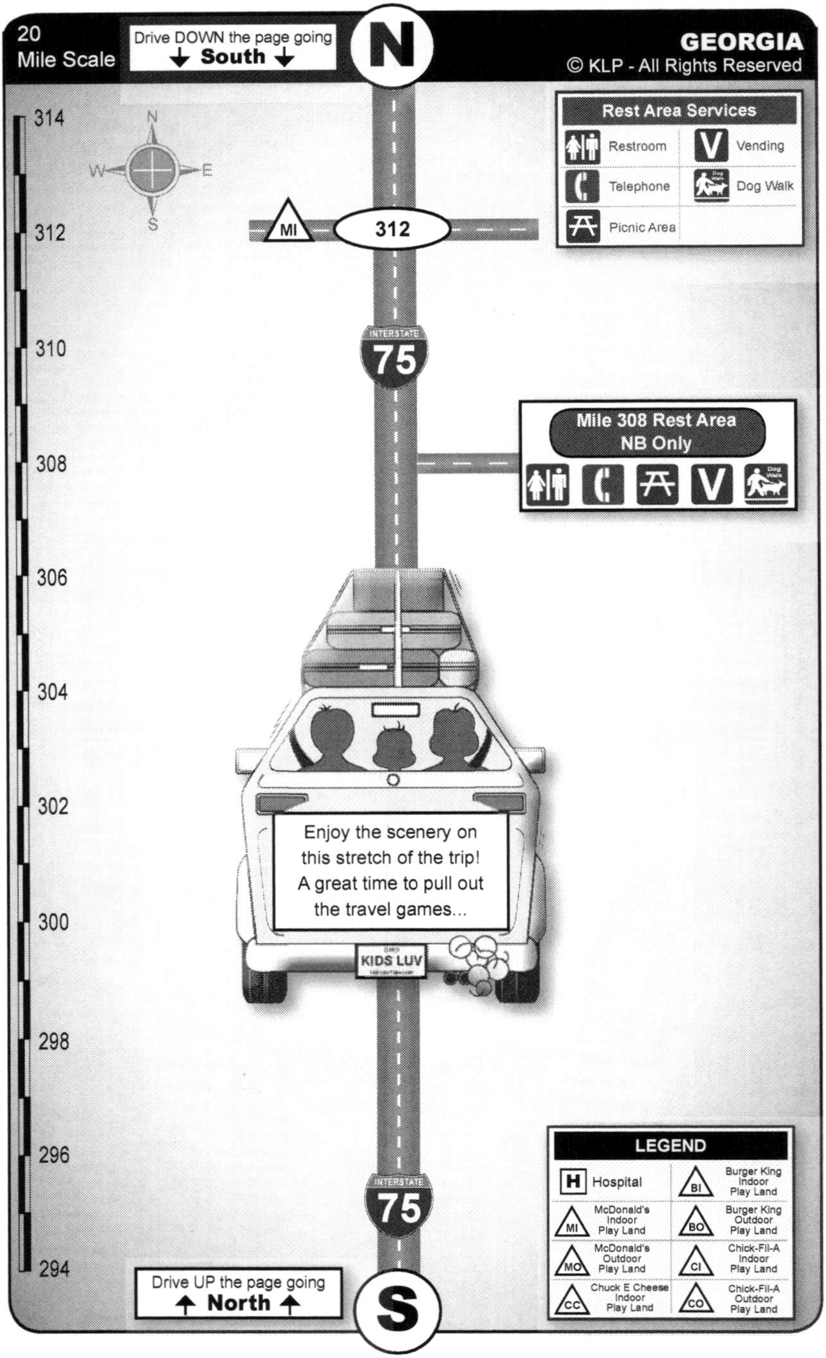
20 Mile Scale
Drive DOWN the page going
South
N
GEORGIA
© KLP - All Rights Reserved
Rest Area Services
Restroom
Vending
Telephone
Dog Walk
Picnic Area
314
312
310
308
306
304
302
300
298
296
294
N
W
E
S
MI
312
75
Mile 308 Rest Area
NB Only
Enjoy the scenery on
this stretch of the trip!
A great time to pull out
the travel games...
KIDS LUV
LEGEND
Hospital
Burger King Indoor Play Land
McDonald's Indoor Play Land
Burger King Outdoor Play Land
McDonald's Outdoor Play Land
Chick-Fil-A Indoor Play Land
Chuck E Cheese Indoor Play Land
Chick-Fil-A Outdoor Play Land
Drive UP the page going
North
S

GEORGIA

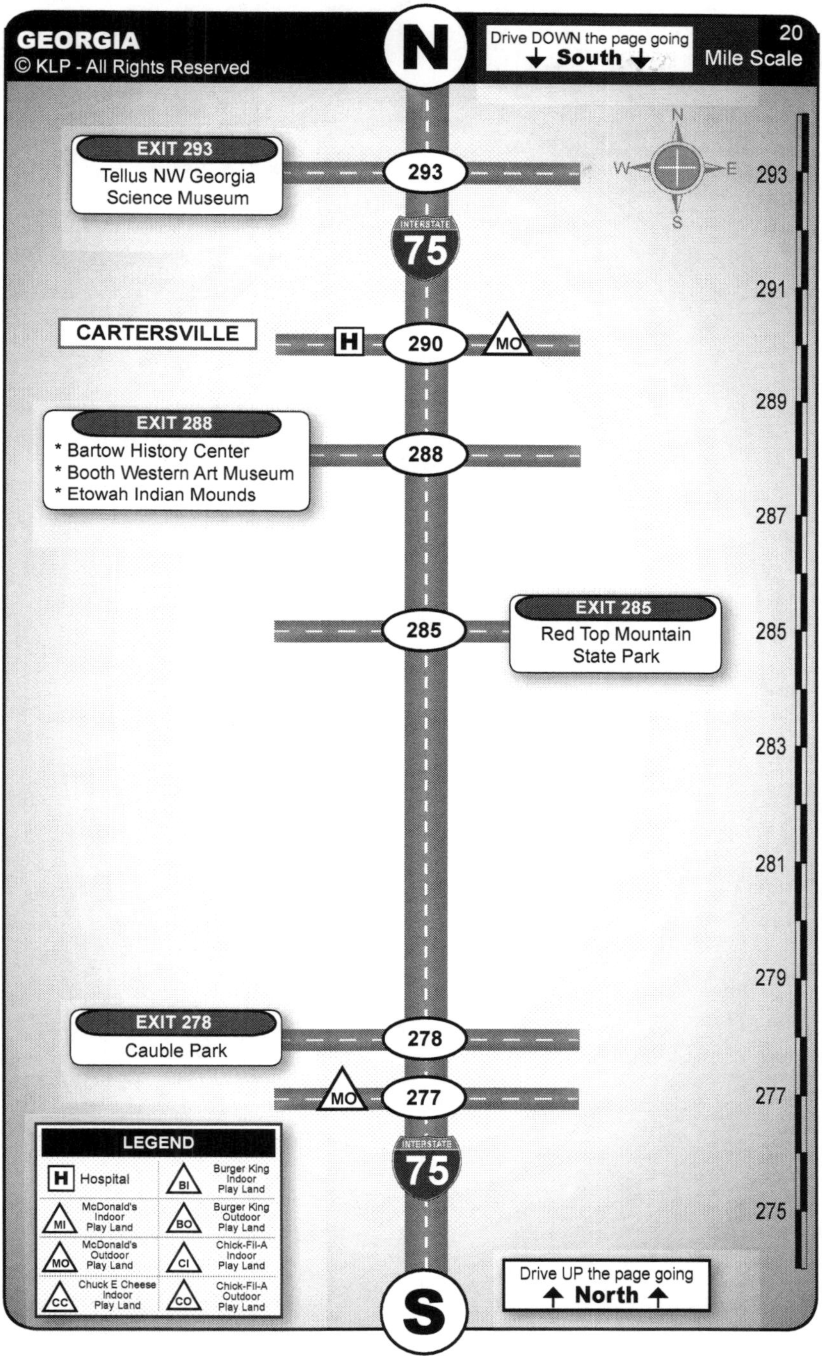
GEORGIA
© KLP - All Rights Reserved
N
Drive DOWN the page going
South
20
Mile Scale
EXIT 293
Tellus NW Georgia
Science Museum
293
N
W
E
S
INTERSTATE
75
291
CARTERSVILLE
H
290
MO
289
EXIT 288
* Bartow History Center
* Booth Western Art Museum
* Etowah Indian Mounds
288
287
285
EXIT 285
Red Top Mountain
State Park
285
283
281
279
EXIT 278
Cauble Park
278
MO
277
277
LEGEND
H Hospital
BI Burger King Indoor Play Land
MI McDonald's Indoor Play Land
BO Burger King Outdoor Play Land
MO McDonald's Outdoor Play Land
CI Chick-Fil-A Indoor Play Land
CC Chuck E Cheese Indoor Play Land
CO Chick-Fil-A Outdoor Play Land
INTERSTATE
75
275
S
Drive UP the page going
North

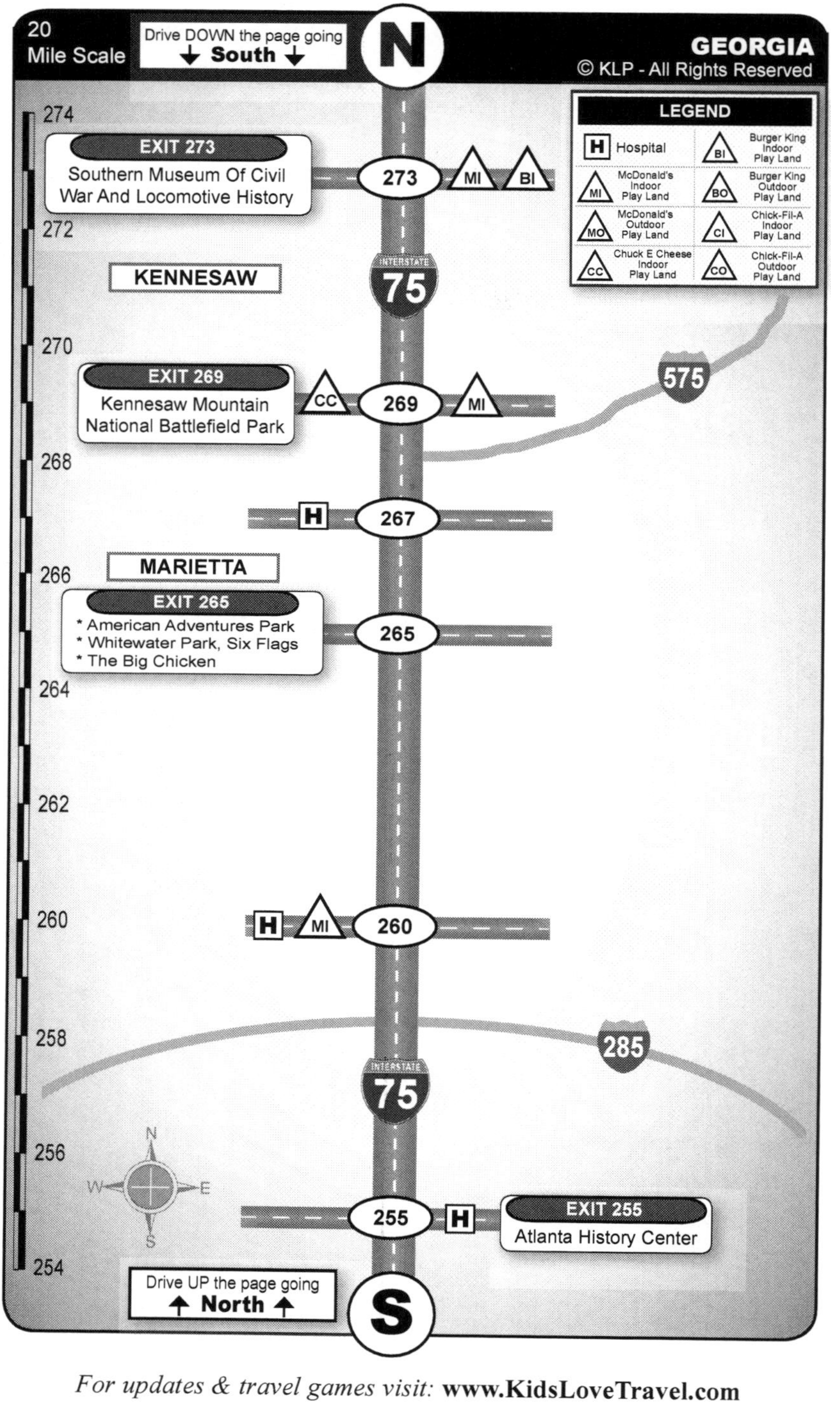
20
Mile Scale
Drive DOWN the page going
South
N
GEORGIA
© KLP - All Rights Reserved
LEGEND
H Hospital
BI Burger King Indoor Play Land
MI McDonald's Indoor Play Land
BO Burger King Outdoor Play Land
MO McDonald's Outdoor Play Land
CI Chick-Fil-A Indoor Play Land
CC Chuck E Cheese Indoor Play Land
CO Chick-Fil-A Outdoor Play Land
274
EXIT 273
Southern Museum Of Civil War And Locomotive History
273 MI BI
272
KENNESAW
75
270
EXIT 269
Kennesaw Mountain National Battlefield Park
CC 269 MI
575
268
H 267
MARIETTA
266
EXIT 265
* American Adventures Park
* Whitewater Park, Six Flags
* The Big Chicken
265
264
262
260
H MI 260
258
285
75
256
N
W
E
S
255 H
EXIT 255
Atlanta History Center
254
Drive UP the page going
North
S

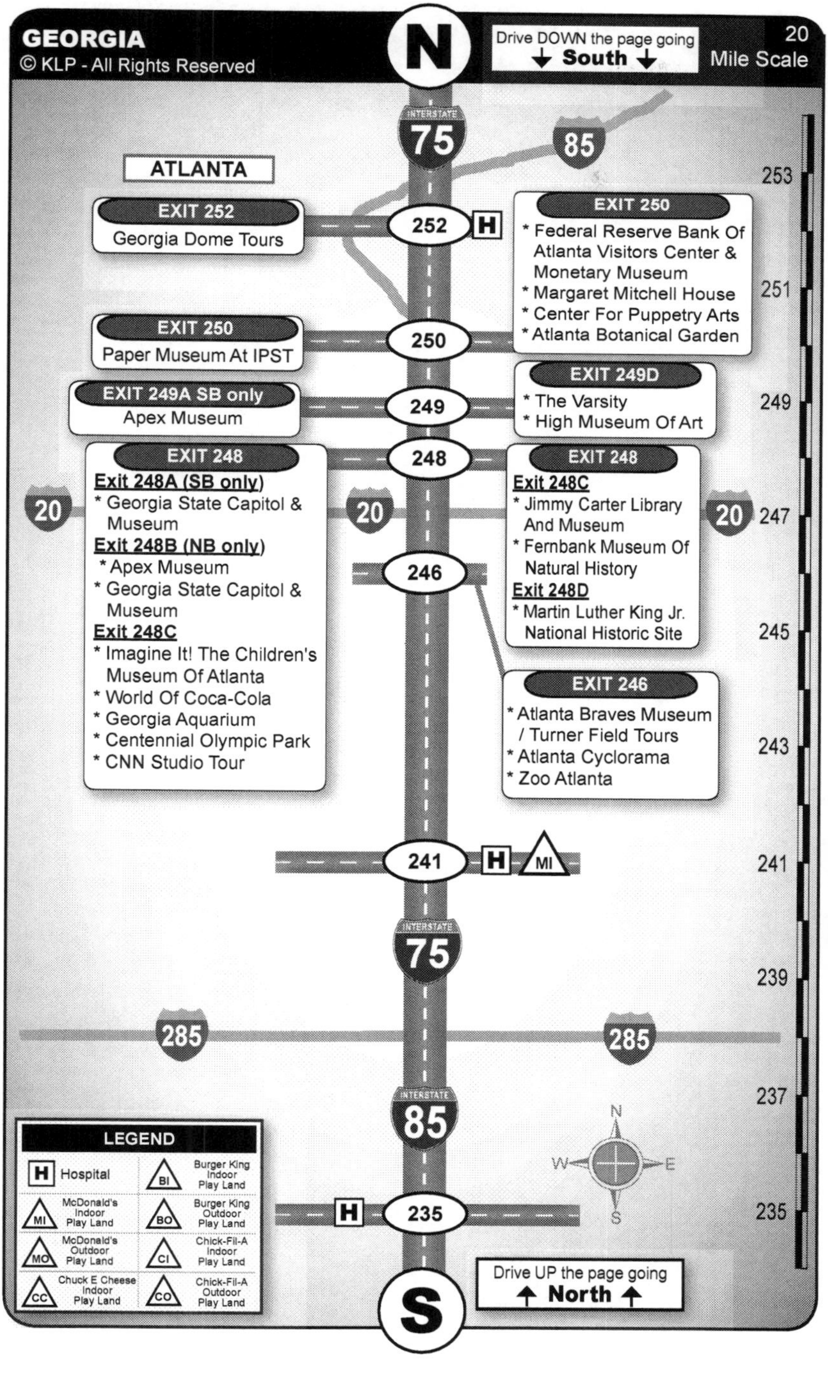
GEORGIA
© KLP - All Rights Reserved
N
Drive DOWN the page going
South
20
Mile Scale
75
85
ATLANTA
EXIT 252
Georgia Dome Tours
252
H
EXIT 250
* Federal Reserve Bank Of Atlanta Visitors Center & Monetary Museum
* Margaret Mitchell House
* Center For Puppetry Arts
* Atlanta Botanical Garden
EXIT 250
Paper Museum At IPST
250
EXIT 249D
* The Varsity
* High Museum Of Art
EXIT 249A SB only
Apex Museum
249
248
EXIT 248
Exit 248A (SB only)
* Georgia State Capitol & Museum
Exit 248B (NB only)
* Apex Museum
* Georgia State Capitol & Museum
Exit 248C
* Imagine It! The Children's Museum Of Atlanta
* World Of Coca-Cola
* Georgia Aquarium
* Centennial Olympic Park
* CNN Studio Tour
EXIT 248
Exit 248C
* Jimmy Carter Library And Museum
* Fernbank Museum Of Natural History
Exit 248D
* Martin Luther King Jr. National Historic Site
20
246
EXIT 246
* Atlanta Braves Museum / Turner Field Tours
* Atlanta Cyclorama
* Zoo Atlanta
241
H
MI
75
285
85
235
H
253
251
249
247
245
243
241
239
237
235
LEGEND
H Hospital
BI Burger King Indoor Play Land
MI McDonald's Indoor Play Land
BO Burger King Outdoor Play Land
MO McDonald's Outdoor Play Land
CI Chick-Fil-A Indoor Play Land
CC Chuck E Cheese Indoor Play Land
CO Chick-Fil-A Outdoor Play Land
N
W
E
S
Drive UP the page going
North
S

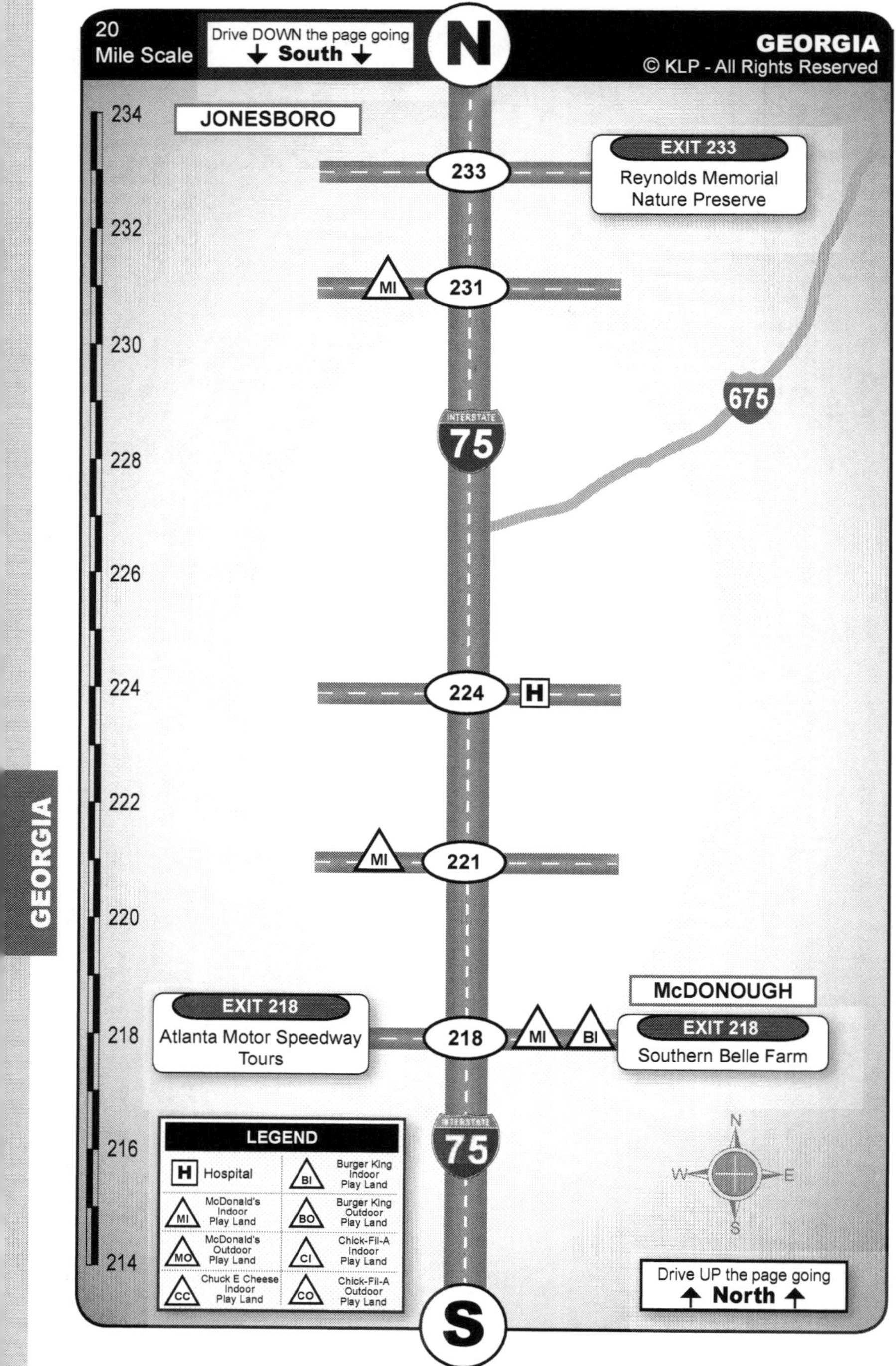
20
Mile Scale
Drive DOWN the page going
South
N
GEORGIA
© KLP - All Rights Reserved
234
232
230
228
226
224
222
220
218
216
214
JONESBORO
EXIT 233
Reynolds Memorial
Nature Preserve
233
MI
231
675
INTERSTATE
75
224
H
221
McDONOUGH
EXIT 218
Atlanta Motor Speedway
Tours
218
BI
EXIT 218
Southern Belle Farm
LEGEND
Hospital
Burger King
Indoor
Play Land
McDonald's
Indoor
Play Land
BO
Burger King
Outdoor
Play Land
MO
McDonald's
Outdoor
Play Land
CI
Chick-Fil-A
Indoor
Play Land
CC
Chuck E Cheese
Indoor
Play Land
CO
Chick-Fil-A
Outdoor
Play Land
W
E
S
Drive UP the page going
North
GEORGIA

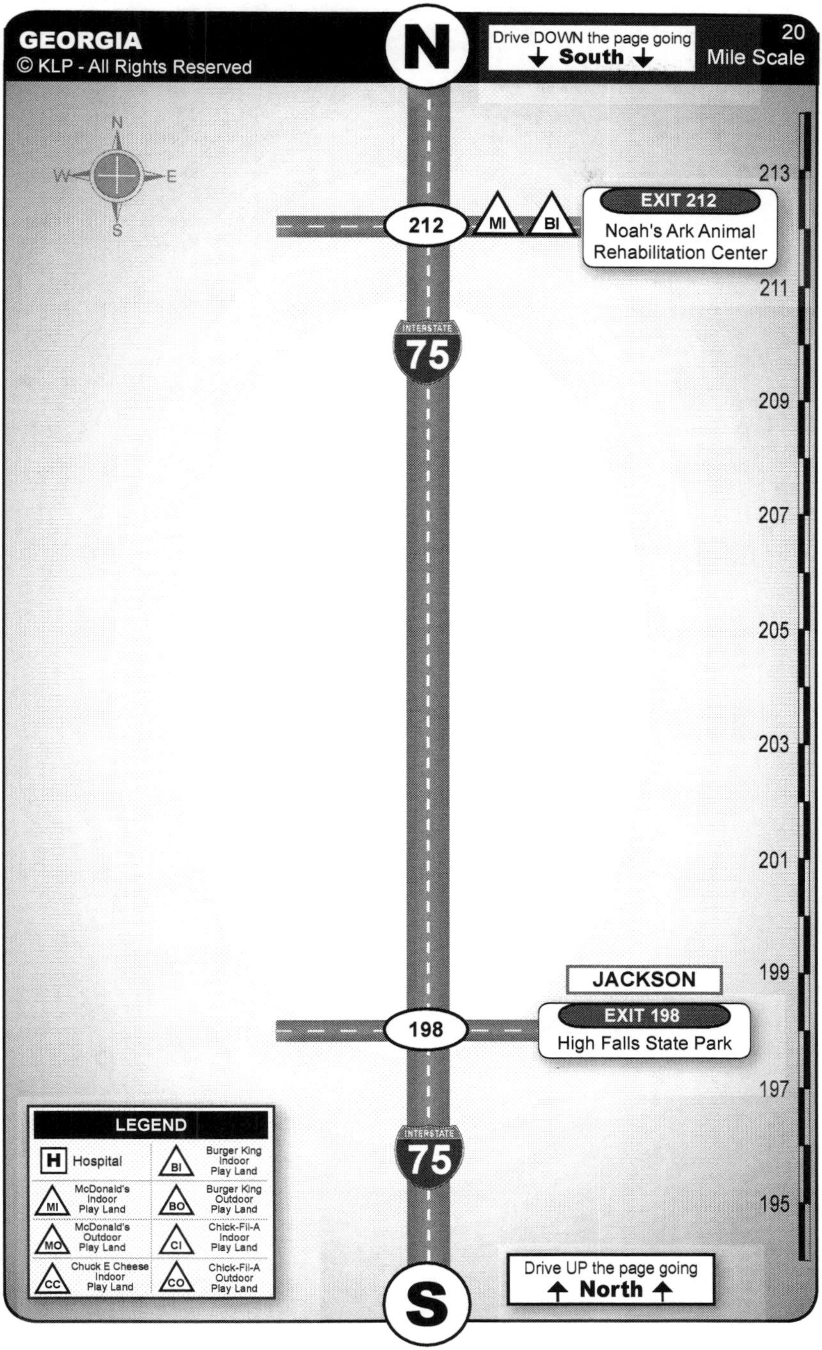
GEORGIA
© KLP - All Rights Reserved
N
Drive DOWN the page going
South
20
Mile Scale
213
212
MI
BI
EXIT 212
Noah's Ark Animal Rehabilitation Center
211
75
209
207
205
203
201
199
JACKSON
198
EXIT 198
High Falls State Park
197
75
195
LEGEND
H Hospital
BI Burger King Indoor Play Land
MI McDonald's Indoor Play Land
BO Burger King Outdoor Play Land
MO McDonald's Outdoor Play Land
CI Chick-Fil-A Indoor Play Land
CC Chuck E Cheese Indoor Play Land
CO Chick-Fil-A Outdoor Play Land
S
Drive UP the page going
North

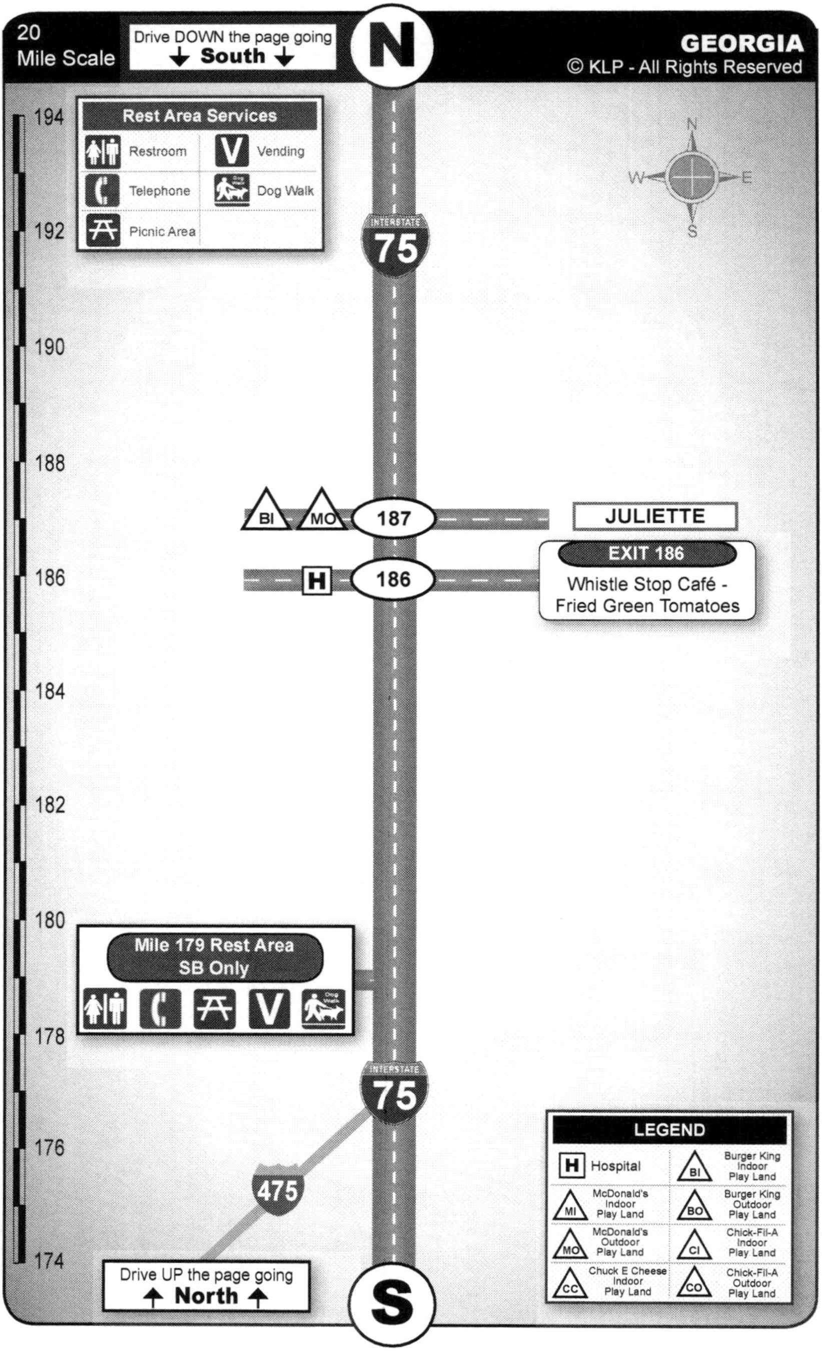
20
Mile Scale
Drive DOWN the page going
South
N
GEORGIA
© KLP - All Rights Reserved
194
192
190
188
186
184
182
180
178
176
174
Rest Area Services
Restroom
Vending
Telephone
Dog Walk
Picnic Area
75
N
W
E
S
BI
MO
187
JULIETTE
H
186
EXIT 186
Whistle Stop Café -
Fried Green Tomatoes
Mile 179 Rest Area
SB Only
75
475
LEGEND
Hospital
Burger King Indoor Play Land
McDonald's Indoor Play Land
Burger King Outdoor Play Land
McDonald's Outdoor Play Land
Chick-Fil-A Indoor Play Land
Chuck E Cheese Indoor Play Land
Chick-Fil-A Outdoor Play Land
Drive UP the page going
North
S
GEORGIA

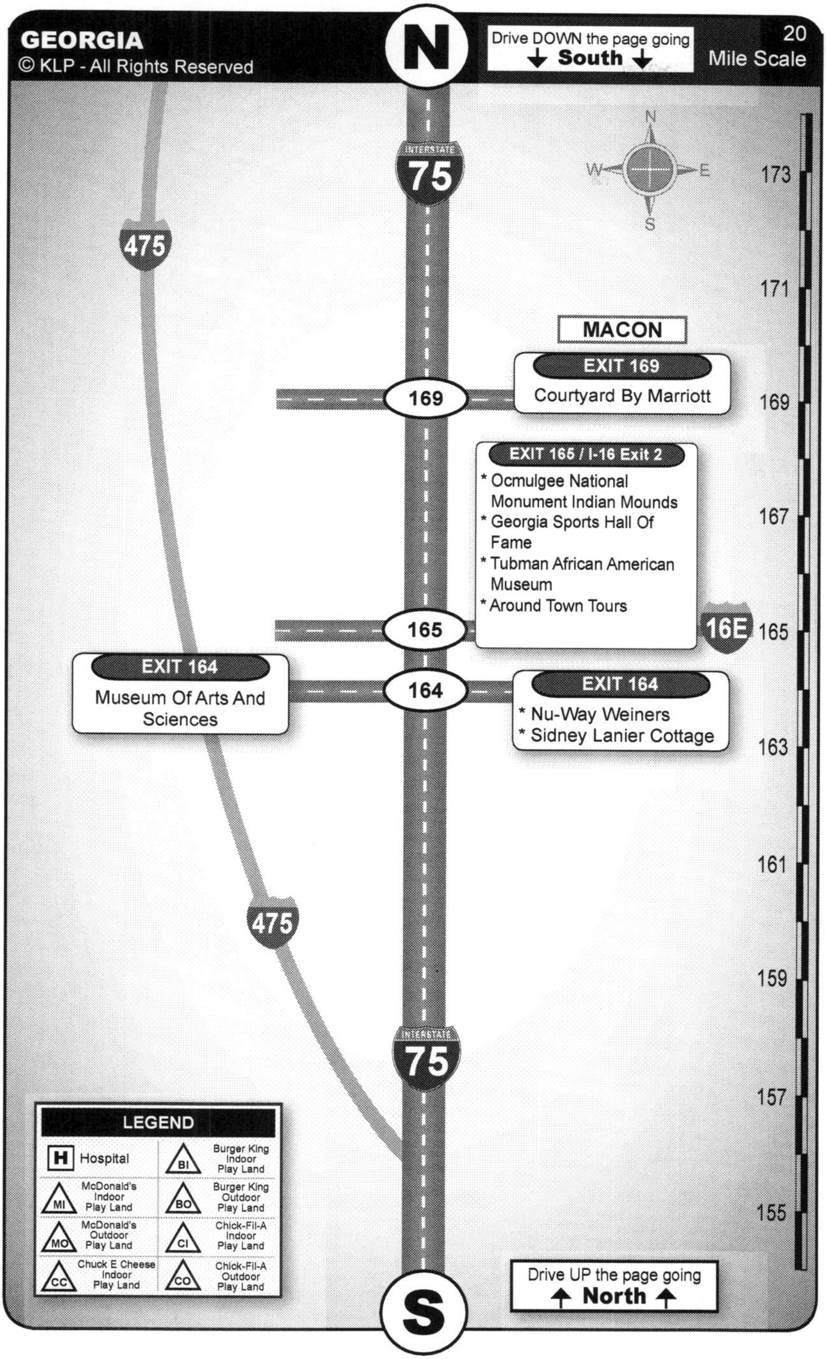
GEORGIA
© KLP - All Rights Reserved
N
Drive DOWN the page going
South
20
Mile Scale
75
475
173
171
169
167
165
163
161
159
157
155
MACON
EXIT 169
Courtyard By Marriott
169
EXIT 165 / I-16 Exit 2
* Ocmulgee National Monument Indian Mounds
* Georgia Sports Hall Of Fame
* Tubman African American Museum
* Around Town Tours
16E
165
EXIT 164
Museum Of Arts And Sciences
164
EXIT 164
* Nu-Way Weiners
* Sidney Lanier Cottage
LEGEND
H Hospital
BI Burger King Indoor Play Land
MI McDonald's Indoor Play Land
BO Burger King Outdoor Play Land
MO McDonald's Outdoor Play Land
CI Chick-Fil-A Indoor Play Land
CC Chuck E Cheese Indoor Play Land
CO Chick-Fil-A Outdoor Play Land
S
Drive UP the page going
North

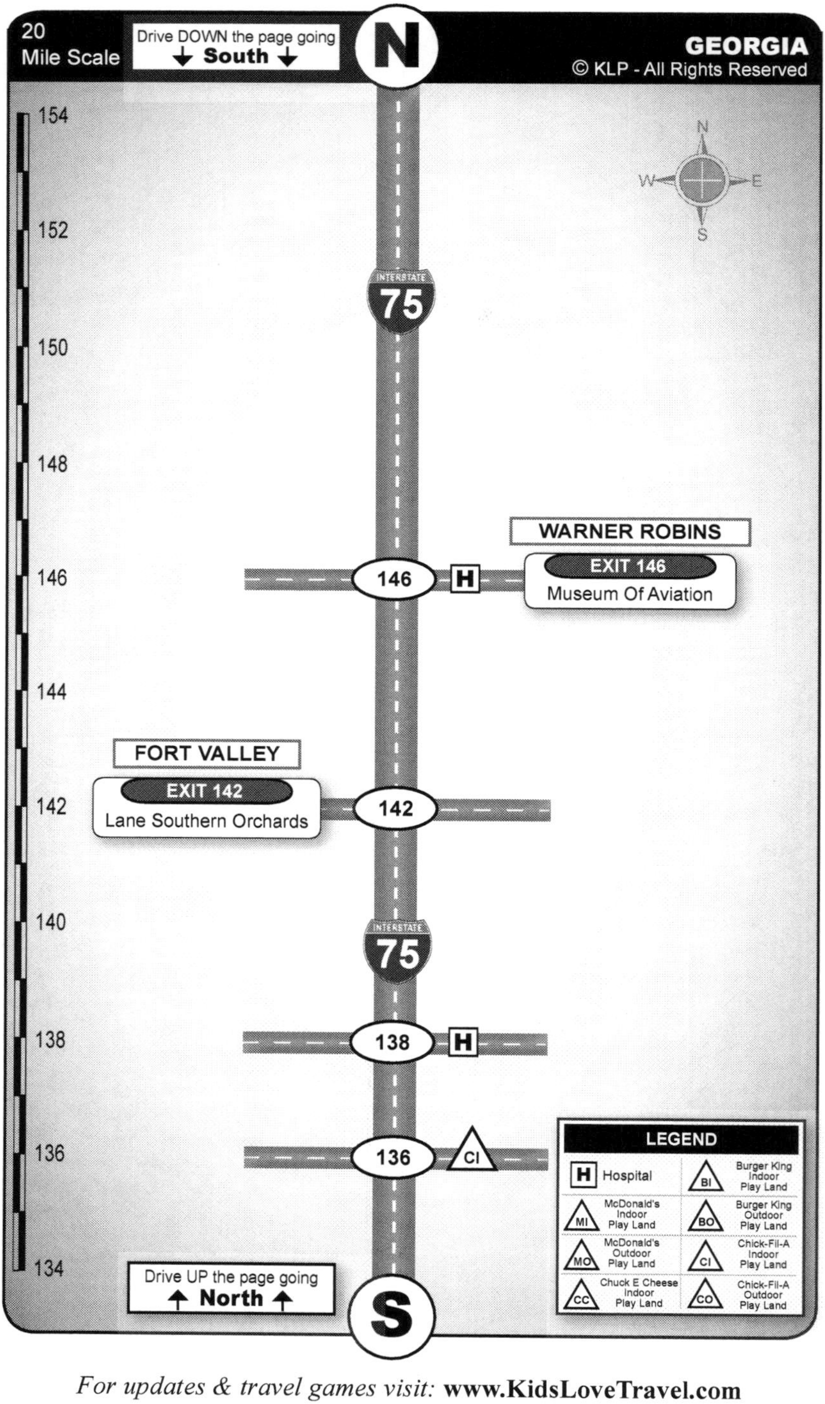
20
Mile Scale
Drive DOWN the page going
South
N
GEORGIA
© KLP - All Rights Reserved
154
152
150
148
146
144
142
140
138
136
134
N
W
E
S
75
WARNER ROBINS
146
H
EXIT 146
Museum Of Aviation
FORT VALLEY
EXIT 142
Lane Southern Orchards
142
75
138
H
136
CI
LEGEND
H Hospital
BI Burger King Indoor Play Land
MI McDonald's Indoor Play Land
BO Burger King Outdoor Play Land
MO McDonald's Outdoor Play Land
CI Chick-Fil-A Indoor Play Land
CC Chuck E Cheese Indoor Play Land
CO Chick-Fil-A Outdoor Play Land
Drive UP the page going
North
S

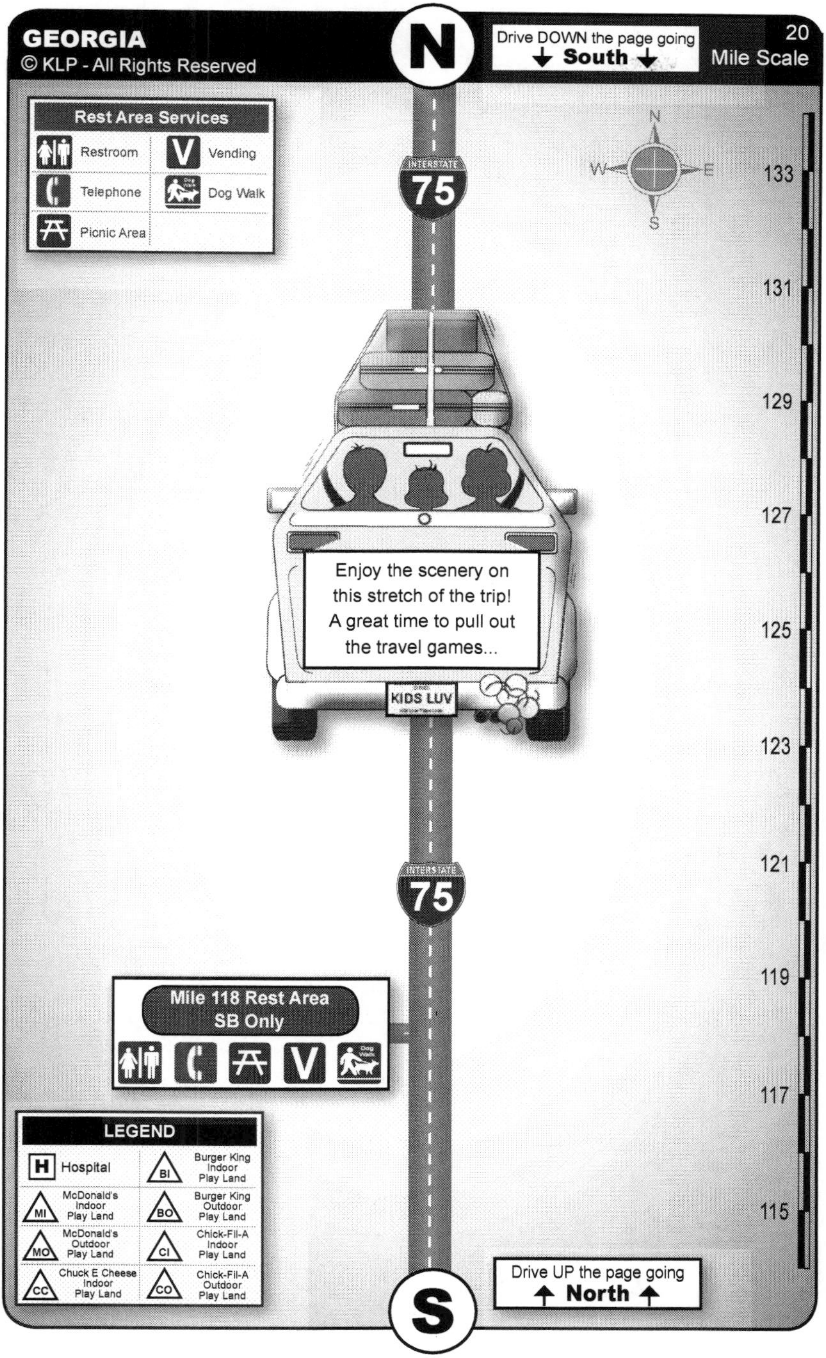
GEORGIA
© KLP - All Rights Reserved
N
Drive DOWN the page going
South
20
Mile Scale
Rest Area Services
Restroom
Vending
Telephone
Dog Walk
Picnic Area
INTERSTATE
75
N
W
E
S
133
131
129
127
125
123
121
119
117
115
Enjoy the scenery on this stretch of the trip! A great time to pull out the travel games...
KIDS LUV
INTERSTATE
75
Mile 118 Rest Area
SB Only
LEGEND
H Hospital
BI Burger King Indoor Play Land
MI McDonald's Indoor Play Land
BO Burger King Outdoor Play Land
MO McDonald's Outdoor Play Land
CI Chick-Fil-A Indoor Play Land
CC Chuck E Cheese Indoor Play Land
CO Chick-Fil-A Outdoor Play Land
S
Drive UP the page going
North

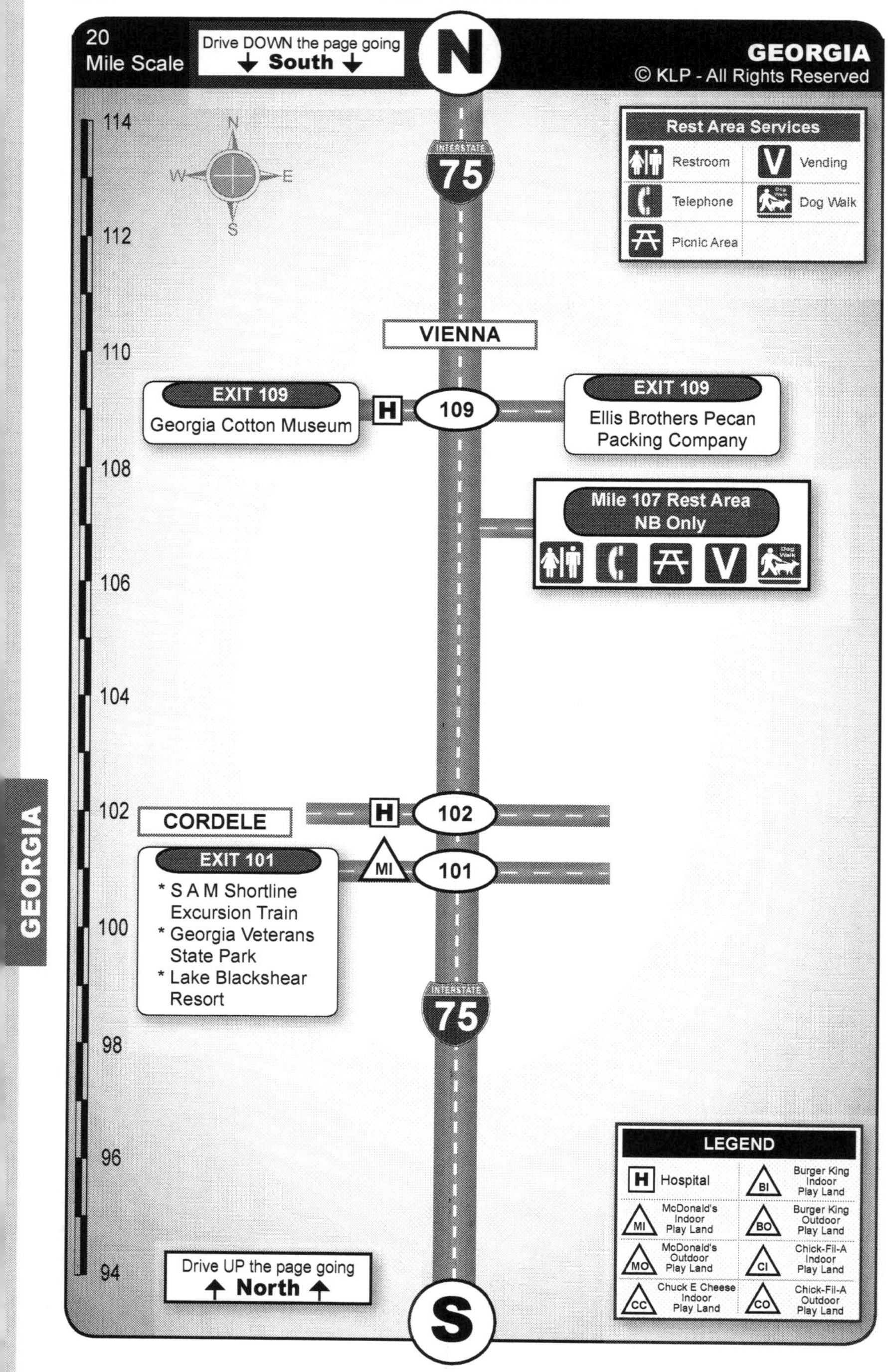
20
Mile Scale
Drive DOWN the page going
South
N
GEORGIA
© KLP - All Rights Reserved
114
112
110
108
106
104
102
100
98
96
94
Rest Area Services
Restroom
Vending
Telephone
Dog Walk
Picnic Area
75
VIENNA
EXIT 109
Georgia Cotton Museum
H
109
EXIT 109
Ellis Brothers Pecan
Packing Company
Mile 107 Rest Area
NB Only
V
CORDELE
H
102
EXIT 101
* S A M Shortline
Excursion Train
* Georgia Veterans
State Park
* Lake Blackshear
Resort
MI
101
75
LEGEND
H Hospital
BI Burger King Indoor Play Land
MI McDonald's Indoor Play Land
BO Burger King Outdoor Play Land
MO McDonald's Outdoor Play Land
CI Chick-Fil-A Indoor Play Land
CC Chuck E Cheese Indoor Play Land
CO Chick-Fil-A Outdoor Play Land
Drive UP the page going
North
S
GEORGIA

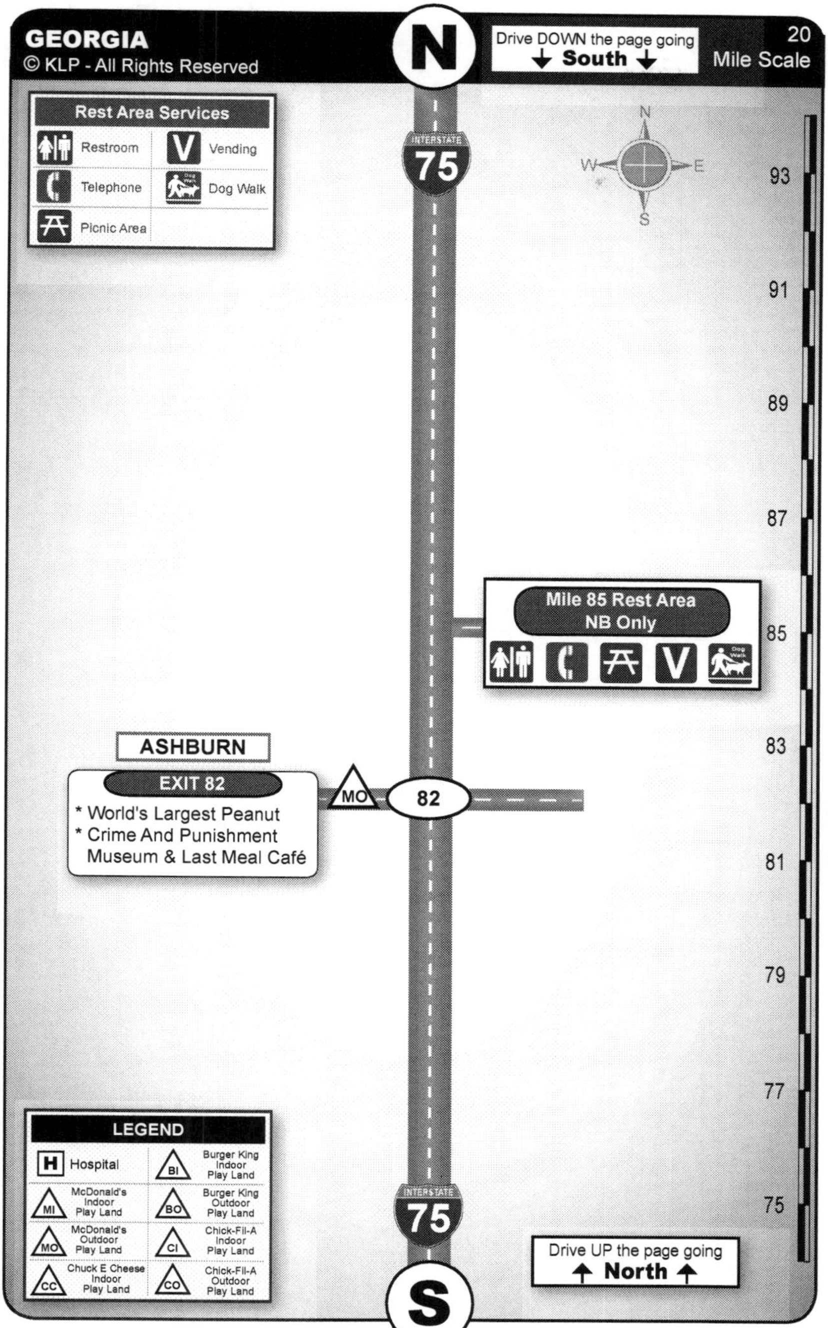
GEORGIA
© KLP - All Rights Reserved
N
Drive DOWN the page going
South
20
Mile Scale
Rest Area Services
Restroom
Vending
Telephone
Dog Walk
Picnic Area
INTERSTATE 75
N
W
E
S
93
91
89
87
85
83
81
79
77
75
Mile 85 Rest Area
NB Only
ASHBURN
EXIT 82
* World's Largest Peanut
* Crime And Punishment Museum & Last Meal Café
MO
82
LEGEND
H Hospital
BI Burger King Indoor Play Land
MI McDonald's Indoor Play Land
BO Burger King Outdoor Play Land
MO McDonald's Outdoor Play Land
CI Chick-Fil-A Indoor Play Land
CC Chuck E Cheese Indoor Play Land
CO Chick-Fil-A Outdoor Play Land
INTERSTATE 75
Drive UP the page going
North
S

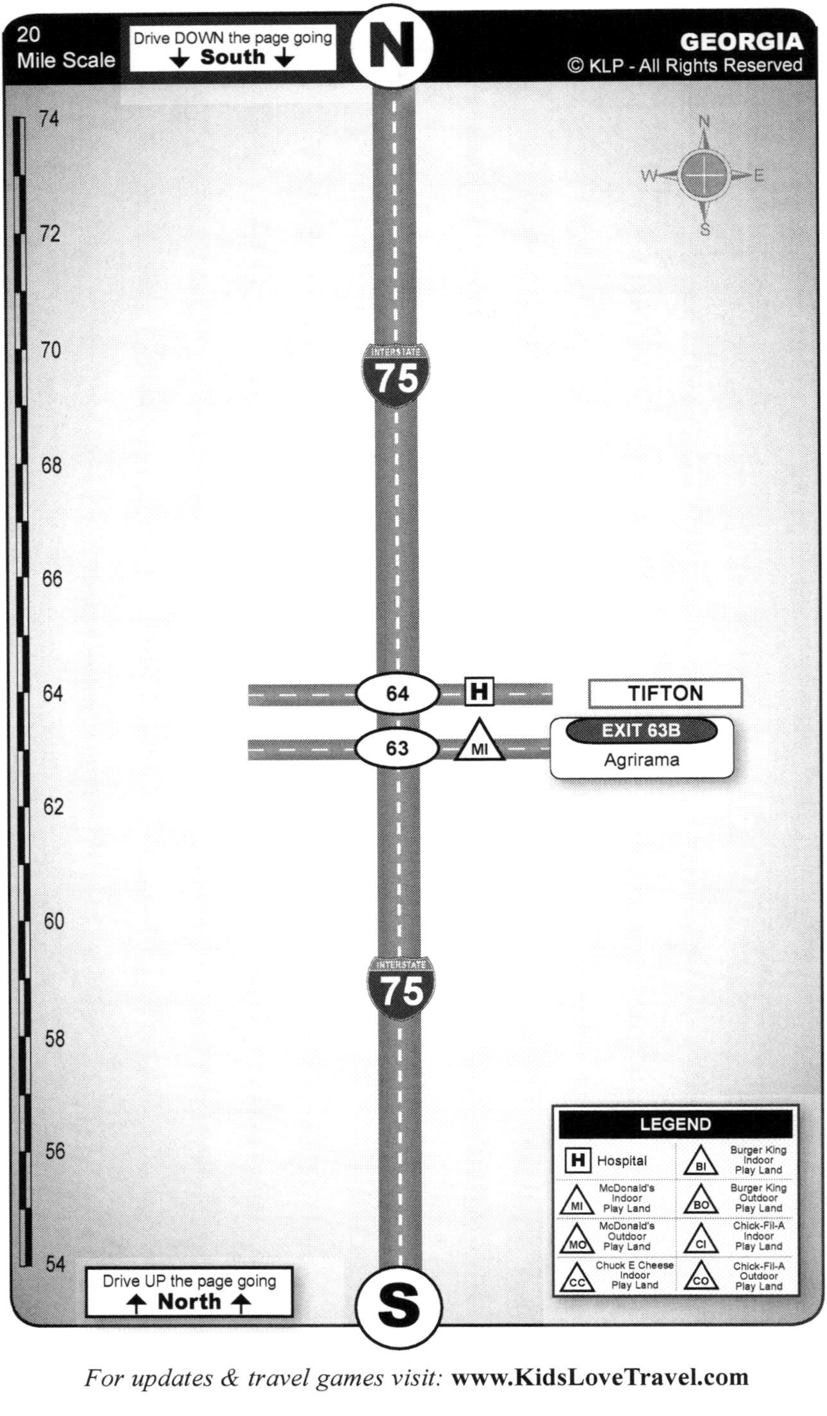
20
Mile Scale
Drive DOWN the page going
South
N
GEORGIA
© KLP - All Rights Reserved
74
72
70
68
66
64
62
60
58
56
54
N
W
E
S
75
64
H
TIFTON
63
MI
EXIT 63B
Agrirama
75
LEGEND
Hospital
Burger King Indoor Play Land
McDonald's Indoor Play Land
Burger King Outdoor Play Land
McDonald's Outdoor Play Land
Chick-Fil-A Indoor Play Land
Chuck E Cheese Indoor Play Land
Chick-Fil-A Outdoor Play Land
Drive UP the page going
North
S

GEORGIA

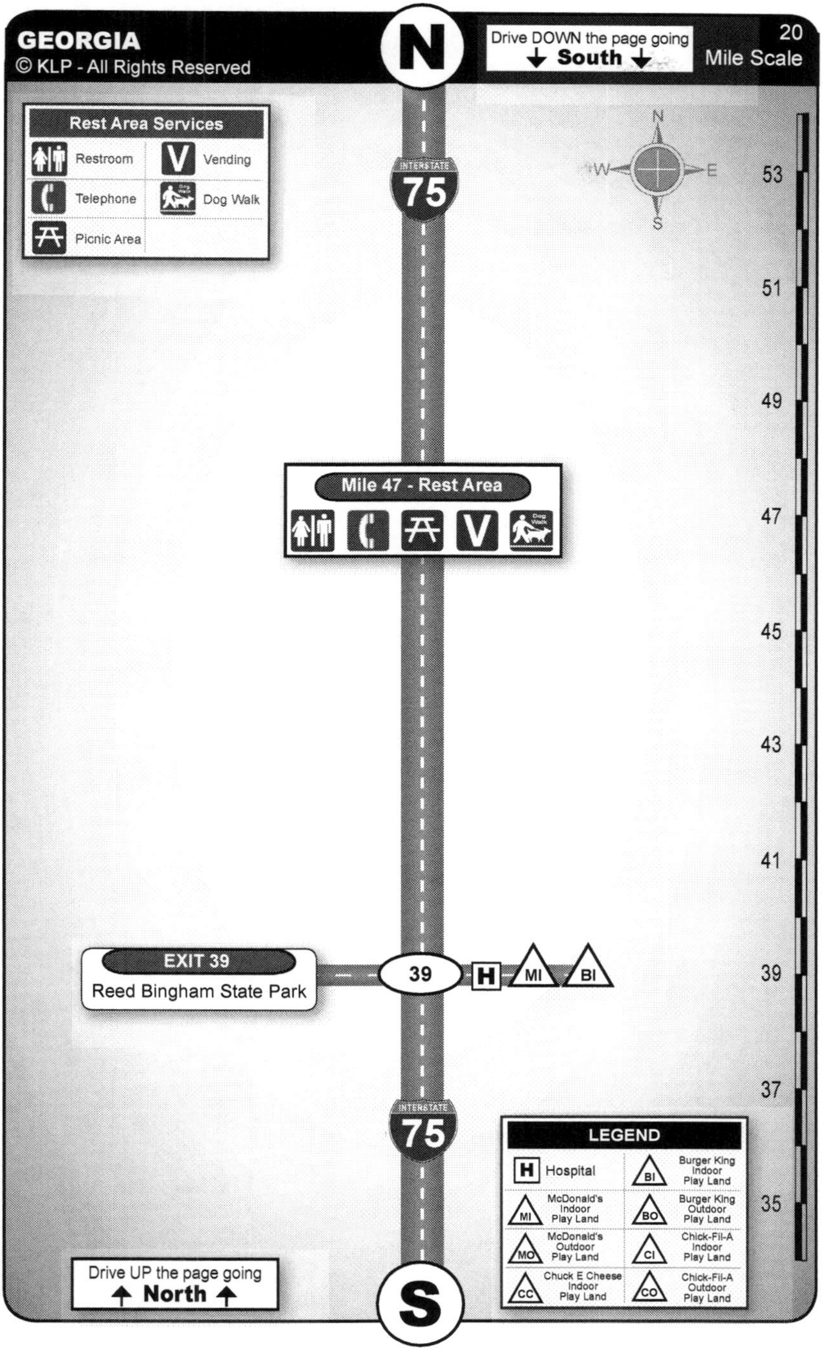
GEORGIA
© KLP - All Rights Reserved
N
Drive DOWN the page going
South
20
Mile Scale
Rest Area Services
Restroom
Vending
Telephone
Dog Walk
Picnic Area
INTERSTATE
75
53
51
49
Mile 47 - Rest Area
47
45
43
41
EXIT 39
Reed Bingham State Park
39
H
MI
BI
37
INTERSTATE
75
LEGEND
H Hospital
BI Burger King Indoor Play Land
MI McDonald's Indoor Play Land
BO Burger King Outdoor Play Land
MO McDonald's Outdoor Play Land
CI Chick-Fil-A Indoor Play Land
CC Chuck E Cheese Indoor Play Land
CO Chick-Fil-A Outdoor Play Land
35
Drive UP the page going
North
S

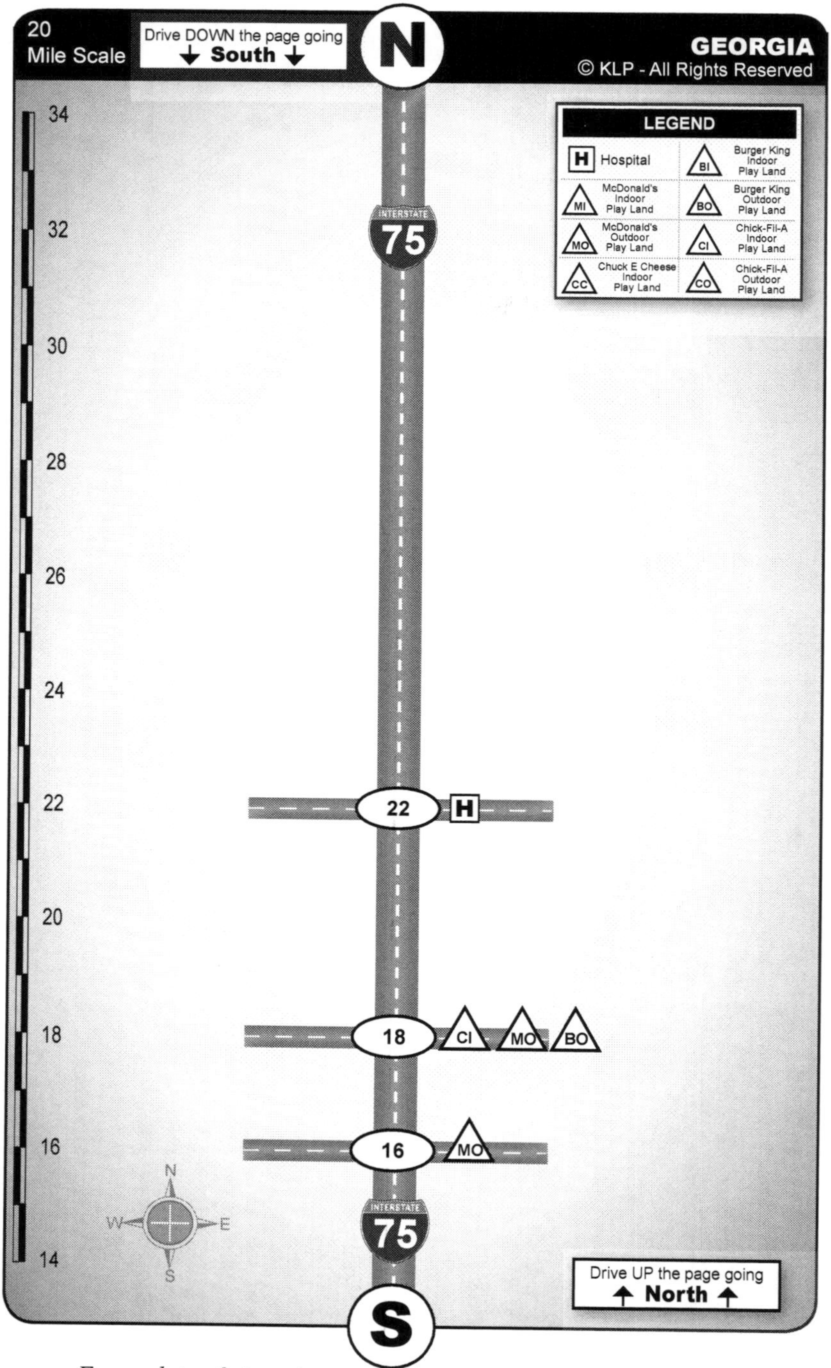
20
Mile Scale
Drive DOWN the page going
South
N
GEORGIA
© KLP - All Rights Reserved
LEGEND
H Hospital
BI Burger King Indoor Play Land
MI McDonald's Indoor Play Land
BO Burger King Outdoor Play Land
MO McDonald's Outdoor Play Land
CI Chick-Fil-A Indoor Play Land
CC Chuck E Cheese Indoor Play Land
CO Chick-Fil-A Outdoor Play Land
34
32
30
28
26
24
22
20
18
16
14
INTERSTATE 75
22 H
18 CI MO BO
16 MO
N W E S
INTERSTATE 75
S
Drive UP the page going
North

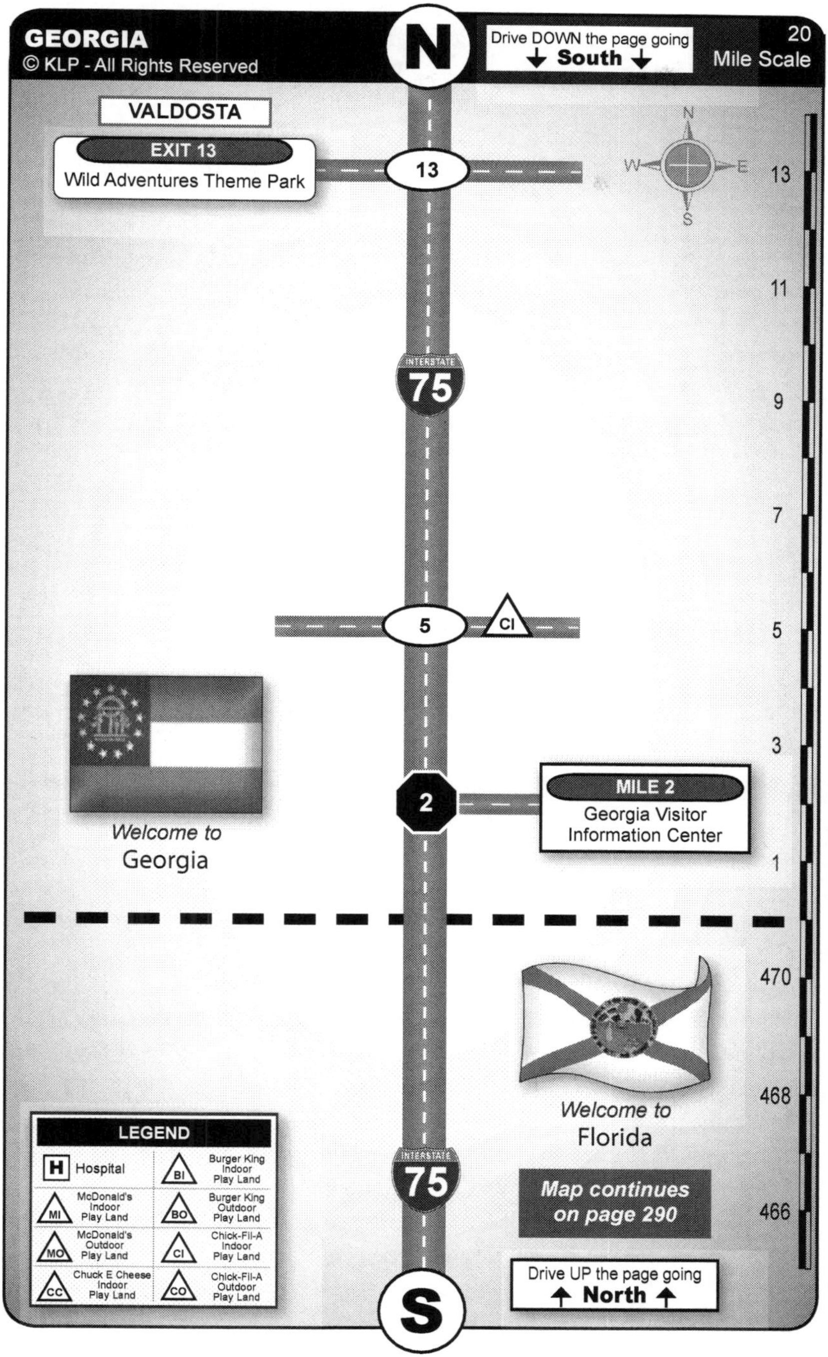
GEORGIA
© KLP - All Rights Reserved
N
Drive DOWN the page going
South
20
Mile Scale
VALDOSTA
EXIT 13
Wild Adventures Theme Park
13
N
W
E
S
13
11
INTERSTATE
75
9
7
5
CI
5
3
2
MILE 2
Georgia Visitor
Information Center
Welcome to
Georgia
1
470
Welcome to
Florida
468
LEGEND
H Hospital
BI Burger King Indoor Play Land
MI McDonald's Indoor Play Land
BO Burger King Outdoor Play Land
MO McDonald's Outdoor Play Land
CI Chick-Fil-A Indoor Play Land
CC Chuck E Cheese Indoor Play Land
CO Chick-Fil-A Outdoor Play Land
INTERSTATE
75
Map continues
on page 290
466
Drive UP the page going
North
S

Sites and attractions are listed in order by Exit Number (North to South) and distance from the exit (closest are listed first). Symbols indicated represent:

Restaurants Lodging

Mile - 352 (west of I-75)

GEORGIA VISITOR INFORMATION CENTER

Ringgold - ***(I-75 just south of GA/TN line and past exit 353) 30736. Phone: (706) 937-4211. www.georgia.org. Hours: Information Services 8:30am-5:30pm daily. Restrooms 7:00am-11:00pm daily. Closed Thanksgiving, Christmas Eve and Christmas Day.***

The staff at the Georgia Visitor Information Centers are there to welcome and assist you with finding your way through Georgia, making lodging reservations, and offer up a friendly smile. In addition, you'll find overnight car and RV parking plus an RV dump here.

Exit - 350 (west of I-75)

CHICKAMAUGA NATIONAL MILITARY PARK

Fort Oglethorpe - ***(I-75 exit 350, then west on Hwy 2, south on 27, follow signs) 30742. Phone: (706) 866-9241. www.nps.gov/chch/index.htm. Hours: Daily 8:00am-5:00pm. Park open till dusk. Closed Christmas Day. Admission: FREE.***

In 1863, Union and Confederate forces fought for control of Chattanooga, the gateway to the deep south. The Confederate's were victorious at nearby Chickamauga in September, but renewed fighting in Chattanooga in November gave Union troops final control. This is the site of the bloodiest two-day battle of the Civil War. In September, 1863, over 100,000 soldiers fought for control of Lafayette Road, resulting in 34,000 casualties. The Cherokee word "chickamauga" means "River of Death." In the Visitor Center watch a multi-media presentation of the battle. Ranger "soldiers" (in costume) present historical talks near the exit to the visitors Center. They may give you some hints as to why this battle was so fierce (rifled muskets-accurate to 350 yards & could shoot every 20 seconds). The seven-mile tour route includes passing/ stopping by: the Gordon-Lee Mansion (home headquarters to US General William Rosecrans - now open by appointment - it's a bed & breakfast); Lee and Gordon's Mill (station for General Braggs Confederate forces before the battle, stronghold station for General Rosecrans during the battle to prevent Confederates from crossing Chickamauga Creek).

Exit - 333 (west of I-75)

DALTON CARPET MILL TOURS

Dalton - *(I-75 exit 333 west one block) 30722. Phone: (706) 270-9960. www.daltoncvb.com. Tours: Groups can schedule a tour of a carpet mill by calling the CVB phone number. See some of Catherine's original hand-tufted spreads, as well as chenille made by machine, visit the Hamilton House Museum in town.*

A wedding gift started the carpet industry. Catherine Evans Whitener made a bedspread designed with a stitch that locked into the fabric when clipped and washed called a "tuft". The bedspread was so liked by those who saw it that, later she began a cottage industry of making them to sell. The Singer Sewing Machine Company in nearby Chattanooga, Tennessee, took an interest and produced a machine to perform the task more efficiently. The product produced by machine were called "Chenille", the French word for "caterpillar", because the rows of machine-tufted threads resembled the creature. Pioneer businessmen experimented with the machines as a way to produce carpet. Their ideas worked. Today carpet mills remain major area employers. See the giant carpet sewing machines that today produce modern carpet styles while on tour.

Exit - 333 (east of I-75)

HAMPTON INN DALTON

Dalton - *1000 Market Street (I-75 exit 333) 30720. www.hamptoninn.hilton.com/dalton. Phone: (706) 226-4333.*

The hotel has a complimentary large hot/cold breakfast with new foods introduced each morning plus fresh fruits. There is also an outdoor pool and an indoor spa. It's located next to an outlet center, Cracker Barrel, Dairy Queen and many other restaurants and shopping within walking distance.

Exit - 333 (east of I-75)

DALTON DEPOT RESTAURANT

Dalton - *110 Depot Street (I-75 exit 333, go east on Walnut to left on Thorton. Right on Crawford, left on Hamilton and then one block to Kings St) 30722. Phone: (706) 226-3160. www.daltondepot.net.*

GEORGIA

The Western & Atlantic Depot of the 1850s served as a Confederate army ordinance depot during the war. It has been converted into a restaurant while maintaining its history. Surrounding the interior is a lengthy mini-railroad track with trains running. Kids can push button control the lobby display. Speaking of trains, you will likely hear a real one go by as you dine (maybe even 3-4 trains!). Upscale Casual. Children's Menu under $5.00, Dinners run $10.00-$16.00. Hours: Open for lunch and dinner, daily.

Exit - 317 (east of I-75)

NEW ECHOTA HISTORIC SITE

Calhoun - ***1211 Chatsworth Highway NE (one mile east of I-75 exit 317 on GA 225) 30701. http://gastateparks.org/info/echota/. Phone: (706) 624-1321. Hours: Tuesday - Saturday 9:00am-5:00pm, Sunday 2:00-5:30pm. Closed Monday (except holidays), Thanksgiving, Christmas and New Years. Closed Tuesday when open Monday. Admission: $2.50-$4.00 per person.***

The Cherokee National group established New Echota as its capital in 1825. This government seat became headquarters for the independent Indian nation that once covered northern Georgia and parts of four other southeastern states. This is the site of the first Native American newspaper office, the signing of a treaty which relinquished Cherokee claims to lands east of the Mississippi, and finally, the sad assembly of Cherokee Indians for the removal along the infamous Trail of Tears. Many artifacts from the original print shop and methods of archeological digs are on display. Today, the site has a museum where you can view a 17-minute video and then take a self-guided tour of historic buildings. The structures include: a print shop, a court house, Council House, a missionary home, Vann's tavern and several homes and farm buildings. Did you know the Cherokee were the most civilized Indian tribe? Learn some Cherokee language with Sequoyah: si-yo = Hello, ga-du = bread, a-ma = water.

GEORGIA

Exit - 293 (west of I-75)

TELLUS NORTHWEST GEORGIA SCIENCE MUSEUM

Cartersville - ***100 Tellus Drive, Hwy 411 (I-75 North to Exit 293 in town of White) 30184. Phone: (770) 606-5700. www.tellusmuseum.org. Hours: Daily 10:00am-5:00pm. Closed most national holidays. Admission: $14.00 adult, $12.00 senior (65+), $10.00 child (3-17) Note: Science In Motion planetarium. Educators: www.tellusmuseum.org/education/pre-and-postactivities.***

Minerals or "rocks" are very important natural resources for this area. Barite is used in the manufacture of rubber for tennis balls, golf balls, brake shoes, eye glasses & much more. The largest exhibit contains a fossil dig filled with real and replicated bones, shark teeth, trilobites, and more. Specimens in the museum are likely to generate questions and comments. When kids look at Okenite (from India), you'll hear comments like "cotton balls" and "fuzzy". Try to find the "fuzzy rock" on your visit to the museum! In My Big Backyard gallery, students have the opportunity to match the life cycle of various insects, match animals to their habitats and to what they eat in the food cycle, and explore other interactive exhibits like the rain and snow simulation. Kids can also "play" with light, magnets and even an electrical "hair-raising" experiment. There's a Little Kids' Science Garden where you can dig for fossils, tromp through Mad Scientists backyard, and travel to the center of earth. The Great Hall features a full scale cast of an Apatosaurus. At nearly 80 feet this was one of the largest dinosaurs to ever walk on North America.

Exit - 288 (west of I-75)

BARTOW HISTORY CENTER

Cartersville - ***13 North Wall Street (downtown, follow signs from I-75 exit 288) 30120. Phone: (770) 382-3818. www.bartowhistorycenter.org. Hours: Monday-Saturday 10:00am-5:00pm, Sunday 1-5pm, plus Thursday evenings. Admission: $2.00-$3.00. Educators: www.bartowhistorycenter.org/school.htm for lesson plans.***

Do you know anything about the Etowah Mounds or DeSoto, the Cherokee or General Sherman? Exhibits at the Bartow History Center focus on the settlement and development of Bartow County, Georgia, beginning with the early nineteenth century, when the Cherokee still inhabited the area. Pioneer life, Civil War strife, post-war recovery, the Great Depression era, early industry, and notable figures are depicted through interactive exhibits in the permanent gallery space. At the History Center, kids can practice penmanship on slate boards, recite lessons, and perform school chores to avoid wearing the dunce cap. Learn map skills with games and puzzles at the History Center. Sit down at the switchboard and explore the history of communication from tin can phones to old radio shows.

Exit - 288 (west of I-75)

BOOTH WESTERN ART MUSEUM

Cartersville - ***501 Museum Drive (I-75 exit 288, Main St. Go west 2.2 miles, follow signs) 30120. Phone: (770) 387-1300. www.boothmuseum.org. Hours: Tuesday-Saturday 10:00am-5:00pm, Sunday 1:00-5:00pm. Open late on Thursday evenings. Admission: $10.00 adult, $8.00 senior, $7.00 student (over 12). Children 12 and under and active military get in free anytime but certain Thursday evenings and Saturday mornings, they have free family admission or themed crafts for $1.00. Note: Gift shop and café.***

Daniel rode into town to see some Western Art...

Explore the West without leaving the South! This place is spectacular! The artwork is certainly emotional, whether its a cowboy checking to see who is riding behind them, or a lifelike bull staring you in the face as you exit the elevator. Start with an orientation film about the history of the West. Then, families are able to check out saddle bags filled with activity sheets and sample artifacts. This "scavenger hunt" method is very engaging and even has a beaded bracelet kit to take home (the rest of the bag's contents remain for the next child). Now, if that wasn't fun enough, head downstairs to Sagebrush Ranch hands-on area. Begin by dressing up as a cowgirl or boy (chaps and all). Take a ride in the rocking stagecoach, sit on a life-size horse or brand a cow. Draw, ride, cook, puzzle or read, too. It's authentic and it's a hoot! Not many art museums are this kid-friendly anywhere - and, such a fun theme - cowboys and Indians. Excellent!

Chuckwagon cookin' with Jenny...

ETOWAH INDIAN MOUNDS HISTORIC SITE

Cartersville - ***813 Indian Mounds Road SE (5 miles SW of I-75 exit 288, follow brown directional signs) 30120. http://gastateparks.org/info/etowah/. Phone: (770) 387-3747. Hours: Wednesday-Saturday 9:00am-5:00pm. Closed Thanksgiving, Christmas and New Years. Admission: $4.00-$5.00 per person. Note: at least once per month, the site holds special themed Indian events on Saturdays. Educators: Online links describe how to create authentic dugout canoes or thatched wattle & daub houses.***

These mounds were the ceremonial center of a town that was home to several thousand Mississippian Indians more than 400 years ago. All the mounds are flat-topped and made from earthen material (dirt). The largest stands 63 acres and appears to serve as the temple for the "Priest-Chief" and as burial sites for Indian nobility. You actually get to climb the 134 steps to walk along the top. In another mound, nobility were buried in elaborate costumes accompanied by items they would need in their after-lives. Many artifacts in the museum show how the natives of this political and religious center decorated themselves with shell beads, tattoos, paint, feathers and copper earrings. You'll see a sample burial site and fish traps. Well-preserved stone effigies and objects made of wood, sea shells and stone are also displayed. This is a mysterious site because these were prehistoric peoples and no one recorded history. The mounds are very well-preserved and fun (but aerobic) to climb.

Exit - 285 *(east of I-75)*

RED TOP MOUNTAIN STATE PARK

Cartersville - ***50 Lodge Road SE (1.5 miles east of I-75 via exit 285) 30121. http://gastateparks.org/info/redtop/. Phone: (770) 975-0055 lodge or (770) 975-4226 center. Hours: Daily 7:00am-10:00pm. Admission: $3.00 daily vehicle parking fee. Miscellaneous: July 4th - Enjoy the lakeside beach or go on a guided hike. Nature programs, a bluegrass concert, fireworks & more. $2.00 parking.***

Named for the soil's rich red color caused by high iron-ore content, Red Top Mountain was once an important mining area for iron. Now, this park is on

Lake Allatoona and is especially ideal for swimming (beach and pool), boating, and fishing. If you don't have a boat, rentals are available. Several hiking trails wind through the park (12 miles of trails, 3/4 mile paved trail behind the restaurant suitable for strollers). One hike spot is a reconstructed 1860s log cabin (open and staffed on Saturdays). The park's lodge and restaurant plus many cottages, offer overnight accommodations. There's also mini-golf and sport courts.

Exit - 278 (west of I-75)

CAUBLE PARK

Acworth - ***(located on Beach Street on the North side of Lake Acworth, I-75 exit 278) 30101. Phone: (770) 917-1234. www.acworth.org/aprd/Parks.html.***

The 25-acre park contains fishing points, public restrooms, a boating ramp (for electric motor driven boats only), a boardwalk, a beach, volleyball net, rental facilities, two playgrounds, and an open play area. Cauble Park opens at 7:00am and closes at 11:00pm. Acworth Beach opens on Memorial Day weekend and closes Labor Day weekend. During the summer Coach's Café is open to meet all of your beverage and food needs. There is no lifeguard on duty and the beach opens at sun up and closes at sun down. There is a $10.00 parking fee on the weekends - only the weekends between Memorial Day and Labor Day.

Exit - 273 (west of I-75)

SOUTHERN MUSEUM OF CIVIL WAR AND LOCOMOTIVE HISTORY

Kennesaw - ***2829 Cherokee Street NW (I-75 exit 273 west) 30144. Phone: (770) 427-2117 or (800) 742-6897. www.southernmuseum.org. Hours: Monday-Saturday 9:30am-5:00pm, Sunday 11am-6:00pm. Closed New Years, Easter, Thanksgiving and Christmas time. Admission: $7.50 adult, $6.50 senior (60+), $5.50 child (6-12). FREEBIES: ask for scavenger hunt.***

The true story behind the old Disney movie, "The Great Locomotive Chase," is what the Southern Museum is all about. The museum's star attraction is The General, a steam locomotive nabbed by Yankee raiders in 1862 just 100 yards from where it stands today.

The daring band of 22 planned to drive The General north to Chattanooga and destroy Confederate supply lines along the way. Rebels manned a locomotive of their own and chased The General, full throttle, for 100 miles until the raiders were forced to abandon ship. Most were captured. Unfortunately for Kennesaw, a few thousand of their friends came back two years later. The Battle of Kennesaw Mountain that followed was one of the bloodiest conflicts fought during the 1864 Atlanta Campaign. But the Museum doesn't end there. Peek into Glover Machine Works: An interactive presentation detailing the train building process, from metallurgy and patterns to casting and construction helping visitors experience life as a factory worker. Other kids interactives include tapping out Morse Code; driving a simulated train; or dressing up in the old-timey village.

Exit - 269 (west of I-75)

KENNESAW MOUNTAIN NATIONAL BATTLEFIELD PARK

Kennesaw - ***900 Kennesaw Mountain Drive (I-75 exit 269, Barrett Pkwy, follow signs) 30152. Phone: (770) 427-4686. www.nps.gov/kemo. Hours: Daily 8:30am-5:00pm. Admission: FREE admission. The mountain road is closed every weekend and on major holidays. They offer a shuttle bus that will provide transportation to the top of the mountain for $1.50-$3.00 per person fee vs. walking.***

The Confederate Army soundly defeated the Union Army here on June 27, 1864. This important battle brought General Sherman's march toward Atlanta to a halt for two weeks. The name Kennesaw is derived from the Cherokee Indian "Gah-nee-sah" meaning cemetery or burial ground. While walking some of the 17.3 miles of interpretive walking trails you will see historic earthworks, cannon emplacements and various interpretive signs. Atop Kennesaw Mountain is an observation platform and memorial to 14 Confederate generals. Inside the Visitor Center, view interpretive showcases and an 18-minute orientation film. Outside, original earthworks and Civil War artillery can be viewed along marked trails.

Exit - 265 (west of I-75)

WHITEWATER PARK, SIX FLAGS

Marietta - ***250 Cobb Parkway, North (off I-75 north exit 265) 30062. Phone: (770) 424-WAVE. www.whitewaterpark.com. Hours: Vary from 10:00am-6:00pm pre-season and post-season to 10:00am-8:00pm peak season. Park open weekends in***

May, daily Memorial Day- mid August, weekends though Labor Day. Admission: $30-$40.00 day tickets. Parking $15. Online discounts.

The South's largest water theme park with nearly 50 water play fun activities. A variety of thrilling water slides, rides, attractions, and special areas for small children are featured at this water park where you will find "The Ocean," a 750,000 gallon pool that whips up four foot waves and "The Cliffhanger," one of the tallest freefalls in the world where the rider is propelled 90 feet straight down at high-speed. Or, try the 735-foot-long Run-a-Way River, a vicious four-person tunnel raft ride. If that's not enough, try the "Tornado" (riders are set in motion down a 132-foot long tunnel and thrown into the giant open-ended funnel), Bermuda Triangle, Gulf Coast Screamer or Banzai Pipeline. For Little Kids (and Chickens): There are other ways to play—splash in Little Squirt's Island and Captain Kid's Cove, or just float down one of two lazy rivers. And everybody loves the 750,000 gallon wavepool, family raft rides and body flumes. For Everyone: The Pirate Invasion Dive Show brings Vegas-show glitz and high-diving heroics to the wavepool most weeknights, followed on summer Fridays by "Dive-In Movies." Float up to the big screen or find a seat on the deck for a family-friendly flick. Never was cinema more refreshing.

THE BIG CHICKEN

Marietta - ***12 N. Cobb Parkway (I-75 exit 265 west to corner of Hwy 120 & US 41) 30062. Phone: (770) 422-4716.***

The Big Chicken is the extraordinary sign for a very ordinary KFC in Marietta. In 1963, the owner of a drive-in wanted to draw attention. And thus, Tubby Davis, owner of Johnny Reb's Restaurant, and an egghead Georgia Tech engineering student built the world's first and only post-modern cubist steel chicken. Using locally milled steel, it stands 50-feet tall. Three decades and several owners later, the Big Chicken still rises proudly above Cobb Parkway. Inside the building is a gift shop with all kinds of Big Chicken memorabilia. Its legacy has even spread to surrounding businesses, many using the nomenclature of "Big Chicken This"...

Exit - 255 (east of I-75)

ATLANTA HISTORY CENTER

Atlanta - ***130 West Paces Ferry Road, NW (I-75 to exit #255, follow signs 2.5 m) 30305. Phone: (404) 814-4004. www.atlantahistorycenter.com. Hours: Monday-Saturday 10:00am-5:30pm, Sunday Noon-5:30pm. Closed most holidays. Admission: $16.00 adult, $13.00 senior (65+) and student (13+), $11.00 youth (4-12). Includes the Atlanta History Museum, Centennial Olympic Games Museum, historic gardens and tours of two Historic Houses, Swan House and Smith Farm AND Margaret Mitchell House. Note: Lots of little theatre rooms with videos here. Ask for the Family Fun brochure. Take a walk outside to visit the Swan House 1928 Mansion or the Tullie Smith Farm. The farmhouse and other related buildings are from the 1840s and are best visited during special event programs. Gift shop and Coca-cola Café. Educators: About a dozen excellent Lesson Plans are online under: School Programs/Educator Resources/Curriculum Resources & Lesson Plans (ex. Farms, Native Americans, Civil War); and History Live! FREEBIES: The Kids Corner onsite has a room full of activity sheet puzzles and coloring that you can do there or take with you.***

Revisit the Civil War, discover southern folk arts and meet famous Atlantans. Kids will gravitate to these areas:

Jenny holding an actual Olympic Torch...

- CENTENNIAL OLYMPIC GAMES: The 1996 Centennial Olympic Games changed Atlanta forever - and accelerated its transformation from southern capital to international city. For seventeen days, Atlanta was the focus of the entire world. The favorite spot - the interactive Sports Lab.
- METROPOLITAN FRONTIERS (1835-present): Journey through four stages of Atlanta history, from early pioneer settlements to today's bustling city of international fame. See an entire 1894 shotgun house (why called that? Hint: long, narrow shape) moved from southwest Atlanta; an 1898 horse-drawn fire engine with a steam-driven pump used by the Atlanta fire department in the city's tragic 1917 fire; a 1920 Hanson car built in Atlanta and one of only two known in existence; a scale model of the "Spaghetti Junction".

- TURNING POINT: THE AMERICAN CIVIL WAR - Explore the stories of both Confederate and Federal soldiers, along with the heartache and hope of loved ones at home. Videos interpret what happened and why. Touch-screen computer learning stations can answer your questions and deepen your understanding. Did you know only 6% of slaves from Africa went to the States? Others went to the Caribbean and South America.
- SHAPING TRADITIONS: FOLK ARTS IN A CHANGING SOUTH - Touch, see, and hear the folk arts that have defined the South for generations. It begins with sections asking "What's folk about folk arts?" and "What's southern about southern folk arts?"

Other Exhibits explore: Barbeque, Rednecks, Bobby Jones, and Native American history.

Exit - 252 (west of I-75)

GEORGIA DOME TOURS

Atlanta - ***One Georgia Dome NW (I-75 exit 252. tours depart between Gates B & C) 30313. Phone: (404) 223-8600. www.gadome.com. Admission: $6.00 adult, $4.00 senior and child (5-12). Individual Tours: Tuesday-Saturday 10:00am-3:00pm during football season (except on days when events occur in the Dome). Tours leave every hour. Call ahead to be sure there's room.***

The world's largest cable-supported dome offers tours. Want to see behind-the-scenes, from the Falcons locker room, to the new turf everyone is talking about (wanna touch it)? Want to see the VIP views from the press box or Dome suites? Get a Falcons eye view of the stadium and then see the TV studio where broadcasted games originate from. Come see the site of the 1994 & 2000 Super Bowls. Visit the venue that hosted gymnastics & basketball for the 1996 Summer Olympics. Every year the Georgia Dome hosts the highest attended and highest rated non-BCS bowl game, the Chick-Fil-A Bowl, which often draws more than 75,000 spectators.

Exit - 250 (west of I-75)

PAPER MUSEUM AT IPST

Atlanta - ***500 10th Street N.W. (I-75/85 exit 250 to IPST Bldg. At Georgia Tech) 30332. Phone: (404) 894-7840. www.ipst.gatech.edu/amp/. Hours: Monday-Friday 9:00am-5:00pm. The Museum is closed on Georgia Tech holidays. Admission: FREE. Suggested donation $3.00 per person. Tours: By Reservation. Grades 3-12. Minimum 10, Maximum 30-40. Fee for tours (see below)***

Trace the history of paper from 4,000 BC to today. Learn how Asians started a fine art and how companies through the ages each developed a way to "watermark" their signature on their product. The gallery showcases the work of contemporary paper artists with special exhibits changing at least twice a year. The permanent exhibit space is FROM HAND TO MACHINE - Follow the path of papermaking that began in ancient China and leads to the advanced technology of today. (self-guided tour is a donation fee)

PAPER TRAVEL - This tour includes the museum as well as "Paper-The Video", a fun and lively video which highlights the history and the uses of paper. The charge for this tour is $5.50 per person. Weekdays at 10:00am. Allow 1 hour.

PAPERWORKS! - This includes a guided tour of the Museum of Papermaking and "Paper-The Video", as well as a hands-on papermaking workshop. Students will enjoy making their own sheets of paper from cotton pulp. The charge for this tour is $8.50 per person. Weekdays at 10:00am. Allow 1½ hours.

Making paper is somewhat of a lost art so this museum may be one of the most unique you'll ever visit.

Exit - 250 (east of I-75)

FEDERAL RESERVE BANK OF ATLANTA VISITORS CENTER & MONETARY MUSEUM

Atlanta - ***1000 Peachtree Street NE (I-75/85, take Exit 250 (10th Street/14th Street/17th Street), turn right onto 10th Street, and left onto Peachtree Street) 30309. www.frbatlanta.org/about/tours/museum.org. Phone: (404) 498-8764. Hours: Monday-Friday 9:00am-4:00pm. Admission: FREE. Tours: Open for scheduled, guided tours only weekdays at 9:30am, 11:00am or 1:00pm. Recommended for pre-teens on up.***

The story of money—from bartering to modern times. In the museum, you'll see examples of rare coins and currency plus displays highlighting noted events in monetary history. After touring the museum, experience the rest of the Visitors Center, where interactive and multimedia exhibits provide in-depth lessons on the role of the Federal Reserve in the U.S. economy. Then, you can take a look inside their cash-processing operations, where millions of dollars are counted, sorted, or shredded daily. You'll also get a glimpse into the bank's automated vault and see the robotic transports that do the heavy lifting.

Exit - 250 (east of I-75)

MARGARET MITCHELL HOUSE & MUSEUM

Atlanta - ***990 Peachtree Street (I-75, 10th Street exit 250 and Peachtree) 30309. Phone: (404) 249-7015. www.gwtw.org. Hours: Open daily 10am-5:30pm, except Sunday Noon-5:30pm. Admission: $13.00 adult, $10.00 senior (65+) and students over 12, $8.50 youth (4-12). Note: Because Margaret was quite a character, ask for the family-friendly version of the apartment tour.***

In the "Gone With the Wind" movie museum, your girls will love to admire the doll collection and everyone will want to "walk thru" the actual doorway to "Tara"! Now, prepare, girls and boys, to be inspired! Tour the historic house and apartment where Margaret Mitchell wrote one of the classic beloved novels "Gone With the Wind". As you learn about the life (and death) of this fascinating woman you'll learn that she wrote short stories as a little girl - she even put on plays with neighborhood children. The girls were always the heroine! Her Dad was a history buff and many characters are based on family and friends throughout Margaret's life history. Touch her lucky stair post or see her battered typewriter where she wrote most of her work. When friends came over, she'd hide her manuscript all over the house. She once forgot the first chapter was hidden in the refrigerator! Amusing stories abound while on tour. We promise, you'll be told a secret or two!

See the famous typewriter where the tale was told...

Although constantly hounded by publishers, Mitchell refused to write a sequel to her novel. She never published another book.

CENTER FOR PUPPETRY ARTS

Atlanta - ***1404 Spring Street, NW (I75 Exit #250 (10th/14th/GA Tech). Turn left on 14th Street, crossing over I-75. At 3rd traffic light, turn left on W. Peachtree Street) 30309. Phone: (404) 873-3391. www.puppet.org. Hours: Tuesday-Friday 9:00am-3:00pm, Saturday 10:00am-5:00pm, Sunday Noon-5pm. Admission: $16.00 per person per performance. Workshop and Museum admission included in single***

show ticket. Tour: special Behind-the-Scenes Tour at the Center and get a peek at how puppet magic is made (weekends at 2pm for groups). Note: Museum and performances change throughout the year. Reservations suggested for activities. FREEBIES: click on Education, then Study Guides for current exhibit activity word finds and coloring pages.

Learning how to make simple puppets...

Many famous puppets have spent the night here (how about Kermit the Frog). Can you imagine the stories this place could tell? So, let's start in the Museum. First of all, it's a little spooky and interactive (even the storage room is animated). The best part - the variety. Asians spend their lifetimes perfecting Shadow puppets and Bunraku puppetry requires three puppeteers to work one figure. Other puppets are much simpler. Kid's imaginations soar seeing household objects like scarves, cloth, and plastic tubing puppets. Now, attend a performance. Their shows are really several notches above any puppet shows elsewhere. Many are based on classic folk tales - some with a "twist". You are encouraged to laugh, giggle, sneer, clap or stomp approval or disapproval at the happenings on stage. The puppeteers greet the audience afterwards to enlighten the crowd and share their "tricks". Next, do a workshop. Learn about different types of puppets - hand, rod, string, marionette, shadow or body. Make your own hand puppet that resembles a character in the performance. Have a short time to perform with your puppet in the mini-stage. What a wonderful way to engage the kids into the art and entertainment of puppetry. This place is a wonderful surprise every visit and worth spending a good part of your morning / afternoon!

ATLANTA BOTANICAL GARDEN

Atlanta - ***1345 Piedmont Avenue (I75/85 exit 250-14th St., left on Piedmont Ave. at The Prado, Midtown) 30309. www.atlantabotanicalgarden.org. Phone: (404) 876-5859. Hours: Tuesday - Sunday 9:00am-5:00pm, open till 7:00pm during Daylight Savings Time. Admission: $18.95 adult, $13.95 child (3 -12). Note: Tropical, desert and endangered plants from around the world are found at Fuqua Conservatory (on the other side of the park). FREEBIES: click on Kids & Schools for fun activity sheets like Critter Crawl or Scavenger Hunt.***

The Atlanta Botanical Garden features one of the world's largest permanent displays of tropical orchids, 15 acres of outdoor display gardens and the Fuqua Conservatory, home to rare and endangered tropical and desert plants. The Children's Garden, alone, is worth the visit here! Greeted by the "Green Man Fountain and "Plants Keep Us Well" atrium, you'll walk into a garden wonderland where plants help us LAUGH, LIVE AND LEARN. Special enclaves include the Laugh Garden, providing a space for little ones to wind through a cocoon tunnel and emerge as a butterfly as they swish around a maze beginning at a colorful caterpillar's mouth and ending at the Butterfly Pavilion. Dig for fossils at the Dinosaur Garden, learn about carnivorous plants in the Soggy Bog, and experience the singing stone at Rocky Pointe. Slide through a leaf, sit around storytime readings of Peter Rabbit, then walk through the story's scenery. Sit in an Indian hut, go to Grandma's House for a visit, play the bee game, and climb in a giant tree house. This is, by far, the best children's garden we've interacted with in the South!

The Children's Garden is sure worth the visit!

Exit - 249D (east of I-75)

THE VARSITY

***Atlanta** - 61 North Avenue, N.W. (I-75/85 exit 249D, the Varsity is immediately on left just over bridge. Pull into first driveway) 30308. www.thevarsity.com. Phone: (404) 881-1706.*

> The Varsity is the world's largest drive-in offering fast-food dining.

An Atlanta institution for over 80 years. You need to know everyone from businessmen to college students frequent here and it's always crowded (they serve over 10,000 customers each day) and noisy - but, it's a must see. You can sit in your car and get car-hop service

or go inside. Whether it's a chili cheese dog, the rings, a Frosted Orange or maybe a fried pie, everyone has their favorites that keep them coming back. Everything is made fresh and all fried items are cooked in Canola Oil w/ No Cholesterol - no trans fat, low saturated fat; and they make their chicken salad and egg salad with Kraft Lite Mayonnaise. If you're just wanting to order for the experience, whatever you order, be sure to add one order of onion rings and a fried pie to split. If you're planning a trip to The Varsity, you should brush up on your Varsity Lingo to make sure you have your "order in your mind". "Walk a Dog" (hot dog to go); Sideways (onions on the side); or P.C. (Plain Chocolate milk always served with ice) are examples of shortcut chants the servers use to call out your order. One of those "you had to be there" diners.

HIGH MUSEUM OF ART

Atlanta - ***1280 Peachtree Street (I-75/85 exit 249D east) 30309. Phone: (404) 733-4400. www.high.org. Hours: Tuesday-Saturday 10:00am-5:00pm, Sunday Noon-5:00pm. Admission: $19.50 adult, $16.50 senior (65+), $12.00 child (6-17). Your ticket includes admission to the permanent collection, all current special exhibitions and family workshops. Walk-up admission is free for Fulton County residents on the first Saturday of each month. Tours: Guided tours Sunday and Wednesday at 1:00pm.***

This museum mostly displays European and American paintings and special exhibits including African, decorative, folk and modern art. The Learning to Look / Looking to Learn interactives are the best way to explore a classic art museum with kids. Learning Gallery: Before or after visiting the galleries, families can play together in five fun activity areas: Building Buildings, Making a Mark, Telling Stories, Sculpting Spaces, and Transforming Treasure. Designed for children ages 5-10 when accompanied by an adult.

Exits - 249A (SB Only)

248B (NB Only) (east of I-75)

APEX MUSEUM

Atlanta - ***135 Auburn Avenue NE (I-75/85 North, take Exit # 248B or heading South, take exit 249A) 30303. Phone: (404) 521-2739. www.apexmuseum.org. Hours: Tuesday-Saturday 10:00am-5:00pm. Admission: $5.00-$6.00 (age 4+).***

The African American Panoramic Experience offers a variety of permanent and temporary exhibits ranging from art to politics. Visit the Yates and Milton Drug Store, one of Atlanta's first Black owned businesses. Hear the stories of early African American pioneers in Atlanta. Learn about the powerful Black Families that helped to make Atlanta great. All Aboard! The Trolley Theater provides the right atmosphere for video presentations on African American experiences.

Exit - 248D (east of I-75)

MARTIN LUTHER KING JR. NATIONAL HISTORIC SITE

Atlanta - ***450 Auburn Avenue, N.E. (I-75 exit 248D, Sweet Auburn district) 30312. Phone: (404) 331-6922. www.nps.gov/malu. Hours: Daily 9:00am-5:00pm. Closed Thanksgiving Day, Christmas and New Years. Summers open until 6:00pm. The Home and Church may have shorter hours, please inquire at the Park Service desk for tour times. Admission: FREE. Tours: No special arrangements are needed since most of the park is self-guided. However, you will need to register to tour the Birth Home of Dr. King. Educators: click on For Teachers/Lesson Plans & Teacher Guides for some excellent exhibit-based activities and problem-solving projects.***

Open the door to see a future leader...

Now a National Historic Site, visit Dr. Martin Luther King Jr.'s Birthplace, Home and Church. Begin in the Visitor Center for orientation. The "Civil Rights Struggle" present emotional exhibits through movie and video clips. Most exhibits encourage children to carry on the dream of freedom, justice and world peace using interactive displays. The exhibits are extremely emotional and capture your attention and your heart. However, it may contain material that is best viewed by children who have studied segregation and Civil Rights beforehand. Otherwise, your children may be terrified how cruel people can be to one another. The Home is located in the residential section of "Sweet Auburn", the center of black Atlanta. Two blocks west of the home is Ebenezer Baptist Church, the pastorate of Martin's grandfather and father. The tour guide at the church "preaches" the church's history from near the pulpit! Here, "M.L." learned about family and Christian love, segregation in the days of "Jim Crow" laws, diligence and tolerance.

GEORGIA

Exit - 248C (west of I-75)

IMAGINE IT! THE CHILDREN'S MUSEUM OF ATLANTA

Atlanta - ***275 Centennial Olympic Park Drive NW (north exit 248C. Turn right onto Baker Street) 30313. Phone: (404) 659-5437. www.childrensmuseumatlanta.org Hours: Monday-Friday 10:00am-4:00pm, Saturday & Sunday 10:00am-5:00pm. Closed WEDNESDAYS and major holidays. Admission: $12.75 per person age 21and above. Note: Vending area. The Museum is also walking distance from The CNN Center, World of Coca-Cola, and other downtown restaurants.***

This is a museum where children can experience the power of imagination and the delight of learning. Primarily designed for ages two to eight, Imagine It! features hands-on, colorful exhibits and activities in which children look, listen, touch and explore. Kids and their adults can learn together where food comes from (and how the body uses it), work construction equipment, explore a barnyard, and make a craft to take home. Make music with bongos and such. The kids especially love the big ball popper that shoots out giant balls on command. You can even walk through a make-believe town and go shopping.

WORLD OF COCA-COLA

Atlanta - ***121 Baker Street (adjacent to Georgia Aquarium at Centennial Olympic Park Drive, I-75 exit 248C) 30313. www.worldofcoca-cola.com. Phone: (800) 676-COKE. Hours: Daily 10:00am-5:00pm. Longer open/close hours during peak season and most weekends. Closed Easter, Thanksgiving, Christmas. Admission: $16.00 adult, $14.00 senior (55+), $12.00 child (3-12). Online discounts. Timed entry tickets. FREEBIES: click on Fun Stuff for downloadable car games and art projects.***

Atlanta is the birthplace of Coca-Cola. The story is told through a bright collection of memorabilia, classic radio and television ads, a fantasy representation of the bottling process and a futuristic soda fountain. It started with a syrup created by a pharmacist. Accidentally, a soda jerk added carbonated water and the customers loved it - Coke was born! Guests are greeted by a enthusiastic guides who direct you to start by viewing the 4-minute audio visual history of the product (later you'll get a chance to watch the Secret Formula 3D movie with moving seats!).

GEORGIA

After that, you are turned loose to explore the many sections of the museum. At Bottle Works you'll view a slow-motion production line so you can see robots in action filling bottles. Really interesting history is found at Milestones of Refreshment. On display- a can that flew on the space shuttle and the original prototype bottle. The highlight of your visit is the last station - taste testing! Try flavors, old and new, plus many found in foreign countries. Some are quite unusual, some very sweet. If you try them all, like we did, you're bound to have a belly-ache - so, be wise, and choose carefully. Don't forget your free Coke as you leave.

> **Top Secret...**
> Did you know the secret formula is still a secret? Where is it kept?

Exit - 248C (west of I-75)

GEORGIA AQUARIUM

***Atlanta** - 225 Baker Street (I-75 exit 248C, follow signs) 30313. Phone: (404) 581-4000. www.georgiaaquarium.org. Hours: Sunday-Friday 10:00am-5:00pm, Saturday 9:00am-6:00pm. Extended hours during peak weekends or school breaks. Admission: $35.95 adult, $31.95 senior, $29.95 child (3-12) includes 4D & Dolphin Tales show. Parking Garage $10.00. Café Aquaria Food Court on premises. Note: Guarantee admission to the Aquarium by making advance reservations. We recommend parents bring a pair of socks for children while playing in the Georgia Explorer gallery's children's play area. Educators: click on Education/teachers online for fact sheets, lesson plans and Ask an Educator Q & A opportunities.*

Beluga whales, whale sharks, 8 million gallons of water - oh my! The world's largest aquarium with more than 100,000 animals is dedicated to the waters of the world, and there's a children's play area with touch tanks for kids to get up close and personal with all kinds of sea critters. Kids love the "pretty colors" in Tropical Diver and the Touch Wall and bubbles and tunnels in Ocean Voyager. Learn about the Whale sharks' journey to Georgia and much more in the Ocean exhibit that cleverly takes you around the same tank of

Getting close with our penguin friends...

water, just from wall, bubble and tunnel views. No one can resist hanging around the giant two-story wall of live fish (it's like you're watching an IMAX film – only it's live)! The Belugas gracefully dance ballet to the music and the Penguins love getting close to humans behind "ice" in Coldwater Quest. Be sure to watch the Octopus action video and make time to be amused by all the Sea Otter and Sea Lion antics in Quest. River Scout and Georgia Explorer have displays of things you might find closer to home – don't be frightened by the Red Piranha or afraid to touch rays or shrimp at the various Touch Tanks in these areas. One of our favorite aquariums, we especially liked the way many paths led you around different sides of the same tank of fish.. .especially amusing to kids as sometimes the fish were above you, below you or right up in your face!

CENTENNIAL OLYMPIC PARK

Atlanta - ***285 International Blvd. (I-75/85 north to exit 248C) 30313. Phone: (404) 223-4412. www.centennialpark.com. Hours: Daily 7:00am-11:00pm. Admission: FREE.***

Look for the Fountain of Rings - the world's largest fountain utilizing the five interconnecting rings of the Olympic symbol with 25 water jets - and you've found the park. The water jets display four 20-minute musical water shows daily beginning at lunchtime, then every three hours. Today, the park features a wide variety of events including Fourth Saturday Family Fun Days, a free event with hands-on activities, April through September. There are also playgrounds, water gardens, a visitors center with Fountainside Cafe, and people-watchers plaza.

CNN STUDIO TOUR

Atlanta - ***One CNN Center (I-75/85 exit International Blvd. exit 248C, left on Olympic Park) 30303. www.cnn.com/tour/atlanta/. Phone: (404) 827-2300 or (877) 4CNN-Tour. Admission: $15.00 adult, $14.00 senior (55+), $12.00 child (4-12). Parking $10.00. Tours: Daily from 9:00am - 5:00pm. Tours depart every 10 minutes from Atrium. Tours last 55 minutes. Advance reservations suggested. The tour is closed on Easter Sunday, thanksgiving day and Christmas Day. Insider's Tip: Don't spend vacation time waiting for an appointment. Make reservations in advance for the 45-minute tour.***

This attraction showcases the CNN Studios. On tour, get a look INSIDE the CNN production studios and newsrooms. Begin by looking at 30+ monitors simulating the CNN control Room. A one-of-a-kind re-creation of CNN's main control room where guests will see and hear the truly behind-the-scenes elements of 24-hour news, live. Look for the monitor with the pre-shot - maybe catch an anchor powdering their nose! An interactive exhibit area follows. This is where guests can view video clips of the top 100 news stories that CNN has covered during the past 20 years, log on to CNN.com, and test their knowledge with the journalism ethics display. Next, see a sample studio - be sure to volunteer to do a short broadcast. Why can't weather people wear blue? Check out the robotic cameras. Great tour to see the glamour and electronic glitz it takes to pull off a 24-hour broadcast.

Exit - 248C (east of I-75)

JIMMY CARTER LIBRARY AND MUSEUM

Atlanta - ***441 Freedom Parkway (I-75/85 exit 248C, Freedom Pkwy) 30307. Phone: (404) 865-7100. www.jimmycarterlibrary.gov. Hours: Monday-Saturday 9:00am-4:45pm, Sunday Noon-4:45pm. Admission: $8.00 adult, $6.00 senior (60+), military and students, Free youth (16 and under). Note: restaurant serving lunch daily except Sunday. Educators: a biography of Jimmy Carter is online under: Information about Jimmy & Rosalynn Carter. Also curriculum under Education.***

The only Presidential Library in the southeast United States features an exact replica of the Oval Office, and the Nobel Peace Prize awarded to President Jimmy Carter. Exhibits change every six months.

GEORGIA

FERNBANK MUSEUM OF NATURAL HISTORY

Atlanta - ***767 Clifton Road NE (I-75/I-85 to downtown exit 248C (GA 10 east). Go 1.7 miles to Ponce de Leon Ave., turn right. Go 1/7 miles to left on Clifton Rd. Follow signs) 30307. Phone: (404) 929-6300. www.fernbankmuseum.org Hours: Monday-Saturday 10:00am-5:00pm, Sunday Noon-5:00pm. Only closed Thanksgiving and Christmas. Admission: $18.00 adult, $17.00 senior (62+) and student, $16.00 child (3-12). IMAX extra $11.00-$13.00. Museum and IMAX combo pricing. Note: IMAX Theatre shows each day. View schedule and features online. Fernbank Café open for lunch. FREEBIE: Three different Scavenger Hunts (detailed, write in answers) are online under: Education/Just for Educators/Online Resources.***

History comes alive at Fernbank Museum of Natural History. Giants of the Mesozoic features the world's largest dinosaurs. This area recreates a snapshot of what life was like years ago during the Cretaceous Period. The exhibit showcases the world's largest meat eater, the 47-foot-long Giganotosaurus as it prepares to make a meal out of the largest dinosaur ever discovered, the 123-foot-long plant-eating Argentinosaurus. Also featured in the exhibition are two species of flying reptiles. Twenty-four in all, the pterosaurs are shown reacting to the scene below. The terrain-like rockwork includes fossils of other animals and plants such as a prehistoric frog, crocodile and Auracaria tree, along with dinosaur tracks. A Walk Through Time in Georgia has gobs of exhibits and realistic dioramas to take you on a journey that begins in the Piedmont, the region in Georgia with the oldest rocks. Then walk in the sand through a marsh or in the muddy swamp. Fish in the Okefenokee Swamp, dock up at the Jekyll Island Pier, encounter native wildlife at Turkey Mountain and more. Other highlights include the Cosmos Theatre, a six-foot sloth that lived during the Ice Age, and the Dinosaur Gallery.

Exits - 248A (SB Only)

248B (NB Only) (west of I-75)

GEORGIA STATE CAPITOL & MUSEUM

Atlanta - ***2 Martin Luther King Dr. (I-75 exit 248A or B, look for the gold domed building, Capitol Hill at Washington Street) 30334. Phone: (404) 656-2846. www.sos.georgia.gov/state_capitol. Hours: Monday-Friday 8:00am-5:00pm. Admission: FREE.***

Native Georgia gold tops the dome of this state capital, an 1889 building that houses a Hall of Flags, Hall of Fame, and a natural science museum. The fourth floor is where you'll spend most of your time on this self-guided tour. Here, you'll be able to peek in the gallery overlooking the Senate and House Chambers - they look serious, don't they? This floor is also host to many displays of the history of Georgia. We learned cotton used to be the cash crop here. When it faded, what three "P's" took over? - peaches, pecans and peanuts.

Exit - 246 (east of I-75)

ATLANTA BRAVES MUSEUM / TURNER FIELD TOURS

Atlanta - *755 Hank Aaron Drive (I-75/85 exit 246, Fulton Street East) 30315. Phone: (404) 614-2310. http://atlanta.braves.mlb.com. Hours: The museum opens two and a half hours before each game and closes in the middle of the seventh inning. Admission: Museum Only: $2.00-$5.00. Tour/Museum: $12.00 adult, $7.00 child. FREE parking in the Green Lot. Tours: On non-game days, tours are offered Monday - Saturday from 9:00a.m. - 3:00p.m, and Sundays from 1:00-3:00p.m. Off season Monday-Saturday 10:00am-2:00pm. Please note that there are no tours offered before any afternoon or Sunday home game. Tours start at the top of each hour and last approximately one hour. No reservations are necessary. Educators: Educational tours of a ball field? Yes, they have tours for Social Studies, Math, Art, etc. for group discounted prices. Just ask.*

THE HALL OF FAME MUSEUM is the starting point of Turner Field Tours and traces the Braves History. The museum features memorabilia commemorating legends of the game and key moments in Braves history from Boston to Milwaukee to Atlanta. On display are artifacts including Hank Aaron's historic 715th home run bat and ball, more than 50 game jerseys, game bats, an actual railroad car from the B&O Railroad used to transport players in the 1950s, the knee brace worn by Sid Bream during his famous slide into home plate that captured the 1992 NLCS pennant for the Braves, and the 1995 World Series trophy and championship rings.

THE TURNER FIELD TOUR is probably the highlight of the visit. See Sky Field, a luxury suite, the press box & broadcast booth, the dugout, and the Plaza with the giant baseballs. But the real behind-the-scenes fun is a peek in the locker room. Look for the "putting green" and the 561 TVs throughout the stadium. They have more TVs here than trash cans! What young, little leaguer wouldn't love this tour?

ATLANTA CYCLORAMA

Atlanta - *800 Cherokee Ave. SE (I-75 exit 246 or I-20 to exit 59a (Boulevard). Follow signs. Located next to Zoo Atlanta in Grant Park) 30315. Phone: (404) 658-7625. www.atlantacyclorama.org. Hours: Tuesday-Saturday 9:00am-4:30pm.*

Thanksgiving,Christmas, New Years Day and Martin Luther King's birthday. Admission: $10.00 adult, $8.00 senior (60+) and child (4-12). Parking free with admission. Tours: Tour guides conduct a 40-minute, two-part educational program on the Battle of Atlanta every hour on the half hour from 9:30am to 4:30pm. The program includes special lighting, sound effects, music and narration. Educators: Scavenger Hunt Packages for 1st-8th grade students are available upon request.

> **Did you know?**
> One of the dying soldiers in the diorama is a portrait of the actor Clark Gable.

Home of the world's largest oil painting, "The Battle of Atlanta". Through spectacular music, art and sound effects, history comes alive as you step back to July 22, 1864 and become part of the eight hour battle. Cycloramas place the spectator in the middle (standing or sitting) as you "follow" the sequence of events. Shows begin with a film that covers the history of the Atlanta Campaign leading up to the battle narrated by James Earl Jones. Tiered central seating is lit as you enter, then the house lights dim. Each section of the painting is viewed from the slowly rotating seating and a guide points out highlights of the painting. Look for General Sherman and Old Abe (the eagle). After the show you may visit a Civil War museum that includes The Texas, a Civil War era train that was engaged in an episode now commonly called "The Great Locomotive Chase."

Exit - 246 (east of I-75)

ZOO ATLANTA

Atlanta - ***800 Cherokee Avenue SE (I-75 exit 246 or I-20 exit 59A. Follow signs east or south.) 30315. Phone: (404) 624-5822. www.zooatlanta.org. Hours: Daily 9:30am-4:30pm (5:30pm on weekends). Grounds remain open 1 hour after admissions close. Closed on Thanksgiving, Christmas. Admission: $21.99 adult (12+), $17.99 senior (65+), military and college student; $16.99 child (3-11). Educators: Educator Loan Boxes are available to rent for classroom use.***

Located near downtown in historic Grant Park, the zoo Atlanta is home to Giant Pandas, as well as many rare and endangered species, including Sumatran orangutans and tigers, black rhinos and African elephants. Don't miss the Giant Pandas of Chengdu (what are their favorite scents? What do they like to eat?) in person or online Panda Cam! See gorillas, lions, giraffes, birds & more in natural habitats. See more than 700 animals representing 200 species from all over the world.

Exit - 233 (east of I-75)

REYNOLDS MEMORIAL NATURE PRESERVE

Atlanta (Morrow) - *5665 Reynolds Road (I-75 exit 233, left onto Jonesboro Road. Go 1.5 miles to Huie Road and turn left) 30260. Phone: (770) 603-4188. www.reynoldsnaturepreserve.org. Hours: The Nature Center is open Monday-Friday 8:00am-5:00pm. Admission: FREE.*

The preserve's primarily hardwood forest boasts ponds, wetlands, streams, designated picnic areas and four miles of well defined foot paths. The paths are laid out in convenient loops which bring visitors back to their starting point. The preserve's gardens include a heritage vegetable and herb garden featuring varieties from the late 1800's, a butterfly and hummingbird garden, and a native plants garden. The Georgia Native Plants Trail is wheelchair accessible. Inside the Nature Center you'll find a collection of native amphibians and reptiles as well as an observation honeybee hive and environmental education exhibits.

Exit - 218 (west of I-75)

ATLANTA MOTOR SPEEDWAY TOURS

Hampton - *1500 Tara Place (I-75 South to Exit #218 and continue on Highway 20 and follow signs) 30228. Phone: (770) 707-7904 or (770) 707-7970 (tours). www.atlantamotorspeedway.com. Tours: daily and run every half hour during operating hours (Monday-Saturday 9:00am-4:30pm, Sunday 1:00-4:30pm). Tours are just $5.00 adult and $2.00 child. Ages 6 and under are free.*

Thrill to the excitement of NASCAR racing and special racing events watched around the world. Twice a year, Atlanta Motor Speedway is the bustling center of the NASCAR Cup world, filled with hundreds of thousands of fans from all over the country. But the rest of the year, this premier racing facility is open to the public for speedway tours and a behind-the-scenes look. TOURS: Official track tours include a brief track history, a visit to Petty Garden, a tour of one the track's luxury suites, a sneak peek at the garages and Victory Lane and two laps in the Speedway van around the same 1.54-mile track where stars like Jeff Gordon and Dale Earnhardt Jr. race.

Exit - 218 (east of I-75)

SOUTHERN BELLE FARM

McDonough - *1658 Turner Church Rd. (I-75 exit 218 take Hwy 81 east thru town, left onto GA 20, follow signs) 30258. www.southernbellefarm.com. Phone: (770)*

898-0999. Hours: vary by season, generally Friday, Saturday and Sunday afternoons. Admission: Generally $8.00-$10.00 for 8-10 farm activities. Tours: pre-arranged group tours offer discounts on activities package and a treat to eat or take home. Picnic at the farm is available, too. Note: Concession Stand. Country Market. We recommend casual attire, very comfy shoes, and maybe a hat for sunny days. FREEBIES: activity sheets on corn, cotton, pumpkin and dairy farming are downloadable online on the School Field Trips/Teaching Resources page.

Start your visit with a Hayride through an 80-acre portion of the farm where you can get the 'lay of the land'. Visit the Barnyard and enjoy the antics of silly farm animals. Kids can pet goats and Holstein calves. Try your hand at the Corn Cannon and see how far you can shoot an ear of corn or a tiny pumpkin! The newest attraction is Pig Races at Oinker Stadium. Watch these little squealers charge around the race track and you'll be howling with laughter! Another funny attraction is the Goat Walk skywalk that the resident goats enjoy climbing on. Experience farm life first hand by trying your hand at picking cotton. Visit the dairy barn to see how cows are milked, then ride on the cow train. Or just come out each Fall and enjoy the maze with all of the other folks who are getting lost and having fun!

Exit - 212 (east of I-75)

NOAH'S ARK ANIMAL REHABILITATION CENTER

Locus Grove - *712 L G Griffin Road (I-75 exit 212) 30248. Phone: (770) 937-0888. www.noahs-ark.org. Hours: Tuesday-Saturday Noon-3:00pm. Closed Thanksgiving time, Christmas week and New Years Day. Admission: FREE. Donations greatly needed.*

This lovingly guided center primarily provides pet therapy as neglected and abused animals and children help to heal each other. The center houses rehabilitated and exotic animals such as lions, tigers, bears and monkeys. Some reptiles and raptors appear on occasion. The general public are invited to visit the nature trails and animal habitats at no charge. Be sure to view their informational video online or in person to understand the good work they are committed to. Maybe consider a family donation to help their cause?

Exit - 198 (east of I-75)

HIGH FALLS STATE PARK

***Jackson** - 76 High Falls Park Drive (nearly 2 miles east of I-75 exit 198) 30233. Phone: (478) 993-3053. www.gastateparks.org/HighFalls/. Hours: Daily 7:00am-10:00pm. Admission: $5.00 vehicle parking fee. Fee for camping.*

This site was a prosperous industrial town with several stores, a cotton gin, a grist mill, blacksmith shop and hotel. Even a shoe factory was in town until a major railroad bypassed it and it became a ghost town in the 1880s. You can enjoy the scenic waterfall or hike to the remaining grist mill foundation. A campground, mini-golf, swimming pool and canoe rental are also available. Boating is allowed, 10 HP limit.

Exit - 186 (east of I-75)

WHISTLE STOP CAFÉ - FRIED GREEN TOMATOES

***Juliette** - 443 McCracken Street (I-75 exit 186 east 9 miles) 31046. Phone: (478) 992-8886. www.thewhistlestopcafe.com. Hours: Daily 11am-4pm.*

In the early 1900s, Juliette was a booming community along the railroad tracks and the Ocmulgee River. As time went on the economy left Juliette a ghost town. Then, in 1991, the town was re-discovered by the producers of the movie "Fried Green Tomatoes". The quaint buildings and the railroad provided just the right ingredients for the movie. Visitors from all over the country now come to taste those famous fried green tomatoes at the real-life café and enjoy walking down the streets of this very small town. After you dine on original tomatoes and southern food, take a walk and look for the burial site of "Buddy's arm" or the Juliette "Little Opry". Cute town...and the trains come through faithfully at noon.

GEORGIA

Exit - 169 (east of I-75)

COURTYARD BY MARRIOTT

Macon - *3990 Sheraton Drive (I-75 exit 169) 31210. Phone: (478) 477-8899. www.marriott.com/hotels/travel/mcnga-courtyard-macon/. Rooms from $99.*

Unwind and relax in one of the 108 spacious and comfortable guest rooms available at this hotel that features large sitting areas, spacious work desks, coffee makers, voice mail, and high speed Internet access in all of the rooms. Amenities on site include a restaurant, a lounge, a seasonal outdoor pool, an indoor whirlpool, an exercise room, guest laundry facilities, and meeting rooms. A breakfast buffet is served daily for around $8.00/$4.00.

Just 2 exits north (I-75 exit 172) is Starcadia Entertainment Complex. www.starcadia.net. They have go-karts, mini-golf, bumper boats, batting cages, arcade, flying swings, junior go-karts, rock climbing, trampoline and even a couple of kiddie rides. Each activity averages around $5.00 per person.

Exit - 165 (east of I-75) / I-16 exit 2

OCMULGEE NATIONAL MONUMENT INDIAN MOUNDS

Macon - *1207 Emery Highway (I-75 exit 165 onto I-16 east to exit 2 on US 80 east) 31217. Phone: (478) 752-8257. www.nps.gov/ocmu. Hours: Daily 9:00am-5:00pm. Closed Christmas and New Years only Admission: FREE. Small admission for events. Note: The Ocmulgee Heritage Trail is near here. Interstate16 East and then exit 2 at Martin Luther King Blvd. The main access point to the Ocmulgee Heritage Trail, the Spring Street (Interstate 16, exit 1A) entrance provides ample parking and the only boat access to the river along the trail. Gateway Park is at the southern end of the trail, at the Martin Luther King Jr. Bridge (Interstate 16, exit 2) on the South side of the river. It features a spectacular overlook with steps down to the water, an interactive fountain, and a 7-foot bronze statue of late soul singer and Macon native, Otis Redding. Street parking is available. FREEBIE: printable Word Find online under: For Kids / Park Fun.*

We made it, now...what's inside?

Between AD 900 and 1100 a skillful forming people lived on this site. They were known as Mississippians - a sedentary people who lived mainly by farming bottomlands for crops of corn, beans, squash, pumpkins, and tobacco. They built a compact town of thatched huts on the bluff overlooking the river. The visitor center houses a museum of items found on site and shows a short film "People of the Macon Plateau" (shown every 30 minutes). Among the artifacts found in the Funeral Mound were a pair of copper sun disks and a copper covered puma jaw, part of a head-dress. Survey the landscape from atop ancient Indian Mounds, listen to tales of the past inside a 1,000 year old ceremonial earth-lodge, hike along nature trails and study archeological remains. Why did they build trenches? Our favorite part? - the earthen lodge and oral program inside. What happens to the lodge twice a year? Would you be comfortable in their "seats"? This is an excellent place to play archeologist or explorer for the day!

Exit - 165 (east of I-75) / I-16 exit 2

GEORGIA SPORTS HALL OF FAME

Macon - ***301 Cherry Street (I-75 to exit I-16 east to MLK, Jr. exit to Cherry St) 31201. Phone: (912) 752-1585. www.gshf.org. Hours: Monday-Saturday 9:00am-5:00pm, Sunday 1:00-5:00pm. Admission: $8.00 adult, $6.00 senior (60+), Military, College Students; $3.50 child (6-16).***

Begin your sports experience in the museum's theater with a high energy, high emotion film about Georgia sports legends. Next, it's on to the exhibit hall, which takes you through sports from prep to professional, including collegiate, amateur, and Olympic achievements such as record home run hitter Henry "Hank" Aaron and football legend Fran Tarkenton. Along the way, you'll have the chance to shoot hoops, kick field goals, throw passes, slam a jump ball, drive a NASCAR simulator and use computers to see how academics like geography, math and history are critical to athletes. There's even an area to be a media announcer and make your own calls on famous ball plays! That was our favorite part - how excited can you sound? Be ready for action as this museum is the most interactive Hall of Fame you'll ever visit!

TUBMAN AFRICAN AMERICAN MUSEUM

Macon - ***340 Walnut Street (I-75 exit 165 to I-16 east to exit 2, MLK, Jr. Blvd. And turn right. Turn right on Walnut) 31201. www.tubmanmuseum.com. Phone: (478) 743-8544. Hours: Tuesday-Friday 9:00am-5:00pm, Saturday 11am-5pm. Admission: $8.00 adult, $4.00 child (age 3-17).***

Along the trolley tour, the Tubman is a wonderful experience to learn about African American art, history and culture. Your visit starts with a 63-foot long mural that documents history from ancient Africa to today's leaders and heroes. Hear the exciting stories of Harriet Tubman, Dr. Martin Luther King, Jr., Otis Redding, Ellen Craft and many more. A hands-on inventors gallery and musical instrument station are favorites for kids of all ages.

AROUND TOWN TOURS - MACON

Macon - ***450 Martin Luther King, Jr. Blvd. (trolley leaves from Welcome Center, Terminal Station. I-75 exit 165 to I-16, exit #2 and turning onto M.L. King, Jr. Blvd.) 31201. Phone: (800) 768-3401. www.visitmacon.org. Hours: Monday-Saturday 9:00am-5:00pm. Admission: $18.00 adult, $8.50 youth (downtown tour). Note: Tickets are available at the Downtown Visitor Center located in the Terminal Station where you'll find free all day parking.***

Around Town Tours offer friendly, local trolley operators who kindly answer questions and give you quick tidbits and access to historical sites around town. The trolley is offered during weekends and events but you can walk it too. It features free trolley transportation & admission into the following attractions:

The DOWNTOWN TOUR ticket includes free admission into the following attractions: GA Sports Hall of Fame and Tubman African American Museum. See separate listings for reviews of each attraction.

Tour INTOWN HISTORIC MACON. You'll feel like royalty at the HAY HOUSE (www.hayhouse.org), also known as "The Palace of the South." This 24-room, 18,000 sq. ft. Italian Renaissance Revival mansion is full of surprises including a secret room where legend has it that Confederate gold was hidden! Next, visit the CANNONBALL HOUSE and imagine seeing an enemy cannonball crashing through your house during a Union Army attack on Macon in 1864! See the cannonball along with the furnishings, lifestyles and clothes of that era. Don't miss the Civil War museum in the old kitchen & servants quarters out back. And, finally, the SIDNEY LANIER COTTAGE - see separate listing.

After dinner get outside and take a stroll through Lights on Macon...Historic Intown Illumination Tour. This safe, self-guided walking tour features over 30 antebellum and historic mansions throughout Macon's historic in-town neighborhood. These homes are dramatically lit up at dusk to showcase their unique architectural features.

Exit - 164 (west of I-75)

MUSEUM OF ARTS AND SCIENCES

Macon - ***4182 Forsyth Road (I-75 exit 164) 31210. Phone: (478) 477-3232. www.masmacon.org. Hours: Tuesday-Saturday 10:00am-5:00pm, Sunday 1:00-5:00pm. Admission: $10.00 adult, $8.00 senior, military; $5.00 students (3-17). Educators: Time Traveler and Holiday themed celebrations change each month.***

At the Museum of Arts & Sciences, a whimsical, three-story Discovery House with interactive exhibits proves that learning about art, science and the humanities can be fun. Take a stroll through the enclosed Back Yard and look for live animals living around a man-made banyan tree, especially the gator in the mini swamp! The museum features daily live animal shows, daily planetarium shows, an observatory, and nature trails. Examine the beauty of original works of art in an artist's garret, peek into a scientist's workshop and then journey into space. Maneuver a robot thru the Great Pyramid, sit in the cockpit of Amelia Earhart's plane, steer a canoe, track elephants, rover the surface of Mars and then search for Blackbeard's pirate ship. In the Inventor's Basement, become a mad scientist for the day or simply enjoy watching nature unfold from the window of winged wonders.

GEORGIA

Exit - 164 (east of I-75)

NU-WAY WEINERS

Macon - ***428 Cotton Avenue, downtown Macon (I-75 exit 164 follow signs to downtown, corner of Cherry & Cotton) 31201. www.nu-wayweiners.com. Phone: (478) 743-6593.***

Nu-Way has been serving up the best hot dogs in Macon for 87 years through three generations of the same family. Recently cited as being among the top 10 in the nation, these Central Georgia restaurants serve up secret-recipe chili sauce and homemade slaw. (10 other locations, include Zebulon Road at I-475; Northside Drive near I-75 and North Avenue at I-16). Hours: 6:00am-7:00pm. Breakfast, lunch and supper. Closed: Sunday. Price range: About $5.00 for a complete lunch. A delectable selection of hot dog toppings, hamburgers, sandwiches and old fashioned chocolate malts can be enjoyed while sitting at a nostalgic stainless lunch counter or booth in the original downtown eatery or at one of ten other locations throughout Macon and Middle Georgia. Kids meals are served in "Dog Houses" and include a treat and toy. For about $1.89 you can order their signature red-colored hot dogs "all the way".

SIDNEY LANIER COTTAGE

Macon - *935 High Street (downtown, I-75 exit 164 into town) 31201. Phone: (478) 743-3851. www.historicmacon.org. Hours: Thursday-Saturday 10:00am-4:00pm. Admission: $3.00-$5.00 per person. Educators: Lanier bio online link.*

Step back in time with a guided tour of this 1840 cottage that is the birthplace of Sidney Lanier (1842 - 1881), famous poet and musician of the Old South, who penned "The Marshes of Glynn" and "Song of the Chattahoochee." He served in the Confederate Army until captured aboard a blockade runner and confined at Fort Lookout, Maryland. Kids' group tours explore 1800s toys and the influences of nature on Lanier's music and poetry. At an early age, Sidney learned to play the flute, violin and many other instruments that imitate sounds in nature (ex. Birds). The museum displays Lanier memorabilia and the gift shop sells books on the Civil War and items on Lanier. Kids with an interest in The Arts are best influenced by sites like this.

Exit - 146 (east of I-75)

MUSEUM OF AVIATION

Warner Robins - *GA Hwy 247 S and Russell Pkwy. (I-75 exit 146. Take US 247C to Robins Air Force Base) 31099. www.museumofaviation.org. Phone: (478) 926-6870 or (888) 807-3359. Hours: Daily 9:00am-5:00pm except Thanksgiving Day, Christmas Day and New Year's Day. Admission: FREE. Tours: pre-arranged guided tours on Tuesday-Saturday $3.00. Note: Victory Café. Freedom Park playground/picnic area. "Transporter." Visitors are transported to virtual reality locations like man's first walk on the moon, Columbus' ships, a volcano, a Grand Prix Race and a fighter jet strike mission (fee per ride).*

GEORGIA

FREEBIES: Scavenger Hunts: www.moaeducation.com/tours.php

This huge, ever-updated museum includes historical displays of military aircraft and the aviation pioneers who "kept them flying" for freedom around the world. Different buildings or hangars house exhibits on artifacts, aircraft, missiles and engines. Kids especially like the Vistascope Theater, "We the People" Theatre, and the Presidential and combat helicopters or wartime planes. The older kids can't wait to have the controls in their hands in the air traffic or fighter plane simulators. With names like "Destroyer" and " StratoFortress," this place appeals to a sense of freedom and strength. Try to catch a presentation, demonstration (posted daily at the reception area) or "dress-up" flight area.

Exit - 142 (west of I-75)

LANE SOUTHERN ORCHARDS

Fort Valley - ***50 Lane Road (I-75 exit 142 west on Hwy 96. Look for the rows and rows of crop trees -you can't miss it) 31030. Phone: (478) 825-3592 or (800) 277-3224. www.lanesouthernorchards.com. Hours: Daily 9:00am-5:00pm. Till dark during Peach season. Admission: FREE. Tours: Individuals can take the free self-guided tour at anytime during the day. Viewing the entire process should take about 30 min. Due to the nature of the peach crop, they cannot guarantee the packing line will run every day. Note: Roadside Market includes the Peachtree Café serving lunch and desserts daily and Just Peachy Gift Shop.***

This fun and educational attraction grows and ships Georgia peaches and pecans. Lane Packing Company farms over 2,700 acres of peach trees and 2100 acres of pecans. Currently, they grow over 30 varieties of peaches. Begin your visit by watching the farm video in the market. How do they make new peach varieties? In the summer, take a self-guided tour of the packing operation from an elevated platform. Informational signs describe each step of the process. See the peaches line up like soldiers to get their baths! It's different and fun to watch.

Exit - 109 (west of I-75)

GEORGIA COTTON MUSEUM

Vienna - ***1321 E. Union Street (I-75 exit 109 west) 31092. Phone: (229) 268-2045. www.cityofvienna.org. Hours: Thursday-Friday 9:00am-4:00pm, Saturday 10:00am-2:00pm. Admission: FREE.***

The history of cotton is told with the aid of farm tools, cotton bolls, a cotton bale, scale and planters desk that kept accurate records of the harvest. It includes the slave issues and how their participation in the production of cotton contributed to the economy. How did farmers deal with insects and poor weather? Ride through the county in the fall to see the beauty of "snow in the south" harvest. The cotton is so thick and so white that it appears to be snow on the ground.

Exit - 109 (east of I-75)

ELLIS BROTHERS PECAN PACKING COMPANY

Vienna - ***1315 Tippettville Road (I-75 exit 109 east) 31092. Phone: (229) 268-9041 or (800) 635-0616. www.werenuts.com. Hours: Retail Store open 8:00am-7:00pm (including holidays). Tours: Guided tours by appointment.***

Ellis Bros. Pecans is a family owned and operated wholesale and retail business. The original pecan grove was started in 1944 by Marvin and Irene Ellis. The shelling plant and retail store are located adjacent to the original pecan grove. Elliott Ellis and his sons manage the operation today. Ms. Irene continues to oversee her candy kitchen. Visitors can view the pecan-and peanut-packing process firsthand by a pre-arranged tour or just watch thru a viewing window (seasonal). Our favorite part - sampling! (and then buying a variety of products made on-site). If you like to stop here for a restroom and ice cream and candied nuts break - try their pecan pie or peach ice cream. Sit a spell on the front porch rocking chairs or take it to go on your travels along I-75.

Exit - 101 (west of I-75)

S A M SHORTLINE EXCURSION TRAIN

Cordele - ***105 East 9th Avenue (I-75 exit 101/Hwy 280 west to Hwy 41. You may also board the train at any of the stops) 31015. Phone: (229) 276-2715 or (877) 427-2457. www.samshortline.com. Admission: Coach Class - Seats are not assigned: $29.99 adult, $19.99 child (2-12). Tours: Walk-ups: first come, first serve. All departures from Cordele at 9:30am, returning around 5:00pm. See online schedule or brochure for Thursday, Friday, Saturday departures (March - December). Note: FLIPS FLOPS and sandals without backs are not allowed on the train for safety purposes. Rain gear is suggested since most depots are not covered and the train runs rain-or-shine. Sandwiches and snacks are ready for purchase aboard the train. Some towns have restaurants.***

Climb aboard the air-conditioned vintage train traveling past pecan groves and scenic country farms, stopping in towns filled with historic attractions, restaurants and shopping. Most tours stop for 45 minutes to 75 minutes at each town. While you can board the Train at any of its stops, the official beginning is at Cordele. The first stop on the route is Georgia Veterans State Park, featuring sparkling Lake Blackshear and fascinating military exhibits (see separate listing). Your next stop may be Leslie, home of the Rural Telephone Museum that showcases antiques, switchboards, classic cars, colorful murals – and, of course, antique telephones ($3.00 adults and $1.00 students). The Victorian town of Americus is next. Tour Habitat for Humanity's Global Village. The small Georgia town made famous by President Jimmy Carter is your next stop. While in Plains, browse President Carter's campaign museum, then buy a bag of peanuts from local merchants. A bit further down the tracks is the community of Archery, featuring the president's boyhood home. The train stops just steps from his old front porch, and you'll have plenty of time to explore the farm before the SAM returns to Cordele. Because this all day trip makes so many stops and allows you to tour highlights of the area - it is the ideal way to tour with kids. This is, by far, one of the best train rides we've ever experienced! All aboard!

TRAIN time is QUALITY family time...

GEORGIA VETERANS STATE PARK

Cordele - ***2459A US 280 West (I-75 exit 101, west to Cordele on US 280) 31015. Phone: (229) 276-2371. http://gastateparks.org/info/georgiavet/. Hours: Daily 7:00am-10:00pm. Admission: $5.00 daily vehicle parking fee.***

Established as a memorial to U.S. veterans, this park features a museum with aircraft, armored vehicles, uniforms, weapons, medals and other items from the Revolutionary War through the Gulf War. Kids gravitate to the outdoor exhibit of real-life wartime tanks and aircraft. We even found a floating tank. They all seem so large to kids. The SAM Shortline Excursion Train runs through the park on its way from Cordele to Plains. Modern camping sites, rental cottages, R/C Model Airplane Flying Field, a seasonal swimming pool and beach, a marina and one-mile Nature Trail add to the site. An 18-hole golf course and pro shop, along with 8,600-acre Lake Blackshear, make this one of Georgia's most popular state parks.

LAKE BLACKSHEAR RESORT

Cordele - ***2459-H US Highway 280 West (I-75 exit 101, west on Hwy 280) 31015. Phone: (229) 276-1004. www.lakeblackshearresort.com.***

The resort is a privately operated resort within Georgia Veterans State Park with 14 hotel rooms, 64 villa rooms, 10 cottages, indoor/outdoor pools and a restaurant. The sunsets are beautiful from your screened-in porch and folks around the pool tell us the boating is excellent, with friendly stations along the way to gas up or dock and grab some chow. Besides the nice pool area, the resort offers bicycle, paddle boat, canoe and kayak rentals. The golf course offers Jr. golf camps. This is a modern oasis in a natural setting. Average Bed & Breakfast package = $130-$140.00 per room/cabin (refrigerator in each room). Resort internet rates start at $89.00. Pets welcome.

Exit - 82 (west of I-75)

WORLD'S LARGEST PEANUT

Ashburn - ***(off I-75 near exit 82) 31714.***

The Georgia State Crop is the Peanut.

Clearly seen beside Interstate 75, this monument is the largest of its kind in the nation. It is a daily reminder of the fact that Georgia's number one cash crop is peanuts. The peanut is approximately 20 feet tall!

CRIME AND PUNISHMENT MUSEUM & LAST MEAL CAFÉ

***Ashburn** - 241 East College Avenue (I-75 exit 82 west. Follow signs to downtown) 31714. Phone: (800) 471-9696. www.jailmuseum.com. Hours: Tuesday-Saturday 10:00am-5:00pm. Café open 11:00am-1:00pm. Admission: $1.00-$3.00.*

Built in 1906, the Turner County Jail resembles a castle outside, but not inside. The original jail cells remain upstairs, the sheriff's family quarters downstairs. Although mature for children, you can see the death cell, Old Sparky electrocution chair, and trap door for hangings. Combine this with heart wrenching stories about infamous criminals, murders, hangings, ghosts and even a love story. Check out the striped prisoner clothes. After the tour, stop in for dessert "to die for" at the Last Meal Café. There is a long standing tradition of death row inmates requesting their last meal with a lavish dessert. Enjoy Southern cobbler, pie, cake or ice cream. Clever theme.

Exit - 63B (east of I-75)

GEORGIA

GEORGIA MUSEUM OF AGRICULTURE (AGRIRAMA)

***Tifton** - 1392 Whiddon Mill Road (I-75, Exit 63B) 31793. Phone: (229) 386-3344 or (800) 767-1875. www.abac.edu/museum. Hours: Tuesday-Saturday 9:00am-4:30pm. Also closed on New Year's Day, Thanksgiving Day, three days prior to Christmas and Christmas Day. Admission: $7.00 adult, $6.00 senior (55+), $4.00 child (5-16). Note: Enjoy the Wiregrass Opry on selected Saturday nights.*

The State's living history museum consists of four distinct areas: traditional farm community of the 1870s, progressive farmstead of the 1890s, industrial

sites complex, and a rural town. Costumed interpreters are on location daily to explain and demonstrate the lifestyle and activities of the period. See bacon and ham curing in the smoke-house and veggies preserved in the canning shed. Ride a logging train into the woods, walk down to the sawmill and turpentine still, see the cooper's shed and the blacksmith's shop before crossing the street to the working print shop. At the Feed and Seed Store and Drug Store, order your favorite refreshments from a working marble top soda fountain. Kids especially love Agrirama's barnyard animals. Because there are over 35 structures relocated to the site, you can meet many different tradesmen and crafters performing different chores. Be careful, they may ask you to help them.

Exit - 39 *(west of I-75)*

REED BINGHAM STATE PARK

Adel - ***542 Reed Bingham Road (6 miles west of town on GA 37 via I-75 exit 39 and 14 miles east of US 319 in Moultrie) 31620. Phone: (229) 896-3551. http://gastateparks.org/info/reedbing/. Hours: Daily 7:00am-10:00pm. Admission: $5.00 daily vehicle parking fee.***

The park has become a major boating and waterskiing attraction in south Georgia. The Coastal Plain Nature Trail and Gopher Tortoise Nature Trail wind through a cypress swamp, sandhill area and other habitats representative of southern Georgia. Watchful visitors may see waterfowl, the threatened gopher turtles and indigo snake, and other creatures. However, the park's most famous residents are the thousands of black vultures and turkey vultures that arrive in late November and stay through early April. Other recreation opportunities include a swimming beach and mini-golf.

Exit - 13 *(west of I-75)*

WILD ADVENTURES THEME PARK

Valdosta - ***3766 Old Clyattville Road (I-75 exit 13) 31601. Phone: (229) 219-7080. www.wildadventures.com. Hours: Open practically year-round at 10:00am. Closing time varies with season (6:00-10:00pm). Admission: $40.00-$45.00 per person. Parking $7.00. Educators: online lesson plans are under: Groups/School Field Trips/Teacher Resources. (science/physics orientation).***

They boast five parks in one place. Through one gate there are wild rides, wild animals and wild entertainment...all with a safari animal theme. The park has 9 roller coasters, 5 water rides, go-karts, over 500 wild animals placed in natural habitats scattered throughout the park, and daily shows plus 50 big-name concerts and special events. Slide into something refreshing at Splash Island Water Park - ride Catchawave Bay or the Double Dip Zip, mist in the Rain Fortress or float Paradise River (seasonal weather-dependent hours).

Entertaining shows feature animals, costumed characters, song, dance, magic and music. Board the safari train where you'll take a cross-continent ride through the open grasslands of Africa and Asia encountering elephants, antelope, zebra, giraffe and more. Walk through the Rain Forest on a journey through a natural wetland featuring birds, monkeys, reptiles and bears. Pet animals in the Wild West Petting Zoo. Evenings provide many eateries, a 3D laser and fireworks show and shopping along with numerous concerts.

Mile - 2 (east of I-75)

GEORGIA VISITOR INFORMATION CENTER

Valdosta - ***(near I-75 GA/FL Line, just north of exit 2) 31601. Phone: (229) 559-5828. www.georgia.org. Hours: Information Services 8:30am-5:30pm daily. Restrooms open 24 hours daily. Closed thanksgiving, Christmas Eve and Christmas Day.***

The staff at the Georgia Visitor Information Center are there to welcome and assist you with finding your way through Georgia, make lodging reservations, and offer up a friendly smile.

Chapter 6 FLORIDA

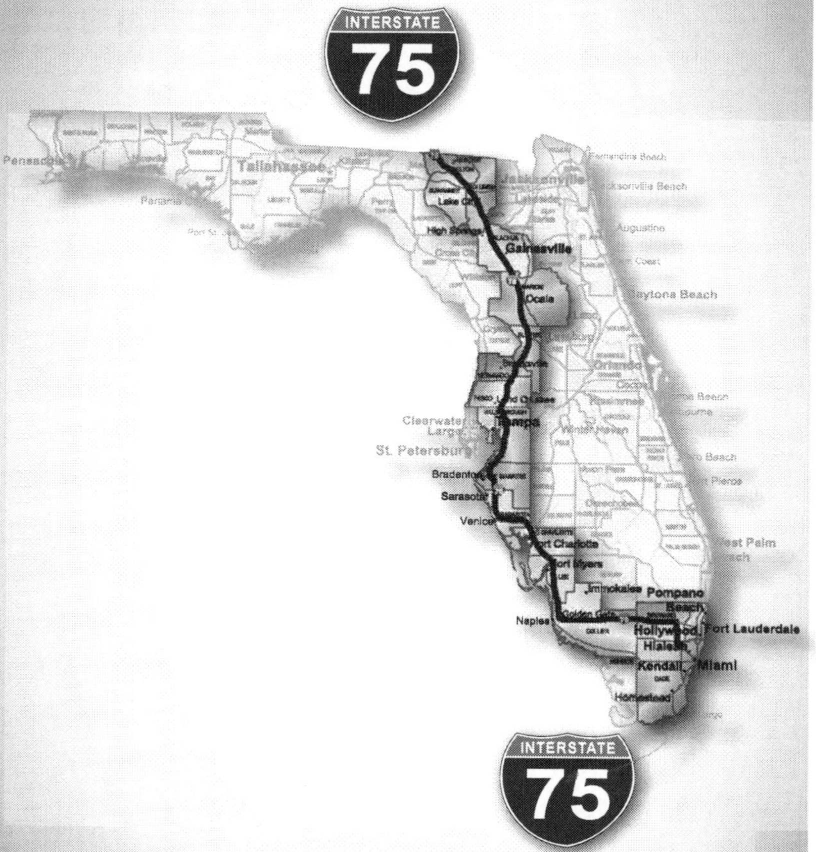

Curious about hundreds of fun places in the lighter gray areas? See <u>*Kids Love Florida*</u>

DEAR FLORIDA TRAVELER:

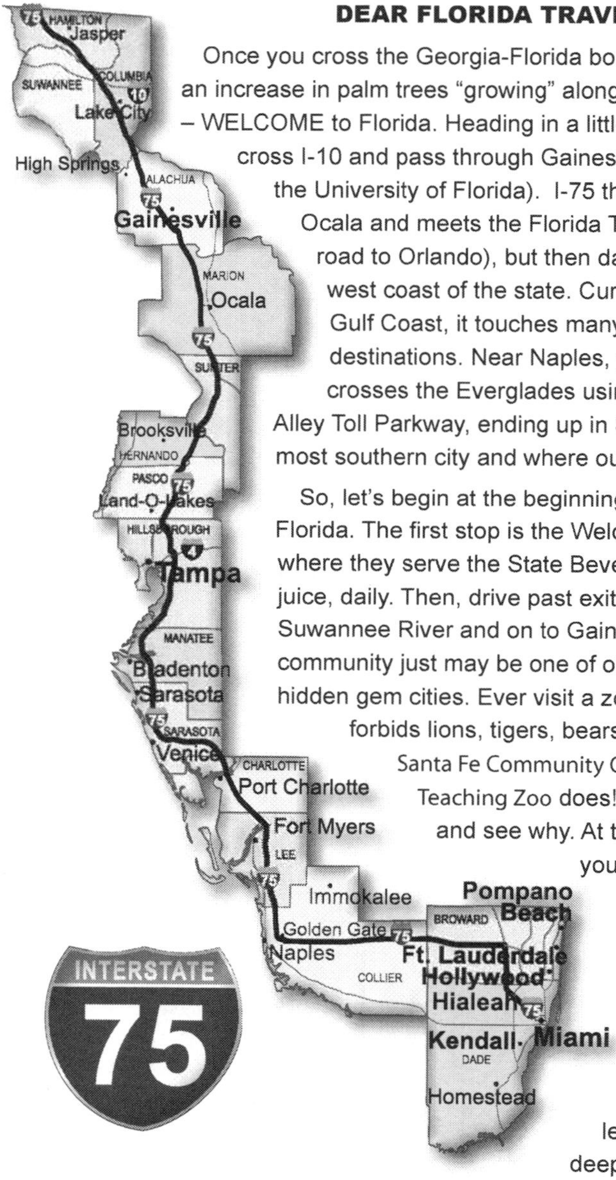

Once you cross the Georgia-Florida border you'll notice an increase in palm trees "growing" alongside the highway – WELCOME to Florida. Heading in a little ways you'll cross I-10 and pass through Gainesville (home of the University of Florida). I-75 then goes through Ocala and meets the Florida Turnpike (the road to Orlando), but then darts towards the west coast of the state. Curving along the Gulf Coast, it touches many popular tourist destinations. Near Naples, your family crosses the Everglades using the Alligator Alley Toll Parkway, ending up in Sunrise – the most southern city and where our I-75 tour ends.

So, let's begin at the beginning – northern Florida. The first stop is the Welcome Center where they serve the State Beverage – orange juice, daily. Then, drive past exits for the Suwannee River and on to Gainesville. This community just may be one of our favorite hidden gem cities. Ever visit a zoo that strictly forbids lions, tigers, bears and giraffes? Santa Fe Community College Teaching Zoo does! Plan a visit and see why. At that same exit you can climb into the Devil's Millhopper State Park sinkhole – the sinking ground gave way suddenly leaving a 120 foot deep and 500 foot wide hole. Take a picture at the bottom as proof of your easy descent and aerobic ascent! At the heart of Gainesville is the pride of the University of Florida – the Gators, but also their intriguing Bat House and the Florida

Museum of Natural History. While the bats only come out at dusk, daylight hours are best to explore scientists recent and ancient discoveries at the museum on the outskirts of campus. Crawl in a cave, wander along a boardwalk, walk "underwater" ancient Florida, move the Earth or investigate habitats of Florida's Indian cultures. Pay the extra fee to enter the Butterfly Rainforest. Think you know butterflies? There's more butterflies here than we've ever seen! After a late lunch, sneak in a peak at the Historic Haile Homestead – the unusual house where they wrote on the walls! Or, be inspired by a famous author, Marjorie Kinnan Rawlings Historic Cracker homestead. This author of works like, "The Yearling" didn't write on walls but she sure banged out a lot of words on her typewriter!

Everybody may know Tampa for its sports teams and Busch Gardens, but there's two museums off the interstate that are well worth the money – if you have time, take about four hours to explore each of them. MOSI (Museum of Science and Industry) is at exit 265 and home to Florida's first IMAX Dome Theater (one show included in admission ticket) and the Southeast's largest science center – we'd call it a science campus. Be sure to take a "ride" safely inside a hurricane and check out every exhibit in Kids In Charge. Did you know the Board of Directors for the design direction of this museum is a bunch of kids? In the downtown area, it's not hard to follow signs leading to the Florida Aquarium. With more than 10,000 aquatic plants and animals and tons of hands-on stations, this place really exhibits some unique creatures around every corner. Play alongside otters, gasp at the size of Goliath Grouper or giggle watching Trumpetfish. Dive shows in the Coral Reefs, sharks in the Bay, swimming with fishes or Explore a Shore outdoor water play areas finish the fun.

As we meander I-75 even further south, you'll notice we get much closer to the Gulf which means more attractions close to the interstate are actually on the water. We start in Bradenton – home to three favorites worth a visit – especially because most are inexpensive stops at exit 220. You may have noticed some orange groves alongside the highway – or at least signs telling you where to get fresh Florida produce. Mixon Fruit Farms is a great place to indulge in citrus heaven. Besides their huge gift shop with everything imaginable that is related to oranges, lemons, grapefruit, etc., they give a wonderful tram tour. The guide takes you out amongst the groves and lets you hold or sample unusual citrus like giant lemons or surprising kumquats. A little further west on SR 64 is the home to Snooty, the oldest living manatee born and nurtured in a man-made, protected environment.

The Parker Manatee Aquarium at the South Florida Museum is actually a complex of buildings with artifacts from prehistoric to the present. When you enter, be sure to coordinate the times for the planetarium show and Snooty feedings so you can get your money's worth. The manatee are so lovable and friendly with staff – they jump right up on the dock to get treats! Just a ways further west of here is the De Soto National Memorial. The park commemorates the legacy of Spanish conquistador, Hernando de Soto, who in 1539 landed near Tampa Bay to begin a four year, four thousand mile trek through the Southeastern United States. Go on the expedition via video, don some conquistador clothes, and try to figure out how to survive! Over one-half of the explorers didn't.

There's far more to Sarasota than white sandy beaches. Stroll through an art museum where the Venetian-style architecture is as much an art form as the masterpieces within. Sarasota's cultural attractions are all gems, but the John and Mable Ringling Museum of Art is its crown jewel. Add the stunning Ringling Estate to your travel plans. This treat for the senses includes the winter residence of John and Mable Ringling called Cà d'Zan, two Circus, a Museum of Art, the Historic Asolo Theater with performances daily and 66 acres of historic grounds and gardens all on beautiful Sarasota Bay. Families wanting to visit an art museum? Yes! Because the Circus Museums alone are worth the admission price. "Ladies and Gentlemen... Step Right Up to the Largest Miniature Circus in the World – the Howard Bros. Circus!" is in the Tibbals Learning Center. Another space has interactives like dress-up and crafts plus colorful and wild clowning costumes and wagons. You can even watch actual woodcarvers on duty making carousel animals.

Besides Fort Myers Beach being one of our favorite Gulf Coast cities to "land" for a while (great shelling in this area), Fort Myers city is also home to some pretty interesting tours. Just east off exit 143 is a farm called **ECHO**. It's not an ordinary farm, but a working demonstration farm where they give HOPE - they teach poor, third world countries how to grow food that adapts to even extreme conditions. As you tour through their Global Village, you will be amazed at how simple, recyclable materials can help create "miracle" plants. So inspiring and you might learn some new gardening techniques! After leaving this enlightening tour, you'll feel the inspiration to visit another famous inventors home – the Edison & Ford Winter Estates at exit 136. The giant Banyan trees invite you to explore the inventor's charming "old-Florida" style home, laboratory and experimental gardens. While the stories told on the tours may be of interest to school-aged kids, most find the Lab & Museum the most kid-friendly. The lab is a mouth-dropper - you can feel the genius' presence! If you truly want to make this a quick stop - opt for the lab and museum only ticket. Maybe have lunch under the Banyan trees, too.

Naples may be the golf capital of the U.S. but it's also a nice place to begin slowing down your pace. See the best of Naples on board a vintage trolley on Naples Trolley Tours. Enjoy a fully narrated tour covering more than 100 points of interest including historic Naples Pier and Tin City. Pass the oldest house, Millionaires Row, an old trading post, the Naples City Dock and many exclusive residences. See something you really like? Just hop off-board and on-board again later at your leisure. Dad doesn't have to do the driving for a while!

For families seeking to explore the outdoors together, Everglades National Park has luscious wetlands and more than 150 miles of canoeing, hiking and bicycling trails. This is the only subtropical preserve in North America and the only place in the world where alligators and crocodiles exist side by side. If you don't want too much adventure, opt for the relaxing boat or tram tours.

One of the strange things you may notice by the end of your trip in this state is that nature is an essential part of the Florida vacation. With an average yearly temperature of around 72 degrees, vibrant wildlife, beautiful foliage and an endless array of outdoor activities, who can blame Florida visitors for wanting to be outside? And, wherever you go in Florida, you're never more than 60 miles from the beach! Enjoy the Sunshine State!

ACTIVITIES AT A GLANCE

AMUSEMENTS

Exit - 265 - *Busch Gardens Africa - Tampa Bay*
Exit - 265 - *Adventure Island*
Exit - 261 - *Dinosaur World*
Exit - 143 - *Shell Factory & Nature Park*
Exit - 136 - *Sun Splash Family Waterpark*

ANIMALS & FARMS

Exit - 390 - *Santa Fe Community College Teaching Zoo*
Exit - 265 - *Lowry Park Zoo*
Exit - 257 - *Florida Aquarium*
Exit - 246 - *TECO Manatee Viewing Center*
Exit - 213 - *Sarasota Jungle Gardens*
Exit - 143 - *ECHO (Educational Concerns For Hunger Organization)*
Exit - 141 - *Manatee Park*
Exit - 105 - *Naples Zoo At Caribbean Gardens*
Exit - 13 - *Flamingo Gardens*

HISTORY

Exit - 387 - *Dudley Farm Historic State Park*
Exit - 387 - *Morningside Nature Center Living History Farm*
Exit - 384 - *Historic Haile Homestead At Kanapaha Plantation*
Exit - 374 - *Marjorie Kinnan Rawlings Historic State Park*
Exit - 314 - *Dade Battlefield Historic State Park*
Exit - 261 - *Ybor City Museum State Park*
Exit - 224 - *Gamble Plantation State Historic Site*

HISTORY *(cont.)*

Exit - 220 - *South Florida Museum / Parker Manatee Aquarium*
Exit - 220 - *De Soto National Memorial*
Exit - 138 - *Southwest Florida Museum Of History*
Exit - 136 - *Edison & Ford Winter Estates*
Exit - 123 - *Mound Key Archaeological State Park*

MUSEUMS

Exit - 256 - *Glazer Children's Museum*

OUTDOOR EXPLORING

Exit - 460 - *Suwannee River State Park*
Exit - 384 - *Gainesville-Hawthorne Trail State Park*
Exit - 265 - *Hillsborough River State Park*
Exit - 240 - *Little Manatee River State Park*
Exit - 220 - *Lake Manatee State Park*
Exit - 205 - *Myakka River State Park*
Exit - 200 - *Oscar Scherer State Park*
Exit - 131 - *Six Mile Cypress Slough Preserve*
Exit - 116 - *Lovers Key State Park*
Exit - 111 - *Delnor-Wiggins Pass State Park*
Exit - 101 - *Florida Panther & Ten Thousand Islands National Wildlife Refuge*
Exit - 101 - *Everglades National Park*
Exit - 80 - *Big Cypress National Preserve*

SCIENCE

Exit - 390 - *Devil's Millhopper State Geologic Site*
Exit - 384 - *Florida Museum Of Natural History*
Exit - 374 - *Paynes Prairie Preserve* State Park

ACTIVITIES AT A GLANCE

SCIENCE *(cont.)*

Exit - 352 - *Silver River State Park*

Exit - 265 - *Museum Of Science And Industry (MOSI)*

Exit - 210 - *Mote Aquarium*

Exit - 138 - *Imaginarium Hands-On Museum*

Exit - 136 - *Calusa Nature Center And Planetarium*

Exit - 13 - *Buehler Planetarium & Observatory*

SPORTS

Exit - 341 - *Don Garlits Museum Of Drag Racing And Classic Cars*

SUGGESTED LODGING & DINING

Exit - 279 - *Saddlebrook Resort*

Exit - 261 - *Columbia Restaurant*

Exit - 220 - *Peaches Restaurants*

Exit - 131 - *Pink Shell Beach Resort*

Exit - 105 - *Naples Beach Hotel Everglades Room Restaurant*

THE ARTS

Exit - 439 - *Stephen Foster Folk Culture Center State Park*

Exit - 213 - *Ringling Museum Complex*

TOURS

Exit - 384 - *University Of Florida*

Exit - 352 - *Silver Springs*

Exit - 257 - *American Victory Mariners Memorial & Museum Ship*

Exit - 229 - *Florida Gulf Coast Railroad Museum*

Exit - 220 - *Mixon Fruit Farms*

Exit - 195 - *Just Ducky Amphibious Tours*

Exit - 131 - *Sun Harvest Citrus*

Exit - 101 - *Naples Trolley Tours*

WELCOME CENTER

Exit - 470 - Florida Welcome Center

GENERAL INFORMATION

Contact the services of interest. Request to be added to their mailing lists.

- Florida Bicycle Association: (407) 327-3941 or www.floridabicycle.org
- Bike Florida: (352) 376-6044 or www.bikeflorida.org
- Office Of Greenways And Trails: www.floridagreenwaysandtrails.com
- Florida State Parks: (850) 488-9872 or www.floridastateparks.org
- Visit Florida: (888) 7FLA-USA or www.visitflorida.com
- National Camping Information: www.gocampingamerica.com
- Sarasota & Her Islands: www.sarasotafl.org
- Naples / Marco Island / Everglades (Paradise Coast): www.paradisecoast.com
- Greater Miami And Beaches: (800) 955-3646 or www.miamiandbeaches.com
- Tampa Bay: (800) 826-8358 or www.visittampabay.com
- Florida Gulf Islands (Anna Maria, Longboat Key, Bradenton): www.floridagulfislands.com
- Alachua County Visitors And Convention Bureau (Gainesville Area). (866) 778-5002 or www.visitgainesville.com
- Fort Myers / Sanibel: (888) 231-6933 or www.fortmyers-sanibel.com

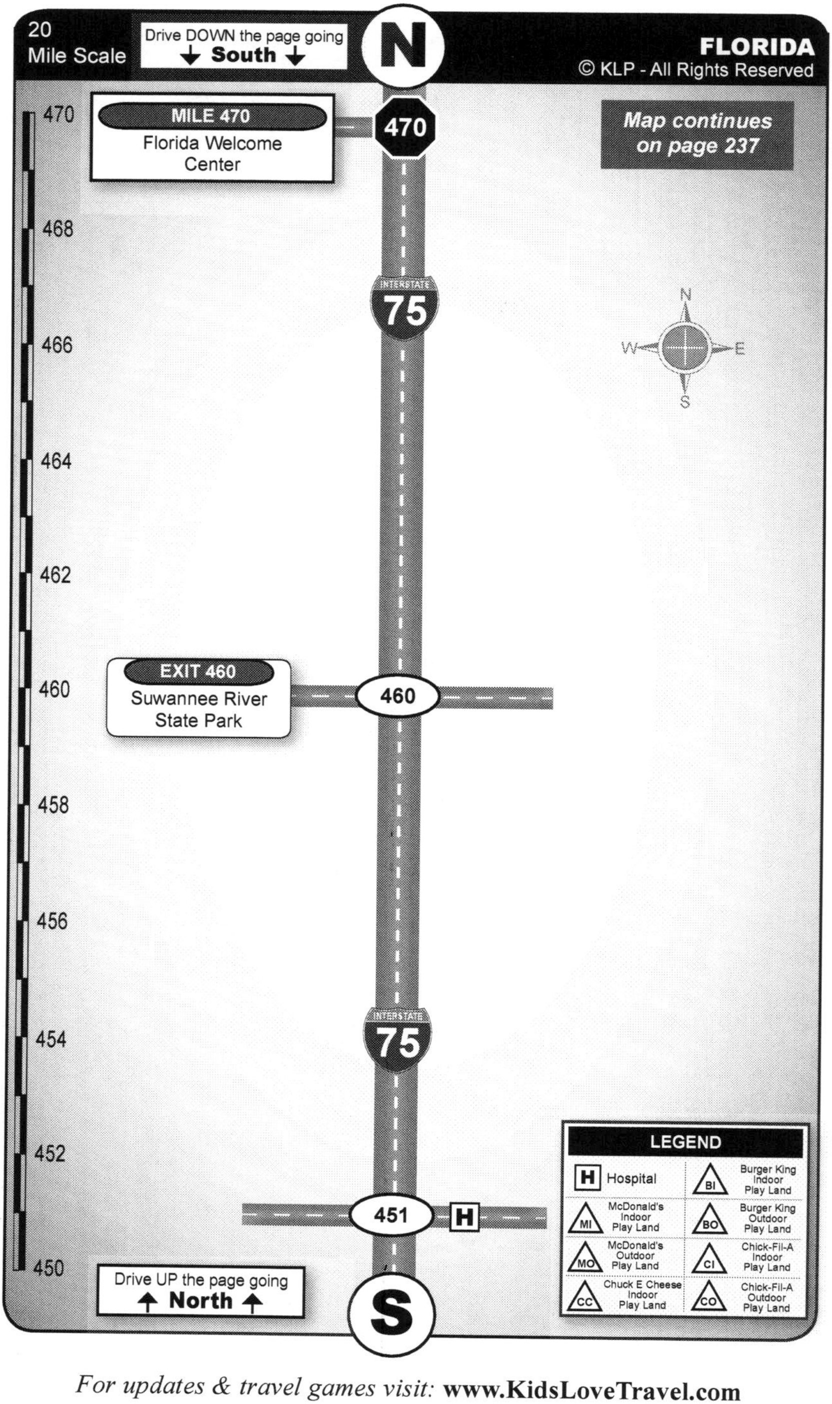
20
Mile Scale
Drive DOWN the page going
South
N
FLORIDA
© KLP - All Rights Reserved
470
468
466
464
462
460
458
456
454
452
450
MILE 470
Florida Welcome Center
470
Map continues on page 237
INTERSTATE 75
N
W
E
S
EXIT 460
Suwannee River State Park
460
INTERSTATE 75
451
H
LEGEND
H Hospital
BI Burger King Indoor Play Land
MI McDonald's Indoor Play Land
BO Burger King Outdoor Play Land
MO McDonald's Outdoor Play Land
CI Chick-Fil-A Indoor Play Land
CC Chuck E Cheese Indoor Play Land
CO Chick-Fil-A Outdoor Play Land
Drive UP the page going
North
S

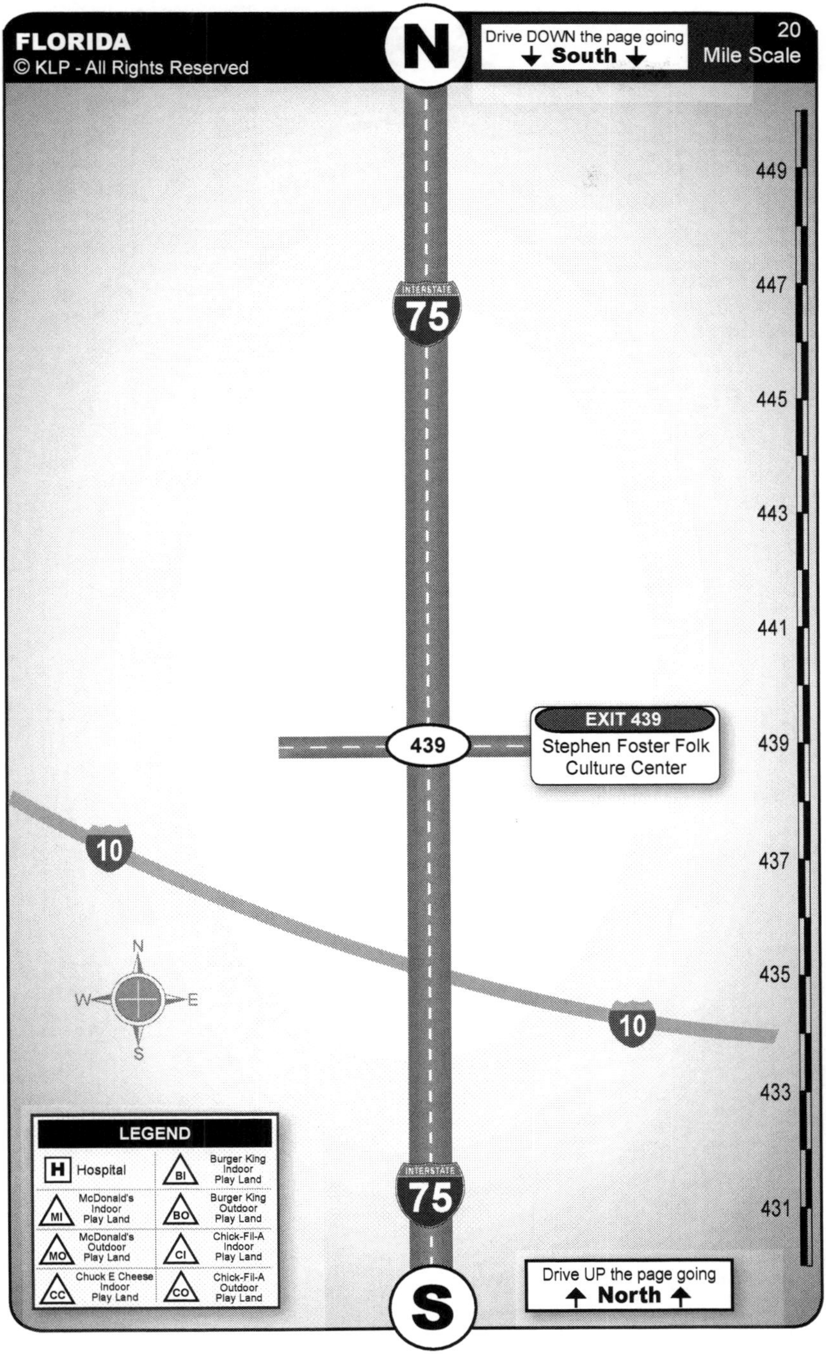
FLORIDA
© KLP - All Rights Reserved
N
Drive DOWN the page going
South
20
Mile Scale
449
447
445
443
441
439
437
435
433
431
INTERSTATE
75
EXIT 439
Stephen Foster Folk
Culture Center
439
10
10
N
W
E
S
LEGEND
H Hospital
BI Burger King Indoor Play Land
MI McDonald's Indoor Play Land
BO Burger King Outdoor Play Land
MO McDonald's Outdoor Play Land
CI Chick-Fil-A Indoor Play Land
CC Chuck E Cheese Indoor Play Land
CO Chick-Fil-A Outdoor Play Land
S
Drive UP the page going
North

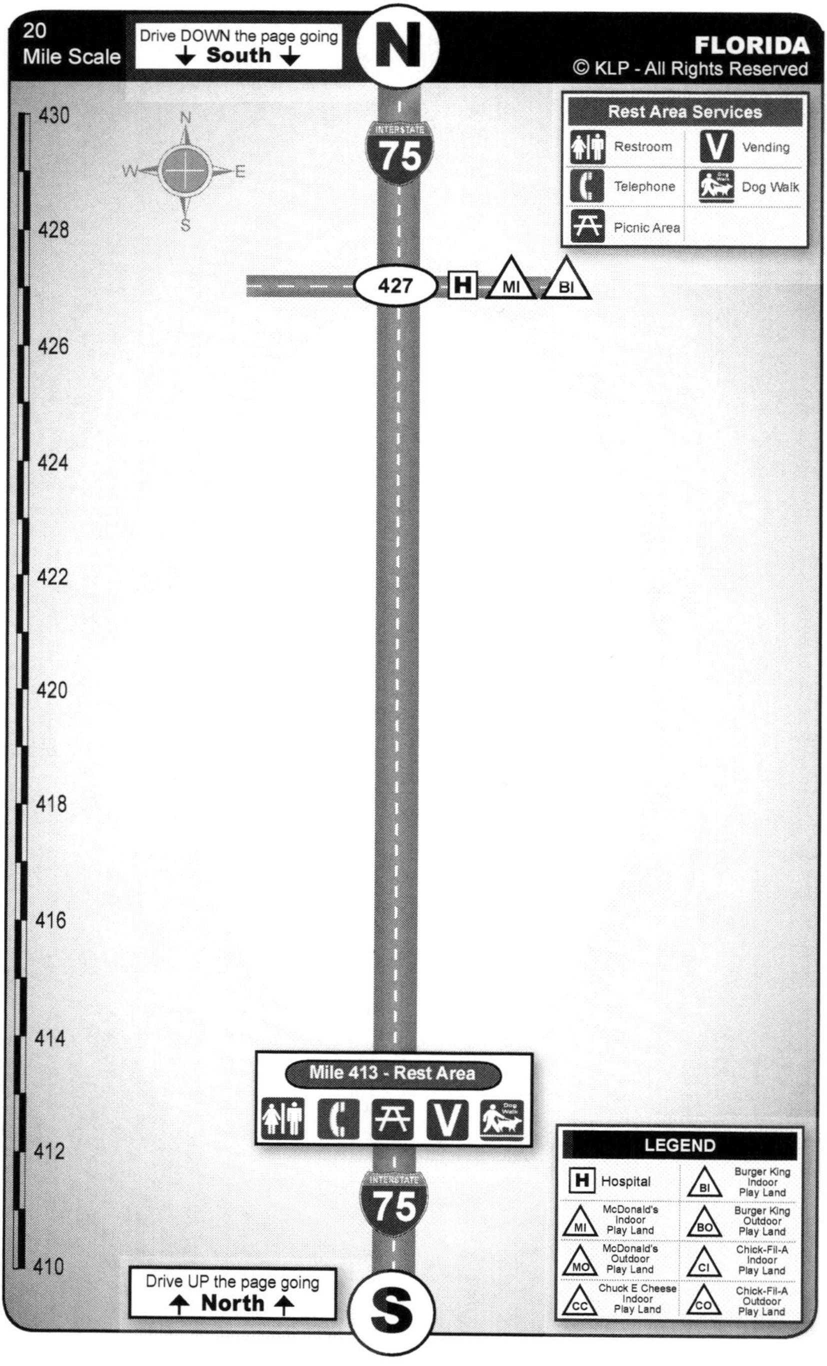

20
Mile Scale
Drive DOWN the page going
South
N
FLORIDA
© KLP - All Rights Reserved
430
428
426
424
422
420
418
416
414
412
410
N
W
E
S
INTERSTATE
75
Rest Area Services
Restroom
Vending
Telephone
Dog Walk
Picnic Area
427
H
MI
BI
Mile 413 - Rest Area
V
INTERSTATE
75
LEGEND
Hospital
Burger King Indoor Play Land
McDonald's Indoor Play Land
Burger King Outdoor Play Land
McDonald's Outdoor Play Land
Chick-Fil-A Indoor Play Land
Chuck E Cheese Indoor Play Land
Chick-Fil-A Outdoor Play Land
Drive UP the page going
North
S

FLORIDA

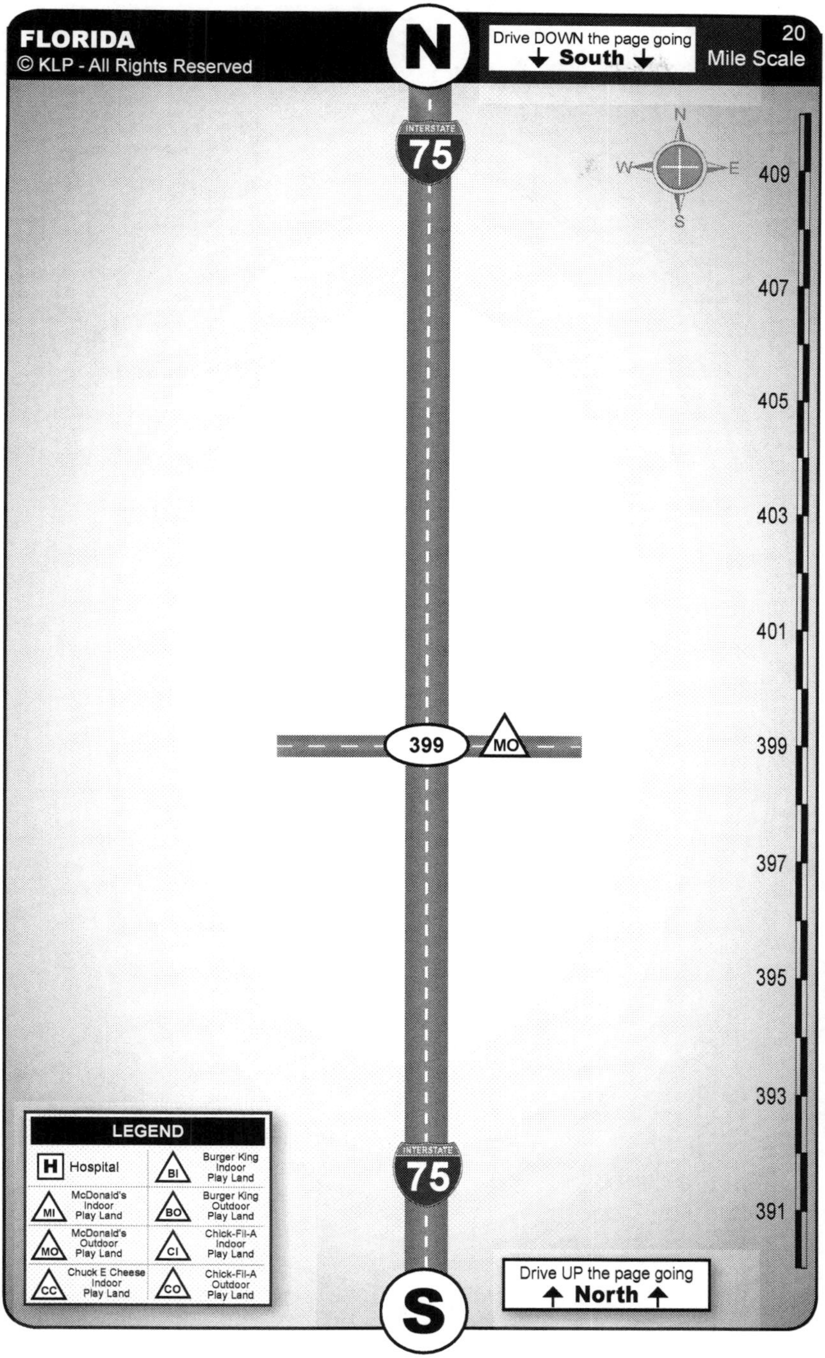
FLORIDA
© KLP - All Rights Reserved
N
Drive DOWN the page going
South
20
Mile Scale
INTERSTATE
75
N
W
E
S
409
407
405
403
401
399
MO
399
397
395
393
391
LEGEND
H Hospital
BI Burger King Indoor Play Land
MI McDonald's Indoor Play Land
BO Burger King Outdoor Play Land
MO McDonald's Outdoor Play Land
CI Chick-Fil-A Indoor Play Land
CC Chuck E Cheese Indoor Play Land
CO Chick-Fil-A Outdoor Play Land
INTERSTATE
75
S
Drive UP the page going
North

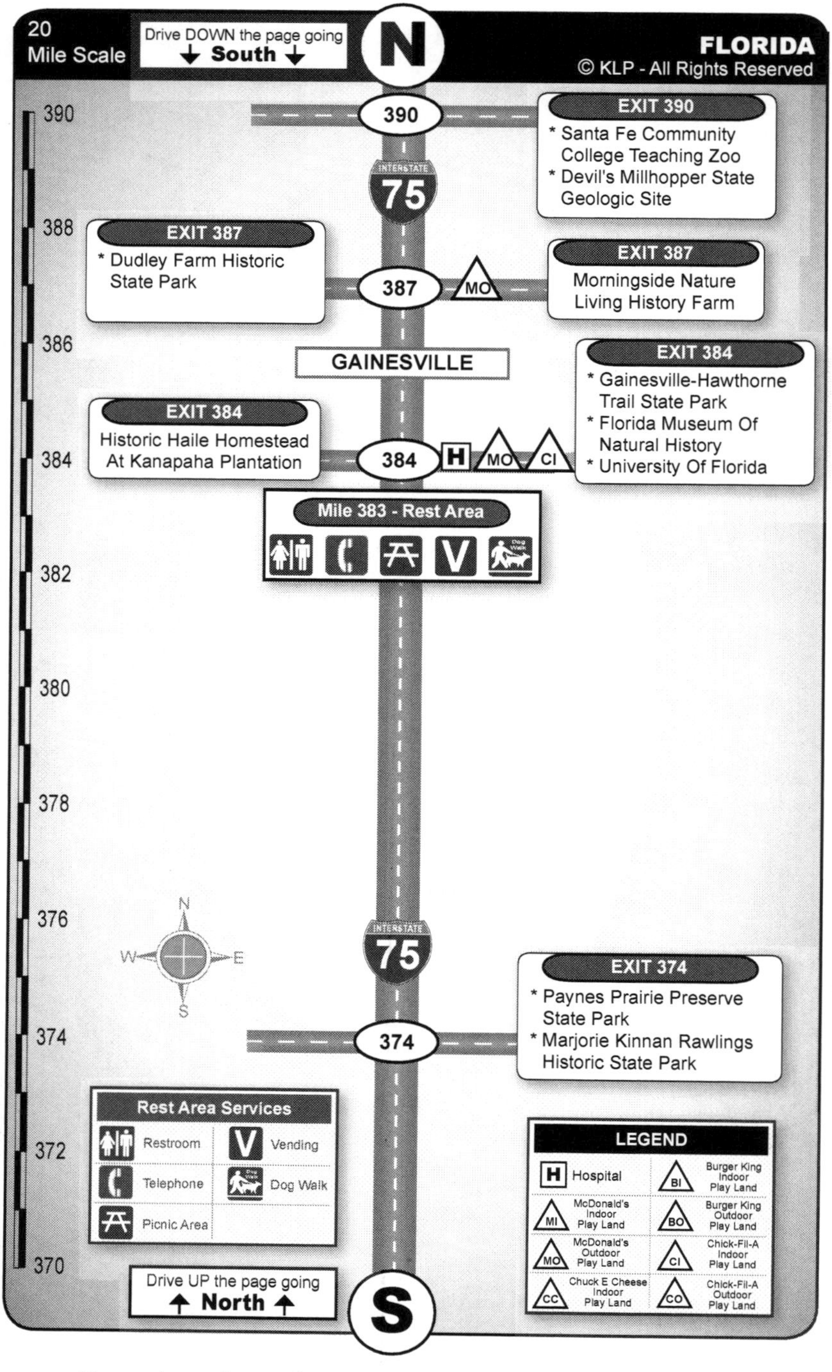
20
Mile Scale
Drive DOWN the page going
South
N
FLORIDA
© KLP - All Rights Reserved
390
388
386
384
382
380
378
376
374
372
370
EXIT 390
* Santa Fe Community College Teaching Zoo
* Devil's Millhopper State Geologic Site
75
EXIT 387
* Dudley Farm Historic State Park
387
MO
EXIT 387
Morningside Nature Living History Farm
GAINESVILLE
EXIT 384
* Gainesville-Hawthorne Trail State Park
* Florida Museum Of Natural History
* University Of Florida
EXIT 384
Historic Haile Homestead At Kanapaha Plantation
384
H
MO
CI
Mile 383 - Rest Area
V
N
W
E
S
75
EXIT 374
* Paynes Prairie Preserve State Park
* Marjorie Kinnan Rawlings Historic State Park
374
Rest Area Services
Restroom
Vending
Telephone
Dog Walk
Picnic Area
LEGEND
H Hospital
BI Burger King Indoor Play Land
MI McDonald's Indoor Play Land
BO Burger King Outdoor Play Land
MO McDonald's Outdoor Play Land
CI Chick-Fil-A Indoor Play Land
CC Chuck E Cheese Indoor Play Land
CO Chick-Fil-A Outdoor Play Land
Drive UP the page going
North
S

FLORIDA

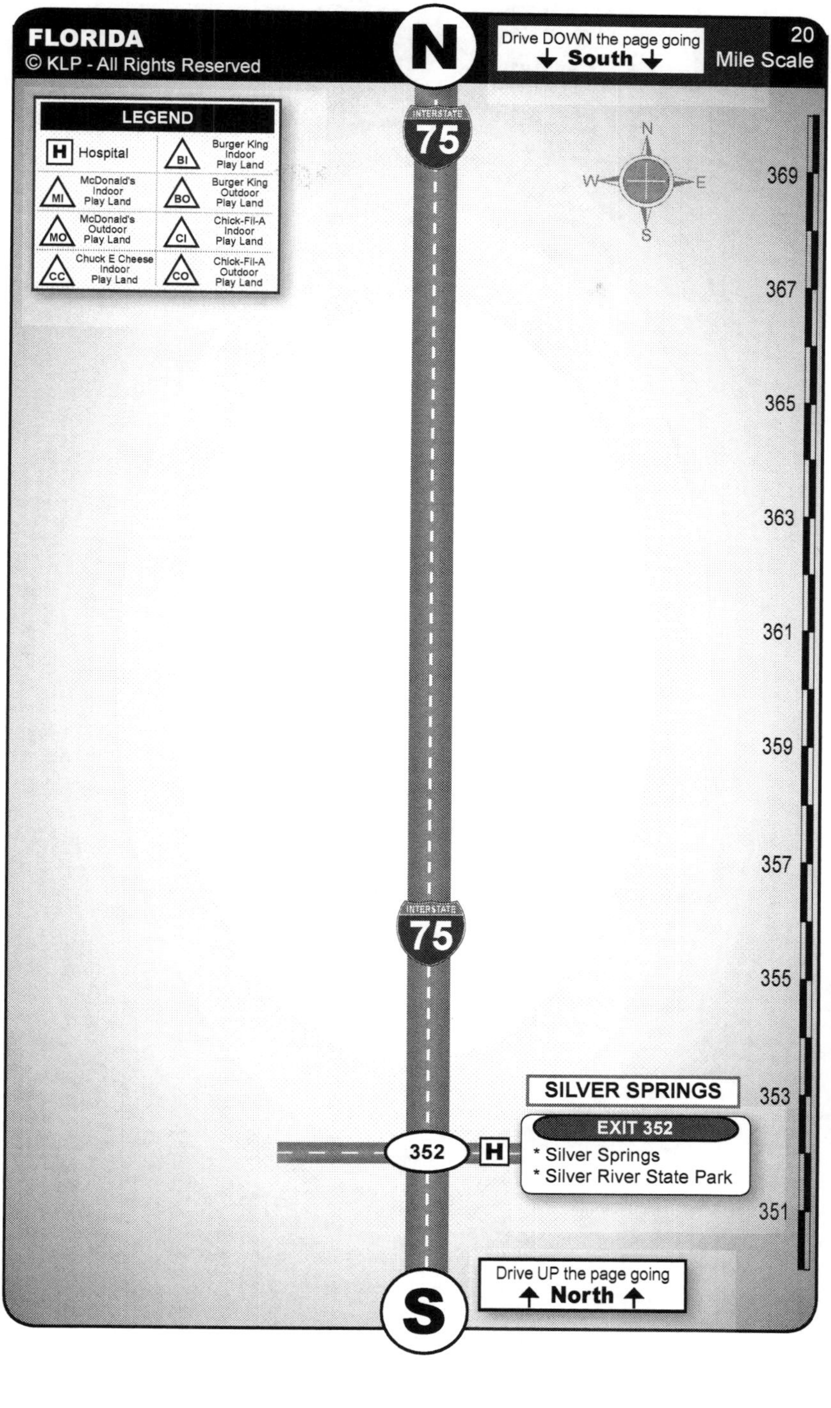
FLORIDA
© KLP - All Rights Reserved
N
Drive DOWN the page going
↓ South ↓
20
Mile Scale
LEGEND
H Hospital
BI Burger King Indoor Play Land
MI McDonald's Indoor Play Land
BO Burger King Outdoor Play Land
MO McDonald's Outdoor Play Land
CI Chick-Fil-A Indoor Play Land
CC Chuck E Cheese Indoor Play Land
CO Chick-Fil-A Outdoor Play Land
INTERSTATE 75
N
W
E
S
369
367
365
363
361
359
357
INTERSTATE 75
355
SILVER SPRINGS
353
EXIT 352
352
H
* Silver Springs
* Silver River State Park
351
Drive UP the page going
↑ North ↑
S

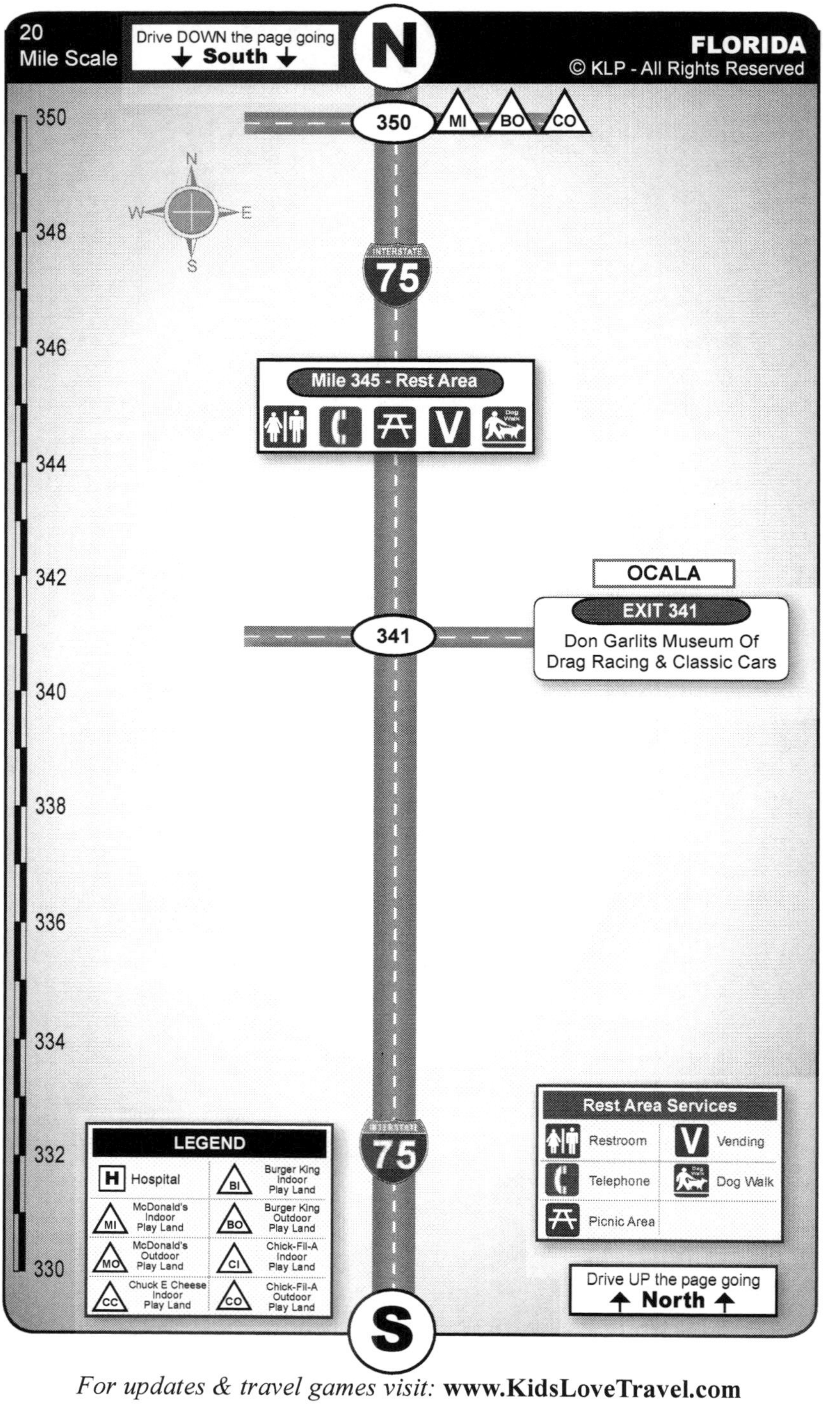
20 Mile Scale
Drive DOWN the page going South
N
FLORIDA
© KLP - All Rights Reserved
350
348
346
344
342
340
338
336
334
332
330
350
MI
BO
CO
N
W
E
S
INTERSTATE 75
Mile 345 - Rest Area
Dog Walk
OCALA
EXIT 341
341
Don Garlits Museum Of Drag Racing & Classic Cars
INTERSTATE 75
LEGEND
H Hospital
BI Burger King Indoor Play Land
MI McDonald's Indoor Play Land
BO Burger King Outdoor Play Land
MO McDonald's Outdoor Play Land
CI Chick-Fil-A Indoor Play Land
CC Chuck E Cheese Indoor Play Land
CO Chick-Fil-A Outdoor Play Land
Rest Area Services
Restroom
Vending
Telephone
Dog Walk
Picnic Area
Drive UP the page going North
S

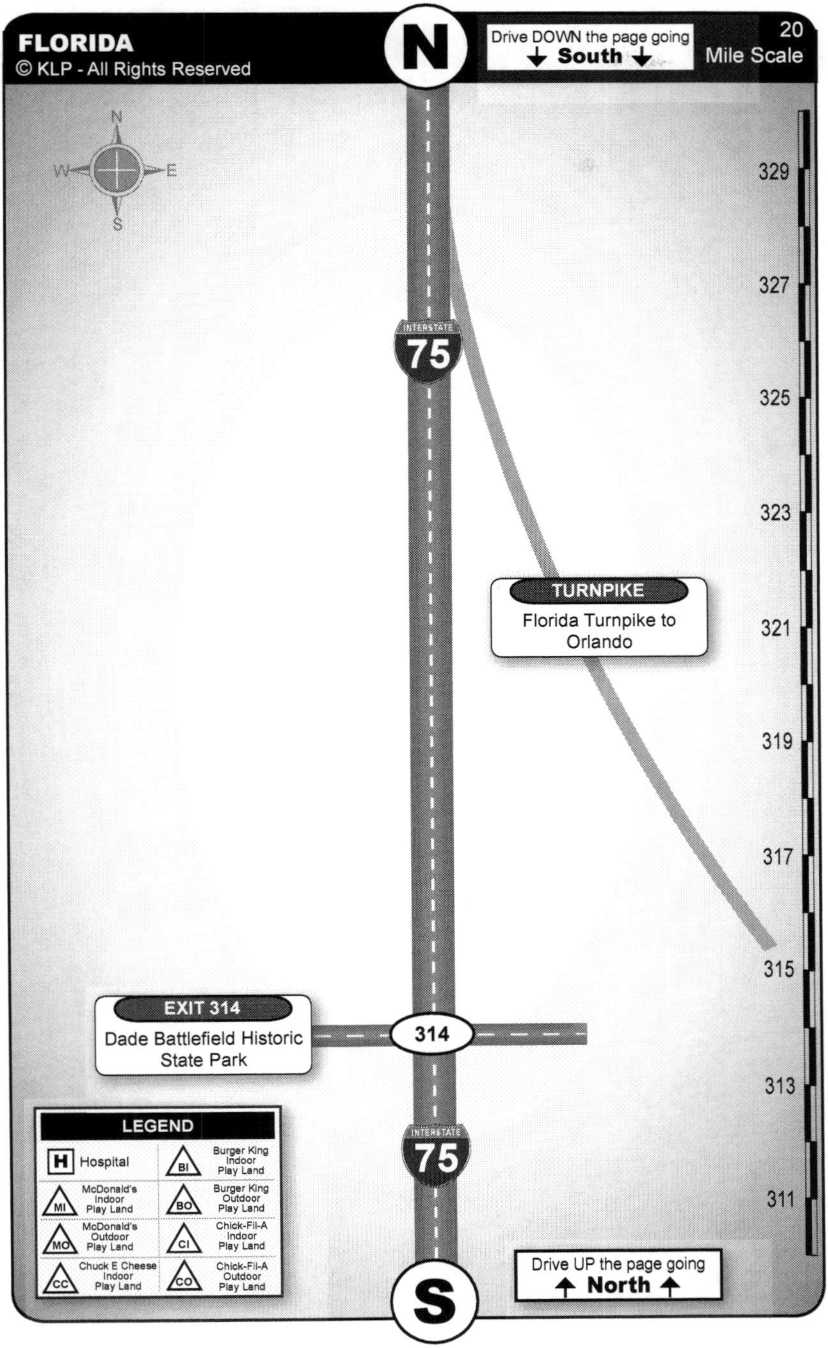
FLORIDA
© KLP - All Rights Reserved
N
Drive DOWN the page going
South
20
Mile Scale
N
W
E
S
329
327
325
323
321
319
317
315
313
311
INTERSTATE
75
TURNPIKE
Florida Turnpike to
Orlando
EXIT 314
Dade Battlefield Historic
State Park
314
INTERSTATE
75
LEGEND
H Hospital
BI Burger King Indoor Play Land
MI McDonald's Indoor Play Land
BO Burger King Outdoor Play Land
MO McDonald's Outdoor Play Land
CI Chick-Fil-A Indoor Play Land
CC Chuck E Cheese Indoor Play Land
CO Chick-Fil-A Outdoor Play Land
S
Drive UP the page going
North

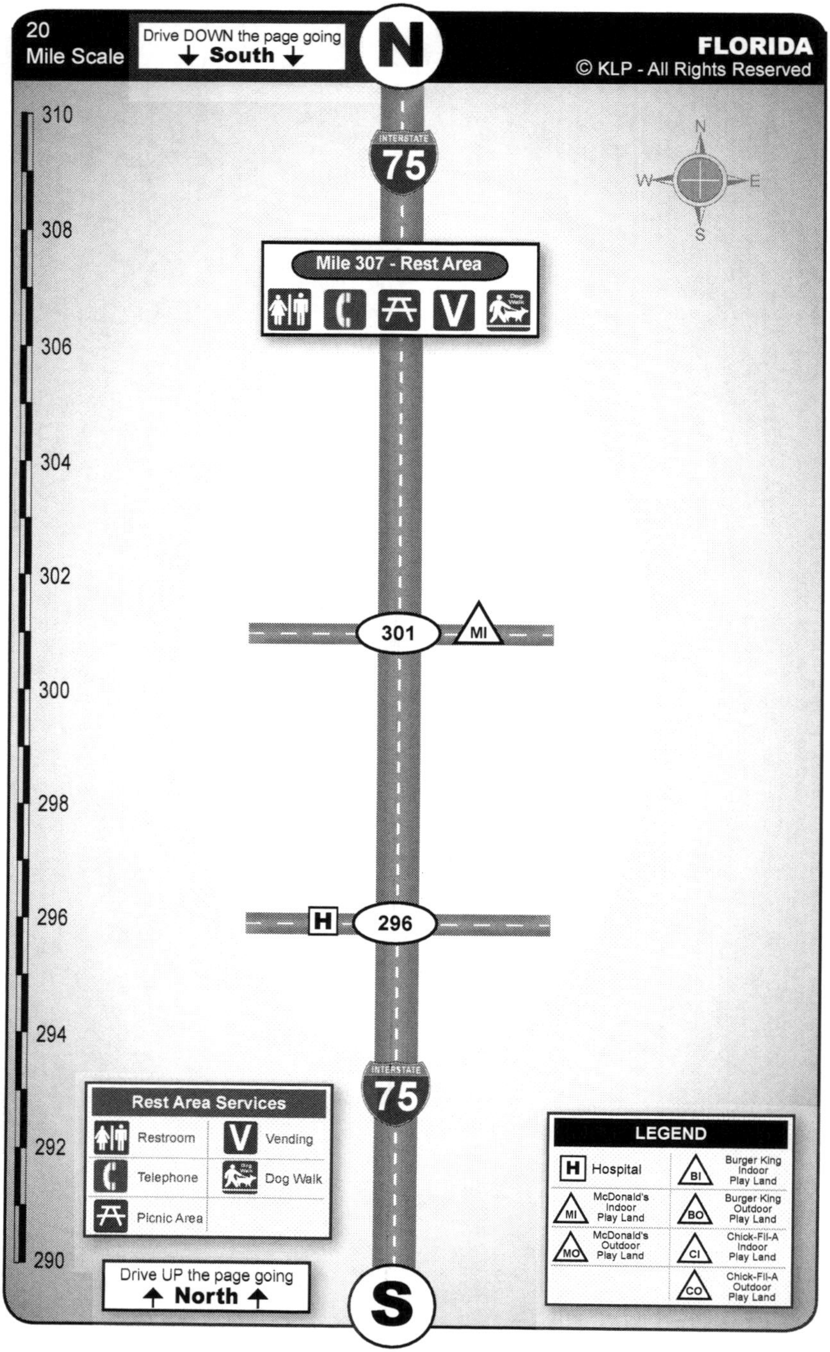
20 Mile Scale
Drive DOWN the page going
South
N
FLORIDA
© KLP - All Rights Reserved
310
308
306
304
302
300
298
296
294
292
290
INTERSTATE 75
N
W
E
S
Mile 307 - Rest Area
Dog Walk
V
301
MI
H
296
INTERSTATE 75
Rest Area Services
Restroom
Vending
Telephone
Dog Walk
Picnic Area
LEGEND
Hospital
BI Burger King Indoor Play Land
MI McDonald's Indoor Play Land
BO Burger King Outdoor Play Land
MO McDonald's Outdoor Play Land
CI Chick-Fil-A Indoor Play Land
CO Chick-Fil-A Outdoor Play Land
Drive UP the page going
North
S

FLORIDA

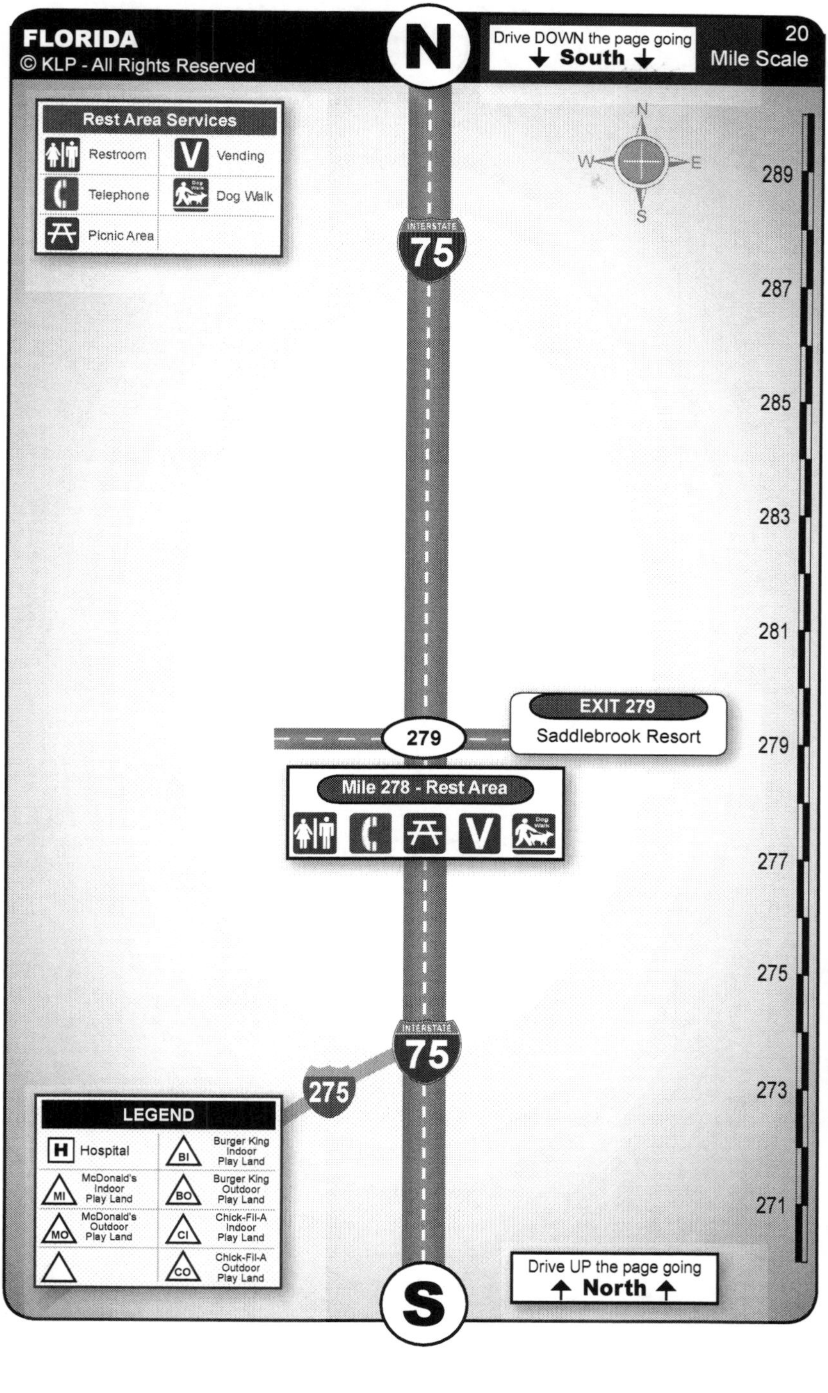
FLORIDA
© KLP - All Rights Reserved
N
Drive DOWN the page going
South
20
Mile Scale
Rest Area Services
Restroom
Vending
Telephone
Dog Walk
Picnic Area
INTERSTATE
75
289
287
285
283
281
EXIT 279
Saddlebrook Resort
279
279
Mile 278 - Rest Area
277
275
INTERSTATE
75
275
273
271
LEGEND
Hospital
Burger King Indoor Play Land
McDonald's Indoor Play Land
Burger King Outdoor Play Land
McDonald's Outdoor Play Land
Chick-Fil-A Indoor Play Land
Chick-Fil-A Outdoor Play Land
S
Drive UP the page going
North

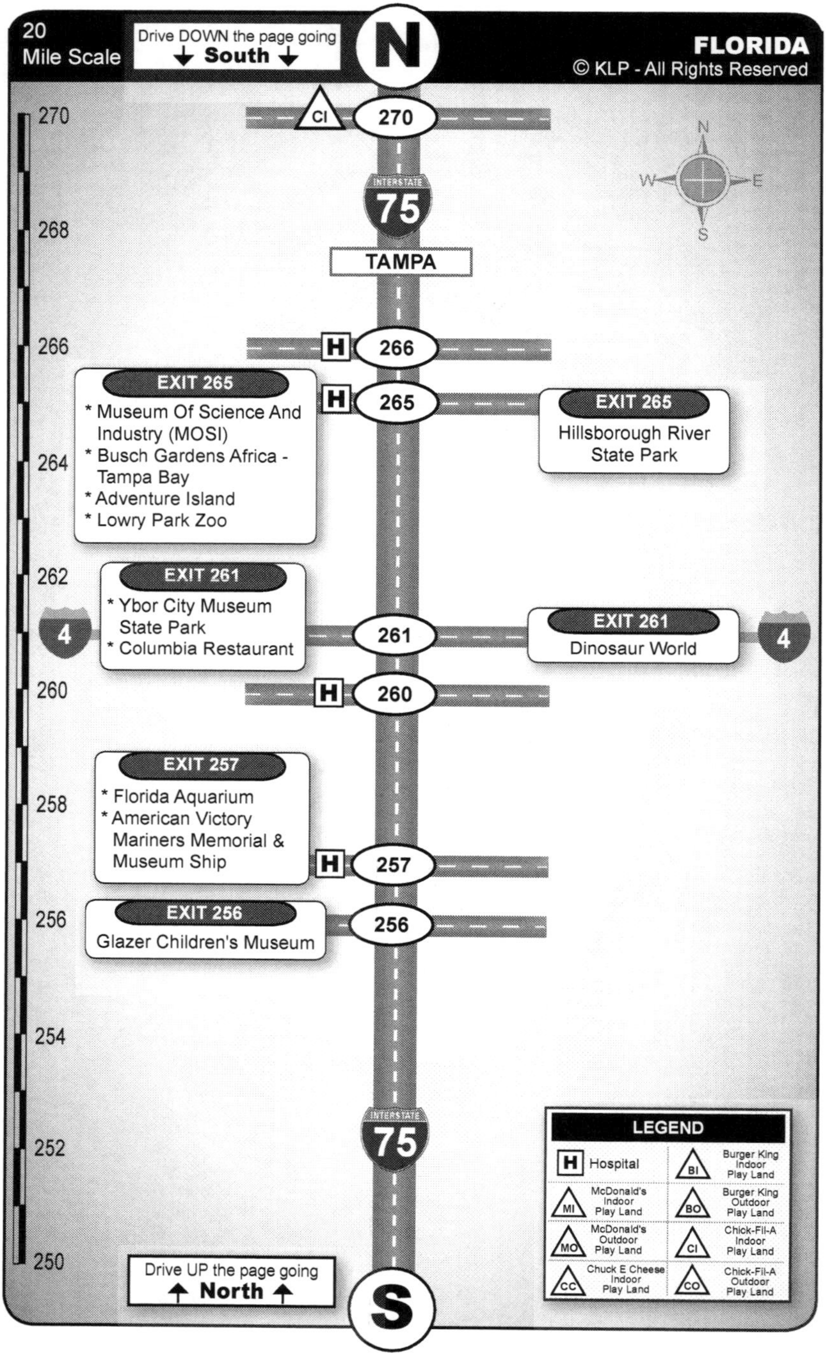
20 Mile Scale
Drive DOWN the page going South
N
FLORIDA
© KLP - All Rights Reserved
270
CI
75
TAMPA
268
266
H
EXIT 265
* Museum Of Science And Industry (MOSI)
* Busch Gardens Africa - Tampa Bay
* Adventure Island
* Lowry Park Zoo
265
EXIT 265
Hillsborough River State Park
264
262
EXIT 261
* Ybor City Museum State Park
* Columbia Restaurant
4
261
EXIT 261
Dinosaur World
260
EXIT 257
* Florida Aquarium
* American Victory Mariners Memorial & Museum Ship
258
257
EXIT 256
Glazer Children's Museum
256
254
252
250
LEGEND
H Hospital
BI Burger King Indoor Play Land
MI McDonald's Indoor Play Land
BO Burger King Outdoor Play Land
MO McDonald's Outdoor Play Land
CI Chick-Fil-A Indoor Play Land
CC Chuck E Cheese Indoor Play Land
CO Chick-Fil-A Outdoor Play Land
Drive UP the page going North
S

FLORIDA

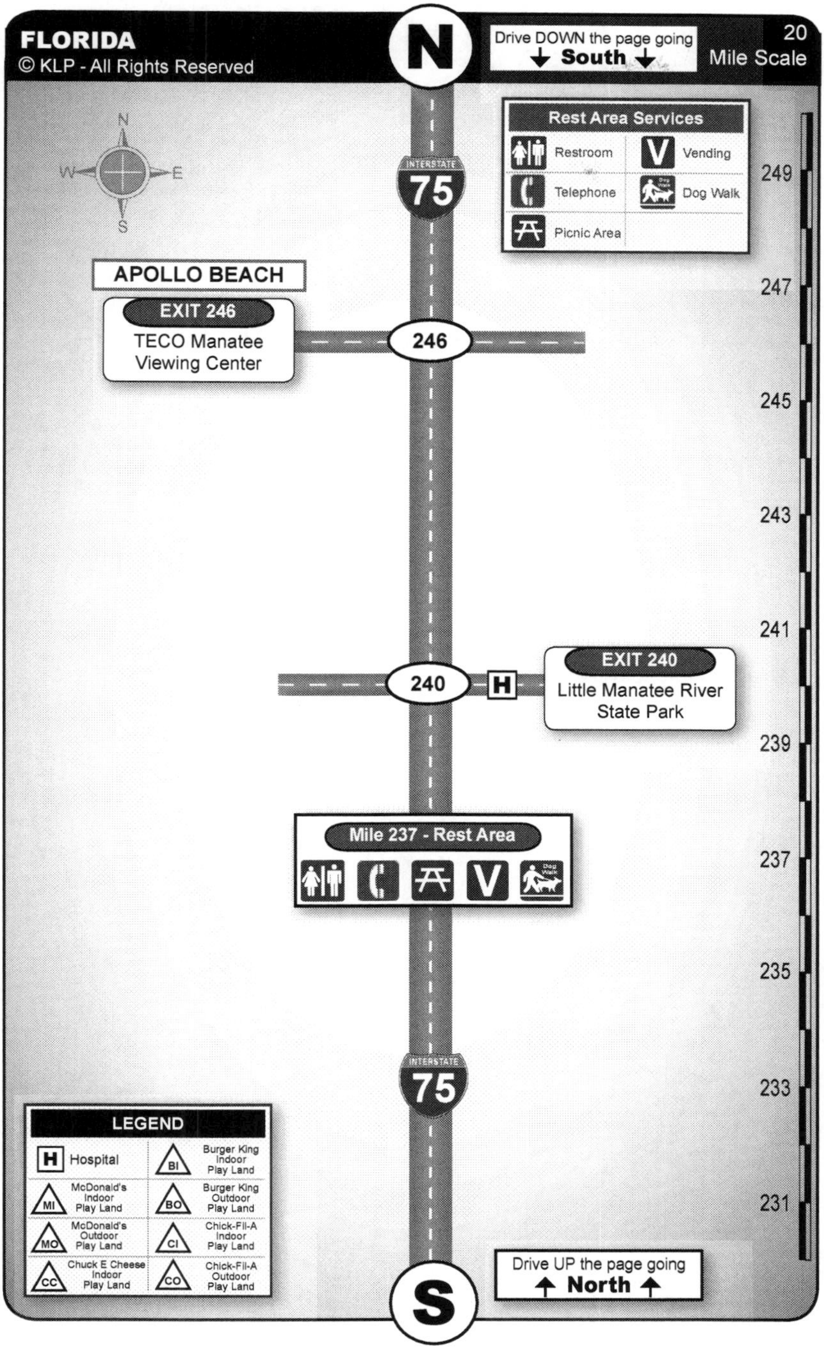
FLORIDA
© KLP - All Rights Reserved
N
Drive DOWN the page going
South
20
Mile Scale
Rest Area Services
Restroom
Vending
Telephone
Dog Walk
Picnic Area
INTERSTATE
75
249
247
245
243
241
239
237
235
233
231
APOLLO BEACH
EXIT 246
TECO Manatee
Viewing Center
246
240
H
EXIT 240
Little Manatee River
State Park
Mile 237 - Rest Area
V
INTERSTATE
75
LEGEND
H Hospital
BI Burger King Indoor Play Land
MI McDonald's Indoor Play Land
BO Burger King Outdoor Play Land
MO McDonald's Outdoor Play Land
CI Chick-Fil-A Indoor Play Land
CC Chuck E Cheese Indoor Play Land
CO Chick-Fil-A Outdoor Play Land
S
Drive UP the page going
North

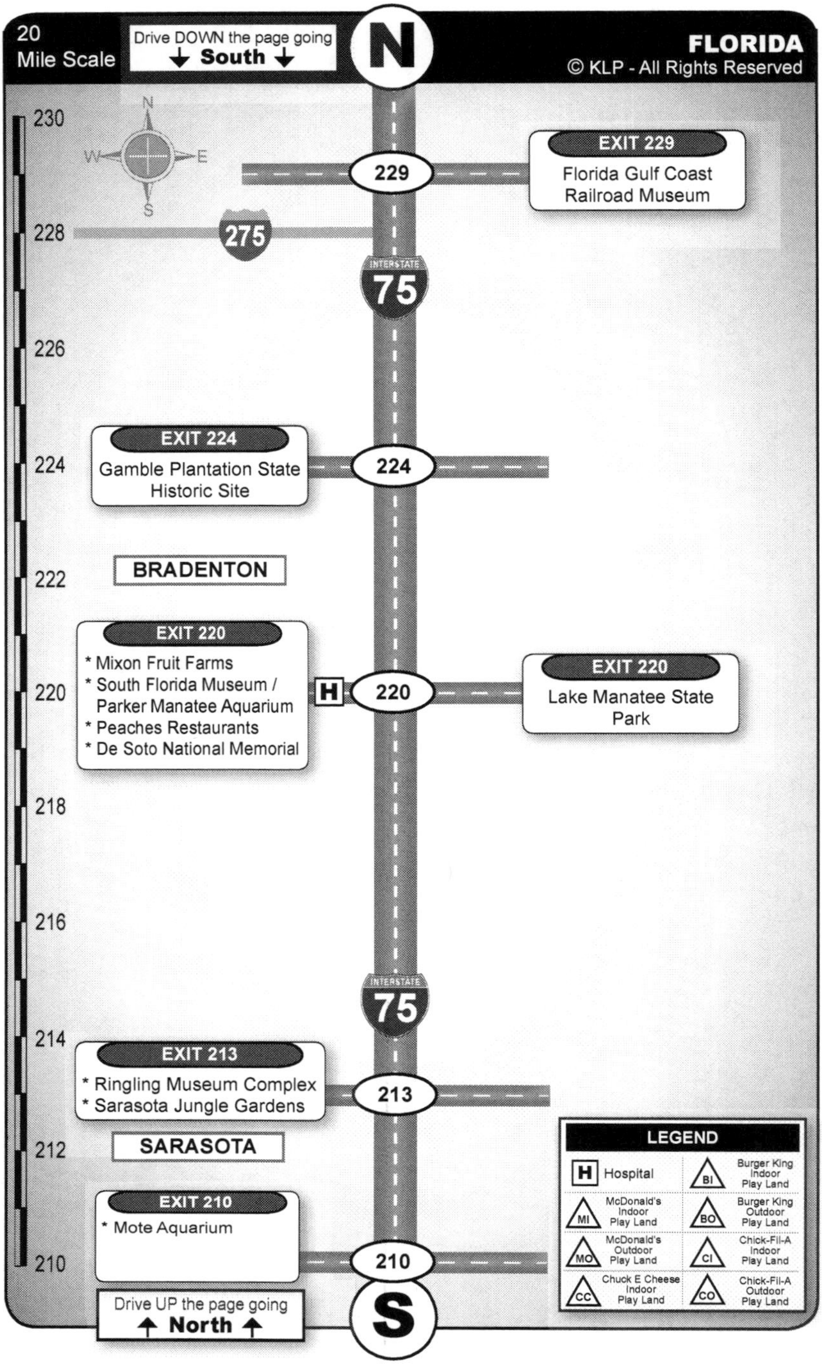
20 Mile Scale
Drive DOWN the page going South
N
FLORIDA
© KLP - All Rights Reserved
230
228
226
224
222
220
218
216
214
212
210
N
W
E
S
275
75
EXIT 229
Florida Gulf Coast Railroad Museum
229
EXIT 224
Gamble Plantation State Historic Site
224
BRADENTON
EXIT 220
* Mixon Fruit Farms
* South Florida Museum / Parker Manatee Aquarium
* Peaches Restaurants
* De Soto National Memorial
H
220
EXIT 220
Lake Manatee State Park
75
EXIT 213
* Ringling Museum Complex
* Sarasota Jungle Gardens
213
SARASOTA
EXIT 210
* Mote Aquarium
210
S
Drive UP the page going North
LEGEND
H Hospital
BI Burger King Indoor Play Land
MI McDonald's Indoor Play Land
BO Burger King Outdoor Play Land
MO McDonald's Outdoor Play Land
CI Chick-Fil-A Indoor Play Land
CC Chuck E Cheese Indoor Play Land
CO Chick-Fil-A Outdoor Play Land

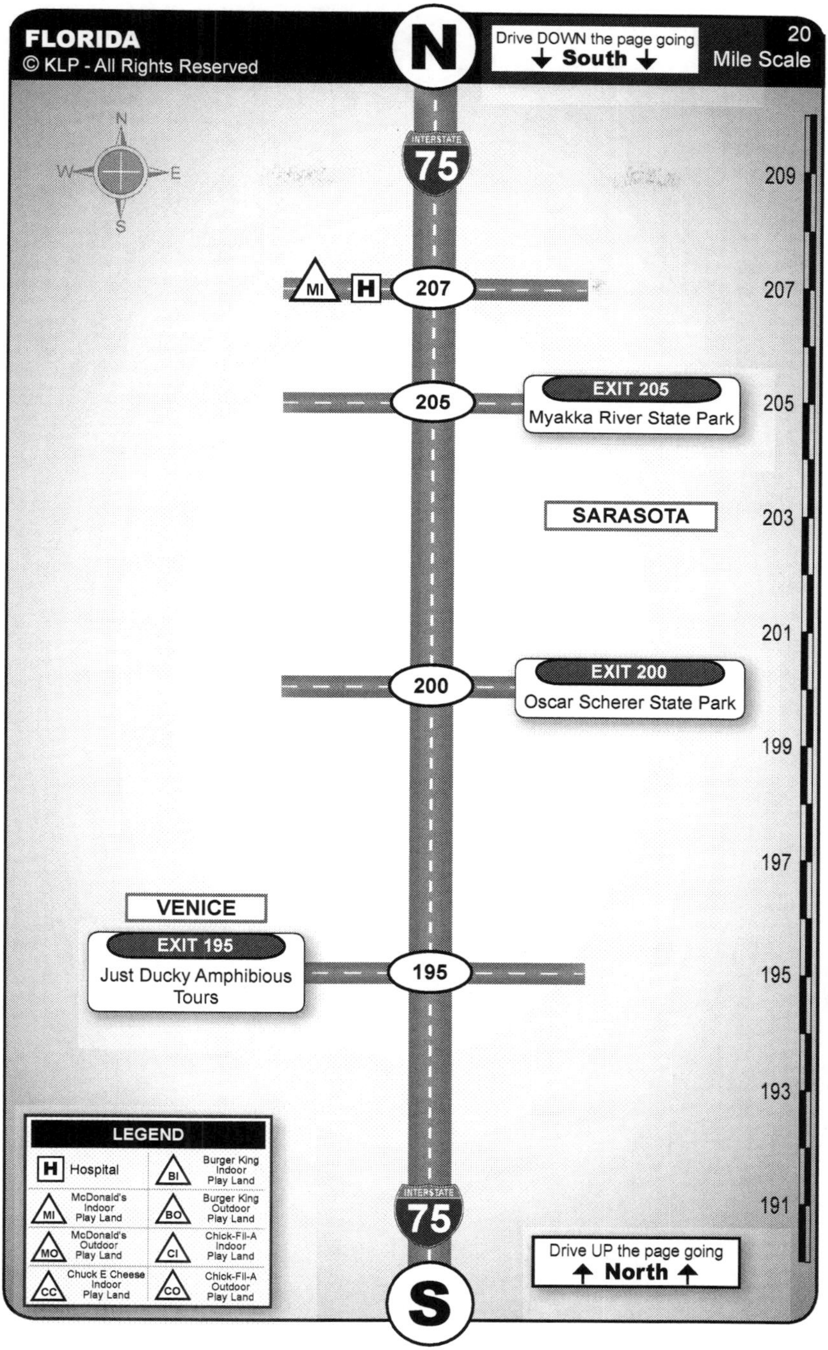
FLORIDA
© KLP - All Rights Reserved
N
Drive DOWN the page going
↓ South ↓
20
Mile Scale
N
W
E
S
75
209
207
207
MI
H
205
205
EXIT 205
Myakka River State Park
SARASOTA
203
201
200
EXIT 200
Oscar Scherer State Park
199
197
VENICE
EXIT 195
Just Ducky Amphibious Tours
195
195
193
191
75
LEGEND
H Hospital
BI Burger King Indoor Play Land
MI McDonald's Indoor Play Land
BO Burger King Outdoor Play Land
MO McDonald's Outdoor Play Land
CI Chick-Fil-A Indoor Play Land
CC Chuck E Cheese Indoor Play Land
CO Chick-Fil-A Outdoor Play Land
Drive UP the page going
↑ North ↑
S

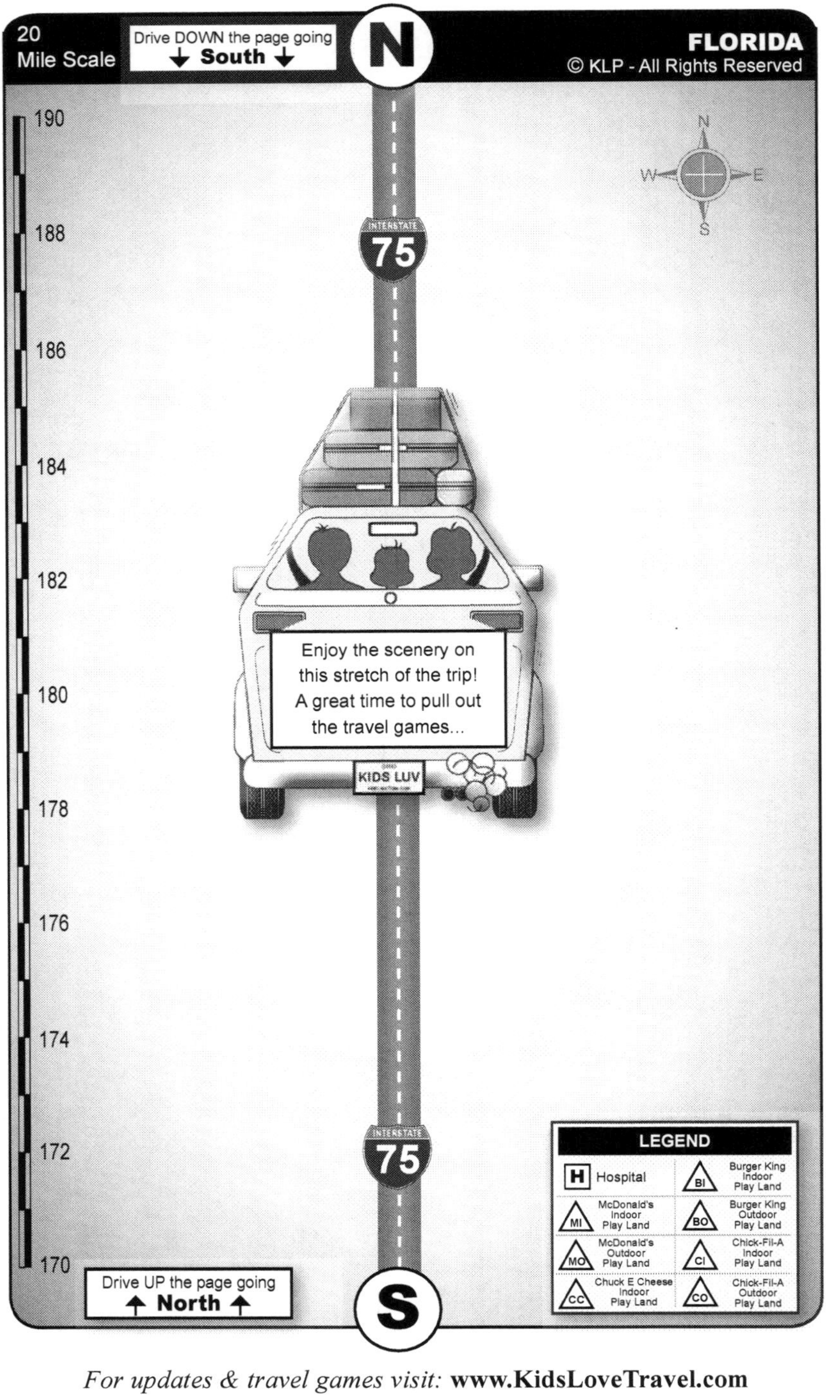
20
Mile Scale
Drive DOWN the page going
South
N
FLORIDA
© KLP - All Rights Reserved
190
188
186
184
182
180
178
176
174
172
170
N
W
E
S
75
Enjoy the scenery on this stretch of the trip! A great time to pull out the travel games...
KIDS LUV
75
LEGEND
H Hospital
BI Burger King Indoor Play Land
MI McDonald's Indoor Play Land
BO Burger King Outdoor Play Land
MO McDonald's Outdoor Play Land
CI Chick-Fil-A Indoor Play Land
CC Chuck E Cheese Indoor Play Land
CO Chick-Fil-A Outdoor Play Land
Drive UP the page going
North
S

FLORIDA

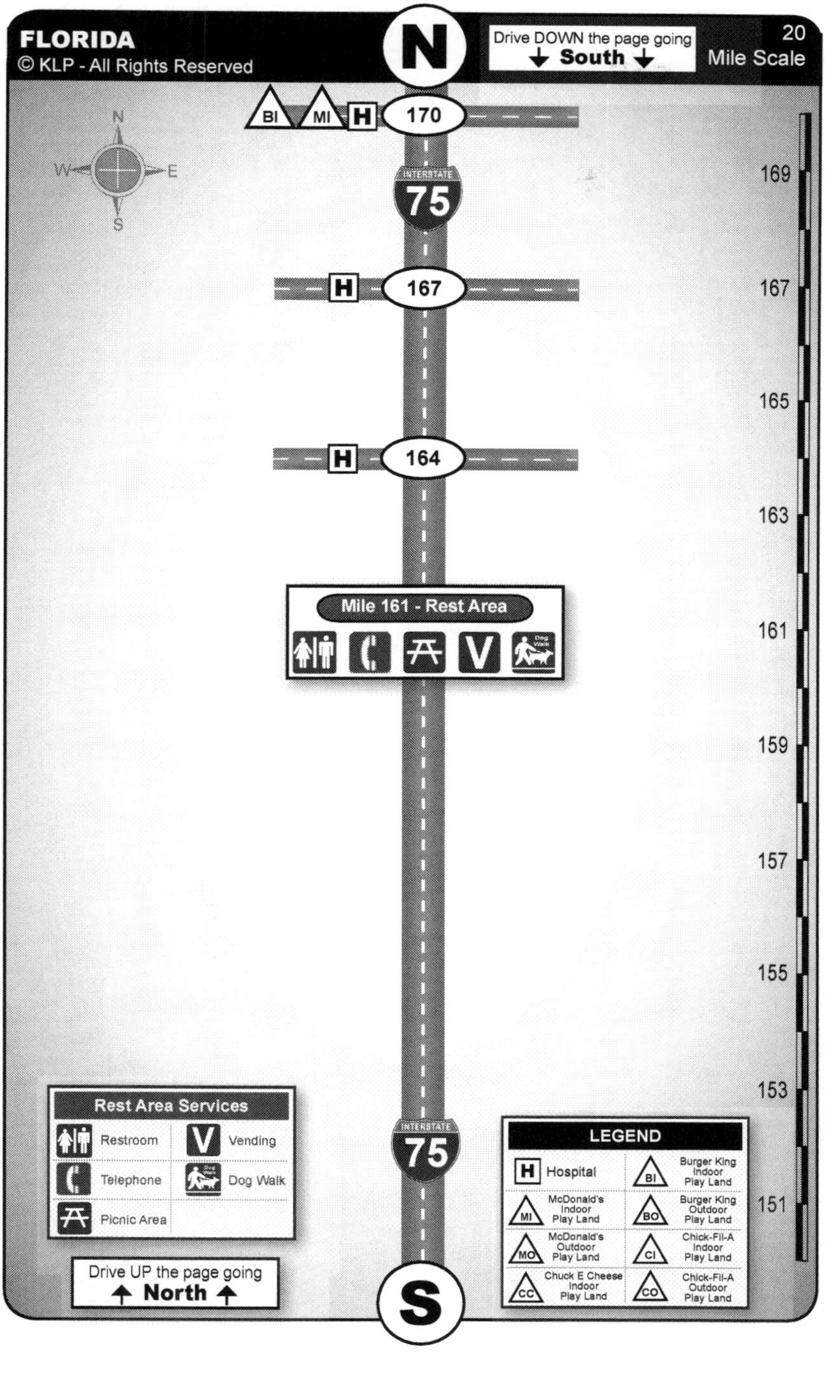
FLORIDA
© KLP - All Rights Reserved
N
Drive DOWN the page going
South
20
Mile Scale
BI
MI
H
170
169
INTERSTATE
75
H
167
167
165
H
164
163
Mile 161 - Rest Area
161
159
157
155
153
151
Rest Area Services
Restroom
Vending
Telephone
Dog Walk
Picnic Area
Drive UP the page going
North
LEGEND
H Hospital
BI Burger King Indoor Play Land
MI McDonald's Indoor Play Land
BO Burger King Outdoor Play Land
MO McDonald's Outdoor Play Land
CI Chick-Fil-A Indoor Play Land
CC Chuck E Cheese Indoor Play Land
CO Chick-Fil-A Outdoor Play Land
S

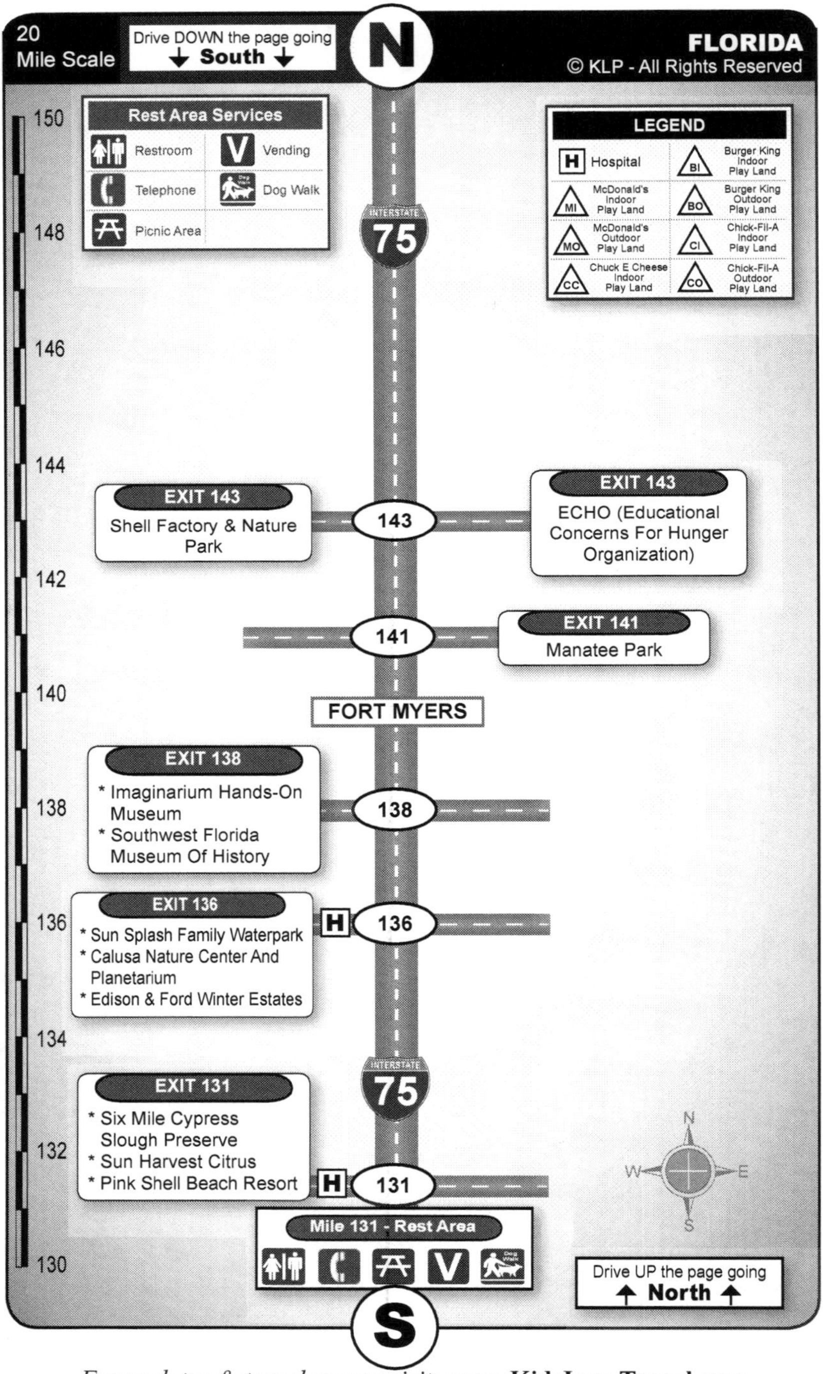
20 Mile Scale
Drive DOWN the page going ↓ South ↓
N
FLORIDA
© KLP - All Rights Reserved
Rest Area Services
Restroom
Vending
Telephone
Dog Walk
Picnic Area
LEGEND
H Hospital
BI Burger King Indoor Play Land
MI McDonald's Indoor Play Land
BO Burger King Outdoor Play Land
MO McDonald's Outdoor Play Land
CI Chick-Fil-A Indoor Play Land
CC Chuck E Cheese Indoor Play Land
CO Chick-Fil-A Outdoor Play Land
INTERSTATE 75
150
148
146
144
142
140
138
136
134
132
130
EXIT 143
Shell Factory & Nature Park
143
EXIT 143
ECHO (Educational Concerns For Hunger Organization)
141
EXIT 141
Manatee Park
FORT MYERS
EXIT 138
* Imaginarium Hands-On Museum
* Southwest Florida Museum Of History
138
EXIT 136
* Sun Splash Family Waterpark
* Calusa Nature Center And Planetarium
* Edison & Ford Winter Estates
H
136
EXIT 131
* Six Mile Cypress Slough Preserve
* Sun Harvest Citrus
* Pink Shell Beach Resort
H
131
Mile 131 - Rest Area
N
W
E
S
Drive UP the page going ↑ North ↑
S

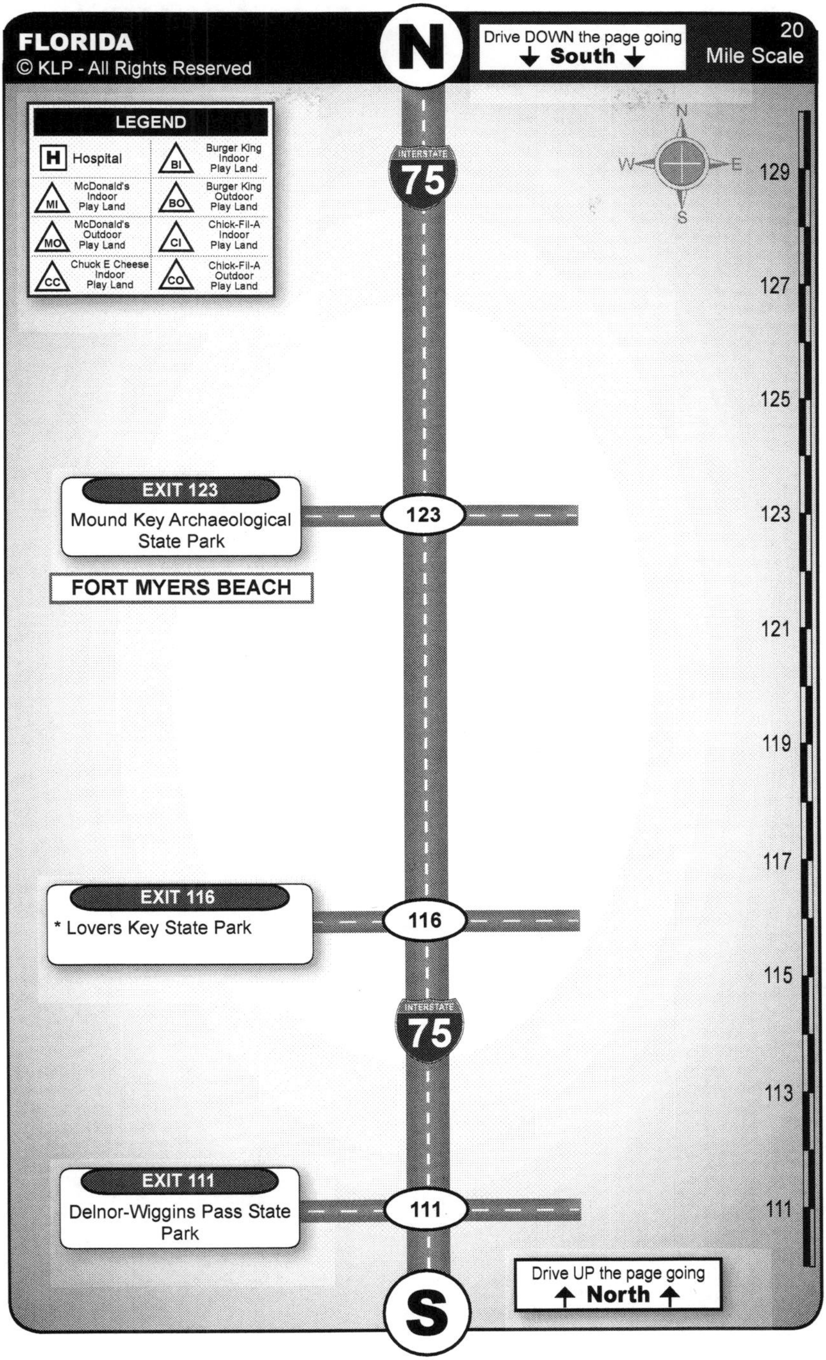
FLORIDA
© KLP - All Rights Reserved
N
Drive DOWN the page going
↓ South ↓
20
Mile Scale
LEGEND
H Hospital
BI Burger King Indoor Play Land
MI McDonald's Indoor Play Land
BO Burger King Outdoor Play Land
MO McDonald's Outdoor Play Land
CI Chick-Fil-A Indoor Play Land
CC Chuck E Cheese Indoor Play Land
CO Chick-Fil-A Outdoor Play Land
INTERSTATE 75
W
E
S
129
127
125
EXIT 123
Mound Key Archaeological State Park
123
FORT MYERS BEACH
121
119
117
EXIT 116
* Lovers Key State Park
116
115
INTERSTATE 75
113
EXIT 111
Delnor-Wiggins Pass State Park
111
Drive UP the page going
↑ North ↑
S

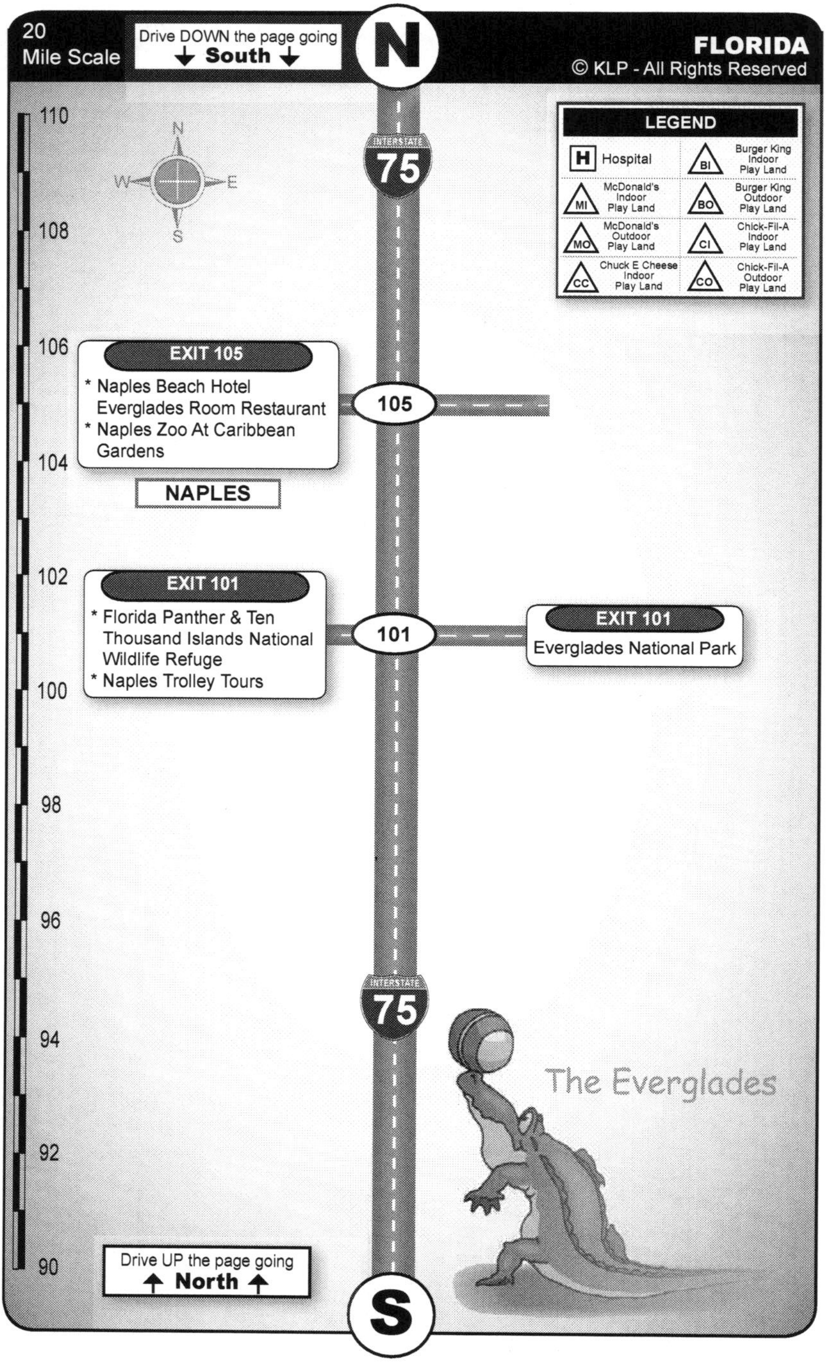
20
Mile Scale
Drive DOWN the page going
↓ South ↓
N
FLORIDA
© KLP - All Rights Reserved
110
108
106
104
102
100
98
96
94
92
90
N
W
E
S
INTERSTATE
75
LEGEND
H Hospital
BI Burger King Indoor Play Land
MI McDonald's Indoor Play Land
BO Burger King Outdoor Play Land
MO McDonald's Outdoor Play Land
CI Chick-Fil-A Indoor Play Land
CC Chuck E Cheese Indoor Play Land
CO Chick-Fil-A Outdoor Play Land
EXIT 105
* Naples Beach Hotel Everglades Room Restaurant
* Naples Zoo At Caribbean Gardens
105
NAPLES
EXIT 101
* Florida Panther & Ten Thousand Islands National Wildlife Refuge
* Naples Trolley Tours
101
EXIT 101
Everglades National Park
INTERSTATE
75
The Everglades
Drive UP the page going
↑ North ↑
S

FLORIDA

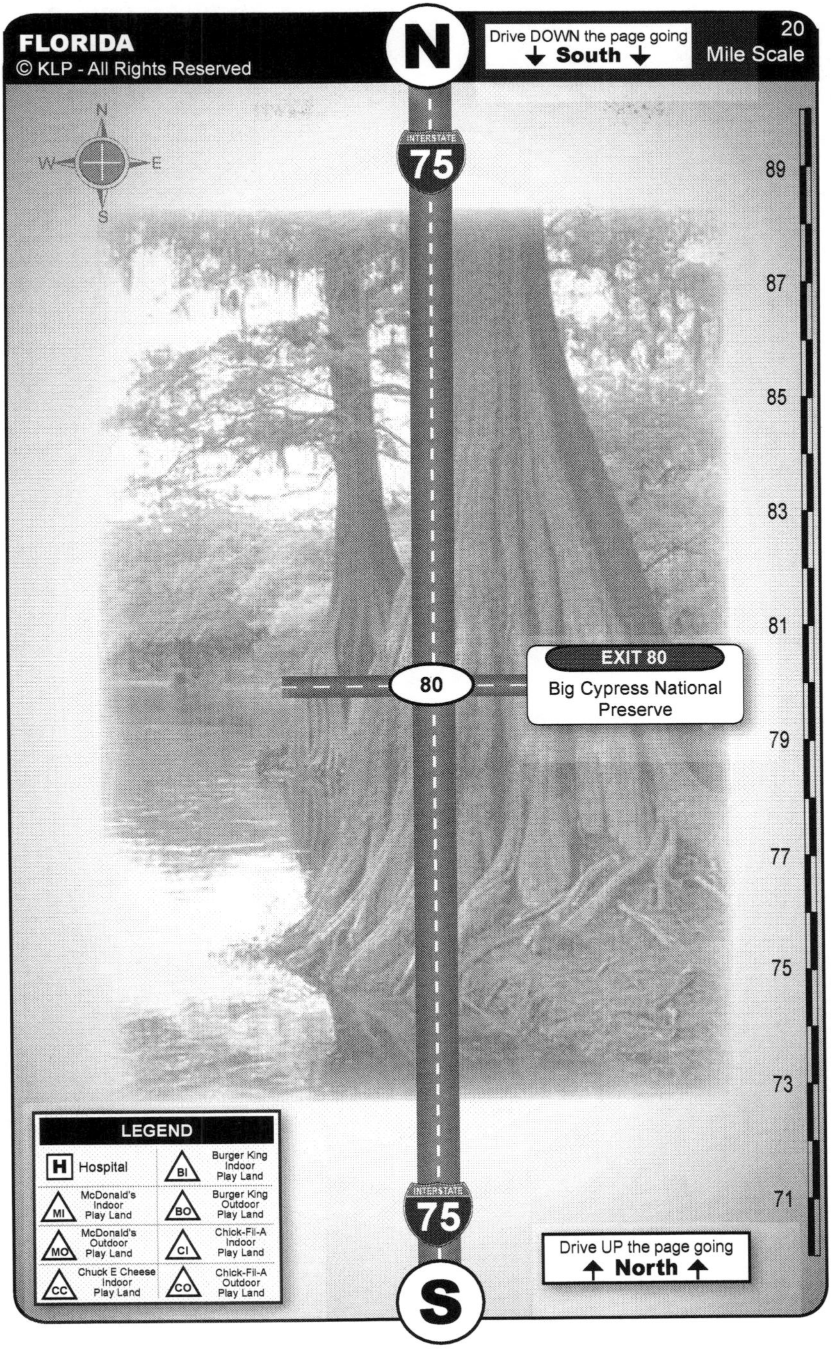
FLORIDA
© KLP - All Rights Reserved
N
Drive DOWN the page going
South
20
Mile Scale
N
W
E
S
75
89
87
85
83
81
EXIT 80
80
Big Cypress National Preserve
79
77
75
73
71
LEGEND
H Hospital
BI Burger King Indoor Play Land
MI McDonald's Indoor Play Land
BO Burger King Outdoor Play Land
MO McDonald's Outdoor Play Land
CI Chick-Fil-A Indoor Play Land
CC Chuck E Cheese Indoor Play Land
CO Chick-Fil-A Outdoor Play Land
75
Drive UP the page going
North
S

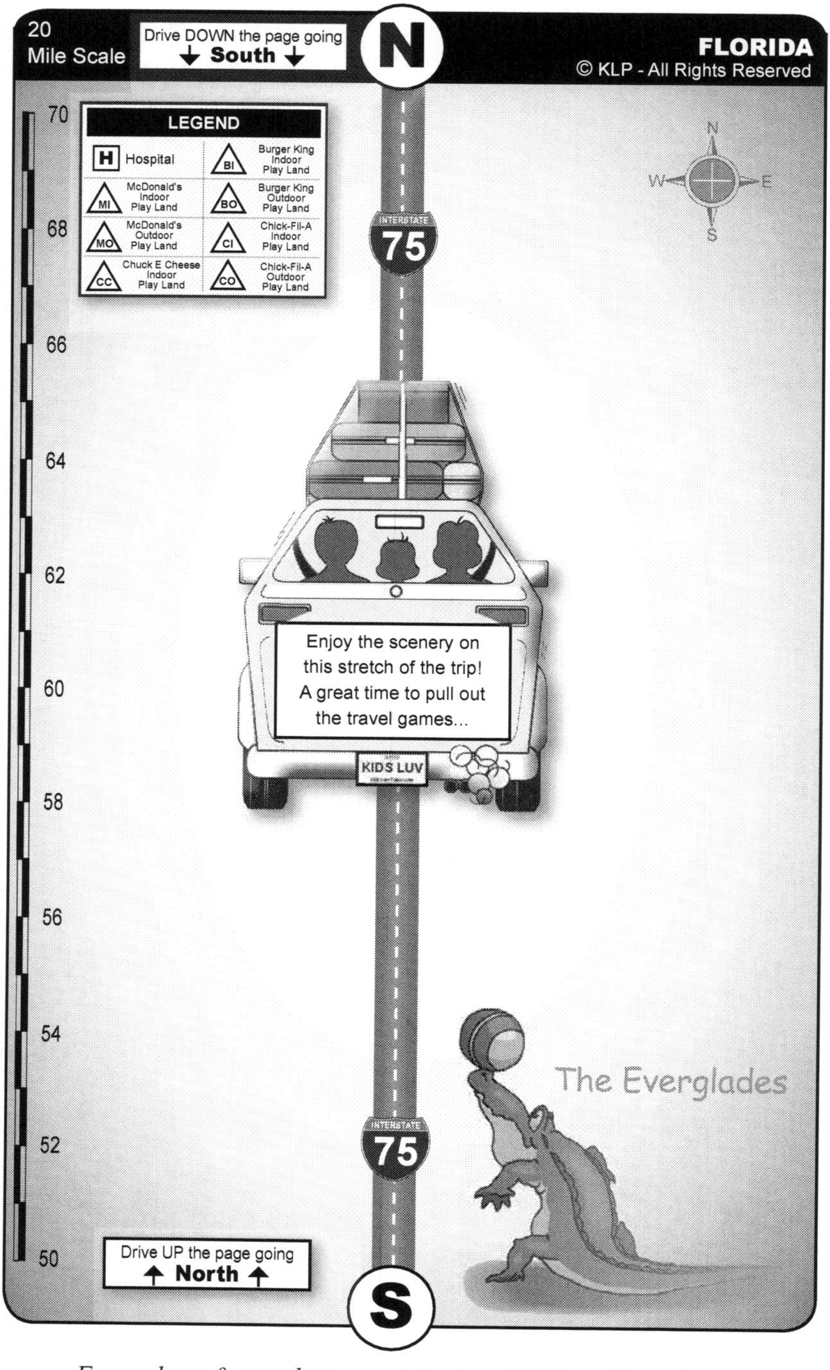
20
Mile Scale
Drive DOWN the page going
South
N
FLORIDA
© KLP - All Rights Reserved
LEGEND
H Hospital
BI Burger King Indoor Play Land
MI McDonald's Indoor Play Land
BO Burger King Outdoor Play Land
MO McDonald's Outdoor Play Land
CI Chick-Fil-A Indoor Play Land
CC Chuck E Cheese Indoor Play Land
CO Chick-Fil-A Outdoor Play Land
70
68
66
64
62
60
58
56
54
52
50
N
W
E
S
INTERSTATE 75
Enjoy the scenery on this stretch of the trip! A great time to pull out the travel games...
KIDS LUV
The Everglades
INTERSTATE 75
Drive UP the page going
North
S

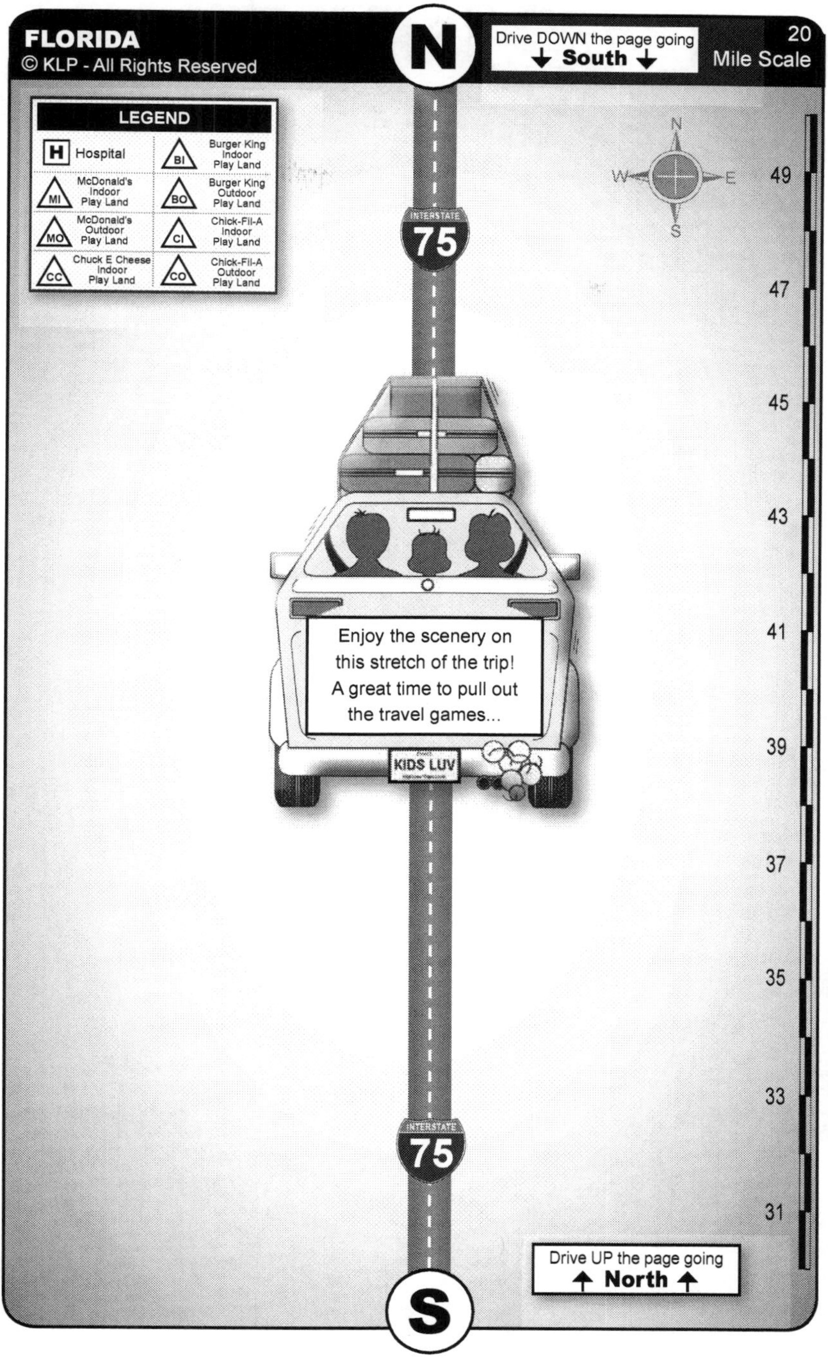
FLORIDA
© KLP - All Rights Reserved
N
Drive DOWN the page going ↓ South ↓
20 Mile Scale
LEGEND
H Hospital
BI Burger King Indoor Play Land
MI McDonald's Indoor Play Land
BO Burger King Outdoor Play Land
MO McDonald's Outdoor Play Land
CI Chick-Fil-A Indoor Play Land
CC Chuck E Cheese Indoor Play Land
CO Chick-Fil-A Outdoor Play Land
N W E S
INTERSTATE 75
49
47
45
43
Enjoy the scenery on this stretch of the trip! A great time to pull out the travel games...
41
KIDS LUV
39
37
35
33
INTERSTATE 75
31
Drive UP the page going ↑ North ↑
S

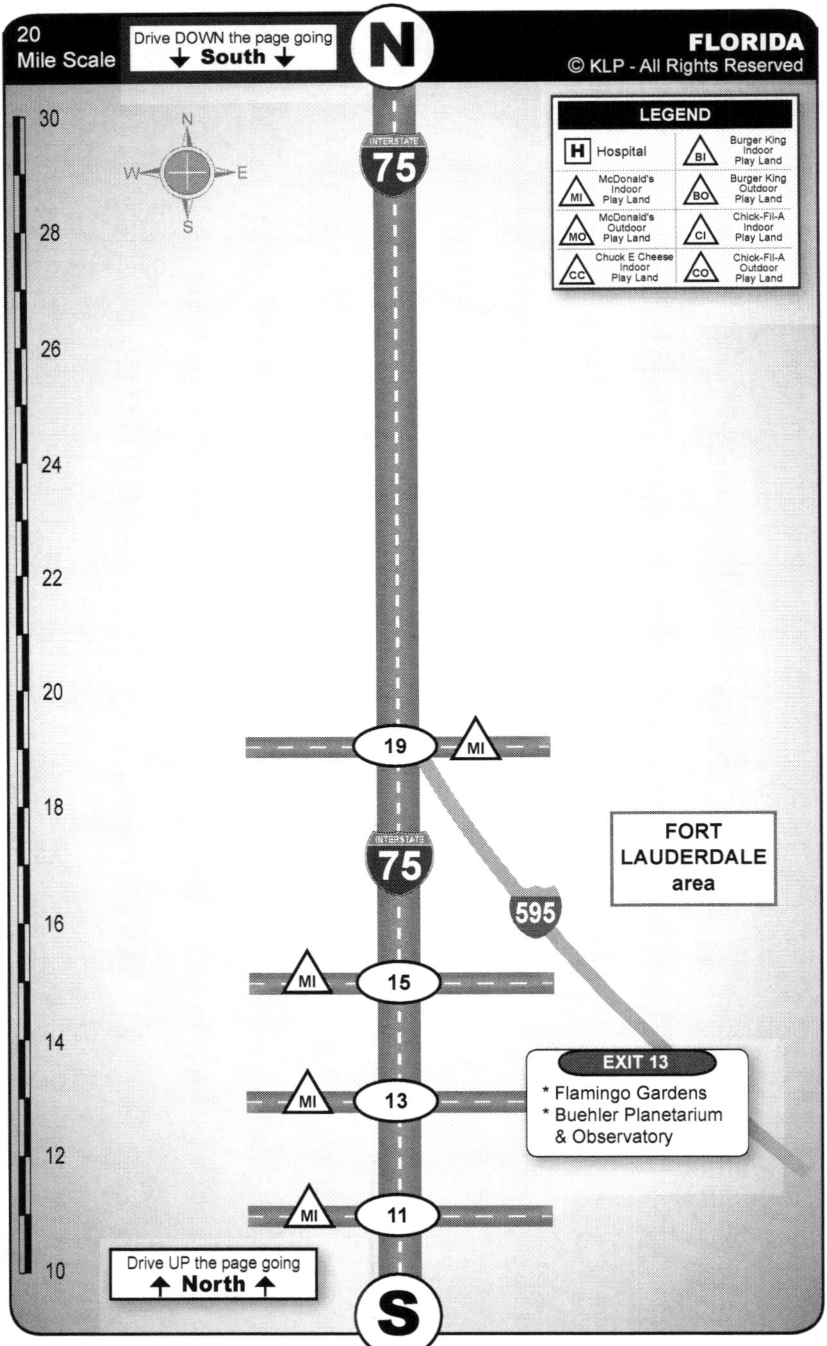
20
Mile Scale
Drive DOWN the page going
South
N
FLORIDA
© KLP - All Rights Reserved
LEGEND
H Hospital
BI Burger King Indoor Play Land
MI McDonald's Indoor Play Land
BO Burger King Outdoor Play Land
MO McDonald's Outdoor Play Land
CI Chick-Fil-A Indoor Play Land
CC Chuck E Cheese Indoor Play Land
CO Chick-Fil-A Outdoor Play Land
30
28
26
24
22
20
18
16
14
12
10
75
19
MI
FORT LAUDERDALE area
75
595
MI
15
EXIT 13
* Flamingo Gardens
* Buehler Planetarium & Observatory
MI
13
MI
11
Drive UP the page going
North
S

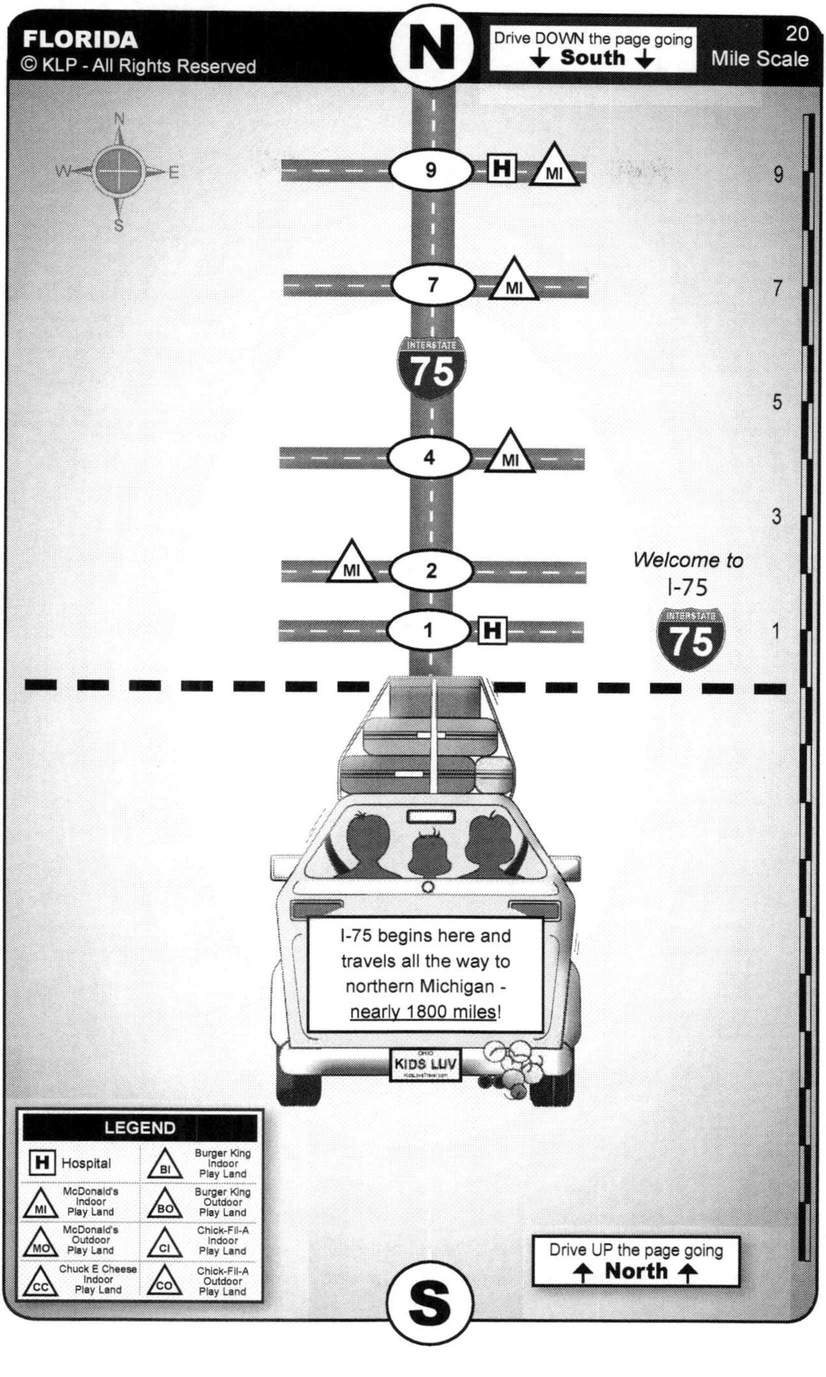
FLORIDA
© KLP - All Rights Reserved
N
Drive DOWN the page going
South
20 Mile Scale
N
W
E
S
9
H
MI
7
MI
75
4
MI
2
MI
1
H
Welcome to
I-75
75
9
7
5
3
1
I-75 begins here and travels all the way to northern Michigan - nearly 1800 miles!
KIDS LUV
LEGEND
H Hospital
BI Burger King Indoor Play Land
MI McDonald's Indoor Play Land
BO Burger King Outdoor Play Land
MO McDonald's Outdoor Play Land
CI Chick-Fil-A Indoor Play Land
CC Chuck E Cheese Indoor Play Land
CO Chick-Fil-A Outdoor Play Land
Drive UP the page going
North
S

Sites and attractions are listed in order by Exit Number (North to South) and distance from the exit (closest are listed first). Symbols indicated represent:

Restaurants Lodging

Exit - 470 (west of I-75)

FLORIDA WELCOME CENTER

Jennings - ***(southbound I-75 guests only). 4 miles north of town. 32053. (386) 938-2981***

Florida's State Wildflower, the Coreopsis, is planted on Florida roadsides for highway beautification. Look for the gold or pink petals.

Tourist information is available in Welcome Centers from 8:00am-5:00pm, seven days a week except holidays. (http://www.visitflorida.com/welcome-centers). This facility is also a Rest Area. The Florida Department of Transportation operates 6 rest areas along Florida's interstate 75 highway to provide safe, secure and comfortable rest stops for Florida travelers. Rest areas are generally located about 45 minutes traveling time apart. The facilities in the Florida Welcome Centers and Interstate Rest Areas are open 24 hours a day, 7 days a week for your comfort and convenience. Facilities are maintained 24 hours a day and nighttime security is provided. Overnight camping is not permitted, but visitors may stay for up to three hours. These rest areas provide restrooms (including family restrooms), picnic areas, pet walk areas, telephones and vending machines to aid travelers seeking a break from a long drive. Ask for your free sample of Florida citrus juice.

Exit - 460 (west of I-75)

SUWANNEE RIVER STATE PARK

Live Oak - ***20185 County Road 132 (I-75 exit 460, SR 6 west to CR141 south. located 13 miles west of town, off US 90) 32060. Phone: (386) 362-2746. www.floridastateparks.org/suwanneeriver. Hours: Florida state parks are open from 8:00am until sundown 365 days a year. Admission: An Honor Fee of $5.00 per car or $1.00 per person is payable at the pay station. Miscellaneous: Falmouth Springs, a short drive from Suwannee River State Park, claims to be the world's shortest river. Falmouth is a fifth magnitude spring.***

The scenic Withlacoochee River joins the legendary Suwannee River within this State Park. An overlook provides a panoramic view of both rivers and the surrounding wooded uplands. When water level is low, visitors can see springs bubbling from the banks of both rivers. Five trails provide great views of both rivers and access to remote springs. Along the river are long mounds of earthworks built during the Civil War to guard against Union gunboats. Other remnants from the past include one of the state's oldest cemeteries, and a paddle-wheel shaft from a 19th century steamboat. Other activities include fishing, picnicking, and canoeing. The park also has a boat ramp, picnic shelters, and a full facility campground and cabins.

Exit - 439 (east of I-75)

STEPHEN FOSTER FOLK CULTURE CENTER STATE PARK

White Springs - ***Post Office Drawer G (I-75 to S.R. 136 (Exit 439), travel east on S.R. 136 for 3 miles. Turn left on U.S. 41) 32096. Phone: (386) 397-2733. www.floridastateparks.org/park/stephen-foster. Hours: Museum, Tower and Gift Shop are open from 9:00:00am - 5:00pm daily. Admission: $5.00 per vehicle. Cabin Fee - $100.00 per night. Camping Fee - $20.00 per night per campsite. Nelly Bly's Kitchen - $125.00 per day.***

Situated on the banks of the legendary Suwannee River, this center honors the memory of American composer Stephen Foster, who wrote "Old Folks at Home," the song that made the river famous. This Cultural Park offers a permanent year-round craft village. In Craft Square, visitors can watch demonstrations of quilting, blacksmithing, stain glass making, and other crafts, or visit the gift shop. Listen to the melodies flowing from the Memorial Carillon Tower, and see 10 wonderfully detailed dioramas illustrating the famous songs of composer Stephen Foster. Rare pianos and priceless musical instruments also are on exhibit. Guided tours of the Museum and Tower are offered daily. Although he never visited the area, his song about the Suwannee River is legendary. The park has wooded trails that are easily accessible for hiking and cycling. Take a canoe or kayak trip on the Suwannee River sure to promise a leisurely adventure. Check into one of the riverside cabins, complete with a kitchenette, outdoor grill and sleeping accommodations for six people. Camp or simply relax and watch the Suwannee River go by...

Exit - 390 (east of I-75)

SANTA FE COMMUNITY COLLEGE TEACHING ZOO

Gainesville - ***3000 NW 83rd Street (I-75 exit 390, east on SR 222 to NW 91st St., follow until sharp left turn) 32606. www.sfcollege.edu/zoo/. Phone: (352) 395-5601. Hours: Daily 9:00am-2:00pm. Closed school holidays and breaks. Admission: $4.00-$5.00 Tours: given approximately every thirty minutes. WEEKDAY TOURS: The Teaching Zoo is OPEN for weekday tours with an appointment scheduled three days in advance.***

Guided tours are led by zoo keepers at the only community college teaching zoo in the nation. The property is the local zoo and the lab for the Zoo Animal Technology Program housing mammals, reptiles, amphibians, birds, and endangered species from Africa, Asia, Australia, Europe and the Americas. Why don't they have lions, tigers and bears? Expense and danger. Because students run this, they learn taking "baby steps" to care for manageable animals on a smaller scale. Some family favorites are the Bald Eagles, Galapagos tortoises, Matschie's Tree Kangaroo (that climb and live in trees), and Cranes with mohawks! A great way to peak interest in kids who may want to pursue careers in zoology. Kids really love the selection of smaller animals and the college students interaction on the tour.

DEVIL'S MILLHOPPER GEOLOGIC STATE PARK

Devil's Millhopper gets its unique name from its funnel-like shape.

Gainesville - ***4732 Millhopper Road (2 miles north of town, off SR 232. I-75 exit 390, CR 222 east. At 43rd St, turn left, then left onto Millhopper) 32653. Phone: (352) 955-2008. www.floridastateparks.org/park/devils-millhopper. Hours: Wednesday-Sunday 9:00am-5:00pm. Admission: $4.00 per vehicle. Note: guided walks with a Park Ranger are available every Saturday at 10:00am. Visitors can enjoy picnicking and learn more about this sinkhole through interpretive displays.***

A significant geological formation, Devil's Millhopper is a National Natural Landmark that has been visited by the curious since the early 1880s. Researchers have learned a great deal about Florida's natural history by studying fossil shark teeth, marine shells, and the fossilized remains of extinct land animals found in the sink (on display in the interpretive center). Legend has it that the millhopper was what fed bodies to the devil, hence the name.

Limestone is the foundation on which the surface of Florida sits. Although this stone is very hard, it is easily dissolved by a weak acid. A sink happens suddenly - the first rain after a drought. Each layer of sediment contains a record of events and animals that lived before. Marine animal shells are in the lower layers, bones and teeth of land animals are found in more "recent" layers. The sinkhole is 120 feet deep and 500 feet across. A one-half mile nature trail follows the rim, and there is a 232-step stairway to the bottom of the sink. Take a picture at the bottom as proof of your easy descent and aerobic ascent!

We made it to the bottom...

Exit - 387 (west of I-75)

DUDLEY FARM HISTORIC STATE PARK

Gainesville (Newberry) - ***18730 W. Newberry Road (I-75 exit SR 26 west 7 miles. Between Newberry & Gainesville) 32669. Phone: (352) 472-1142. www.floridastateparks.org/park/dudley-farm. Hours: Wednesday-Sunday 9:00am-4:00pm. Admission: $5.00 per vehicle.***

A 19th century working farmstead features a visitor center, picnic area and a guided or self-guided tour of the 18 historic structures that make up an authentic (no reproduction) farm complex. Staff and volunteers in authentic farm clothing carry on chores and activities much the same as they were in the late 1800s. Buildings include the old general store, a dairy shed, canning house, smokehouse, syrup house, hay barn, tobacco barn, stables and an 1880s kitchen. Livestock includes mules, cracker cows, horses, turkeys, and Barred Rock chickens. You might notice gardens, grape arbors, pecan and fruit trees, pastures, pinewoods, and croplands of peanuts, field peas, and sweet potatoes growing. In the fall, you can experience harvesting, grinding, boiling and bottling of sugar cane. Year-round, you can feed the chickens, walk on the nature trail or enjoy sitting in the rocking chairs on the spacious porches as you watch time go by.

Sidetrippers who like short hikes: The picnic area is located on the west side of the parking lot across from the visitor center and is equipped with 6 tables and 3 grills. Picnic Area Loop - A pleasant 15 minute walk that wanders through a hammock with many live oaks and sinkholes. The Pause and Ponder Trail - Enjoy this .3 mile loop nature trail at Dudley Farm's Visitor Center. This is your chance to take a quiet, meditative walk through the diverse habitat of Dudley Farm's woodlands. There is mystery here as the trail slopes downhill and curves out of sight. The trail climbs to high ground with a view out over pasture land where the Dudleys once grew cotton and where cows still graze. A hand-hewn cedar bench is made for resting or bird-watching. Pileated woodpeckers can be heard calling; native magnolias and live oaks create a majestic canopy. The trail begins and ends at the park's picnic area.

Exit - 387 (east of I-75)

MORNINGSIDE NATURE CENTER LIVING HISTORY FARM

Gainesville - ***3540 East University Ave (I-75 exit 387, head east on SR26 about 8 miles) 32641. Phone: (352) 334-2170. www.natureoperations.org. Hours: Farm is open Tuesday-Saturday from 9:00am-4:30pm, with live interpretive experiences offered every Saturday (September-May). Admission: Small admission fee during festivals & reenactments.***

At Morningside Nature Center, 278-acres of remnant forest is preserved along 5 miles of nature trails. Morningside's Living History Farm recreates the single-family rural farm that typified north central Florida during the late nineteenth century. Hogan's Cabin, a long-leaf pine cabin built in 1840, was the centerpiece of a project put at Morningside as part of Alachua County's bicentennial celebration in 1976. Other buildings include Clark's Kitchen, with a wood-burning cook stove, a log twin-crib barn from the late 1800s, a smoke-house, composting privy, and the Half-Moon one-room schoolhouse, built in the 1880s and one of the oldest schoolhouses in Alachua County. The farm is used as a re-enactment most Saturdays, where visitors can view costumed interpretive staff growing crops such as cotton and tobacco in the Cash Crop Field and medicinal herb, fruits, and vegetables in the Heirloom Garden. On site workers prepare the annual supply of syrup from sugar cane grown on property, care for live farm animals, leach lye from oak ashes to make soap, spin and weave cotton and wool, hook up the windmill to pump water, split wood for the fireplace, and perform other chores that were a part of turn-of-the-century living.

Exit - 384 (west of I-75)

HISTORIC HAILE HOMESTEAD AT KANAPAHA PLANTATION

Gainesville - *8500 Archer Road (I-75 exit 384, SR 24 west of town) 32608. Phone: (352) 336-9096. www.hailehomestead.org. Hours: Saturday 10:00am-2:00pm and Sunday Noon-4:00pm. Open for tours during the week by special appointment. Admission: $5.00 adult, under 12 free.*

One of the oldest houses in Alachua County, this historic home was once Thomas Evans Haile's and his family. The Hailes came here from Camden, South Carolina in 1854 to establish a 1,500 acre Sea Island Cotton plantation which they named Kanapaha. The Homestead later became the site of house parties attended by some of Gainesville's most distinguished citizens. The unusual thing about this family is: they wrote on the walls! Start your tour on the front porch. Kids like to sit on the Boggle Bench - what does it do? Once inside, you can't help but notice the assorted writings on the wall - mostly about parties held here. Why were kids and guests allowed to write on the walls? Whose name appears the most? Look for poems and math problems. Measure yourself against the growth chart of the owner's kids (15 of them). Many furnishings are original (like the nursery crib used by all the kids). There's a rock tablet outside you can write on - just to get it out of YOUR system. Although the furnishings are sparse, the student tour slowly introduces you to the "characters" that lived here versus what they owned. This makes for curious questions from kids. And, really, the highlight of the tour are those 12,500 assorted words on the walls! Very interesting...

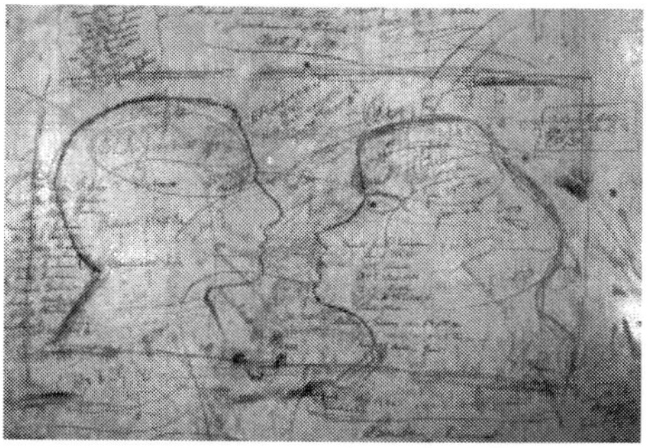

A family was allowed to write on the walls?

Exit - 384 (east of I-75)

GAINESVILLE-HAWTHORNE TRAIL STATE PARK

Micanopy - *100 Savannah Boulevard 32667. Phone: (352) 466-3397. Notes: Parking is provided at three locations, Boulware Springs Park in Gainesville (Mile 0), Lochloosa Trailhead (Mile 15), and the Hawthorne Trailhead (Mile 16.2). www.floridastateparks.org/park/gainesville-hawthorne. Bicycling and skating are permitted everywhere in the park except on La Chua trail. Admission: FREE.*

Gainesville-Hawthorne Trail State Park stretches 16 miles from the City of Gainesville's Boulware Springs Park through the Paynes Prairie Preserve State Park and the Lochloosa Wildlife Management Area. The old rail bed-turned-greenway is both a recreational surface and a grassy path for equestrians. Family bike riding is recommended. The entire trail is a pleasure to ride, and there are even a few hills to climb and speed down. If you take your time, park your bikes and visit La Chua trail in Paynes Prairie, you might even have an opportunity to see bison, wild horses and sandhill cranes.

FLORIDA MUSEUM OF NATURAL HISTORY

Gainesville - *University of Florida Cultural Plaza, Southwest 34th St. and Hull Road) (I-75 exit 384, follow signs - off SR 121) 32611. www.flmnh.ufl.edu. Phone: (352) 846-2000. Hours: Monday-Saturday 10:00am-5:00pm, Sunday 1:00-5:00pm. Closed Thanksgiving and Christmas. Admission: General Admission is FREE, although donations are gladly accepted and suggested ($2.00-6.00). There is a cover charge for special exhibits and the Butterfly Rainforest: $10.50 adult, $9.00 senior (62+) and students, $6.00 child (3-17). Parking: Reserved parking for museum visitors - excluding University holidays - is $3.00 per day (cash only), 8:45am-4:30pm., Monday through Friday. The reserved parking area is immediately east and north of the Harn Museum of Art in the UF Cultural Plaza. Please see attendant in gated booth. Parking is free on weekends and State holidays. Note: Due to the limited width of paths, backpacks and strollers are not permitted in the Butterfly Rainforest.*

Giant fossil shark jaws...

While exploring the natural history of Florida and ancient times, museum scientists made discoveries of mammoths

FLORIDA

and miniature horses in Northern Florida, to pre-colonial settlements in Haiti. The museum showcases and shares these finds. The Northwest hardwood hammock features a life-sized limestone cave and is patterned after the forest at Florida Caverns State Park early spring (walk thru an amazingly realistic cave - indoors!) Lift up a log and look for fossils and creatures; crawl in the cave-Look for the Spelunker; and Listen to bird sounds. The pitcher plant bog (coastal), Indian trading scene (river), and boardwalk coastal marsh (barrier islands) showcase many waterways and wildlife. Walk thru time beginning when Florida was underwater (scaled to 12 times larger!) to fossils and bones of ancient animals. Move the Earth or see a 15-foot-tall ground sloth and a two-foot-tall horse. Investigate South Florida Peoples (Calusa, Miccosukee and Seminole Indians) as you walk thru a full-scale mangrove forest, underwater scene and a Calusa leader's house. The theatrical lighting and recreated environs are spectacular! Engaging and entertaining.

Finally, the BUTTERFLY RAINFOREST. At any one time, over 2,000 butterflies delicately flutter around. Look for the state butterfly - the Zebra Longwind, or the large, almost neon, Blue Morpho. More butterflies than we've ever seen! The four-story outdoor screened enclosure has waterfalls, a walking trail, lush subtropical and tropical plants and hundreds of live butterflies. Their "Wall of Wings" reaches nearly three stories high. Kids can observe scientists working in labs. Think you know butterflies? What temperature do butterflies prefer? Where do they go when it rains?

As you leave the Rainforest, check in the mirror for "hitchhikers."

Exit - 384 (east of I-75)

UNIVERSITY OF FLORIDA

Gainesville - ***Visitors Passes at UF's main entrance at Southwest 13th Street (US441) and Southwest 2nd Avenue (I-75 exit 384, follow signs - off SR 121) 32611. Phone: (352) 392-3261. www.ufl.edu.***

Gatorade was named for the University of Florida Gators football team, where the drink was first developed.

The Historic Campus contains many buildings on the National Register of Historic Places such as University Auditorium. Above the Auditorium, visitors will find Century Tower, a 49-bell carillon that rings on quarter hours (maps available at the gated entrances). Florida Field at Ben Hill Griffin Memorial Stadium is located directly east of the O'Connell Center and seats 85,000 fans. Affectionately nicknamed "The Swamp" - the Stadium is home to the National Champ "Fightin Gators" football team.

BAT HOUSE: (just past the Natural History Museum, left onto Museum, immediate left into parking lot, walk left to Bat House). They sleep 60,000 plus by day but at sunset - out they all come for a drink and an eating frenzy (eating 30 million bugs each night)! Your family can watch and learn from thousands of live bats. Be sure to be there right at sunset (any night over 60 degrees) for the overwhelming view!

Exit - 374 (east of I-75)

PAYNES PRAIRIE PRESERVE STATE PARK

Gainesville (Micanopy) - ***100 Savannah Blvd. (I-75 exit 374. East on CR 234. Left onto US 441) 32667. www.floridastateparks.org/park/paynes-prairie. Phone: (352) 466-3397. Hours: Visitors Center open daily 9:00am-5:00pm. Park open 8:00am to sunset. Admission: $6.00 per vehicle. $2.00 for trails.***

Watch the video, "The Level Green Plain," view the exhibits, and enjoy panoramic views of the prairie from the 50' observation tower. You may even catch a glimpse of some of recent spring additions, including 2 bison calves, wild "cracker" horse foals, turkey chicks, and young eagles. From late November to early March, sandhill cranes and migrating waterfowl winter at the prairie basin. Buffalo and wild horses roam. The wild horses are descendants of those brought over by the Spanish in the early 1500s. For a closer look, explore the 30 miles of trails for equestrians, hikers and bicyclists. Fishing and boating (canoes, kayaks and small boats) and full campground amenities.

Rawling's favorite writing place...

MARJORIE KINNAN RAWLINGS HISTORIC STATE PARK

Gainesville (Cross Creek) - ***18700 S County Road 325 (Exit 374, off SR 20 east, follow signs) 32640. www.floridastateparks.org/park/marjorie-kinnan-rawlings. Phone: (352) 466-3672. Hours: Rawlings' farmyard, grove, and nature trails***

(2 short ones) are open 9:00am-5:00pm daily, throughout the year. Admission: $3.00 per vehicle. Guided tours are $2.00-$3.00 per person (age 6+). Tours: Public guided tours given Thursday-Sunday at 10:00am, 11:00am and each hour from 1:00-4:00pm (October-July only). 10 person max. on each tour. Note: Your pet is welcome to the park on a hand-held leash (so they won't chase the chickens and the ducks!), but if you take the tour of the house you need to be able to carry it. And remember, it's the 1930s and they are not air-conditioned or heated, so dress for the weather.

Famed author, Marjorie Rawlings came to Cross Creek in 1928 where she settled into her new life in this "half-wild, backwoods country," growing oranges, cooking on a wood-burning stove, running a small animal farm, and writing down her impressions of the land and her Cracker neighbors.. Visitors may tour the house - kept the way it was in the 1930s - with a ranger in period costume. The ranger will invite you in and quote Miss Rawlings, "bring an open mind and an overnight bag." She sat most often on the wide veranda at her typewriter, writing the books that would endear her to the world and capture the beauty of Florida and the spirit of its people. Rawlings' clunky black typewriter still rests on a table on the front porch (good photo op). Also, look for the giant dictionary and Moe, the dog. "The Yearling" an American classic and winner of the Pulitzer Prize, is the story of young Jody Baxter's coming of age in the big scrub country forest (a pet deer sounds like fun but there is a sad ending). Learn about the author's life, including her famous dinners with guests such as Ernest Hemingway or her party in the bathroom. The kitchen is a favorite room - did you know Miss Rawlings wrote a cookbook, too? Inspiring and authentic tour. After your tour, remember to wander through the citrus grove and see the newly restored tenant house, or wander the paths deeper into the woods.

The adjacent county park, which has a boat ramp, playground and picnic facilities, is the site where MKR kept her milk cow.

Exit - 352 (east of I-75)

SILVER SPRINGS & WILD WATERS

Ocala - ***5656 E. Silver Springs Blvd. (I-75 exit 352 east of Ocala on SR 40) 34488. Phone: (352) 236-2121. www.silversprings.com. Hours: Daily 10:00am-6:00pm. Check web calendar for details. Admission: $8.00 per carload. Basic Boat Tours: $11.00 adult, $10.00 senior (55+) and youth (3-17).***

Start your day with this enchanting tour of 7 major parts of the spring. The glass-bottom allows everyone to see the changes in water color and wildlife below. Look for turtle, fish, movie props and hidden caves. The Lighthouse Ride combines a carousel and gondola ride with a telescoping outer tower that quietly rises 98 feet above Silver Springs. This ride is a good way to see an overview of the park. Guests enjoy a panoramic view of the park, the pristine Silver River and the area's bird life, fish and other animals. The Extended Cruise (weekends, double fees, 90 minutes)showcases Silver Springs' history through scenes on the riverbanks featuring period props, sound and even some funny living history characters. Guests encounter a working archeological dig site, homestead and a typical movie set representing the classic films and television shows that have been filmed at the park (ex. Tarzan). ***WILD WATERS outdoor waterpark***: Open summers for $32.99 adults, $27.99 child. Dry Rides are $2 each.

See the underwater scenery - the glass bottomed boat was invented here in 1878!

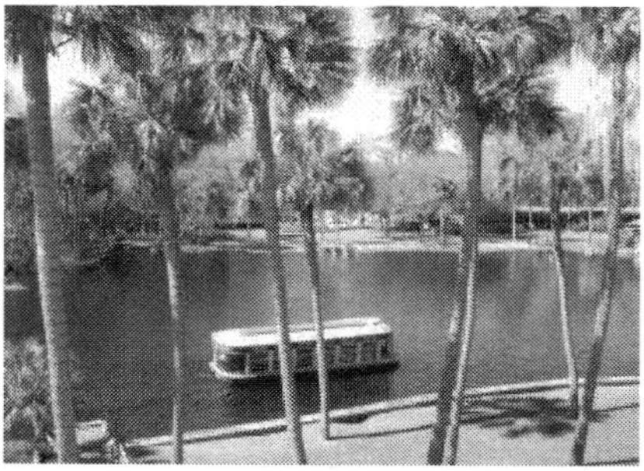

Silver Springs, famous for its Glass-Bottom Boat ride, encompasses the largest artesian limestone spring in the world.

SILVER SPRINGS STATE PARK

Ocala - ***1425 N E 58th Avenue (SR 35) (east of Ocala, one mile south of State Road 40 on State Road 35) 34470. www.floridastateparks.org/park/silver-springs. Phone: (352) 236-5401. Hours: Museum/Center: Weekends & major holidays 9:00am-5:00pm. Park open daily 8:00am-sunset. Admission: Museum: $2.00 per person, children 6 and under are FREE. $8.00 per carload entrance fee. Cabin & Camping Fees. Note: Visitors can canoe down the crystal clear river, hike or bike along one of the nature trails, or just sit and watch for the wide variety of birds and wildlife. For overnight stays, the park has a full facility campground and 10 luxury cabins.***

Visitors to the museum take a journey through Silver River's past. Everything from mammoths to movies are included in the exhibits. Upon entering the museum, you come nose to tusk with a Columbian Mammoth skeleton. This cast is one of the few full size mammoth skeletons on display in Florida. Be awe struck by the giant jaw and teeth of the Megalodon (prehistoric shark) that swam over Florida so many years ago. A young mastodon skull and an adult skull are both displayed. A variety of fossils are found throughout the museum. Artifacts from some of Florida's first human inhabitants are also found within the museum. You can see tools and weapons constructed from native materials dating as far back as 12,000 years ago. The shells of other, smaller creatures living in Florida's prehistoric seas, called Foramnifera, formed the basis of the Floridian Aquifer, our modern day water source. An interactive exhibit informs visitors about some of the current issues affecting local water supply. The collection in the second half of Silver River Museum illustrates a period of time spanning over 500 years, beginning with the initial Spanish exploration. It's a nice display of cultural and natural history in Central Florida.

Exit - 341 (east of I-75)

DON GARLITS MUSEUM OF DRAG RACING AND CLASSIC CARS

Ocala - ***13700 SW 16th Avenue (I-75 exit 341, one block east on CR 484) 34473. Phone: (877) 271-3278. www.garlits.com. Hours: Daily (except Christmas) from 9:00am-5:00pm. Admission: $20.00 adult, $15.00 senior (60+) and youth (13-18), $10.00 child (5-12). Note: they have a covered pavilion outside. Sonny's BBQ is right around the corner & offers catering.***

Mention the name "Big Daddy" around anyone familiar with auto sports and one name comes to mind, "Don Garlits". A legend in Top Fuel Drag racing, Don has inspired generations to reach for their best in the ¼ mile. In recent years, Don even borrowed a car and still ran over 300 MPH to prove he could still do it! See the Museum of Classic Cars (Vintage Cars, Early Fords, Hot Rods, and '60s & '70s muscle cars) and the Museum of Drag Racing (many of the record-breaking "swamp rat" cars) that will inspire both young and old alike.

Exit - 314 (west of I-75)

DADE BATTLEFIELD HISTORIC STATE PARK

Bushnell - *7200 CR 603 (off I-75 exit 314, west of US 301) 33513. Phone: (352) 793-4781. www.floridastateparks.org/park/dade-battlefield. Hours: Daily 8:00am-sunset. The center is open 9:00am-5:00pm daily. Admission: $3.00 for up to 8 people per car.*

Dade Battlefield offers a peaceful setting away from the hustle and bustle of the city. One can explore the natural beauty of the wildflowers along the park's nature trail or walk along the Old Fort King Road where Major Dade and his command encountered 180 Seminoles. The battle that started the Second Seminole War is commemorated in January each year under the oaks of Dade Battlefield. On December 28, 1835, Seminole Indian warriors ambushed 108 soldiers at this site-only three soldiers survived. The park protects not only a historic battlefield, but also the natural communities as they existed when the soldiers and Seminoles battled over 180 years ago. Strolling a half-mile nature trail through pine flatwoods, visitors might see gopher tortoises, woodpeckers, songbirds, hawks, and indigo snakes. The park has a playground, picnic area with covered shelters, and a recreation hall. The visitor center has information and displays about the battle and visitors can watch a twelve-minute video history, This Land, These Men.

Exit - 279 (east of I-75)

FLORIDA

SADDLEBROOK RESORT

Tampa (Wesley Chapel) - *5700 Saddlebrook Way (one mile east of I-75 exit 279) 33543. Phone: (813) 973-1111 or (800) 729-8383. www.saddlebrookresort.com.*

Saddlebrook Resort is a secluded retreat that offers service and comfort. In the heart of the resort, the Walking Village includes all recreation and dining facilities surrounding the heated SuperPool. Wait till your kids see the Super Pool! Guest accommodations border the Walking Village, making transportation needless (valet parking is provided so you're not tempted to "drive" the property). The resort is comprised of 800 deluxe guest rooms, and one-two-

and three bedroom suites. Suites include a spacious living/dining room and fully equipped kitchen. Every day is different for children staying at Saddlebrook: Animal Mondays, Dinosaur Tuesdays, Weather Wednesdays, Underwater Thursdays, Finally Fridays, Sports Saturdays and Science Sundays. Open to kids ages 4-12, S'Kids Club offers a place for young resort guests to meet others their age while allowing mom and dad free time for meetings, golf, tennis or the Spa. Babysitting is provided for kids under age 4. Saddlebrook also offers a variety of other activities for children including the SuperPool featuring racing lanes, water volleyball and basketball. Additional equipment is available for check out at the Swim Shop including board games, bicycles, water toys and fishing gear. Two whirlpools, the Poolside Café and a child's play area surround the pool. Nearby are Junior tennis and golf opportunities. Rates range $100.00-$200.00 per person (age 16+), per night. All nightly rates include breakfast and dinner.

We loved waking up to an "al fresco" breakfast ...

Exit - 265 (west of I-75)

MUSEUM OF SCIENCE AND INDUSTRY (MOSI)

Tampa - *4801 E. Fowler Avenue (I-75 exit 265, Fowler Avenue westbound about 2.5 miles) 33617. Phone: (813) 987-6000 or (800) 995-MOSI. www.mosi.org. Hours: Monday-Friday 10:00am-5:00pm; Saturday-Sunday 10:00am-6:00pm. Admission: $22.95 adult, $20.95 senior (60+), $18.95 child (3-12). Parking is FREE. Ticket includes admission into MOSI, Kids in Charge, one Planetarium show and one standard IMAX film. New Sky Trail Ropes or Zip Line extra $5-$10.*

Safely inside a hurricane...

Home to Florida's first IMAX Dome Theater and the Southeast's largest science center, the Museum was designed with input from kids. The scientific playground is filled with over 450 hands-on activities and interactive traveling exhibits. Highlights include the "Gulf Coast Hurricane Chamber" which allows visitors to experience 74 mile per hour winds, and the "Challenger Learning Center" where guests can assume the role of astronaut or engineer. We absolutely loved the hurricane wind chamber experience! MOSI's "High Wire Bicycle" is the longest high wire bike in a U.S. museum. The Kids In Charge building was so well done - you can tell local kids really have input. The exhibits not to miss are Bed of Nails (we really laid on a real bed of nails!) and the Rope Maze (spider web puzzle). Other features: "BioWorks Butterfly Garden," "The Amazing You: An Exhibition of the Human Body," plus an Avionics Flight simulator, a planetarium and two Diplodocus dinosaurs that stand three stories tall and are the largest articulated dinosaurs ever discovered. This campus is huge.

BUSCH GARDENS - TAMPA BAY

Tampa - ***3605 East Bougainvillea (I-75 exit 265, take SR582 west to SR581 south. Follow signs) 33612. www.buschgardens.com. Phone: (813) 987-5000 or (888) 800-5447. Hours: Basically 10:00am-6:00pm. Extended morning and evenings hours during peak Tampa season. Admission: $65.00-$95.00 (age 3+). Discounts for Florida residents and online ticket purchases. Adventure tours are extra (ex. Safari is $29-$39 extra). Tours: Serengeti Safari is a must for giraffe lovers. Your flat-bed gated jeep allows you to feed fresh veggies and fruit to several animals found in Africa but most importantly you can hand-feed tall giraffe as they sweep down their long purple tongues! What a photo!***

A family adventure park featuring a combination of world-class animal habitats, thrill rides, and live entertainment. The park provides guests with four steel coasters and two newer coasters: Cheetah Chase - cat and mouse style and Shiekra, the country's first "dive coaster" that goes up, down, down and loops around in Stanleyville town. The park has been recognized among the top zoos in North America providing more diverse ways to get up-close to animals than any other place outside of Africa. Guides take families on a Rhino Rally in customized SUVs to see rhinos the size of pick-up trucks, buffalo, elephant and others in the Serengeti Plain. You'll pass under a waterfall and get washed away in a storm on a fun thrill ride. In Sesame Street Safari, children find an area just for them filled with a three-story tree house, an enchanted forest, and wonderful rides. Set in the Congo area, Jungala, the 4-acre attraction invites guests to discover exotic creatures, explore a village hidden deep in the jungle and connect with the inhabitants of the lush landscape through up-close animal interactions, multi-story family play areas, rides and live entertainment. Entertainment includes a 4-D family adventure film and Broadway caliber musicals that takes guests to the heart of the jungle. Each month, several venues throughout the park present live music and dance with different themes (ex. Irish dancers). Regular "fair rides" are found scattered throughout the park. Congo River Rapids is a "wet" family raft ride.

Exit - 265 (west of I-75)

ADVENTURE ISLAND

Tampa - ***10001 Malcolm McKinley Drive (I-75 exit 265, take SR582 west to SR581 south - adjacent to Busch Gardens) 33612. Phone: (813) 987-5600 or (888) 800-5447. www.adventureisland.com. Hours: Open daily mid-March through early-September and weekends only mid-September through late October. Admission: $40.00 plus per person (age 3+). Note: Leave your wallet in the locker and forget soggy cash. Use the bar-coded waterproof wristbands.***

Thirty acres of water-drenched fun in the sun feature the ultimate combination of high-speed thrills and an inviting tropical surrounding of a Key West setting. Corkscrew slides, waterfalls, outdoor cafes, a wave pool and children's play area round out the assortment of rides. The complex includes other family attractions such as outdoor cafes, picnic and sunbathing areas, gift shops, and a championship white-sand volleyball complex.

LOWRY PARK ZOO

Tampa - ***1101 W. Sligh Avenue (off I-275, look for exit signs) 33604. Phone: (813) 935-8552. www.lowryparkzoo.com. Hours: Daily 9:30am-5:00pm. Admission: $24.95 adult, $22.95 senior (50+), $19.95 child (3-11). Mini-amusement rides are now included in zoo admission. Add $5 extra for live animal rides.***

This 26-acre open-air natural habitat zoo is ranked as one of the top three mid-sized zoos in the country. Home to more than 1,500 animals in lush tropical settings, the zoo includes a free flight lorikeet aviary, children's petting zoo and educational center. One of the zoo's highlights is its "Manatee and Aquatic Center," one of only three rehab facilities in the state of Florida for gentle sea cows. The world's largest living lizard species, the legendary Komodo dragon, is featured in the zoo's Asian Domain. Newer attractions take visitors to Australia and Africa. "Wallaroo Station" is home to Palm cockatoos, kookaburra, dangaroos and wallabies while "Safari Africa" & "Ituri Forest" have habitats for elephants, giraffes, bongo, warthogs and camels. And, probably your kids favorites: the interactive exhibits - Giraffe-feeding, White Rhino feeding, Camel Safari, the Petting Zoo, Penguin Beach, Free-Flight aviaries and StingRay Bay.

Exit - 265 (east of I-75)

HILLSBOROUGH RIVER STATE PARK

Tampa (Thonotosassa) - ***15402 N US 301 (I-75 exit 265 east, six miles south of Zephyrhills on U.S. 301) 33592. www.floridastateparks.org/park/hillsborough-river. Phone: (813) 987-6771. Hours: Daily 8:00am-sunset. Admission: $4.00 for up to 8 people per car. $20.00 camping fee. Note: The concession is open for breakfast and lunch daily from 9:00am-4:00pm. Canoes and bikes can be rented from 9:00am-3:00pm and all rental equipment must be returned by 4:00pm. The pool is open daily, weather permitting from 9:00am-5:00pm.***

Built in 1936 by the Civilian Conservation Corp. Hillsborough River State Park is steeped in history and natural beauty. Many activities are available at the park by which visitors can access and enjoy this area. Fort Foster, a replica of an original Second Seminole War military fort, is open for guided tours on Saturdays and Sundays. A visit to the Fort allows visitors to step back in time to the days of when Florida was being settled by pioneers. The Fort Foster Visitor Station houses a display of artifacts from the time period, and provides the visitor with information about the operation of the Fort.

Hikers can walk over seven miles along four nature trails. The Wetlands Restoration Trail accommodates bicyclists and hikers. A popular trail is the Rapids Nature Trail. It meanders through oak hammocks to the edge of the Hillsborough River at the point where an outcropping of limestone rocks has created rapids. If you want to enjoy the river by being on it, the park has canoe rentals for visitor's convenience. Hillsborough River State Park also offers 111 campsites, picnic areas, pavilions, and the Spirit of the Woods Pool Side Café and Gift Shop. A swimming pool with a capacity of 216 swimmers is also within the park.

Exit - 261 (west of I-75)

YBOR CITY MUSEUM STATE PARK

Tampa - ***1818 E 9th Avenue (I-4 exit 1 - 21st/22nd Street, head east a few blocks) 33605. Phone: (813) 247-1434. www.ybormuseum.org. Hours: Daily 9:00am-5:00pm. Closed Thanksgiving, Christmas and New Years Day. Admission: $4.00 (age 6+) Tours: Visitors can also take self-guided tours using maps from the Museum & Information Center. Note: TECO LINE STREETCARS (replicas) transport passengers from downtown Tampa through the Channel District/port, the Florida Aquarium, and into Ybor City (stops at 7th Avenue, Centro Ybor and Centennial Park). Traveling 6.5 mph, the streetcars take approximately 20 minutes to make 11 stops on the 23 mile track. $5 unlimited ride fare.***

This Historical Park's exhibits tell the story of the immigrant life and Ybor's cigar making history. The State Park complex covers approximately one-half city block and includes a garden, the original Ferlita bakery, and multiple restored cigar workers' houses called casitas (meaning little houses). Visitors can tour the interior of one of the casitas to learn about the shot-gun style houses and the families that resided there. A cigar roller works at the Ybor City Museum State Park from 11:00am-1:00pm on Friday, Saturday and Sunday. Although we don't want to promote smoking to youth, chatting (in Spanish) with the cigar maker was interesting and interactive. La Casita is open from 10:00am-3:00pm (except Sunday). The workers were not allowed to leave for coffee breaks, so the restaurant next door would bring café con leche to them. What were readers? Why were they so important?

Inside a Cuban stone baking oven

COLUMBIA RESTAURANT

Tampa (Ybor City) *- 2117 E. 7th Avenue. (I-4 exit 1 - 21st/22nd Street, head east a few blocks) 33605. Phone: (813) 248-4961. www.columbiarestaurant.com.*

This 100 year old plus eatery has old-world charm serving authentic, flavorful Spanish/Cuban cuisine since 1905. The Columbia continues to be owned and operated by the 4th & 5th generation of the Hernandez Gonzmart family and has remained the oldest restaurant in Florida and the largest Spanish restaurant in the world. Kids Menus ($4.95) items offer: steak, Cuban sandwich, grilled cheese or chicken tenders, but the adult menu is what's special. Daily lunch (avg. $13) and dinner (avg. $20) are served. Try Cuban sandwiches, grouper, Cuban bread, deviled crab, guava dessert, Spanish bean soup and Crema Catalana with café con leche for dessert. Really, if you want to try several dishes like Mama Gonzmart would cook, try their combos. Our favorites were the gravy, black beans and empanadas on the combo plate. We love when eating can become a cultural education. To get the feel for how this eatery fits into this old city space, take a peek through the Columbia Museum next door.

Exit - 261 (east of I-75)

DINOSAUR WORLD

Plant City *- 5145 Harvey Tew Road (I-4 exit 17, 20 minutes from Tampa) 33565. Phone: (813) 717-9865. www.dinosaurworld.com Hours: Daily 9:00am-6:00pm. Admission: $11.95-$16.95 (age 3+). Fossil Dig tickets are included in the child admission price for ages 3-12. Active duty U.S. military personnel receive FREE ADMISSION to Dinosaur World with an active military ID shown at time of ticket purchase. Note: Enjoy a museum, gift shop, and picnic area, playground and hands-on activities for children. There is no food service at Dinosaur World, however, they have excellent picnic areas. Bring a picnic lunch or enjoy one of the local fast food or dine in restaurants and bring the food back to the park picnic areas. Pizza delivery is also available.*

The world's largest dinosaur attraction is located in Plant City. The sight will turn heads as you approach viewing a dinosaur poking out from the foliage beside the highway. In this subtropical garden, visitors can mingle with 160 models of prehistoric beasts. The 12-acre outdoor-educational museum has figures of scaled-down, scientifically accurate models of Brachiosaurus, T-Rex with fiery eyes, Brontosaurus, Stegosaurus and his bumpy backbone, Iguanodon, Triceratops and such. There are little dinos no bigger than a turkey; others rise 25 feet above the ground. Each specimen is identified on a plated description highlighting it's habits and habitats. Dinosaur Mountain houses a video theater and an exhibit on how the dinosaur models were made. Families can examine fossils and learn why dinosaur remains are not found in Florida. Then, try your paleontologist skills out digging through the Fossil Dig or Boneyard areas. The simulated sand pit or rock cave areas provide tools to uncover hidden little fossils and one big, life-size Stegosaurus skeleton. Many photo ops here - especially the head of a T. rex with its mouth open.

Exit - 257 (west of I-75)

FLORIDA AQUARIUM

Tampa - ***701 Channelside Drive (I-75 exit 257 west on SR60 to Channelside Dr. (left) 33602. Phone: (813) 273-4000 or (800) FLFISH-1. www.flaquarium.org. Hours: Daily 9:30am-5:00pm. Closed Thanksgiving and Christmas. Admission: $23.95 adult, $20.95 senior (60+), $18.95 child (2-12). Online discounts. Tours: Wild Dolphin Cruises take the Aquarium experience out onto the bay on a catamaran in search of bottlenose dolphin and other Florida wildlife. (additional $10.00-$14.00, afternoons daily). Behind the Scenes tours: Ever wondered how they feed the fish, or the sharks? How they make sea water? You'll especially like the Fish Kitchen.***

With more than 10,000 aquatic plants and animals and tons of hands-on stations, this place really exhibits some unique creatures around every corner. Be sure to watch for the white alligator with blue eyes; play alongside otters; unbelievable Goliath Grouper (800 lbs); and our favorite - Trumpetfish - they look like feathers instead of fish. Look for the sea dragon habitat, sea urchin touch tank and Sea Hunt shark exhibit.

The downtown waterfront attraction also offers a number of daily shows including dive shows in the "Coral Reefs Gallery" and the Shark Show. You'll encounter creatures with long-range sensors, shape-shifting abilities and bone-crushing teeth. Shark Bay is a 93,000-gallon saltwater exhibit that is home to shark species from around the world including sand tiger sharks, zebra sharks, nurse sharks, black tip reef sharks and a green sea turtle. Try to catch the show labeled from "Fear to Fascination." New adventures at the aquarium allow visitors to put on a wetsuit and "Swim with Fishes" like angelfish and parrotfish. And, the newest gallery: Ocean Commotion! Allows guests to walk through a fog screen and enter a gallery of ocean lights, sounds and Raldo, an intrepid reporter as he interviews nominees for the golden Gill Award. The "Explore a Shore," an adorable outdoor children's play area with water cannons and slides, is just outside the back of the aquarium.

AMERICAN VICTORY MARINERS MUSEUM SHIP

Tampa - ***705 Channelside Drive (adjacent to Florida Aquarium) 33602. Phone: (813) 228-8766. www.americanvictory.org. Note: Passengers can park in the Florida Aquarium Parking Lot or the Port Authority Parking Garage.***

SELF GUIDED TOURS - The ship's popular Self-Guided Tours allow visitors to view first hand the on-going work to restore this 60-year old icon of America's merchant maritime might. If you haven't visited in a while, do so soon! Explore the cargo holds, radio room, hospital, galley, weaponry, mess halls, crew cabins, the Captains quarters, and the fl ying bridge. Restoration Tours are available Tuesday - Saturday, 10:00am-5:00pm and Sundays & Mondays, Noon-4:00pm. The last self-guided tours begin at 4:00pm, all days. Tour costs are $10.00 adults, $5.00 for kids 4-12; kids 3 and under are free. Seniors/students/vets $8.00.

FLORIDA

Exit - 256 (west of I-75)

GLAZER CHILDREN'S MUSEUM

Tampa - ***Downtown 33604. Phone: (813) 935-8441. www.glazermuseum.org. Hours: Monday-Friday 10am-5pm, Saturday 10am-6pm, Sunday 1-6pm. Admission: $15.00 adult, $12.50 senior & military, $9.50 child.***

The Glazer Children's Museum's mission is to inspire children and families by creating learning ops around innovative play and discovery. The new facility's centerpiece is a giant "web" called Waters Journey where kids pretend to be a drop of water and features lots of windows which allow the children playing to look out over the Hisslborough River. Passersby are able to see the children at play emphasizing the interconnectedness of the world. Because water is an important part of Tampa, kids here have their own giant water play port and tots have their own Tugboat area too.

Most of the rest of the museum is a miniature city offering hands-on activities for children. Complete with streets, sidewalks, park benches, shade trees, picnic tables and buildings representing various businesses found in a typical city - a library, restaurant, bank, supermarket, veternarian's offi ce, TV station, hospital, fi rehouse and apartments - can be explored by little hands and wide eyes. Kids pretend and role-play what they want to be when they grow up in Kid City.

Exit - 246 (west of I-75)

TECO MANATEE VIEWING CENTER

Apollo Beach - ***6990 Dickman Road (I-75 exit 246. Turn west on Big Bend Rd-CR 672-for 2.5 miles) 33572. Phone: (813) 228-4289. www.tampaelectric.com/company/mvc/. Hours: Daily 10:00am-5:00pm (November thru mid-April). Admission: FREE. Note: No pets. The Manatee Viewing Center is home to a 40-panel, 7,000-watt photovoltaic (PV) solar panel array. Installed atop the Center's education building, visitors can see this impressive system from the main parking lot and learn more about how solar power is generated. The center also features a gift shop, the South Shore Cafe, and a web cam that is in operation during the center's open season.***

To observe endangered Florida manatees in their real homes, head to Tampa Electric's Big Bend Power Station, where the manatee are attracted by the power plant's warm water discharge. The Manatee Viewing Center's observation platform allows close-up views of the graceful sea cows. Inside, look for an authentic manatee skeleton and an 11.5 foot fiberglass reproduction, with various exhibits, videos, etc. providing insight into the manatee's physical characteristics.

> Observers have spotted more than 300 manatees in this canal at one time.

Exit - 240 (east of I-75)

LITTLE MANATEE RIVER STATE PARK

Wimauma - ***215 Lightfoot Road (I-75 exit 240, head east on SR674 then five miles south of Sun City, off U.S. 301 on Lightfoot Road) 33598. Phone: (813) 671-5005. www.floridastateparks.org/park/little-manatee-river. Hours: Daily 8:00am-sunset. Admission: $5.00 per vehicle.***

The Little Manatee River begins in a swampy area near Fort Lonesome and flows almost 40 miles before emptying into Tampa Bay. Visitors can fish along the banks of the river or rent canoes at the ranger station. Wildlife enthusiasts can enjoy hiking a six-and-a-half mile trail through the park's northern wilderness area. For those who prefer their hikes on horseback, the park has 12 miles of equestrian trails and four equestrian campsites. Campers can spend the night in a full-facility campground or hike out to a primitive campsite along the trail. The scenic picnic area along the river has tables, grills, and pavilions.

Exit - 229 (east of I-75)

FLORIDA GULF COAST RAILROAD MUSEUM

Parrish - ***12210 83rd St East (I-75 exit 229, head east on 97th St to US301, turn right (south) 34219. Phone: (941) 776-0906. www.FGCRRM.org. Admission: $14.00 adult, $10.00 child (3-11). Additional fees charged for specials like Train Robberies and The Little Engine. Museum Hours: Weekends 10am-4pm. Tours: Saturday and Sunday 11:00am and 2:00pm.***

Many visitors ask, "Where are the displays?" The answer includes the museum's rolling equipment, and the historical items found in these cars. Instead of just looking at items, the museum takes you for a 13 mile round trip ride aboard the exhibits. The 1.5 hour train ride in vintage passenger cars goes through rustic Manatee County.

Exit - 224 (west of I-75)

GAMBLE PLANTATION STATE HISTORIC SITE

Bradenton (Ellenton) - ***3708 Patten Avenue (Exit 224 from I-75. Head west for 1 mile on US 301) 34222. www.floridastateparks.org/park/gamble-plantation. Phone: (941) 723-4536. Hours: Thursday-Monday 9am-5pm. Admission: FREE. Tours are charged. Tours: Guided tours are offered twice in the morning and four***

times in the afternoon (Thursday-Monday). $6.00 adult, $4.00 child (6-12). Note: picnic tables on the grounds.

This antebellum mansion was home to Major Robert Gamble and headquarters of an extensive sugar plantation. It is the only surviving plantation house in South Florida. It is believed that Confederate Secretary of State, Judah P. Benjamin, took refuge here after the fall of the Confederacy, until his safe passage to England could be secured. As you enter the mansion, it feels as though you stepped through a time portal that transported you back into the 1850s. The tour guide takes you into the first room, the parlor. There you see an extravagant piano, dating over 140 years old, that was purchased for only $25.00. You enter the next room and are introduced to picture molding.

Exit - 220 (west of I-75)

MIXON FRUIT FARMS

Bradenton - ***2712 26th Avenue East (I-75 South to exit 220/SR 64 west for 5 miles. Just past the 2nd bridge turn left onto 27th St. East) 34208. Phone: (800) 608-2525. www.mixon.com. Hours: Store hours Monday-Saturday 10:00am-5:00pm. Admission: Adults: Tour only $10.00. ChildrenTour only $5.00. Tours: By appointment, several times daily. Orange Blossom Tram Tours are at 11:00, 1:00 and 3:00. Closed Christmas and New Year's. Just call ahead and be sure there's room for your family on the next tour. Note: Browse the giant gift shop.Wildlife Care and Education Center and Children's Magical Maze, too.***

Let Mixon's treat you to a FREE cup of fresh squeezed Orange or Grapefruit Juice.

Come take a ride on the Orange Blossom Express! It's affordable family fun and you'll learn all the secrets of citrus while discovering a new world inside the live groves. Tours are packed full of educational tidbits and trivia. Learn Florida's history & cultural heritage, citrus origins, growth and industry – did you know citrus groves love bees and water vapor? Try a fresh kumquat right off the vine. Roll it and pop the whole thing in your mouth!

Be sure to try the "surprising" kumquat...

Now that's a lemon...

Learn about the Good, the Bad and the Ugly. Witness Ponderosa lemons as big as grapefruit or oranges mixed with grapefruit in the shape of a bell. Take a peek in the packinghouse and juice processing facilities. Have a "ham" in the family? Take photos in the Grove's fun caricature photo stands. You'll also get to sample homemade fudge, fresh squeezed citrus juice and sliced oranges and grapefruit. Stay for one of Mixon's Famous "Orange Swirl" Ice Cream Cones (made from fresh squeezed orange juice) and sit out on Grandma Rosa's front porch. Add lunch and enjoy deli sandwiches, soups or salads. A bright, friendly and fun place to definitely put in your travel plans.

SOUTH FLORIDA MUSEUM / PARKER MANATEE AQUARIUM

Bradenton - ***201 10th Street West (I-75 exit 220, head west on SR 64 about 7miles into downtown. Turn right on 10th St. west. 34206. www.southfloridamuseum.org. Phone: (941) 747-2556. Hours: Monday-Saturday 10:00am-5:00pm; Sunday Noon-5:00pm. Closed Mondays (May, June & August-December). Closed Thanksgiving Day, Christmas Day & New Year's Day and for annual maintenance the first two weeks in September. Admission: $19 adult, $17 senior (60+), $14 child (4-12). Includes Museum, Aquarium and one Planetarium Show.***

Discover Florida's story from the prehistoric to the present with life-sized casts of Ice Age mammals that roamed in Southwest Florida 12,000 years ago, realistic dioramas, and fossil exhibits that explain how Florida was formed. See materials collected from Florida archeological digs. Make time to explore Discovery Place - an area with some hands-on activity. Or, journey back to 16th century Spain in their Spanish Plaza with a replica of a 16th century chapel.

PARKER MANATEE AQUARIUM - is home to Snooty, the oldest living manatee (over 55 years old!) born and nurtured in a man-made, protected environment. The pool holds approximately 60,000 gallons of water and includes both deep and shallow water to provide continuity for Snooty's feeding habits. Several aquarium shows occur each day. You must meet Snooty - he is so loveable and friendly with staff - he jumps right up on the dock to get treats! It's easy to see why Florida has fallen in love with this mammal.

Snooty comes up for a little treat

FLORIDA

PLANETARIUM - A state-of-the-science, all digital full dome planetarium/ theater. Features astronomy presentations, sound and light shows and wide-screen large format programming featured daily.

Exit - 220 (west of I-75)

PEACHES RESTAURANTS

Bradenton (Ellenton), ***nine locations.***

Daily 6:00am-2:30pm. Breakfast and lunch menu with Mom's home cooking. A cozy, country home setting is the venue for fresh baked goods and homemade soups at this no-fuss diner. Hungry patrons favor the chicken salad platter served with fresh fruit. The real hit is the peaches and cream coffee cake.

DE SOTO NATIONAL MEMORIAL

Bradenton - P.O. Box 15390 (I-75 follow State Road 64 west (also Manatee Avenue), follow signs to 75th Street West. Turn right (north) onto 75th Street West) 34280. Phone: (941) 322-1000. www.nps.gov/deso/. Hours: Daily 9:00am-5:00pm except major winter holidays. Admission: FREE. Note: A ten table picnic area is located adjacent to the parking lot and is available for visitors on a first come basis. Grills are not allowed within the park. Several small beaches are located within the park. The De Soto Point Beach is located west of De Soto Point and northwest of the Visitor Center. This beach is exposed to the current of the Manatee River and the waves of Tampa Bay. The Cove Beach located on the south side of De Soto Point and is more popular because it is sheltered from most current and waves. No life guards are on duty. Swimmers use park beaches at their own risk. Dogs are permitted within the park only when on a hand held leash.

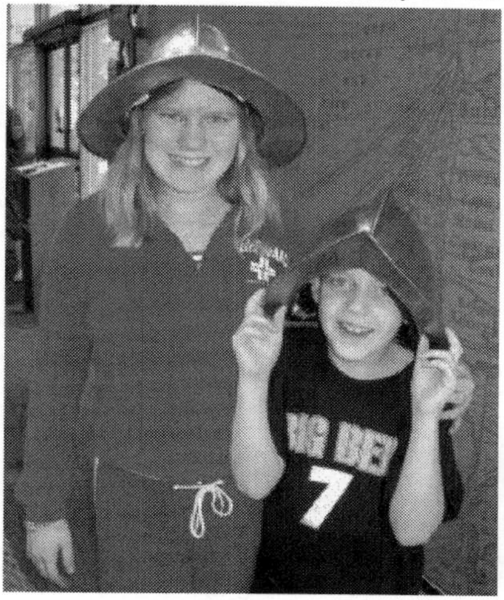

Try on a "steel" explorer hat!

The park commemorates the legacy of Spanish conquistador, Hernando de Soto, who in 1539 landed near Tampa Bay to begin a four year, four thousand mile trek through the Southeastern United States.

Begin with a 22-minute movie as actors re-enact scenes from this expedition (shown every half hour). Go on the expedition viavideo and survive! Over one-half of the explorers didn't. The presentation is necessary to orient your family to this time in early North American history. This expedition would never yield the gold and treasure these men so desperately sought and the Spanish began to re-think their desire to conquer it. Now, go outside and attend living history demonstrations (mid-December thru mid-April) in the replica Spanish Camp, try on pieces of armor (great photo ops), or walk the nature trail through a Florida coastal landscape similar to the one encountered by conquistadors almost five hundred years ago. We really learned a lot here and the interpreters and rangers are very helpful and interesting.

> **Did You Know?**
> Hernando de Soto died on May 21, 1542, 3 years after his conquest of La Florida began. His men buried him in the Mississippi River so that Native Americans would not know that he was not the immortal god he claimed to be. His remains have never been found.

Exit - 220 (east of I-75)

LAKE MANATEE STATE PARK

Bradenton - ***20007 State Road 64 (9 miles east off I-75 exit 220) 34202. Phone: (941) 741-3028. www.floridastateparks.org/park/lake-manatee. Admission: $5.00 per vehicle for up to 8 people.***

Located east of I-75, this 556-acre recreation area extends along the shores of Lake Manatee. A boat ramp provides easy access to the lake; boat motors must be less than 20 horsepower. Canoeing and kayaking are also popular activities. The lake offers excellent freshwater fishing, and anglers can fish from their boats or from the park's fishing dock. Swimming is permitted in a designated area of Lake Manatee; a facility with showers is located nearby. A large picnic area is nestled in a sand pine scrub area near the lake. Nature trails are available.

Exit - 213 (west of I-75)

RINGLING MUSEUM COMPLEX

Sarasota - ***5401 Bay Shore Road (I-75, Exit 213 West on University Parkway) 34243. Phone: (941) 351-1660. www.ringling.org. Hours: Daily 10:00am-5:00pm. Closed thanksgiving, Christmas and New Years. Admission: $25.00 adult, $23.00 senior (65+) & Military, $5.00 child (6-17) and teachers. Tours: For an extra $5.00 admission you can reserve a guided tour of Cà d'Zan Mansion. Tours***

are scheduled every 15 minutes through out the day starting at 9:45am. Note: What are your children interested in? Family guides are available to help you plan your visit around their interests. Download family guides from their Family Programs page. Strollers can be brought into all Museum buildings! The Banyan Café is located across from the Circus Museum and offers family-friendly fare like hot dogs, chicken fingers, and salads in a cafeteria setting. It is open 11:00am-4:00pm daily. If you'd rather pack a snack, picnic tables are available between the Banyan Café and the Rose Garden. Tables are available on a first come, first served basis. Please remember that no food or drinks are allowed in the galleries.

On your way over towards the mansion, be sure to check out the Banyan trees where the roots grow down from the branches!

The John and Mable Ringling Museum of Art is home to several art attractions. The Art Museum features significant holdings in European, American and non-Western art. Ca d'Zan is the Ringlings' magnificent, 32-room Venetian-Gothic mansion on the bay. The Circus Museum displays art and artifacts from the Ringling Circus enterprise. You can begin in the InterActive Area where kids pretend to be in the circus or watching a circus. Art takes the form of a Woodcarvers Studio with carousel animals in stages of production and crafters actively working on a new project while you watch. Kids light up in the wildly colorful Circus Wardrobe Room and the "warehouse" Wagon Room full of life-size circus carts. "Ladies and Gentlemen...Step Right Up to the Largest Miniature Circus in the World – the Howard Bros. Circus!". The mini-circus is an authentic replica of Ringling Bros. and Barnum & Bailey Circus during the height of the tented

A circus king's home...

circus era (early 1900s). The ¾-inch-to-the-foot model covers 3,800 sq. feet and boasts a 55-car train, 152 wagons, 1,500 circus artists and staff, a 200-animal menagerie and eight main tents. Our kids comments -"I wish I could play with this!" This is worth the admission price alone! What a wonderful, colorful museum complex - don't miss it!

Exit - 213 (west of I-75)

SARASOTA JUNGLE GARDENS

Sarasota - ***3701 Bayshore Road (I-75 exit 213 University Parkway West. 2 miles south of airport off US 41) 34234. www.SarasotaJungleGardens.com. Phone: (941) 355-5305 or (877) 861-6547. Hours: Daily 9:00am-5:00pm. Closed Christmas and Thanksgiving Day. Admission: $15.00 adult, $14.00 senior (60+), $10.00 child (3-12). Coupon online.***

The area's only Zoological Gardens combines lush gardens and colorful macaws, pointy-tooth alligators and gentle flamingos that eat out of your hands (of course, the flamingos eat out of your hand, not the alligators). Traverse along 10 acres of cool, jungle trails and take in a show on this self-guided tour. Shows include subjects like Birds of Prey, Critters and Reptiles (hold a python if you dare). Also enjoy the Kiddie Jungle, Reptile World, and Flamingo Café.

Exit - 210 (west of I-75)

MOTE AQUARIUM

Sarasota - ***1600 Ken Thompson Parkway, City Island (exit 210 off I-75 west to US 41, turn left. Right at Gulfstream Ave. across Causeway to St Armands Circle. Exit circle at Blvd of Presidents) 34236. Phone: (941) 388-2451. www.mote.org. Hours: Daily 10:00am-5:00pm. Lab Hours: 8:00am-5:00pm weekdays. Admission: $19.75 adult, $14.75 child (4-12). Website coupon. General admission includes access to Mote Aquarium, the Marine Mammal Center and Mote's new Immersion Cinema. Note: Dining: The Deep Sea Diner- retro '50s-style diner offers a fun, affordable, family-style menu.***

From the original focus on sharks, Mote research has expanded to include seven major areas of concentration, organized into seven research centers. Mote scientists are committed to that process of discovery: Advancing our understanding of the sea and what is needed to sustain it. Sometimes, they research hazards to the water, study shark behavior or maybe try to bring a species back to its native waters. Their Dolphin & Whale Hospital provides critical care for stranded dolphins and whales. In the aquarium, you can't miss the giant squid, octopus or the real seahorses (collected from nearby Bays). Think it's cool to see a shark? Find out what it feels like to BE the shark in the exciting 12-minute movie shown in Shark Attack Theater. Learn how sharks use their senses to catch their prey. Viewable working labs and high-tech interactive exhibits showcase the world-renowned research of Mote Marine Laboratory. There is also a 135,000-gallon shark habitat, stingray touch pool, and manatee and turtle exhibits.

Exit - 205 (east of I-75)

MYAKKA RIVER STATE PARK

Sarasota - ***13207 State Road 72 (9 miles east of I-75 exit 205, on SR 72) 34241. Phone: (941) 361-6511. www.floridastateparks.org/park/myakka-river. Hours: Daily 8:00am-sunset. Admission: Entrance fee - $6.00 per vehicle. Separate fees for tours, camping. Tours: Saturday morning ranger-guided walks.***

This is one of Florida's oldest and largest state parks. The Myakka River flows through tens of miles of wetlands, prairies and woodlands. Myakka is popular for hiking, fishing, camping, bicycling, and wildlife observation. Explore the treetops on the canopy walkway, and climb the 70-foot tower for an awesome view. MYAKKA WILDLIFE TOURS: (941) 365-0100. Call for schedules and rates. Enjoy Safaris traveling on one of the world's largest airboats or on the land tram. During these informative tours, you will learn about Florida's natural wonders and animals. See alligators in the wild.

Exit - 200 (east of I-75)

OSCAR SCHERER STATE PARK

Sarasota (Osprey) - ***1843 S. Tamiami Trail (US 41, two miles south of Osprey) 34229. Phone: (941) 483-5956. www.floridastateparks.org/park/oscar-scherer. Hours: Florida state parks are open from 8:00am until sundown 365 days a year. Admission: $5.00 per vehicle for up to 8 people. FREEBIES: Cell Phone Audio Tours: call 941-926-6813 for education messages.***

Along with the wildlife easily observed at Oscar Scherer State Park, there are a number of recreational activities available. A small freshwater lake provides visitors with a perfect location for swimming. Fishing is enjoyed in South Creek with freshwater species found above the dam and saltwater species found below the dam. A Florida freshwater fishing license is required for all persons 16 years of age or older. A saltwater license may be required. See a park ranger for specific license requirements. Visitors with a sense of adventure will find South Creek ideal for canoeing. Canoes may be rented at the ranger station. You may want to join a park ranger for a guided canoe program and learn more about the park's history and plant and animal life.

Exit - 143 (west of I-75)

SHELL FACTORY & NATURE PARK

Fort Myers, North - ***2787 North Tamiami Trail (I-75:Take Exit 143 and turn left onto State Road 78 (Bayshore Road). Go 5 miles to US 41; turn right) 33903. Phone: (239) 995-2141 or (888) 4-SHELLS. www.shellfactory.com. Hours: Shell Factory & Nature Park: Daily 10:30am-6:30pm. Waltzing Waters at sunset each night. Admission: Shell Factory: FREE. Nature Park: $8.00-$10.00 per person (age 4+). All fun park activities carry a fee, also. Tours: of the factory and warehouse are at 11:00am and 2:00pm daily. Note: Dine at Southwest Florida's largest seafood restaurant—Capt'n Fishbones for a moderately priced lunch or dinner. Rosie's Gourmet Fudge.***

The Shell Factory is billed as the "world's largest collection of rare shells, sponges, coral, fossils and sea life specimens" with more than 5 million shells. A gift shop visit is like a treasure hunt. Ever seen a shell priced at $2,300 or octopus coral? You can pick a pearl from an oyster or watch master glass blower and potter demonstrations.

FUN PARK & ARCADE: You can play arcade games, miniature golf, test the speed of your pitch at their pitching cage, bump into friends at the Bumper Boat lagoon, stop by The Patio for live entertainment from 7-10PM most evenings, or come for karaoke from 6:00-9:00pm Sundays.

The newly renovated NATURE PARK features a Petting Zoo, Environmental Education Center, and a Botanical Trail. Bobcats, raccoons, and llamas, oh my! Watch playful prairie dogs as they greet each other by touching their teeth together, the “prairie dog kiss”. You can even feed them a treat – remember bring quarters, as they always have a healthy appetite! Keep cool while you feed the turtles and fish that live in the misty ponds below the waterfalls. Next to the waterfalls, the Primate Pavilion currently houses ring-tailed lemurs. Come see Big Bertha, a 10-foot long female alligator, and her large friends at the Slough. (It's pronounced "sloo" or "slew") On the weekends the alligators are fed. Feedings are usually around 2:30pm but call ahead as feeding times can vary. Soar high above the zoo on the zip line.

Exit - 143 (east of I-75)

ECHO GLOBAL FARM

Fort Myers, North - ***17391 Durrance Road (off of SR 78, one mile east of I-75 exit 143) 33917. Phone: (239) 543-3246. www.echonet.org. Hours: Nursery open mornings, daily except Sunday. Admission: Guided tours cost $10.00 adult, $5.00 child (6+). Tours: 1 1/2 hour guided tours to the public Tuesday thru Friday 10:00am, noon & 2:00pm; Saturday at 10:00am & noon (December-March) and Tuesday, Friday and Saturday only at 10:00am (April-November). For groups of 8 or larger, please make a reservation.***

Working to fight world hunger, ECHO (a non-profit Educational Concerns for Hunger organization) invites you for a tour of its working demonstration farm. They give HOPE - they teach poor how to grow food that adapts to even extreme conditions. And guess what? You may learn some new garden techniques yourself! ECHO's farm shows collections of tropical food plants in Florida, as well as herb gardens and animals in the Global Village. Tilapia - why are they easy and great to grow? Ever tasted Pummelo fruit - buy some at their store and try it. Bamboo really does "shoot" up fast. Visitors can see the useful plants and farming systems that interns are cultivating in urban rooftop plantings, rice fields, hillside farming systems (even some growing in car tire terraces), rain forest clearings, semi-arid tropics, hot humid lowlands and monsoon tropics. We discovered and bought seeds to plant a Moringa bush. This miracle plant is possibly the best source of nutrients in the world - it even contains protein! And, you can sample some - one salad a day of this stuff and you'll be able to keep the doctor away! What an amazing, heart-felt place to explore.

Grinding plants to sprinkle on food for better nutrition...

Exit - 141 (east of I-75)

MANATEE PARK

Fort Myers - ***10901 SR 80 (SR 80, 1.5 miles east of I-75 exit 141) 33905. Phone: (239) 694-3537 or (239) 461-7477. www.leeparks.org (click on Facilities). Hours: Daily 8:00am-sunset. Visitors Center open daily 9am-4pm. Admission: Parking fee of $1.00 per hour or $5.00 daily maximum. No Pets. Observation area is FREE. Note: Picnic areas & shelters, fishing cove & pier on the Orange River, canoe/kayak launch to the Orange River, program amphitheater and playground. FREEBIES: Manatee Worksheets & Games on Park Details page.***

What a great quick stop along your journeys in Florida! Visitors can observe endangered West Indian manatees in their non-captive habitat from three observation areas during "Manatee Season." Manatee Park officially opens for "season" around mid-December as visitors are able to view several manatees daily in the Florida Power & Light (FPL) discharge canal. Please monitor gulf temperatures as best viewing occurs when it dips below 68 degrees. Best known for the Winter home for the Florida Manatee, this park is also the year round home for Florida native plants & butterflies. "All About Manatees" program daily at 11:00am and 2:00pm - November through March. Free guided walk through the native plants habitats at 9:00am every Saturday. Who will be the first in your group to spot the manatee's back or snout? It's a thrill to find them!

Baby & Momma Manatee in the wild...

FLORIDA

Exit - 138 (west of I-75)

IMAGINARIUM SCIENCE CENTER

Fort Myers - ***2000 Cranford Avenue (historic downtown) (Interstate 75: Exit 138, west on Dr. Martin Luther King, Jr. Boulevard (State Road 82) for four miles and left on Cranford Avenue) 33916. www.imaginariumfortmyers.com. Phone: (239) 337-3332. Hours: Monday-Saturday 10:00am-5:00pm, Sunday Noon-5:00pm. Admission: $12.00 adult, $10.00 senior (55+), $8.00 child (3-12). Admission includes 3D film, animal encounters, touch tank, hurricane and exhibits.***

Interactive learning in the sciences. A giant Pipe-O-Saurus greets visitors at the entrance to the Florida wetlands zone. Once inside, one can stand in a Florida thunderstorm without getting wet, watch Eelvis, the live eel, slither through the coral in one of three 900-gallon aquariums, get blown away in the HurricanExperience, and broadcast the weather from a TV weather studio. Outside, visit the lagoon where fish, turtles, swans and alligators live beside a reptile retreat with iguanas, tortoises and more. Theater in the Tank video presentations and 3-D shows, too.

SOUTHWEST FLORIDA MUSEUM OF HISTORY

Fort Myers - ***2300 Peck Street (I-75 south exit 138 west on MLK. One block south on Jackson) 33901. Phone: (239) 332-5955. www.swflmuseumofhistory.com/. Hours: Tuesday-Saturday 10:00am-5:00pm. Admission: $9.50 adult, $8.50 senior, $5.00 child (3-12) and students w/ id.***

Housed in the restored Atlantic Coastline railroad depot, the museum features displays and exhibits of the history of southwest Florida from prehistory through the present. Displays include graphic depictions of ancient Florida: Paleo, Archaic, Calusa, and Seminole Indians; Spanish explorers; a Pullman rail car or an authentic replica pioneer "Cracker house." The first tourist to visit southwest Florida was Spanish explorer Ponce de Leon, who visited Pine Island in 1513 and was later mortally wounded in these same waters by a Calusa Indian arrow. One of the southernmost land battles of the American Civil War was fought in Fort Myers in early 1865 over cattle, with both sides claiming victory. Explore the World War II airfield exhibit, which includes a recently excavated P-39 bomber that crashed into Estero Bay during the war and a restored AT-6 training plane.

Exit - 136 (west of I-75)

SUN SPLASH FAMILY WATERPARK

Cape Coral - ***400 Santa Barbara Blvd (I-75 exit 136, turn west and cross the Midpoint Memorial Bridge. Turn north on Santa Barbara Blvd.) 33991. Phone: (239) 574-0557. www.sunsplashwaterpark.com. Hours: Long Weekends only (mid-March to mid-June); daily 10:00am-6:00pm, some 8:00pm (mid-June to mid-August); weekends only 10:00am-5:00pm (mid-August to mid-October). Admission: $17.95 adult, $15.95 child (3-12 and seniors (60+), Note: Lounge chairs, life jackets, changing rooms and rental lockers are available.***

Slide into a million gallons of fun at a waterpark that offers 12-acres of watery adventure. Free fall up to 40 feet per second on the X-celerator, the park's fastest and most extreme slide; Face your fears on the Terror Tube. Dare to catch air on the Thunder Bum open chute with speed bumps. Enjoy other waterslides, the popular Main Stream River inner tube ride, Lily Pads and a Tot Spot kiddie area featuring interactive squirt works, sand volleyball, a game arcade, and more.

CALUSA NATURE CENTER AND PLANETARIUM

Fort Myers - ***3450 Ortiz Avenue (I-75 exit 136, head west on SR884 a little, then north on Ortiz) 33906. Phone: (239) 275-3435. www.calusanature.com. Hours: Monday-Saturday 10:00am-5:00pm, Sunday 11:00am-5:00pm. Admission: $1-.00 adult, $5.00 child (3-12) includes admission to the nature center, trails and all planetarium shows that day.***

Outside, rustic boardwalks lead visitors on a tour of 105 acres of subtropical environment. Inside, permanent and changing exhibits of the natural history of southwest Florida are on display. There are more than 100 Florida native animals to see. Alligator and snake demonstrations hold visitors' interest twice daily. Naturalists guide walks and aviary tours several times a week. Changing planetarium starlit astronomy and laser light shows occur in the relaxing 90-seat theater. Discover, explore, touch, and learn about Florida's estuary animals up-close when you visit their interactive 1,000 gallon estuary touch tank. How many eyes does a Horseshoe crab have? How does a sea star eat?

Exit - 136 (west of I-75)

EDISON & FORD WINTER ESTATES

Fort Myers - ***2350 McGregor Blvd. (Interstate 75 (Exit #136) travel West on Colonial boulevard (SR 884). Turn right onto McGregor Boulevard (SR 867) 33901. Phone: (239) 334-3614. www.efwefla.org. Hours: Daily 9:00am-5:30pm. Closed Thanksgiving and Christmas. Last tour leaves promptly at 4:00pm. Admission: Combined ticket for both homes is $20.00 adult, $11.00 child (6-12). Lab & Museum only: $12.00 & $5.00. Active military FREE. Tours: Young Inventors Family Tour Saturdays at 11am. While the stories***

Edison among the Banyan trees....

FLORIDA

told on the tours may be of interest to school-aged kids, most find the Lab & Museum the most kid-friendly. If you truly want to make this a quick stop - opt for the lab and museum only ticket. Maybe have lunch under the trees, too. Note: Banyan Café (tables underneath the giant banyan tree groves) from 10:00am-4:00pm.

In 1885, Thomas Edison first visited Florida and purchased property along the Caloosahatchee River where he built a vacation home. The 1886 "Seminole lodge" served as a winter retreat and work place for the prolific inventor until his death in 1931. The inventor's charming "old-Florida" style home, laboratory and experimental gardens have been authentically maintained. Rare antique automobiles and Edison phonographs fill some spaces, the Laboratory where Edison turned goldenrod (a weed!) to rubber (yes!) another. Look for the pool made with Edison Portland Cement - and it has never leaked. The lab is a mouth-dropper - you can feel the genius' presence! Throughout the laboratory, all of his things are just as they were in his lifetime, including his "cat-nap" cot. Because of his deafness, Edison's sleep was undisturbed and relaxed him so much that 15 minute sleep to him was as good as is several hours to anyone else. Some might say he invented the "Power Nap"! Be sure the kids get to spend time in the Whiz Inventors Room of the Museum. Here they play a Charlie Brown Inventor video while looking over giant prototypes of Edison's inventions. There's even a worksheet to take home and make your own homemade light bulb!

His lab...as Edison left it...

Did you know Edison invented the first Talking Dolls?

Edison's good friend Henry Ford followed close behind and purchased the neighboring property in 1915. "The Mangoes" was the winter getaway for the Fords. A 1914 Model T, 1919 Model T, 1917 Ford Truck and 1929 Model A are on display. Ford used General Electric appliances. Henry would ask guests to "take a seat" - it didn't mean sit - it meant take a chair and move it aside so they could clear the floor for square-dancing - a Ford family passion. Edison and Ford spent many winters working, talking and even relaxing together in tropical southwest Florida. Can you imagine what those brilliant minds talked about?

Exit - 131 (west of I-75)

SIX MILE CYPRESS SLOUGH PRESERVE

Fort Myers - ***7751 Penzance Blvd., Six Mile Cypress Parkway (1.5 miles north of Daniels Pkwy, exit 131 off I-75) 33912. www.sloughpreserve.org. Phone: (239) 432-2004. Hours: Spring/Summer 8:00am-8:00pm, Fall/Winter 8:00am-5:00pm. No entry one hour prior to the closing. Interpretive Center: Tuesday-Friday 10:00am-4:00pm, Saturday 10:00am-2:00pm, Sunday Noon-4:00pm. Admission: FREE. Parking costs $1.00 an hour. $5.00 daily maximum. Freebies: Parents, print off activity sheets and games online on their "Just for Kids" page.***

Visitors journey through this 2,500-acre wetland ecosystem on a mile-long boardwalk trail, where southwest Florida's diverse plant and wildlife are found. See subtropical ferns and bromeliads. Watch for birds like herons, egrets, ibis and anhingas. Guided walks daily in the winter. Wednesdays only in the summer and fall. Smoking, fishing, jogging, pets, bikes and roller blades are not permitted along the trail.

Exit - 131 (west of I-75)

SUN HARVEST CITRUS

Fort Myers - ***14810 Metro Pkwy (I-75 exit 131, head east on Daniels Pkwy, southwest on Six Mile Cypress to Metro Parkway on the way to the airport) 33912. Phone: (239) 768-2686 or (800) 743-1480. www.sunharvestcitrus.com. Hours: Store open Monday-Saturday 8:00am-7:00pm, Sunday 10:00am-6:00pm. Admission: FREE. Note: They also have soft-serve ice cream, fruit smoothies, candies and baked goods for sale. Playground on premises.***

"Squeeze" in a stop to this huge green packinghouse and retail store that offers in-season Indian River citrus fruit, five varieties of freshly squeezed juices year-round, and in-season gift fruit shipping. Watch as fresh juice is made while enjoying free samples of juices and fruit. Get a behind-the-scenes look at their state-of-the-art packinghouse operations. See for yourself how the hand-picked citrus is cleaned, graded and packed — all within hours after leaving the family's Indian River groves.

PINK SHELL BEACH RESORT

Fort Myers - ***275 Estero Blvd. (I-75 at Daniels Pkwy (Exit 131). At Summerlin Rd, turn left and follow signs to Fort Myers Beach. Directly after Sky Bridge, turn right) 33931. Phone: (239) 463-6181 or (888) 309-2913. www.pinkshell.com.***

Pink Shell Beach Resort & Spa has been an American beach tradition for more than 50 years, catering to the needs of generations of families with children. One of the amenities is the "Octopool" at the new luxury condos at White Sands Villas. It's a zero-entry and undersea fantasy, featuring waving sea grasses, colorful tropical fish, coral reefs, starfish, seahorses, sculpted sea sponges, a coral encrusted archway with waterfall, a life-size octopus with illuminated eyes and a large conch shell fountain. Bongos restaurant is right off the pool and has the most kid-friendly menu and atmosphere. KiddsKampp is an adult-supervised child's (4-11) program designed to offer kid-friendly

activities, while providing parents with free time to enjoy the spa, watersports or fishing. And get this, young adults 12 and over are invited to help and become a member of the Junior Recreational Attendant Program. The Resort offers a family Sand Dollar Package full of extras for families (starts at $305.00 per night). Daily recreational activities for families (like ours) seeking to spend quality time TOGETHER range from creating shell picture frames, to design a t-shirt, to ice cream buffets, poolside bingo, conch shell blowing contests and sandcastles. The Recreation Center offers Junior fishing pole rentals (used at the resort's own fishing pier) and movie and board game rentals, too. Accommodations range from efficiencies, one-or two-bedroom suites and deluxe beach villas (every room has a fully equipped kitchen/kitchette). Enjoy quick access to the sandy shores, great balcony views and spacious, kid-friendly rooms. They have a 3 nice, heated waterfront pools, tennis courts and watersport rentals are available. And the rooms are so comfortable...

Exit - 123 (west of I-75)

MOUND KEY ARCHAEOLOGICAL STATE PARK

Fort Myers (Estero) - ***3800 Corkscrew Road (just east of Lovers Key in Estero Bay) 33928. Phone: (239) 992-0311. www.floridastateparks.org/park/mound-key. Hours: Daily 8:00am-sunset. Admission: FREE. Note: The only access to the island is by boat; there are no facilities...a true deserted island.***

Framed in forests of mangrove trees, the shell mounds and ridges of Mound Key rise more than 30 feet above the waters of ESTERO BAY.

Prehistoric Native Americans are credited with creating this island's complex of mounds with an accumulation of seashells, fish bones, and pottery. Mound Key is believed to have been the ceremonial center of the Calusa Indians when the Spaniards first attempted to colonize Southwest Florida. In 1566, the Spanish governor of Florida established a settlement on the island with a fort and the first Jesuit mission in the Spanish New World. The settlement was abandoned three years later after violent clashes with the Indians. Interpretive displays can be found along a trail that spans the width of the island. Located in Estero Bay, several miles by boat from Koreshan State Historic Site or Lovers Key State Park.

Exit - 116 (west of I-75)

LOVERS KEY STATE PARK

Fort Myers Beach - ***8700 Estero Blvd., Black Island, just south of Fort Myers Beach (head west at exit 116 for 10 miles) 33931. Phone: (239) 463-4588. www.floridastateparks.org/park/lovers-key. Tours: Admission, including the tram ride, is $8.00 per vehicle.***

A delightful tram transports visitors along a rustic boardwalk, crossing picturesque Oyster Bay and a scenario of mangrove isles, to one of the most private public beaches anywhere. Lovers Key claims a section of unspoiled beach where one can cast at surf line, picnic with raccoons, bird watch and search the shoreline for seashells. The park's concession offers boat and fishing tours, as well as bicycle, canoe, and kayak rentals.

Exit - 111 (west of I-75)

DELNOR-WIGGINS PASS STATE PARK

Naples - ***11135 Gulfshore Dr. (I-75 Exit 111 west 6 miles) 34108. Phone: (239) 597-6196. www.floridastateparks.org/park/delnor-wiggins. Hours: Florida state parks are open from 8:00am until sundown 365 days a year. Admission: $6.00 for up to 8 people per car. NOTE: To avoid overcrowding during the busy winter season, the park closes its gates when it reaches maximum capacity.***

This small barrier island on the Gulf of Mexico is a real unspoiled Florida beach with coastal hammock for shade and picnicking. Many go shelling, swimming, fishing and boating. At the north end of the island, a tower gives visitors a bird's-eye view of Wiggins Pass and the surrounding coastal habitat. A concession is located in the parking lot. One of the best beaches in the nation, the mile long park is a popular seashore destination in Naples for canoeing and snorkeling, too.

Exit - 105 (west of I-75)

NAPLES BEACH HOTEL EVERGLADES ROOM RESTAURANT

Naples - 851 Gulf Shore Blvd North (beachfront) (take Golden Gate Parkway west towards beachfront, follow signs south to hotel (before you get to downtown) 34102. www.naplesbeachhotel.com.

This resort property has been named Naples' Best Family Resort. As you enter the lobby notice the seawater aquarium. The Everglades Room is a traditional dining room offering an elaborate breakfast buffet, as well as a la carte selections. Enjoy old Florida elegance and tremendous Gulf views. In season, a traditional (and very freshly prepared) Sunday brunch is served. If you're staying overnight, the resort offers complimentary year-round "Beach Klub 4 Kids" programs entertaining children ages five to 12 daily with activities such as swimming, arts and crafts, beach walks, sandcastle construction and games. A "Kids Night Out" complete with dinner, a movie and games, is available on weekend evenings for a nominal charge. This is a great place to breakfast before boarding the trolley to tour town. They have a stop in front of the hotel.

NAPLES ZOO AT CARIBBEAN GARDENS

Naples - ***1590 Goodlette-Frank Road (I-75 exit 105, head west on golden Gate Pkwy 4 miles to Goodlette-Frank Rd, head south one block) 34102. Phone: (239) 262-5409. www.napleszoo.com. Hours: Daily 9:00am-5:00pm. Last ticket sold at 4:00pm. Admission: $19.95 adult, $18.95 senior (65+), $11.95 child (3-12). Deep discounts for Florida residents & military. Note: Coolers and picnic lunches are welcome. Cafe & gift shop on premises.***

Discover a world of wildlife just outside of downtown. Explore a day of fun shows, a cruise or two, plus get close to animals from alligators to zebras. Interpretive information overlooks a nearby island that is home to several species of lemur, native to Madagascar. Another eye-catching area is in Reptiles featuring a multimedia show on Serpents: Fangs & Fiction. Animals in residence at the zoo include several giraffe you can hand-feed to Africa's moustached monkeys and Asia's reticulated python. Our favorite part was gliding past Islands of Monkeys, Lemurs, and Apes off the shores of Lake Victoria on a Primate Expedition Cruise. As the catamarans float next to the islands, the expedition guide narrates the interesting details about these fascinating animals. You can also take the tour more than once as the cruise is included in your admission. (each cruise is about 15-20 minutes long)

Exit - 101 (west of I-75)

FLORIDA PANTHER & TEN THOUSAND ISLANDS NATIONAL WILDLIFE REFUGE

Naples - ***(refuge headquarters is in east Naples at Exit 101 of Interstate 75) 34114. http://floridapanther.fws.gov/. Phone: (239) 353-8442.***

The Refuge has two public hiking trails - the first public access to this important wildlife habitat refuge in its 16 years of existence. The Duncan Memorial Trail is .3 miles and is wheelchair accessible with a raised, shell-paved trail bed. An additional unimproved loop trail winds 1.3 miles through the refuge. Both trails open daily from sunup to sundown, closed after dark. Panthers are extremely rare and shy so sightings are unlikely, however, panther tracks may appear on the unimproved loop trail. Best chances to spot wildlife are early morning and late afternoon - watch for deer, bear, wild turkey and many species of birds. Another boardwalk should lead to a wetlands area, kiosks with interpretive information and more. Parking is available at the trail entrance on State Road 29 just north of I-75.

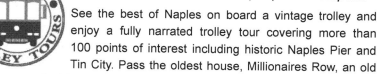

NAPLES TROLLEY TOURS

Naples - ***1010 6th Avenue South (I-75 exit 101, head west on SR84 into downtown. Follow signs for Visitors Center. 2 blocks west of Tin City) 34102. Phone: (239) 262-7300. www.naplestrolleytours.com. Hours: Eight full trips beginning at 8:30am until about 5:00pm. Tours: lasts approx. 1 hour, 45 minutes. $25.00 adult, $12.50 child (4-12). Online coupons.***

See the best of Naples on board a vintage trolley and enjoy a fully narrated trolley tour covering more than 100 points of interest including historic Naples Pier and Tin City. Pass the oldest house, Millionaires Row, an old trading post, the Naples City Dock, the disguised parking garage, and many exclusive residences. The tours are hosted by knowledgeable guides who not only know the history of Naples but also have a pulse on current events and activities explorers can soak up after the tour. FREE Reboarding - Deboard the Trolley at any convenient stop to shop, dine, or sightsee, then reboard the Trolley and it's on with the tour. Tour at your own pace. Think Naples is for seniors? The average age is 25-41 - surprised?

Exit - 101 (east of I-75)

EVERGLADES NATIONAL PARK

Everglades City - ***(most northern part begins in Naples area, take U.S. 41 (Tamiami Trail) east to Shark Valley) 34139. Phone: Visitor Information (305) 242-7700. www.nps.gov/ever. Admission: $10.00 per private vehicle for a 7 day pass. Freebies: FREE Family Fun Packs. Available for loan from the Flamingo, Shark Valley and Gulf Coast Visitor Centers, the packs are filled with story books, field guides and binoculars. Educators: www.nps.gov/ever/forteachers/curriculummaterials.htm.***

Everglades National Park is the only subtropical preserve in North America and is part of the largest wetlands ecosystem in the United States. The western gateway to the Park is in Everglades City. Along the outskirts of the national park, numerous private tour operators provide airboat and swamp buggy excursions through the sawgrass plains, swamps and hardwood hammocks of this ecosystem. There is also a daily guided boat trip into the mangrove estuaries of the Ten Thousand Islands section of the Park. Look for wood storks and great blue herons wading, or watch for frequent encounters with dolphins and manatees.

High atop a GIANT Swamp Buggy

__VISITOR CENTER__ GULF COAST - Open All Year at 9:00am-4:30pm. Phone: (239) 695-3311. The Center is located in the northwest corner of the park. It is the gateway for exploring the Ten Thousand Islands, a maze of mangrove islands and waterways that extends south to Flamingo and Florida Bay. The visitor center has natural history exhibits, educational displays, and orientation films. Restaurants, stores, lodging, and campgrounds are located nearby. Boat tours and canoe rentals are available at the marina, as well as nearby. These boat trips run daily, approximately every half hour Canoes may be rented to explore Chokoloskee Bay and the Turner River. Backcountry permits are required for camping.

Exit - 80 (east of I-75)

BIG CYPRESS NATIONAL PRESERVE

Everglades - ***33100 Tamiami Trail East (I-75, state road 29, and U.S. 41 all travel through the preserve) 34141. Phone: (239) 695-1201. www.nps.gov/bicy. Hours: Oasis Center open Daily 9:00am-4:30pm, except Christmas. Rest of preserve is open daylight hours unless weather closes portions. Admission: FREE. Note that some Visitor Center and Headquarter offices are deep into the Preserve and may require more than a 10 mile ride from I-75. Educators: click on Teachers for curriculum and online games - www.nps.gov/bicy/forkids/online-games.htm.***

Big Cypress has a mixture of pines, hardwoods, prairies, mangrove forests, cypress strands and domes. White-tailed deer, bear and Florida panther can be found here along with the more tropical liguus tree snail, royal palm and cigar orchid. This meeting place of temperate and tropical species is a hotbed of biological diversity. Hydrologically, the Preserve serves as a supply of fresh, clean water for the vital estuaries of the ten thousand islands area near Everglades City. Visitors will find a recreational paradise with camping, canoeing, kayaking, hiking and birdwatching opportunities. Recently, the Preserve opened several new pedestrain boardwalks to enhance the visitor experience in the preserve. Travelers can pull off the Tamiami Trail Scenic Highway at the Kirby Storter Roadside Park and take a short walk into the quiet coolness of an ancient cypress forest, or watch for alligators at new viewing boardwalks at Turner River Road and at the park's Oasis Visitor Center. The visitor center offers a 15-minute movie about the preserve, a wildlife exhibit and book sales.

FLORIDA

Exit - 13 (east of I-75)

FLAMINGO GARDENS

Fort Lauderdale (Davie) - ***3750 S. Flamingo Road (I-75 exit 13, head east on SR818, then north on SR823 a little ways) 33330. www.flamingogardens.org. Phone: (954) 473-2955. Hours: Daily 9:30am-5:30pm. Closed Mondays June thru mid-November. Admission: $18.00 adult, $10.00 child (4-11). Discounts for seniors, military and students w/ id. Tours: Tour by Tram: $3.00-$4.00 per person. Narrated tram ride through the tropical rainforest, native hammock, wetland areas, and groves. The tour is fully narrated, lasting approximately 25 minutes. Note: Flamingo Café.***

Once a spectacular estate, this Garden is now a refuge housing a free flight aviary, alligators, flamingos, bobcats and injured animals. Rare, exotic and native plants, a 200-year old oak hammock, citrus groves, wetlands and a tropical flowering tree walk balance out the botanical gardens. If you're not in the mood to walk it, take the tram tour. Otherwise, put the kiddies in the stroller and let them get close to all the "pretty colors". A nice living example of Florida's natural history.

BUEHLER PLANETARIUM & OBSERVATORY

Fort Lauderdale (Davie) - ***3501 SW Davie Road (Broward Community College, central Campus) 33314. Phone: (954) 201-6681. www.iloveplanets.com. Admission: Adult & Children FREE entrance at Observatory on public viewing nights. Planetarium Themed Shows: $4.00-$5.00 per person.***

Explorations through all of space. Enjoy programs that explore the wonders of the Universe. Most of the public programs involve the stars and folklore with themes like: Secret Rockets, Explorers, Marvelous Backyard, Egypt and Clouds of Fire. Observatory open to Public Wednesday, Friday, and Saturday 8:00pm-10:00pm for free.